Settler Australia, 1780-1880

Volume 1: Settlement, Protest and Control

Richard Brown

Published by Authoring History

http://richardjohnbr1066.wordpress.com/

© Richard Brown, 2013

All rights reserved. No part of this publication may be reproduced in any form, stored in or re-introduced into a retrieval system, or transmitted, in any form or by any means, electronic, mechanical, photocopying, recording or otherwise without the prior consent of the author.

The moral right of Richard Brown to be identified as the author of this work has been asserted in accordance with the Copyright, Designs and Patents Act 1988.

ISBN-13: 978-1479362783

ISBN-10 : 1479362786

Printed by CreateSpace

Contents

Contents	i
Acknowledgements	iii
Abbreviations	iv
Series Preface	vi
Creating a colonial state	1
1 Why Botany Bay?	10
2 Three Fleets	19
3 Autocracy and consent	31
4 Military rule to responsible government	89
5 Secretaries and Colonial Secretaries 1788-1856	123
6 A Very British Coup: A 'Rum' Rebellion	136
7 Federal or not?	179
8 Settling the land	196
Violence and protest	263
9 A convict society	273
10 Establishing the rule of law	282
11 Policing	310
12 Bushrangers and women in rebellion	332
13 Hell in Paradise	358
14 Fearing the Irish, 1800-1807	384
15 Irish Political Prisoners, 1790-1876	413
Appendix: Who ran colonial government?	462
Further Reading	467

Index 469
About the Author 485

Acknowledgements

Although many of the papers in this volume were revised and re-written after I retired from full-time teaching, most were originally drafted during my last two years of teaching. I began work on the Eureka Rebellion before domestic circumstances led me to retire from teaching several years earlier than I had intended. Some of the papers were simply sketches of ideas and issues that I explored in greater depth in the published work while others from the outset were more substantial pieces that, in some cases, did not figure in the published work at all. I must particularly thank the many students who over three decades listened patiently to my ideas on history, demonstrated the beginnings of historical thinking and understanding and who made me think about the subject far more than they will ever know. It was this process of grappling with the past, for me as much as for them, that made teaching such a joy. It is only by interrogating the past that we can come to understand what happened and why people acted as they did and how events and people have been seen by succeeding generations. The past is always refracted through the prism of what we now regard as important and what is remembered. Such is our condescension of the past.

Words are inadequate to express my thanks to my wife Margaret for her support across all the years. Research and writing are, by their nature often solitary activities and without her forbearance I could never have begun let alone finished this project.

Richard Brown
Dunstable, 2013

Abbreviations

ADB: *Australian Dictionary of Biography*, 17 Vols. (Melbourne University Press), 1966-.
Clark, *Select Documents* 1: Clark, C. M., *Select Documents in Australian History 1788-1850*, (Angus and Robertson), 1950.
Clark, *Select Documents* 2: Clark, C. M., *Select Documents in Australian History 1851-1900*, (Angus and Robertson), 1955.
Brown, Richard, *Three Rebellions*: Brown, Richard, *Three Rebellions: Canada 1837-1838, South Wales 1839 and Victoria, Australia 1854*, (Clio Publishing), 2010.
Brown, Richard, *Famine, Fenians and Freedom*: Brown, Richard, *Famine, Fenians and Freedom, 1840-1882*, (Clio Publishing), 2011.
Brown, Richard, *Resistance and Rebellion*: Brown, Richard, *Resistance and Rebellion in the British Empire, 1600-1980*, (Clio Publishing), 2013.
HRA, Series I: *Historical Records of Australia*, Series I, Governors' despatches to and from England, 1788-1848, 26 Vols. (Government Printer), 1914-1925, also available as a searchable CD, (Archive CD Books Australia), 2009.
HRA, Series III: *Historical Records of Australia*, Series III, Despatches and papers relating to the settlement of the states, 6 Vols. (Government Printer), 1921-1923, also available as a searchable CD, (Archive CD Books Australia), 2012.
HRA, Resumed Series III: *Historical Records of Australia*, Resumed Series III, 3 Vols. (Melbourne University Press), 1997-
HRA, Series IV: *Historical Records of Australia*, Series IV, Legal papers, 1 Vol. (Government Printer), 1922.
HRNSW: *Historical Records of New South Wales*, 7 Vols. (Charles Potter, Government Printer), 1892-1901, also available as a searchable CD, (Archive CD Books Australia), 2010.
HRNZ: *Historical Records of New Zealand*, 2 Vols. (J. Mackay, Govt. Printer), 1908-1914.
Melbourne: Melbourne, A. C. V., *Early Constitutional Development in Australia*, (University of Queensland Press), 1963.

NSW: New South Wales.
NZ: New Zealand.
Serle: Serle, Geoffrey, *The Golden Age: A history of the colony of Victoria 1851-1861*, (Melbourne University Press), 1963.
Sweetman: Sweetman, Edward, *Constitutional Development of Victoria 1851-6*, (Whitcombe & Tombs Limited), 1920.
VDL: Van Diemen's Land.
WA: Western Australia.

Series Preface

Whilst researching *The Rebellion Trilogy* I drafted a series of papers on different aspects of colonial rule in Australia that contributed, some more than others, to the published works. [1] This was part of the process of drafting the books into a form that combined a narrative of the key events, their causation and consequences with a critique of that narrative through examining linkage and remembrance. This collection of essays brings together some of those jottings, with their inevitable repetition, and considers various aspects of the history of Australia from its beginnings as a penal colony at Botany Bay through the advent of responsible government in the mid-1850s to the 1880s. I have taken the opportunity to rewrite most of the original papers in the light of further research aided especially by the availability of the Trove website at the National Library of Australia.

The two volumes in *Settler Australia, 1780-1880* are published in two formats: two printed volumes and a single Kindle volume that contains both printed volumes. *Settlement, Protest and Control* examines the way in which Australia developed. It is divided into two parts: establishing a colonial state and violence and protest. Uniquely in Britain's growing empire, the colonies in New South Wales and Van Diemen's Land were established as penal settlements. Why the British government decided to settle Australia and the problems encountered by the first three fleets in transporting convicts to the other side of the globe demonstrate the scale of the endeavour. Between 1788 and 1823, the two colonies were ruled by a naval and then military autocracy largely unaccountable for their actions to the growing number of free settlers and emancipated convicts who had completed their sentences and, because of their distance from London, accountable with difficulty to the Colonial Office in London. This was, for instance, evident in the Rum Rebellion in 1808 not a

---

[1] Brown, Richard, *Three Rebellions: Canada 1837-1838, South Wales 1839 and Australia 1854*, (Clio Publishing), 2010, *Famine, Fenians and Freedom, 1840-1882*, (Clio Publishing), 2011, and *Resistance and Rebellion in the British Empire, 1600-1980*, (Clio Publishing), 2013.

populist uprising but a coup within the governing elite for whom Governor William Bligh's 'tyranny' challenged its political and economic hegemony.

By the 1820s, there were calls from the British Parliament for a more responsive system of government for New South Wales and Van Diemen's Land that reflected demands from settlers in Australia. The result was a gradual process of constitutional evolution away from an autocratic system of government towards one that was more responsive to local inhabitants, a process completed in the 1850s with the introduction of responsible government, a devolved system of rule that combined local hegemony over colonial issues within an overarching and developing notion of imperial sovereignty. This process of constitutional change occurred at the same time as the territories of New South Wales were divided and new colonies founded: Western Australia in the late 1820s, South Australia from 1836, belatedly Victoria in 1851 and Queensland in 1859. The ways in which the land was settled concludes the first part of the book.

State violence accompanied the birth of New South Wales and Van Diemen's Land and was a constant presence during the following century. Nowhere was this more evident than in the punishment settlement on Norfolk Island, 'Hell in Paradise' as it was termed by contemporaries, where those already transported were re-transported for further transgressions. So brutish was it that convicts in New South Wales often preferred to be hanged than submit to its regime. Convict society was often volatile and resistance to the arbitrary character of colonial rules was widespread as the attitude of women prisoners amply demonstrates. Rebellion or the threat of rebellion was infrequent although New South Wales experiences a spate of rebellious conspiracies in the first decade of the nineteenth century including the rebellion at Castle Hill in 1804 and rebellion on Norfolk Island was an endemic problem. Those convicted of political offences such as Swing rioters in 1830 and Chartists in the 1830s and 1840s were, from the 1790s through to the end of transportation in 1868, frequently dispatched to the Australian colonies. This was particularly the case with political prisoners from Ireland with Young Irelanders and later Fenians exiled to the colonies to serve their sentences. The violent and militarised character of New South Wales and Van

Diemen's Land was gradually diluted with the establishing of the rule of law and the emergence of colonial policing though this could be as arbitrary and harsh as the use of the military to control the population.

The second volume, *Eureka and Democracy*, is also divided into two parts. The constitutional separation of New South Wales and the Port Phillip District in 1851 and the establishment of Victoria as a separate colony coincided with the discovery of large deposits of gold. Although the established colonial administration in New South Wales coped relatively well with the ensuing influx of immigrants in search of success on the gold diggings, developments in Victoria were less auspicious. Coping with setting up the new colony and the rapid growth in population proved difficult for Charles La Trobe, the colony's Lieutenant-Governor leading to growing protest from diggers who, not without justification, felt oppressed by colonial taxation and the colonial police. With widespread protest in 1851 and 1853, matters came to a head in Ballarat in the final months of 1854 when a combination of colonial mismanagement, locally and in Melbourne, and a burgeoning sense of in justice and tyranny led to the formation of a rebel stockade on the Eureka gold field and its brutal repression by British troops and colonial police. It proved a pyrrhic victory for the authorities that was damned for the heavy-handed nature of its actions during and after the attack on the Stockade and was unable to convict any of those brought to trial for high treason the following year.

How far Eureka was responsible for political change in Victoria in the mid-1850s is debatable. The process of establishing responsible government in the colony took place parallel to the increasing intensity of protest on the goldfields and would have occurred whether there were protests or not. Nonetheless, the 'spirit' of Eureka played an important role in developing a new system of colonial government that was aware of and responsive to populist demands and Eureka was and still is regarded as the midwife of democracy in Australia. It became, though initially its memory was 'whispered', one of the defining events in the formation of Australian nationalism.

The second section of the book contains papers linked broadly to the theme of democracy. They explore the different ways in which working people struggled to define their rights within the framework of changing notions of the colonial state and maintain those rights against assault from those who favoured an anti-democratic state and from immigrant labour. Paradoxically, the Australian state that emerged from the 1870s was both inclusively democratic in character and also exclusively racist and 'white' in its cultural attitudes leading to the espousal of a 'White Australia' policy after Federation in 1901. For most of the nineteenth century, according to Richard White, there was no strong evidence of a distinctively Australian identity: 'Australians saw themselves, and were seen by others, as part of a group of new, transplanted, predominantly Anglo-Saxon emigrant societies'. It is significant that a sense of national distinctiveness only grew stronger towards the end of the century and that this was accompanied by 'a more explicitly racial element', based on being Anglo-Saxon or, as confidence in the new society grew, 'on being the most vigorous branch of Anglo-Saxondom'. [2] White settlers may have been deeply attached to freedom for themselves but they opposed freedom for others. The result was that to be free, individuals needed to be of British or at least European origins. However, these colonial freedoms were not freely given to settlers who had to extract recognition of their rights by persuasion, resistance and even rebellion from metropolitan and colonial authorities that wished to maintain centralised control over colonial activities. [3]

---

[2] White, Richard, *Inventing Australia*, (Allen & Unwin), 1985, p. 47.
[3] McLaren, John, 'The Uses of the Rule of Law in British Colonial Societies in the Nineteenth Century', in Dorsett, Shaunnagh, and Hunter, Ian, (eds.), *Law and Politics in British Colonial Thought: Transpositions of Empire*, (Palgrave Macmillan), 2010, pp. 71-90.

Creating a colonial state

Six years after James Cook landed at Botany Bay in 1770 and gave the territory its English name of 'New South Wales', the American colonies declared their independence and the revolutionary war with Britain began. Access to America for transported convicts ceased and overcrowding in British gaols soon raised official concerns. In 1779, Joseph Banks, the botanist who had travelled with Cook to NSW, suggested Australia as an alternative place for transportation, a proposal repeated four years later by James Matra, who had also sailed on the *Endeavour*. [1] Alongside the opportunity NSW offered as a new home for the American Loyalists who had supported Britain in the War of Independence and who found themselves dispossessed, he raised the potential returns of trade with Asia and the Pacific. Eventually the Government settled (although not without criticism) on Botany Bay as the site for a colony. Secretary of State Lord Sydney chose Captain Arthur Phillip of the Royal Navy to lead the fleet there and to be its first Governor. He was responsible for keeping law and order, entitled to grant land, raise armed forces for defence, discipline convicts and military personnel and issue regulations and orders. As the colony grew, he could raise taxes through customs duties.

The critical question facing those who arrived in Australia in 1788 was how do you establish a society from scratch and how far was it possible to transport political and social structures as well as convicts? What the members of the First Fleet found shocked them. The colony represented an inversion of the accepted order of things. It was to be built by Britain's discards. They seem to have been unprepared for the changed seasons, but creatures like the black swan, both the same as, and yet opposite to, the northern white swan, neatly conformed to some of the early theories about what a world upside down might contain.

---

[1] Frost, Alan, *The Precarious Life of James Mario Matra: Voyager with Cook, American Loyalist: Servant of Empire*, (Miegunyah Press/Melbourne University Press), 1995, and Christopher, Emma, *A Merciless Place: The Fate of Britain's Convicts after the American Revolution*, (Oxford University Press), 2011 pp. 330-332.

Similarly, being dark-skinned unlike the pale Europeans, it was assumed that the indigenous peoples also had the opposite of 'civilised' European values. For them the arrival of an entirely alien culture represented disaster. Transformed from custodians of their ancestral lands, enjoying a rich material and spiritual culture, to dispossessed 'savages', their world was indeed turned upside down. Creatures like the kangaroo and platypus, however, were much more disturbing, hinting at perverted rather than inverted forms of nature. Interestingly, John Hunter attributed these supposed freaks of nature to a 'promiscuous intercourse' between species that served to infect the country and he compared it with the moral contagion represented by the cargo of convicts. [2] Those who planned the colony at Botany Bay paid little attention to the nature of the society they were creating. It was assumed that Britain's social structures and social prejudices would be transposed to NSW as they had been to the American colonies where felons became part of an already established society. This was not the case in NSW where felons or ex-felons were in the majority until the 1820s and where the 'proper' order of society was soon challenged as convicted felons became founding members of a new society. While few became as prosperous as the emancipist merchant Simeon Lord, many former convicts came to hold positions of authority and to enjoy greater prosperity than they could ever have known in Britain. [3]

Many convicts began their servitude during transportation. They entered into a 'repressive penal system' that began with their incarceration in the hulks while waiting transportation. [4] The problem with this journey was that 'no vessel was specially designed and built as a convict ship'. [5] Usually the voyage, during which many convicts died, 'took eight months, six of them at sea and two

---

[2] Bach, John, (ed.), *An Historical Journal, 1787-1792, by John Hunter: An Historical Journal of the Transactions at Port Jackson and Norfolk Island*, (Angus and Robertson), 1968, pp. 47-48.
[3] Hainsworth, D. R., 'Lord, Simeon (1771-1840)', *ADB*, Vol. 2, pp. 128-131.
[4] Connah, Graham, *The Archaeology of Australia's History*, (Cambridge University Press), 1988, p. 50.
[5] Bateson, Charles, *The Convict Ships 1787-1868*, (Brown), 1959, p. 68.

in ports for supplies and repairs'. [6] During the voyage of the Second Fleet, '26% had died, and 488 were landed sick from scurvy, dysentery, and infectious fever' and after landing, 'the total of deaths increased by fifty'. [7] Though this was an extreme example, typically conditions during early voyages were poor. Many of the weak died before they reached the penal settlements. John White saw 'a great number of them lying, some half and others nearly naked, without either a bed or bedding, unable to turn or help themselves'. Often if convicts survived the voyage, 'coming into contact with fresh air, men fainted and died when being taken on shore to the inadequate hospital'. [8]

The 1828 census claimed that 'emigrants were so far a small minority...that New South Wales had fewer than 5,000 people who had come voluntarily in a population of 36,598'.[9] However, within twenty years, this situation dramatically changed and the 1851 census showed that there were 'about 80,000 convicts and former convicts still alive and living in Australia but that they were only about one in five of the white population.' [10] This trend was intensified by the gradual ending of transportation after 1840 and especially by the influx of immigrants in search of gold in the 1850s. Despite the shift from convict to free settlers, around 400 convicts were sent to Australia each year between 1793 and 1810 and more than a thousand a year by 1815. This increased to some 2,600 a year from 1816 to 1825 and nearly 5,000 a year from 1826 to 1835. [11] During the eighty years this policy operated between 150,000 and 160,000 convicts were transported; about sixty per cent were English, thirty-four per cent Irish and five per cent Scots. 60,000 were transported to NSW from 1788 to 1840 and again briefly in 1847, 75,000 to VDL (1803-1853), 1,750 to Victoria (1844-1849) and 10,000 to WA (1850-1868).

---

[6] Inglis, K. S., *The Australian Colonists: An Exploration of Social History 1788-1870*, (Melbourne University Press), 1974, p. 6.
[7] O'Brien, Eris, *The Foundation of Australia: A Study in English Criminal Practice and Penal Colonisation in the Eighteenth Century*, (Sheed and Ward), 1937, rep., (Greenwood Press), 1970, p. 168.
[8] Ibid, O'Brien, Eris, *The Foundation of Australia*, pp. 168-169.
[9] Ibid, Inglis, K. S., *The Australian Colonists*, p. 14.
[10] Ibid, Inglis, K. S., *The Australian Colonists*, p. 15.
[11] Ibid, Inglis, K. S., *The Australian Colonists*, p. 8.

Governor Phillip established a system in which people were employed according to their skills. Educated convicts were given relatively easy administrative work while initially female convicts were assumed to be most valuable as wives and mothers. Although convicts had always been seen as a cheap source of labour from 1810, they were used more widely as a means of advancing and developing economic frontiers in both NSW and VDL. Once the convicts reached Australia, they were assigned to one of two types of services depending on the severity of the crime committed and the skills they had. If convicts survived the journey, they were retained in either 'government service' or 'assigned as labour to a private land owner'. Those in government service either entered a 'labour gang in which a variety of tasks on public works' were completed or were in an 'iron gang which is forced labour while wearing chains fastened to the ankles and waist'. [12] They were housed by the government in camps where accommodation sometime consisted of 'small sheds on wheels in which twenty men slept' that could be 'moved elsewhere when the immediate job was finished'. Both the labour gang and the iron gang were employed in areas known as 'stockades', which were 'surrounded by a high stacked fence' and usually 'deep in the bush and guarded'. [13] The public work achieved by these 'convict gangs' was substantial. These gangs did more than build roads and in the 1840s 'carried away the whole of the top of Pinchgut Island in Sydney Harbour and prepared the site on which Fort Denison was subsequently constructed'.[14]

Convicts assigned to private land holders held different jobs from those in government service. This was expanded in the 1820s and 1830s, the decades when most convicts were sent to the colonies, and became a major source of employment. Many convicts were sent to farms to help landowner cultivate and increase the value of his land. They worked as 'agricultural labourers, they cleared land, constructed bridges, made salt, produced bricks and mined

---

[12] Ibid, Connah, Graham, *The Archaeology of Australia's History*, p. 51.
[13] Ibid, Connah, Graham, *The Archaeology of Australia's History*, p. 55.
[14] Ibid, Connah, Graham, *The Archaeology of Australia's History*, p. 57.

coal'. [15] These convicts often learned a trade that could be useful once they were freed. Convicts assigned to farm labour were not necessarily treated better and worked just as hard as the convicts in governmental servitude.

Much of the operational administration of the penal system was in the hands of the guards. [16] Unfortunately, 'the almost total absence of a properly qualified class of persons to fill the situation of superintendents and overseers of probation gangs' left the colony with many unqualified guards.[17] They came from a 'lower class of society, from the slums of the cities' and often used their position as a way of making money and emigrating to a new society. In many respects, the guards were 'no better and no worse than the men they guarded' and were 'victims among victims' since their lives were also ones of servitude as guards of the convicted. [18] The convicts lived under almost constant 'scrutiny' and often the 'convicts worked and sweated inside as the guards remained outside' watching over them.[19] Exploited, abused and subject to arbitrary injustice, it is hardly surprising that some convicts fought back while others 'bolted' swelling the ranks of the bushrangers.

Governor King (1800-1804) first issued tickets of leave in 1801 to any convicts as a reward for good behaviour and who were able to support themselves to save providing them with food from government stores. Macquarie later ordered that convicts had to serve three years before being eligible and in the early 1820s Governor Brisbane finally established regulations governing tickets of leave. Freedom was usually granted to those who had either good behaviour or completed their sentence. Those who were not eligible for a pardon were issued with a Certificate of Freedom on the completion of their sentence. There were two kinds of pardons that a convict could receive. The first pardon was 'absolute' meaning the sentence was finished and the

---

[15] Ibid, Connah, Graham, *The Archaeology of Australia's History*, p. 51.
[16] See, Robbins, W. M., 'The Supervision of Convict Gangs in New South Wales 1788-1830', *Australian Economic History Review*, Vol. 44, (1), (2004), pp. 79-100.
[17] Brand, Ian, *The Convict Probation System: Van Diemen's Land 1839-1854*, (Blubber Head), 1990, p. 14.
[18] Lagrange, Francis, *Flag on Devil's Island*, (Doubleday), 1961, pp. 174-175.
[19] Ibid, Lagrange, Francis, *Flag on Devil's Island*, p. 191.

convict was free to go. The second was 'conditional pardon' meaning a convict was free on condition that he or she never returned to the British Isles. [20] In *Great Expectations*, Abel Magwitch was granted conditional freedom and knew that his return to London to see Pip would eventually lead to his death. [21]

> I was sentenced for life. It's death to come back. There's been over much coming back of late years, and I should certainly be hanged if took. [22]

This created a distinction within the convict community between those still under sentence and those who had been pardoned who could leave the colony and return to Britain and those who had been pardoned and could not. This created a chasm between the emancipated felon and the free settler in the early and mid-nineteenth century. Then, 'respectable people worried about the future of a community composed so largely of men and women who belonged in it because they had been caught stealing.' The idea behind this belief was the morals or lack of morals of the free convict. This is definitely a legitimate concern and Macquarie declared in 1821:

> New South Wales should be made the home and a happy home to every emancipated convict who deserves it and that once a man is free, his former state should no longer be remembered. [23]

In fact, the word convict was to be 'forbidden from general discourse' as freed convicts did not want to be reminded of their former servitude. [24] In the 1828 census, freed convicts accounted for nearly half of the free population and Australia was in serious need of free immigrants. The imperial government decided in 1831 to stop giving land away to settlers, to sell it at not less the five

---

[20] Ibid, Connah, Graham, *The Archaeology of Australia's History*, p. 51.
[21] Reid, K. M., 'Exile, Empire and the Convict Diaspora: The Return of Magwitch', in Hanne, Michael, (ed.), *Creativity in Exile*, (Rodopi), 2004, pp. 57-70.
[22] Dickens, Charles, *Great Expectations*, (T. B. Peterson), 1861, p. 118
[23] Ibid, Inglis, K. S., *The Australian Colonists*, p. 13.
[24] Ibid, Inglis, K. S., *The Australian Colonists*, p. 14.

shillings an acre and to use the money from land sales to subsidise or 'assist' the fares of some immigrants. [25] This began a process of encouraging settlement that persisted until the 'Ten Pound Poms' from 1945 to 1973 when the cost of assisted passage was increased to £75.

From 1788 until 1823, NSW was a penal colony although free settlers started to arrive in 1793. [26] Law courts may have been established when the colony was founded, but, for thirty-five years successive governors were absolute rulers. A growing number of colonists were unhappy with total control in the hands of one person and urged the British Parliament to allow the colony to establish a legislature. The result was significant territorial and governmental changes: the British government separated VDL followed, four years later in 1829 with the addition of WA; there was a second subdivision of NSW to create South Australia founded in 1836, and, in parallel, the development of the Port Phillip District founded in 1835 though it did not gain separation from NSW until 1851.

The problems of governing NSW and the other emergent colonies can be illustrated by the question of land. From the foundation of the colony in 1788, all lands were vested in the Crown. Prior to 1856, the whole responsibility for government rested with the residing Governor under direction from the British Parliament. In that time, NSW could almost be classed as a department of the Colonial Office in London, with the Colonial Secretary in Sydney holding the position of permanent Under-Secretary and acting the official link between all other officials and the Governor. The Governor was the supreme authority in the colony with autocratic and personal powers though, almost from the outset these were challenged and defined in the courts. All important correspondence that required either decisions or action on the part of the governor was addressed to the Colonial Secretary. Matters of minor importance or mere detail were directed to the relevant offices.

In Australia, both the Imperial Government and the various colonial legislatures tried to direct the pace and character of settlement expansion by various modes of land

---

[25] Ibid, Inglis, K. S., *The Australian Colonists*, p. 16.
[26] Melbourne, pp. 8-46, remains useful on the governance of NSW under autocratic rule.

disposal. [27] According to Jeans, the bureaucratic structure above shows

> ...a basic unit or segment of political organization, stretching from the highest reaches of policy-making to the most subordinate officials who carry out policy by contact with the public. A government may be seen as composed of many such segments, each dealing with its special sphere of administration. Surrounding the components of the segment are external institutions and individuals whose views and needs impinge on the decisions being made at some level within the segment. [28]

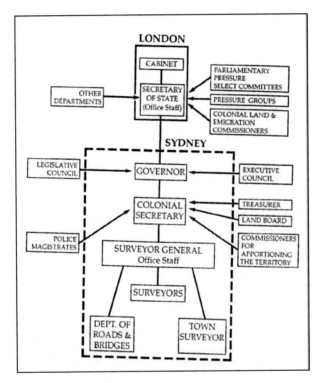

---

[27] Powell, J. M., *The Public Lands of Australia Felix: Settlement and Land Appraisal in Victoria 1834-1891 with Special Reference to the Western Plains*, (Oxford University Press), 1970.

[28] Jeans, D. N., 'The impress of central authority upon the landscape: south-eastern Australia 1788-1850', in Powell J. M., and Williams, M., (eds.), *Australian Space, Australian Time: Geographical Perspectives in Australia, 1788-1914*, (Melbourne: Oxford University Press), 1975, p. 5.

Between 1788 and 1850, public business was not separated into different departments and many branches of the public sector were involved in selling, leasing and granting Crown Land. Much of the work was routine and many tasks were duplicated. Delays stemming from confusion over responsibilities saw land administration fall further and further into arrears. [29] As the colonies expanded, centralised administration under imperial authority became increasingly ineffective and public business became so vast and complex that the Governor and Colonial Secretary could not cope with the demands of the administration. This was particularly evident in Victoria under Sir Charles Hotham in 1854 when his relationship with his Colonial Secretary broke down and he attempted to rule alone. In 1851, the Australian Colonies Government Act passed by the Imperial Parliament and gave authority to the colonial Legislative Councils to prepare democratic constitutions for the colonies but the problems confronting colonial administrators in NSW and the newly established Victoria were compounded by the onset, development and legacies of the Gold Rush that began in 1851. [30]

In 1855 and 1856, by imperial legislation, responsible government was granted to the Australian colonies. That Act vested in the colonial legislature the entire management and control of waste lands belonging to the Crown.[31] The establishment of responsible government marked a significant departure from the previous administrative framework for Crown Land decision-making and policy-making and the outcomes and impacts of Crown Land legislation and policy of this early period in Australian settlement influenced land settlement patterns for many decades after the colonies was granted responsible government.

---

[29] New South Wales Commission of Inquiry into the Surveyor General's Department, *Report from the Commissioners Appointed to Inquire into the Surveyor General's Department, with Minutes of Evidence and Appendix*, (William Hanson, Government Printer), 1855.
[30] Williams, M., 'More and smaller is better: Australian rural settlement 1788-1914', in ibid, Powell J. M., and Williams, M., (eds.), *Australian Space, Australian Time: Geographical Perspectives in Australia, 1788-1914*, pp. 61-103.
[31] For the debate on waste lands see, *Hansard*, House of Commons, Debates, Vol. 138, (1855), cc719-736.

1 Why Botany Bay?

Several misconceptions have arisen about whether the colony of New South Wales was actually established to solve Britain's convict problem in the late eighteenth century leading to a tendentious 'Botany Bay debate'. The history is actually far more complex and the convict problem had been an issue since Tudor times. The transportation of thousands of convicts abroad after 1597 provided a good source of cheap labour in Africa, the Caribbean and India, and from 1666 North America, although the latter destination came to an abrupt end after 1776 with the American War of Independence.[1] It was only then that Australia gained in importance. However, historians have agreed that the decision to transport large numbers of convicts to eastern Australia in the late-eighteenth century was unexpected and sudden.

Why Australia? America was no longer an option. Canada refused to take any more convicts owing to poor previous experiences, although this time the convicts were to be guarded and this might have made a difference. British Honduras was not an option as the settlers preferred coloured slaves to convicted white slaves. The West Indies were not viable as the influential slave traders did not want their profitable slave market, already in decline, to be further weakened by competition from the English gaols. Western Africa already had sufficient cheap labour and so the state could not send its convict labour there. A survey ship was sent to Das Voltas Bay on the south-west coast of Africa in the hope that its strategic position on a major trade

---

[1] Innes, Joanna, 'The role of transportation in seventeenth and eighteenth century English penal practice', in Bridge, Carl, (ed.), *New Perspectives in Australian History*, (Sir Robert Menzies Centre for Australian Studies, Institute of Commonwealth Studies, University of London), 1990, pp. 1-24. Ekirch, A. Roger, *Bound for America: The Transportation of British Convicts to the Colonies, 1718-1775*, (Oxford University Press), 1987, and Morgan, Gwenda, and Rushton, Peter, *Eighteenth-Century Criminal Transportation: The Formation of the Criminal Atlantic*, (Palgrave Macmillan), 2004, provide a detailed account of the operation of the transportation system.

route could be made profitable.[2] However, the investigation found its climate and fertility unsuitable. As Africa and America were inappropriate, the whole of the South-West Pacific was available. New Zealand was disregarded owing to Joseph Banks' dislike of the area. This left the area including Australia. The argument that Australia was chosen as no alternative could be found has been stated by Shaw,[3] David Mackay[4] and Mollie Gillen[5]. They argue that convicts were unwanted and a remote site was advantageous. Gillen has suggested that NSW had always been a back-up plan since 1786. Blainey, by contrast, argues there were closer alternatives, such as the uninhabited islands of the Bermudas or the West Indies and the availability of other lands implies that there was deeper reasoning to the decision.[6]

So what were the real reasons for the British Government's plans to establish a colony there? The traditional view maintains that desperation played a major role in the decision to send convicts to Australia. The mounting numbers of convicts in gaols and hulks was at a dangerous level. Ernest Scott pronounced in 1933:

> It is clear that the only consideration which weighed seriously with the Pitt Government was the immediately pressing and practical one of finding a suitable place for a convict settlement.[7]

---

[2] Christopher, Emma, *A Merciless Place: The Fate of Britain's Convicts after the American Revolution*, (Oxford University Press), 2011, examines the available if abortive alternatives especially in West Africa.
[3] Shaw, Alan, *Convicts and the colonies: a study of penal transportation from Great Britain and Ireland to Australia and other parts of the British Empire*, (Faber), 1966.
[4] Mackay, D., *A Place of Exile: European Settlement of New South Wales*, (Oxford University Press), 1985.
[5] Gillen, Mollie, 'The Botany Bay decision, 1786: convicts not empire', *English Historical Review*, Vol. 97, (1982), pp. 740-766, but see also her *The Search for John Small: First Fleeter*, (Library of Australian History), 1988, and *The Founders of Australia, A Biographical Dictionary of The First Fleet*, (Library of Australian History), 1989.
[6] Blainey, G. C., *The Tyranny of Distance: How Distance Shaped Australia's History*, (Macmillan), 1977, pp. 20-39.
[7] Scott, Ernest, 'British Settlement in Australia, 1783-1806', in Scott, Ernest, (ed.), *Cambridge History of the British Empire:*

Although even in 1933, this view was questionable it quickly established itself as the convenient traditional view repeated on any occasion that Australian colonisation was mentioned. Martin has suggested that the attempted assassination of the King by Margaret Nicholson in August 1786 played a part in hastening the decision. [8] Though this may not have been crucial, the influence of pressures at home cannot be underestimated. There was increasing parliamentary pressure on Pitt's government to find a solution to the convict problem that had been debated on several occasions since 1779. Most historians accept this was critical in forcing a decision; for example, a survey ship was not sent to investigate Botany Bay before settlement as there simply was not enough time. On 18 August 1786, Lord Sydney issued instructions to the Treasury to provide the ships necessary to carrying 750 convicts of Botany Bay. The traditional view in the debate is that Botany Bay was chosen as a 'dumping ground' for convicts and in 1976 Norman Bartlett wrote:

> There is no evidence that either William Pitt or any member of his cabinet thought of Botany Bay as anything more than a convenient place distant enough for the safe disposal of social waste. [9]

This traditional approach is also supported by Atkinson who believes that 'Botany Bay was chosen as a convict settlement not because of, but in spite of the possibility that it might become a trading post.' [10]

Yet when the decision to transport convicts to Botany Bay was first announced in late 1786, London newspapers identified James Matra and Sir Joseph Banks as the authors of the plan adopted by the government.

---

volume VII (part I) Australia, (Cambridge University Press), 1933, reprinted with a new introduction, 1988, p. 58.

[8] Martin, Ged, 'The founding of New South Wales', in Statham, P., (ed.), *The Origins of Australia's Capital Cities*, (Cambridge University Press), 1988, pp. 37-51.

[9] Bartlett, Norman, *1776-1976: Australia and America through 200 years*, (Ure Smith), 1976, p. 2.

[10] Atkinson, Alan, 'A Counter-Riposte' in Martin, Ged, (ed.), *The Founding of Australia: The Argument about Australia's Origins*, (Hale and Iremonger), 1978, pp. 265-269.

Mr. Matra, an Officer of the Treasury, who, sailing with Capt. Cook, had an opportunity of visiting Botany Bay, is the Gentleman who suggested the plan to Government of transporting convicts to that island. [11]

Although David Mackay [12] rejected the notion that Banks and Matra were directly consulted by the government and that it is misleading to draw conclusions about government intentions from the private plans of these private individuals, Banks' role in the Botany Bay scheme went back to March 1779 when he proposed the idea to a House of Commons Select Committee. [13] The idea of establishing a colony at Botany Bay was extended in the 'Matra proposal' in August 1783, even before the end of the War of Independence between America and England. [14] James Matra who travelled with Cook to the South Seas in 1770, spoke of NSW as having good soil, advantages of flax cultivation, the possibility of trade with China, the availability of timber for ships masts and had Sir Joseph Banks' support. [15] His idea was that the new colony could be used by 'those Americans who had remained loyal to Britain in the War of Independence' such as himself; this idea was, however, rejected. Initially Matra did not mention convicts, but later amended his proposal to 'include transportees among the settlers but as cultivators in their own right rather than as forced labour' after an interview with the Home Secretary Lord Sydney who had already made plans to settle loyalists in Canada. The Cabinet memorandum of December 1784 shows that Matra's plan formed the basis

---

[11] *London Chronicle*, 12 October 1786.
[12] Ibid, Mackay, David, *A Place of Exile: European Settlement of New South Wales*, p. 37.
[13] Banks gave evidence to the Bunbury Committee on 10 April 1779 and proposed Botany Bay as a possible solution to the convict problem. His description of Botany Bay as 'sufficient to support a very large number of people' made no reference to his observations in 1770 about its sandy soil. Matra also exaggerated the fertility of Botany Bay's soil.
[14] Matra, James Mario, 'Proposal for establishing a Settlement in New South Wales', 23 August 1783, *HRNSW*, Vol. 1, (2), pp. 1-8, in ibid, Martin, Ged, (ed.), *The Founding of Australia: The Argument about Australia's Origins*, pp. 9-15.
[15] Tink, Andrew, 'The Role of Parliamentary Committee Witnesses in the Foundation of Australia', *Australasian Parliamentary Review*, Vol. 20, (2), (2005), pp. 33-38, at pp. 34-36.

for the scheme of colonisation. The London newspapers announced in November 1784:

> A plan has been presented to the [Prime] Minister, and is now before the Cabinet, for instituting a new colony in New Holland. In this vast tract of land....every sort of produce and improvement of which the various soils of the earth are capable, may be expected.

An abridged version of Matra's proposal was published in *The General Advertiser* in October 1786. These and many other articles in the English press discussing the forthcoming colonisation were promptly republished in other European countries and in America.

Did the British government consider the type of labour force that would be required to establish a colony or was Botany Bay just seen as a solution to the ever growing number of convict hulks along the River Thames? Soon after arriving in 1788, Governor Phillip requested 'carpenters, masons, bricklayers' to help with the setting up of the colony along with many tools of the trades. Yet the proposal for the establishment of the new colony in the 'Heads of a Plan' addressed the effective disposing of the convicts to the new colony, along with the cultivation of flax, required stores and provisions, clothing for convicts, how the objective of the convict colony overrides the costs involved, naval staff and such. [16]

However, the tools sent with the First Fleet were of poor standard, with only twelve carpenters among the initial convicts. Women's clothing was also of poor quality and quantity plus aged and ailing convicts were sent. Poor planning does not support the belief of the non-traditional view of the reasons behind the decision to colonise Botany Bay: The 'great southern port' and the 'development of a flax industry for naval use' suggested by revisionist historians as the reason for the settlement rather than for the disposal of unwanted convicts seem to have been somewhat negated by the account of inadequate supplies of even the most elementary equipment. The traditionalist may well ask that if Botany Bay was planned to be the 'great southern port' why then did free settlers not arrive until

---

[16] 'Heads of a Plan', *HRNSW*, Vol. 1, (2), pp. 17-20, in ibid, Martin, Ged, (ed.), *The Founding of Australia: The Argument about Australia's Origins*, pp. 26-29.

1793 on the *Bellona*, five years after the arrival of the First Fleet. Governor Phillip was given instruction to cultivate flax

> And as it has been humbly represented to us that advantages may be derived from the flax-plant which is found in the islands not far distant from the intended settlement...excellence of a variety of maritime purposes...an article of export...that you do send home...samples of this article...instruct you further upon this subject. [17]

Norfolk Island, a thousand miles east of Botany Bay, offered the prospect of both a timber and flax industry. These orders form part of the non-traditionalist justification for their point of view. Traditionalist historians feel the possibility of the flax industry at Botany Bay was just an additional benefit to England when options for the convicts were being decided. Yet contracted tradesmen were still being sent to NSW in 1792 to help with the colony at Norfolk Island and others. Sparse flax producing equipment was sent out with the First Fleet 'which hardly indicates strong encouragement for any flax enterprise or faith in the success of the new venture'. [18]

Traditionalists stand firm to the opinion that Botany Bay was only colonised to 'rid the nation's (Britain) prisons and hulks of convicts'. Frost believes the opposite is true approaching the Botany Bay debate from a broader perspective and arguing that there were strategic considerations in Pitt's Cabinet decision in 1784 to set up the colony; naval trade, supply of flax and naval timber from Norfolk Island and the fact the use of Britain's excess convict labour might serve these purposes. [19] Botany Bay had already been surveyed by Cook in 1770 with its

---

[17] Phillip's Instructions, 25 April 1787, *HRNSW*, Vol. 1, (2), p. 89.
[18] Abbott, G. J., 'Staple theory and Australian economic growth', *Business Archives and History*, Vol. 5, (1965), pp. 142-154 and 'The Botany Bay decision', *Journal of Australian Studies*, Vol. 16, (1985), pp. 21-41, are particularly useful on this issue.
[19] Frost, A., *Convicts and Empire: A Naval Question 1776-1811*, (Oxford University Press), 1980, but see also his 'The Decision to Colonise New South Wales', Mulvaney, D., and White, Peter, (eds.), *Australians to 1788*, (Fairfax, Syme & Weldon Associates), 1987, *Botany Bay Mirages: Illusions of Australia's Convict Beginning*, (Melbourne University Press), 1994, and his synoptic *Botany Bay: The Real Story*, (Black Inc.), 2011.

supposed ability to shelter a fleet of ships. By colonising NSW, Britain would protect Cook's 'right of possession' over Botany Bay from the French and Dutch, thus giving them more positional power over the seas and any possible trade.

The loss of the American colonies came as a great shock, especially to George III who had never taken the threat seriously. In order to re-establish itself as a great power, Britain needed to consolidate its empire and the acquisition of a new colony could do this. In the 1770s, France, keen on becoming a world power, allied itself with every other major nation in Europe, including Russia, against Britain. The threat to Britain and its empire, particularly to its colonies in the Far East and India, forced the government to consider options that would allow Britain to maintain its position and continue to compete on the world stage. A strategic location needed to be secured from that could support its empire from French invasion. A safe harbour was also needed for the British fleet in the Pacific Ocean and Indian Ocean, from where, at short notice, supplies of food and other materials to its colonies could be obtained cheaply. In addition, plantations were needed to grow hemp to supply rope to the Navy and a new source of wood to counteract the effects of depleted English supplies, primarily for naval mast and spar repairs. The strategic argument is perhaps supported by the choice of Phillip as the first governor and Frost points out that both Phillip and his two successors were naval officers.

In 1952, Ken Dallas suggested that Britain wanted to establish a trading post to spearhead British penetration of the Pacific and to service an alternative sea route to China.[20] In his subsequent book, he maintained that it was the fur trade of the north Pacific, trade opportunities with China and South America and the development of sealing and whaling in the Pacific that combined to make British settlement of Australia a viable economic project. There is evidence to support his case: demand for whale and seal oil was in big demand in Britain and many of the shops from

---

[20] Dallas, K. M., 'The First Settlement in Australia; considered in relation to sea-power in world politics', *Papers and Proceedings of the Tasmanian Historical Research Association*, number 3 (1952), pp. 1-12, reprinted in ibid, Martin, Ged, (ed.), *The Founding of Australia: The Argument about Australia's Origins*, pp. 39-49. His ideas were extended in *Trading Posts or Penal Colonies*, (Richmond and Son), 1969.

the Second Fleet were converted whalers that were reconverted to their original use after the voyage. This has been criticised, but the work of Margaret Stevens [21] and H. T. Fry [22] indicated that the British were concerned over the security of trade routes to China and that Pitt's policies in the 1780s were dictated primarily by commercial considerations. David Mackay disputes this arguing that the First Fleet was not sufficiently equipped to provide the protection and manpower necessary to defend the strategic position of Botany Bay. [23] Mackay has also argued against the strategic position of Botany Bay in relationship to naval trade. Like many, he feels that the establishment of the colony was rushed and poorly done and 'crisis orientated' not a good start if the motives were really for naval trade and timber supply. After viewing many of what seems to be a circle of comments and opinions that formed the Botany Bay debate, he then accused the non-traditionalists of: 'Distorting our records of the past, and sought to create a myth of a better national origin.' They have also overestimated the capacity of governments in the late-eighteenth century. Mackay stills acknowledges that regardless of the 'shoddy' way in which Botany Bay was set up that 'from such inauspicious beginnings Australia grew to maturity and nationhood'.

Geoffrey Blainey shared Dallas' belief that there was a positive reason for the choice of colony. He emphasised Lord Sydney's announcement that the choice of colony was to be 'reciprocally beneficial'. This is the only reason given in official documents to explain why such a remote land was chosen. This dearth of official information has greatly fuelled the debate surrounding the Botany Bay decision. He reported that an export trade was to be started in flax, hemp, and in wood for mainmasts. This would strengthen

---

[21] Stevens, M., *Trade, Tactics and Territory: Britain in the Pacific 1783-1823*, (Manchester University Press), 1983.
[22] Fry, H. T., 'Captain James Cook: the historical perspective', in *The significance of Cook's 'Endeavour' voyage: Three Bicentennial Lectures*, (James Cook University of North Queensland), 1970, pp. 1-23, and "Cathay And The Way Thither': The Background To Botany Bay', in ibid, Martin, Ged, (ed.), *The Founding of Australia: The Argument about Australia's Origins*, pp. 136-149.
[23] Ibid, Mackay, David, *A Place of Exile: European Settlement of New South Wales*.

Britain's naval power in the event of a Baltic blockade preventing England getting flax from its usual supply in Russia. Blainey even suggested that the convicts were a convenient smokescreen for gaining strategic materials. The validity of sources used to formulate this hypothesis has been questioned. It has led to Alan Frost's modified theory[24] that the British sought supplies for their ships in eastern waters that needed to refit without sailing home if they were to defend British lands in India against the French. Another commercial advantage was that the empty convict ships could carry cargoes of tea back, although whether this was realised before the decision-making or not has been disputed. However, during the debates in the 1960s, the fact that NSW was almost entirely a convict settlement tended to be overlooked. Both the 'flax and timber' theorists and the 'China route' party have had to admit that the early years of the NSW colony did not triumphantly vindicate their arguments.

In reality, it is likely that there was a jumble of motives. Transportation resolved the convict problem by expelling them from England. It helped the whaling industry that needed a secure base in the Pacific and secured a route for those who wanted to expand trade with China. It limited the territorial ambitions of the French and the claims of the Spanish and Dutch to the continent. It helped repair the damage done to British imperial prestige by the debacle in America. Above all, it was economical since convict labour was expected to become self-funding after initial financial help from the Exchequer. For British politicians, colonising Australia appears to have satisfied many of the different interests that were clamouring for action.

---

[24] Frost, A., 'Botany Bay: An Imperial Venture of the 1780s', *English Historical Review*, Vol. 100, (1985), pp. 309-330.

2 Three Fleets

The First Fleet consisted of six convict ships (*Alexander, Charlotte, Lady Penrhyn, Friendship, Prince of Wales* and *Scarborough*), three food and supply transports (*Fishburn, Borrowdale* and *Golden Grove*) and two Royal Navy escorts (*HMS Sirius* and *HMS Supply*). [1] This was to be a public-private partnership with the government providing the warships, private contractors the convict vessels and the East India Company the three supply transports that would offset some of the costs by sailing on to China to collect teas for the return journey. Arthur Phillip had been central to the planning of the voyage since he was given his first Commission in October 1786 making heavy and persistent demands on the Treasury, Admiralty and Home Office especially over security on the convict ships and better medical supplies. Central to his success was the unequivocal support he received from Lord Sydney.

---

[1] On the First Fleet, see ibid, Gillen, Mollie, *The Founders of Australia: A Biographical Dictionary of the First Fleet*, Frost, Alan, *The First Fleet: The Real Story*, 2nd ed., (Black Inc.), 2012, and ibid, Bateson, Charles, *The Convict Ships 1787-1868*, pp. 94-119. Among the more important accounts published by officers of the First Fleet are Phillip, Arthur, *The voyage of Governor Phillip to Botany Bay: with an account of the establishment of the colonies of Port Jackson & Norfolk Island*, (John Stockdale), 1790, White, John, *Journal of a voyage to New South Wales with sixty-five plates of nondescript animals, birds, lizards, serpents, curious cones of trees and other natural productions*, (J. Debrett), 1790, Tench, Watkin, *A Narrative of the Expedition to Botany Bay: With an Account of New South Wales, Its Productions, Inhabitants, &c. To which is Subjoined, a List of the Civil and Military Establishments at Port Jackson*, (printed for Messrs. H. Chamberlaine, W. Wilson, L. White, P. Byrne, A. Gruebier, Jones, and B. Dornin), 1789, ibid, Hunter, John, *An historical journal of events at Sydney and at sea, 1787-1792*, London, 1793, and Collins, David, *An account of the English colony in New South Wales from its first settlement in January 1788, to August 1801: with remarks on the dispositions, customs, manners, &c., of the native inhabitants of that country*, (T. Cadell and W. Davies), 1798. See also, Irvine, Nance, (ed.), *The Sirius Letters: The Complete Letters of Newton Fowell, midshipman and Lieutenant aboard the Sirius, Flagship of the First Fleet on its voyage to New South Wales*, (Fairfax Library), 1988.

Phillip first attempted to sail on 10 May 1787 but was prevented by the refusal of sailors on the transport *Fishburn* who refused to unmoor the ship until they received 'three guineas apiece'. Once this was resolved, the Fleet, consisting of 11 ships and 1486 convicts, marines and sailors, finally left England on 13 May. Apart from a failed convict plan to take over the *Scarborough* just over a week after it sailed, the voyage proceeded without major interruptions. The first leg of the voyage from Portsmouth to Rio de Janeiro, a distance of 6,100 miles, took three months. Stopping at Tenerife on 3 June[2], the Fleet reached Rio de Janeiro on 5 August and remained there until 3 September. [3] Phillip, who had served in the Portuguese navy, knew the Viceroy of Brazil and this was instrumental in establishing Rio until the opening of the Suez Canal in 1869 as a critical staging post for future voyages out to Botany Bay via the Cape of Good Hope and back to London via Cape Horn.

Phillip then took advantage of the westerly winds for the second leg of the voyage to Cape Town, a distance of 3,300 miles, and where he arrived in mid-October.[4] Food supplies were replenished and the Fleet was stocked up on plants, seeds and livestock for its arrival in Australia. The final leg of the voyage, some 6,500 miles through parts of the treacherous Southern Ocean previously unexplored, took a further three months. Assisted by the gales of the latitudes below the fortieth parallel, the heavily-laden transports surged through the violent seas vindicating Phillip's decision to split the Fleet at Cape Town to allow the faster transports to establish an advance camp at Botany Bay. A freak storm struck as they began to head north around VDL, damaging the sails and masts of some of the ships. In November, Phillip transferred to *Supply*. With *Alexander*, *Friendship* and *Scarborough*, the fastest ships in the Fleet and carrying most of the male convicts, *Supply* hastened ahead to prepare for the arrival of the rest. Phillip intended to select a suitable location, find good water, clear

---

[2] Phillip to Lord Sydney, 5 June 1787, Phillip to Under Secretary Evan Nepean, 5 June 1787, *HRNSW*, Vol. 1, (2), pp. 106-108.
[3] Phillip to Lord Sydney, 2 September 1787, Phillip to Under Secretary Evan Nepean, 2 September 1787, *HRNSW*, Vol. 1, (2), pp. 109-117.
[4] Phillip to Lord Sydney, 10 November 1787, *HRNSW*, Vol. 1, (2), pp. 118-119.

the ground and perhaps to build some huts and other structures before the other ships arrived.5 However, the *Supply* reached Botany Bay on 18 January 1788 only hours before the rest of the Fleet, so no preparatory work was possible. The three fastest transports in the advance group arrived on 19 January; slower ships, including the *Sirius* arrived the following day. Eleven vessels carrying over 1,400 people and stores had travelled more than 15,000 miles in 252 days without losing a ship. Forty-eight people had died on the journey, a death rate of just over three per cent. Given the rigours of the voyage, the navigational problems, the poor condition and sea-faring inexperience of the convicts, the primitive medical knowledge, the lack of precautions against scurvy, the crammed and fetid conditions of the ships, poor planning and inadequate equipment, this was a remarkable achievement.

During the voyage there were seven births, while 69 people either died or were discharged or deserted (61 males and 8 females). As no complete crew musters have survived for the six convict transports and three supply ships, there may have been as many as 110 more seamen. The number of people directly associated with the First Fleet will probably never be exactly established and all accounts of the event vary slightly. Mollie Gillen gives the following statistics.[6]

	Embarked at Portsmouth	Landed at Port Jackson
Officials and passengers	15	14
Ships' crews	324	269
Marines	247	245
Marines' wives and children	46	54
Convicts (men)	579	543
Convicts (women)	193	189
Convicts' children	14	18
Total	1403	1332

It was soon realised that Botany Bay did not live up to the glowing account that Captain James Cook had given in 1770 or the later embellishments of Sir Joseph Banks. The bay was open and unprotected, fresh water was scarce and

---

[5] Phillip to Lord Sydney, 15 May 1788, *HRNSW*, Vol. 1, (2), pp. 121-136 considers the first three months at Sydney Cove.
[6] Ibid, Gillen, Mollie, *The Founders of Australia: A Biographical Dictionary of the First Fleet*, p. 445.

Phillip considered the sandy soil around Botany Bay was poor for growing crop. The area was studded with enormously strong trees. When the convicts tried to cut them down, their tools broke and the tree trunks had to be blasted out of the ground with gunpowder.[7] On 21 January, Phillip and a party that included John Hunter left Botany Bay in three small boats to explore other bays to the North. Phillip discovered that Port Jackson, immediately to the North, was an excellent site for a colony with sheltered anchorages, fresh water and fertile soil. Cook had seen and named the harbour, but had not explored it. Phillip's impressions of the harbour were recorded in a letter he sent to England later; 'the finest harbour in the world, in which a thousand sail of the line may ride in the most perfect security...'[8] The party returned on 23 January and was startled when two French ships, a scientific expedition led by Jean-François de La Pérouse came into sight and entered Botany Bay.[9] The French remained until 10 March and had expected to find a thriving colony where they could repair ships and restock supplies, not a newly arrived fleet of convicts worse off than themselves.

On 26 January 1788, the fleet weighed anchor and by evening had entered Port Jackson. The site selected for the anchorage had deep water close to the shore, was sheltered and had a small stream flowing into it. Phillip named it Sydney Cove, after Lord Sydney the Home Secretary. The female convicts remained on board ship while most of the 560 male convicts and 210 marines cleared the ground and built primitive shelters. However, when the women were landed on 6 February, briefly all semblance of order dissolved in a night of drunkenness and indiscriminate sex. The primitive huts built for the officers and officials quickly collapsed in rainstorms. The marines had a habit of getting drunk and not guarding the convicts properly and their commander, Major Robert Ross was arrogant and lazy and this caused some difficulties for Phillip.[10] Crucially, Phillip

---

[7] *HRNSW*, Vol. 1, (2), pp. 121-122, 348 gives Phillip's assessment of Botany Bay and his reasons for choosing Sydney Cove.
[8] *HRNSW*, Vol. 1, (2), pp. 67-70.
[9] Dyer, Colin, *The French Explorers and Sydney*, (University of Queensland Press), 2009, draws on French observations of the British convict settlement at Sydney Cove.
[10] Moore, John, *The First Fleet marines, 1788-1792*, (University of Queensland Press), 1987. See also, Macmillan, David S., 'Ross,

worried that his fledgling colony was exposed to attack from the local indigenous people, the Eora, who seemed curious but suspicious of the newcomers or foreign powers.

It was to be almost two and a half years before other ships arrived with their cargo of new convicts and provisions. From the start the settlement was overwhelmed with problems. Very few convicts knew how to farm and the soil around Sydney Cove was poor. Instead of Cook's lush pastures, well watered and fertile ground, suitable for growing all types of foods and providing grazing for cattle, they found a hot, dry, unfertile land unsuitable for the small farming necessary to make the settlement self-sufficient. Everyone, from the convicts to Captain Phillip, was on rationed food. Shelter was also a problem. They had very little building material and the government had provided only a very limited supply of poor quality tools. [11] Extra clothing had been forgotten and, by the time the Second Fleet arrived, convicts and marines alike were dressed in patched and threadbare clothing. [12] By July 1788, all the ships except the *Sirius* and *Supply* had left and the settlement was isolated.

On 2 October, John Hunter in the *Sirius* was despatched to Cape Town to purchase provisions.[13] Until her return on 2 May 1789 with barely enough flour to supply the colony for four months, rations were cut back and this reduced work on farming and building. In early 1788, the *Supply* had taken a small contingent of convicts and marines led by Second Lieutenant Philip Gidley King, Phillip's protégé, to Norfolk Island to set up another penal colony. The land proved more fertile than Sydney Cove and the timber of better quality, but the rocky cliffs surrounding the island meant that it could not be loaded on the ship for transport to Sydney Cove. The *Supply* brought a few green turtles back on its voyages from Norfolk Island that helped to supplement the food in the colony.[14] For Phillip survival

---

Robert (1740?-1794)', *ADB*, Vol. 2, pp. 397-398. Tensions between Phillip and Ross were evident from the founding of the settlement.
[11] *HRNSW*, Vol. 2, p. 388 lists the articles sent with the First Fleet
[12] Phillip to Evan Nepean, 5 July 1788, Phillip to Lord Sydney, 5 July 1788, *HRNSW*, Vol. 1, (2), pp. 142-144, 145-151.
[13] Phillip to Lord Sydney, 30 October 1788, *HRNSW*, Vol. 1, (2), pp. 207-209.
[14] Phillip to Lord Sydney, 28 September 1788, *HRNSW*, Vol. 1, (2), pp. 185-193.

and exploration were inextricably linked and journeys to the west of Sydney Cove resulted in the location of better land on the Parramatta River and exploration of the Hawkesbury River as far upstream as Richmond Hill. A settlement, called Rose Hill was developed on the Parramatta and agriculture, although on a small scale at first, was eventually successful.[15] In an attempt to deal with the food crisis, Phillip in 1789 granted James Ruse, a convict the land of Experiment Farm at Parramatta on the condition that he developed a viable agriculture and became the first person to grow grain successfully in Australia.[16] Lack of transport initially meant that crops, when harvested, could not be readily available for Sydney though the launching of a locally built vessel on 5 October 1789 made a regular service between Sydney and Rose Hill possible. [17] By December 1789, the optimism engendered by successful and economically beneficial exploration came to an end when Lieutenant Dawes reported that the Blue Mountains seemed impassable. Despite the problems of surviving in these conditions in early 1790 Phillip could report than only 73 of those who arrived on the First Fleet had died while 87 had since been born.

In February 1790, the *Sirius* was ordered to proceed to China to purchase further supplies. This was delayed as she and the *Supply* were needed to take more convicts and marines to Norfolk Island in an attempt to reduce pressure on the dwindling supplies in Sydney. On 19 February the *Sirius* ran aground and was wrecked off Norfolk Island

---

[15] On the early development of Rose Hill see, *HRNSW*, Vol. 1, (2), pp. 198, 209-217.
[16] An account of Ruse's methods is given in Tench, Watkin, *A Complete Account of the Settlement at Port Jackson*, (Nicol and Sewell), 1793, pp. 80-81. See also, Fitzhardinge, L.F., 'Tench, Watkin (1758?-1833)', *ADB*, Vol. 2, pp. 506-507 and Wood, G. A., 'Lieutenant William Dawes and Captain Watkin Tench', *Journal and Proceedings*, (Royal Australian Historical Society), Vol. 10, (1), (1924), pp. 1-24.
[17] The problem of the lack of artisans and farmers identified by Phillip was quickly acknowledged in London and 'it is advisable that twenty-five of those confined in the hulks...who are likely to be the most useful should be sent out in the ship [*Lady Juliana*] intended to convey provisions and stores': see Lord Sydney to the Lords of the Admiralty, 29 April 1789, *HRNSW*, Vol. 1, (2), pp. 230-231.

leaving the colony with just one ship.[18] The *Supply* returned in April and on 17 April left to sail to Batavia to get supplies as the situation was becoming desperate with only three months' supply left of some foods.[19] On 3 June, the *Lady Juliana*,[20] a transport with 222 female convicts arrived at Sydney Cove followed on 20 June by the *Justinian* with provisions for the colony. Rations were immediately increased and, with the arrival of further ships carrying convicts, the old labour hours were restored. New buildings were planned and large areas of land near Rose Hill were cleared for cultivation. In October 1790, the *Supply* returned safely from its voyage to Batavia, and eight weeks later, a Dutch ship, the *Waaksamheyd*, which Lieutenant Ball had hired, arrived with a full cargo of rice flour and salted meat. It turned out though, that much of the food was of such poor quality, as to be inedible, and after only a few months, the colony was once again on the verge of starvation.

In his first despatches to Lord Sydney, which he did not receive until late March 1789, Phillip asked that plans to transport further large numbers of convicts should be suspended until the colony was on a more stable footing. Sydney agreed but, after he retired on 4 June, Lord Grenville his successor seized on Phillip's description of the fertility of Norfolk Island to justify sending a further 1,000 convicts 'with the least expense to the public'. Unlike the First Fleet, where great efforts were taken to ensure the health of the convicts, the Second Fleet[21] was contracted to the slave-trading firm Camden, Calvert & King who

---

[18] Captain John Hunter had expressed concerns over the soundness of the ship the previous year especially 'that the copper has not been taken off her bottom...between eight and nine years': Hunter to Secretary Stephens, 18 February 1789, *HRNSW*, Vol. 1, (2), p. 227. See also, Ross to Phillip, 22 March 1790 and Phillip to Lord Sydney, 11 April 1790, *HRNSW*, Vol. 1, (2), pp. 319-321, 326-327, Harris to Clayton, *HRNSW*, Vol. 1, (2), pp. 340-342 on the loss of the ship and Lieutenant Fowell to his father, *HRNSW*, Vol. 1, (2), 31 July 1790, pp. 373-386.
[19] Phillip to Evan Nepean, 15 April 1790, 16 April 1790, *HRNSW*, Vol. 1, (2), pp. 330-331.
[20] Phillip to Evan Nepean, 17 June 1790, *HRNSW*, Vol. 1, (2), pp. 346-351.
[21] William Grenville to Phillip, 24 December 1789, *HRNSW*, Vol. 1, (2), pp. 284-286 informed Phillip of the new batch of convicts.

undertook to transport, clothe and feed the convicts for a flat fee of £17 7s 6d per head, [22] half the price changed by contractors in 1787, whether they landed alive or not.[23] Unlike the slave trade where deaths in transit reduced profits, the contractors had little incentive to worry about conditions. Upon arrival the sickly convicts were a drain on the already struggling colony. The only agents of the Crown in the crew were the naval agent, Lieutenant John Shapcote, who died on the voyage and Captain William Hill, commander of the NSW Corps, all other crew were supplied by the firm. Hill afterwards wrote a strong criticism of the ships' masters stating that

> ...the more they can withhold from the unhappy wretches the more provisions they have to dispose of at a foreign market, and the earlier in the voyage they die, the longer they can draw the deceased's allowance to themselves.[24]

The fleet was comprised of six ships, one Royal Navy escort, four convict ships and a supply ship. The *Lady Juliana* sailed on 29 July 1789 arriving at Port Jackson after a voyage lasting 309 days on 3 June 1790 before the other convict ships and is not always counted as a member of the Second Fleet.[25] The store ship *Justinian* did not sail with the convict ships on 19 January 1790 (it left the following day)

---

[22] While the contract for the First Fleet had been a generous £54,000 for seven ships carrying a thousand convicts and marines, Camden, Calvert & King were paid £22,370 for four ships. Hill argued that the appalling conditions were a consequence of the contract with slaver-traders.

[23] Flynn, Michael, *The Second Fleet: Britain's Grim Convict Armada of 1790*, (Library of Australian History), 1993, ibid, Bateson, Charles, *The Convict Ships 1787-1868*, pp. 120-131.

[24] Captain Hill to Wathen, 26 July 1790, *HRNSW*, Vol. 1, (2), p. 367. The recipient of the letter was the abolitionist William Wilberforce. The anguished nature of the complete letter suggests that he tried but failed to alleviate the suffering of the convicts though it was perhaps Hill's intervention that resulted in his ship, the *Surprize* losing only 14 per cent of its cargo while the *Neptune* and *Scarborough* lost twice as many. See also, the extract from a letter, Rev R. Johnson to Mr Thornton, *HRNSW*, Vol. 1, (2), pp. 386-389.

[25] On the *Lady Juliana* see, Rees, Siân, *The Floating Brothel: the extraordinary true story of an eighteenth-century ship and its cargo of female convicts*, (Hodder), 2001.

and arrived before them on 20 June 1790. *HMS Guardian* set out before the convict ships on 12 September 1789 but struck ice after leaving the Cape of Good Hope. [26] The *Surprize*, *Neptune* and *Scarborough* had previously been involved in transporting slaves to North America and left England on 19 January 1790, with 1,006 convicts (928 male and 78 female) on board. They made only one stop on the way, at the Cape of Good Hope. Here 20 male convicts, survivors from *Guardian*, were taken on board. The three vessels made a faster trip than the First Fleet, arriving at Port Jackson in the last week of June 1790, three weeks after *Lady Juliana* and a week after the *Justinian*.

The voyage was relatively fast, but the mortality rate was the highest in the history of transportation to Australia. Among those who sailed on the Second Fleet were D'Arcy Wentworth and his convict mistress Catherine Crowley, on *Neptune* and John Macarthur, then a young lieutenant in the NSW Corps and his wife Elizabeth, on *Scarborough*. Of the 1,026 convicts who embarked, over a quarter, 267 (256 men and 11 women), died during the voyage. On *Neptune* they were deliberately starved, kept heavily ironed and frequently refused access to the deck. Scurvy could not be checked. On *Scarborough*, rations were not deliberately withheld, but a reported mutiny attempt led to the convicts being closely confined below decks. On arrival at Port Jackson, half naked convicts were lying without bedding, too ill to move. Those unable to walk were slung over the side. At least 488 sick were landed (47 per cent of those embarked). The remainder were described as 'lean and emaciated' and exhibiting 'more horrid spectacles than had ever been witnessed in this country'. [27] Phillip took immediate steps to send the healthiest arrivals to the fertile settlements at Parramatta and Norfolk Island and wrote to Grenville requesting settler farmers rather than further

---

[26] Commanded by Lieutenant Edward Riou, it struck an iceberg off the African coast. Riou, after parting with as many of his men as the boats would hold, not only successfully navigated his half-sinking ship 400 miles to the Cape of Good Hope but kept order amongst the panic-stricken convicts, an achievement that has few parallels in naval history. See, Riou to Stephens, 20 May 1790, *HRNSW*, Vol. 1, (2), pp. 336-340.

[27] Phillip's initial response can be found in Phillip to Grenville, 13 July 1790, *HRNSW*, Vol. 1, (2), pp. 354-356.

convicts until the colony was self-supporting. [28] Grenville ignored this was planned a Third Fleet to carry 2,000 more convicts.

When news of the horrors of the Second Fleet reached England, both public and official opinion was shocked. An enquiry was held but no attempt was made to arrest Donald Traill, master of *Neptune* and described as a demented sadist or bring a public prosecution against him, the other masters, or the firm of contractors. They had already been contracted by the government to prepare the Third Fleet for sailing to Port Jackson in 1791. Traill, along with his Chief Mate William Ellerington, were privately prosecuted for the murder of an un-named convict and also a seaman named Andrew Anderson and a cook named John Joseph. But, after a trial lasting three hours before Sir James Marriott in the Admiralty Court, the jury acquitted both men on all charges 'without troubling the Judge to sum up the evidence.'[29]

The Third Fleet consisted of 11 ships that set sail from United Kingdom in February, March and April 1791 bound for the Sydney penal settlement, with over 2,000 convicts.[30] The first ship to arrive in Sydney was the *Mary Ann* with its cargo of 169 female convicts and provisions on the 9 July 1791. The *Mary Ann* could only state that more ships were expected to be sent. The *Mary Ann* had sailed on her own to Sydney Cove, and there is some argument about whether she was the last ship of the Second Fleet, or the first ship of the Third Fleet. The ships that make up each Fleet, however, are decided from the viewpoint of the settlers in Sydney Cove. For them the second set of ships arrived in 1790 (June), and the third set of ships arrived in 1791 (July-October). The *Mary Ann* was a 1791 arrival. The next ship to arrive just over 3 weeks later on 1 August 1791 was the *Matilda*. With the *Matilda* came news that there were another nine ships making their way for Sydney, and which

---

[28] *HRNSW*, Vol. 2, pp. 179-181.
[29] *Admiralty Proceedings on the Sessions held 7th and 8th June 1792 before Sir James Marriott and others, Trials of Kimber, Traill, Ellerington and Hindmarch for murder and Berry and Slack for piracy*, London, 1792
[30] Ibid, Bateson, Charles, *The Convict Ships 1787-1868*, pp. 131-139 and Ryan, R. J., *The Third Fleet Convicts: an alphabetical listing of names, giving place and date of conviction, length of sentence, and ship of transportation*, (Horwitz Grahame), 1983

were expected to arrive shortly. The final vessel, the *Admiral Barrington*, did not arrive until the 16 October nearly eleven weeks after the *Matilda*, and fourteen weeks after the *Mary Ann*. 195 male convicts and 4 female convicts died during this voyage.[31] Though this death rate was high, it was nowhere near as bad as that which had occurred on the Second Fleet. Although the Third Fleet brought much needed supplies, it also brought despatches informing Phillip that there would in future be two embarkations a year supported by the necessary stores and provisions.

Phillip now had more mouths to feed and to avert another famine, hired the transport *Atlantic* to sail to Calcutta for a cargo of rice.[32] She sailed late in October and with good sailing was expected to return by the following April or May. By early 1792, food stocks were down to dangerous levels.[33] The grain harvest at Parramatta had been above expectations, but still too small to feed the colony for more than a few weeks. Phillip had no choice but to reduce the ration yet again. Food shortages lead to desperation and food stealing became common. Discontent became so close to revolt that the Governor refused close assembly in numbers for any reason. A numbers count revealed that 44 men and women were missing. Most had wandered into the bush, believing that they could find a better place; few were ever found or returned. In April 1792, with no sign of the *Atlantic*, Phillip reduced the ration again to near starvation level with flour down to 1½ pounds and 2 pounds of maize and some pork. The mortality rate had reached desperate proportions and a general air of despair was everywhere. 'Distressing as it was to see the poor wretches dropping into the grave', David Collins wrote,

> ...it was far more afflicting to observe the countenance and emaciated persons of many who remained, soon to follow their miserable companions...It was not hard labour that destroyed them; it was an entire want of strength in the constitution to

---

[31] *New Holland Morning Post*, 18 October 1791.
[32] The problem was evident in a letter from Phillip to Lord Grenville, 5 November 1791, *HRNSW*, Vol. 1, (2), pp. 532-541.
[33] See, Phillip to Henry Dundas, 19 March 1792, Phillip to Evan Nepean, 29 March 1792, *HRNSW*, Vol. 1, (2), pp. 596-599, 610-613.

receive nourishment, to throw off the debility that pervaded their whole system.[34]

The *Atlantic* finally returned from Calcutta with a cargo of rice and other food including pork; the latter found to be 'for the most part putrid' and had to be thrown out. Phillip though, had good reason to believe that the worse was over. *HMS Gorgon* had returned from England with assurances from authorities that regular shipments of food and other supplies would be forthcoming. The first sign of this promise was the arrival in July, of the supply ship *Britannia* with four months of flour and eight months of beef and pork 'for every description of persons in the settlement at full allowance.' It also carried a year's supply of clothing and the news that two more ships were on the way. The full standard ration was thereby restored.

When Phillip left the colony in December 1792, its population was 4,222, of which 1,256 were at Sydney, 1,845 at Parramatta and 1,121 at Norfolk Island. The colony was still short of many necessities and livestock. However, 1,703 acres of land were under cultivation or cleared of timber for cultivation and of the 3,470 acres that had been granted to settlers, 470 acres were being cultivated. Many settlers were self-sufficient and some had surpluses of grain and vegetables to sell. Phillip introduced regular private markets to trade, fish, livestock, grain and clothing in 1792. The harvest before Phillip's departure had yielded 4,800 bushels and within another year, Grose optimistically but prematurely reported that the colony was virtually independent of outside supply.

---

[34] Ibid, Collins, David, *An account of the English colony in New South Wales*, p. 207.

3 Autocracy and consent

Captain James Cook made three voyages to the South Pacific between 1768 and 1779 and on each occasion carried 'Secret Instructions' from the British Admiralty. These contained an outline of the route of the voyage, described the activities he and his men were to undertake, and the manner in which he was to report his progress. They were secret in that they held the real intentions and plans for the voyage, while other papers issued would be made available on demand to show Cook's authority for his command and the enterprise. On his first voyage, Cook sailed in the *Endeavour* to Tahiti to assist in the scientific observation of the transit of the planet Venus and then sailed south in search of the fabled 'Great Southern Continent'.[1]

The Secret Instructions, dated 30 July 1768 contained in the Letterbook carried on the *Endeavour*, included Additional Instructions authorising James Cook to take possession of 'a Continent or Land of great extent' thought to exist in southern latitudes and instructed him 'with the Consent of the Natives to take possession of Convenient Situations in the Country in the Name of the King of Great Britain'.[2] These provided that, if he found the Continent, he should chart its coasts, obtain information about its people, cultivate their friendship and alliance and annex any convenient trading posts in the King's name. Cook followed the coast of New Zealand showing that Abel Tasman had been wrong to conclude that it formed part of the southern

---

[1] Beaglehole, J. C., *The Life of Captain James Cook*, (Stanford University Press), 1974, and his editions of Cook's journals, *The Journals of Captain James Cook: The Voyage of the Endeavour,1768-1771*, (Cambridge University Press), 1955, *The Journals of Captain James Cook: The Voyage of the Resolution and Adventure, 1772-1775*, (Cambridge University Press), 1961, and *The Journals of Captain James Cook: The Voyage of the Resolution and Discovery, 1776-1780*, 2 Vols. (Cambridge University Press), 1967, are the standard works. Edwards, Philip, (ed.), *James Cook: The Journals*, (Penguin Books), 2003, is an abridged version.

[2] This Letterbook contains the only surviving set of Cook's original Secret Instructions. See, *HRNSW*, Vol. 1, (1), pp. 398-402, for the secret instructions for Cook's third voyage.

continent and then turned west, reaching the southern coast of NSW on 20 April 1770.[3] He sailed north, landing at Botany Bay one week later[4], before continuing to chart the Australian coast all the way north to the tip of Queensland. There, on Possession Island, just before sunset on 22 August 1770, he declared the coast a British possession:

> Notwithstand[ing] I had in the Name of His Majesty taken possession of several places upon this coast, I now once more hoisted English Coulers and in the Name of His Majesty King George the Third took possession of the whole Eastern Coast . . . by the name New South Wales, together with all the Bays, Harbours Rivers and Islands situate upon the said coast, after which we fired three Volleys of small Arms which were Answerd by the like number from the Ship.[5]

Over eight days and nights in late April 1770, Captain Cook and the men of the *Endeavour* made their first extended landfall on the east coast of New Holland. Cook had recorded signs that the coast was inhabited during the voyage north noting as he returned to the ship the large number of fires on all the land and islands about them, 'a certain sign they are Inhabited'.[6] Both Cook and Joseph Banks wrote accounts of the attempts to 'form a connection with the natives', but this was largely downplayed by later historians of the expedition to such an extent that a common misconception is that there was no interaction with the locals or so little that it was not worthy of sustained comment. The problem, as Nugent clearly demonstrates, was how both sides read the encounter. For example, what might have appeared as potentially aggressive behaviour to Cook, especially weapon waving, loud shouting and body

---

[3] Ibid, Edwards, Philip, (ed.), *James Cook: The Journals*, pp. 120-121.
[4] Ibid, pp. 122-123.
[5] Ibid, pp. 170-171.
[6] Unlike Cook's interaction with other peoples in the Pacific and New Zealand, his contacts with the peoples in Australia have been relegated to a footnote in history perhaps because they were so brief. See, Nugent, Maria, *Captain Cook Was Here*, (Cambridge University Press), 2009, for a detailed examination and critique of Cook's eight days at Botany Bay in late April-early May 1770 and the original encounter on land between the British explorers and the first Australians that has become one of Australia's founding legends.

decoration, was in fact a description of customary behaviour when local Aboriginal groups came into contact with strangers, whether they were native peoples or explorers.

Cook then sailed through Torres Strait, returning to England in May 1771. Cook's Secret Instructions represented the first official expressions of British interest in Australia combining the pursuit of scientific discovery with the desire to find exploitable natural resources and to expand Britain's control of strategic trading posts around the globe and assumed that these varied interests could be made compatible with a respect for the native populations in those countries. Cook's observations along the NSW coastline on his first voyage formed the foundation for Britain's decision to establish the colony at Botany Bay in 1788.[7]

Cook's second and third voyages involved a fuller exploration of the Pacific and Atlantic, including the search for a north-west passage through the Pacific to the Atlantic. He was instructed to make scientific observations and collect natural specimens, and to show 'every kind of civility and regard' to the natives, at the same time taking care not 'to be surprized by them'. With their consent, he was to take possession in the name of the King of any convenient situations in any country he might discover. Cook eventually reached the north-west passage, but the Bering Strait was ice-bound and he was unable to cross it. Returning through the South Pacific, he was killed in the Sandwich Islands on 14 February 1779.

Founding a colony: Phillip

Although law courts were established when the colony was founded, for the first thirty-five years, the Governors were absolute rulers. The British Parliament could control their authority, but England was 12,000 miles and eight months away by sea: by the time a complaint was heard and decided, nearly two years might have gone by. Phillip's first and second Commissions, dated 12 October 1786 and 2 April 1787, appointed him as the representative of the Crown in an area embracing roughly the eastern half of

---

[7] *HRNSW*, Vol. 1, (1), contains extracts from Cook's private log and the log book of the *Endeavour*. However, the volume is perhaps most valuable for the journals of officers, pp. 175-298.

Australia together with adjacent Pacific islands.[8] Although Major Robert Ross, commander of the Marines, was appointed Lieutenant-Governor, it was Captain John Hunter, commander of the Fleet's flagship *Sirius*, who had a dormant commission to replace Phillip as Governor should he become incapacitated. Before he left for NSW, Phillip received his Instructions (composed by Lord Sydney) from King George III, 'with the advice of his Privy Council'. The first Instructions included Phillip's Commission as Captain-General and Governor-in-Chief of New South Wales. An amended Commission, dated 25 April 1787, designated the territory of New South Wales as including 'all the islands adjacent in the Pacific Ocean' and running westward to the 135th meridian, that is, about mid-way through the continent. [9] The Instructions advised Phillip about managing the convicts, granting and cultivating the land, and exploring the country.

He was also instructed to 'conciliate' the indigenous people, '...and if any of our subjects should wantonly destroy them...', then punishment would follow. [10] The Aborigines' lives and livelihoods were to be protected and friendly relations with them encouraged, but the Instructions make no mention of protecting or even recognising their lands. It was assumed that Australia was *terra nullius*, that is, land belonging to no one, an assumption that shaped land law and occupation for more than 200 years. It was hoped that the land would be seized without bloodshed and with the cooperation of the native people. This proved impossible to achieve and Broome argued that 'Contradiction lay at the heart of British policy', and conciliation was doomed from the beginning. [11] The land was simply seized and, as a result, Aborigines immediately lost any rights without being compensated. This was reinforced after Phillip began to issue grants of

---

[8] *HRNSW*, Vol. 1, (2), pp. 24-25, 61-67, *HRA*, Series I, Vol. 1, pp. 1-2.

[9] *HRNSW*, Vol. 1, (2), pp. 84-91, *HRA*, Series I, Vol. 1, pp. 2-9.

[10] Gumbert, M., *Neither Justice Nor Reason*, (University of Queensland Press), 1984, p. 11. Phillip was given two commissions before he left England: *HRA*, Series I: Vol. 1, pp. 1-9. It was the second commission, dated 25 April 1787 that provided Phillips with instructions on the Aboriginal question.

[11] Broome, R., *Aboriginal Australians: a history since 1788*, 4th edition, (Allen & Unwin), 2010, p. 22.

land to officers and freed convicts who warned the Aborigines to stay off 'their land'. [12] The early British residents of Australia exhibited a far greater contempt for the Aborigines than British colonists showed toward native peoples in other places. Settlers in North America made their share of disparaging remarks about Indians, but they also praised Indian technology, social life and political organisation. Comments on the Aborigines, by contrast, were mainly variations on a single theme. Aborigines were not regarded as human equals and any interaction between them was tainted by this misconception. Although the Aborigines had their own moral code and law, for the early convicts and free settlers in NSW they were regarded as 'savages'. For Phillip and a few of his officers, there was an acceptance of the Romantic notion of the 'noble savage', but this idea soon faded with the realities of contact. By 1809, the naturalist George Caley, sent to NSW by Joseph Banks to gather botanical specimens, summed up two decades of British observations. He told Banks, 'I believe it is universally said that the natives of New South Wales are the most idle, wretched and miserable beings in the world.' [13]

Phillip [14] was responsible solely to his superiors in London and was expected to carry out their orders as embodied in his first Instructions of 25 April 1787, his 'additional' Instructions of 20 August 1789 and official dispatches. [15] Within these limits his powers were absolute. The Crown vested him with complete authority over the

---

[12] Phillip's instructions on land grants, 22 August 1789: *HRA*, Series I: Vol. 1, pp. 124-128.

[13] George Caley to Joseph Banks, 16 February 1809, in Currey, J. E. B., (ed.), *George Caley, Reflections on the Colony of New South Wales*, (Lansdowne Press), 1966, pp. 177-178.

[14] Fletcher, B. H., 'Phillip, Arthur (1738-1814)', *ADB*, Vol. 2, pp. 326-333, Mackaness, G., *Admiral Arthur Phillip*, (Angus & Robinson), 1937, Thea, Stanley, *Arthur Phillip: Australia's Founding Governor*, (Movement Publications), 1985, and Frost, Alan, *Arthur Phillip: His Voyaging 1738-1814*, (Oxford University Press), 1987, provide contrasting biographical material. See also, Stockdale, John, *The voyage of Governor Phillip to Botany Bay: with an account of the establishment of the colonies of Port Jackson & Norfolk Island*, 3rd ed., (Printed for J. Stockdale), 1790. Clune, David, and Turner, Ken, (eds.), *The Governors of New South Wales, 1788-2010*, (Federation Press), 2009, pp. 30-125, considers governors from Phillip to Macquarie.

[15] *HRNSW*, Vol. 1, (2), pp. 256-259, *HRA*, Series I, Vol. 1, pp. 9-16.

inhabitants and gave him the right to promulgate regulations touching practically all aspects of their lives. As Tench commented, 'He is left to act entirely from his own judgement.' [16] Phillip combined executive and legislative functions and from September 1791 could remit sentences imposed by the Civil and Criminal Courts established under a warrant issued on 2 April 1787 and three convicts were soon sentenced to hang by Judge-Advocate David Collins for stealing food, though Phillip commuted the sentence and only one was eventually executed. Only the crimes of treason or wilful murder were exempt from this provision, but even here he could grant a reprieve while awaiting advice from London. Distance from Britain and the relative indifference of the Home Office towards the affairs of the infant colony enlarged even further the scope of the governor's initiative and increased his responsibilities.

The New South Wales Courts Act 1787 established a legal system, providing for the establishment of the first New South Wales Court of Criminal and Civil Jurisdiction by executive action. [17] It ensured that British law landed with the First Fleet in 1788 [18] and that the convict colony had the basis for law enforcement. The Act also allowed for a more 'summary' legal proceeding than was usual, adapting court procedures to the conditions of the new convict colony. The Court was established by the Letters Patent of 2 April 1787. [19] The Charter of Justice 2 April 1787 provided the authority for the establishment of the first New South

---

[16] Ibid, Tench, Watkin, *A Narrative of the Expedition to Botany Bay*, p. 28.
[17] House of Lords Record Office: 27 George III, 1787; *HRNSW*, Vol. 1, (2), pp. 67-70.
[18] '8th February 1788: The criminal court, consisting of six officers of his Majesty's forces by land or sea, with the judge advocate, sat for the first time, before whom several convicts were tried for petty larceny. Some of them were acquitted, others sentenced to receive corporal punishment, and one or two were, by the decision of the court, ordered to a barren rock, or little island, in the middle of the harbour, there to remain on bread and water for a stated time.' Ibid, White, John, *Journal of a Voyage to New South Wales*, pp. 126-127.
[19] Letters Patent are written instrument granting authority from the Crown, not enclosed but open to view, with the seal of the sovereign at the bottom. As the provision for establishing a Civil Court had not been included in the Act there was no legislative basis for its foundation.

Wales Courts of Criminal and Civil Jurisdiction. [20] The Charter of Justice is in the form of Letters Patent providing for a Deputy Judge-Advocate and six court officers to be appointed by the Governor and the establishment of a Civil Court. The governor was required to give his permission to any death sentence imposed by the Court and was empowered to give pardons. The Civil Court had the power to deal with disputes over property and had jurisdiction over wills and estates. Although the British intended to transport English law and legal proceedings along with the convicts, in practice there were significant departures from English law in the new and distant Colony. Notably, the first civil case heard in Australia, in July 1788, was brought by a convict couple. They successfully sued the captain of the ship in which they had been transported, for the loss of a parcel during the voyage. [21] In Britain, as convicts, they would have had no rights to bring such a case. In reaching this decision, the Judge-Advocate, David Collins, ignored the English common law rule of felony attaint. [22] Under that rule, those who had been sentenced to death for felony were unable to hold property, give evidence or sue in the courts. Henry and Susannah Cable had been sentenced to death and their attaint should have followed them for the full period of their transportation. Thus the ambivalent relationship between Australian and English common law began with the very first case. [23]

---

[20] States Records, New South Wales: SRNSW: X24, *HRNSW*, Vol. 1, (2), pp. 70-76.
[21] Cable/Kable v Sinclair, July 1788, was the first civil action brought in Australian legal history. In it, two convicts successfully sued the master of one of the first fleet ships for the loss of their baggage on the voyage. In doing so, commentators argue, the colony began with the rule of law rather than the simple rule of the lash. See, Kercher, B., *Debt, Seduction and Other Disasters: the Birth of Civil Law in Convict New South Wales*, (Federation Press), 1996, pp. xviii-xix, and Neal, David, *The Rule of Law in a Penal Colony: Law and Politics in Early New South Wales*, (Cambridge University Press), 1991, pp. 1-8.
[22] 'Collins, David (1756-1810)', *ADB*, Vol. 1, pp. 236-240. See also, Currey, John, *David Collins: a colonial life*, (Miegunyah Press), 2000.
[23] On the early development of a legal system in NSW, see, Nagle, John F., *Collins, the courts & the colony: law & society in colonial New South Wales 1788-1796*, (Indiana Press), 1996.

Far from being able to fall back on his aides in the initial trying years, Phillip had to struggle against widespread defeatism and occasional opposition. [24] The attitude of the marine officers and especially Major Ross affected their men and possibly the convicts who had least cause of any to feel content with their lot. [25] The officers, construing their duties as being primarily military, caused Phillip much trouble. They refused to help in supervising the activities of the convicts even though, through the oversight of the British authorities, few suitable persons were available and they objected to having to sit on the Criminal Court.

Officers decline the least interference with the convicts, unless when they are immediately employed for their (the officers) own conveniency...they did not suppose that they were sent out to do more than garrison duty, and these gentlemen...think the being obliged to sit as members of the Criminal Court as hardship... [26]

They then resented Phillip's decision to appoint convict overseers and night watchmen. Their discontent was heightened by the fact that unlike emancipated convicts they were denied free grants of land and lacked the opportunity to secure any of the advantages traditionally associated with colonial service. Ross made matters worse by his high-handed actions, such as the arrest of five of his officers who refused when asked by Ross to reconsider a sentence they imposed on a private. This created friction in the mess and prompted Lieutenant Ralph Clark [27] to describe him as 'the most disagreeable commanding officer I ever knew'. [28] Although at first on reasonable terms with Phillip, Ross soon became quarrelsome, acting both as a focus of discontent and a major irritant. He supported and

---

[24] Egan, Jack, *Buried alive: Sydney 1788-1792: eyewitness accounts of the making of a nation*, (Allen & Unwin), 1999, contains valuable accounts from the early years of settlement.
[25] See, for example, *HRNSW*, Vol. 1, (2), pp. 262-265. See also, *HRNSW*, Vol. 2, pp. 383-384, for Ross' instructions dated 2 March 1787.
[26] *HRNSW*, Vol. 1, (2), p. 153.
[27] Hine, Janet D., 'Clark, Ralph (1762-1794)', *ADB*, Vol. 1, pp. 225-226.
[28] Cit, Egan, Jack, *Buried alive: Sydney 1788-1792: eyewitness accounts of the making of a nation*, p. 76.

encouraged his fellow officers in their conflicts with Phillip, engaged in clashes of his own and complained of the governor's actions to the Home Office. Phillip for his part was anxious in the interests of the community as a whole to avoid friction between the civil and military authorities. Though firm in his attitude he endeavoured to placate Ross, but without effect.[29] The execution of six marines who had been court martialled for systematically stealing Government stores infuriated Ross who left that marines were punished more severely than convicts who were judged in the ordinary criminal court.

Phillip solved the problem by ordering Ross to Norfolk Island on 5 March 1790 to replace Philip Gidley King, the commandant there, whom he had previously decided to send to England to report personally on the establishment. This was, in part, necessary because of Phillip's complete isolation from his superiors in London. Until the increase in voyages between Britain and Sydney in the mid-1790s, communications with London were sparse and slow. Two years elapsed between the sailing and return of the First Fleet's ships during which nothing officially had been heard from Phillip and this pattern persisted throughout his tenure as Governor. His final despatch to Lord Sydney was dated 15 April 1790, almost a year after Sydney had left office and his letter of 14 June 1790 congratulating Lord Grenville, Sydney's successor at the Home Office was answered by Dundas, Grenville's successor on 10 January 1792.

Partly to counter criticism by Ross and others, Phillip highlighted favourable developments in his despatches and concealed the personal doubts that he periodically experienced. Not the least of his accomplishments was to help to keep faith in the venture alive in official circles in London and to provide the optimism as well as the leadership without which morale in NSW might have

---

[29] This was evident in Phillip to Sydney, 16 May 1788, *HRA*, Series I, Vol. 1, pp. 36-48, detailing the court martial of Joseph Hunt. Phillip stated that he 'was not informed of the courts being under arrest till the next morning, when he came to inform me, and I used every means in my power to prevent a general court-martial, the inconveniences of which were obvious. Any accommodation being declined...'

crumbled completely. [30] Phillip's enthusiasm is all the more remarkable in view of the fact that during his five year term of office the colony assumed a shape that was not in accord with his wishes. Instead of the free settlers whom he sought to encourage with grants of from 'five hundred to one thousand acres' and the assistance of 'not less than twenty men' maintained at government expense for two years, only convicts arrived. This was not surprising. When the Home Office finally dispatched Instructions to Phillip in August 1789 authorising him to give grants to migrants it was on terms far less generous than he had contemplated. People leaving England lacked any real incentive to come to NSW and preferred the more accessible parts of the empire untainted by the stigma of convictism. Only thirteen free settlers left for Sydney in the first five years and none of these landed until after Phillip's departure. [31] The governor had expected a variety of advantages to flow from the presence of settlers. Besides forming the basis for the kind of settlement he hoped would emerge, he thought they would also prove of practical value for the penal standpoint by assisting in administration and convict control, by employing the prisoners and by setting an example for them to follow. Inspired by the profit motive, they would quickly make the settlement self-sufficient in basic foodstuffs. Their failure to materialise forced Phillip to depend on methods which he would have preferred to drop and that further increased his problems.[32]

---

[30] For example, Phillip to Sydney, 9 July 1788, *HRA*, Series I, Vol. 1, p. 51, 'I could have wished to have given your Lordship a more pleasing account of our present situation; and am persuaded I shall have that satisfaction hereafter; nor do I doubt but that value of this country will prove the most valuable acquisition Great colony. Britain ever made; at the same time no country offers less assistance to the first settlers than this does ; nor do I think any country could be more disadvantageously placed with respect to support from the mother country, on which for a few years we must entirely depend.'
[31] *HRNSW*, Vol. 2, p. 15, lists five who arrived on the *Bellona* in early February 1793.
[32] The lack of free settlers is a persistent theme in Phillip's correspondence: see, *HRNSW*, Vol. 1, (2), pp. 153, 177, 191, 207, 299, 347, 470, 534, 557, and 597. Letters from G. Matcham, *HRNSW*, Vol. 1, (2), pp. 590, 615, indicate that there was some interest in Britain in exploiting the agricultural deficit in the colony but that the response from government was tardy.

Between 1788 and 1792 about 3,546 male and 766 female convicts were landed at Port Jackson and handed over by the contractors to the Governor, who faced the task of deciding how their sentences were to be served. Anxious to keep costs low the British government insisted that they be disposed of in such a way as to involve the Treasury in a minimum of expenditure. Previously, in the American colonies, settlers had taken them into employment, but in the absence of private employers in NSW most convicts remained in government hands throughout the first five years and Phillip found himself responsible for directing their energies. The task was not made easier by the characteristics of the convicts themselves and many were unfit subjects for an experiment in colonisation. Not unnaturally they resented being wrenched from their homeland and taken to a harsh, hostile and uncivilised land. Phillip found them lazy and anxious to escape work by any means possible. Few were mechanics [33] or knew anything of agriculture and each of the fleets that arrived up to 1792 contained a high proportion of aged and sick who were unfit for work. [34] Worst of all was the Second Fleet that arrived in June 1790 after losing more than a quarter of its 'passengers' *en route* through sickness. Phillip's reports on the unscrupulous behaviour of the private contractors helped to produce improvements, but not until after the Third Fleet had arrived bearing convicts whose physical condition appalled him once more.

The crisis reached a peak in 1790 after the wreck of the supply ship *Guardian* off the Cape of Good Hope; although the situation eased in 1791, it remained uncertain and even when the full ration could be issued it was generally

---

[33] There was, for example, a lack of carpenters; see, *HRNSW*, Vol. 1, (2), pp. 146, 183. See also comments in *HRA*, Series I, Vol. 1, p. 81, about individuals as 'indifferent carpenters' and 'tollerable sawyers'.

[34] The problem of the lack of artisans and farmers identified by Phillip was quickly acknowledged in London and 'it is advisable that twenty-five of those confined in the hulks...who are likely to be the most useful should be sent out in the ship [*Lady Juliana*] intended to convey provisions and stores': see Lord Sydney to the Lords of the Admiralty, 29 April 1789, *HRNSW*, Vol. 1, (2), pp. 230-231.

unappetising and often of poor quality.[35] Under such conditions the health of the convicts deteriorated and they found prolonged manual labour difficult. Faced with a lack of suitable personnel to act as supervisors Phillip selected superintendents from among the better-behaved convicts, placed them under the few free men in the settlement, ex-marines, a few from the ships' crews, and some whose sentences had expired. He encouraged gardening. [36] He had dispatched a party to Norfolk Island under Philip Gidley King within a month of his arrival, and constantly reinforced it when he found that the island was more fertile than the land around Sydney. [37] He exercised great care in distributing rations and insisted on equality for all regardless of their standing. The governor based his actions on no particular set of beliefs except a broad humanitarianism. By nature self-sacrificing he was not prepared to inflict greater suffering on others than on himself and he felt that gradations in the ration were unfair in time of scarcity. As a result, he transferred his personal supply of flour to the general store making it clear that he would survive on the same ration as everyone else, a gesture that Collins said did his 'immortal honour'.

Phillip's measures helped to keep the settlement alive in its early years and a pattern of slow consolidation was evident. By 1791, only 213 acres were under crop and the number of farm animals amounted to only 126 head, for some of the cattle brought out had strayed, while others had died or been slaughtered. The building programme, by contrast, had advanced more satisfactorily with combined brick and tile production at 46,000 units a week by mid-1791, resulting in the erection of dwelling places for the governor, the officers, the convicts and some of the troops, together with several store-houses. Having completed these and other essential tasks Phillip was able to give more attention to farming. The area cultivated by government

---

[35] The problem of feeding the population at Sydney Cove as persistent until 1792, see *HRNSW*, Vol. 1, (2), pp. 173, 223, 299, 326-327, 377, 382, 557, 570, 596, 644, 654.

[36] Gardens were given to marines and convicts: *HRNSW*, Vol. 1, (2), pp. 189, 362.

[37] Phillip to Dundas, 4 October 1792, *HRNSW*, Vol. 1, (2), p. 661, contained an enclosure with details of land grants. 104 had been made at Norfolk Island and this contrasted with only 66 at Parramatta.

labour expanded much more rapidly after 1791 and by October 1792 some 1,017 acres were under crop on the public domain; although livestock was still scarce important advances had been made towards the attainment of self-sufficiency in grain. The community was still vitally dependent on overseas supplies for most of its needs, but no longer was survival thought to be impossible.

In 1791 the marines were replaced by the New South Wales Corps. [38] In the light of what was to come this may appear unfortunate and Phillip's relations with the Corps were marked by growing disagreement over rations, granting of land and assigning convicts to provide the necessary labour. Its officers had quickly acquired the economic interests that led to conflict with later governors.[39] Effective discipline was vital in an isolated community where convicts far outnumbered their gaolers and where it was impracticable to segregate them behind bars. Phillip housed the convicts in a series of huts so arranged that they could be policed at night; but the watch of necessity had to be drawn mainly from among the better convicts, and this caused further trouble with the marines who complained bitterly on the odd occasion when a convict policeman detected one of their number breaking the law. Offences committed within the colony were, if only minor, tried by the magistrates, or when more serious by the Civil and Criminal Courts. Phillip sat on neither bench, but he was able within limits to determine their composition and to vary their sentences, thereby influencing the course of justice.[40] Before leaving England he had stated his opposition to the death penalty save for murder and sodomy, which crimes he felt best punished by handing guilty persons over to be eaten by 'the natives of New

---

[38] On the establishment of the NSW Corps, see *HRNSW*, Vol. 1, (2), pp. 249-251; see also Grenville to Phillip, 24 December 1789, *HRA*, Series I, Vol. 1, pp. 132-133.

[39] Phillip to Sydney, 20 February 1789, *HRA*, Series I, Vol. 1, p. 106, contained the following prophetic statement: 'When this circumstance is laid before Lord Sydney, I doubt not but his Lordship will see that the civil Government of this colony may be very materially affected by directions of such a nature being given to the commandant of the detachment, and by him carried into execution without the knowledge or consent of the Governor, and which I presume never was intended by Lord Howe.'

[40] Phillip to Sydney, 5 June 1789, *HRA*, Series I, Vol. 1, pp. 107-111.

Zealand'. This harsh sentence was never imposed, but there were some executions, particularly for the theft of food in time of scarcity.[41] More usual was the lash, then a standard punishment in the army and navy, or committal to a gaol-gang.[42]

Phillip's second Commission dated 2 April 1787 had given him the power of granting land to approved persons, defined in his first Instructions as former convicts. The British government was anxious to encourage people of this kind to remain at Port Jackson and for this reason offered them small plots of land and full maintenance during the early months of operations. The Home Office also indicated its willingness to make grants to the non-commissioned officers and privates of the marines who might elect to remain after completing a tour of duty, and to any migrants who might arrive. Phillip was ordered to examine the soil, report on its quality and suggest terms on which it might be alienated. Without fully waiting for his advice, however, the Secretary of State dispatched on 22 August 1789 fresh Instructions on the granting of land. The only residents not permitted to own land were the civil staff and military officers, whose pleas for this concession were not satisfied until after Phillip had departed. The governor himself had viewed their requests with no great enthusiasm. While willing to allow them to grow foodstuff in time of shortage or run livestock on plots of Crown Land he was not happy at the thought of their becoming property owners. He feared their attention might be distracted from their duties. He realised that they would wish to employ convicts, and these he thought might be left too much to their own devices. Shortly before leaving England he stressed that insufficient convicts were available to make it possible for the officers' likely demands to be met. Phillip was also reserved in his attitude towards the issuing of land grants to emancipated convicts, for he rightly felt that many would never succeed at farming.

In September 1791, Philip Gidley King returned from London with the Great Seal for the colony and a

---

[41] The number of executions was relatively small; four in 1788 and two in 1789: Phillip to Lord Sydney, 12 February 1790, *HRNSW*, Vol. 1, (2), p. 298.

[42] Phillip was given the authority to remit sentences in November 1790, *HRA*, Series I, Vol. 1, pp. 208-212.

Commission empowering Phillip to remit the sentence of any convict. King returned to Norfolk Island as Lieutenant-Governor while Ross and Hunter returned to England. Ross' replacement, Major Francis Grose, Commandant of the New South Wales Corps and Lieutenant-Governor arrived early in 1792. Despite concerns expressed by Grenville about Phillip returning to England, on 11 December 1792 he sailed on the *Atlantic* to seek medical attention for a pain in his side which had involved him in constant suffering. [43] His work in NSW has been widely commended and, given the circumstances under which he was obliged to operate, it is difficult to see how he could have accomplished more than he did. Many of his hopes, including those for the encouragement of whaling off the coast which he recommended very strongly, were not realised. [44] Despite these frustrations he retained his optimism, displaying a resilience and sense of duty that carried him through periods of great difficulty and physical pain. However, he left when two developments loomed that were to dismantle much of his work. One consequence of the discovery of the settlement by overseas merchants was that increasingly they brought cargoes including liquor for sale. This may have given regularity to the supplies brought to the colony but Phillip recognised the dangers of permitting the convicts to obtain spirits. The one occasion, in October 1792, when he allowed it to be sold to the other residents confirmed his fears, for there was widespread drunkenness and disturbance. [45] The episode was not repeated but, had he stayed much longer, it is doubtful Phillip could have countered the many problems that were to arise from the liquor trade. Similarly his departure preceded by only two months the arrival from London of

---

[43] Chief-Surgeon Knox to Sir A. S. Hamond, (one of the Commissioners of the Navy), *HRNSW*, Vol. 1, (2), p. 675; see also, pp. 329-330, 422 and 483, for requests for leave of absence.

[44] For Phillip's observations on the potential of whaling, see *HRNSW*, Vol. 1, (2), pp. 612-613, 665.

[45] Phillip's initially supported the import of rum; see, Phillip to Dundas, 2 October 1792, *HRNSW*, Vol. 1, (2), p. 648, '...for it is a bounty which many of the people deserve and to the undeserving it never will be given...'

orders allowing civil and military officers to own land, [46] an event that provided these men with an opportunity to promote their interests and heightened the possibility of their conflict with a governor anxious to favour no single element in the community. It was perhaps fortunate that Phillip was unable to follow his original intention of returning to Port Jackson once his health was restored, but medical advice compelled him formally to resign on 23 July 1793. [47]

Military interlude: Grose and Paterson

Until Captain John Hunter, Phillip's replacement arrived in NSW in September 1795, the colony was administered first by Major Francis Grose [48] (11 December 1792 to 12 December 1794) and then by Captain William Paterson [49] (12 December 1794 to 11 September 1795). Grose had arrived in Sydney on 14 February 1792 with the remaining 340 soldiers of the New South Wales Corps. Grose had been allowed to sell officers' commissions and also to make a profit on each recruit. This meant that the Corps was, from the outset, a commercial venture as much as a fighting unit. Phillip had introduced regular private markets in 1792 where settlers could sell their surpluses but they were soon superseded by the Corps that, against Phillip's wishes, hired the *Britannia* to bring supplies from Cape Town that it could sell in Sydney. This marked the beginnings of tensions between government and private enterprise.

The inhabitants were quick to take advantage of Grose's unassertive, affable and indolent nature. [50] On assuming command, he replaced civil magistrates with military officers, gave the senior officer at Parramatta control over the convicts there when he was not present, and appointed Lieutenant John Macarthur as Inspector of

---

[46] Grose to Dundas, 16 February 1793, *HRNSW*, Vol. 2, p. 15. See also Dundas' instruction concerning land grants in his letter to Grose, 30 June 1793, *HRNSW*, Vol. 2, pp. 50-51.
[47] Phillip to Dundas, 23 July 1793, *HRNSW*, Vol. 2, pp. 59-60.
[48] Fletcher, B. H., 'Grose, Francis (1758?-1814)', *ADB*, Vol. 1, pp. 488-489.
[49] Macmillan, David S., 'Paterson, William (1755-1810)', *ADB*, Vol. 2, pp. 317-319.
[50] Dundas to Grose, 30 June 1793, *HRNSW*, Vol. 2, p. 51, expressed concern about the secret sale of spirits.

Public Works. [51] Some historians suggest that the military officers deeply influenced his moves and one has asserted that Macarthur became the real ruler of NSW. Grose showed a greater concern for the welfare of his troops than Phillip had displayed. He increased the weekly ration to give them more food than the convicts and he improved their housing conditions. Without specific instructions and initially without authorisation, he issued land grants of about 100 acres to serving members of the Corps who requested them. [52] In accordance with Home Office instructions, he provided the officers with farms and, despite orders to the contrary, allowed each the use of ten convicts provisioned at government expense. [53] The civil staff was treated in the same ways as the military hierarchy. Some emancipated convicts and the handful of migrants who arrived were encouraged to take up small holdings on less favourable terms than previously laid down by the British government. The opening of the rich Hawkesbury River region, for which Grose must take some of the credit, induced large numbers to settle there. [54]

Behind these moves lay the conviction that the community stood to benefit far more from the exertions of private individuals than from government enterprise. Public farming had failed to produce sufficient food for the settlement's needs and although it was not abandoned, it was reduced. Unimpressed with the quality of small holders, Grose placed great trust in the officer farmers whose exertions, he felt, promised quickly to make NSW self-sufficient in foodstuff. This belief, as well as the desire to promote their well-being, led him to help their pursuits. Partly through their efforts, partly through a rapid expansion in the number of small settlers, the number of acres farmed and livestock grazed increased during his

---

[51] On Macarthur's appointment, see *HRNSW*, Vol. 2, pp. 14, 226. See also, Grose to Dundas, 16 February 1793, *HRA*, Series I, Vol. 1, p. 416.
[52] *HRA*, Series I, Vol. 1, p. 438, lists the grants made by 31 May 1793 including four of 100 acres to serving officers.
[53] See, *HRNSW*, Vol. 2, pp. 209, 302-303, 324, 328.
[54] On developments in the Hawkesbury region, see *HRNSW*, Vol. 2, pp. 210, 238, 254, 307, 346. See also, Barkley-Jack, Jan, *Hawkesbury Settlement Revealed: A new look at Australia's third mainland settlement 1793-1802*, (Rosenberg), 2009.

regime. [55] By December 1794, NSW was still importing essential supplies and the threat of famine still hung over the settlement. The British government disliked the means by which Grose had helped the settlement's progress. The reduction of public farming forced him to draw on the Treasury to buy food that convicts might have raised for nothing; his practice of providing maintenance for the officers' convict servants increased the burden on the stores and troubled Home Office officials who thought that such people should be supported by their employers.

Some of the civil and military staff began to engage in trade, especially in spirits at substantial profit to themselves. Although Grose derived no personal benefit from these practices, he was responsible for failing to curb them. Perhaps his advisers persuaded him to turn a blind eye to abuses that were to their advantage; but, since spirits proved an excellent incentive payment for convict labourers, it probably explains why he allowed the officers to acquire it. Assessments of the other aspects of his rule have been strongly coloured by the critical writings of contemporaries such as Richard Johnson, [56] Samuel Marsden [57] and Thomas Arndell but it is unlikely that NSW in this period experienced murder, drunkenness and disorder on the scale they indicated. The charges against Grose of making indiscriminate grants of land to his friends and fellow officers also appear without foundation, as the grants made were in accordance with his instructions and only to those officers who requested them. Smallholders were not exploited by the officers to the extent often suggested though Grose reduced the size of their land grants, but the picture drawn by contemporaries was not entirely untrue. [58] By encouraging the officers' farming

---

[55] On the land under cultivation, see *HRNSW*, Vol. 2, pp. 209, 302, 311, 482.
[56] Grose to Dundas, 4 September 1793, *HRNSW*, Vol. 2, pp. 64-65, described Johnson as 'a very troublesome, discontented character'. Johnson's response to Grose's comments are contained in a letter to Dundas 8 April 1794, *HRNSW*, Vol. 2, pp. 201-204, in which he explains the origins of his dispute with Grose.
[57] *HRNSW*, Vol. 2, p. 209, Grose expressed some concerns over Marsden.
[58] Grose to Dundas, 30 April 1794, *HRA*, Series I, Vol. 1, p. 474, stated that of the 59 grants made 1793-1794 seven were 25 acres

pursuits and allowing them to engage in trade, Grose enabled them to secure a hold over the colony that they were soon to exploit in their own interests. The Corps' officers grew wealthy from large land grants, the preferential sale of farm produce to the Government Store and an unlimited supply of convict labour. This led to the rapid clearing of land and the establishment of productive new settlement on the Hawkesbury River and resulted in an increase in food production. After Grose returned to England in December 1794, this situation continued under William Paterson who granted 4,965 acres of land and made no attempt, either then or after Hunter assumed office, to check or to control the trading and farming activities of his officers. This entrenched the economic and political power of military officers in the colony making it difficult for Hunter, King or Bligh as naval governors to check their influence. Unwittingly Grose and Paterson had helped to create problems that their immediate successors were unable to resolve. [59]

Restoring naval authority: Hunter

Hunter faced three major problems in running the colony. [60] There was a division of responsibility between different institutions in London. As Governor, Hunter was responsible to the King through the Duke of Portland, Secretary of State for the Home Office.[61] Since NSW had no

---

and two 20 acres but the overwhelming majority, thirty four, were for 30 acres.
[59] Grose to Dundas, 8 December 1794, *HRNSW*, Vol. 2, pp. 274-276, indicated his resignation and his decision to appoint Paterson as his replacement until Hunter arrived.
[60] Hoyle, Arthur, *The Life of John Hunter, Navigator, Governor, Admiral*, (Mulini Press), 2001, Auchmuty, J. J., 'Hunter, John (1737-1821)', *ADB*, Vol. 1, pp. 566-572. See also, Wood, G. A., 'Governor Hunter', *Journal and Proceedings* (Royal Australian Historical Society), Vol. 14, (6), (1928), pp. 344-362. For Hunter's commission and instructions, see *HRNSW*, Vol. 2, pp. 110-117, 227-234, and *HRA*, Series I, Vol. 1, pp. 513-527.
[61] William Henry Cavendish-Bentinck, 3rd Duke of Portland (1738-1809) was a Whig politician for the first thirty years of his political career but as a conservative Whig was Portland was deeply uncomfortable with the French Revolution, and ultimately broke with Fox over this issue, joining Pitt's government as Home Secretary in 1794, a position he held until 1801. Briefly an MP,

means to express public opinion, Portland was influenced by private correspondence from discontented residents such as Macarthur and the governor was rarely aware of the entire information at the disposal of the government when it made its decisions.[62] Although the Home Office was responsible for the convicts and the colony, it had to rely on the Admiralty for transport to convey prisoners to Sydney Cove. The military were the responsibility of the Secretary at War and the Commissariat and the Ordnance Department was responsible for military buildings. The Treasury, the Mint and two audit officers were concerned with the financial interests of the colony and the Post Office had the relatively easy task of dispatching mail whenever opportunity arose. Within NSW itself, the relationship between the civil and military establishments had been problematic since 1788 and the establishment of the NSW Corps and the decision by Grose to grant them land and their monopolistic attitude to the spirit trade made existing tensions even more difficult.[63]

Every day convinces me more and more that many of those people, if they cannot be prevail'd on to make their public office their first consideration, shou'd be remov'd. Their private concerns occupy all their time, and £50 per annum seems to be no object when £300, £400, or £500 is to be gained by trade. [64]

Portland succeeded to the title in 1762 but did not make his maiden speech in the House of Lords until 1783; one of his claims to fame is that he rarely spoke in parliament. See, Wilkinson, David, *The Duke of Portland: politics and party in the age of George III*, (Palgrave), 2003, pp. 108-136, for his period at the Home Office.

[62] Hunter expressed his concern about Macarthur in a letter to Portland on 14 September 1796, *HRNSW*, Vol. 3, pp. 129-131, in which he made clear that '...this officer's conduct...[was] impertinent, indirect and highly censurable interference in the dutys and department of the Governor of this colony...'

[63] The problem of spirits concerned Hunter from the outset. His general order of 23 January 1796 prohibited the making of spirits in the colony: *HRNSW*, Vol. 3, p. 10; general order 11 July 1796 took action over the unlimited sale of spirits, *HRNSW*, Vol. 3, pp. 58-59; general order 12 December 1796, *HRNSW*, Vol. 3, pp. 185-186, on the link between crime and spirits.

[64] Hunter to Portland, 20 June 1797, *HRA*, Series I, Vol. 2, p. 22.

There were also the beginnings of the division between convicts, emancipated convicts and free settlers and between public and private sectors. Finally, the outbreak of war with France in 1793 had exacerbated this situation calling into question excessive government spending in NSW and, although the colony was not forgotten, it inevitably was not viewed as important a priority as had been the case before 1793. The potential for tensions between these different elements had existed from the founding of the colony but grew in significance from the mid-1790s when the survival of the colony was assured and food shortages became less common. Even so, Hunter complained in his first letter of Portland of the scarcity of salt and that the colony was 'destitute of every kind of tool used in agriculture'. [65] As late as September 1798, Hunter was concerned that the people were 'literally speaking, nearly naked and a great number without a bed or blanket to lie upon'. [66]

Hunter's first impressions on his return to NSW, as recorded in his official dispatches, [67] were largely favourable, though he privately confessed later in a letter to Sir Samuel Bentham that he had little understanding of the nature of his 'irksome command' when he solicited the appointment.[68] By October 1795, he had become aware of the enormity of his task commenting to Portland on the extent to which the settlement had expanded and the problems this had created for effectively maintaining its security and administration. [69] This is reflected in the flurry of government and general orders he issued in the remainder of 1795 including one preventing the indiscriminate felling of timber on the Hawkesbury. [70] Hunter had a resident civil establishment of thirty-one including medical staff and superintendents of convicts, master carpenters and the like, but less than a third could

---

[65] Hunter to Portland, 11 September 1795, *HRNSW*, Vol. 2, p. 318.
[66] Hunter to Portland, 25 September 1798, *HRNSW*, Vol. 3, p. 493.
[67] Hunter to Portland, 11 September 1795, *HRNSW*, Vol. 2, pp. 318-319, stated that 'agriculture...far exceeds any expectation...and does great credit to the arrangements made by...Grose and...Paterson'.
[68] Hunter to Bentham, 20 May 1799, *HRNSW*, Vol. 3, pp. 673-675.
[69] Hunter to Portland 25 October 1795, *HRNSW*, Vol. 2, pp. 328-329.
[70] Hunter to King, 5 December 1795, *HRNSW*, Vol. 2, p. 341.

be considered serious official advisers.[71] The number of officers on duty with the NSW Corps was seventeen. [72] There was considerable difference in age between the newly arrived Governor, approaching his sixtieth year and those who might be called on to act as his advisers. Macarthur, as Inspector of Public Works on whom Hunter relied in the early months of his governorship until the Baughan affair, was 28. [73] Captain Paterson, the Corps Commandant was 40; Captain Joseph Foveaux was 30; almost everyone else was younger. [74] Hunter was an experienced officer and accustomed to naval discipline and expected to see it reflected in NSW. Instead, he faced an entrenched military force and an increasingly dispersed body of settlers largely dependent at the mercy of the monopolistic trading practices of the military hierarchy and other officials. His instructions would have been difficult to implement even if he had a loyal and competent public service with reliable military support but he did not. [75]

The population of NSW in 1795 was 3,211 of whom 1,908 or 59 per cent were convicts. The remainder were largely military and administrative personnel and prisoners

---

[71] The civil establishment is listed in *HRNSW*, Vol. 2, pp. 331-332.
[72] They are listed in *HRNSW*, Vol. 2, p. 330.
[73] Initially Hunter retained the services of Macarthur see, Hunter to Portland, 25 October 1795, *HRNSW*, Vol. 2, p. 327, but their relationship quickly deteriorated into acrimony, see correspondence between Macarthur and Hunter between 24 and 29 February 1796 printed in *HRNSW*, Vol. 3, pp. 26-29, that resulted in Macarthur's resignation as inspector of public works. Macarthur became increasingly critical of Hunter's administration, see, Macarthur to Portland, 15 September 1796, *HRA*, Series I, Vol. 2, pp. 89-93.
[74] Fletcher, B. H., 'Foveaux, Joseph (1767-1846)', *ADB*, Vol. 1, pp. 407-409, and Whitaker, Ann-Maree, *Joseph Foveaux: power and patronage in early New South Wales*, (University of New South Wales Press), 2000. Promoted to major in 1796, as senior officer in the absence of Lieutenant-Colonel William Paterson between August 1796 and November 1799 he controlled the NSW Corps during a period when some of its officers were making their fortunes from trading and extending their landed properties. Whether Foveaux was a trader is unclear but he certainly turned his hand to stock-raising. By 1800, he had 1,027 sheep on the 2,020 acres of land he had been granted, making him the largest landholder and stock-owner in the colony.
[75] For Hunter's instructions, see *HRNSW*, Vol. 2, pp. 227-234

whose terms of servitude had ended. These expirees posed a problem for Hunter [76] and in June 1797 there were about 700 men supporting themselves, generally through casual labour, without government aid. [77] There were only a dozen or so free settlers and the settlement was confined to a small region close to the coast, with its economic centre at Parramatta and much of the economic advances in the 1790s came from those expirees who successfully turned to agriculture. Although the colony was almost self-sufficient in grain if the harvest was good, it was dependent on overseas supplies for nearly all other essentials and the need to import cattle and sheep was stressed more strongly in Hunter's instructions than in Phillip's. Between the departure of Phillip and the arrival of Hunter, private enterprise had supplanted that by government as the main form of economic activity. In December 1792, the government cultivated by far the larger proportion of land and most people spent their days working under its direction either on the public farm or on the construction of roads and buildings. By late 1795, however, officers and small farmers combined cropped an acreage far exceeding that belonging to the government, produced the greater part of the grain supply and owned most of the livestock in the settlement. Many convicts were privately employed and insufficient were left for limited public works. [78] Hunter claimed that the labour shortage was so acute that at least a further thousand workers could be absorbed. [79] NSW was becoming increasingly colonial in character with its penal role one of several often conflicting dimensions.

The problem facing smallholders was that if the government produced sufficient food on its own lands for those fed from government stores, then the farmers would

---

[76] This is evident in Hunter's general orders concerning robberies; see, the order for 26 September 1796, for example, *HRNSW*, Vol. 3, p. 139, and Portland to Hunter, 2 March 1797, *HRNSW*, Vol. 3, pp. 195-196, where Portland asks Hunter to take immediate action against bush-rangers.

[77] Hunter to Portland, 20 June 1797, *HRNSW*, Vol. 3, p. 226.

[78] The problem of labour shortages is evident in setting rates of pay for free labourers in general order 14 January 1797, *HRNSW*, Vol. 3, pp. 189-190. That this proved difficult to enforce is clear from subsequent general orders.

[79] Hunter to Portland, 25 October 1795, *HRNSW*, Vol. 2, p. 328.

have no market for their produce and it would be impossible to develop a self-reliant colony.

> ...if it is the wish or intention of Government to have this colony increase to a state of respectability, some encouragement must be held out to respectable settlers and industrious people of all descriptions. This can never be the case if it be the intention of Government to cultivate land enough for the maintenance of all the convicts sent here. The farmer will be labouring for a mere subsistence; he can never cloath himself and family if he has no market for his surplus corn, and if Government does not become his purchaser he can have no market. What then, my Lord, must be the consequence? A general indolence, a total inattention to farming, dissatisfaction with their situation, and a desire to quit the country by every opportunity which offers...[80]

However, the British government, though anxious to encourage private farming, was determined that the financial burden of the settlement on the Treasury should be limited. Portland insisted that Hunter should pursue a policy that in the long run could only harm local farmers. Hunter's first action as governor was to disobey his instructions and to continue the practice established by Grose of allowing ten convict servants for agricultural and three for domestic purposes to each officer occupying ground. Other farmers were provided with from one to five assigned convicts. Hunter started from the position that government farming was wasteful and inefficient and was also initially impressed with the success achieved by some of the officers whose efforts he thought might prove the basis for future prosperity. It is easy to blame Hunter for disobeying his instructions, and Portland had no difficulty in doing so, but Hunter recognised that the changes envisaged in London could only be effected at the expense of those who potentially were his principal supporters.[81]

The actions of the NSW Corps were not without parallel in other parts of Britain's colonies. Macarthur's profits as regimental paymaster were far less than those often accumulated by similar officers in India. The difference between the commercial activities of Macarthur and his fellow officers in NSW and equivalent operations

---

[80] Hunter to Portland, 28 April 1796, *HRA*, Series I, Vol. 1, p. 559.
[81] Portland was especially critical in a despatch to Hunter, 31 August 1797, *HRA*, Series I, Vol. 1, pp. 108-109.

elsewhere was that in NSW they almost achieved a monopoly, whereas in other colonies this was rarely possible. The result was growing tensions between Hunter and the military. Hunter soon ended his association with Macarthur telling Portland that 'scarcely nothing short of the full power of the Governor' would satisfy him. [82] It also became obvious that the soldiers of the NSW Corps resented the authority of the civil power.

> Continually thwarted and worthless characters encourag'd almost into a state of resistance by those whose schemes might have been in some degree effected by the changes I was about to make, and which in few words may be said to be *order and regularity for confusion and licentiousness*. [83]

Yet if Hunter failed as a governor, and Portland judged him a failure, the Secretary of State was equally culpable. He was slow to answer dispatches and failed to understand Hunter's position as an increasingly isolated individual with little physical or moral support thousands of miles from his home. Portland severely criticised Hunter for allowing more than two assigned servants to any military officer. [84] He directed that these servants should be fed and clothed by their masters and not from the government store, and particularly required that the officers should cease to trade in spirits. Yet Portland also paid attention to letters from Macarthur, a known dealer in spirits, vehemently attacking Hunter for refusing him 100 labourers instead of the two allowed by law.

By 1798, Hunter was clearly aware that trading by the officers had to be controlled sending a detailed account of the settlers' grievances about inflated prices.[85] This showed differences of as much as 700 per cent between the landing costs and the price of sale to the public. The problem was that his solutions, though satisfactory in a convict prison,

---

[82] Hunter to Portland, 14 September 1795, *HRA*, Series I, Vol. 1, pp. 661-663.

[83] Hunter to Portland, 12 November 1796, *HRA*, Series I, Vol. 1, p. 670. See also Hunter to Portland, 25 July 1798, *HRA*, Series I, Vol. 2, pp. 160-171, for further criticism of Macarthur.

[84] Government and General Order, 29 June 1796, reduced the number of assigned convicts to two: *HRNSW*, Vol. 3, p. 57.

[85] Settlers' petition to Hunter, 18 February 1798, *HRNSW*, Vol. 3, pp. 367-370.

were impractical in a developing free community. As government control of wages, prices and hours of work proved increasingly ineffective, Hunter called on a small group of supporters, Dr Thomas Arndell, the clergymen, Richard Johnson [86] and Samuel Marsden, [87] to prove to the British government that the deterioration in the public morals and economic progress of the colony was entirely due to the nature of the military government between 1792 and 1795. Although Hunter's analysis was correct that a definite increase in economic momentum and of political development had taken place in that period, neither the convict records nor the surviving letters from residents in 1793-1795 supported charges of increased crime, especially theft and excessive drunkenness, at that time. [88]

> Extensive cultivation and good crops, speaking generally, but not a barn, granary, or storehouse, wherein to preserve those crops even thought of yet. No mechanics in the colony to erect them; most of the convicts out of their time, and discontented at being hinder'd a single day from providing for themselves; in short, I am apprehensive that great part of our bountiful harvest may be lost. Our boats gone to ruin and decay; butts or houses, formerly the property of Government, leas'd away, and continual applications making to me to furnish others for those who are intitled to them. But I will not fatigue you. I only hint those few circumstances to satisfy you that there does exist great ground and cause for vexation. [89]

Grose's and Patterson's rule seemed very profitable for the agricultural community and the majority of contemporaries commented positively on the material progress, something mirrored in Hunter's early dispatches. Hunter's first attempt to reduce the military power saw a return to a civil regime. Hunter's return of the chaplains

---

[86] *HRA*, Series I, Vol. 2, pp. 178-183.
[87] *HRA*, Series I, Vol. 2, pp. 185-188.
[88] It was one of Macarthur's criticisms of Hunter that '...the interest of Government is utterly disregarded, its money idly and wantonly squandered, whilst vice and profligacy are openly countenanced.' Macarthur to Portland, 14 September 1796, *HRNSW*, Vol. 3, p. 133.
[89] Hunter to Portland, 20 August 1796, *HRA*, Series I, Vol. 1, p. 589.

and the medical men to the bench of magistrates,[90] even though they were in a minority, was regarded as a limitation on the military power and, in Hunter's words led to:

> ...frequent indirect and some direst attempts have been made to annoy the civil officers officiating as magistrates, with a view to the lessening that respect and influence over the minds of the lower orders of the people so highly necessary in our situation. [91]

In the military-civil struggle for power, Portland reserved his strongest criticism of Hunter for his behaviour in the case between John Baughan and the NSW Corps. [92] Portland:

> ...could not well imagine anything like a justifiable excuse for not bringing the four soldiers who were deposed against to a court-martial and punishing them with the utmost severity.[93]

Baughan had been transported in 1787 on the First Fleet and by the early 1790s had established himself as a master carpenter and builder especially of mills. [94] On 4 February 1796, overhearing himself being abused by a sentinel who apparently bore him a grudge, Baughan slipped out of his workshop, collected the soldier's arms from his deserted post and handed them to the guard. The sentinel was immediately arrested. Next morning, as an act of reprisal, Baughan's cottage was stormed and extensively damaged by a military rabble. He and his wife 'suffered much personal outrage' and Hunter expressed himself forcibly about this 'daring violation of the public peace'. [95]

---

[90] Hunter to Portland, 12 November 1796, *HRNSW*, Vol. 3, pp. 171-172, explains Hunter's change from a military to civil regime.
[91] Hunter to Portland, 12 November 1796, *HRNSW*, Vol. 3, p. 171.
[92] Hunter to Portland, 26 August 1796, *HRNSW*, Vol. 3, p. 87: '...I strongly suspect there are some person or persons in this colony (whose situations are probably respectable) extremely inimical to the necessary influence and authority of the civil power, and to that respect which is due from the public to the civil magistrates.'
[93] Portland to Hunter, 31 August 1797, *HRNSW*, Vol. 3, p. 294.
[94] Gray, A. J., 'Baughan, John (1754? -1797)', *ADB*, Vol. 1, p. 74.
[95] The attack on Baughan led to an immediate response in a general order issued on 5 February 1796 and Hunter's immediate response: *HRNSW*, Vol. 3, pp. 15-16. Hunter's letter to Captain Paterson on 7 February 1796 and his general order a week later illustrated his clear anger at the situation: *HRNSW*, Vol. 3, pp. 17,

The offenders, through Captain John Macarthur, expressed 'their sincere concern for what had happened' and agreed to indemnify the sufferer.[96] That Hunter accepted this showed that he grasped the realities of the situation, whilst his Government and General Order together with his dispatches clearly revealed a full appreciation of the problems created by a disorderly soldiery though he did not include the officers in his sweeping denunciations. [97]

Although Hunter was concerned by the troublesome nature of the Irish sent out as a result of the United Irishmen's conspiracy and rebellion, he showed much sympathy and humanity, by the standards of the day, towards the convicts in general, and especially towards their wives and children. [98] Much of his strong feelings against the 'rum' trade and the prevalence of private stills were based on these humane sentiments. [99] The severe criticism of his failure to control the rum trade, to keep down prices, to lower government expenditure and to control the trading of the military officers was grossly unfair, especially since with the dismissal of Richard Dore [100] in January 1799, Hunter had to act as his own private secretary. [101] In addition, his aide-de-camp, Captain George Johnston, although at one time in temporary command of the NSW Corps, was arrested in 1800 for refusing a general court martial in the colony on a charge of forcing spirits on a sergeant as part of his pay at an improper price. Whilst he was probably no more censurable than any other officer of the Corps save Paterson, nevertheless the charge implied habits at Government House similar to those elsewhere in the colony. When Paterson returned from overseas leave in

---

18-19. Hunter to Portland, 10 April 1796, *HRA*, Series I, Vol. 1, pp. 573-577, includes two enclosures on the Baughan affair.

[96] See undated memorandum written after 7 March 1796 by Hunter, *HRNSW*, Vol. 3, pp. 19-22.

[97] See Hunter to Portland 28 April 1796, *HRNSW*, Vol. 3, pp. 41-42 but especially Hunter to Portland, 10 August 1796, pp. 64-67.

[98] See Hunter to Portland, 15 February 1798, *HRNSW*, Vol. 3, pp. 359-361.

[99] 'Rum' was the colloquial term used by contemporaries in NSW for spirits.

[100] Allars, K. G., 'Dore, Richard (1749-1800)', *ADB*, Vol. 1, pp. 313-314.

[101] On Dore's dismissal, see Hunter to Portland 21 February 1799, *HRNSW*, Vol. 3, pp. 547-575, *HRA*, Series I, Vol. 2, pp. 244-278.

November 1799 he arrived with strict instructions to prevent further trading by the Corps, especially in spirits, and he assured the governor that he was being obeyed. It was odd that the opportunity to make an example of one of the officers should be seized at the expense of the governor's aide-de-camp.

There had been a persistent, often anonymous campaign against Hunter almost from the start of his period as governor. This was evident in Portland's letter to Hunter in early 1799 stating that certain charges had been made anonymously against Hunter and that he needed to satisfy the government that these were false. [102] The letter reached Hunter in November 1799 and he replied immediately not knowing that the decision had already been made to replace him. His recall was in a stern dispatch from Portland dated 5 November 1799 that he did not receive until 16 April 1800.[103] It was acknowledged by Hunter on 20 April 1800 and he handed over the government to the Lieutenant-Governor Philip Gidley King on 28 September. His final months in the colony were poisoned not only by his feelings of failure and undeserved blame, but also by the obvious eagerness of his successor to assume office. Portland's actions can hardly be called just since Hunter had been condemned unheard with no opportunity to answer the criticisms that had been made of him.

Why Hunter was recalled is not difficult to explain, though whether the reasons were justifiable remains a matter of debate. Hunter was regarded as an honest individual, but he was seen, especially by King as lacking in firmness and was too willing to accept the advice of individuals who used their influence for their own advantage. King believed he was 'sadly duped and deceived' by his friends. [104] Perhaps more damaging was his unwillingness to implement his Instructions from London where they clashed with the interests of the major colonists, especially the officers of the NSW Corps. While Hunter rightly argued that his decision reflected the particular

---

[102] Portland to Hunter, 26 February 1799, *HRNSW*, Vol. 3, p. 636, *HRA*, Series I, Vol. 2, pp. 338-340.
[103] Portland to Hunter, 5 November 1799, *HRNSW*, Vol. 3, pp. 733-738, *HRA*, Series I, Vol. 2, pp. 387-392.
[104] King to Under Secretary King, 8 November 1801, *HRNSW*, Vol. 4, p. 613.

circumstances in NSW, it led to tensions with Portland that Hunter's opponents in the colony were able to exploit. It is hardly surprising that Hunter sought to restore his reputation after 1800 and that, to some extent, he was successful. [105]

Towards rebellion: King and Bligh

It was Arthur Phillip who chose King as second lieutenant on HMS *Sirius* for the expedition to establish a convict settlement in NSW. [106] King had served with Phillip before the First Fleet and was regarded as his protégé. Phillip certainly had a high opinion of King and consciously promoted his interests throughout the late 1780s and 1790s. Despite his lowly rank, soon after the settlement was established at Sydney Cove, King was selected to lead a small party of convicts and guards to set up a settlement at Norfolk Island. [107] On 14 February 1788, King sailed for his new post with a party of twenty-three, including fifteen convicts.[108] On 6 March 1788, King and his party landed

---

[105] Hunter, John, *Governor Hunter's Remarks on the Causes of the Colonial Expense of the Establishment of New South Wales. Hints for the Reduction of Such Expense and for Reforming the Prevailing Abuses*, (S. Gosnell), 1802, represented a vindication of his conduct, associated with his consistently useful advice on all that concerned NSW, the realisation that his successors faced equal or greater difficulties and that the government was regularly misinformed of conditions in the colony, led to a reappraisal of his position.

[106] For biographical information, see Shaw, A. G. L., 'King, Philip Gidley (1758-1808)', *ADB*, Vol. 2, pp. 55-61; King, J. and J., *Philip Gidley King: a biography of the third governor of New South Wales*, (Methuen), 1981.

[107] See, Hoare, Merval, *Norfolk Island; an outline of its history 1774-1968*, (University of Queensland Press), 1969, Hazzard, Margaret, *Punishment Short of Death: A History of the Penal Settlement at Norfolk Island*, (Hyland House), 1984, and Treadgold, M. L., *Bounteous bestowal: the economic history of Norfolk Island*, (Australian National University), 1988.

[108] Crittenden, Victor, *King of Norfolk Island: The Story of Philip Gidley King as Commandant and Lieutenant-Governor of Norfolk Island*, (Mulini Press), 1993. For King's appointment and instructions see, *HRNSW*, Vol. 1, (2), pp. 136-138. Fidlon, P. G. and Ryan, R. J., (eds.), *The Journal of Philip Gidley King: Lieutenant, R.N., 1787-1790*, (Australian Documents Library),

with difficulty, owing to the lack of a suitable harbour and set about building huts, clearing the land, planting crops and resisting the ravages of grubs, salt air and hurricanes.[109] More convicts were sent and these proved occasionally troublesome. Early in 1789, King prevented a mutiny when some of the convicts planned to take him and other officers prisoner and escape on the next boat to arrive.[110] Despite the lack of a safe harbour, of lime and timbered land, there was plenty of fish, the stock flourished and the soil was good. It could maintain 'at least one hundred families', King told Phillip. Impressed by his work, the governor several times recommended his subordinate for naval promotion, but this would have raised difficulties because of King's lack of seniority. To solve the problem the Secretary of State announced in December 1789 that King would be appointed Lieutenant-Governor of Norfolk Island at a salary of £250.[111]

Following the wreck of *Sirius* at Norfolk Island in March 1790, King left and returned to England to report on the difficulties facing the settlements in NSW. During his twenty months' absence the island had been under the command of Lieutenant-Governor Robert Ross[112] but Ross was not an easy commandant and convicts, settlers, soldiers and officials had become discontented under his rule.[113]

1980, provides King's view of his governance of Norfolk Island until 1790.
[109] Phillip to Sydney, 28 September 1788, *HRNSW*, Vol. 1, (2), pp. 185-187, provides analysis of the resources of Norfolk Island. Ross to Phillip, 11 February 1791, gives a detailed discussion of problems encountered, *HRNSW*, Vol. 1, (2), pp. 434-450.
[110] Phillip to Sydney, 12 February 1790, *HRNSW*, Vol. 1, (2), pp. 293-294. Since Phillip had corresponded with Sydney during 1789, it is difficult to explain why he left it a year before informing him of the mutiny.
[111] For King's commission dated 28 January 1790, see, *HRNSW*, Vol. 1, (2), pp. 287-288.
[112] For Ross' instruction dated 2 March 1790, see, *HRNSW*, Vol. 1, (2), pp. 314-316. See also his observations on the island in December 1790, *HRNSW*, Vol. 1, (2), pp. 416-420, and the contrast with King's observations in January 1791 when he was in London, *HRNSW*, Vol. 1, (2), pp. 428-431.
[113] He had introduced martial law almost as soon as he arrived at Norfolk Island because of the loss of the *Sirius*; see, Ross to Phillip, 22 March 1790, *HRNSW*, Vol. 1, (2), pp. 319-320; see also the enclosures pp. 321-323, in which Ross laid down the standards

King found 'discord and strife on every person's countenance' and was 'pestered with complaints, bitter revilings, back-biting'. [114] Tools and skilled labour were both very short. Thefts were common and there was still no criminal court on the island, despite the representations he had made in London on the need for better judicial arrangements.[115] However, King's able and enthusiastic guidance helped to improve conditions. The regulations he issued in 1792 encouraged the settlers, who were drawn from ex-marines and ex-convicts, and he was willing to listen to their advice on fixing wages and prices and other things. By 1794, the island was self-sufficient in grain, and had a surplus of swine that it could send to Sydney. The numbers 'off the store' were high and few of the settlers wanted to leave, but unfortunately King had had no success with the growing of flax that so interested the British government. [116] In February 1794, King was faced with unfounded allegations by members of the NSW Corps on the island that he was punishing them too severely and ex-convicts too lightly when disputes arose. As their conduct became for mutinous, he sent twenty of them to Sydney for trial by court-martial. [117] There Lieutenant-Governor Francis Grose censured King's actions in going to NZ without first informing him, something with which Portland the new Secretary of State in London later concurred and issued orders that gave the military illegal authority over the

---

that would now operate on the island. Phillip informed Grenville in a letter dated 14 July 1790, *HRNSW*, Vol. 1, (2), pp. 357-358. Food shortages on Norfolk Island led Ross to introduce draconian measures in proclamations on 7 August 1790, *HRNSW*, Vol. 1, (2), pp. 390-393.
[114] King to Under Secretary Evan Nepean, 23 November 1791, *HRNSW*, Vol. 1, (2), p. 562; see also King to Phillip, 29 December 1791, *HRNSW*, Vol. 1, (2), pp. 572-580.
[115] See Phillip to Dundas, 4 October 1791, *HRNSW*, Vol. 1, (2), p. 655, on the inconveniences of the lack of a criminal court on Norfolk Island. Legislation was finally passed in London establishing a criminal court on Norfolk Island on 9 May 1794, *HRNSW*, Vol. 2, pp. 235-236.
[116] King to Dundas, 19 November 1793, *HRNSW*, Vol. 2, pp. 86-98, details the voyage to NZ to obtain Maori help with flax production. This failed and the natives returned to NZ, *HRNSW*, Vol. 2, p. 174.
[117] King to Grose, 30 January 1794, *HRNSW*, Vol. 2, pp. 103-110.

civilian population. [118] Grose later apologised, but conflict with the military continued to plague King.

Suffering from gout, King returned to England in October 1796, and after regaining his health, he resumed his naval career. [119] Phillip had wanted King to be appointed governor of NSW in 1792 and had continued to advocate King's cause after Hunter had been preferred in 1794. In January 1798, it was decided that he should return to NSW with a dormant commission as Governor-General to succeed Hunter in the event of the latter's death or absence from the colony, though at that time there was no question of Hunter being recalled. [120] The commission was issued on 1 May. [121] However, King was delayed in England for a further year and when he finally sailed in a whaler, the *Speedy* on 26 November 1799 the situation had changed and he carried the dispatch recalling Hunter. [122]

Authorised to assume office as soon as Hunter could arrange his departure and already irritated by the delays in England, King was anxious to set in motion radical reforms in the colony and worried about his pay. During the

---

[118] Grose to King, 25 February 1794, *HRNSW*, Vol. 2, pp. 125-131; King to Dundas, 10 March 1794, *HRNSW*, Vol. 2, pp.135-173, detailed the mutiny and Grose' response. For King's response to Grose's reprimand see, King to Grose, 19 March 1794, *HRNSW*, Vol. 2, pp. 173-192.

[119] King provided a summary of his career in King to Portland, 15 June 1797, *HRNSW*, Vol. 3, pp. 221-223. In this, he emphasised that he had been commended by Phillip and by Henry Dundas, the previous Secretary of State.

[120] This was agreed on 27 January 1798, *HRNSW*, Vol. 3, p. 353.

[121] This is printed in *HRNSW*, Vol. 3, p. 381 and *HRA*, Series I, Vol. 2, p. 605, and announced in *The Star*, 19 May 1798.

[122] The initial plan was for him to sail on the *Porpoise*, but initial trials showed the ship to be unseaworthy, see King to Sir Joseph Banks, 6 February 1799 and George Caley to Sir Joseph Banks, 9 February 1799, *HRNSW*, Vol. 3, pp. 533-538, and King to Sir Andrew Hamond, Comptroller of the Navy Board, 14 February 1799, *HRNSW*, Vol. 3, pp. 544-546. Once modifications had been made and after a significant delay, the *Porpoise* sailed in September 1799 but problems with the steering gear led to its return to England: King to Sir Joseph Banks, 17 September 1799, and King to Sir A. Hamond, 18 September 1799, *HRNSW*, Vol. 3, pp. 718-721. By early October 1799, the *Porpoise* had been declared unfit for service: Portland to the Admiralty Commissioners, 5 October 1799, *HRNSW*, Vol. 3, p. 723.

transition King's previously good relationship with Hunter became strained and his correspondence suggests that Hunter thought that King had an 'unbecoming impatience' for him to leave.[123] King did not assume command until 28 September 1800, [124] but had earlier assured Under-Secretary John King that his taking over was 'well-liked and anxiously looked for'. [125] King wrote gloomily of existing conditions, insisted that 'nothing less than a total change in the system of administration' was necessary, and forecast that 'discontent will be general' when this took place. [126] His task would be 'laborious and highly discouraging' but he would not be 'at all intimidated' and, although he had no formal instructions until raised from the status of Lieutenant-Governor to Governor in 1802, [127] he improvised them for himself from the dispatches to Hunter [128] and elaborated them in the orders he gave to Major Joseph Foveaux whom he appointed to replace himself as Lieutenant-Governor of Norfolk Island in June 1800. [129]

---

[123] See, for example, Hunter to King, 11 July 1800, *HRNSW*, Vol. 4, pp. 175-176.
[124] King to Portland, 28 September 1800, *HRNSW*, Vol. 4, pp. 177-195, is his first despatch where he used the title 'Acting Governor'.
[125] King to Under-Secretary King, 3 May 1800, *HRNSW*, Vol. 4, p. 83.
[126] King to Under-Secretary King, 3 May 1800, *HRNSW*, Vol. 4, p. 84.
[127] Hunter embarked on board *H.M.S. Buffalo* on 28 September, 1800 and King assumed the administration on the same day by virtue of a dormant commission issued to him in May 1798. It was not until 20 February 1802 that Hunter's commission was revoked and King appointed Captain-General and Governor-in-Chief. For King's Commission and Instructions dated 20 February 1802, see, *HRNSW*, Vol. 4, pp. 697-711, *HRA*, Series I, Vol. 3, pp. 384-398.
[128] Hunter made his commission and instruction available to King on 19 April 1800, *HRNSW*, Vol. 4, p. 80 but, according to Hunter to King, 11 July 1800, King did not replicate, *HRA*, Series I, Vol. 2, p. 662.
[129] See, King to Portland, 29 April 1800, *HRNSW*, Vol. 4, p. 79, makes clear King's decision and King to Foveaux, 26 June 1800, *HRNSW*, Vol. 4, pp. 96-108, details Foveaux's appointment and instructions.

King's first task was to attack the misconduct of monopolist traders and traffickers in spirits.

> Cellars from the better sort of people to the blackest characters among the convicts are full of that fiery poison.[130]

In March 1799, the commander-in-chief had ordered Colonel William Paterson, when he was leaving England to re-join his corps, to inquire into his officers' trading activities.[131] This gave King the opportunity, even before Hunter had left, to ask Paterson to act.[132] As soon as he assumed command King issued orders that he had already prepared, including a new set of port and price regulations intended to curb exploitation and the liquor traffic.[133] He felt compelled to allow Surgeons William Balmain[134] and D'Arcy Wentworth[135] to sell 4,359 gallons of spirits that they had on hand,[136] but was able to reduce the rate of spirit imports to about a third that of the last months of Hunter's administration. He tried to persuade the government in Calcutta and British consuls in the United States to discourage the shipping of liquor to NSW to offer the colonists an alternative beverage and began the construction of a brewery.[137] It only began production in 1804, and in his efforts to reduce spirit drinking, he faced the refusal of most convicts to work 'in what they

---

[130] King to Sir Joseph Banks, 3 May 1800, *HRNSW*, Vol. 4, pp. 82-83.

[131] Horse Guards to Lieutenant-Colonel Paterson, 6 March 1799, *HRNSW*, Vol. 3, pp. 639-640. Paterson arrived in Sydney in November 1799.

[132] King to Paterson, 8 September 1800, *HRNSW*, Vol. 4, pp. 139-140.

[133] Regulations were issued on 10 September 1800, *HRNSW*, Vol. 4, pp. 144-146, and in greater detail on 1 October 1800, *HRNSW*, Vol. 4, pp. 220-222.

[134] Fletcher, B. H., 'Balmain, William (1762-1803)', *ADB*, Vol. 1, pp. 51-52.

[135] Auchmuty, J. J., 'Wentworth, D'Arcy (1762-1827)', *ADB*, Vol. 2, pp. 579-582.

[136] On this decision see the correspondence in September 1800, *HRNSW*, Vol. 4, pp. 141-143.

[137] King received support from London in the form of hop plants: Hobart to King, 24 February 1803, *HRNSW*, Vol. 5, p. 48; Hobart to King, 9 May 1803, *HRA*, Series I, Vol. 3, p. 79, stated that a brewery was being established.

emphatically call their own time for any other mode of payment', but he cut spirit consumption per adult male in 1801-1804 to about two and a half bottles a month. [138] Despite this, King found increasing difficulty in suppressing illicit local distilling or sly-grogging, even though he issued repeated orders against it. He imposed a duty of 5 per cent on imports to raise revenue, as Hunter had suggested in 1798, but did not anticipate the later policy of reducing the profits of illegal grog-selling by allowing unrestricted imports of spirits subject to a moderately heavy duty.

In June 1800, King had protested to Hunter against the 'exorbitant demands of creditors' in the colony. [139] He felt that the poorer settlers could best be protected by price control and by the 'establishment of a public warehouse', such as he had advocated for Norfolk Island in 1796 and Hunter had also referred to but then had not told the authorities in London what goods were needed. [140] King's detailed requests were at once acted on and merchandise was sold through it at a price only 50 per cent above the costs necessary to cover transport and selling charges. The increasing quantities imported commercially weakened the monopolists' grip on the colony's economy and improved the colonists' means of obtaining supplies. King tried to control, not always with success, prices, wages, hours of work, the employment of convicts, baking, butchers, interest rates, weights and measures and the value of all the many kinds of currency circulating in the colony. [141] He sought to reduce forgeries by introducing printed forms for promissory notes, but they were usually ignored. He recalled all the officers' servants in excess of two each reducing the number victualed by the Crown from 356 to 94. [142] The position of the Colonial Office was clear:

---

[138] King to Portland, 10 March 1801, *HRA*, Series I, Vol. 3, pp. 7-8, for King's concerns about spirits brought from the United States and, despite instructions from London to the contrary, from India. See also, *HRNSW*, Vol. 6, p. 150.

[139] See, King to Hunter, 6 July 1800, and subsequent correspondence, *HRNSW*, Vol. 4, pp. 170-177.

[140] *HRNSW*, Vol. 4, p. 377.

[141] See, for example, King's general orders on 2-3 October 1800, *HRNSW*, Vol. 4, pp. 222-224.

[142] Government and General Order, 11 June 1801, *HRNSW*, Vol. 4, pp. 402-403, re-established the notion of only two assigned convicts for military officers.

I entirely approve the measures you have taken for reducing the expenses of the settlement, by discharging from the stores all those convicts who are not altogether employed in the service of the Crown, with the exception of two convicts allowed as servants to each civil and military officer; but it should be understood by those officers, that in all cases where they themselves cultivate lands and raise stock that they are to feed *all* the convicts allowed to them, without any exceptions whatever. The five convicts allowed to each magistrate, appears to me to be too many, but knowing your attention to publick economy, I am willing to leave it to your local experience and discretion to diminish that number in such degrees as you may think proper. [143]

King increased the number of convicts on the public farms from 30 to 324 and had quadrupled their cultivated acreage by 1803. Later he allowed public farms to decline, following orders from London for an increase in private agriculture.[144] He helped private farmers by land grants, by the issue of seed, tools, sheep and rations and by hiring oxen. Contrary to his instructions, he postponed the purchase of grain by tender and kept its price up to 8s a bushel, by ordering the government stores to buy direct from the grower and by distributing government breeding stock as a reward 'to those whose exertions...appeared to

---

[143] Portland to King, 19 June 1801, *HRA*, Series I, Vol. 3, p. 99. The number of assigned servants (not convicts employed as labourers) for magistrates was reduced to four, Government and General Order, 16 December 1801, *HRA*, Series I, Vol. 3, pp. 467-468. Hobart to King, 5 April 1803, *HRA*, Series I, Vol. 4, p. 63, increased the salaries of civil officials (but not military) and removed assigned servants from both: 'I have received His Majesty's commands to direct you to withdraw from all the officers of the civil and military establishment of the settlement the two convicts who have hitherto been allowed to them by Government. The augmentation of the salaries of the civil officers will enable them to pay for the services of such convicts as they may choose to employ, in lieu of the two hitherto allowed them, and the military officers can have no claim, in the present advanced state of the colony, to any aid of this kind, beyond what is allowed to military officers serving in other colonies.'
[144] Hobart to King, 24 February 1803, *HRNSW*, Vol. 5, p. 45: 'I observe that the quantity of land cultivated for Government has been of late considerably increased...I am inclined to think it would not be advisable to augment it to any considerable extent beyond that proportion.'

merit that encouragement'.[145] He also increased the size of land grants and made reservations for pasturage adjacent to them. The result was that only 56 out of 646 farmers were 'on the stores' in 1806, compared with 110 out of 401 in 1800. Smallholders had done much better than before, particularly during the first half of his administration and the colony seemed to be self-sufficient in grain though the disastrous Hawkesbury floods in 1801[146] and 1806 [147] postponed King's hopes in this regard. [148]

King had a shrewd understanding of the importance of economic development and during his administration the government's flocks and herds quintupled. [149] He bought cattle from India to improve the quality of the government stock. [150] Although rejecting direct government involvement with 'fine-woolled sheep', and alert to the importance of the 'weight of Carcase' to the small settlers, he was able by careful breeding to produce 'a total change in Government Flock from Hair to Wool' [151] and to distribute ewes to settlers to improve flocks of the colony. [152] He began the mining of coal, which he hoped would be a profitable

---

[145] King to Hobart, 14 November 1801, *HRA*, Series I, Vol. 3, pp. 324-325, saw prices rise to 15s a bushel though by January 1802 prices had returned to 8s a bushel, *HRA*, Series I, Vol. 3, p. 607. In early 1803, this was further reduced to 7s 6d at Sydney and Parramatta and 7s at Hawkesbury, King to Hobart, 1 March 1804, *HRA*, Series I, Vol. 4, pp. 518-519.
[146] *HRA*, Series I, Vol. 3, pp. 134-136, details a petition from Hawkesbury settlers on 21 August 1801 and King's response.
[147] The most extensive report was in *Sydney Gazette*, 30 March, 1806. There had been floods previously in 1799 and 1800 and later in 1809. This led to later Macquarie townships being built on higher land and remained largely dry in the floods in 1816 and 1819. However, the area remains prone to flooding.
[148] On King's assessment of the state of the colony on 31 December 1801 and 30 October 1802, see *HRNSW*, Vol. 4, pp. 651-670, 866-880.
[149] King's perceptive remarks on Macarthur's livestock showed his grasp of the need to improve government cattle and sheep, *HRNSW*, Vol. 4, pp. 114-115.
[150] *HRA*, Series I, Vol. 3, pp. 29-32, *HRNSW*, Vol. 4, pp. 312-315, *HRNSW*, Vol. 5, pp. 113-114.
[151] *HRNSW*, Vol. 5, p. 556. See also Macarthur's comments, *HRNSW*, Vol. 5, pp. 173-175.
[152] On sheep farming in 1805 see, King to Camden, 2 October 1805, *HRA*, Series I, Vol. 5, pp. 555-568.

export, was interested in timber cutting and encouraged experiments in growing vines, tobacco, cotton, hemp and indigo. [153] Although in the opening sentence of the first journal of his experiences from 1787 to 1790, published with minor revisions as an appendix to Hunter's *Historical Journal of the Transactions at Port Jackson and Norfolk Island* in 1793, King had affirmed the contemporary opinion that Botany Bay was founded simply as a penal settlement. By 1791, he was expressing great hopes for it as a Pacific base for flax cultivation and for whaling. Flax was not a success but whaling was, and both it and later sealing owed much to King's encouragement. He was a friend of whale fleet owner Samuel Enderby and advised the British government to allow the whalers to carry merchandise to NSW. [154] He encouraged sealers to go to Bass Strait and for whaling ships to visit New Zealand and the Pacific.[155] By 1792, there was a whaling industry off the south coast of NZ

---

[153] King to Portland, 8 July 1801, *HRA*, Series I, Vol. 3, p. 116, stated that coal was already being exported to India at £3 a ton
[154] Dallas, K. M., 'Enderby, Samuel (1756-1829)', *ADB*, Vol. 1, p. 357.
[155] As early as 1792, Sydney Cove was the centre for the profitable whale and seal trade around the southern coasts. Under Governor King, if not necessarily because of him, the colony made great strides. Whaling brought profit to its shores, for the ships came into Sydney to refit. King referred to whaling as the only 'staple' and saw visions of secondary profits. The American whalers provided a market for foodstuffs, water and timber. By 1800, London was unloading 300 tons of sperm oil fished off the coast of NSW. The whaling and sealing industry was quite unregulated and King recognised that this uncontrolled slaughter would ruin the industry and on 9 May 1803 he wrote to Nepean, *HRA*, Series I, Vol. 4, p. 249, 'Although a vast quantity of Sea Elephants and Seals have been taken and still abound about Hunters Island and Kings Island, yet from the different communications I have received I shall find it expedient to restrain individuals from resorting there in too great numbers, and to fix certain times for their visiting these places, to prevent the destruction of that commercial advantage. Since I took command 16,000 gallons of oil and 27,800 seal skins have been imported from thence by individuals, 1,063 tuns of spermaceti oil have also been procured by the south whalers, all which I need not point out as a rising nursery for Seamen.'

and by 1800 whaling and sealing had extended into the Bass Strait.[156]

In 1804, King encouraged Robert Campbell to send a shipment of oil and skins from Sydney to London in the *Lady Barlow* in contravention of the monopoly of the East India Company that he had constantly urged the government to modify.[157] Campbell believed that it was time for a more generous and freer definition of the commercial rights of NSW as the colony lacked established staples and was hampered by trade monopolies. Though the *Lady Barlow* was duly seized for illegal entry to the Port of London, her position was resolved with little commercial loss to Campbell. With the support of Sir Joseph Banks, he secured permission for a second colonial cargo to follow the *Lady Barlow*. Under this impetus a bill was drawn up to recognise NSW as a regular colony with valuable trade concessions, but the Grenville ministry lost office in March 1807 before it could be passed. King sought permission at the same time to open up trade between NSW and China [158] and decided that VDL was preferable to Port Phillip as a further penal settlement.[159]

King could, of course, never forget that he was in charge of a convict colony. He had to keep the prisoners in subjection, but at the same time he could not ignore the

---

[156] On the development of the South Sea whale-fishery, see, minutes of the Board of Trade, 4 December 1801, *HRNSW*, Vol. 4, p. 630. See also, Little, B., 'Sealing and Whaling in Australia Before 1850', *Australian Economic History Review*, Vol. 9, (1969), pp. 109-127.

[157] King to Hobart, 14 August 1804, *HRA*, Series I, Vol. 5, p. 9, 20-22, 53-63. Steven, Margaret, 'Campbell, Robert (1769-1846)', *ADB*, Vol. 1, pp. 202-206, and the more detailed *Merchant Campbell 1769-1846*, (Melbourne University Press), 1965. King had a high regard for Campbell commenting to Bligh that he had been 'the greatest services to the inhabitants...that the price of his merchandise was the same in time of scarcity as in abundance, that he had advanced a great sum of money, and protected the poor and distressed settler; and that in fact he was the only private pillar which supported the honest people of the Colony'.

[158] King to Camden, 30 April 1804, *HRNSW*, Vol. 5, p. 603, King to Hobart, 14 August 1804, *HRA*, Series I, Vol. 5, p. 9. East India Company to Sir Stephen Cottrell, *HRNSW*, Vol. 5, pp. 644-645, gave its response to King's proposal.

[159] King to Lieutenant-Governor Collins, 26 November 1803, *HRNSW*, Vol. 5, pp. 263-268.

growing number of emancipated convicts, and firmly reminded Major George Johnston that the British government had not intended the prisoners to be consigned 'to Oblivion and disgrace for ever'.[160] King appointed emancipated convicts to his bodyguard and enrolled them in the Loyal Associations, as had been done in the NSW Corps. Apart from the rather special case of appointing as military engineer, George Bellasis,[161] a former officer in the East India Company who had killed an opponent in a duel, he placed men like Richard Fitzgerald,[162] James Meehan,[163] David Mann,[164] Andrew Thompson,[165] Rev. Henry Fulton[166] and Father James Dixon[167] in administrative positions. He took firm measures to regulate the position of assigned servants, even if at first they were often disobeyed and laid the foundation of the future ticket-of-leave system by granting 'annual certificates' to prisoners deserving indulgence. Though he granted pardons to about 50 per cent more convicts every year than Hunter, he had about 30 per cent more to deal with including many political prisoners. King was at first perhaps unduly alarmed by them and especially by the Irish, perhaps because he had been in England during the disturbances in Ireland from 1797 to 1799.[168] However, after initial forebodings, in both 1801 and 1802 he was able to report their 'regular and orderly behaviour' and to compare their conduct most favourably with that of the military officers. Deeply

---

[160] *HRNSW*, Vol. 5, p. 28.
[161] 'Bellasis, George Bridges (- 1825)', *ADB*, Vol. 1, p. 83. See also, King to Hobart, 9 May 1803, *HRA*, Series I, Vol. 4, pp. 173-174.
[162] MacLaurin, E. C. B., 'Fitzgerald, Richard (1772-1840)', *ADB*, Vol. 1, pp. 383-384.
[163] Perry, T. M., 'Meehan, James (1774-1826)', *ADB*, Vol. 2, pp. 219-220.
[164] Parsons, Vivienne, 'Mann, David Dickenson (1775?-1811?)', *ADB*, Vol. 2, pp. 201-202.
[165] Byrnes, J. V., 'Thompson, Andrew (1773?-1810)', *ADB*, Vol. 2, pp. 519-521.
[166] Cable, K. J., 'Fulton, Henry (1761-1840)', *ADB*, Vol. 1, pp. 421-422.
[167] Parsons, Vivienne, 'Dixon, James (1758-1840)', *ADB*, Vol. 1, p. 309.
[168] Hunter to Officers, 4 September 1800, *HRNSW*, Vol. 4, pp. 119-130, details the inquiry into an Irish plot in 1800 and King to Banks, 8 October 1800 on a threatened rebellion by United Irishmen at Parramatta, *HRNSW*, Vol. 4, p. 229 and pp. 235-238

concerned by the Irish conspiracy in 1804, he seems to have felt more secure after it had been suppressed and he had divided the ring-leaders between the different settlements, including Newcastle, which he re-established in 1804 largely in order to take them. When war with France resumed in 1804, to supplement the battery on Dawes Point King began to build the citadel at Fort Phillip as a place of refuge in case of an internal rising, but it turned out to be of little strategic value.[169]

King was faced with the British government's persistent demands to reduce the costs of the colony.[170] The general success of his policies enabled him to cut the proportion of the population drawing government rations from 72 per cent in 1800 to 32 per cent in 1806 and the colony's indebtedness to the government was reduced. Fortunately trouble with the Treasury over his expenditure when on Norfolk Island made him meticulous in keeping accounts and he drew Treasury bills for stores at a rate about 20 per cent less than Hunter had between 1796 and 1798 for three-quarters the number of people. In June 1802, King imposed a 5 per cent duty on imported spirits and on merchandise brought from east of the Cape and not of British manufacture. [171] This decision was not legally authorised but this was not questioned and by using the revenue raised for the gaol and orphan funds, he began the appropriation of colonial revenue for local purposes. He was interested in the girls' Orphan School, and though he regretted that he could not establish a similar institution for boys, he took several day-schools 'under the protection of Government' and used apprenticeship to teach convict boys to become skilled tradesmen. He asked the British government to send out supplies of smallpox vaccine, and

---

[169] King to Hobart, 14 August 1804, *HRA*, Series I, Vol. 5, p. 2. King to Camden, 20 July 1805, *HRA*, Series I, Vol. 5, p. 529, indicated the state of work on Fort Phillip and its armaments.

[170] This is evident particularly in correspondence between Hobart and King, for example, Hobart to King, 30 November 1803, *HRNSW*, Vol. 5, pp. 271-272: 'I approve the exertions you have made to effect this desirable object [reduction of Treasury Bills]....at the same time [I] remark that the supplies of all descriptions which have been sent to the colony...have been extremely liberal...'

[171] Government and General Order, 14 June 1802, *HRNSW*, Vol. 4, pp. 789-790.

so enabled the surgeons to perform the first successful vaccination in the colony. [172] In March 1803, he permitted the government printer, George Howe [173] to establish the *Sydney Gazette*, allowing him use of the government press and type. [174] He was sympathetic to the missionaries who visited the colony, welcomed Maori and Tahitian visitors to Sydney and sought to keep peace with Aborigines. These, he told Governor William Bligh, he 'ever considered the real Proprietors of the Soil'. He refused to allow them to be worked as slaves, tried to protect their persons and their property and to preserve a 'good understanding' with them; but he found them 'very capricious', often 'sanguinary and cruel to each other', and like his contemporaries failed to understand what he called their 'most ungrateful and treacherous conduct'. [175]

King had always aimed to promote 'the prosperity of the colony, and giving a permanent security to the interests of its inhabitants'. He knew he could not satisfy all, and had faced 'scurrility and abuse, clothed with darkness and assassination'. This abuse has harmed his reputation that is undeservedly lower today. In the end, he was defeated by the officers of the NSW Corps. He knew that he would have to confront them when he arrived in Sydney in 1800 and even before he had assumed office he was regretting that Hunter had allowed Captain George Johnston to return to England for his trial on charges of trading in spirits. Johnston soon returned untried, but trials in the colony were not successful and King found the military intransigence that he had faced at Norfolk Island was now exacerbated by his policies that threatened the military elite's economic position. He badly needed capable law officers and a change in the personnel of the NSW Corps, but the British government ignored his requests. He was faced with frequent disobedience and insolence that early in

---

[172] King to Hobart, 9 May 1803, *HRNSW*, Vol. 5, p. 115. Vaccinations occurred at Norfolk Island, in Sydney and on the Derwent in VDL.
[173] Byrnes, J. V., 'Howe, George (1769-1821)', *ADB,* Vol. 1, pp. 557-559. King to Hobart, 9 May 1803, *HRA*, Series I, Vol. 4, p. 85.
[174] King to Hobart, 9 May 1803, *HRNSW*, Vol. 5, p. 118.
[175] King to Bligh, n.d., 1807, Mitchell Library, Philip Gidley King Papers, C189, p. 273, cit, Banner, Stuart, *Possessing the Pacific: land, settlers, and indigenous people from Australia to Alaska*, (Harvard University Press), 2007, p. 31.

1803, immediately after he had refused to allow a cargo of spirits to be landed from the *Atlas*, culminated in the circulation of libellous 'pipes' against him and his officials.[176] The investigations and courts martial that followed revealed the animosity that existed between the Governor and the Corps. King declared that 'for the prosperity of His Majesty's subjects in this territory...some change is absolutely necessary in our criminal courts'. With this Colonel Paterson entirely agreed, asserting that 'most of the disquiet that has agitated this settlement...is chiefly to be attributed to the unfortunate mixture of civil and military duties'. [177]

In November 1801, King had repeated Hunter's action and sent home an accused officer, John Macarthur, charged with fighting a duel with his commander, Paterson, itself the result of a quarrel with the Governor. [178] But in July 1805, Macarthur returned without being court-martialled. He had resigned his commission and obtained an order for 5,000 acres of the best land in the colony for his sheep-breeding.[179] Although King recognised the economic importance of Macarthur's proposals for sheep farming for the colony and supported them, he had received little political support in London. The same occurred when he complained of the proceedings of the local courts martial as vitally affecting the peace of the colony, the Judge-Advocate

---

[176] The deteriorating relationship between King and the military in early 1803 is detailed in *HRNSW*, Vol. 5, pp. 22-37. Some of these libels are printed in *HRNSW*, Vol. 5, pp. 123-127; see also, King to Hobart, 9 May 1803, *HRA*, Series I, Vol. 4, pp. 159-160, 167-173.

[177] Paterson to War Office, 24 August 1801, *HRA*, Vol. 3, p. 292.

[178] King to Portland, 25 September 1801, *HRNSW*, Vol. 4, pp. 529-533, 559-582, considers the duel between Paterson and Macarthur; King to Portland, 5 November 1801, *HRNSW*, Vol. 4, pp. 609-610, *HRA*, Series I, Vol. 3, pp. 280-286, 296-298, on the duel, its causes and on sending Macarthur to England for trial. However Adjutant-General Calvert to Under-Secretary Sullivan, 31 January 1803, *HRNSW*, Vol. 5, pp. 11-13, made clear the impossibility of trying Macarthur in England and remitted the trial back to NSW.

[179] Camden to King, 31 October 1804, *HRA*, Series I, Vol. 5, pp. 161-162, detailed the land and convicts Macarthur was to receive. King to Camden, 20 July 1805, *HRNSW*, Vol. 5, pp. 660-662, *HRA*, Series I, Vol. 5, pp. 510-512, suggest King and Macarthur were reconciled as King was prepared to give him assistance with his land grant and sheep farming.

in London in January 1804 coldly told him that 'for the sake of harmony' he would 'pass over any seeming irregularity'.[180] Disputes with the NSW Corps and a recurrence of gout led King to ask for leave of absence in May 1803 while an inquiry was held into the state of the colony.[181] In November, the Secretary of State received King's request and immediately accepted what he was quick to interpret as an offer of resignation.[182] After King received Hobart's reply in June 1804 his activities slowed down. However, he was not relieved until August 1806 [183] and in the interval he suspected that other critics especially Maurice Margarot, Henry Hayes, Michael Robinson and William Maum were blackening his reputation in England.[184] This negative view of King remained and Watson concluded on 1915:

> ...it is difficult to trace any direct influence of the governor [King] in the improvement of the conditions of life in the colony. The colony made considerable progress, but probably all the development was due to automatic and general causes, unaided by the personality or direction of the administrator.[185]

The problems faced by Hunter and especially by King have tended to be seen in terms of the breakdown in relations between their successor, William Bligh and the NSW Corps. This judgement is particularly unfair for King since he made a significant contribution to the economic development of the colony especially the move away from a government-led economy to one in which private enterprise played an increasingly important role.

---

[180] Judge-Advocate Morgan to King, 4 January 1804, *HRNSW*, Vol. 5, pp. 301-302.
[181] King to Hobart, 9 May 1803, *HRNSW*, Vol. 5, p. 130.
[182] Hobart to King, 30 November 1803, *HRNSW*, Vol. 5, pp. 273-274.
[183] Castlereagh to King, 20 November 1805, *HRNSW*, Vol. 5, p. 735, *HRA*, Series I, Vol. 5, p. 489, informed King that Bligh was his replacement.
[184] King's concerns about Margarot and Hayes were initially expressed in a letter to Under-Secretary Sullivan, 21 August 1804, *HRNSW*, Vol. 5, pp. 450-451. King to Under-Secretary Cooke, 20 July 1805, *HRNSW*, Vol. 5, pp. 663-667, detailed his concerns about what he saw as their 'vile assassinating acts'.
[185] Watson, Frederick, 'Introduction', *HRA*, Series I, Vol. 5, p. xiii.

Initially a colony of convicts and guards, under Phillip, Hunter and King NSW was ruled by a military government though there was an element of civilian rule in the person of civil magistrates and, from the outset, an embryonic notion of the rule of law. The persistent problem of a colony faced with endemic shortages and the real threat of periodic starvation was far from resolved by 1806 when the disastrous floods again demonstrated just how precarious survival could be. [186] Successive governors were increasingly faced by the changing nature composition of colonial society as convicts gained their freedom and free settlers began to arrive. This, combined with the growing power of the NSW Corps that exploited the colony in its own economic interests, created growing problems with military rule. Colonists had access to the courts but those courts were dominated by military personnel who often had little sympathy for the plight of either emancipated convicts or free settlers. The need to rein in the power of the NSW Corps and especially its officers led to a division within the ruling elite as Hunter and then King sought to assert their gubernatorial authority. Faced by a military elite with sympathetic access to the decision-making process in London and the problem of retaining support from successive secretaries of state whose policies were rarely consistent, neither Hunter, who was recalled or King, who 'resigned' made any permanent inroads into the power of the Corps. When Governor William Bligh (1806-1810) [187] vigorously challenged the near-monopoly of trade and land grants being exercised by the Corps' officers and their associates amongst the leading landowners, he was arrested by the army in 1808 in Australia's only military coup.

Change under Macquarie

Phillip, Hunter, King and Bligh were naval officers and all had faced problems controlling military personnel and all had been largely unsuccessful. For Phillip, the problem with

---

[186] On the Hawkesbury flood, March 1806, see, King to Camden, 7 April 1806, *HRNSW*, Vol. 6, pp. 59-65. Over 23,000 bushels of wheat and 3,500 livestock plus 7 lives were lost and over 36,000 acres of land inundated.

[187] For Bligh's commission and instructions, dated 26 May 1804, see, *HRNSW*, Vol. 5, pp. 628-641.

Major Ross and the Marines was largely the result of different expectations of their role in the new colony. For Hunter, King and in the case of Bligh disastrously, tensions with the NSW Corps were a consequence of the growing division between government and private enterprise and the expectation of profit that pervaded the ethos of the Corps, ordinary soldiers as well as officers. The appointment of Major-General Lachlan Macquarie as the fifth Governor of NSW represented a shift away from naval to military appointees as Governor. [188] He held office from April 1809 taking up his commission as governor on 1 January 1810 and remained in the colony until his resignation in 1821. [189] As Governor of NSW, he also assumed control of the North Island of NZ with the appointment of a Justice of the Peace for the Bay of Islands.[190] After the military coup in 1808, the British Government decided to recall the NSW Corps and replaced them with the 73rd Regiment.[191] As officer commanding the 73rd Regiment, Macquarie was at a distinct advantage to his predecessors as senior officer of the garrison as well as Governor. Like previous governors, Macquarie was given absolute authority to make and implement laws. [192] His first exercise of authority was to

---

[188] McLachlan, N. D., 'Macquarie, Lachlan (1762-1824), *ADB*, Vol. 2, pp. 187-195, Ellis, M. H., *Lachlan Macquarie: His Life, Adventures and Times*, (Dymock's Book Arcade) 1947, 2nd ed., (Angus & Robertson), 1952, and Ritchie, John, *Lachlan Macquarie: a biography*, (Melbourne University Press), 1986, are valuable biographies. Macquarie, Lachlan, *Journal of his Tours of New South Wales and Van Diemen's Land 1810-1822*, (Trustees of the Public Library of New South Wales), 1956, provides his own view of governing NSW and VDL. Ibid, Atkinson, Alan, *The Europeans in Australia*, Vol. 1, pp. 317-342.
[189] Macquarie's arrival and his proclamation on 1 January 1810 are dealt with in *HRNSW*, Vol. 7, pp. 252-253, *HRA*, Series I, Vol. 7, pp. 226-227.
[190] New Zealand was part of NSW from 1788 until 1840 when it was proclaimed as a separate colony.
[191] Castlereagh to the Admiralty, 2 May 1809, and Under-Secretary Cooke to Quartermaster-General Gordon, 11 May 1809, *HRNSW*, Vol. 7, pp. 112-113, 141, cover the recall of the NSW Corps.
[192] T. W. Plummer to Macquarie, 4 May 1809, *HRNSW*, Vol. 7, pp. 113-124, provides a detailed critique of the situation in NSW and the need for reform. Macquarie's commission and instructions dated 9 May 1809 are printed in *HRNSW*, Vol. 7, pp. 126-140,

revoke all the controversial actions of the rebel regime including government appointments, land grants, leases, sentences and pardons. [193] His Instructions were

> To improve the Morals of the Colonists, to encourage marriage, to provide for Education, to prohibit the Use of Spirituous Liquors, to increase the Agriculture and Stock, so as to ensure the Certainty of a full supply to the Inhabitants under all Circumstances. [194]

Macquarie insisted on morality, virtue and temperance closing 55 inns and increasing the tax on imported liquor.[195] He remodelled the Commissariat [196] and the organisation of the Police Fund as the basis of colonial revenue, [197] levied customs duties, opened a new market place, [198] created a coinage in 1813 to replace barter, (particularly the 'rum currency') and established the first bank in 1817. [199] He opened schools for the young so that the children would become better citizens than their parents. [200] He used emancipist settlers as teachers and eventually at his request, qualified teachers were sent out from England. He allowed ex-convicts to be re-admitted to the rank in society they had forfeited including appointing three emancipated convicts (D'Arcy Wentworth, Andrew Thompson and Simeon Lord)

HRA, Series I, Vol. 7, pp. 183-197. See also Castlereagh to Macquarie, 14 May 1809, *HRNSW*, Vol. 7, pp. 143-147
[193] See the two proclamations issued on 4 January 1810, *HRNSW*, Vol. 7, pp. 255-259, *HRA*, Series I, Vol. 7, pp. 227-231.
[194] See, *HRNSW*, Vol. 7, p. 137.
[195] See Proclamation, 24 February 1810, *HRA*, Series I, Vol. 7, pp. 278-279. Government and General Order, 16 February 1810, *HRNSW*, Vol. 7, pp. 289-290.
[196] Macquarie to Castlereagh, 30 April 1810, *HRNSW*, Vol. 7, pp. 353-354, *HRA*, Series I, Vol. 7, p. 248.
[197] Macquarie to Liverpool, 18 October 1811, *HRA*, Series I, Vol. 7, pp. 385-386.
[198] Macquarie to Liverpool, 18 October 1811, *HRA*, Series I, Vol. 7, p. 386.
[199] The formation of a bank was first raised in Macquarie to Castlereagh, 30 April 1810, *HRA*, Series I, Vol. 7, p. 264-266, and again 27 October 1810, *HRA*, Series I, Vol. 7, p. 343. The issue continued to be raised in correspondence, see, Liverpool to Macquarie, 26 July 1811, *HRA*, Series I, Vol. 7, p. 365.
[200] Macquarie to Castlereagh, 27 October 1810, *HRA*, Series I, Vol. 7, p. 246.

as magistrates in 1810. [201] Macquarie founded new towns at Richmond, Castlereagh, Pitt Town, Wilberforce and Windsor now referred to as the five 'Macquarie towns' to the west of Sydney and expanded the settlement. He visited VDL twice, [202] Newcastle and Illawarraand founded Port Macquarie. [203] He encouraged exploration including the crossing of the Blue Mountains in 1813 opening access to western lands and was responsible for the extension of the colony. [204] Macquarie was also responsible for 265 public

---

[201] Macquarie to Castlereagh, 30 April 1810, *HRNSW*, Vol. 7, p. 356-357, *HRA*, Series I, Vol. 7, p. 276.

[202] Macquarie's first tour of VDL occurred in 1811: Macquarie to Liverpool, 18 October 1811, *HRA*, Series I, Vol. 7, pp. 378-280, Macquarie to Liverpool, 17 November 1812, *HRA*, Series I, Vol. 7, pp. 581-589, contained Macquarie's report on the administration of VDL not contained in the *Journal*. Macquarie announced his intention to tour VDL a second time in Macquarie to Bathurst, 21 March 1821, *HRA*, Series I, Vol. 10, p. 492. The tour is reported in Macquarie to Bathurst, 17 July 1821, *HRA*, Series I, Vol. 10, p. 500. Macquarie stated that he has published a Government and General Order, 16 July 1821, giving an account of his 'Observations and remarks and that he enclosed a copy', pp. 501-507. Mitchell Library: A777 *Journal to and from Van Diemen's Land 1811* and A784 *Journal of A Tour of Inspection in Van Diemen's Land 1821*, are more detailed. See also *Sydney Gazette*, 11 January 1812, pp. 1-2, and *Sydney Gazette* 21 July 1821.

[203] Macquarie refers to the Northern Settlements at Port Macquarie and Newcastle 1821 in Macquarie to Bathurst, 30 November 1821, *HRA*, Series I, Vol. 10, p. 573: 'I have lately made Tours of inspection to the Northern Settlements at Newcastle and Port Macquarie, and afterwards to Bathurst and Illawarra or Five Islands; all of which are fine rich fertile Districts, and promise at no distant period to prove most valuable acquisitions to the Parent Colony. The result of My Observations on these Tours of Inspection I shall do myself the honor of reporting to Your Lordship in Person, on my arrival in England.' Macquarie must have completed this Despatch some weeks after the date 30 November 1821. He returned to Sydney from the tour to the Northern Settlements on 21 November 1821, travelled to Bathurst and back 15-26 December 1821 and travelled to Illawarra and back 9-17 January 1822. Macquarie's journals are Mitchell Library: A781 *Journal to and from Newcastle*, A783 *Journal of A Tour of Inspection to Bathurst in Decr. 1821*, and A786 *Journal of a Tour to the Cow Pastures and Illawarra/in January 1822*.

[204] On his tour of the interior in 1810, see, Macquarie to Liverpool, 18 October 1811, *HRA*, Series I, Vol. 7, pp. 378-380, and of the Bathurst Plains, Macquarie to Bathurst, 24 June 1815, *HRA*, Series

works of varying scale during his administration, many the work of his chief architect Francis Greenway, an ex-convict.[205] They included general post office and a new general hospital, [206] new army barracks and three new barrack buildings for convicts, roads to Parramatta and across the Blue Mountains, castle-like stables and five planned towns built out of reach of floodwaters along the Hawkesbury River. Central to Macquarie's administration was his concern for public morality. In some of his earliest orders the prevailing habit of cohabiting without marriage was denounced, [207] constables were directed to enforce laws against Sabbath breaking [208] and a regular church parade was introduced for convicts in government employment. [209] It seemed that he was successful in increasing 'Religious Tendency and Morals' as both church-going and the marriage rate increased. [210]

As the strongest inducement to reform Macquarie decided that ex-convicts, when they had shown that they deserved the favour, should be readmitted to the rank in

---

I, Vol. 8, p. 557. Macquarie wrote in Government and General Order 10 June 1815, pp. 568-576, 'For further Particulars...I take the Liberty to refer Your Lordship to the Accompanying Printed Report of my Tour, which I had published in the *Sydney Gazette* for the information of the Public (whose Curiosity was all alive on the Subject), soon after my return hither.' Mitchell Library: A778 *Journal of a Tour of Governor Macquarie's first Inspection of the Interior of the Colony, commencing on Tuesday the 6th of Novr. 1810*, and A779 *Tour to the New Discovered Country in April 1815*, is his detailed record. See also, *Sydney Gazette* 15 December 1810, p.1, *Sydney Gazette* 10 June 1815, *The Naval Chronicle*, Vol. 35, (January-June 1816), pp. 105-112, *The Colonial Journal*, Vol. 1, (January-July 1816), pp. 69-76, and *New Monthly Magazine and Universal Register*, Vol. 5, (25), 1 February, 1816, pp. 14-19.

[205] Herman, Morton, 'Greenway, Francis (1777-1837)', *ADB*, Vol. 1, pp. 470-473. See also Ellis, M. H., *Francis Greenway: His Life and Times*, (Angus and Robertson), 1953.

[206] Government and General Order, 23 June 1810, *HRNSW*, Vol. 7, p. 389.

[207] Proclamation, 24 February 1810, *HRNSW*, Vol. 7, pp. 292-294.

[208] See, Government and General Order, 27 January 1810, and 26 May 1810, *HRNSW*, Vol. 7, pp. 280-281, 382.

[209] Government and General Order, 19 May 1810, *HRNSW*, Vol. 7, p. 381.

[210] On economic growth under Macquarie see, Becket, Gordon, *A Collection of Essays on the Colonial Economy of New South Wales*, (Trafford Publishing), 2012, pp. 226-233.

society they had forfeited. Initially this policy was approved by Lord Liverpool, the Prime Minister as well as by William Wilberforce and the Select Committee on Transportation in 1812, but it aroused immediate indignation among immigrant settlers and military officers and alienated the very classes whose co-operation Castlereagh had advised him to foster. By 1818, he went so far as to suggest the cessation for three years of all immigration apart from 'respectable Monied Men'. He had found many of the free immigrants unsatisfactory settlers and disapproved of their reluctance to fraternise with ex-convicts.

Macquarie's support of emancipated convicts resulted in sustained opposition almost from the beginning of his governorship. Early in 1810 the senior chaplain, Samuel Marsden, [211] refused outright to serve with the emancipist justices, Simeon Lord[212] and Andrew Thompson on the turnpike board for the new Parramatta Road. In 1811, Macquarie flatteringly named a street in Parramatta after Marsden, but despite Wilberforce's attempts to mediate there was further controversy between them in 1814, and finally in January 1818 Marsden was summoned to Government House and denounced as a 'secret enemy'. Since the chaplain probably had more influential friends in England than any other colonist, he proved a dangerous antagonist. Jeffery Bent, judge of the Supreme Court created under the new Charter of Justice granted in 1814 also proved a vehement opponent. He kept his court closed rather than admit ex-convict attorneys to practise even though there was only one free lawyer in the colony. The governor's growing rift with both Bent brothers led to their recall. Ellis Bent died before this decision arrived, but his brother returned to England and assisted H. G. Bennet in mounting the campaign against Macquarie in the House of Commons that led to the appointment of a Select Committee on Gaols and of John Thomas Bigge as commissioner to enquire into the affairs of the colony.

Macquarie's emancipist policy also led to his falling out with his old friend of Indian days, Colonel George Molle who arrived with the 46th Regiment early in 1814 as

---

[211] Yarwood, A.T., 'Marsden, Samuel (1765-1838)', *ADB*, Vol. 2, pp. 207-212.
[212] Hainsworth, D. R., 'Lord, Simeon (1771-1840)', *ADB*, Vol. 2, pp. 128-131.

Lieutenant-Governor. [213] Soon after their arrival Molle and his officers complained of high prices and asked for higher pay. They disliked the favour shown by Macquarie to the emancipated convicts, whom they excluded from the regimental mess, even in cases when the governor looked on them with favour. In 1816, William Charles Wentworth insulted Molle in a 'pipe' or lampoon. Next year, during the investigation of its authorship, some of the officers of the regiment insulted Macquarie who felt that his 'old and Much liked Acquaintance' Molle, on whose 'Friendship and Candour' he had relied, had not seriously tried to check the opposition of his juniors to the Governor. Molle insisted that D'Arcy Wentworth, William's father, was responsible for his son's libels and demanded that he be court-martialled. To end all this bickering, Macquarie asked that the regiment be removed. Fortunately in August 1817 the 48th replaced Molle and the 46th that left for Madras the following month.

In the immediate aftermath of the French Wars, the British government faced with mounting public debts and economic depression adopted a programme of retrenchment. In 1817, Lord Bathurst, Secretary of State for the Colonies decided to examine the effectiveness of transportation as a deterrent to criminals. [214] Reform of the convict assignment system promised to stimulate colonial economic development but also to reduce state spending by shifting convict labour from the public to private sector. Bathurst's decision was also motivated by the dramatic growth in the numbers transported after 1815: between 1788 and 1815, some 15,000 convicts had seen sent to Australia but between 1815 and 1820, just over 13,000 men and women were transported and between 1815 and 1840 an average of 3,737 convicts arrived in NSW and VDL annually. John Thomas Bigge's commission to NSW reflected Bathurst's concern that Macquarie's humane and liberal policies were undermining the effectiveness of the transportation system as a means of criminal punishment.

---

[213] Macmillan, David S., 'Molle, George James (1773-1823)', *ADB*, Vol. 2, p. 243.
[214] Ritchie, John, *Punishment and Profit: the reports of Commissioner John Bigge on the colonies of New South Wales and Van Diemen's Land, 1822-1823*, Heinemann), 1970, examines the reasons for Bigge being sent to New South Wales.

Bigge arrived in Sydney on 26 September 1819 with sweeping inquisitional powers. From the outset, Bigge's relations with Macquarie were difficult. Macquarie had been given little warning of the official inquiry and received humiliating orders that he regarded as an affront to his authority according Bigge precedence next to himself as governor. Macquarie was a professional soldier of humble origins who understood the particular problems of governing NSW while Bigge, an aristocratic, professional lawyer who judged issues by English standards had no understanding of governing a penal colony. Private differences of opinion soon became embarrassing public arguments. [215]

Bigge felt that Macquarie's public works policy was 'absurd' and they disagreed over Macquarie's appointment of William Redfern, an emancipist, as a magistrate. [216] Bigge could see no advantages in either the aims or achievements of Macquarie's emancipist policy. For him, the policy was incompatible with Tory views of the purpose of the criminal law and reflected attitudes developed during his time in slave colonies in the West Indies. The basic difference between Bigge and Macquarie was that they saw NSW in different ways. Macquarie viewed it as 'a Penitentiary or Asylum on a Grand Scale' though he believed that one day it must be one of the greatest and most flourishing Colonies belonging to the British Empire'. By contrast, Bigge was influenced by people such as John Macarthur who saw its potential as a free settlement and wool growing area. Tension turned to antipathy and Bigge found himself more in sympathy with the exclusives of the squattocracy than with the Governor. Bigge was assiduous in assembling evidence in NSW and VDL, though this was often given in private with no distinction being made between sworn and unsworn testimonies, witnesses were not cross-examined, no rules of evidence were observed and he was far from impartial in the conclusions he drew. Although Macquarie strongly contested Bigge's conclusions, his position had already been fatally weakened by the changed attitudes of the Colonial Office. Bennett concluded:

---

[215] Bennett, J. M., 'Bigge, John Thomas (1780-1843)', *ADB*, Vol. 1, pp. 99-100.
[216] Ford, Edward, 'Redfern, William (1774-1833)', *ADB*, Vol. 2, pp. 368-371.

His analysis was unfairly prejudiced against an administration superior to any previously known in the colony and that enjoyed widespread popular support among the inhabitants.[217]

Bigge's reports were important for the future constitutional and political development of Australia. He emphasised that the population of the colony had grown enormously and now included many free settlers. His three reports, published in 1822 and 1823, questioned the autocratic style of government that had existed since Governor Phillip's administration.[218] As a result, clauses were inserted in the New South Wales Act (4 Geo. IV, c. 96) to set up limited constitutional government through a Legislative Council, to establish VDL as a separate colony, to enable widespread legal reforms and to make new provisions for the reception of convicts from England. Bigge's first report, *The State of the Colony of New South Wales*, focused on four main issues: general colonial conditions, the convict system, relations between social classes and Macquarie's programme of public works. Much was made of the alleged mismanagement of convicts but Bigge was unconcerned that the convict system was working very effectively in the colony, that Macquarie's methods had produced and maintained 'peace if not harmony' and that he had ended most brutality and violence. Bigge also criticised Macquarie's emancipist policy and disapproved of the status emancipated convicts were allowed in society. He thought the Governor's building programme was wastefully expensive and used his authority to discontinue some projects. Macquarie's opinion that the report 'gave no knowledge of the present state of the colony' was justified by the commissioner's lack of balance. Bigge failed adequately to explain the colony's history or contrast the

---

[217] Ibid, Bennett, J. M., 'Bigge, John Thomas (1780-1843)', p. 99.
[218] On his return to England, Bigge presented three reports to the House of Commons: *The State of the Colony of New South Wales*, (19 June 1822); *The Judicial Establishments of New South Wales and of Van Diemen's Land*, (21 February 1823); and *The State of Agriculture and Trade in the Colony of New South Wales*, (13 March 1823). Facsimile editions of the three reports were published in 1966. See also, Ritchie, J., (ed.), *The Evidence to the Bigge Reports: New South Wales under Governor Macquarie*, 2 Vols. (Heinemann), 1971.

orderly society that he found to the virtual anarchy existing before Macquarie took office. Bigge exposed inefficiency in district constables, theft of government medical stores, blemishes in the ticket-of-leave system for convicts, shortfalls in country education, poor accommodation for female convicts and poor regulation of liquor traffic, but he failed to acknowledge the very real achievements of government.

If the first report was candid, the second report, *The Judicial Establishments of New South Wales and of Van Diemen's Land*, was equivocal in character. Its analysis of the colonial legal establishments was superficial and he reserved his most valuable conclusions for private despatch to Bathurst. Bigge's supplementary instructions allowed him to report privately on matters of this kind but, having elected to do so, he allowed the public report to become a vehicle of insidious attack on Governor Macquarie. In his public report, he relied on statements by Mr Justice Barron Field [219] and Judge-Advocate (Sir) John Wylde [220] who attacked Macquarie but privately admitted that he had little confidence in their testimony. Bigge's lengthy treatment of the old libel case *Marsden v. Campbell* was calculated to discredit Macquarie since John Campbell had been the Governor's secretary from 1810 to 1821. [221] Most of the recommendations in the report affecting the civil

---

[219] Currey, C. H., 'Field, Barron (1786-1846)', *ADB*, Vol. 1, pp. 373-376.
[220] Mckay, R. J., 'Wylde, Sir John (1781-1859)', *ADB*, Vol. 2, pp. 627-628.
[221] Holder, R. F., 'Campbell, John Thomas (1770?-1830)', *ADB*, Vol. 1, pp. 199-201. The 'Philo Free' letter was published on 4 January 1817 in the *Sydney Gazette*, of which Campbell was official censor. This elaborately sarcastic review of the missionary activities of the 'Christian Mahomet' of the South Seas was obviously directed at Samuel Marsden who instituted a criminal charge against Campbell. He was found guilty of allowing the libel to appear, but no sentence was passed. Marsden then brought successful civil action and obtained £200 damages. Campbell, in his official apology sent to the Colonial Office by the governor, said that the 'hasty and inconsiderate Letter' was inspired by his indignation at Marsden's 'marked disrespect' to the governor's orders in not attending the meeting of Aboriginals at Parramatta a few days before. Undoubtedly this indignation had been growing for some time over the clergyman's open defiance of and devious attacks on the governor's authority and policy.

jurisdiction originated from Field and, while Bigge suggested reforms in criminal jurisdiction, Bigge simply supported submissions from the colonial lawyers, and especially the earlier recommendations of Judge-Advocate Ellis Bent and opposed popular demands for legal redress such as the introduction of jury trials or the modification of the military tribunals that composed the criminal courts. [222] Despite being the first lawyer of any distinction in the colony, he made surprisingly little personal contribution to founding a sound legal system. His concern was to draw attention to Macquarie's abuses of his limited legislative and prerogative powers and to condemn the governor's 'insensibility to the controlling power of the law'. This may have been a valid conclusion in terms of the letter of the law, but did not acknowledge that the rule of law was still in an embryonic form in NSW.

The third report, *The State of Agriculture and Trade in the Colony of New South Wales*, was the most unprejudiced and least contentious. It gave a generally clear picture of farming and grazing in the Sydney district and west of the Blue Mountains but failed to acknowledge the important developments of the Illawarra district and suggested incorrectly that agriculture had stagnated under Macquarie. Otherwise it was well presented and included useful accounts of the state of revenue, trade and the country's economic position.

Macquarie was the first to see beyond the limits of the convict settlement or the opportunities for self-enrichment that had characterised the early colony. [223] His vision, by 1821, was shown in a public building and town-planning programme that had established a solid infrastructure for the colony. [224] Exploration had reached deep into the inland and settlement and agriculture were following, north and south along the coastline and inland beyond Bathurst. Agriculture was, in fact, creating the conditions for the colony to become almost economically self-sufficient. The

---

[222] See Judge-Advocate Bent to Under-Secretary Cooke, 7 May 1810, and Judge-Advocate Bent to Earl Liverpool, 19 October 1811, *HRNSW*, Vol. 7, pp. 310-377, 621-630.

[223] Macquarie to Bathurst, 27 July 1822, *HRA*, Series I, Vol. 10, pp. 671-684, provides a justification for Macquarie's policies written after he returned to England.

[224] Ibid, pp. 684-701, Macquarie lists his public works in NSW and VDL as an appendix to his letter to Bathurst.

non-Aboriginal population of the colony including VDL was approximately 37,000, of whom at least 8,000 were free settlers or had been born in the colony. However, frustration and recurring bouts of illness led him to submit his resignation on several occasions. A serious illness in 1819 almost proved fatal, and the pressures of Bigge's commission of inquiry reinforced his desire to return home to defend the charges made against his administration. Finally at the end of 1820, he learned that his third application for resignation had been accepted though it was not until 12 February 1822 that he and his wife and son departed for England. What Bigge had not understood was that Macquarie had converted NSW from a rebellion-torn penitentiary to a settlement of substance.

By 1822, NSW had begun to evolve away from its penal origins. Although free settlers had begun to arrive in the colony in the early 1790s, it was not until after 1815 that in both NSW and VDL, there was sustained growth and new land was brought into cultivation. [225] Constitutionally, NSW was founded as an autocracy run by the governor, although the early governors effectively ruled by consent, with the advice of military officers, officials and leading settlers and exercised their powers within the restraints of British law. By the early 1820s, it was widely believed that the deterrent effect of transportation had declined and there had been a blurring between the respective positions of emancipated convicts and free settlers. Bigge's reports sought to restore transportation as 'an object of real terror' by calling for greater severity in the treatment of convicts, an end to free grants of land at the end of their sentences and a continuance of their subordinate status by not admitting them to positions of social responsibility. For Bigge, the future of the colony lay with the free settlers who would possess the land, employ the convicts and produce wool. Free immigration was no longer secondary to the purposes of settlement and this meant that the autocratic system needed to be modified and a system of government more suitable for free subjects of the Crown introduced. This, for Bigge, meant a legislature to curb the autocratic tendencies of governors and a judicial system that safeguarded the rule

---

[225] In 1809, there were an estimated 300 free settlers in NSW and VDL though this figure does not include children. By 1820, there were 1,307 free immigrants.

of law. This restraint on rule by decree exacerbated the existing tensions between exclusives and emancipated convicts and opened up a three-way contest for power between successive governors and these two groups that dominated colonial politics until the 1850s.

4 Military rule to responsible government

Under Macquarie's successors, Sir Thomas Brisbane, Sir Ralph Darling, Sir Richard Bourke and Sir George Gipps, three major developments impacted on the ways in which NSW was governed. [1] From 1823 there was a shift from military to civilian rule in the colony that placed constraints in the authority of Governors. Of especial importance were the introduction of representative legislative bodies and the increasing power of the courts to hold governors legally accountable for their decisions. The social balance in the colony shifted from transported convicts to free settlers and emancipated convicts and the contemporary perspective of NSW as simply a penal colony gradually changed. The exploration of Australia in the 1810s and 1820s resulted in growing British territorial ambitions in Australia as a whole. In part economic, the growing need to define 'Australia' was also motivated by the potential threat from other nations with ambitions in the South Pacific. There had been a French presence that was sufficiently threatening at the beginning of the nineteenth century to induce Governor King to establish VDL as a colonial adjunct of NSW. Russia also had ambitions in the Pacific though this tended to be focused on the northern ocean. Finally, the United States already had important economic interests especially in whaling in the southern ocean and, although its imperial ambitions were as yet undeveloped, the potential for extending economic into territorial ambitions was viewed as possible. The need to maintain British hegemony in Australia led to NSW losing its colonial primacy with the creation of separate colonies in VDL, the nascent settlements in WA, Port Phillip District and the creation of South Australia. Although it may have

---

[1] See ibid, Clune, David, and Turner, Ken, (eds.), *The Governors of New South Wales, 1788-2010*, pp. 126-202, on Brisbane, Darling, Bourke and Gipps. Callaghan, Thomas, *Acts and Ordinances of the Governor & Council of New South Wales and Acts of Parliament Enacted for, and Applied to the Colony with Notes & Index*, 3 Vols. (William John Row, Government Printer), 1847, provides details of legislation passed between 1824 and 1846.

yearned to retain its colonial position as 'primus inter pares', these new communities developed independently and had their own ways of doing things even if their political institutions mirrored those in NSW.

Emancipists and Exclusives

Early accounts of Australia's colonial history pitted two groups against each other: the hierarchical, largely landed and pseudo-aristocratic 'exclusives' and the 'emancipists', of lower social status, possessing 'considerable solidarity' and politically sound in their democratic aspirations supported respectively by 'bad' and 'good' governors. It was a contest that the 'exclusives' lost, perhaps because they had to lose, and from which democratic liberalism emerged triumphant. The problem with these accounts is that 'emancipist' did not enter usage as a noun until 1822, before that ex-convicts had been termed 'emancipated convicts', while 'exclusives' was first used in 1836 and only then as a term of derision. [2]

The social pretentions and prejudices of Britain were transported to NSW with the First Fleet and the colony was founded as a society of clearly distinguished ranks. As a penal colony it consisted of free settlers and convicts but the colonial administration recognised that just as there were gradations in the social status of free settlers, the same gradations existed among the convict population. Phillip thought that the skills that individuals had employed in Britain, for instance as artisans, should be encouraged in the new colony and those who were literate were quickly subsumed within the colonial administration as clerks. This pragmatic solution to the skills shortage was continued by subsequent governors. Being a convict was a temporary condition and once emancipated or at the completion of their sentence, in some cases convicts were free to return to Britain, though may have chosen to remain in the colonies while others, whose pardon was conditional, had to remain in Australia. [3] Almost from the beginning of NSW, there were distinct groups in the colonial society: free settlers, convicts and emancipated convicts divided by the nature of

---

[2] *Colonist*, 28 January 1836: 'Our *Pure Merino*, our *Exclusive* contemporaries have been abusing the Governor.'
[3] Bathurst to Brisbane, 29 July 1823, *HRA*, Series I, Vol. 11, pp. 91-92, provided instruction on the treatment of emancipated convicts.

their pardon or whether they had completed their sentence. To see colonial society in terms of the anachronistic and polarised emancipists and exclusives neglects its more nuanced character. 4

Colonial societies were almost always more fluid and volatile than society in Britain and this was particularly the case in NSW and VDL when convicts or emancipated convicts were in a majority. The critical question was what their status should be as now free men and women. Although it may have been difficult to hide their penal origins, connections always existed between free and emancipated colonists as, for instance, in business or commerce and it was easy, as Bigge did in his three reports, to misrepresent or exaggerate their relationships exacerbating social divisions that had probably softened in the 1810s. Yet Macquarie's decision to place a handful out of the thousands of emancipated convicts in important and high status government positions was met with widespread resentment from free settlers especially those within its political and economic elite. Macquarie may have believed that having served their sentence emancipated convicts were free to resume their place in society. At a private level contact between free and emancipated settlers was a personal matter but whether ex-convicts could be truly rehabilitated and accepted back into public society was another matter. Bathurst concluded in his letter to Brisbane in July 1823:

> ...you will not appoint any person [to the magistracy] who has been a Convict to that important situation, until he shall have acquired weight and consideration by the meritorious discharge of other civil employments...[and also] by the consideration of the private character which he had obtained since his return to Society and which naturally requires some interval of time before any fair estimate could be formed of it. 5

For emancipated men and women of whatever social status, it was critical to gain colonial respectability and

---

4 Connor, Michael, *The Politics of Grievance: Society & political controversies in New South Wales 1819-1827*, (Mirimar Books), 2012, based on his PhD thesis, (University of Tasmania), 2002, considers the question of vocabulary and society in its opening part.
5 Bathurst to Brisbane, 29 July 1823, *HRA*, Series I, Vol. 11, p. 92

possessing respectability was important for them and their children. Some emancipated convicts became extremely wealthy and could purchase respect but that was not the same thing as respectability. [6] Despite his commercial acumen, Simeon Lord may not have been regarded as a 'gentleman' because of his convict experience but he successfully established respectable credentials for his family. His eldest son, Simeon, was a successful pastoralist and fathered two members of parliament, the founder of the Victoria Downs station and a daughter who married a Queensland Surveyor-General. Francis, Lord's second son, was a legislative councillor in 1843-1848, 1856-1861 and finally 1864-1892. Edward was city treasurer of Sydney and mayor of St. Leonards while George William was a member of the Legislative Assembly after 1856, Colonial Treasurer in 1870-1872, a legislative councillor between 1877 and 1880 and a prominent company director.

At one level colonial society sought to emulate society in Britain but there were clear limitations to how far this emulation could progress. There was no hereditary aristocracy that monopolised economic and political power and there were opportunities for social advancement that were largely unknown in nineteenth century Britain. Emancipated convicts might marry widowed landowners and become neighbours of free settlers. Free emigrants who came to the colony as artisans might branch out on their own, become successful businessmen and end up patronising their former masters. Individuals who little prospect of political advancement at home could become important and well-paid colonial officials. NSW and VDL, as well as the later colonies, were all places of social opportunity in which distinctions of rank could easily become blurred and where social advancement through labour or luck were not uncommon. After being in the colony several months, Fanny Macleay decided:

> The people here are half mad – They are for ever quarrelling with each other & are as angry with one as possible unless one

---

[6] The question of colonial respectability is examines in McKenzie, Kirsten, *Scandal in the Colonies: Sydney & Cape Town, 1820-1850*, (Melbourne University Press), 2004, and Baxter, Carol, *An Irresistible Temptation: The true story of Jane New and a colonial scandal*, (Allen and Unwin), 2006.

embraces their prejudices & refrains from speaking to those with whom they are offended. 7

It was, however, still a society in which social class played a significant role. Settlers sorted themselves into upper-, middle- and working-classes but within each of those classes there were gradations based on skills, education and gender, respectability and non-respectability, colonial and British born, as well as free and emancipated. This was not a society of social absolutes.

The 'long' decade, 1821-1837: establishing a civic society

Between 1823 and 1830, the legislative and judicial framework for NSW and VDL was established through a combination of legislation passed by the British Parliament and its application to the specific circumstances in the colonies. This reflected the conclusions reached in Bigge's three reports and was largely motivated by the need to achieve some accommodation between the powers of the governor and the calls from free settlers for some form of representative government and more clearly defined legal structures. Parallel to these constitutional developments but similarly caused by calls from free settlers for territorial expansion, were attempts to define and delimit the extent of British involvement in Australia. In this process, it was gubernatorial proclamation, albeit supported by the Colonial Office, rather than British legislation that characterised this process of 'empire-building'.

The Supreme Court of Civil Judicature, the first superior court of NSW, was established by the Letters Patent dated 2 April 1814. This Second Charter of Justice of NSW provided that there should be a Supreme Court constituted by a Judge appointed by the King's commission and two Magistrates. The charter also created the Governor's Court and the Lieutenant-Governor's Court. The jurisdiction of the Governor's Court and the Supreme Court extended to VDL. All three courts were concerned with civil matters only. In 1823, the New South Wales Act defined a

---

[7] Earnshaw, Beverley, and Hughes, Joy, (eds.), *Fanny to William: The Letters of Frances Leonora Macleay, 1812-1836*, (Historic Houses Trust of New South Wales: Macleay Museum, University of Sydney), 1993, 28 May 1826, p. 56.

new structure for the courts and the role of judges. [8] The legislation repealed the New South Wales Courts Act 1787 and authorised the establishment of a Legislative Council and Supreme Court in NSW and a Supreme Court in VDL. It also provided that VDL could become a separate colony. [9]

The Supreme Court in both NSW and VDL would hear all pleas, civil, criminal or mixed and had the same powers as the common law courts of King's Bench, Common Pleas and Exchequer in England and also the Courts of Equity and Chancery. The new Supreme Courts were also given ecclesiastical jurisdiction to decide such matters as probate and letters of administration. Section 8 of the Act authorised the King to introduce trial by jury, if so advised by the Privy Council. Civil cases were normally heard before the Chief-Justice and two magistrates, but if all parties agreed, the magistrates could be replaced by a jury of 12 men. Appeals from civil cases decided in the Supreme Court could go to a Court of Appeal comprising the Governor and Chief-Justice. An appeal to the Privy Council was possible when more than £500 was involved. In criminal cases, a jury of seven military or naval officers would be assembled. Courts of Quarter Sessions were set up to try crimes not punishable by death (s19). These procedures resembled those of the existing Courts of Criminal and Civil Judicature abolished by this Act. The legislation was implemented through the Charter of Justice published on 13 October 1823 that took effect in NSW on 17 May 1824. [10] This provided for the creation of a Supreme Court of NSW, with a single Chief-Justice and if necessary four extra judges, for the appointment of Court officers and the admission of solicitors and barristers to practice. Unlike

---

[8] House of Lords, Record Office: 4 Geo. IV c.96, An Act to provide, until the First Day of July One thousand eight hundred and twenty-seven, and until the End of the next Session of Parliament, for the better Administration of Justice in New South Wales and Van Diemen's Land, and for the more effectual Government thereof and for other Purposes relating thereto.

[9] Section 44 of this Act authorised the separation of VDL from NSW that took place under an Order-in-Council (a command or direction from the Privy Council) in 1825. Bathurst to Brisbane, 28 August 1823, *HRA*, Series I, Vol. 11, pp. 109-113, detailed Brisbane's responsibilities in relation to VDL under the newly appointed Sir George Arthur as its Lieutenant-Governor.

[10] States Records, New South Wales: SRNSW: X22

earlier Charters, it ruled out the admission of ex-convicts to the legal profession while judges ruled out ex-convicts sitting on juries, although in practice this was not always adhered to.

In 1823, the British Government did not considered NSW to be ready for representative government but the Legislative Council provided a first step towards a 'responsible' Parliament. The legislation (s24) created a Legislative Council with appointed members, 'not exceeding seven and not less than five' councillors appointed by Britain's Secretary of State. [11] They were all public officials and even though they had very little power as councillors, they had considerable influence in their official positions and had the power to advise the governor in the exercise of his legislative powers. Councillors' opposition could, in normal circumstances defeat a law proposed by the governor. In addition, the Council had control over local appropriation of revenue. Decisions of governor and Council remained subject to veto by the Crown and the Chief-Justice of the Supreme Court also had a limited power of veto. The Act prevented the Governor for submitting any bill to the Council unless the Chief-Justice had certified that the proposed measure was not repugnant to the laws of England and each proposed law had to be set before the British Parliament (s29).

The Legislative Council first met on 25 August 1824 and was presided over by Governor Brisbane. Its members were: Chief-Justice Francis Forbes, Colonial Secretary Frederick Goulburn, Principal Surgeon, James Bowman and the Surveyor-General, John Oxley. Lieutenant-Governor, Colonel William Stewart was not present at the first meeting. Brisbane thought it unwise to attend subsequent sittings that were chaired by the Chief-Justice. The Governor initiated its business and had the power to overrule it when he thought this was necessary. In 1825, Ralph Darling's Commission provided for the creation, by prerogative act of an Executive Council that the Governor was directed to consult and was to act on its advice. [12] The number of Legislative Councillors was also increased to seven including some councillors not holding public office.

---

[11] Bathurst to Brisbane, 19 January 1824, *HRA*, Series I, Vol. 11, pp. 195-196.
[12] *HRA*, Series I, Vol. 12, pp. 99-126.

The Executive and Legislative Councils shared the same premises, had common members and shared the same Clerk (the Clerk of the Councils) until the positions were separated in July 1843.

The 1823 Act was a temporary measure and there was a 'sunset clause' that it was to terminate in five years (s.45). It was replaced by the Australian Courts Act of 1828 (9 Geo IV, c.83). [13] This strengthened the role of both Supreme Courts by ending appeals from Supreme Court decisions to the Governor, although appeals to the Privy Council could still only come from the Governor. Jury trials in the Court of Quarter Sessions were abolished until established in the Supreme Court, but a Supreme Court judge could allow juries in civil actions, if either party applied.[14] It empowered the Governor to introduce general trial by jury in criminal matters. Trial by jury for people charged under criminal law was finally established in 1833 in NSW and, in limited circumstances, the following year in VDL. Existing courts were to be retained apart from the Governor's Court, the local Court of Appeal. The Act put beyond legal doubt that the laws of England current when the Act came into operation would be applied in VDL as well as in NSW setting the date of this invisible transfer or 'Reception Day' as 25 July 1828 (s24). Later parliamentary legislation did not apply unless it was specifically passed for the colonies. This provided Australian statute law with a firm legislative foundation and allowed it to evolve according to its own conditions and needs.

The 1828 Act further increased the size of the Legislative Council to fourteen, seven of them non-official, but all nominated by the governor. The governor retained his initiative in introducing measures, but councillors could submit their own bills and, if refused, record their dissent. The governor was also required to preside in the Council even while his bills were being discussed, and to abide by its majority decision, though he had a casting vote. The veto of the Chief-Justice on legislation was abolished. Each new

---

[13] House of Lords Record Office: 9 Geo. IV c.83, An Act to provide for the Administration of Justice in New South Wales and Van Diemen's Land, and for the more effectual Government thereof, and for other Purposes relating thereto.

[14] In 1830, an amendment to the Jury Act 1829 (NSW) permitted ex-convicts to serve on juries.

enactment was now sent to the Supreme Court to be enroled but any of the judges could state its repugnancy to the laws of England and so compel its amendment. The Act strengthened the legal and civil standing of legislative and judicial institutions in NSW and VDL from the perspective of colonists but also of Britain.

The 1828 Act was of particular importance for VDL and put beyond doubt that it was a civil colony, even if its continuing penal functions and a strong quasi-military character made it an unusual one. [15] VDL was now seen as a British colony of settlement and the corpus of English law was accessible to British subjects in the colony. [16] Even Lieutenant-Governor George Arthur recognised that the colony was on the path to a civic society. While VDL was, for the present, 'an extensive Gaol to the Empire', he wrote to Earl Bathurst in 1826, that he was 'laying the foundations of a free Colony'.

> As, when the rugged scaffolding and rubbish is removed, a magnificent and well-proportioned Building delights the Eye, so here, when transportation shall cease, and all its chains and trammels disappear, a flourishing country will be at once exhibited.[17]

The Act envisaged the issuing of a new Charter of Justice for VDL. This second Charter arrived in 1831 and with other local legislation established the basis for the

---

[15] A persistent issue for Tasmania and the eastern Australian colonies was how far the legislative power of the Colonies was delimited by British statutes either preceding or following Reception Day. This issue was largely settled when the British Parliament passed the Colonial Laws Validity Act 1865 (28 & 29 Victoria c. 63) by which only colonial legislation voided on the ground of repugnancy was inconsistent with British statutes directed to that specific Colony (ss2 and 3).

[16] A later step towards Tasmanian legislative independence from Britain was the 1907 British legislation, the Australian States Constitution Act. Only legislation that altered the Constitution of the Tasmanian Parliament could be reserved for Royal Assent to those. Tasmanian legislative independence was achieved with the Australia Act 1986, concurrently enacted by the Commonwealth, State and United Kingdom Parliaments.

[17] Arthur to Bathurst, 21 April 1826, *HRA*, Series 3, Vol. 5, pp. 152-153.

operation of the Supreme Court for the remainder of the century.

Sir Thomas Brisbane succeeded Macquarie as Governor on 1 December 1821. [18] Macquarie had been a highly visible Governor, living in Government House in Sydney and travelling throughout the colony. Brisbane, by contrast lived and worked at Parramatta, coming in to Sydney a day or two a week, rarely travelled outside the Sydney district and had little contact with colonial society outside occasional vice-regal social functions. [19] Much of what he did during his four years in the colony was based on Bigge's reports and the instructions deriving from them, modified to take account of his view of local circumstances.[20] For instance, he conscientiously carried out Bigge's instructions of the 'necessity for creating a dread of transportation' and that the too lenient approach adopted by Macquarie should be tightened up. [21] He reduced the prevalence of premature tickets-of-leave, reduced the number of road gangs, whose members were prone to criminal activities and established new centres of secondary punishment first at Moreton Bay and then on Norfolk Island. [22] But he opposed excessive corporal punishment, reprieved many prisoners condemned to death and granted

---

[18] Heydon, J. D., 'Brisbane, Sir Thomas Makdougall (1773-1860)', *ADB*, Vol. 1, pp. 151-155, and Brisbane, Sir Thomas Makdougall, *Reminiscences of General Sir Thomas Makedougall Brisbane*, (T. Constable), 1860, pp. 43-60.

[19] Brisbane was able to continue his passion for science at Parramatta, see, 'Observations Made at Paramatta in New South Wales by Sir Thomas Brisbane to Which Are Annexed Observations Made by Charles Rumker at Stargard', *Memoirs of the Astronomical Society*, Vol. 2, (1826), pp. 277-284, and Schaffer, Simon, 'Keeping the Books at Paramatta Observatory', Aubin, David, Bigg, Charlotte and Sibum, H. Otto., (eds.), *The Heavens on Earth: Observatories and Astronomy in Nineteenth-Century Science and Culture*, (Duke University Press), 2012, in pp. 118-147.

[20] His Commission and Instructions are printed in *HRA*, Series I, Vol. 10, pp. 589-603.

[21] Bathurst to Brisbane, 9 September 1822, *HRA*, Series I, Vol. 10, pp. 784-790, outlines Bigge's conclusions about transportation and convict treatment. Bathurst to Brisbane, 22 July 1824, ibid, Vol. 11, pp. 321-322, proposed the re-occupation of Norfolk Island.

[22] See Brisbane to Bathurst, 28 April 1823, *HRA*, Series I, Vol. 11, pp. 74-80, outlining his policy towards convicts.

a large number of pardons for which he was criticised by Lord Bathurst. [23] He also hired out convicts with tickets-of-leave to colonists reducing the shortage of labour in the colony. [24] This reduced the cost of feeding them by the colonial government as well as providing revenue to the Colonial Office and resulted in an increase in the land under cultivation from 25,000 acres to 54,000 acres by 1825. [25]

Brisbane was cautiously liberal in his approach to governing NSW and stated at a public meeting just before he left that he believed that free institutions could be safely established in the colony. He supported trial by jury, a competitive uncensored press and favoured liberal changes to the New South Wales Act. He did not censor William Charles Wentworth's *Australian* when it began publication in 1824, despite its criticism of the authorities over, for instance the problem of women in the colony [26] and removed control of the *Sydney Gazette* from government control: the press in NSW was considerably freer under Brisbane than it was in Britain. [27] He established Courts of Quarter Sessions that allowed trial by jury, a successful experiment that ended in 1828 and the new Legislative Council operating effectively from 25 August 1824 producing legislation that was a serious attempt to establish an orderly basis for colonial administration. [28] Brisbane

---

[23] Bathurst to Brisbane, 18 March 1824, *HRA*, Series I, Vol. 11, pp. 545-546.
[24] This was, for instance, evident in Brisbane to Bathurst, 29 October 1824, *HRA*, Series I, Vol. 11, p. 387. Frederick Goulburn, NSW's Colonial Secretary stated in early October that shortages in the convict work force included 35 sawyers, 70 carpenters, 151 'farming men' and 98 labourers.
[25] Ibid, Brisbane, Sir Thomas Makdougall, *Reminiscences of General Sir Thomas Makedougall Brisbane*, p. 44.
[26] *Australian*, 7, 21 April 1824. See also criticisms of Brisbane and his responses contained in the *Morning Chronicle*, 21 August 1824, printed *HRA*, Series I, Vol. 11, pp. 606-614.
[27] Brisbane to Bathurst, 12 January 1824, *HRA*, Series I, Vol. 11, pp. 470-471, in which he states that 'I consider it most expedient to try the experiment of the full latitude of the freedom of the Press' and also lifted any censorship over the *Sydney Gazette*.
[28] For his legislative record see, *Acts and Ordinances of the Governor and Council of New South Wales Under the Authority of the Act of the Imperial Parliament of the Fourth of George IV, Cap. 96 and Passed During the Administration of His Excellency Sir T. Brisbane, 1824-1825*, (Robert Howe, Government Printer),

recognised, unlike Macquarie and his successor Sir Ralph Darling, that the growing size of the colony meant that governors had to delegate power to their officials. To his critics, this appeared as weakness and they unfairly accused him of lack of interest in the colony. He was regarded, in John Dunmore Lang's words as

> ...a man of the best intentions...but being constitutionally disinclined to business, he was at the same time singularly deficient of that energy of mind which was requisite to carry his purposes into action; and the consequence was, that though possessing for a considerable period the delegated powers of royalty, his good intentions were seldom realised and his promises too frequently forgotten. [29]

Brisbane was Governor at the cusp of constitutional change in Australia that he navigated with commendable skill. He never came to terms with the superior and pugnacious behaviour of the NSW magistracy, was ill-served by disloyal and factious officials and found himself caught up in the internecine divisions in colonial society between immigrant settlers and emancipated convicts who sought a greater say in the future direction of the colony and the established elite that resisted this. Heydon argued that it was 'an unhappy period in Brisbane's life' while Wellington commented on his recall 'there are many brave men not fit to be governors of colonies'. [30] This was not the view of many others in the colony for whom his had been 'a mild, an impartial and firm administration...all orders of the people have been equally protected and equally recognised...' [31]

1827. See also, Brisbane to Bathurst, 3 November 1824, *HRA*, Series I, Vol. 11, pp. 406-408, on the first two meetings of the Legislative Council.

[29] Lang, John Dunmore, *An Historical and Statistical Account of New South Wales*, 2 Vols. 2nd ed., (A. J. Valpy), 1837, Vol. 1, p. 192.

[30] Ibid, Heydon, J. D., 'Brisbane, Sir Thomas Makdougall (1773-1860)', *ADB*, Vol. 1, p. 154.

[31] Address, 1825, printed in ibid, Brisbane, Sir Thomas Makdougall, *Reminiscences of General Sir Thomas Makedougall Brisbane*, pp. 54-59, at p. 55. Further favourable addresses can be found at pp. 114-120.

Brisbane's successor Sir Ralph Darling was an individual on whom there were extreme views. [32] For many he was unpleasant, cold and authoritarian while others have seen him as a governor 'maligned'. [33] His only previous experience of colonial rule was between 1819 and 1820 when he had been military commander of Mauritius during which time he had dissolved the local council when it criticised him and had incurred the wrath of local planters in his determination to end the slave trade. This had not prepared him for the more arduous and socially complex task of governing NSW. Darling's own social position came not from birth but from army promotions and marriage and this made him extremely sensitive to social etiquette, the public expression of gentility. He introduced a formality previously lacking into the conduct of both business and entertainment at Government House to protect him and his family from wealthy emancipated convicts and 'the vulgar and impertinent'. [34] For Darling effective government was based on strict observance of regulations, unhesitating personal loyalty of his subordinates and respectability, essential he believed 'not only for the character of Government, but that the moral improvement of the people mainly depended on it'. [35]

Initially, Darling proved an effective and hard-working governor introducing much-needed reform of the machinery of local government and introducing much-needed banking and monetary reforms [36] and he brought the public accounts under control. [37] Colonial revenue

---

[32] For Darling's Commission and Instructions, see *HRA*, Series I, Vol. 12, pp. 99-126.

[33] 'Sir Ralph Darling (1772-1858), *ADB*, Vol. 1, pp. 282-286, and Fletcher, Brian, *Ralph Darling: A Governor Maligned*, (Oxford University Press), 1984, provide biographical material.

[34] Wright, Christine, *Wellington's Men in Australia: Peninsular War Veterans and the Making of Empire c. 1820-40*, (Palgrave Macmillan), 2011, pp. 40-42, for Darling and etiquette.

[35] For Darling's legislative achievement see, *The Public General Statutes of New South Wales from 5th Geo IV to 8th Will, IV, inclusive, (1824-1837)*, (Thomas Richards), 1861, pp. 46-248.

[36] See, Darling to Bathurst, 20 May 1826, *HRA*, Series I, Vol. 12, pp. 296-308, on his banking and monetary reform that had begun under Brisbane.

[37] Brisbane's appointment of William Lithgow as Auditor-General of all colonial revenue in NSW was central to this: see, Brisbane to Bathurst, 2 October 1824, *HRA*, Series I, Vol. 11, p. 379. For

doubled during his administration without additional taxes and this funded the entire cost of the civil government. [38] However, Darling found himself having to work with and take into account the advice of newly established Executive and Legislative Councils and his power to initiate legislation was restricted until 1829 by having to obtain a certificate from the Chief-Justice that it was not 'repugnant to the Laws of England'. This led to tensions between Darling and Sir Francis Forbes, the Chief-Justice who defended the principle of the rule of law and prevented executive incursions into the power of the judiciary. [39]

Darling's military attitudes were increasingly resented and he found himself facing concerted opposition from self-appointed champions of civil liberties such as William Wentworth. The 1823 Act had not satisfied the calls by reformers for popular government since it left the Executive Council under oligarchic control and left the governor with extensive autocratic powers. This was particularly the case with land and convict labour, areas in which settlers had important vested interests that brought them into conflict with Darling. After Bigge's reports, Lord Liverpool's Tory government recognised that Crown Land in NSW was a valuable asset for raising revenue; land sales had been introduced by Brisbane and large grants were restricted to those who undertook to maintain one convict labourer for every hundred acres. Soon after arriving in NSW Darling established a Land Board to examine the claims of applicants and land was only granted to genuine settlers in proportion to their capital and alienation within seven years was forbidden. [40] This did not reduce the demand for land and withholding grants appeared as arbitrary as earlier practices, but Darling's administration laid the foundations for a uniform land system. His approach to the convict assignment system was also unpopular and, although he established an Assignment Board to facilitate the operation

---

Darling's reorganisation see, Darling to Under Secretary Hay, 2 February 1826, *HRA*, Series I, Vol. 12, pp. 148-153.
[38] Becket, Gordon, *Financing the Colonial Economy 1800-1835*, (Trafford Publishing), 2012, pp. 258-257, considers financial management under Darling and Bourke.
[39] On the tensions between Darling and Forbes, see pp. 297-307.
[40] Darling to Bathurst, 5 May 1826, *HRA*, Series I, Vol. 12, pp. 266-268, on the creation of the Land Board that Darling had been authorised in his Instructions to establish.

of the system, he also arbitrarily penalised his critics by removing their convict servants. [41]

There is no doubting Darling's commitment to effective colonial rule in NSW, something that was recognised among his critics such as Forbes but he was unfortunate in being Governor at a time when NSW was rapidly transforming from a penal into a free colony and when, between 1827 and 1831, the British government itself was undergoing change. What had been an acceptable way of ruling NSW before 1823 was increasingly subject to criticism in Parliament and in the colony itself. In that respect, Darling was, for all his organisational abilities, temperamentally unsuited to respond to colonial pressure for constitutional and political change.

During the 1820s and 1830s, NSW became an increasingly politicised society. Questions of religious tolerance, education and constitutional reform that led to political fissures in Britain between Whigs and Tories were translated into colonial terms in NSW. Although the penal character of NSW introduced political and social nuances absent in Britain, broadly settlers who were Tories in Britain sided with the conservative elitist faction in the colony that argued for a hierarchical and exclusive definition of polity while those who were Whigs or radicals associated themselves with 'colonial liberals' in their calls for greater colonial constitutional definition and inclusive democratic freedoms.

Like his predecessor, Sir Richard Bourke was one of Wellington's officers during the Peninsula War and had previous experience of colonial government in South Africa.[42] A relative of Edmund Burke, Bourke was a Protestant Irish landowner from Limerick, part of a tightly knit group of landed Limerick families linked by marriage, patronage and liberalism in religion and politics. Bourke's

---

[41] For regulations for the distribution of assigned servants see, Darling to Bathurst, 1 May 1826, *HRA*, Series I, Vol. 12, pp. 251-253.

[42] For biographical material see, King, Hazel, 'Bourke, Sir Richard (1777-1855), *ADB*, Vol. 1, pp. 128-133, and *Richard Bourke*, (Oxford University Press), 1971. See also, King, Hazel, 'Richard Bourke and his Two Colonial Administrations: A Comparative Study of Cape Colony and New South Wales', *Journal and Proceedings of the Royal Australian Historical Society*, Vol. 49, (5), 1964, pp. 360-375.

liberalism sought mediation between the conservative Irish Protestant minority and the Roman Catholic minority and, even though he supported the Act of Union, he retained a strong sense of being Irish and favoured a tolerant, non-sectarian sense of citizenship, something reflected in his approach to imperial governance. [43] Unlike Darling, his liberalism led to persistent conflict with the 'conservative' faction within the Executive and Legislative Councils that impeded some of his plans to improve NSW and finally led to his resignation in 1837. He was, however, supported by 'colonial liberals' such as Forbes and Wentworth and was well-regarded by 'the people' as shown by the ovation that the crowd gave him on his departure.

Bourke responded more positively than Darling to the changing political tone of colonial politics and actively sought help from his Legislative Council with government affairs. Both held office for about six years, yet Bourke called his Council to 223 sittings compared to Darling's 85, and its printed reports ran to 691 pages under Bourke, but only 152 under Darling. Despite this, Bourke's record of reform in NSW was patchy not because he lacked colonial vision or reforming energy but because he faced resistance from the conservative colonial establishment within his Legislative Council and beyond. With the support of most of the judiciary and legal profession and with the agreement of the Colonial Office, he proposed the extension of trial by jury and the substitution of civil for military juries in criminal cases. Despite opposition from those who objected to ex-convicts serving on juries, in 1832 the existing Jury Act expired and was renewed in a slightly more liberal form.[44] A year later, strengthened by a petition signed by some 4,000 persons for the extension of civil juries, Bourke submitted a bill to the Legislative Council that was passed only by his casting vote, and even so he had to accept the continued use of military juries in criminal cases if the accused demanded it. He also introduced the Summary Punishment Bill reforming the criminal law in relation to

---

[43] Laidlaw, Zoe, 'Richard Bourke: Imperial liberalism tempered by Empire', in Lambert, D., and Lester, A., *Colonial Lives Across the British Empire: Imperial Careering in the Long Nineteenth Century*, (Cambridge University Press), 2006, pp. 113-144.
[44] Ibid, *The Public General Statutes of New South Wales from 5th Geo IV to 8th Will, IV, inclusive, (1824-1837)*, pp. 251-260.

convicts consolidating the law and reducing magistrates' power to inflict punishment to reduce the bias shown against convicts in more remote districts. [45] Although the bill was passed unanimously by the Legislative Council, the law continued to meet bitter resistance from some magistrates especially those in the Hunter River District where settlers had a justifiable fear of assigned convicts committing atrocities and where the Castle Forbes revolt occurred in 1833. James Mudie, an odious magistrate in the Hunter River orchestrated opposition among landowners to Bourke's administration that, he argued, had encouraged convicts to expect lenient treatment.[46] In reality, Bourke's reputation for leniency was misplaced. He was severe in his punishment of convicts but recognised that there was a fine line between the deterrent and reformative effects of punishment and that it should be administered with stern impartiality. What he did was to introduce greater order and predictability to the penal system not necessarily to make it more humane. Bourke successfully introduced church reform. Although Anglicans formed the largest denomination in NSW, about a fifth of the population was Roman Catholic and Presbyterians and other Nonconformists formed an important minority. To decision to dissolve the Church and Schools Corporation that controlled land used to produce funds for the Anglican Church, was taken before Bourke became Governor. The Church's leader in Australia, Archdeacon Broughton, argued that the land should still be used for the exclusive use of Anglicans while Bourke believed that all denominations were entitled to share in the proceeds. As an Irishman, he had seen the impact of sectarian intolerance and proposed to give public funds to the major denominations in proportion to the number of adherents. Despite the objections of the Anglican Church to becoming dependent on an annual grant, the Church Act was passed in 1836 with Anglicans covered by separate legislation. [47] This legislation proved highly successful and all denominations experienced

---

[45] Ibid, *The Public General Statutes of New South Wales from 5th Geo IV to 8th Will, IV, inclusive, (1824-1837)*, pp. 324-334.
[46] For the Castle Forbes revolt in 1833 and Mudie's attacks on Bourke, see pp. 414-420. See also, Mudie, James, *The Felonry of New South Wales*, (Whaley and Co.), 1837.
[47] Ibid, *The Public General Statutes of New South Wales from 5th Geo IV to 8th Will, IV, inclusive, (1824-1837)*, pp. 658-661.

growth in the number of churches and clergy and continued to keep pace with rising population. Bourke was less successful in his education reforms that, faced with Broughton's more assertive opposition, were abandoned after he twice attempted to establish a general system of education completely controlled and paid for by government. Some districts had no schools while had only poor quality Anglican parochial schools. Bourke believed that the government ought to establish schools and appoint trained teachers but had to abandon his efforts when faced with widespread opposition from the Protestant churches that was intensified by the support Bourke received from the Roman Catholic Church. [48]

In 1833, Bourke proposed elected government for the colony with the immediate introduction of a single chambered legislature, half elected and half nominated. This was shelved by the Colonial Office largely because of the difficulty of finding a solution that would be acceptable to Parliament in London and to the different political groups in NSW. However, a decision could not be delayed indefinitely since the New South Wales Act of 1828 was due to expire in 1836. Conservatives in the colony wanted elected representation to be delayed until free settlers outnumbered emancipated convicts and attacked Bourke's regime as lax on convict discipline pointing to the increase in levels of crime. Liberal colonists, by contrast, wanted the immediate introduction of elective institutions and denied that there had been any increase in the incidence of crime. The Colonial Office postponed any decision in 1836 by renewing the 1828 Act for a year, then did the same in 1837 and finally postponed any further constitutional change until after transportation to NSW ended. As a result, it was not until 1842 that the colony obtained a Legislative Council on the lines Bourke had originally proposed six years earlier. [49]

---

[48] Burton, William Westbrooke, *The State of Religion and Education in New South Wales*, (J. Cross), 1840, pp. 112-268, surveys the state of education in the 1830s geographically. See also, *Sessional Papers Printed by Order of the House of Lords, Volume 8, Accounts and Papers*, 1838, pp. 385-416.

[49] Macarthur, James, *New South Wales, Its Present State and Future Prospects: Being a Statement with Documentary Evidence*, (D. Walther), 1837, provides an excellent snapshot of NSW under Bourke.

From the 1820s, NSW's economic prosperity increasingly depended on wool because of easy access to land and the cheap labour provided by assigned convicts. Bourke's years as Governor saw the ending of the restricted settlement of Australia with the creation of the Port Phillip District and the founding of Melbourne. This, combined with the construction of roads between NSW and Port Phillip and the unofficial occupation of land by squatters, led to a significant expansion of settlement and population.[50] Even though the number of convicts in the colony increased from 21,000 in 1831 to 32,000 six years later, during the 1830s debates in both London and Sydney resulted in the end of transportation to NSW in 1840. This prospect led to the introduction of a scheme in 1832 paid for from the sale of Crown Lands by auction but managed in London for assisting free settlers. However, the unsatisfactory nature of many of the settlers caused widespread criticism in NSW. To address colonial concerns, in 1835 the Legislative Council established a Select Committee to examine the issue that recommended the introduction of a 'bounty' system of immigration organised and controlled from within the colony and which had the support of both conservative and liberal colonists. The consequence was a dual system of free immigration: the assisted passage scheme based in London supplemented by the bounty scheme introduced by Bourke. This had the desired effect and while population of NSW rose from about 51,000 in 1831 to over 97,000 in 1837, the proportion of convicts to free people declined.

Darling and Bourke were imperial administrators and represented a new cadre of military and civil officials who undertook imperial service across the globe in the 'British World'. Bourke had proved to be a more effective if controversial governor of great personal charm whose rule in NSW was humane, just and forward-thinking. His enthusiasm for reform was frequently not replicated by his more conservative opponents and his ideas for a more tolerant, educated society in which elected institutions played a central role ran ahead of political thinking in both London and Sydney. In addition, many of the critical

---

[50] For the significance of the recognition of the Port Phillip District, see Brown Richard, *Settler Australia, 1780-1880, Volume 2: Eureka and Democracy*, (CreateSpace), 2013, pp. 6-11.

changes in land and emigration policy were made by others and his actual achievements in the legal system and in church reform were modest. Nonetheless, Bourke's reputation remains high perhaps because he had a vision of NSW not as an inferior version of England but rather an overseas British community able to negotiate with the imperial government on its own behalf and acted as a benevolent ruler applying known and well-defined rules with equity. Although he resigned in 1837, unlike Brisbane and Darling, Bourke retained the support of the Colonial Office. The Colonial Secretary Lord Glenelg wanted him to take over the government of Cape Colony and in 1839 he was offered the governorship of Jamaica and commander-in-chief of military forces in India. He declined them all and the offer to stand for Parliament in 1841 largely because of declining health.

Governor Phillip's Commission established the boundary of NSW 135 degrees east longitude, a convenient line that included only the eastern one-third of the future Northern Territory. This provision continued in the Commissions of the Governors until in 1824 the British government decided to establish a military and trading post on the northern coast of Australia. This was established at Fort Dundas on Melville Island, some five degrees west of the established boundary of British interests. [51] To resolve this situation when a Commission issued by Letters Patent of 16 July 1825 to Ralph Darling, the next Governor of NSW, the Colonial Office extended the western boundary of NSW to 129 degrees east longitude. [52] This longitude later became the frontier dividing WA and South Australia. To the south, everything beyond Wilson's Promontory, the south-eastern 'corner' of the continent, ceased to be under the control of NSW and was placed under the authority of the Governor of VDL. The decision to extend the boundary of NSW further west marked the beginning of the imperial acquisition of the remainder of Australia as first WA in 1829

---

[51] Three British military/trading posts were set up on the north coast (Fort Dundas, 1824-1828; Fort Wellington, Raffle's Bay, 1827-1829; Victoria, Port Essington, 1838-1849) and emphasised Britain's claim to the whole of the Australian continent but were mainly concerned with British commercial and strategic interests in the Indian Ocean. They were temporary and not intended to promote colonisation in the Northern Territory.
[52] State Records New South Wales: SRNSW: X23.

and then South Australia in 1836 and finally Victoria in 1851 were established as separate colonies.

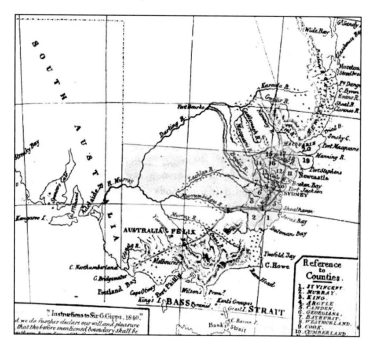

Eastern Australia, c1840

Between 1821 and 1837, the nature of colonial expansion in Australia changed radically. Although NSW retained its primacy, VDL was already an independent colony and the Swan River settlement had been tentatively established in WA. Australia was now a much larger colonial enterprise that was rapidly outgrowing its penal origins. This was also reflected in the significant constitutional innovations introduced in the 1820s that limited the untrammelled executive authority of the governor with Legislative and Executive Councils institutionalising the notion of government with consent and the initial powers of veto of the Chief-Justice limiting gubernatorial legislative autonomy. Political actions in NSW and increasingly in VDL were now accountable through the courts and enshrined in judicial decisions that established a colonial rule of law. Transportation had created a penal society but the developments in the 1820s and 1830s established the basis for a civic culture.

Towards responsible government, 1837-1856

Bourke's successor as Governor, Sir George Gipps had also served with Wellington in Portugal and Spain. [53] He had previous colonial experience in the West Indies in the 1820s and as a member of the Gosford Commission that enquired into French-Canadian dissatisfaction with British rule in Lower Canada in the mid-1830s. [54] Although a major in the British army, he did not have the rank to become military commander in NSW, a position held by Major-General Maurice O'Connell, and is generally considered to be the first civil Governor of the colony. Bourke had enjoyed considerable economic prosperity during his tenure but Gipps was faced with an intense slump soon after he arrived in the colony that lasted until the mid-1840s. He also had to deal with the prickly issues of land, relations between settlers and Aborigines, the suspension of the convict system in 1840 and calls for the separation of the Port Phillip District from the control of Sydney.

Gipps inherited a highly centralised system for managing the colony. His imprimatur was necessary for an inordinate number of minor decisions and although he sought to decentralise some decision-making, this remained a problem until the establishment of responsible government in the 1850s. His instructions from the Colonial Office were clear: he was to reduce colonial expenditure, something he did with some success and which did not win him many friends in the colony. He also had to address the demands for great colonial political

---

[53] McCulloch, S. C., 'Sir George Gipps (1791-1847), *ADB*, Vol. 1, pp. 446-453; Barker, Sydney, 'The Governorship of Sir George Gipps', *Journal of the Royal Australian Historical Society*, Vol. 16, (1930), pp. 169-263, and Gipps, J., *Every Inch a Governor: Sir George Gipps Governor of New South Wales 1838-1846*, (Hobson Bay Publishing), 1996, the only detailed study of his time in office. See also, Shaw, A. G. L., (ed.), *Gipps-La Trobe Correspondence, 1839-1846*, (Melbourne University Press at the Miegunyah Press), 1989.
[54] On Gipps' contribution to the Gosford Commission, see Brown, Richard, *Rebellion in Canada, 1837-1885, Volume 1: Autocracy, Rebellion and Liberty*, (CreateSpace), 2012, pp. 195-196, 200.

responsibility. Initially Gipps gained an unjustifiable reputation as a liberal. He had extended trial by jury soon after arriving in the colony in 1838, admitted the public to the Legislative Council by building a public gallery and also instructed that its proceedings should be published. [55] In fact, he was no democrat and favoured a restricted franchise excluding especially those with convict antecedents. He thought that control of the colony should remain centralised in the Governor and a small executive group but supported the decision to make the Legislative Council a partly elected body.

Calls for responsible government in Australia were informed by experiences elsewhere in the British Empire and were part of a global constitutional dialogue in different parts of the Empire as settlers sought to assert the political rights had brought with them from Britain. The politicised colonists in NSW carefully followed global events, drawing comparisons between experiences in one colony and another and considering the ways the Colonial Office reacted to constitutional demands. As early as 1819, William Charles Wentworth had noted that Britain had introduced elective franchises in the West Indies and Canada. [56] The essence of colonial constitutionalism in Australia was not a rejection of Britishness but a declaration of the principle of freedom from arbitrary or despotic rule. The problem was how to apply the principle to something as large as the British Empire. Edmund Burke had emphasised that ties within the Empire should be 'light as air but strong as iron'.[57] His solution was to let the colonies govern themselves without interference from imperial authorities. Yet, as Peter Lalor commented three months after Eureka, 'a British Government can never bring forth a measure of reform without having first prepared a font of human blood

---

[55] See, for instance, Macarthur, Edward, *Colonial Policy of 1840 and 1841: As illustrated by the Governor's Despatches, and Proceedings of the Legislative Council of New South Wales*, (J. Murray), 1841, pp. 27-70.

[56] Wentworth, W. C., *A Statistical, Historical and Political Description of the Colony of New South Wales and its dependent Settlements in Van Diemen's Land*, (G. & W. B. Whittaker), 1819, pp. 295-300, 356-357.

[57] Cochrane, Peter, *Colonial Ambition: Foundations of Australian Democracy*, (Melbourne University Press), 2006, pp. 7-10.

in which to baptise that offspring of their generous love'. [58] As in the Canadas, it took the Colonial Office time to recognise that colonial autonomy could strengthen not weaken the Empire by affirming a shared history. It was the idea that 'breaking away was coming together'. [59]

So long as NSW and VDL were largely populated by convicts, London was unwilling to listen to colonial demands for self-government. Nevertheless, the demands of free citizens for a stake in government increased. From 1835, the Australian Patriotic Association, with Wentworth as Vice-President, aimed to win representative government for NSW, albeit on behalf of propertied interests. [60] Charles Buller was employed by the Association as their London agent in 1838 and proved an able advocate for the citizens of NSW. [61] Canadian precedents were important for Australian democrats in their fight to secure self-government and parliamentary democracy but they were also important in justifying the Colonial Office's refusal. [62] The imperial government was unwilling to add to its difficulties by replicating constitutional conflict in Australia. Australian advocates of self-government read in the colonial press of the rebellions in the Canadas in 1837 and 1838 caused by 'an arbitrary, arrogant, vindictive and fraudulent oligarchy'.[63] Durham's *Report* was serialised in the pages of the *Sydney Gazette* from 27 June to 12 September 1839 [64]

---

[58] Peter Lalor's letter to the *Argus*, 10 April 1855, reprinted in 'Eureka Documents', *Historical Studies: Eureka Supplement*, (December 1954), p. 12.
[59] Ibid, Cochrane, Peter, *Colonial Ambition*, p. 9.
[60] Irving, Terry, *The Southern Tree of Liberty: The Democratic Movement in New South Wales before 1856*, (The Federation Press), 2006, pp. 26-36.
[61] Sweetman, p. 97.
[62] Sweetman, p. 19; Wright, Raymond, *A Blended House: The Legislative Council of Victoria 1851-1856*, (Department of the Legislative Council), 2001, pp. 46-47; Oldfield, Audrey, *The Great Republic of the Southern Seas: Republicans in Nineteenth-Century Australia*, (Hale & Iremonger), 1999, p. 44.
[63] Benjamin Wait quoted in ibid, Oldfield, Audrey, *The Great Republic of the Southern Seas*, p. 42.
[64] Nadel, George, *Australia's Colonial Culture: Ideas, Men and Institutions in Mid-Nineteenth Century Eastern Australia*, (F. W. Cheshire), 1957, p. 103. On the influence of Durham's *Report* on Australian thinking see, McKenna, M., *The Captive Republic: A*

and Gipps declared in the NSW Legislative Council that 'every man would do well to read it'. [65] Durham's *Report* and particularly its view of responsible government would influence the development of the Australian constitutions of the 1850s, but before that it was adopted the British government gave elements of self-government to NSW. [66]

The NSW Constitution Act 1842 created Australia's first semi-representative legislature, and while it did not grant full responsible government, it was an acknowledgment of the growing maturity of colonial society.[67] The Legislative Council that had been established after 1823 consisted of nominated members only and this only briefly satisfied the political demands of the colony as it emerged from its penal origins. When James Macarthur visited London in 1842, with Buller's help he drafted a document that formed the basis for a 'blended house' with one third nominated, two thirds elected members, but with no concept of ministerial responsibility. [68] This was a concept unique in the Empire, a single legislative chamber that blended appointed and elected representatives. Such an assembly was considered quite liberal by British standards, avoiding the problems of an 'appointed for life' upper house used in Canada. [69] The Legislative Council consisting of 36 members, 12 appointed by the Governor and the rest elected. Eligibility to vote was based upon ownership or occupation of property and only 9,315 out of a male population of 76,147 had sufficient property to vote in the first general election in June and July 1843. [70]

The Act did not establish 'responsible government' as the governor still had overriding authority and Ministers of

---

History of Republicanism in Australia, 1788-1996, (Cambridge University Press), 1996, pp. 29-31.
[65] Sweetman, p. 10.
[66] For example, Hunt, Thornton Leigh, *Canada and South Australia: A Commentary on that part of the Earl of Durham's Report which relates to the Disposal of Waste Lands and Emigration*, (A. Gole & Co.), 1839.
[67] House of Lords Record Office: 5 & 6 Vic. C.76, An Act for the Government of New South Wales and Van Diemen's Land
[68] Sweetman, p. 10.
[69] Ibid, Wright, Raymond, *A Blended House*, pp. 3-4.
[70] Thompson, M. M. H., *The Seeds of Democracy: Early Elections in Colonial New South Wales*, (Federation Press), 2006, pp. 1-168, provides a detailed analysis of the 1843 elections.

State were not members of the Legislative Council. However, Gipps ceased to be a member of the Council and was represented there by six officials (with portfolio) and his six nominees but they were easily outvoted by the elected representatives. There was a strong British interest in protecting the Governor from the consequences of including elected members that was enshrined in the 1842 Act. He was financially independent, having control over the money raised from the control of Crown Land and from fines and penalties. Although the Governor had lost his monopoly to initiate legislation, he could compel the Council to consider his legislative proposals and could refer back any bills that the Council passed with suggested amendments. Gipps and the British government were seen as responsible for the economic depression in NSW and the electors blamed the government and its policies for their economic and financial problems and punished it in the polls. Only one government minister and one nominee from the former Council were re-elected in 1843. Adopting the model of the 'blended house' created a legislature over which colonial government had limited control. Gipps was pleased that a number of alleged 'placemen' had been returned for rural constituencies, but with the exception of Edward Deas Thomson, the Colonial Secretary and John Plunkett, the Attorney-General, the nominated members lacked effective and talented spokesmen. [71] By contrast, the oppositionist members, though they could not dismiss the government and agreed on little, contained individuals, including Wentworth and Lang, of considerable political and tactical ability and powers of oratory that developed into an effective political force calling for responsible government.

The new Legislative Council was adversarial in character from the outset and a vocal anti-government caucus opposed Gipps on virtually every issue. Arguments over the colonial budget were endemic during the last three years of his administration. Much of the cost of colonial government was not subject to legislative scrutiny, but in 1843 Gipps requested extra funds for the administration of

---

[71] Biographical material can be found in Osborne, M. E., 'Sir Edward Deas Thomson (1800-1879)', *ADB*, Vol. 2, pp. 523-527, while Foster, S. G., *Colonial Improver: Edward Deas Thomson, 1800-1879*, (Carlton), 1978, is more detailed.

justice resulting in oppositionist councillors examining the entire spending on justice and making cuts. This presaged bitter clashes between Gipps and the Council over attempts by oppositionist legislators to extend their control over public finances and government. Just as in Lower Canada in the 1820s, the 'power of the purse' was an issue behind which elected members could unite especially during a depression. Although there were cries of no taxation without representation, the landowning elite sought to entrench its privileged position in society if a limited form of responsible government was introduced. Gipps could have countered the trend towards social elitism if he had been prepared to accept emancipists on the Legislative Council but his inherent conservatism about colonial self-government precluded this. Attacked vehemently by the colonial press and berated by his conservative opponents desperate to maintain their privileges and by colonial liberals who saw him as an obstacle to democratic reform, his eight years in NSW were difficult. Whether Gipps was a successful governor is a matter on which contemporaries and later historians disagree. Although he was an effective and conscientious administrator, his manner was brusque and aloof. More importantly, he lacked the political skills necessary to manage the competing economic and social interests in the colony while 'the blended house' failed to deliver the political support he needed to accomplish this.

Oppositionist politicians used the Council as a forum to demand liberal reforms of the colonial administration and further moves towards responsible government from Britain. Wentworth and landowners called for greater security of tenure but much of the most effective work was done in Select Committees. Committees chaired by Wentworth and Charles Cowper came to different conclusions about the reintroduction of transportation to fill the labour shortage in the colony. Cowper's committee opposed this move and won the argument. Another committee called for railway construction but the most important recommendation came from Robert Lowe's Select Committee on education that called for the establishment of a national system of elementary education.[72] Critical of the denominational system as

---

[72] Knight, Ruth, *Illiberal Liberal: Robert Lowe in New South Wales, 1842-50*, (Melbourne University Press), 1966, pp. 130-147,

leaving 'the majority uneducated in order thoroughly to imbue the minority with peculiar tenets' and for being uneconomic 'wherever one school is founded, two or three others will arise, not because they are wanted, but because it is feared that proselytes will be made', it proposed to allow the system to continue in areas where population was concentrated such as Sydney and the larger towns. But, it called for a system of national education for 'the lower classes in the community' within which there was separate religious education, a teacher training school, a system of inspection in Sydney and funding from the Legislative Council. Similar to Bourke's proposals a decade earlier, in 1848 a National School Board was formed but with a separate board for denominational schools to contain sectarian opposition. Generally, however, reformers felt that there had been little progress in making the executive more accountable and, with high levels of absenteeism among councillors many approached the 1848 election in a growing atmosphere of disillusion and apathy.

Nonetheless, the Council's legislative record between 1843 and 1848 was significant. Economic measures included regulation of trade and customs, legislation on banks, friendly societies and joint-stock companies and questions of insolvency, bankruptcy and small debts took up considerable time while the abolition of the use of debtors' prison occurred. Questions of public order resulted in legislation restricting public processions especially on divisive issues such as temperance and religion and greater police powers to cope with the rising scourge of bandits on country roads. There were also significant reforms in criminal law with a reduction in those crimes carrying the death penalty and detailed regulation of both trial by jury and the laws of evidence.

Sir Charles FitzRoy succeeded Gipps as governor in August 1846 and remained in office until January 1855. He was a junior officer at the Battle of Waterloo in 1815. Between 1818 and 1831, he served in Canada and the Cape of Good Hope and became Governor of Prince Edward Island in Canada in 1837 and the Leeward Islands from

---

Patchett Martin, A., *Life and Letters of the Right Honourable Robert Lowe Viscount Sherbrooke*, 2 Vols. (Longman, Green and Co.), 1893, Vol. 1, pp. 211-231, 241-267; report of Lowe's Committee on Public Education is printed on pp. 225-231.

1841 until 1845 when he was chosen to succeed Gipps in NSW. His promotions were largely due to the influence of his family rather than the support of the officials in the Colonial Office who thought he was 'indolent', a judgement confirmed by Earl Grey and the Duke of Newcastle, Colonial Secretaries after 1846. [73] His years as governor coincided with major constitutional and demographic changes in Australia but his critics suggested that his leadership lacked enterprise and drive. [74] His was a hands-off approach to colonial government, rule by procrastination. It is true that he avoided controversy, delegating responsibility to capable subordinates especially Thomson and allowing events to take their course rather than intervening. J. M. Ward, however, takes the view that, even if there was some truth in these criticisms, FitzRoy proved an effective conciliator who believed in moderation even when the Colonial Office took a different view. For instance, he resolved the problem of tensions between the Legislative Council and Government House that had rumbled on over the Council's asserted right to scrutinise details of the financial estimates presented by the Governor by simply yielding. He recognised the value of conceding a point that had been granted in some other colonies and prized good relations between the legislature and the executive far above the niceties of constitutional law. This led to strong criticism from the Colonial Office but when Earl Grey became Colonial Secretary in 1847 he approved FitzRoy's decision. [75]

FitzRoy took an ambivalent position on responsible government approving a bicameral legislature but opposing the transfer of the colony's policies and legislation from London to Sydney. He accepted that the colonists had a strong case for reform but feared that their lack of unity

---

[73] FitzRoy has proved a difficult subject for biographers as he did not keep a diary, few of his personal letters survived and he did not publish any memoirs. See, Ward, J. M., 'FitzRoy, Sir Charles Augustus', *ADB*, Vol. 10, pp. 384-389.

[74] For FitzRoy's response to the discovery of gold in NSW in 1851 and his and Thomson's effective administrative solutions, see Brown, Richard, *Settler Australia, 1780-1880, Volume 2: Eureka and Democracy*, (CreateSpace), 2013, pp. 24-30.

[75] *The Public General Statutes of New South Wales from 11 Victoriae to 15 Victoriae, inclusive, (1847-1851)*, (Thomas Richards), 1861, details legislative developments in the opening years of FitzRoy's tenure as Governor.

might result in a bitter contest for power. He favoured a limited form of self-government arguing that neither the Legislative Council nor the public were anxious for responsible government as it existed in Canada. The resulting Australian Constitutions Act passed in 1850 followed FitzRoy's views dismissing calls for responsible government. NSW, VDL, South Australia and WA continued to be governed separately and independently.[76] Grey favoured a federation of the Australian colonies as early as 1847 largely because of his belief in free trade and the legislation made FitzRoy Governor-General of the Australian Colonies in 1851, an empty title as things transpired. Although the Colonial Office was enthusiastic about federation, colonists could see no advantage in it and it was abandoned when faced with strong parliamentary opposition in London.

The legislation separating Victoria from NSW and naming and providing a Constitution for the new Colony, it was signed by Queen Victoria on 5 August 1850. [77] The NSW Parliament passed the necessary enabling legislation before separation took effect on 1 July 1851. This formally established Victoria as a separate colony from NSW. For NSW, the Act not only reduced its territory, but provided for changes to government. It liberalised the franchise qualifications for the NSW Legislative Council (s4) and empowered the governor and the Legislative Council, with Britain's approval, to establish a Parliament of two Houses, either appointed or elected (s2). The Act authorised a number of important changes for VDL creating a Legislative Council with two-thirds of its members elected (s7) and empowered the governor, with its advice and consent to make laws 'for the Peace, Welfare and good Government' of the colony, with the proviso that such laws not be repugnant to the law of England (s14). The new Legislative Council could make further provision for the administration of justice, including juries (s29). It also received the power to prepare legislation altering the constitution of the Legislative Council by varying the qualifications of electors

---

[76] House of Lords, Record Office: 13 & 14 Vic. No. 156, An Act for the better Government of Her Majesty's Australian Colonies.

[77] For the constitutional development of Victoria to 1851, see Brown, Richard, *Settler Australia, 1780-1880, Volume 2: Eureka and Democracy*, (CreateSpace), 2013, pp. 6-18.

and elected members and could replace itself with a Legislative Council and 'House of Representatives' whose members might be appointed or elected (s32). The way was paved for creating a colonial version of the two chambers of the Imperial Parliament.

WA had just begun to receive convicts and was subject to special provisions in the Act providing that, upon the petition of not less than one-third of the householders of the colony, and when the colony ceased to depend on grants from the United Kingdom, a Legislative Council (to consist of members of whom two-thirds might be elected) could be established by the existing Council. Householders petitioned for greater representation in 1865 and although the petition was rejected, six additional members were added to the Council. In 1867, the West Australian governor agreed to nominate those elected on the basis of adult suffrage. Two years after transportation ended in 1868, a Legislative Council with two-thirds of its members elected was established. WA moved to establish a bi-cameral legislature and responsible government in 1889 and this was enacted in the Constitution Act 1890.

In NSW and Victoria, where transportation of convicts virtually ceased after 1840, the Australian Constitutions Act was widely welcomed. The eventual goal for many was responsible government, with colonial premiers and ministries more closely resembling the British Prime Minister and ministries. The colonial governor's role would be broadly similar to that of the monarch in Britain, to appoint head of government, whoever commanded a majority in the legislature. The immediate effect of this Act for VDL was partly representative government on the model in operation in NSW since 1842. [78] In this model, the Governor remained, in an active and practical sense, the chief executive as well as the vice-regal representative in the Colony.

Continuing transportation of convicts from Britain meant 'responsible government' for VDL was a remote prospect in 1850. Systematic criticism developed from 1844. Anti-transportation became a socio-political movement of fervent strength, comparable to the Anti-Corn Law agitation in contemporary Britain. By 1850, the Tasmanian anti-

---

[78] Townsley, W. A., *The Struggle for Self-Government in Tasmania, 1842-1856*, (Tasmanian Government Printer), 1951

transportation movement had developed into a crusade for 'social freedom', the phrase of prominent Launceston anti-transportationist, the Reverend John West. The crusade quality of this movement found expression at mass meetings in VDL and Victoria. In 1851 that situation changed. The discovery of extensive alluvial gold in NSW and Victoria from 1851 persuaded the British government that sending convicts to a colony close to probably the richest goldfield in the world was bad policy. The Colonial Secretary in Britain, Sir John Pakington, on 14 December 1852 wrote to Lieutenant-Governor Denison, a resolute defender of transportation, foreshadowing its end. The Duke of Newcastle, Pakington's successor, confirmed the demise in a despatch of 22 February 1853. [79] Cessation of transportation was confirmed by an Order-in-Council of 29 December 1853 that repealed an 1847 designation of VDL as a penal colony. 'Van Diemen's Land' became 'Tasmania' coincident with responsible government in 1855-1856.

In December 1852, Pakington, and the following year his successor Newcastle wrote to the governors of NSW, Victoria and South Australia encouraging them to draft constitutions under the 1850 Act. He suggested these embody a bicameral legislature with an elected Lower House, control over Crown Lands, something previously retained by the British Parliament and, in effect, responsible government. Denison wrote to Newcastle on 25 August 1853 requesting that VDL receive the same invitation. Newcastle agreed on 30 January 1854. However the Island was already on track to responsible government and on 1 September 1853, Thomas Daniel Chapman moved in the Legislative Council for the introduction of a Bill which became the Constitution Act 1855.

In NSW, the 1850 legislation was criticised for providing insufficient local control of revenue and for failing to give the Legislative Council full powers even though it was extended to 54 members of whom two-thirds were elected. The Act did not satisfy growing demands for self-government and a draft Constitution for New South Wales was prepared by a Legislative Council committee headed by William Wentworth. After amendment in the Council, it was adopted on 9 August 1853 and taken to Britain. Wentworth, in his desire to follow the English political model, planned

---

[79] National Archives, CO 408/37

for a hereditary Upper House, like the House of Lords but this did not receive FitzRoy's support. This idea was treated with derision with claims that hereditary peers in Australia would be a 'bunyip aristocracy'. [80] The British authorities thought it went too far in the direction of self-government and they amended it, before the New South Wales Constitution Act received the Royal Assent on 16 July 1855.

The New South Wales Constitution Act 1855 was an amended version of the legislation passed by the New South Wales Parliament in 1853. [81] The British Act established the structures and lasting institutions of parliamentary democracy in Australia with a bi-cameral parliament consisting of a Legislative Assembly or Lower House made up of 54 elected members elected on a broad property franchise and an appointed Legislative Council or Upper House of no fewer than 21 members nominated by the Governor on the advice of his Executive Council initially for five years and thereafter for life. It provided for wide powers over domestic matters, including revenue raising and land. Britain still retained the power to disallow colonial legislation. The Act also provided for the NSW governor, acting on the advice of the Executive Council, to make appointments to public office. While 'responsible government', with Ministers of State drawn from and accountable to the Parliament, was not expressly included, this was clearly intended.

From 1856, NSW gained a fully responsible system of government. The Legislative Assembly was not fully representative because there were still property qualifications for voters. However, in 1858, the Electoral Reform Act gave NSW virtual manhood suffrage and secret ballot. Electoral boundaries were changed almost totally in 1858, to be more in line with population, but there were still great disparities between electorates. Pastoral districts sent one Member for approximately 3,000 voters, while Sydney elected one Member for 5,900 voters. Although most male residents had the right to vote by 1858 and almost all of

---

[80] On this issue, see Brown, Richard, *Settler Australia, 1780-1880, Volume 2: Eureka and Democracy*, (CreateSpace), 2013, pp. 401-414.
[81] House of Lords, Record Office: 18 & 19 Vic. No. 183, An Act to enable Her Majesty to assent to a Bill, as amended, of the Legislature of New South Wales, 'to confer a Constitution on New South Wales, and to grant a Civil List to Her Majesty'.

those with that right could, in theory, stand for Parliament, very few could afford to, since Members were not paid until 1889. This placed NSW among the world leaders in the introduction of parliamentary democracy.[82] There were still two significant groups in the community who could not vote: women and Aborigines. Women were granted the right to vote in NSW in 1902, but Aboriginal people had to wait for formal recognition until 1962. Since 1856, the role of the Legislative Council has remained unchanged as an Upper House of review and a check on the Lower House where the government is formed. Responsible government changed the role of the Sovereign but did not replace it. Under the devolved system, the British Parliament kept its overall authority, but it no longer interfered in colonial affairs.

---

[82] Scalmer, Sean, 'Containing Contention: A Reinterpretation of Democratic Change and Electoral Reform in the Australian Colonies', *Australian Historical Studies*, Vol. 42, (3), (2001), pp. 337-356, argues widespread collective action stimulated political change and that electoral reforms were introduced to contain further contention.

5 Secretaries and Colonial Secretaries 1788-1856

That the British Government showed little interest in the administrative details of the convict settlement at Botany Bay is not surprising. Distance simply made direct administration impossible and although the imperial authorities in London may have established the parameters for effective administration, operational decisions were left to the colonial authorities. As NSW developed, London on occasions acted as arbiter between the different interests that emerged in its fledgling communities and the interests of colonial government. It considered petitions and judicial appeals but preferred that as many decisions as possible should be made by the colonial authorities and its confidence in the Governor was crucial for good colonial governance.

Powers, largely unaccountable until 1823, were delegated to the Governor to regulate almost all aspects of the convicts' and free settlers' lives. Phillip and his successors regulated the supply of rations and granted lands and allotted convicts to those who could employ them. They gave assistance to settlers and established Government stores fixing prices of commodities, rates of wages and hours of labour. They imposed tolls and duties, gave and withdrew licences to trade and established and controlled markets. They checked weights and measures, struck a currency and fixed rates of interest. They made provision for the maintenance of public order and examined and modified the penalties that the courts imposed.[1] These activities were carried out through the Governor's senior officers, the colony's developing bureaucracy: the Deputy Judge-Advocate; the Commissary; the Principal Surgeon; the Chaplain; the Surveyor General; the Principal Superintendent of Convicts; the commander of the forces and the senior naval officer and especially by the Governor's Secretary.

Phillip did not have a secretary when he arrived in Botany Bay but soon recognised the need for a confidential subordinate who could relieve him of some of the details of

---

[1] Melbourne, p. 11.

administration and appointed the Commissary Andrew Miller to do the extra duty. It was one of the first of many dual appointments that initially plagued the colony because of the lack of available talent. Running the Commissariat proved a full-time duty and, after less than five months, Miller was relieved of his secretarial role. Phillip then appointed David Collins, the Deputy Judge-Advocate in his place.[2]

Collins, an officer of Marines, was an important choice and he was vital in establishing the role and function of the Secretary to the Governor or Secretary to the Colony. For the next eight years, quietly and efficiently, he proved indispensable to administering NSW keeping detached from local factions and earning the confidence of Phillip and his successors. As early as November 1788, Major Ross complained to Under-Secretary Evan Nepean that the Governor 'communicates nothing to any person here but to his secretary' and it is indicative of the importance already attached to the position that Ross spoke of Captain Collins as Secretary rather than as Judge-Advocate.[3]

Collins left Sydney in September 1796 and for the next twenty-one months Hunter acted as his own secretary, aided by unreliable clerks. The post remained vacant until Richard Dore, the first attorney to settle in the colony arrived in May 1798 as the new Judge-Advocate. Dore immediately solicited appointment to the 'confidential situation' of Secretary. Hunter agreed, with some reluctance, appointing Dore as his Secretary under his order of 22 June 1798. The new Secretary, however, tampered with the despatch reporting his appointment in order to give a favourable account of himself to the Secretary of State in London and his subsequent behaviour showed similar disloyalty.[4] Serious differences arose between the Governor and the Secretary initially from Dore's

---

[2] Richardson, G. D., 'The Early Archives of New South Wales; Notes on their Creation and their Keepers', *Journal of the Royal Australian Historical Society*, Vol. 59, (2), (1973), pp.86-87. See also, Richardson, G. D., *The Archives of the Colonial Secretary's Department, 1788-1856*, MA thesis, University of Sydney 1951: ML [MSS.832])

[3] Major Ross to Under Secretary Evan Nepean, 16 November 1788, *HRNSW*, Vol. 1, (2), p. 212.

[4] Ibid, Richardson, G. D., 'The Early Archives of New South Wales; Notes on their Creation and their Keepers', p. 87

awkwardness and what Hunter called his 'improper innovations' and his determination 'to be govern'd by his own views and interests in the line of his profession, and to follow, or rather to establish, such rules as best suited those objects'. Dore was a sick man, but Hunter complained, those objects 'ill-accorded with his situation here, either as an officer on public service, paid by the Crown, or the confidential situation in which he stood with me'. [5] Hunter had no authority to dismiss Dore as his only legal officer but he could dismiss him as Secretary doing so on 23 January 1799. He subsequently managed the affairs of the colony without a Secretary.

Governor King who took office in September 1800 had had learned from his predecessor's difficulties and immediately appointed Neil MacKellar, a subaltern and acting Adjutant of the NSW Corps to act as his Aide-de-Camp and Secretary. [6] MacKellar restored some order into the secretarial administration, but his responsibilities to the NSW Corps resulted in him being succeeded in April 1801 by William Neate Chapman, another of King's Norfolk Island officers, and a loyal family friend. When Chapman went home on leave in March 1804 King, with Hunter's experience in mind, was determined not to do without a Secretary emphasising that 'it is impossible for the official Duty being dispensed with'. Although dual appointments continued under King, he recognised the growing importance of the Secretary as central to the administrative efficiency of the colony itemising his administrative duties in the following terms

Secretary--Has the custody of all official papers and records belonging to the colony; transcribes the public despatches; charged with making out all grants, leases, and other public Colonial instruments; also the care of numerous indents or lists sent with convicts of their terms of conviction, and every other official transaction relating to the colony and Government; and is a situation of much responsibility and confidence.'[7]

---

[5] Hunter to the Duke of Portland, 21 February 1799, *HRA*, Series I, Vol. 2, pp. 244-245.
[6] Government and General Order, 29 September 1800, *HRA*, Series I, Vol. 2, p. 621.
[7] 'Statement of the duties of the respective officers on the Civil Establishment of His Majesty's Colony in New South Wales', 1 March 1804, *HRA*, Series I, Vol. 4, p. 538.

He further expanded on his own duties:

> **Governor--**As chief magistrate of the colony and Commander-in-Chief, he has the direction and the superintending control of every act and person — civil, military, settlers, and convicts — under his government, in executing which, he has to attend to the duty of every civil officer. His attention must be particularly directed to regulating and controlling the occasional expenses of the colony, investigating and deciding on appeals in civil causes; and from the peculiar nature of this colony, a constant attention is required of him to keep the prisoners in order, attend to wants of all descriptions, fixing settlers, allotting lands, and the personal inspection of every species of public work going forward in the colony, added to which, he has every responsibility and care attached to him of the settlements at Norfolk Island, and now the addition of Lieut't-Governor Collins's Government—all which, and his correspondence with the different departments of Government, occasions the most arduous exertions of the mind.[8]

King therefore appointed Garnham Blaxcell, formerly acting purser in *HMS Buffalo* and latterly, like Chapman, a Deputy-Commissary, as his acting Secretary in April 1804 and he remained in office until his appointment lapsed with Governor Bligh's assumption of command in August 1806.

William Bligh established a new precedent by bringing his own Secretary with him to the colony and was therefore able to make himself independent of whatever local talent might become available for that duty. Edmund Griffin served Bligh faithfully in very trying circumstances. The governor frequently consulted Griffin on public affairs and apparently valued his advice. His influence as well as the importance of his position was apparent during and after the Rum Rebellion. The rebels, once Bligh was safely under arrest, lost no time in seizing Griffin and subjecting him to a rigorous examination in their attempt to extract suitable evidence against Bligh, though with relatively little success. Griffin remained with Bligh at Government House, still serving and recognised as his Secretary, although he no longer had access to the Secretary's office or to the official papers. He went with Bligh to the Derwent and later with him to England.

---

[8] 'Statement of the duties of the respective officers on the Civil Establishment of His Majesty's Colony in New South Wales', 1 March 1804, *HRA*, Series I, Vol. 4, p. 538.

Between Bligh's deposition in January 1808 and Macquarie's arrival as the new governor in late 1809, a succession of individuals held power in NSW. Major Johnston, in wresting the government from Bligh, clearly appreciated the importance of a Secretary who was sufficiently implicated in the coup to remain loyal and appointed Nicholas Bayly to the position the day after Bligh's removal. [9] He wrote much of the correspondence with the deposed governor and was deeply involved in the general maladministration of the regime. Under the new administration, the dominant figure in the rebellion John Macarthur, had no official position. In his own interests Johnston needed to give some semblance of legality to their relationship, or, as he put it, 'finding I should require the aid of some Gentleman in whose integrity I should have confidence, I requested Mr McArthur to assist me', and accordingly, 'As there was no Office vacant to which I could appoint him, and as it was necessary he should have some public character, I created an Office which has never before existed here, and I appointed him Secretary to the Colony.'[10] The designation 'Secretary to the Colony' had been used before, if without official sanction, but now, for the first time, there was a division between private and public offices.

Foveaux, when he arrived to take command on 28 July 1808, brushed the whole secretarial structure aside and appointed Lieutenant James Finucane of the NSW Corps as Secretary, with the usual instruction that all correspondence on public business was to be addressed to him. Paterson, the next commander during the interregnum, assumed office as Lieutenant-Governor on 9 January 1809 and appointed Alexander Riley as Secretary. Riley thus became the first person to hold important office after Bligh's downfall who had not been an officer of the NSW Corps or one of its close associates in Sydney. Riley had arrived as a free settler in 1804 and became storekeeper and subsequently acting Deputy-Commissary at Port Dalrymple. His post as Secretary was of doubtful advantage to Riley's mercantile ambitions and he resigned in March. Finucane

---

[9] Ibid, Richardson, G. D., 'The Early Archives of New South Wales; Notes on their Creation and their Keepers', pp. 89-90.
[10] Major Johnston to Viscount Castlereagh, 11 April 1808, *HRA*, Series I, Vol. 6, p. 219.

was therefore reappointed and stayed in office until December 1809. [11]

Altogether, ten different men served as Secretary to the Governor, or to the colony, or 'to Government', in the twenty-two years before Governor Macquarie arrived with an average tenure of office of less than two years, allowing for vacancies. This was not conducive to good administration. The arrival of Governor Macquarie at the end of 1809 brought to the office of Secretary to the Governor probably the ablest and most experienced man who had yet filled it, one who was to hold it for the longest period, and who, as its last occupant under the old style, was to be the link between the older casual system of court appointments and the new method of permanent appointment by commission from the Crown. In his eleven years of office, the methodical John Thomas Campbell greatly improved the situation in respect of the public records of the colony and most of the early records to survive are from this period.

Macquarie, assisted by Campbell, set about restoring order in the colony and regulating the style in which the public business would be conducted. The Governor issued a General Order stating that petitions and memorials would only be received on the first Monday of each month, those for land and cattle on the first Monday in June and those from convicts for indulgences on the first Monday in December.

> 9. His Excellency will receive the Civil and Military Officers of Government on Business each Day in the Week (Sunday excepted) between the hours of Ten and Twelve in the forenoon; and no Letters of Business are to be sent to His Excellency on Sundays, nor out of the hours he has assigned to Public Duties on the other Days of the Week; nor are any Letters of Business to be sent to His Excellency's Secretary but during his Office hours, and on Week Days. Letters, sent either to His Excellency or his Secretary contrary to these orders (unless on occasion of real necessity and pressing Emergency), will be returned unanswered to the Persons who wrote them. His Excellency's Hours for the

---

[11] Ibid, Richardson, G. D., 'The Early Archives of New South Wales; Notes on their Creation and their Keepers', pp. 90-91.

Despatch of Public Business are from Ten in the forenoon to Three in the Afternoon; and his Secretary's hours are the same.[12]

Generally, order and regularity was established in the performance of the public business during the twelve years of Macquarie's administration. He was succeeded by Sir Thomas Brisbane on 1 December 1821.

Frederick Goulburn succeeded Campbell, taking office as Secretary and, for the first time also as Registrar of the Records on 1 February 1821. He was the first such officer officially called Colonial Secretary and was appointed by a Commission dated 13 June 1820. [13] He also held the position of Private Secretary to the Governor. Although this represented a change in the method of appointment and his commission did not detail his duties. Initially, the relationship between Brisbane and Goulburn was extremely cordial but disagreement developed over the nature and scope of the Goulburn's duties. Brisbane accused Goulburn of acting contrary to his express instructions, withholding correspondence and information from him and exceeding his authority.[14] In May 1824, Major Ovens was officially appointed Brisbane's Private Secretary although he had in fact been acting in this capacity since the middle of 1823. Consequently the two offices were separated.[15] Many of the records prior to the establishment of the separate office were retained by the Colonial Secretary but others were transferred at the end of 1825.[16]

Before 1823, all inwards correspondence for the Governor was addressed to the Governor, although filed in the office of the Secretary to the Governor and, after 1821, that of the Colonial Secretary. In 1823, a notice appeared in the *Sydney Gazette* directing that letters and memorials intended for the Governor were to be addressed to the

---

[12] Government and General Order, 9 July 1813, *HRA*, Series I, Vol. 7, p. 784.
[13] Commission of Frederick Goulburn as Colonial Secretary, *HRA*, Series I, Vol. 10, p. 664.
[14] Liston, C. A., *New South Wales under Governor Brisbane, 1821-25*, PhD thesis, University of Sydney, 1980, pp.71-86.
[15] Brisbane to Bathurst, 1 May 1824, *HRA*, Series I, Vol. 11, pp. 256-258.
[16] 'Memorandum of the Papers handed over from the Private to the Colonial Secretary at the end of the year 1825' (NRS 903, [5/2333.3])

Colonial Secretary. [17] Although Brisbane had intended this order to refer only to applications for land grants, he did not wish, at that time, to risk alienating his most essential administrative official by repealing the notice. [18] The following year, Goulburn maintained that he was the only channel through which the Governor could give directions to the various members of the civil establishment and that documents not passing through his Office were 'informal'.[19] This claim led to the final breach between the two men. [20] Brisbane was recalled and left the colony late in November 1825 and Goulburn was relieved of the position of Colonial Secretary but continued to serve in that capacity until 7 January 1826.

The cause of the dispute between the governor and the Colonial Secretary had been the lack of an authoritative statement as to their relative positions. This was largely remedied in 1825 when Darling was given additional instructions on this matter:

> ...in addition to those functions which under your general Instructions are specially committed to the Colonial Secretary, he is to conduct, under your direction, all Official Correspondence in the Colony, and is to act on all occasions as the general medium of Communication, through which your orders are to be signified either to the community at large, or to private persons. [21]

The duties of the various Government offices were revised by Governor Darling and notified in a Government and General Order dated 5 January 1826. This also ordered that

> 12th. The Public Correspondence in the Colony is to be carried on generally through the medium of the Colonial Secretary. The Heads of Departments and Commandants of Stations (except when the subject relates to the Military Branch of the Service) will

---

[17] *Sydney Gazette*, 29 May 1823 p. 1a.
[18] Ibid, Liston, C. A., *New South Wales under Governor Brisbane, 1821-25*, pp. 76-77.
[19] Secretary Goulburn to Governor Brisbane, 19 April 1824, *HRA*, Series I, Vol. 11, p. 258; reply, 26 April 1824, *HRA*, Series I, Vol. 11, p. 260.
[20] Ibid, Liston, C. A., *New South Wales under Governor Brisbane, 1821-25*, p. 80
[21] Earl Bathurst to Governor Darling, 14 July 1825, *HRA*, Series I, Vol. 12, p. 18.

address their Applications and Reports to that Officer for the information or decision of the Governor. [22]

Prior to this the Governor received many papers direct as the Memorandum of papers handed over at the end of 1825 shows. Further instructions changing the channels of communication in the colony were given by Darling in a Government Order dated 1 September 1829. Persons having:

Occasion to make any Application upon Subjects relating to any particular Department' were to 'address themselves in the first instance to the Head of that Department, who in all Matters of unquestionable regulation, will at once afford such information as may be required. In Cases where it may be necessary to bring the Subject under the Consideration of the Governor, the Head of the Department will forward the Application with every necessary Information, accompanied by his own remarks to the Colonial Secretary'.[23]

A *List of Periodical Returns required to be furnished by the various Departments of the Government* dated about 1831 provides some indication of the amount of information the Colonial Secretary required from government offices at that time and the amount of detail that may be found in his records.

Between 1826 and 1856, Alexander McLeay and Edward Deas Thomson successively held the position of Colonial Secretary establishing continuity in colonial administration during the demographic and geographical expansion of NSW. Their relationships with Darling, Bourke, Gipps and Fitzroy lacked the antagonism between previous governors and Colonial Secretaries though this did not prevent disagreements on specific issues. As a result of the introduction of representative government in the 1820s and the inclusion of elected representatives after 1842, the Colonial Secretary acted as the 'prime minister' of colonial government with responsibilities for managing the government's legislative programme. After responsible government in 1856, the Colonial Secretary (at times known as the Principal Secretary, or Chief Secretary) frequently

---

[22] Government and General Order, 5 January 1826, *HRA*, Series I, Vol. 12, p. 152.
[23] *Sydney Gazette*, 5 September 1829 p. 1b.

acted as Premier or Prime Minister prior to the establishment of the Premier's Department in 1907. The diversity of the functions and duties of the Colonial Secretary are clearly shown in the administrative arrangements published in 1856

...legislative matters; naval and military establishments, including the Volunteer Corps; foreign correspondence; postal arrangements and contracts; immigration; Police, including Petty Sessions; gaols and penal establishments; medical establishments, including quarantine, vaccination and lunatic asylums; registration and statistics; municipal institutions; Government printing; proclamations, commissions, and other instruments under the Great Seal; naturalization of aliens; ecclesiastical establishments; public education; literary and scientific institutions; hospitals and charitable institutions; Aborigines; remission and execution of sentences; and all other matters of internal arrangement not confided to any other Minister. [24]

In the further administrative arrangements notified by the Governor on 4 October 1859, the Colonial Secretary was referred to as the 'Colonial Secretary or Chief Secretary to the Government'. During the nineteenth century the Colonial Secretary's Department continued to be the most important administrative unit in New South Wales. It had dealings with other public offices on nearly all major developments and activities, as well as having responsibility for a wide and varied range of functions.

---

[24] *New South Wales Government Gazette*, No. 155, 9 October 1856

Appendices

Secretaries to the Governor 1788-1824

Date	Name
January - June 1788	Andrew Miller [25]
June 1788 - 29 September 1796	David Collins [26]
30 September 1796 - 21 June 1798	Governor Hunter without a secretary
22 June 1798 - 23 January 1799	Richard Dore [27]
24 January 1799 - 28 September 1800	Hunter again without a secretary
29 September 1800 - 1 April 1801	Neil MacKellar (Captain), Acting-Secretary [28]
2 April 1801 - 16 March 1804	William Neate Chapman [29]
20 April 1804 - 12 August 1806	Garnham Blaxcell, Acting-Secretary [30]
13 August 1806 - 26 January 1808	Edmund Griffin (remained Bligh)
27 January 1808 - 29 July 1808	Nicholas Bayly, Private Secretary to Major Johnston [31]
12 February 1808 - 29 July 1808	John Macarthur 'Secretary to the Colony' [32]
30 July 1808 - 9	James Finucane, Secretary to

---

[25] George Parsons, 'Miller, Andrew (-1790)', *ADB*, Vol. 2, p. 229.
[26] 'David Collins, (1756-1810)', *ADB*, Vol. 1, pp. 236-240.
[27] Allars, K. G., 'Dore, Richard (1749 - 1800)', *ADB*, Vol. 1, pp. 313-314.
[28] Austin, M., 'MacKellar, Neil (-1802)', *ADB*, Vol. 2, pp. 170-171.
[29] 'Chapman, William Neate (1773? -1837?)', *ADB*, Vol. 1, p. 218.
[30] Dunlop, E. W., 'Blaxcell, Garnham (1778-1817)', *ADB*, Vol. 1, p. 115.
[31] Fletcher, B. H., 'Bayly, Nicholas (1770-1823)', *ADB*, Vol. 1, p. 76.
[32] Steven, Margaret. 'Macarthur, John (1767-1834)', *ADB*, Vol. 2, pp. 153-159.

January 1809	Lieutenant-Colonel Foveaux
9 January 1809 - March 1809	Alexander Riley, Secretary to Lieutenant-Governor Paterson [33]
19 March - 31 December 1809	James Finucane, Secretary to Lieutenant-Governor Paterson
1 January 1810 - 21 January 1821	John Thomas Campbell [34]
1 February 1821 - 11 May 1824	Frederick Goulburn, also Colonial Secretary [35]

Where the date for the end of office is unknown, the date preceding that of the next appointment is assumed.

Colonial Secretaries 1824-1856

Dates of Office	**Name**
1 January 1821 - 7 January 1826	Frederick Goulburn
8 January 1826 - 2 January 1837	Alexander McLeay [36]
2 January 1837 - 6 June 1856	Edward Deas Thomson [37]
6 June 1856 - 25 August 1856	Stuart Alexander Donaldson [38]
26 August 1856 - 2	Charles Cowper [39]

---

[33] Conway, Jill, 'Riley, Alexander (1778?-1833)', *ADB*, Vol. 2, pp. 379-381.
[34] Holder, R. F., 'Campbell, John Thomas (1770?-1830)', *ADB*, Vol. 1, pp. 199-201.
[35] Parsons, Vivienne, 'Goulburn, Frederick (1788-1837)', *ADB*, Vol. 1, pp. 463-464.
[36] 'McLeay, Alexander (1767-1848)', *ADB*, Vol. 2, pp. 177-180.
[37] Osborne, M. E., 'Thomson, Sir Edward Deas (1800-1879)', *ADB*, Vol. 2, pp. 523-527, and Foster, S. G., *Colonial Improver: Edward Deas Thomson, 1800-1879*, (Carlton), 1978.
[38] Draper, Sandra, 'Donaldson, Sir Stuart Alexander (1812-1867)', *ADB*, Vol. 4, pp. 84-86.
[39] Ward, John M., 'Cowper, Sir Charles (1807-1875)', *ADB*, Vol. 3, pp. 475-479.

| October 1856 | |

6 A Very British Coup: A 'Rum' Rebellion

His Excellency the Governor laments at finding, by his late visits through the colony, that the most calamitous evils have been produced by persons bartering or paying in spirits for grain of all kinds... [1]

Just before sunset on 26 January 1808, the twentieth anniversary of the arrival of the First Fleet in Australia, over 300 soldiers of the New South Wales Corps, the 102nd Regiment of the British army expressly created to protect the new colony, gathered on the parade ground in front of their barracks in what is now Wynyard Square. The officers of the Corps who had held a rare full dress dinner at the barracks two nights earlier, had decided the following day, to arrest and depose Governor William Bligh, fourth Governor of the colony. [2] The soldiers were led in formation from the parade ground by their commander, Major George Johnston, with drawn sword in one hand and the other arm in a sling, an injury caused when he fell out of his carriage drunk on the way home after the regimental dinner. [3] Guns loaded, bayonets fixed, sweltering in their scarlet woollen coats, with banners flying and the regimental band playing *The British Grenadiers*, the column marched down High Street, across the new stone bridge spanning the Tank Stream and up Bridge Street to Government House, a show of force designed to impress and more importantly intimidate the general populace. There was no possibility of resistance. Bligh's personal guard had already been suborned and the two naval vessels under his command were out of port. Bligh was taken by surprise and kept under house arrest for a year and it was a further year before Governor Lachlan Macquarie arrived

---

[1] *HRNSW*, Vol. 6, p. 253-254.
[2] Mackaness, G., *The Life of Vice-Admiral William Bligh*, 2 Vols. (Farrar & Rinehart), 1937, Vol. 2, pp. 95-334, covers his rule in NSW, the rebellion and its aftermath. See also, Shaw, A. G. L., 'Bligh, William (1754-1817)', *ADB*, Vol. 1, pp. 118-122.
[3] Lemcke, Geoffrey, *Reluctant Rebel: Lt. Col. George Johnston, 1764-1823*, (Willoughby), 1998, and Yarwood, A. T., 'Johnston, George (1764-1823)', *ADB*, Vol. 2, pp. 20-22

with his own 73rd Regiment to enforce the removal of the NSW Corps. The events were unusual as they occurred within the colonial élite. This was the so-called 'Rum rebellion'.[4]

Under what circumstances is resistance to established authority permissible? The founders of the colony in NSW thought in terms of the Lockean model of the formation of government. Locke maintained that individual liberties were paramount but that in the progression from a state of nature to civil society some of these liberties would be sacrificed in return for the protection that government could give especially in relation to life, liberty and property. If government acted in a despotic way, the governed could reclaim their original rights through resistance and rebellion. What happened in Sydney at the beginning of 1808 is replete with contrasting personalities and vested interests in open conflict but it is sometimes difficult to avoid a sense of people squabbling over very little, an impression that the British government in London appears to have had. However, for those involved, the disagreements were not about issues of little importance but went to the heart of how they believed a colony should be governed.[5]

Bligh as Governor

In the early years of the settlement, particularly during the three years between the first Governor Arthur Phillip's retirement in December 1792 and the arrival of John Hunter his successor in mid-1795, when Major Francis Grose and then Captain William Paterson administered the colony, alcohol (generically referred to as 'rum') was readily tradable in the barter-based economy operating beyond the bureaucratic, requisition system at the government store.

---

[4] Brown, Richard, *Resistance and Rebellion*, pp. 547-576, also examines Bligh's second mutiny.
[5] Karskens, Grace, and Waterhouse, Richard, "Too Sacred to Be Taken Away': Property, Liberty and the 'Rum' Rebellion', *Journal of Australian Colonial History*, Vol. 12, (2010), pp. 1-22, re-assesses the Rum Rebellion in order to understand its real causes. It is observed that the rebellion resulted from a notion of Bligh's alleged tyrannical move to take away the property and liberty of NSW citizens, fuelled by the lack of a representative form of government in NSW.

Rum became a substitute for currency. The shortage of currency in the colony was aggravated by the fact that William Bassett Chinnery, [6] the agent appointed by the British Government to operate the colony's accounts from London was in the process of embezzling some £80,000. [7] The NSW Corps officers' early trading success was based on the fact that they were paid in London and could draw bills there that would be honoured. They alone had access to sterling for purposes of trade and a trading cabal that operated as an extension of the officers' mess was able profitably to exploit its monopoly position in rum and other goods. They vigorously defended this position under both Hunter and King. This was no longer the case in 1808 as competition now ensured that monopoly profits were substantially reduced, although high prices were retained by the penumbra of illegality that surrounded the trade.

The relationship between the civil and military establishments had been difficult since 1788 and the decision by Major Francis Grose, acting-Governor between late 1792 and late 1794, to grant land to the NSW Corps and their monopolistic attitude to the spirit trade made existing tensions even more difficult when John Hunter took over as Governor in September 1795. [8]

---

[6] William Bassett Chinnery, who was appointed Agent for New South Wales on 1 May 1787, was enabled to embezzle more than £80,000 of Treasury funds prior to his dismissal on 17 March 1812. For Chinnery's private life and his love of music, see, Yim, Denise, *Viotti and the Chinnerys: a relationship charted through letters*, (Ashgate), 2004. Chinnery was able to avoid detection for a long time because the accounting and control systems used at the British Treasury and the function and operation of the Audit Office established in 1785 were inadequate.

[7] See Scorgie, Michel E., Wilkinson David J., and Rowe, Julie D., 'The Rise and Fall of a Treasury Clerk: William Bassett Chinnery', paper presented to the Conference of the British Accounting Association, April 1998; compare with Scorgie, Michel E., 'The rise and fall of William Bassett Chinnery', *Abacus*, Vol. 43, (2007), pp. 76-93. See also ibid, Whitaker, Anne-Maree, *Joseph Foveaux: Power and Patronage in Early New South Wales*, pp.155-156.

[8] Hoyle, Arthur, *The Life of John Hunter, Navigator, Governor, Admiral*, (Mulini Press), 2001, Auchmuty, J. J., 'Hunter, John (1737-1821)', *ADB*, Vol. 1, pp. 566-572. See also, Wood, G. A., 'Governor Hunter', *Journal and Proceedings of the Royal Australian Historical Society*, Vol. 14, (6), (1928), pp. 344-362.

> Every day convinces me more and more that many of those people, if they cannot be prevail'd on to make their public office their first consideration, shou'd be remov'd. Their private concerns occupy all their time, and £50 per annum seems to be no object when £300, £400, or £500 is to be gained by trade. [9]

The activities of the NSW Corps were not unknown in other British colonies. John Macarthur's profits as regimental paymaster were far less than those often accumulated by similar officers in India. [10] The difference between the commercial activities of Macarthur and his fellow officers in NSW and equivalent operations elsewhere was that in NSW they almost achieved a monopoly, whereas in other colonies this was rarely possible. The result was growing tensions between Hunter and the military with Hunter quickly informing Portland, his superior in London that 'scarcely nothing short of the full power of the Governor' would satisfy him.[11] It also became obvious that the soldiers of the NSW Corps resented the authority of the civil power.

> Continually thwarted and worthless characters encourag'd almost into a state of resistance by those whose schemes might have been in some degree effected by the changes I was about to make, and which in few words may be said to be *order and regularity for confusion and licentiousness.*[12]

Hunter's replacement as Governor in 1800, Philip Gidley King was equally ineffective in controlling the

---

[9] Hunter to Portland, 20 June 1797, *HRA*, Series I, Vol. 2, p. 22. The problem of spirits concerned Hunter from the outset. His general order of 23 January 1796 prohibited the making of spirits in the colony: *HRNSW*, Vol. 3, p. 10; general order 11 July 1796 took action over the unlimited sale of spirits, *HRNSW*, Vol. 3, pp. 58-59; general order 12 December 1796, *HRNSW*, Vol. 3, pp. 185-186, on the link between crime and spirits.
[10] Steven, Margaret. 'Macarthur, John (1767-1834)', *ADB*, Vol. 2, pp. 153-159, Ellis, M. H., *John Macarthur*, (Angus & Robertson), 1978.
[11] Hunter to Portland, 14 September 1795, *HRA*, Series I, Vol. 1, pp. 661-663.
[12] Hunter to Portland, 12 November 1796, *HRA*, Series I, Vol. 1, p. 670. See also Hunter to Portland, 25 July 1798, *HRA*, Series I, Vol. 2, pp. 160-171 for further criticism of Macarthur.

activities of the NSW Corps.[13] He badly needed capable law officers and a change in the personnel of the NSW Corps, but the British government ignored his requests. He was faced with frequent disobedience and insolence that early in 1803, immediately after he had refused to allow a cargo of spirits to be landed from the *Atlas*, culminated in the circulation of libellous 'pipes' against him and his officials.[14] The investigations and courts martial that followed revealed the animosity that existed between the governor and the Corps. The need to rein in the military establishment and especially its officer élite led to a division within the ruling élite as Hunter and then King sought to assert their gubernatorial authority. Faced by a military élite with sympathetic access to the decision-making process in London and the problem of retaining support from successive secretaries of state whose policies were rarely consistent, neither Hunter, who was recalled or King, who 'resigned' made any permanent inroads into the power of the Corps.

Asserting authority

William Bligh was selected by the British Government as governor in part because of his reputation as a strict but fair disciplinarian. The critical figure in his appointment was Sir Joseph Banks who had accompanied Captain James Cook on his first voyage and was the government's unofficial adviser on matters relating to Australia. Banks had formed an intense dislike of John Macarthur in 1801 when the latter, already one of the wealthiest men in the colony, applied for permission to export some of the king's merino sheep to NSW and for an enormous land grant to help establish a wool industry. Banks did not favour a large land grant to one person but thought the wool industry should be developed by an English company. He also knew that Macarthur, due to a thrusting desire for personal

---

[13] For biographical information, see Shaw, A. G. L., 'King, Philip Gidley (1758-1808)', *ADB*, Vol. 2, pp. 55-61; King, J. and J., *Philip Gidley King: a biography of the third governor of New South Wales*, (Methuen), 1981.

[14] The deteriorating relationship between King and the military in early 1803 is detailed in *HRNSW*, Vol. 5, pp. 22-37. Some of these libels are printed in *HRNSW*, Vol. 5, pp. 123-127; see also, King to Hobart, 9 May 1803, *HRA*, Series I, Vol. 4, pp. 159-160, 167-173.

enrichment, was a disruptive force in the colony. When Macarthur's requests for sheep and land were granted, Banks was upset and recommended Bligh for the job of governor because he thought he could manage Macarthur. On 15 March 1805, he wrote to Bligh requesting he consider the post commenting that King's successor must have the following qualities:

> ...one who had integrity unimpeached, a mind capable of providing its own resources in difficulties without leening on others for advice, firm in discipline, civil in deportment and not subject to whimper and whine when severity of discipline is wanted to meet emergencies. [15]

Banks proceeded to offer a number of inducements to persuade Bligh to accept. The Governor's salary would be doubled from £1,000 to £2,000 and, in addition, Banks believed Bligh need spend less than half of this because he would have 'the whole of the Government power and stores' at his disposal. His seniority and pension rights would continue. Banks even added that there would be better marriage prospects for his six daughters in NSW. He was not simply using his influence to help Bligh; he was exerting pressure on Bligh to accept the Governorship. He was not ignorant of Bligh's reputation as a disciplinarian: he chose him for that reason. Bligh, Banks believed, stood a good chance of standing up to and reining in the maverick NSW Corps, something his predecessors had been unable to do. So did Earl Camden, Secretary of State for War and the Colonies, who wrote to Banks that he was recommending Bligh for appointment because of Bligh's 'merit & ability & of the character he bears, for firmness & Integrity'. [16] Bligh was persuaded and left for Sydney with his daughter, Mary Putland, and her husband who died on

---

[15] This crucial letter was first quoted, in full, in the *HRNSW*, Vol. 6, pp. xxxv–xxxvi. The editor gave no specific location for this letter, but stated that he had had access to manuscripts in the possession of W. R. Bligh of Sydney, William Bligh's grandson. Bligh presented some of these to the Public (now State) Library of New South Wales in 1902 and they were transferred to the Mitchell Library (ML) in 1910. This letter was not amongst the collection and its present location is unknown.

[16] Camden to Bligh, 18 April 1805, ML, Banks Papers, Series 59:01.

4 January 1808 of tuberculosis. Bligh's wife remained in England. [17]

Even before his arrival, Bligh's style of governance led to problems with his subordinates. The Admiralty gave command of the *Porpoise* and the convoy to the lower ranked Captain Joseph Short and Bligh took command of a transport ship. [18] This led to quarrels that eventually resulted in Captain Short firing across Bligh's bow in order to force Bligh to obey his signals. When this failed, Short tried to give an order to Lieutenant Putland, Bligh's son-in-law to stand by to fire on Bligh's ship. Bligh boarded the *Porpoise* and seized control of the convoy. When it arrived in Sydney, Bligh, backed up by statements from two of Short's officers, [19] had Short stripped of the captaincy of the *Porpoise* that he gave to his son-in-law. [20] He also cancelled the land grant Short had been promised as payment for the voyage [21] and shipped him back to England for court martial, at which he was acquitted. [22] The president of the court, Sir Isaac Coffin, wrote to the Admiralty and made several serious accusations against Bligh, including that he had influenced the officers to testify against Short. Bligh's wife obtained a statement from one of the officers denying this and Banks and other supporters of Bligh lobbied successfully against his recall. The Secretary of State thought the dispute arose from 'very trivial causes' and:

---

[17] Bligh's commission, instructions and additional instructions are in *HRA*, Series I, Vol. 6, pp. 1-19.
[18] Short to Secretary Marsden, 12 March 1806, *HRNSW*, Vol. 6, pp. 31-34, Bligh to Secretary Marsden, 30 May 1806, *HRNSW*, Vol. 6, pp. 81-84, and Bligh to Castlereagh, 1 April 1806, *HRNSW*, Vol. 6, pp. 55-57, provide the protagonists' stances. Short to Bligh, 15 May 1806, *HRNSW*, Vol. 6, pp. 74-75, explains Short's position and his offer of an apology.
[19] Lieutenant Tetley to Bligh, 15 November 1806, *HRA*, Series I, Vol. 6, p. 40, and Daniel Lye to Bligh, 22 November 1806, 9 December 1806, *HRA*, Series I, Vol. 6, pp. 41-42.
[20] Bligh to Secretary Marsden, 12 December 1806, *HRNSW*, Vol. 6, pp. 208-221, details the enquiry.
[21] Bligh to Windham, 5 November 1806, *HRA*, Series I, Vol. 6, p. 30.
[22] Rear-Admiral Isaac Coffin to W. W. Pole, 13 December 1807, *HRNSW*, Vol. 6, p. 388.

>...proceeded to a length to which it could not possibly have advanced had you both been impressed with a just sense...of the propriety...of preserving a good understanding with each other. [23]

Soon after his arrival at Sydney on 13 August 1806, Bligh was given an address of welcome signed by Major Johnston for the military, by Richard Atkins for the civilian officers and by John Macarthur for the free settlers. [24] However, not long after, he also received addresses from the free and freed settlers of Sydney and the Hawkesbury River region, with a total of 369 signatures, many made only with a cross, complaining that Macarthur did not represent them.[25]

>...We beg to observe that had we deputed anyone, John Macarthur would not have been chosen by us, we considering him an unfit person to step forward upon such an occasion, as we may chiefly attribute the rise in the price of mutton to his withholding the large flock of wethers he now has to make such price as he may choose to demand. [26]

This only confirmed what Bligh would have been told by Banks about Macarthur.

One of Bligh's first actions [27] was to use the colony's stores and herds to provide relief to farmers who had been severely affected by flooding on the Hawkesbury River, a situation that had disrupted the barter economy in the colony. [28] Supplies were divided according to those most in need and provisions were made for loans to be drawn from the store based on capacity to repay. Bligh offered to take

---

[23] Windham to Bligh, 31 October 1807, *HRA*, Series I, Vol. 6, p. 80.
[24] Address to Governor Bligh, 14 August 1806, *HRNSW*, Vol. 6, pp. 165-166.
[25] Sydney Settlers' Address to Governor Bligh, 22 September 1806, *HRNSW*, Vol. 6, pp. 189-189; see also, Hawkesbury Settlers' Address, undated, 1806, *HRNSW*, Vol. 6, pp. 190-192.
[26] *HRNSW*, Vol. 6, p. 189.
[27] See, Government and General Order, 23 August, 30 August 1806, *HRNSW*, Vol. 6, pp. 173-174, 176.
[28] Samuel Marsden to King, 28 March 1806, *HRNSW*, Vol. 6, pp. 53-54, provides valuable details about the flood while King to Camden, 7 April 1806, *HRNSW*, Vol. 6, pp. 59-61, considers its effects. See also, *HRNSW*, Vol. 6, pp. 176, 186, 237, 823-831. Newspaper coverage of the floods can be found in, *Sydney Gazette*, 30 March, 6 April 1806.

wheat from the next crop into the Government stores at 15s per bushel. [29] This delighted the settlers, resulting in strong loyalty to Bligh even after the events of 1808 but it earned the enmity of traders in the Corps who had been profiting greatly from the situation. [30] This was evident in an address to Bligh on 17 February 1809:

> That your memorialists had no hand, act, or part in the rebellion that now exists in this colony. That they do abhor and detest the said act, its aiders, and abettors, and were every way fully satisfied and content under His Excellency's administration. His Excellency was doing all that public virtue or private worth could accomplish to correct abuses, re-establish discipline, protect and encourage sobriety and industry. That your memorialists believe the following causes principally led to the rebellion; - That the officers had been (and still continue) merchants, traders, and dealers, which was carried on by employing convicts as their agents in different parts of the colony, by which means a great number of the inhabitants are in debt to them or their agents, which gave them a dangerous influence...The officers were interested in impeding agriculture: the more settlers were ruined the cheaper they could purchase estates; the less grain grown by the settlers, the better prices they had for their own... [31]

Bligh was under instructions from the Colonial Office to normalise trading conditions in the colony by prohibiting the use of spirits as payment for commodities. Bligh was determined to stamp out the barter of spirits for goods or labour, commenting on 7 February 1807:

> It is absolutely necessary to be done to bring labour to a true value and support the farming interest... In addition to the reasons already given to prohibit the barter of spirits, is the strong temptation it holds out to the settlers and other inhabitants to erect private stills, which tend to destroy not only the grain but the industry and morals of the people. [32]

---

[29] *Sydney Gazette*, 21 December 1806.
[30] See, Fletcher, Brian H., 'The Hawkesbury settlers and the Rum Rebellion', *Journal of the Royal Australian Historical Society*, Vol. 54, (3), (1968), pp. 217-237, for a detailed discussion of the relationship between Bligh and the Hawkesbury settlers.
[31] Hawkesbury Settlers' Address to Bligh, 17 March 1809, *HRNSW*, Vol. 7, pp. 78-80.
[32] Bligh to Marsden, 7 February 1807, *HRNSW*, Vol. 6, pp. 246-252.

This was followed on 14 February 1807 by a further proclamation:

> His Excellency the Governor laments at finding, by his late visits through the colony, that the most calamitous evils have been produced by persons bartering or paying in spirits for grain of all kinds...In order to remedy these grievous complaints, and to relieve the inhabitants who have suffered by this traffic, he feels it his duty to put a total stop to this barter in future, and to prohibit the exchange of spirits or other liquors as payment for grain, animal food, labour, wearing apparel, or any other commodity whatever, to all descriptions of persons in the colony and its dependencies. [33]

Between October 1806 and February 1807, he introduced further measures to carry out his instructions. On 4 October 1806, Bligh banned departing ships from leaving crew members behind [34] and issued new port regulations securing government control of ships and boat building and on 28 February 1807 declared that all goods shipped to NSW should only be unloaded at Port Jackson.[35] On 1 November, he issued general orders forbidding barter in goods. [36] On 3 January 1807, he proclaimed all promissory notes should be payable only in sterling, not kind [37] and the following month he outlawed the importation of stills for alcohol production and bartering with spirits. [38] Bligh communicated his policy to the Colonial Office in 1807, advising that it would be met with resistance. Castlereagh, Secretary of State for War and the Colonies wrote back to Bligh, giving instructions to stop the barter of spirits that were received on 31 December 1807 and H. V. Evatt later commented:

---

[33] Government and General Order, 14 February 1807, *HRNSW*, Vol. 6, pp. 253-254.
[34] Regulations respecting Vessels: Foreign and English, 4 October 1806, *HRNSW*, Vol. 6, pp. 193-197.
[35] Government and General Order, 28 February 1807, *HRNSW*, Vol. 6, p. 258.
[36] Government and General Order, 1 November 1806, *HRNSW*, Vol. 6, p. 198.
[37] Proclamation, 3 January 1807, *HRNSW*, Vol. 6, p. 236.
[38] Government and General Order, 14 February 1807, *HRNSW*, Vol. 6, pp. 253-254.

...Bligh was authorised to prevent free importation, to preserve the trade under his entire control, to enforce all penalties against illegal import, and to establish regulations at his discretion for the sale of spirits. [39]

Bligh had come to administer a penal settlement not facilitate private enterprise. [40] Evatt argues that the enmity of the monopolists within the colony stemmed from this and other policies that attacked the power of the rich and promoted the welfare of the poor settlers. Free settlers such as John and Gregory Blaxland claimed that Bligh had no interest in supporting their enterprises and did not give them the assistance that the British Government had promised. [41] People came to NSW to make money and Bligh seemed oblivious to this. He ceased the practice of handing out large land grants to the powerful in the colony and during his term granted just over 2,180 acres of land, half of it to his daughter and himself. [42] One thousand acres were at the Hawkesbury that he farmed as a 'model farm' for private gain. He allocated himself publicly victualed convicts and animals from the public herds and erected buildings at government expense. This was, to say the least, insensitive, but Bligh was never known for his tact. He was 'making hay while the sun shines as fast as he can', as Surgeon John Harris wrote. [43]

---

[39] Evatt, H. V., *Rum Rebellion: A Study of the Overthrow of Governor Bligh by John Macarthur and the New South Wales Corps*, (Angus & Robertson), 1938, p. 72.
[40] Karskens, Grace, & Waterhouse, Richard, "Property is too sacred to be taken away...merely at the will of a Governor': Property, Liberty, Tyranny and the Rum Rebellion', *Journal of Australian Colonial History*, Vol. 12, (2010), pp. 1-22.
[41] This is evident in Gregory Blaxland to Under-Secretary Chapman, 15 October 1807, and John Blaxland to ?, 16 October 1807, *HRNSW*, Vol. 6, pp. 301-304, 308-313. See also, Castlereagh to King, 13 July 1805, *HRA*, Series I, Vol. 5, pp. 490-491, on what the Blaxlands were promised.
[42] The question of the land grant at Parramatta dragged on after Bligh's death into the 1820s. See Bathurst to Darling, 18 January 1827, *HRA*, Series I, Vol. 13, pp. 17-22.
[43] Harris to Anna Josepha King, 25 October 1807, *HRNSW*, Vol. 6, p. 347. Bligh has earlier dismissed Harris from the magistracy: Government and General Order, 2 May 1807, *HRNSW*, Vol. 6, p. 266.

Bligh also upset some people by allowing a group of Irish convicts to be tried for revolt by a court that included their accusers and then when six out of the eight were acquitted, he kept them in custody. Soon after his arrival he replaced most of the officials, many of them from the military, with his own appointments. This did not play well in a small community and did not endear him to the Corps.[44] He dismissed D'Arcy Wentworth [45] from his position of Assistant Surgeon to the Colony and sentenced three merchants to a month's imprisonment and a fine for writing a letter that he considered offensive. Bligh also dismissed Thomas Jamison [46] from the magistracy, describing him in 1807 as being 'inimical' to good government. [47] Jamison the highly capable, if devious Surgeon-General of NSW had accumulated significant personal wealth as a maritime trader and was also a friend and business partner of Macarthur. Jamison, who never forgave Bligh for sacking him as a magistrate and interfering with his private business activities, supported his later deposition.

Governor Phillip had intended to reserve the land between, roughly, Hunter Street and the water for public purposes. Cutting into this reserved area, during Phillip's time, was a track formed by the passage of traffic behind the row of tents that the officers of the First Fleet had pitched on arrival, soon replaced by rudimentary huts, on the western bank of the Tank Stream that flowed into Sydney Cove, now Circular Quay. [48] That track became

---

[44] On Bligh's early appointments, see Government and General Orders, 15, 16 August 1806, *HRNSW*, Vol. 6, pp. 167-169.

[45] Bligh to Windham, 31 October 1807, *HRA*, Series I, Vol. 6, pp. 188-190, stated the Bligh suspended Wentworth on 25 July for 'extreme misconduct': 'it has been a practice to allow them [sick men] to remain victualed as Hospital Patients requiring care, applying their use to private advantage.' D'Arcy Wentworth to Castlereagh, 17 October 1807, *HRNSW*, Vol. 6, pp. 313-328, gives Wentworth's response.

[46] Parsons, Vivienne, 'Jamison, Thomas (1753?-1811)', *ADB*, Vol. 2, pp. 12-13.

[47] Bligh to Windham, 31 October 1807, *HRNSW*, Vol. 6, p. 355; see also, Nicholas Bayly to Jamison, 12 February 1808, *HRNSW*, Vol. 6, pp. 518-519, indicates the cause of his dismissal.

[48] Ibid, Atkinson, Alan, *The Europeans in Australia, A History*, Vol. 1, (Oxford University Press), 1997, p. 273. Bligh to Windham,

George Street and this, rather than Phillip's conception, proved to be the model for the grand Sydney tradition of urban planning. Phillip's successors gradually abandoned his plan. Leases were granted, at first only for short periods. However, Governor King attempted to regularise the haphazard system and to establish clearly defined property rights by creating a register of dealings, quadrupling the rent and granting a large number of leases, many for periods of fourteen years.[49] Bligh, wanted to return to critical aspects of Phillip's original plan by clearing grand spaces around Government House and the church, but King's leases stood in the way. Bligh used his wide discretionary powers to achieve his objective refusing to issue further leases, announcing that he would not approve building on existing leases, ordering residents to surrender possession of homes and demolishing structures built without approval. Intending to revoke the leases, but unsure of his power to do so, he sought instructions from London.[50]

The wife of a commercially successful emancipist wrote complaining:

> From some he took good houses and gave them bad ones. From others he took their houses and turned them into the street and made them no recompense whatever. Some he stopped building. Others he made make improvements against their inclinations and on the whole endeavoured to crush every person as much as possible.[51]

When one occupant of a leasehold residence in the environs of Government House objected to Bligh's order to remove it, asserting that he could not be forced to do so by the laws of England, Bligh allegedly exploded:

---

31 October 1807, *HRA*, Series I, Vol. 6, pp. 155-156, lists the leases under question.

[49] See generally Atkinson, Alan, 'Taking Possession: Sydney's First Householders', in Aplin, Graeme, (ed.), *A Difficult Infant: Sydney before Macquarie,* (University of NSW Press), 1988, especially pp. 76, 79-82, 83-84.

[50] Ibid, Atkinson, Alan, 'Taking Possession: Sydney's First Householders', pp. 84-87; *HRA*, Series I, Vol. 6, pp. 155-156, 714-715. See also, Government and General Order, 23 July 1807, *HRNSW*, Vol. 6, pp. 275-276.

[51] Ibid, Atkinson, Alan, *The Europeans in Australia,* Vol. 1, p. 273.

Damn your laws of England! Don't talk to me of your laws of England. I will make laws for this colony, and every wretch of you, son of a bitch, shall be governed by them. Or there (pointing over to the gaol) is your habitation! [52]

Bligh had quickly made enemies of some of the most influential people in the colony and also antagonised some of the less wealthy who had leases on government land within Sydney. Even if these measures affected relatively few, they represented an assault on private property that was construed by some as the beginnings of the rebellion.

The New South Wales Corps

The NSW Corps was a powerful Sydney institution. In 1808, its members comprised 10 per cent of the white population of 4,000 that included their families and a large number of former soldiers. The Corps owned a considerable amount of property and ran many businesses in Sydney, including one-third of the town's pubs. The numbers of Corps and ex-Corps members, therefore, formed a substantial and influential group, exhibiting what Governor King had called 'the jealousy but too often attendant on professional *esprit de corps*'. [53] The rank-and-file members of the Corps were not recruited from the dregs of society as has often been claimed. Over a third were skilled men. [54] Their life in NSW was a vast

---

[52] Ritchie, John, *A Charge of Mutiny: The Court Martial of Lieutenant Colonel George Johnston for Deposing Governor William Bligh in the Rebellion of 26 January 1808*, (National Library of Australia), 1988, p. 365.

[53] King to Under-Secretary Cooke, 18 June 1808, *HRNSW*, Vol. 6, p. 656.

[54] McAskill, Tracey, 'An asset to the Colony: The social and economic contribution of Corpsmen to early New South Wales', *Journal of the Royal Australian Historical Society*, Vol. 82, (1), 1996, pp. 40-59, Montague, R. H., 'The Men of the New South Wales Corps: a Comparison?', *Journal of the Royal Australian Historical Society*, Vol. 62, (4), (1977), pp. 217-233, and Stratham, P., 'A new look at the New South Wales Corps, 1790-1810', *Australian Economic History Review*, Vol. 24, (1), 1984, pp. 20-33. Information on the NSW Corps and the trading conducted by its officers, is available in, Statham, Pamela, (ed.), *A Colonial Regiment: New Sources relating to the New South Wales Corps, 1789-1810*, (Australian National University), 1992.

improvement on what they would have had in Britain and they would fight to retain it. They were used to power and influence but Bligh did not treat them with respect. In October 1807, Major George Johnston wrote a formal letter of complaint to the Commander-in-Chief of the British Army, stating that Bligh was abusive and interfering with the troops of the NSW Corps. Before the rebellion, this was the only official complaint sent to London. However, the burden of his letter was that Bligh did not treat the Corps with the dignity it deserved. He spoke roughly to it, criticised and insulted it: 'his abusing and confining the soldiers without the smallest provocation', 'his casting the most undeserved and opprobrious censure on the Corps'. [55]

Some officers had built up financial capital during the 1790s and early 1800s when profits were high and also through their preferential access to land grants, cheap labour by assignment of convicts and supply of provisions, livestock and equipment delivered for government purposes at the cost of the British taxpayer. In 1808, many officers retained an interest in trade, which had become more diverse and much more competitive, but their principal economic interest now lay in agricultural grants and in urban leaseholds in Sydney, where one sub-divided block, for instance, changed hands for £900 just before Bligh's arrival. Although those adversely affected by Bligh's policies included many with no association with the NSW Corps, no coup could have occurred without the united resolve of its officers. Bligh had stirred the acute anxieties of these men by challenging their individual and collective reputation and status. This was a serious affront under the code of honour that they regarded as the most important social bond of their lives. [56] He also offended members of this caste by his conduct and bearing and perhaps most of all, by his language. Devoid of tact, quick tempered, infuriated by insubordination or incompetence, incapable

---

[55] Johnston to Sir James Gordon, military secretary to the Duke of York, 8 October 1807, *HRNSW*, Vol. 6, p. 652.
[56] The emphasis on the code of honour as a critical factor in the coup was first put forward by Parsons, George, 'The Commercialisation of Honour: Early Australian Capitalism 1788-1809', in ibid, Aplin, Graeme, (ed.), *A Difficult Infant: Sydney Before Macquarie*, pp. 18-41. The theme was developed by ibid, Duffy, Michael, *Man of Honour: John Macarthur, Duellist, Rebel, Founding Father*, (Macmillan), 2003.

of compromise, prone to indulge in mockery and abuse, he failed to respect the boundary between criticism and derision. [57] Manning Clark described him in the following terms:

> If anyone dared to object or remonstrate with him, he lost his senses and his speech, his features became distorted, he foamed at the mouth, stamped on the ground, shook his fist in the face of the person so presuming, and uttered a torrent of abuse in language disgraceful to him as a governor, an officer and a man. [58]

The officers of the NSW Corps, as well as most free settlers, were attracted to the colony precisely because their social origins did not allow them to live as gentleman in the land of their birth. It was commonplace to buy commissions in the army and for those not able to afford one in the more fashionable and prestigious regiments, the NSW Corps proved a good alternative. The economic and, therefore, the social status of the officers were never secure. Bligh not only attacked their commercial and agricultural interests, he challenged the core of their personal identity.

Whatever his formal powers may have been, Bligh undermined what the local élite regarded as property rights, especially with respect to the urban leases. This was fundamentally inconsistent with contemporary understanding of the rights of free Englishmen. Bligh, of course, relied on his formal authority and had the personal strength to exercise powers that his two predecessors, Hunter and King, had compromised by permitting private men to grow wealthy at the expense of the Crown. He was determined to reassert the public interest as he saw it and to act strictly in accordance with his instructions. In most respects, his approach to governing was disciplined and purposeful. However, in a small settlement like Sydney, effective and purposive government required an understanding of communal expectations and an element of consent. Bligh proved as oblivious to the fears and aspirations of the Sydney élite as he had earlier been to the delights that the crew of *The Bounty* had experienced in Tahiti. The scene was set for a conflict of institutional

---

[57] See, Denning, Greg, *Mr Bligh's Bad Language: Passion, Power and Theatre on the Bounty*, (Cambridge University Press), 1992.
[58] Clark, C. M. H., *A History of Australia*, Vol. 1, (Melbourne University Press), 1962, p. 216.

cultures between that of the navy, where authority was typically exercised in the confined autocracy of a ship and that of the army, where the exercise of authority often involved interaction with a broader community.

Although Bligh had returned to England a hero in 1790 after the mutiny on the *Bounty*, he was on his second breadfruit voyage on *HMS Providence* between 1791 and 1793, when some of the mutineers captured at Tahiti were placed on trial in September 1792 and could not defend himself. As a result of the campaigns launched by Fletcher Christian's brother and others to justify the actions of the mutineers, the view took hold in certain quarters that it was Bligh's tyranny that had caused the mutiny. This reputation made Bligh politically vulnerable in NSW and according to Surgeon Edward Luttrell before:

> Governor Bligh [came] into the colony a clamour [had] been raised against him, and an opposition formed to counteract his government. [59]

The old rhetoric about monarchical tyranny could be revived and intensified against Bligh. The accusations were long on rhetoric but short on evidence. For instance, when Elizabeth Macarthur wrote to a female friend in England in January 1807 she described Bligh in such a fashion:

> The Governor has already shewn the inhabitants of Sydney that he is violent — rash — tyrannical. No very pleasing prospect at the beginning of his reign. [60]

Lieutenant William Minchin commented:

> ...a deluge worse than that of the Hawkesbury has since swept off every path to...industry and happiness...if a Military Officer might be allowed to use the words Tyranny and oppression, I would inform you that until now I never experienced their weight.[61]

---

[59] Surgeon Luttrell to Under-Secretary Sullivan, 8 October 1807, *HRNSW*, Vol. 6, p. 296.
[60] See, Elizabeth Macarthur to Miss Kingdon, 29 January 1807, ML, A2908, Vol. 2.
[61] William Minchin to Philip Gidley King, 20 October 1807, ML MSS 681/2, pp. 397-399.

John Harris, the Corps' surgeon, who had been dismissed from his positions of naval officer and magistrate, reported:

> ...it is completely the reign of Robertspere, or that of Terror...I have heard much said of Bounty Bligh before I saw him, but no person could conceive that he could be such a fellow...Caligula himself never reigned with more despotic sway than he does. [62]

In October 1807, a verse with direct reference to the *Bounty* mutiny was circulating in Sydney:

> Oh tempora! Oh Mores! Is there no Christian in New South Wales to put a stop to the Tyranny of the Governor. [63]

Macarthur and Bligh

John Macarthur, attributed as the progenitor of the Australian wool industry – although his wife Elizabeth arguably deserves the title more – precipitated the crisis. Macarthur had arrived with the NSW Corps in 1790 as a lieutenant and by 1805 had substantial farming and commercial interests in the colony. [64] He had quarrelled with governors Hunter and King, and fought two duels. Michael Duffy regards his acute sense of honour as the key to his character and actions. He challenged Bligh to what was, in effect, a political duel in defence of both his honour and his money. Macarthur was as offensive, domineering, short-fused and arrogant as Bligh, but had an unscrupulous shrewdness, indeed subtlety that Bligh both lacked and could not discern in others. Clearly, from the beginning of Bligh's rule, Macarthur saw him as a powerful obstacle to the realisation of his ambitions and their interests clashed in a number of ways.

---

[62] John Harris to Anna Josepha King, 25 October 1807, ML A1980, pp. 237-248.
[63] John Harris to Philip Gidley King, 25 October 1807, ML MSS 681/2, pp. 401-408.
[64] Craig, R. J., and Jenkins, S. A., 'The Cox and Greenwood ledger of the New South Wales Corps 1801-1805: the account of Captain John Macarthur', *Journal of the Royal Australian Historical Society*, Vol. 82, (2), (1996), pp. 138-152.

Macarthur's wealth was regarded by Bligh as the most offensive example of private profit at public expense and determined to reduce it. On one occasion he refused to make a major land grant that Macarthur believed had been negotiated in London. Bligh's tone was dismissive: 'Are you to have such flocks of sheep and such herds of cattle as no man ever heard before. No sir!' [65] Macarthur was right to stress the shortage of herdsmen. Convict labour was scarce. No prisoners had arrived in 1805 and only about 550 males in 1806 and 1807, fewer than those freed by passage of time; but the shortage never affected the farm that Bligh had bought on the Hawkesbury. Bligh stopped Macarthur from cheaply distributing large quantities of wine to the Corps and also halted his allegedly illegal importation of brewing stills. In March 1807, a still for Macarthur arrived in Sydney, sent unannounced by his London agent. Bligh impounded it as illegal. Macarthur successfully argued to have the copper body, with goods inside, sent to his private store. [66] In October 1807, Naval Officer Robert Campbell sent his nephew to retrieve the still from Macarthur's store for return to England under Bligh's order. However, his nephew had no official status and Macarthur successfully sued for wrongful seizure.

Macarthur's interest in an area of land granted to him by Governor King conflicted with Bligh's town-planning interests. In December 1807, Bligh challenged Macarthur's lease on Church Hill, given by Governor King despite Phillip's order of no private leases in Sydney town and on 20 January 1808 ordered the demolition of the fence on the lease Macarthur had begun six days earlier. [67] Macarthur and Bligh were also engaged in other disagreements,

---

[65] Ibid, Duffy, Michael, *Man of Honour: John Macarthur-Duellist, Rebel, Founding Father*, p. 255, n 10.
[66] Bligh to Windham, 31 October 1807, *HRA*, Series I, Vol. 6, pp. 160, 164-178, details the question of Macarthur's still.
[67] Surveyor-General Grimes to Macarthur, 13 January 1808, *HRNSW*, Vol. 6, pp. 413-414, ordered Macarthur not to build on the lease on Church Hill with Macarthur's response reluctantly resigning the land to please Bligh if Bligh allocated him as alternative lease. The matter escalated the following day with correspondence between Grimes and Macarthur in which Grimes made it clear that Macarthur's proposal was unacceptable and that he was unwilling to receive further correspondence on the issue: *HRNSW*, Vol. 6, pp. 416-417.

including a conflict over landing regulations. In June 1807, John Hoare a convict had stowed away and escaped to the Pacific Islands on the *Parramatta*, one of Macarthur's vessels. [68] In December 1807, when that vessel returned to Sydney, the £900 bond to the NSW government for assisting escape was deemed to be forfeited. The ship was consequently impounded. Macarthur now refused to pay or victual the crew, forcing them on 14 December to come ashore illegally breaching the landing regulations. In effect, he abandoned a ship worth £10,000 rather than pay a fine of £900.

Bligh instructed the Judge-Advocate, Richard Atkins to issue an order for John Macarthur to appear on the matter of the bond on the 15 December 1807. [69] Outraged, Macarthur sent an angry reply declaring his contempt for Atkins and the government. The following day, Atkins issued warrant for Macarthur's arrest. Macarthur demanded to be brought before bench of magistrates that granted him bail on condition he appeared again the following day where magistrates, including George Johnston, commit Macarthur to criminal trial and he was bailed to appear for trial at the next sitting of the Sydney Criminal Court on 25 January 1808. However, the Court did not define the charges. [70] The court was constituted of Atkins and six officers of the NSW Corps: Anthony Fenn Kemp, John Brabyn, William Moore, Thomas Laycock, William Minchin and William Lawson. Macarthur objected to Atkins sitting in judgement of him because he was his debtor[71] and inveterate enemy and read from a lengthy

---

[68] Macarthur's ship and the runaway, 27 June 1807, *HRNSW*, Vol. 6, p. 270.
[69] Bennett, J. M., 'Atkins, Richard (1745-1820)', *ADB*, Vol. 1, pp. 38-40.
[70] See Macarthur to Atkins, 20 January 1808, *HRNSW*, Vol. 6, p. 418, and subsequent correspondence on the imprecise nature of the charge, *HRNSW*, Vol. 6, pp. 418-420.
[71] During January 1808, Macarthur had tried to recall debt he held against Atkins but Bligh refused Macarthur's requests to assist his recovery of debt. See Macarthur to Bligh, 29 December 1807, *HRNSW*, Vol. 6, pp. 395-396, and Macarthur to Bligh, 1, 12 January 1808, *HRNSW*, Vol. 6, pp. 411-412, 413. On Macarthur's 'trial', see the succinct discussion in ibid, Woods, Gregory D., *A history of criminal law in New South Wales: the colonial period 1788-1900*, pp. 33-34.

document declaiming in Lockean terms towards the conclusion:

> You will now decide, gentlemen, whether law and justice shall finally prevail...You have the eyes of an anxious public upon you, trembling for the safety of their property, their liberty, and their lives. To you has fallen the lot of deciding a point which perhaps involves the happiness or misery of millions yet unborn. I conjure you in the name of Almighty God, in whose presence you stand, to consider the inestimable value of the precious deposit with which you are entrusted.[72]

This was grossly exaggerated but then gave the Corps its rallying call:

> It is to the Officers of the New South Wales Corps that the administration of Justice is committed; and who that is just has anything to dread? [73]

Macarthur's ranting about the defence of liberty and property that were never in danger, gave Johnston excuse to claim that 'insurrection and massacre' were imminent because Bligh was planning 'to subvert the laws of the country' and 'to terrify and influence the Courts of Justice'.[74]

Atkins rejected this, but Macarthur's protest had the support of the other six Corps members of the court. Atkins threatened to gaol Macarthur. Kemp retaliated by threatening to gaol Atkins who left for Government House, declaring that there was no court without him. A similar manoeuvre had been tried in 1803. Kemp was defendant in a court case and this time Johnston, the acting commanding officer of the Corps, demanded that the Governor, King, replace the Judge-Advocate, John Harris. King buckled and replaced Harris. Bligh, however, stood firm. During the day, messages went back and forth between the court and Government House over Atkins'

---

[72] Johnston to Castlereagh, 11 April 1808, *HRA*, Series I, Vol. 6, p. 227.
[73] Johnston to Castlereagh, 11 April 1808, *HRA*, Series I, Vol. 6, p. 227.
[74] For Macarthur's trial on 25-26 January 1808 see, *HRNSW*, Vol. 6, pp. 422-433, and Johnston to Castlereagh, 11 April 1808, *HRA*, Series I, Vol. 6, pp. 221-234.

position. Around 12.30 pm, Bligh made it clear that he had no power to remove Atkins and without Atkins there was no validly constituted court. The officers nevertheless refused to serve with Atkins. Three hours later Macarthur sought military protection due to unspecified threats and at 5.30 pm, Bligh wrote to Johnston with the request that he attend Government House. [75] It is noteworthy that Bligh wrote to Johnston in order to attempt to resolve this impasse rather than immediately resorting to action. Johnston sent a message to say he was indisposed, as he had wrecked his 'chaise' on the evening of the 24 January on his way back home to Annandale after dining with officers of the Corps. It was increasingly clear that stalemate had been reached.

Overthrowing Bligh

Events escalated on the morning of 26 January 1808. First, Bligh ordered Provost-Marshall William Gore to arrest Macarthur and again called for the return of the court papers that were now in the hands of officers of the Corps.[76] Then, at 10 am, the officers requested the appointment of a new Judge-Advocate and the release of Macarthur on bail. They had received no reply by 3.00 pm and adjourned the court. After this, Bligh sent a note to the officers summoning them to Government House at 9 am the following morning, indicating that Atkins had charged them with certain crimes, but not revealing what these were. [77] Finally, an hour later, Bligh informed Johnston of his action and additionally told him that the actions of his officers were considered treasonable. [78] As the officers were to appear before Bligh and all the magistrates, this would be a charge under criminal not military law and the charge, if proven, was a capital offence. [79] To make this threat

---

[75] Secretary Griffin to Johnston, 25 January 1808, *HRA*, Series I, Vol. 6, p. 234.
[76] King, Hazel, 'Gore, William (1765-1845)', *ADB*, Vol. 1, pp. 459-460.
[77] *HRNSW*, Vol. 6, p. 433.
[78] *HRNSW*, Vol. 6, p. 433, *HRA*, Series I, Vol. 6, p. 236.
[79] See, McMahon, John, 'Not a Rum Rebellion but a military insurrection', *Journal of the Royal Australian Historical Society*, Vol. 92, (2006), p. 135.

against officers was an intemperate and extreme move. There could be no greater slur on their honour.

Bligh's threat of the charge of treason may have been the turning point. This is certainly the view of McMahon and of Fitzgerald and Hearn who stated that Johnston was motivated because of 'potential danger to his officers (and ... [the] Corps)'. [80] Johnston appears to have felt his relationship with Bligh had broken down so much that there was no point in talking to him. It was unlikely that Bligh would have executed the officers; but very likely they might be sent to gaol pending further advice. If this action had been taken it would have left only two remaining officers in Sydney, aside from Johnston and one of these, Cadwallader Draffin, was deemed mentally unstable. [81] Johnston later maintained that if the officers had been gaoled, the soldiers would have rioted and perhaps killed Bligh as well as prejudicing internal security in the colony. He arrested Bligh for his own protection. Johnston was not particularly close to Macarthur and had in fact been one of the magistrates who ordered the latter be arrested over the incident leading to the court case. He was an experienced officer, had been in the Colony since 1788 and was apparently highly regarded by his men. What Macarthur had started, Johnston would finish in a way perhaps Macarthur never imagined, though Macarthur certainly supported it.

Later that afternoon at 5.00 pm, Johnston went to the barracks and ordered Macarthur's release and assumed, with no vested legal authority, the title of Lieutenant-Governor. [82] After discussion with fellow officers, a number of wealthy civilians and the newly-released Macarthur, the decision was taken to depose Bligh. Macarthur duly drafted a petition for Bligh's arrest as a tyrant, and for powers to pass to Johnston. [83] According to Evatt, those who signed the petition probably only agreed

---

[80] Fitzgerald, Ross and Hearne, Mark, *Bligh, Macarthur and the Rum Rebellion*, (Kangaroo Press), 1988, p. 120.
[81] Duffy, Michael, *Man of honour: John Macarthur, duellist, rebel, founding father*, (Macmillan), 2003, p. 295.
[82] *HRNSW*, Vol. 6, p. 433.
[83] *HRNSW*, Vol. 6, p. 434, *HRA*, Series I, Vol. 6, p. 240. Apart from Macarthur and the Blaxland brothers, the petition was signed by James Mileham, James Badgery, Nicholas Bayly and by S. (Simeon) Lord.

to this action once reassured that Bligh was safely under house arrest. [84] An order was duly issued stating that Bligh was charged: 'by the respectable inhabitants of crimes that render you unfit to exercise the supreme authority another moment in this colony; and in that charge all officers under my command have joined'. Johnston went on to call for Bligh's resignation and submission to arrest. [85]

At 6.00 pm the Corps, with full band and colours, marched to Government House to arrest Bligh. They were hindered by Bligh's recently widowed daughter and her parasol at the gates but Captain Thomas Laycock finally found Bligh after an extensive search, in full dress uniform, behind his bed where he claimed he was hiding papers. Bligh was painted as a coward for this but Duffy argues that if Bligh was hiding it would have been to escape and thwart the coup. [86] Stephen Dando-Collins suggests that Bligh was attempting to travel to the garrison at Hawkesbury from where he could lead the fight against Johnston. [87] Bligh said later at Johnston's court martial that he hid:

> ...to defeat their object, and to deliberate on means to be adopted for the restoration of my authority, which in such a critical situation could only be accomplished by my getting into the interior of the country adjacent to the Hawkesbury, where I knew the whole body of the people would flock to my standard. [88]

It is apparent from this statement that Bligh was contemplating a form of civil conflict by raising a militia to oppose the military. While Fletcher casts doubt the level of support Bligh may have had from settlers in the Hawkesbury, he nevertheless concludes 'a balance of probability...seems weighted in favour...that there was

---

[84] For discussion of petitions on 26 and 27 January to Johnston, see Donohoe, J., *Captain Bligh's Petticoat Mutiny*, (J. S. Shaw North Publishing), 2011

[85] Johnston proclaimed martial law, *HRNSW*, Vol. 6, p. 434, *HRA*, Series I, Vol. 6, pp. 240-241, and sent Bligh a letter calling on him to resign, *HRNSW*, Vol. 6, p. 434, *HRA*, Series I, Vol. 6, p. 241.

[86] Ibid, Duffy, Michael, *Man of honour: John Macarthur, duellist, rebel, founding father*, pp. 297-298.

[87] Dando-Collins, Stephen, *Captain Bligh's Other Mutiny: the true story of the military coup that turned Australia into a two-year rebel republic*, (Random House), 2007.

[88] Ibid, Ritchie, John, *A Charge of Mutiny: The Court Martial of Lieutenant Colonel George Johnston for Deposing Governor William Bligh in the Rebellion of 26 January 1808*, p. 9

strong support for Bligh at the Hawkesbury'. [89] An alternative scenario suggests that Bligh, as naval commodore with command of the *Porpoise* that had just returned to Sydney, could have sailed to VDL, where he might have sought support from either Lieutenant-Governor Collins at Hobart or from Lieutenant-Colonel Paterson at Port Dalrymple. This would certainly have given encouragement to his supporters in Sydney. It is not surprising that Johnston had been greatly concerned that the soldiers under his command had initially failed to arrest Bligh.

On 27 February, with Bligh confined at Government House, Johnston revoked martial law and dismissed officers of Bligh's government including Atkins and Provost-Marshall Gore. There were all-night celebrations across Sydney that included drinking and dancing around bonfires, burning of effigies, satirical posters, oil-lamp transparencies in windows and 'Bligh under the bed' cartoon displayed in soldiers' homes. Throughout 1808, Bligh was confined to Government House refusing to leave for England until lawfully relieved of his duty. [90] Johnston had no prospect of material advancement from dismissing Bligh; in fact, he was putting his future income as an army officer at grave risk. Bligh's evidence to the court martial in 1811 suggests that Johnston was hesitant in his actions and showed his lack of self-confidence by marching the whole NSW Corps against the undefended Government House. Johnston was in no way Macarthur's tool. This has been obscured by the enthusiasm of both Macarthur's supporters and his detractors to place him more fully in the centre of the rebellion than his actions deserve. He was a competent and independent official, whose motive in removing Bligh was to resolve a crisis in the colony's administration and preserve public order. [91] This was not a rebellion in the sense of people grabbing power and possessions for themselves. A mutiny is much more restricted with the aim of removing a bad leader. There was a strongly held belief

---

[89] Ibid, Fletcher, B. H., 'The Hawkesbury Settlers and the Rum Rebellion', p. 234.
[90] Atkinson, Alan, 'The British Whigs and the Rum Rebellion', *Journal of the Royal Australian Historical Society*, Vol. 66, (2), (1980), pp. 73-90.
[91] Johnston to Castlereagh, 11 April 1808, *HRA*, Series I, Vol. 6, pp. 208-221, provides Johnston's justification for rebellion.

in the early-nineteenth century that gentlemen had the right to overthrow leaders who abused their power. In this context, George Johnston's action becomes much more principled and this was acknowledged during his court martial in 1811 when the leniency of his sentence was justified by reference to Bligh's 'impropriety and oppression'. In the days following the 1808 insurrection Daniel McKay, a publican who had once been employed as a gaoler but dismissed by Bligh as too brutal, took relish in erecting a sign outside his establishment. On one side it depicted a Highland officer thrusting his sword through a snake, whilst the female figure of Liberty presents him with a cap. On the other side emblazoned in large type was the dedication: 'The Ever Memorable 26th January 1808'. [92]

There is some debate over the nature of the 'rebellion' and the degree to which it was planned. Some historians argue that had Johnston been in sufficiently good health to meet Bligh on 25 January 1808, the rebellion would perhaps not have occurred. Or had he already decided that Bligh would have to be removed and calculated that ill-health was a good tactic to escalate matters? Johnston consistently represented himself as an agent of the popular will claiming to have found the townsfolk of Sydney on his arrival from Annandale on 26 January 1808 in a state of tumult and apprehension, with no man's life or property safe against a tyrannical governor. The same question could be asked of Macarthur's actions on his trial. The problem is that, while both Johnston and Macarthur had grave doubts about Bligh's method of ruling, there is no evidence to suggest that they colluded in precipitating rebellion, something that would anyway have proved difficult as Macarthur was under arrest for much of 25 and 26 January. The meeting between Johnston, Macarthur and the group of wealthy citizens on 26 January has been mooted as indicative of conspiracy, but arguably its significance lies rather more in giving civilian legitimacy to military action. In fact, the rebellion did not require a great deal of planning and the NSW Corps was willing to support

---

[92] For Bligh's account of the rebellion, 30 June 1808, *HRNSW*, Vol. 6, p. 670. See also, Bligh to Castlereagh, 30 April 1808, *HRA*, Series I, Vol. 6, pp. 420-440.

Johnston's order to arrest Bligh. For the rebellion to succeed all that was necessary was to apprehend Bligh. [93]

An interregnum

Removing Bligh has been achieved with relative ease but he legally remained Governor and the *de facto* administration that had been established lacked any constitutional legality.[94] Although there was no breakdown of law and order, there was a division among the colonists and especially within the governing élite between those who supported the rebel administration and those who remained loyal to Bligh. Until a superior officer to Johnston arrived six months after the coup, John Macarthur was effectively in control of civil administration and was not constrained by the operation of the rule of law. During that period the rudimentary legal system was abused, where not suspended and the courts used as a tool of political revenge.[95] Magistrates loyal to Bligh were dismissed. [96] Other loyalists were subject to a parody of justice. Gore and George Crossley, the dubious ex-lawyer who had some role in advising Bligh on the rebellion were convicted on bogus charges and transported to the coal mines at Newcastle for seven years. [97] In March 1809, John Palmer, Bligh's Commissary who was charged with sedition for distributing Bligh's Proclamation that the Corps was in a state of mutiny, denied the competency of the court and refused to plead but was unlawfully gaoled for three

---

[93] Gore to Castlereagh, 26 April 1808, *HRNSW*, Vol. 6, pp. 602-606, gives an account of Bligh's arrest by a supporter. Bligh to Castlereagh, 30 April 1808, *HRNSW*, Vol. 6, pp. 607-629, gives his first account of the rebellion.

[94] Johnston did not inform Castlereagh of Bligh's arrest until 11 April 1808, *HRNSW*, Vol. 6, pp. 575-589. For correspondence between Bligh and the rebels see, Johnston to Castlereagh, 11 April 1808, *HRA*, Series I, Vol. 6, pp. 242-271, and Johnston's General Orders, *HRA*, Series I, Vol. 6, pp. 271-276.

[95] *HRNSW*, Vol. 6, pp. 435-453, Johnston to Castlereagh, 11 April 1808, *HRA*, Series I, Vol. 6, pp. 276-291, print the Colonial Secretary's Papers of the examination of officers after Bligh's arrest.

[96] Government and General Order, 27 January 1808, *HRNSW*, Vol. 6, p. 453.

[97] Allars, K. G., 'Crossley, George (1749-1823)', *ADB*, Vol. 1, pp. 262-263.

months and fined £50. [98] The civil court processes were also abused. [99] However, with the exception of politically motivated cases, the legal system continued to operate more or less as before. Commerce was adversely affected as it was uncertain whether the negotiable bills payable in sterling that had traditionally been used for transactions with the government, would be honoured in London. [100] No one who lived through these months was in little doubt that the rule of law was severely compromised.

Atkins was replaced [101] and Johnston initially appointed the Surveyor-General Charles Grimes as Judge-Advocate and ordered that Macarthur and the six officers be tried. [102] On 2 February, they were found not guilty. [103]

---

[98] Steven, Margaret, 'Palmer, John (1760-1833)', *ADB*, Vol. 2, pp. 309-311. See also, Palmer to Bligh, 2 March 1808, *HRNSW*, Vol. 6, pp. 530-531, in which he reaffirmed his support for Bligh. Palmer was reinstated by Governor Lachlan Macquarie but failed to receive any official compensation for deprivations suffered in the rebellion. Though the secretary of state instructed Macquarie to examine the commissariat accounts and see that the office was placed on a proper footing, he observed that as the complaints against Palmer 'have been chiefly brought forward since the arrest of Governor Bligh, it is probable they are exaggerated'. Palmer's examiners at the Comptroller's Office in London held that the charges 'seemed to have arisen as much from private pique as from zeal for the public service' and were too vague to justify a formal inquiry. However, they thought it inexpedient to restore Palmer because of his long tenure in office (since 1791) and recommended the appointment of another commissary. On 25 July 1811, Palmer was demoted to assistant commissary and placed on half-pay and next year the entire commissariat system was reorganised.
[99] Kercher, B., *Debt, Seduction and Other Disasters: The Birth of Civil Law in Convict New South Wales*, (Federation Press), 1996, pp. 41-42.
[100] Curry, J. E. B., *Reflections on the Colony of New South Wales: George Caley*, (Lansdowne), 1966, p. 157.
[101] He was, however, reinstated as Judge-Advocate on 13 December 1808. Aitken's conversion to the rebel cause was motivated largely by financial considerations, the capacity of the Corps to pander to his alcoholic tastes and a free grant of 500 acres in the Minto District.
[102] Dowd, Bernard T., 'Grimes, Charles (1772-1858)', *ADB*, Vol. 1, pp. 487-488, and 'Charles Grimes: The Second Surveyor-General of New South Wales', *Journal of the Royal Australian Historical Society*, Vol. 22, (4), (1936), pp. 247-288.

By contrast, Bligh supporters were sentenced harshly with Provost-Marshall Gore receiving seven years for causing the arrest of Macarthur. [104] On 3 April, Grimes resigned after George Johnston, in his role as Acting-Governor, criticised some 'extraordinary' proceedings in his court. Although Grimes' comments were partly due to his ignorance of the law or, as Johnston said, 'errors of judgment more than of design', Grimes was regarded as one of the opponents of his administration. Macarthur was then appointed as the so-called 'Secretary' and ran the business affairs of the colony. [105] Another prominent opponent of Bligh, Macarthur's ally Thomas Jamison, was made the colony's Naval Officer, the equivalent of Collector of Customs and Excise and was also reinstated as a magistrate, which enabled he and his fellow legal officers to scrutinise Bligh's personal papers for evidence of wrong-doing. In June 1809, Jamison sailed to London to bolster his business interests and give evidence against Bligh in any legal prosecutions that might be brought against the mutineers. He never had the opportunity to testify at

---

[103] *HRNSW*, Vol. 6, pp. 465-510 and *HRA*, Series I, Vol. 6, pp. 291-352, detail the trial. Johnston then appointed Anthony Fenn Kemp to the post. Aitkens and especially Kemp and Grimes were incompetent but more importantly made judicial decisions unfavourable to Macarthur. Foveaux had little choice but to reinstate Aitkens: Foveaux to Castlereagh, 20 February 1809, *HRA*, Series I, Vol. 7, p. 2, 'I had no choice left but to restore Mr Atkins, or expose the public to the serious inconveniences which must inevitably have followed from leaving so indispensable a department vacated.' See also, *The Trial of John McArthur, Esq. before a court of criminal judicature, assembled at Sydney, in New South Wales, on February the 2nd, 1808, and four following days*, (Wood & Innes), 1808.

[104] Gore denied the authority of the rebel court that would not give bail and refused to plead; he was kept in gaol without trial for more than two months, and in a letter to Bligh unfavourably compared his treatment by the NSW rebels with that by the Irish rebels ten years before. On 30 May, Gore was again brought before a rebel court and again refused to plead. He was sentenced to transportation for seven years and was sent to Coal River (Newcastle) where he laboured with ordinary convicts. See, *HRA*, Series I, Vol. 6, pp. 555-563, for a statement of Gore's refusal to recognise the court, his defence and correspondence with Bligh.

[105] Government and General Order, 12 February 1808, *HRNSW*, Vol. 6, p. 519.

Johnston's court martial dying in London at the beginning of 1811. Within a few months of Bligh's arrest, divisions emerged within the rebel leadership. [106] Johnston and Macarthur fell out with Blaxland [107] and Macarthur even managed to alienate the NSW Corps, previously his staunchest supporters. [108]

Foveaux, Paterson and Macquarie

Following Bligh's overthrow Johnston had notified his superior officer, Colonel William Paterson who was in VDL establishing a settlement at Port Dalrymple (now Launceston) of events. [109] Paterson was reluctant to get involved until clear orders arrived from England. [110] When he learned that Lieutenant-Colonel Joseph Foveaux was returning to Sydney with orders to become acting Lieutenant-Governor, Paterson left Foveaux to deal with the situation. [111] Foveaux arrived on 28 July and immediately took over the colony but left Bligh under house arrest. He felt that Bligh's behaviour had been insufferable but, personal feelings apart, restoring the deposed governor was impractical since the NSW Corps

---

[106] Macarthur to Captain Piper, 24 May 1808, *HRNSW*, Vol. 6, pp. 643-644, indicated that unity was short-lived: '...some of our old acquaintances have behaved most scurvily...'
[107] Johnston to Castlereagh, 30 April 1808, *HRA*, Series I, Vol. 6, pp. 453-516, provides details for the reasons behind the rift between the Blaxlands and Johnston and Macarthur.
[108] Johnston to Castlereagh, 30 April 1808, *HRA*, Series I, Vol. 6, pp. 518-520.
[109] Macmillan, David S., 'Paterson, William (1755-1810)', *ADB*, Vol. 2, pp. 317-319. Johnston's letter is lost but Paterson's reply on 12 March 1808 is printed in, *HRNSW*, Vol. 6, pp. 536-538.
[110] Paterson to Castlereagh, 12 March 1808, *HRNSW*, Vol. 6, pp. 538-539. Bligh to Paterson, 8 August 1808, *HRA*, Series I, Vol. 6, pp. 601-601, was the first direct contact between Bligh and Paterson since the coup in which Bligh asked Paterson 'to use your utmost endeavours to suppress this Mutiny of the Corps under your command, that I may proceed in the Government of the Colony according to the powers delegated to me by our Gracious Sovereign.'
[111] Ibid, Whitaker, Anne-Maree, *Joseph Foveaux: Power and Patronage in Early New South Wales*, pp. 103-116, deals with his months in charge. See also, Fletcher, B. H., 'Foveaux, Joseph (1767-1846)', *ADB*, Vol. 1, pp. 407-409.

would certainly have opposed such a move. [112] He at once took secure hold of the reins of government, dispensing with the services of John Macarthur who as 'Secretary' had been the power behind Johnston. The broad outlines of his policy were influenced by the same desire for cheap and efficient government that had guided his work on Norfolk Island and he sought to make his administration acceptable to London by pursuing objectives it had long favoured. He attacked the liquor trade and tried to reduce expenditure, reform the administration of the commissariat and improve public works turning his attention to improving the colony's roads, bridges and public buildings. Efforts were made to encourage the raising of beef and mutton, while he tried to persuade smallholders to breed additional swine, so providing an outlet for their surplus maize. His land policy was moderate and he made few grants, though he did alienate some town land that was properly available only for lease.

Little exception can be taken to these aspects of Foveaux's rule. However, his treatment of the pro-Bligh faction was severe and sometimes unfair. The troublesome Bligh refused to depart and was bitterly criticised in Foveaux's dispatches. [113] George Suttor and a group of his associates were imprisoned for challenging his authority for refusing to attend a muster. [114] He disallowed Robert

---

[112] Bligh appealed to Foveaux to be reinstated: Bligh to Foveaux, 29 July 1808, *HRNSW*, Vol. 6, p. 713, but Foveaux refused to interfere. His justification can be found in Foveaux to Castlereagh, 4 September 1808, *HRNSW*, Vol. 6, pp. 728-735, and *HRA*, Series I, Vol. 6, pp. 623-631.

[113] This was particularly evident in a private letter from Foveaux to Under-Secretary Chapman (?), 10 September 1808, *HRNSW*, Vol. 6, pp. 749-754, and in Foveaux to Under-Secretary Cooke, 21 October 1808, pp. 783-784, where he suggested that Bligh was conspiring with settlers to support his restoration.

[114] Parsons, Vivienne, 'Suttor, George (1774-1859)', *ADB*, Vol. 2, pp. 498-500. Suttor was a firm supporter of Bligh and a leader among the settlers. In May 1808, he was instrumental in drawing up an address of welcome to Paterson, anticipating his arrival in Sydney and asking him to take action against the rebels; but as Paterson did not come it was not presented. In November, Suttor drew up another petition to be sent to the Colonial Office and with Martin Mason was chosen for a mission to London to explain the abuses in the colony and ask for the reinstatement of Bligh: Settlers' Petition to Castlereagh, 4 November 1808, *HRNSW*, Vol.

Campbell's contract with David Collins to import cattle to the Derwent, criticised Campbell's assistance to Bligh and accused Campbell and John Palmer of benefiting greatly from the liquor trade. [115] It has been argued that advice from officers who were jealous of Campbell's trading position underlay these moves and that Foveaux, acting as their tool, sought to destroy the merchant. If true, it was a serious flaw in what was quite an enterprising administration.

When there was still no word from England, he summoned Paterson to Sydney on 9 January 1809 to sort

---

6, pp. 802-804. In the meantime, however, Suttor was imprisoned for six months for failing to attend Foveaux's general muster and for impugning his authority. In 1810, Bligh took Suttor with him in the *Hindostan* as a witness against Colonel George Johnston.

[115] Steven, Margaret, 'Campbell, Robert (1769-1846)', *ADB*, Vol. 1, pp. 202-206, and *Robert Campbell and the Bligh rebellion, 1808*, (Canbara & District Historical Society), 1962. During the events that culminated in the deposition of Bligh, Campbell publicly and privately supported the governor's attempts at reform, convinced that it was his liberalising economic measures that had goaded his opponents into open rebellion. In Campbell's opinion Bligh 'wished to administer justice to all ranks of people'. This exposed him to the hostility of the rebels and had such adverse effects on his business interests that he claimed he was never fully able to repair. When Bligh was deposed, Campbell was put under military arrest and subsequently was dismissed as treasurer, Naval Officer and collector of taxes. On the grounds that he was suspected of trying to establish a trading monopoly in collusion with Bligh, the rebel faction supervised the activities of Campbell & Co., supporting without investigation any damaging allegations concerning irregularities in its trade. In June 1809, Campbell was tried for disobedience in refusing to officiate as coroner. He argued that as he had been charged officially with certain offences he deemed himself incompetent to hold any civil position until such charges had been disproved; but the court, whose authority Campbell refused to acknowledge, found him guilty and fined him £50. Although his business partner and his brother-in-law, Commissary John Palmer, were both gaoled by the rebels, Campbell openly remained a supporter of their victims and a focus for Bligh's allies. In January 1810, he was one of the first of those reinstated in their former offices by Macquarie. On 12 May, Campbell, with his family, sailed unwillingly for England in the *Hindostan* to appear as a witness for Bligh at Lieutenant-Colonel George Johnston's trial.

out matters. [116] Paterson sent Johnston and Macarthur to England for trial [117] and confined Bligh to the barracks until he signed a contract agreeing to return to England. [118] His opinion of Bligh was not high and he certainly regarded Bligh as culpable in causing the rebellion:

> He bore the most rancorous ill-will to every Officer and Inhabitant who he conceived could possibly in the remotest manner interfere with a matured plan of exercising the high command with which he was honoured in the purposes of gratifying his insatiably tyrannic Disposition and advancing his pecuniary interest. [119]

Paterson, whose health was failing, then retired to Government House at Parramatta and left Foveaux to run the colony. In January 1809, Bligh was given the control of HMS *Porpoise* on condition that he returned to England. [120] However, he sailed to Hobart in late March seeking the support of the Tasmanian Lieutenant-Governor David Collins to retake control of the colony. [121] Collins did not support him [122] and on Paterson's orders Bligh remained

---

[116] In poor health and drinking heavily, Paterson was a weak ruler. He spent most of the year at Parramatta as an invalid and the clique that had overthrown Bligh had the real control of affairs. Macquarie reported later, Paterson was 'such an easy, good-natured, thoughtless man, that he latterly granted Lands to almost every person who asked them, without regard to their Merits or pretensions'. Foveaux to Castlereagh, 20 February 1809, *HRA*, Series I, Vol. 7, p. 3.
[117] On 29 March 1809, Macarthur, Johnston and others sailed for England to participate in Johnston's court-martial for mutiny arriving on 9 October.
[118] Like Foveaux, Paterson refused to intervene in the Bligh affair, Paterson to Bligh, 21 January 1809, *HRNSW*, Vol. 7, pp. 8-9.
[119] Paterson to Castlereagh, 12 March 1809, *HRA*, Series I, Vol. 7, p. 18.
[120] Agreement between Bligh and Paterson, 4 February 1809, *HRNSW*, Vol. 7, pp. 17-18, *HRA*, Series I, Vol. 7, pp. 45-46.
[121] Bligh's Proclamation of his authority at the Derwent, 29 April 1809, *HRNSW*, Vol. 7, pp. 108-110, *HRA*, Series I, Vol. 7, pp. 96-99.
[122] Collins to Bligh, 4 May 1809, *HRNSW*, Vol. 7, p. 125 with Bligh's response, 7 May 1809, *HRNSW*, Vol. 7, pp. 125-126.

cut off on board the *Porpoise* and moored in Hobart until January 1810. [123]

It was two years before the rebellion was finally quenched. The threat of Napoleon was more important and there was also growing tension between Britain and the United States that eventually led to war in 1812. After considerable delay, the Colonial Office decided that sending further naval governors to rule the colony was untenable. Instead the NSW Corps, now known as the 102nd Regiment of Foot, was to be recalled to England and replaced with the 73rd Regiment of Foot, whose commanding officer would take over as Governor. [124] Bligh was to be reinstated for twenty-four hours and then recalled to England. Johnston was to be sent to England for court martial and Macarthur tried in Sydney though both were already on their way to London. Major-General Lachlan Macquarie [125] was put in charge of the mission after Major-General Miles Nightingall fell ill before departure. [126] He took over as Governor with an elaborate ceremony on 1 January 1810. [127]

Macquarie reinstated all the officials who had been sacked by Johnston and Macarthur and cancelled all land and stock grants that had been made since Bligh's deposition, though to calm things down he then restored

---

[123] See Paterson's Proclamation against Bligh, 19 March 1809, *HRNSW*, Vol. 7, p. 81.

[124] Duke of York to Castlereagh, 30 October 1808, *HRNSW*, Vol. 6, pp. 782-783. Although tainted by mutiny, the 102nd, after a period in England and Guernsey, served creditably in Bermuda and on active service in the war against the United States, returning from Canada in 1817, before being disbanded on 12 March 1818.

[125] McLachlan, N. D., 'Macquarie, Lachlan (1762-1824), *ADB*, Vol. 2, pp. 187-195, Ellis, M. H., *Lachlan Macquarie: His Life, Adventures and Times*, (Dymock's Book Arcade) 1947, 2nd ed., (Angus & Robertson), 1952, and Ritchie, John, *Lachlan Macquarie: a biography*, (Melbourne University Press), 1986, are useful biographies.

[126] Nightingall to Castlereagh, 6 December 1808, *HRNSW*, Vol. 6, pp. 810-811; he accepted the commission. Nightingall to Castlereagh (?), 20 March 1809, *HRNSW*, Vol. 7, p. 64, on the onset of the illness that prevented him from taking up his commission.

[127] Macquarie's Commission, 8 May 1809, *HRNSW*, Vol. 7, pp. 126-133 and his Instructions, 9, 14 May 1809, *HRNSW*, Vol. 7, pp. 122-140, 143-147.

grants that he thought appropriate and prevented any settling of scores. [128] When Bligh received the news of Macquarie's arrival, he sailed from Hobart to Sydney, arriving on 17 January 1810 to collect evidence for the forthcoming court martial of Major George Johnston. [129] He departed for the trial in England on 12 May aboard the *Hindostan*, with recalled NSW Corps soldiers and witnesses including Atkins and Paterson, who died en route, for the trial against Johnston arriving on 25 October 1810. Mary Putland, recently married to Lieutenant-Colonel Maurice O'Connell remained in Sydney. Macquarie investigated the mutiny and reported finding no evidence that the insurrection resulted from any direct fault on Bligh's part. Nor did he attribute the blame to any incident in the prolonged power struggle between the naval 'Captain-General and Governor-in-Chief' and the military force under his orders. In May 1810, Macquarie wrote to the Secretary of State in London that it was:

> ...extremely difficult to form a just Judgement on this delicate and mysterious subject... in justice to Governor Bligh...I have not been able to discover any Act of his which could in any degree form an excuse for, or in any way warrant, the violence and Mutinous Proceeding pursued against him. [130]

Given that he did not respect Blight and regarded him as a 'most unsatisfactory Man to transact business with', Macquarie's statement appears unbiased. [131] However, he refrained from negative comment possibly deliberately as he had served with George Johnston in North America in 1777, on who, or what set of circumstances was responsible for the mutiny.

The ambiguity in this investigation was perpetuated in the subsequent court martial in England. On 3 April 1811, the newly appointed Prince Regent ordered the court martial of Johnston and on 7 May 1811, fifteen high-ranking officers and Judge Advocate General convened a court martial. The trial lasted thirteen days, with twenty-

---

[128] Proclamation, 4 January 1810, *HRNSW*, Vol. 7, pp. 255-257, *HRA*, Series I, Vol. 7, pp. 227-231.
[129] Bligh to Castlereagh, 9 March 1810, *HRNSW*, Vol. 7, pp. 309-312.
[130] Macquarie to Castlereagh, 10 May 1810, *HRNSW*, Vol. 7, p. 378.
[131] *HRA*, Series I, Vol. 7, p. 331.

two witnesses plus Bligh for Crown and eighteen witnesses for Johnston. Having informally heard arguments from both sides, the government authorities in England were not impressed by either Macarthur's or Johnston's accusations against Bligh or by Bligh's ill-tempered letters accusing key figures in the colony of unacceptable conduct. Against the patent fact of mutiny was set nothing more substantial than the governor's temper and unproven and irrelevant allegations of cowardice at the time of the arrest. [132] On 6 June, Johnston was found guilty and cashiered from the military 'for suffering to be led by Macarthur', the lowest penalty possible. [133] His barrister, John Adolphus who held the view that Johnston was a misled man, wrote after the trial:

> I always considered and indeed understood that the parties who led you into your present most unpleasant and unfortunate situation, would, at least, have taken off your shoulders the expense of the present prosecution, but as you refer in your letter to the smallness of your means, I beg you will consider me as entirely satisfied. [134]

A similar note was struck by Johnston himself when he wrote in June 1820:

> Every person that promised [at the time of the deposition of Bligh to support me with their lives and fortunes] has risen upon my ruin. I alone am the sufferer, having lost my commission, and upwards of 6000 pounds for conceding to their requests. [135]

He was then able to return as a free citizen to Annandale his estate in Sydney.

---

[132] Ibid, Yarwood, A. T., 'Johnston, George (1764-1823)', p. 21.
[133] Ibid, Ritchie, John, *A Charge of Mutiny: The Court Martial of Lieutenant Colonel George Johnston for Deposing Governor William Bligh in the Rebellion of 26 January 1808*, is the most detailed account. On 12 November 1811, Bligh published his account of the court martial: *Account of the rebellion of the New South Wales Corps: communicated to the Rt. Hon. Lord Castlereagh and Sir Joseph Banks, Bart*, (Banks Society Publications), 2003.
[134] Cit, ibid, Yarwood, A. T., 'Johnston, George (1764-1823)', *ADB*, Vol. 2, p. 21.
[135] Cit, ibid, p. 22.

Legal opinion was that none of the civilians involved could be tried for treason in England. Macquarie received instructions from Lord Castlereagh:

> ...as Gov'r Bligh has represented that Mr McArthur has been the leading Promoter and Instigator of the mutinous Measures...you will, if Examinations be sworn against him...have him arrested thereupon and brought to Trial before the Criminal Court of the Settlement.

Macarthur's obvious course was to remain in England and exert every influence to have this obstacle removed. Because of the uncertainty of his position, he toyed with the idea of taking 'a small Farm of about a Hundred a Year' to help to balance his living expenses. At the same time he tried to resolve the problem of returning to NSW at personal risk and the alternative of withdrawing his family from 'plenty and affluence' in the colony to a life of 'pinching penury' in England. He became increasingly convinced that unless their colonial property would yield the £1,600 a year necessary to support the family and educate and establish his sons, he would have to return. Initially, none of Macarthur's efforts in England clarified his position and it was not until early in 1817 that he received permission to return to NSW on condition that he should not become involved in public affairs. Exile itself was some sort of punishment.

Bligh's promotion to Rear Admiral was delayed until the end of Johnston's trial. Afterward it was backdated to 31 July 1810 and Bligh took up a position that had been kept for him. He continued his naval career in the Admiralty in unspectacular fashion and died in 1817. Macquarie had been impressed with Foveaux's administration. He put Foveaux's name forward to succeed Collins as Lieutenant-Governor of VDL because he could think of no one more fitting and considered that he could not have acted otherwise with regard to Bligh. [136] However, when Foveaux returned to England in 1810, he narrowly escaped court-martial for assenting to Bligh being deposed

---

[136] Foveaux to Earl Liverpool, 6 July 1811, *HRNSW*, Vol. 7, pp. 553-554, wishes to succeed Collins in VDL but in Liverpool's response, 11 July 1811, *HRNSW*, Vol. 7, p. 555, his application was refused. On 18 July, Foveaux then asked Liverpool that arrears in pay owing him should be paid, *HRNSW*, Vol. 7, pp. 556-557.

and imprisoned and Macquarie's recommendation was ignored. [137] Foveaux was taken back into active service and given command of a light regiment in 1811 and pursued an uneventful military career after that, rising to the rank of Lieutenant-General. [138]

Conclusion

The 'Rum' Rebellion had nothing to do with rum. Almost no one at the time of the rebellion thought it was about rum. Bligh briefly tried to give it that interpretation to smear his opponents, but there was no evidence for it and he quickly abandoned it. The label was conferred some fifty years after the event by William Howitt, [139] a writer with teetotal sympathies and popularised by H. V. Evatt as the title of the series of lectures he delivered at the University of Queensland for its 150th anniversary.[140] Officers of the NSW Corps had monopolised the rum trade in the 1790s, but this ended years before the rebellion, with the arrival on the commercial scene of successful former convicts such as Simeon Lord and free traders like Robert Campbell. The name seems to have persisted partly due to the power of alliteration and partly because it allowed left-leaning writers to blame the event on Australia's proto-

---

[137] Martin Mason to Earl Liverpool, 26 January 1811, *HRNSW*, Vol. 7, pp. 490-491, recounted charges against Foveaux.
[138] Ibid, Whitaker, Anne-Maree, *Joseph Foveaux: Power and Patronage in Early New South Wales*, pp. 162-194, considers his career after 1812.
[139] Howitt, William, *Land, labour, and gold: or, Two years in Victoria: with visits to Sydney and Van Diemen's Land*, 2 Vols. first edition, (Longman, Brown, Green, and Longmans), 1855, p. 118, second edition, (Longman, Brown, Green, Longmans, and Roberts), 1858, Vol. 2, p. 78.
[140] Ibid, Evatt, H. V., *Rum Rebellion: A Study of the Overthrow of Governor Bligh by John Macarthur and the New South Wales Corps*, remains useful because, although partisan in favour of Governor Bligh, it was written by an eminent Australian lawyer. Ellis, M. H., *John Macarthur*, (Angus & Robertson), 1955, is partisan in the opposite direction. A more balanced account is ibid, Fitzgerald, Ross, and Hearne, Mark, *Bligh, Macarthur and the Rum Rebellion,* though it does contain errors in military detail. Davis, Russell Earls, *Bligh in Australia: A New Appraisal of William Bligh and the Rum Rebellion*, (Woodslane Pty Limited), 2010, is the most recent narrative.

capitalists. Neither was it really a 'rebellion'. Contemporaries thought of it as a mutiny or military insurrection though it might more accurately be described as a *coup d'etat* in that, once the NSW Corps had seized power by arresting Bligh, it was its leaders who ruled the colony and, in the case of Paterson and Foveaux refused to reinstate Bligh, until replaced by Macquarie.

With Macquarie's inconclusive investigation in 1810 and the ambivalence of the court martial findings on the basic cause of the mutiny, there has been a diversity of theories as to why it occurred and these have polarised into two distinct and divergent perspectives. At one extreme, historians argue that the rebels had been granted large tracts of land that they successfully exploited in their own interests and that Bligh's policies threatened their wealth. John Macarthur is cast as a conniving puppet master and Bligh's personal defects are played down. This interpretation appeals to those who have faith in government enterprise and an egalitarian inclination to support, as Bligh did, the small farmers of the settlement on the Hawkesbury flood plain.

At the other extreme, the primary focus is on the part played by the officers of the NSW Corps in providing much of the entrepreneurial drive in trade and agriculture that was necessary to enable the colony to succeed. Bligh's policies threatened that success. His was a static vision of a government-dominated society serviced by yeoman farmers that starkly contrasted with the dynamic Sydney-based commerce. Adherents to this approach emphasise the defects in Bligh's character and policy and play down the greed and cunning of the rebels. Certainly those involved in the coup were quick to put their interpretation on events. A picture of Bligh being pulled from beneath the bed where he had hidden for two hours was possibly produced and put on display within hours of the event. It was part of a campaign to brand Bligh a coward and reduce support for him in the colony and in Britain. This seems to have been at least partly successful. Following the rebellion, the NSW Corps was withdrawn, Johnston was cashiered and Macarthur had to stay out of the colony for many years for fear of prosecution had he returned. Yet the outcome could have been far worse for the rebels, but for the antipathy that existed towards Bligh in England at the time of Johnston's trial in 1811. The perspective appears also to have been the judgement of the only systematic contemporary investigation of the events, the court martial that simply cashiered Johnson, a punishment universally regarded as exceptionally lenient.

Both perspectives are plausible because the available contemporary evidence consists largely of assertions by those with a vested interest in the outcome, perhaps inevitable with an event that polarised a small community.[141] Three issues are important when assessing this event. Any explanation of why the coup occurred can look like justification or condemnation. However, it is important not to project today's values backwards to judge the corruption of the officers. Early-nineteenth century British politics and public administration was, by today's standards, profoundly corrupt and the early Sydney colony was no different. Finally, this was an age in which conduct was defined by the code of honour to which all gentlemen had to subscribe. This code is expressed through the tradition of duelling that was already evident in colonial NSW and that provides part of the explanation for the military coup of 1808.

Evatt turned Bligh into a proto-democrat overturned by the corrupt capitalists of the NSW Corps, Ellis claimed the capitalist Macarthur as heroic in his establishment of viable wool and other farming in the colony while Fitzgerald and Hearns explain that both men were on the make, desperate to set themselves up during their time in Australia. The coup was the result of a range of factors including various aspects of commercial self-interest. The traffic in rum was of little if any significance, except to some of the non-commissioned officers. Much more important, amongst multiple causes, was the conflict between real estate developers and the public interest over the exploitation of prime urban land near the water. The tension over urban leases was one of a number of conflicts in which Bligh sought to reverse practices permitted by his less resolute predecessors. He made only three land grants in eighteen months and issued no leases; he only pardoned two convicts; he cracked down on profiteering and enforced import restrictions. His policies undermined the wealth

---

[141] This is particularly evident in the correspondence in *HRA*, Series I, Vol. 6, where Bligh, Johnston, Foveaux and Paterson and pro- and anti-Bligh factions placed their positions on the record.

and the prospects of that part of the local élite with access to capital. On a number of occasions he deployed his authority over the rudimentary judicial system to attack those he opposed and intervened directly in court cases to achieve his ends.

This kind of untrammelled executive power was unacceptable to 'free-born Englishmen'. Government by whim in the exercise of an absolute discretion was tyranny, typical of Continental nations and anathema to the English. Jeremy Bentham maintained that military rule breached the Enlightenment tenet of liberty since there was no separation of powers to prevent the executive becoming excessively powerful and that the colonies reflected the spirit of French absolutism rather than British constitutionalism. [142] Broad discretionary powers may have been necessary for NSW governors to deal with convicts, but when applied to free settlers and emancipated convicts, they challenged the dominant Lockean ideology of eighteenth century Britain and the principles of the rule of law that provided the civic discourse of early Sydney. [143] Bligh's conduct may have been acceptable on a ship where a culture of authority created an expectation of unquestioning and immediate execution of orders. However, such conduct was unacceptable when applied to free subjects, who made up the majority of the 7,000 persons in the colony. Indeed there were serious doubts,

---

[142] Benton, Laura, *A Search for Sovereignty: Law and Geography in European Empires, 1400-1900*, (Cambridge University Press), 2010, pp. 191-197, examines the development of Bentham's view of the illegality of governance in NSW.

[143] See Neal, David, *The Rule of Law in a Penal Colony: Law and Power in Early New South Wales*, (Cambridge University Press), 1991, pp. 92-94, 97-98; Braithwaite John, 'Crime in a Convict Republic', *Modern Law Review*, Vol. 64, (2001), p. 11; Gascoigne, John, *The Enlightenment and the Origins of European Australia*, (Cambridge University Press), 2002, pp. 39-44; Krygier, Martin, 'Subjects, Objects and the Colonial Rule of Law', in Krygier, Martin, *Civil Passions: Selected Writings*, (Black Inc), 2005, pp. 56-91; Thompson, E. P., *Whigs and Hunters: The Origin of the Black Act*, (Pantheon), 1975, pp. 265-266; Hay, Douglas, 'Property, Authority and the Criminal Law', in ibid, Hay, Douglas et al, (eds.), *Albion's Fatal Tree: Crime and Society in Eighteenth Century England*, pp. 17-63; Cole, D. H., "An Unqualified Human Good': E. P. Thompson and the Rule of Law', *Law and Society Review*, Vol. 28, (2001), p. 117.

privately expressed by Bentham but known to some settlers, about whether, in the absence of express parliamentary authority, the Governor could lawfully exercise such authority over free men and women at all. [144]

The sense of personal security of citizens, indeed the existence of social order, is determined in large measure by the extent to which people can arrange their personal affairs and their relationships with associates, friends, family and neighbours on the assumption that basic standards of propriety are met and reasonable expectations are satisfied. All forms of social relationships, including economic interaction, are impeded by the degree to which personal and property rights are subject to unpredictable and arbitrary incursion, so that people live in fear or act on the basis of suspicion, rather than on the basis that others will act in a predictable way. The rule of law provided the central legitimising discourse of eighteenth century England. It was firmly established in Australia by the experience of the coup itself and, perhaps more significantly, by the experience of government under a military regime. Bligh had united a number of disparate interests. His removal took away that unity.

The absence of a clearly legitimate authority enabled those with a grievance to seek vengeance and anyone with access to power to abuse it. After the coup, the sense of personal security was lost to a substantial degree and the rule of law compromised and, on occasions, set aside. Later, the courts appeared to operate more normally and fairly. However, throughout the two years between the deposition of Bligh and the arrival of Macquarie, the colony was controlled by an illegal government. Every appointment, including to judicial office and every governmental decision was invalid. Personal and property rights were institutionally insecure and the residents of NSW welcomed the restoration of legitimate authority under Lachlan Macquarie. In accordance with his instructions, he invalidated the appointments and the decisions of the rebel administration, including appointments to and decisions by the courts. Completed court orders were not reopened on the basis of necessity,

---

[144] Atkinson, Alan, 'Jeremy Bentham and the Rum Rebellion', *Journal of the Royal Australian Historical Society*, Vol. 64, (1), (1978), pp. 1-13, at p. 1.

perhaps most poignantly applied in the case of the invalid death sentences that had been carried into effect. Nevertheless, some redress was available for the past illegal exercise of governmental power. One of those banished to the coal mines sued successfully for false imprisonment. [145] The rule of law was emphatically restored.

---

[145] Ibid, Kercher, B., *Debt, Seduction and Other Disasters: The Birth of Civil Law in Convict New South Wales*, p. 40.

7 Federal or not?

Although free settlers started to arrive in 1793, for its first thirty-five years, NSW was a penal colony and successive governors were absolute rulers. [1] The British Parliament could control their authority, but was eight months away by sea. A sense of belonging to a new nation was encouraged in 1817 when Governor Macquarie recommended adopting the name 'Australia' for the entire continent instead of New Holland. Continued colonial expansion resulted in the separation of VDL from NSW followed, four years later in 1829 with the addition of WA. There was a second subdivision of NSW to create South Australia in 1836, and, finally, the genesis of the Port Phillip District from 1835 into Victoria in 1851.

Britain transposed its unitary constitutional structure of government to NSW but was then forced by conditions to decentralise power to newly established colonies. This departure from British unitary ideas led naturally, but only later, to federal ideas of an Australian nation. Britain was not 'forced' to accept territorial fragmentation but adopted federalism as a deliberate strategy and that, in the course of the first four divisions British colonial policy swung back towards a more unitary territorial plan. This helps to explain why the distinctly federal ideas of the 1820s fell apart over the future of Port Phillip District which, unlike its predecessors was not initially established as a new colony. [2]

VDL was settled in 1803 as a military outpost of the Sydney prison colony largely to limit French interest in NSW's southern approaches. [3] Legal separation did not occur until December 1825. The island had achieved relative prosperity in its two decades as part of NSW growing to

---

[1] Melbourne, pp. 8-46, remains useful on governance under early governors.
[2] What follows draws on ideas put forward in Brown, A. J., *The Frozen Continent: The fall and rise of territory in Australian constitutional thought 1815-2003*, Ph.D. thesis, (Griffith University), 2003, especially chapters 1-3.
[3] Foster, Colin, *France and Botany Bay: The Lure of a Penal Colony*, (Melbourne University Press), 1996, considers French interest in Australian settlement and its influence on the development of their own penal policy.

over 12,000 Europeans and Sydney's jurisdiction did not prove incompatible with good government. Separation was the result of a shift in British colonial policy and occurred in the same legislation that established civil government in NSW in 1823. [4] The NSW Act dealt mainly with structure of the legal system though it established a nominated Legislative Council. This had been recommended in the 1819-1823 Bigge's colonial enquiry but was also part of the broader debate on how to manage the British Empire after the French Wars. [5] Bigge argued that Australia should cease to be 'the mere resort of felons' and move to civil government generating raw materials, markets and investment and paying its own way. Transportation would continue but to encourage free settlement, convicts would be removed into pastoral service or new remote penitentiaries.

There were four reasons for the shift in colonial policy.[6] The new focus on free settlement meant that people and investment needed to be attracted to areas other than Sydney and the Van Diemen's Land Company promoted the economic benefits of the island. Civil government needed public institutions available closer to their population. For VDL the priority was for independent local judges to resolve disputes rather than legislative representation. [7] Separation also reflected local political needs and echoed demands from 'landowners, merchants and other inhabitants' who petitioned George IV to use his powers to 'elevate VDL into a separate and independent Colony' in April 1824 after the 1823 Act was passed. Finally, territorial separation was part of a broader constitutional shift by the British Government. Since 1783, colonial policy had been based on retaining the loyalty of existing colonies, especially Canada and limiting all new settlement to strategic military posts governed largely through royal prerogative powers as in the case of Australia. The constitutional options available with the ending of military rule in NSW and VDL reflected the developing relationship between Britain and the newly

---

[4] Melbourne, pp. 98-103, considers the Act and its ramifications.
[5] Bennett, J. M., 'John Thomas Bigge (1780-1843)', *ADB*, Vol. 1, 1966, pp. 99-100, is a short biography. Melbourne, pp. 74-87, examines his reports.
[6] Ibid, Brown, A. J., *The Frozen Continent*, pp. 36-42.
[7] Melbourne, pp. 104-162, considers constitutional developments from 1823 to the 1828 Act.

independent United States. American federal expansion after 1783 was an important consideration in Britain but also in Australian settlements already linked directly to America's orbit as part of the emerging 'Pacific economy'. Hobart, for example, was an important American fishing and trading outpost. The American experience had a direct influence on the British colonial policy and the Australian constitutional plan certainly had strong federal elements.

The architect of the 1823 Act was James Stephen who played a central role in developing colonial policy until he retired in 1847. [8] For Stephen, colonial policy included building a new British South Pacific nation. This involved resuming the pattern of multiple colonies from which the American federal nation had developed and VDL was simply the first of the new 'branches' necessary to form a nation. This federal position challenges two basic features of Australian history. It is generally assumed that British constitutionalism in Australia began from the position of the unitary nation and that it maintained this position until forced to do otherwise. There is a common belief that new Australian colonies were created as autonomous units with their constitutional status defined solely by imperial membership and that no formal inter-colonial links predated the first subdivisions of NSW.

'Federal' ideas are usually dated to the 1840s when officials in Sydney proposed the appointment of an Australian Governor-General to regulate trade followed by British ideas for an inter-colonial general Assembly in 1846-1850. Yet, the legal basis of separation in 1823 was to some degree federal in that Sir George Arthur, the Lieutenant-Governor of VDL was constitutionally junior to NSW's new Governor Ralph Darling who saw himself as 'Captain-General' of both colonies. The British approach to the separation of VDL recognised federal structures as a

---

[8] Sainty, J. C., *Office-Holders in Modern Britain, Vol. VI, Colonial Office Officials 1794-1870*, (Institute of Historical Research), 1976, provides details on Stephen's role as permanent under-secretary between 4 February 1836 and 3 May 1848. Knaplund, Paul, *James Stephen & The British Colonial System 1813-1847*, (University of Wisconsin Press), 1953, is an excellent biography but see also Ward, C. J. M., 'The Retirement of a Titan: James Stephen 1847-50', *Journal of Modern History*, Vol. 31, (1959), pp. 189-205, and Foden, Norman Arthur, *James Stephen, architect of empire*, (New Zealand Historical Bulletins), 1, Auckland, 1938.

strategy for colonisation. Central to this were ideas canvassed before the American Revolution that a federal union could facilitate colonial expansion. Benjamin Franklin recognised in his 1754 'Albany Plan' that 'a single old colony does not seem strong enough to extend itself otherwise than inch by inch' but that an inter-colonial union could resolve this by working as a 'commonwealth for increase'. [9] Whether the Colonial Office in the late 1820s and 1830s had a clear idea of how to achieve its new 'commonwealth for increase' is far more debatable. VDL had two clear advantages over most of the territories to which Britain's new colonial policy applied: a viable colonial population and a clear natural boundary. These did not exist in the next two colonial divisions, WA in 1829 and South Australia five years later resulting in a gradual shift away from the federal towards a unitary constitutional solution. [10]

The creation of WA in 1829 resulted from the need to provide some governance for rapidly acquired land.[11] In 1824, Britain extended its Australian military outposts to Melville Island and the Coburg Peninsula on the extreme north coast to deny trading posts to Holland, France and the United States and declared a 700 kilometre extension of NSW. In 1826, a further convict camp was established at King George's Sound (Albany) but it was not until 1829 that the final third of the continent was declared legally British and led to the setting-up of a civilian settlement at Swan River by Captain James Stirling [12] WA was enormous: at 25

---

[9] Labaree, Leonard, (ed.), *Papers of Benjamin Franklin*, Vol. 5, (Yale University Press), 1962, pp. 387-392; Newbold, Robert C., *The Albany Congress and the Plan of Union of 1754*, (Vantage Press), 1955, Shannon, Timothy J., *Indians and Colonists at the Crossroads of Empire: The Albany Congress of 1754*, (Cornell University Press), 2000.

[10] Melbourne, pp. 163-221, details constitutional change from 1828 to 1836.

[11] Stannage, C. T., (ed.), *A New History of Western Australia*, (University of Western Australia Press), 1981, especially Statham, Pamela, 'Swan River Colony 1829-1850', pp. 181-210, and Clark, pp. 79-89.

[12] On Stirling see, Crowley, F. K., 'Sir James Stirling (1791-1865)', *ADB*, Vol. 2, pp. 484-488, and Statham, Drew P., *James Stirling: Admiral and Founding Governor of Western Australia*, (University of Western Australia Press), 2003.

million hectares more than fifty times VDL. The creation of the new territory was not determined by constitutional principles but was the result of two things. It was acquired by the Admiralty rather than the Colonial Office, and as a result, the founding legislation of 1829 and 1831 was unclear whether WA was a 'colony' of similar status to NSW and VDL and the extent to which all the territory was within the jurisdiction of the Swan River settlement. Also, the Colonial Office had no say in what was a political decision to approve Stirling's proposal for Swan River. There was an additional argument for Swan River to be separate because, as a convict-free environment, it was significantly different from NSW. Unlike VDL, WA was acquired because of Britain's strategic need to maintain legal authority over the western third of the continent and was not conceived as a branch of the new British 'commonwealth for increase'.

Unlike VDL and Swan River, South Australia was a novel development: a colony looking for somewhere to colonise. [13] Edward Wakefield's National Colonisation Society had a more detailed vision than Swan River. [14] Nevertheless, requests for a chartered company were refused though a compromise was found in a Colonisation Commission, governmental in character but largely under the Society's control. This raised its own political problems but was far more effective in delivering colonisation than the Swan River proposal. In addition, its constitutional position was far clearer since colonists were united by their aspiration to create a 'paradise of dissent'. Wakefield intended that South Australia would be different with a society 'most favourable as to morality' as opposed to the 'pre-eminently vicious' nature of the convict colonies.

---

[13] Jaensch, Dean, (ed.), *The Flinders History of South Australia: Political History*, (Wakefield Press), 1986, pp. 1-94, looks at developments from 1834 to 1857. Price, A. Grenfell, *The Foundation and Settlement of South Australia 1829-1845*, (F. W. Preece), 1924, and Pike, D. H., *Paradise of Dissent: South Australia 1829-57*, (Melbourne University Press), 1957, remain useful.

[14] On Wakefield, see Bloomfield, P., *Edward Gibbon Wakefield: builder of the British Commonwealth*, (Longman), 1961, and the broader study by Temple, Philip, *A Sort of Conscience: The Wakefields*, (Auckland University Press), 2002. Prichard, M. F. Lloyd, (ed.), *The Collected Works of Edward Gibbon Wakefield*, (Collins), 1968, contains his important writings.

Parliament approved the plan in 1834 with, for the first time, the promise of an Australian representative legislature when its population reached 50,000. The 1834 Act authorised the creation of 'a British province or provinces', a term used in Canada but now for the first time in Australia with essentially federal connotations. As with VDL, this status involved less than total separation since, though South Australia was administratively independent, the province would be described for its first decade as still officially part of NSW. [15]

The establishment of South Australia suggested a return to a more coherent but ill-defined territorial approach but ironically the well-planned South Australia was based on no territorial logic at all. There was no real inspection of the site and the experiences of Colonel William Light, its first Surveyor-General confirmed in 1836 just how uninformed its location had been. [16] In late 1830, accounts reached London of Charles Sturt's 1828-1829 descent of the Murray River and when Sturt backed the suitability of areas he had never visited, the result was a speculative boom. [17] Subscribers rushed to join the scheme and pastoralists from VDL were reportedly ready to start seizing the land. The National Colonisation Society's case was based on combination of anecdotes and the suppression of other information. From June 1831, the Colonial Office repeatedly asked for information that it never obtained and for this and other reasons opposed the final 1834 legislation. South Australia owed its existence to political pressure brought by Wakefield and his supporters. The Colonial Office was not simply unsure about the plan but actively opposed it.

The change in colonial policy was clearly demonstrated by Port Phillip that was resettled in 1834-1835, just ahead of South Australia, but did not achieve territorial independence for sixteen years. Swan River and South

---

[15] On Wakefield's theory of systematic colonisation see, Mills, R. C., *The Colonization of Australia (1829-42), The Wakefield Experiment in Empire Building*, (Sidgwick & Jackson Ltd), 1915, pp. 90-139
[16] Dutton, G. P. H., *Founder of a City: the Life of Colonel William Light*, (Chapman & Hall), 1961, is a concise biographical sketch.
[17] Parker, Derek, *Outback: The Discovery of Australia's Interior*, (Sutton Publishing), 2007, pp. 8-35, considers the notion of the Great Inland Sea and Sturt's expedition.

Australia attracted investment and settlers direct from Britain but Port Phillip District was the result of a moving frontier within Australia itself. Pastoralists in VDL had applied as early as 1827 for permission to establish sheep runs on the northern coast of the Bass Strait. This provides a clear indication of the rapid economic and population growth of the island. In 1834, the Henty family established a pastoral run for their cattle and sheep at Portland and the following year John Batman's Port Phillip Association triggered a land rush by using the American frontier tactic of 'buying' 600,000 acres from their Aboriginal owners. [18] In many respects, this simply looked like 'squatting' and completely disregarded the official land districts established by NSW in 1829. The 'frontier' has long been viewed as an insignificant force in Australian history yet the dramatic expansion of the American frontier influenced the actions of those crossing the Bass Strait in 1835. They were making political as well as economic statement in two respects. By making retrospective authorisation of their land grants their main concern, they were directly copying American methods. They also immediately called for a formal new political community and by March 1836 the Port Phillip Association's supporters in London asked the Colonial Office to proclaim a new colony. [19]

Historians have presumed that Port Phillip achieved territorial separation in 1851 and only then developed a strong interest in federalism. [20] In reality, political ideas were secondary to territorial autonomy until it was finally achieved. Demands for separation at Port Phillip clearly showed that some communities argued that they should receive their own territory but within a federalist framework

---

[18] Bassett, Marnie, *The Hentys: An Australian Colonial Tapestry*, (Oxford University Press), 1954, and Peel, Lynette, (ed.), *The Henty Journals: A Record of Farming, Whaling and Shipping in Portland Bay, 1834-1839*, (Melbourne University Press), 1996, examine this entrepreneurial family.
[19] Shaw A. G. L., *A History of the Port Phillip District: Victoria Before Separation*, (Miegunyah Press), 1996, is an excellent study of the period to 1851. *The Foundation Series of Historical Records of Victoria*, Vols. 1-7, (Melbourne University Press), 1981-1998, Vol. 8, *Cumulative Index*, (Melbourne University Press), 2002, reproduce official documents that survive from 1835 to 1840.
[20] Brown, Richard, *Settler Australia, 1780-1880, Volume 2*, (CreateSpace), 2012, pp. 6-17, explores developments to 1851.

in which separation, economic and demographic development and nationalism worked together. [21] This was evident in the importance of American influences. The early Melbourne Chamber of Commerce was reportedly dominated by Americans and when Tocqueville's *Democracy in America* appeared in 1835, it was immediately translated and widely disseminated throughout the Empire. [22] Though he questioned the morality of the economic and political effects of frontier, Tocqueville was struck by the boundless elasticity of federalism with America's growing number of states working smoothly together. The Port Phillip separation campaign gained important support from Sydney's John Dunmore Lang who visited Port Phillip for the first time in November 1841 and was soon speaking to separatist audiences about his experiences from a recent ten-week trip to the eastern United States. [23] He assured his audiences that their campaign paralleled the driving force of American frontier development and its division into small democratic states. [24]

Nonetheless, despite extending colonial status to struggling West and South Australia, Port Phillip's treatment represented a shift in British colonial thinking. On the one hand, the British authorities treated the settlement as a separate unit by appointing its own police magistrates and a judge, directing that it followed South Australian land policy and making initial efforts to keep it convict-free. Nevertheless, in 1839 it was decided not to separate Port Phillip as a 'colony', 'settlement' or 'province' but to establish a new territorial unit: a 'district' headed by a superintendent, Charles La Trobe leaving Port Phillip still legally part of NSW. [25] This seemed to be 'a clear case of the Governor you have when not having a Governor, and Port

---

[21] Clark, *Select Documents* 1, pp. 338-361, 362-364, printed petitions for separation in 1844 and 1849; pp. 361-362, prints the case against separation from the *Sydney Herald*, 6 February 1841.
[22] Brown, Richard, *Settler Australia, 1780-1880*, Volume 2, (CreateSpace), 2012, pp. 374-378.
[23] Melbourne, pp. 331-346, explores the separation movement.
[24] Baker, D. W. A., 'John Dunmore Lang (1799-1878)', *ADB*, Vol. 2, pp. 76-83.
[25] Drury, Dianne Reilly, *La Trobe: The Making of a Governor*, (Melbourne University Press), 2006, pp. 132-236, examines his role in Port Phillip.

Phillip the colony you have when not having a colony'. [26] This decision confirmed what the territorial decisions on West and South Australia had only intimated: British colonial policy was confused.

Traditionally, Port Phillip's passage to separation between 1835 and 1851 was delayed not by British colonial policy but the political problems in NSW. From the early 1840s, Port Phillip's destiny became directly linked to conflict with Sydney's pastoral and commercial interests through its association with colonial land, labour and emigration policy. The land problem was not new and the British Government had been attempting to systematise land policy in the Sydney districts since 1829 but with only limited success. [27] In early 1840, the conflict intensified with the Colonial Office plans for a representative legislature in NSW but also ending the transportation of convict labour. Conflict between Sydney's interests and the Colonial Office included a battle over the size of the Port Phillip District. In December 1840, the NSW Governor Sir George Gipps issued land instructions extending the Port Phillip land district from the 36th Parallel to the more natural boundary along the Murrumbridgee and Murray rivers. [28] Though defended in Melbourne, the new boundary was vigorously attacked in Sydney and London as part of a Colonial Office plan to help 'land-jobbing South Australians' injure the original colony. The debate faded after the new instructions were cancelled in 1841. Yet, when the British Government re-examined the territorial question in 1842, the result was the same as in 1839. The NSW Constitution Act 1842 gave the Port Phillip District six seats in the new two-thirds elected representative legislation, but refused to give either separation or land. [29] The reason for this lay less with Sydney's political campaign but in the Colonial Office where plans for a new approach not only in Australia but in British North America was being developed.

---

[26] Ibid, Brown, A. J., *The Frozen Continent*, p. 51.
[27] Melbourne, pp. 245-257.
[28] McCulloch, S. C., 'Sir George Gipps (1791-1847), *ADB*, Vol. 1, pp. 446-453; Barker, Sydney, 'The Governorship of Sir George Gipps', *Journal of the Royal Australian Historical Society*, Vol. 16, (1930), pp. 169-263, remains the only detailed study of his period in office.
[29] Melbourne, pp. 258-276, examines events leading to the 1842 Act.

The 1791 Constitutional Act determined that the best way of retaining Canada was to separate it into two provinces. French-speaking Lower Canada posed a political problem almost from the outset while difficulties in Upper Canada grew in significance after 1815. The result, in the 1820s, was unsuccessful British proposals for union, a reverse trend to that operating in Australia. Rebellion in 1837-1838 galvanised Britain into action and the 1840 Union Act saw the reunification of the Canadas. The argument, expressed forcefully in Durham's *Report*, was that a unitary legislature allowed all to be represented fairly but ensured unity by allowing the majority to prevail on provincial issues. [30] Yet, in Australia, the principles of colonial responsible government laid out in the *Report* were given greater prominence than its territorial solution, for in contrast to Canada, the source of political difficulties was not the minority Australian provinces but the majority Sydney 'squattocracy'. Official resistance to separation cannot be seen as a victory for the squatters nor was it intended to disadvantage the Port Phillip community but reflected growing British policy concerns about the political problems of multiple colonies. The federal territorial path remained an option, but it was no longer the preferred alternative.

The development of a new constitutional path for Australia occurred parallel to efforts to find solutions for the Canada problem that the Colonial Office and especially James Stephen had been working on since 1836. In the next ten years, Stephen attempted on three occasions to introduce his decentralised-unitary model to Australia. His first attempt began in 1838 with parallel efforts in all existing mainland colonies: in NSW, a Constitution Bill was successfully negotiated with its leading spokesmen though it languished pending a decision on convict transportation; and in the setting-up of Australia's first formal representative institutions as town trusts and councils in WA in 1838 and Adelaide the following year. The creation of local institutions resolved two major problems. In NSW, new constitutional arrangements were needed but neither the majority emancipated convicts nor the self-interested

---

[30] Brown, Richard, *Rebellion in Canada, 1837-1885, Volume 1: Autocracy, Rebellion and Liberty*, (CreateSpace), 2012, pp. 529-537, on Durham's *Report*.

squatter élite were able to take over colonial legislation while transportation remained. In addition, there were growing demands for services and infrastructure to support the growing population that could not realistically be funded from London. In North America, settlers rapidly developed decentralised village and town organisations but in NSW all public services remained centralised and dependent on the Crown. Stephen's model solved these problems by establishing a two-tiered system in which a colonial legislature would be created by secondary election from elected local institutions with a wide democratic franchise. In spite of this, the strategy had only limited success. WA barely established the first tier while in South Australia the first tier was successfully created but financial difficulties suspended debate on the second. In NSW, with the Constitution Bill in limbo, Gipps introduced a Local Government bill in May 1840 into the still-appointed legislature but this was withdrawn amid conflict over the franchise. As a result, Gipps began slowly to issue individual council charters.

Stephen's second attempt was in the 1842 NSW Constitution Act that conspicuously failed to separate Port Phillip. [31] It proposed a system of district councils as the new base unit of territorial organisation. [32] The system worked in Port Phillip with councils formed at Melbourne in 1842 and Geelong in 1849 but they proved to be the only ones to survive and in the Sydney district and elsewhere, the attempt failed. By late 1845, all but one council was bankrupt since the Legislative Council removed their ability to collect local taxes on which they depended. The scheme had fallen victim to the new alliance between pastoralists and emancipated convicts that campaigned against any local rates as 'taxation without representation', really meaning 'taxation without responsible government'. Stephen concluded in January 1846 that the mistake in 1842 was to break the legislature's electoral dependence on the municipal institutions designed to keep it in check. The

---

[31] Clark, *Select Documents* 1, pp. 335-340 prints the legislation.
[32] On local government see Melbourne, pp. 317-324, and the more extensive studies by Larcombe, F. A., *The origin of local government in New South Wales, 1831-58*, (Sydney University Press), 1973, pp. 26-52, and Golder, Hilary, *Politics, Patronage and Public Works: The Administration of New South Wales Vol. 1 1842-1900*, (UNSW Press), 2005, especially pp. 3-86.

result was his third and final attempt to apply the unitary model by re-establishing the secondary election structure in the 'Australian Charter' sent by the Earl Grey, the Colonial Secretary, in July 1847. [33] The Charter updated Stephen's initial scheme with Grey's plan for creating a free-trade national union, reclassifying the existing four colonies as 'provinces', whose secondarily-elected legislatures would then choose delegates for a national assembly. This was abandoned in early 1848 following Sydney's predictable attacks on the local institutions as 'cumbrous and expensive'. [34]

Stephen's constitutional model was a coherent strategy for rebuilding Australian colonial structures on a constitutional path less aligned to federalism and more within the British unitary tradition. It was a progressive solution intended to minimise territorial separation by actively providing for political and economic decentralisation within a unitary structure. Yet, it failed not because unitary principles were inadequate but because Australia's political leaders killed it off. The district councils failed because they challenged the power of the existing legislators by fragmenting their demands for responsible government and demonstrated that different political communities had different views on how territory should be organised. Those who sought political autonomy used the new unitary institutions where they could but did not see them replacing their major goal of territorial separation. The Sydney squatter élite fought to maintain its position and opposed both federal and unitary decentralisation.

By the mid-1840s, the question of what type of nation Australia was to be and how it was to be organised remained unresolved. The practical outcome was that the twenty-five year search for a coherent plan for the allocation of Australian territory had come to a grinding halt. There was now a three-sided debate between separatists, the Sydney legislative élite and the Colonial Office in London over the nature of Australia's future constitutional

---

[33] Ward, John M., *Earl Grey and the Australian Colonies 1846-1857*, (Melbourne University Press), 1958, pp. 37-44. See, Clark, *Select Documents* 1, pp. 367-370, and Grey to FitzRoy, 31 July 1847, *HRA*, Series I, Vol. 25, pp. 698-703, on Grey's thinking in 1847.

[34] Clark, *Select Documents* 1, p. 371.

development. [35] Gipps argued that if the Sydney élite took notice of Port Phillip's call for separation and reversed its opposition to local government, further separation of NSW's territory might be avoided. If not, Port Phillip would be the first of several small colonies into which NSW would be divided. [36] However, in 1850, the decentralised unitary model was finally abandoned. The Privy Council Committee on Trade and Plantations reported that further subdivision of NSW, WA and South Australia would occur though in reality the return to subdivision proved more problematic. Grey's decision to proceed with Victoria's separation in July 1847 took four years to implement as the British Government sought an agreed constitutional formula for the colonies. This was evident not only over Port Phillip but in the debates over separation of NSW's northern districts in 1846-1848 and 1849-1852.

The return to colonial subdivision came in February 1846 when the British Government established Australia's fifth colony, the vast 'North Australia'. The colony had an official settlement numbering over two hundred convicts, soldiers and families at Port Curtis but lasted only twenty-six months. It was the last colony proposed entirely from London, the creation of William Gladstone, briefly Colonial Secretary from December 1845 to July 1846 and was designed as a new convict colony to relieve prison overcrowding caused by the ending of transportation to NSW in 1840. [37] North Australia and Port Curtis were abandoned after the Colonial Office passed back into Whig control in July 1846. [38]

Gladstone's successor Grey also needed to find a short-term solution to the convict problem and deliberately provoked a new wave of separation agitation. In mid-1849, his plan to resume transportation to Sydney and Melbourne

---

[35] Irving, Terry, *The Southern Tree of Liberty: The Democratic Movement in New South Wales before 1856*, (The Federation Press), 2006, provides a radical focus on constitutional developments in the 1840s.

[36] On this issue and the response of the Colonial Office see ibid, Ward, John M., *Earl Grey and the Australian Colonies 1846-1857*, pp. 122-133.

[37] Shaw, Alan, *Gladstone at the Colonial Office 1846*, (Australian Studies Centre), 1986.

[38] On the renewal of transportation, see Melbourne, pp. 357-365.

was met with widespread colonial opposition. [39] However, he also received representations for separation from New England north though these initially did not directly request convict labour, Grey believed that labour shortages in the north would enable transportation to occur to the new colony. His response in late 1849 was to include a clause in the then draft Constitution Bill inviting all 'inhabitant householders of any such of the territories...northward of the thirtieth degree of South latitude' to petition for 'a separate colony or colonies'. This had the desired effect with leading towns and pastoral communities petitioning for separation, led by the convict-seeking squatters of New England and Darling Downs and backed by coastal communities seeking separation without convicts. Despite having incited the debate, two years later Grey decided that separation was not justifiable.

Grey's *volte face* is conventionally put down to advice from the Colonial Office that it would be better to wait. Yet, it is clear that the whole separation tactic was a political manoeuvre to force local legislators to agree to his demands for the restarting of transportation to NSW as a whole. Had Grey wanted to establish a northern colony, he had no need to abandon North Australia, but his transportation policy was different and aimed at releasing minor offenders and assisted immigrants into areas of existing large population. If the NSW legislators had agreed to his demands, separation would have been unnecessary but when they did not there was little point in separation since it did not solve the convict problem. Either way, ultimately the debate had been a farce.

Grey's bluff, nevertheless, had three important effects on the Australian debate. Although no such 'right' existed, Grey's 'clause' raised expectations that the 'right' to territorial self-determination had been established and colonists came to believe that all they had to do was ask for separation and the Crown was obliged to act. Grey also encouraged Australians to believe that as well as being receptive to 'bottom-up' demands, the British Government had a comprehensive 'top-down' plan for continued sub-division. The separation of Victoria under the 1850 Act and the debate on the northern colonies suggested a coordinated

---

[39] On attitudes to transportation, see ibid, Ward, John M., *Earl Grey and the Australian Colonies 1846-1857*, pp. 197-226.

process where no such policy existed. Finally, British interest in sub-division was a short-term political strategy, something that the separatist communities only grasped to a limited extent. Grey's treatment of the northern districts between 1849 and 1852 indicated that the Colonial Office sought to limit its involvement to vital colonial political problems. The 1850 Constitution Act paved the way, and by late 1852 the influx of gold miners allowed Grey's Conservative successor Sir John Pakington to promise responsible government within months of taking office. [40] What is clear is that by the early 1850s there was a growing gap between the expectations of the colonists and the realities of colonial policies.

When separation demands failed, blame was placed not with the Colonial Office but with the more immediate opposition of Sydney. This was now a well-established view, a natural progression from Sydney's reputation for corruption and venality. Sydney was blamed for the tardiness of Port Phillip's metamorphosis into the state of Victoria and later in the northern districts in 1852-1853 and again in 1856 when the final separation boundary was moved to the McPherson Ranges. Much anti-Sydney feeling was exaggerated, though the NSW legislature was vocal in its opposition to separation in its campaign for responsible government. By the early 1850s, the debate between separatists, the NSW legislature and the Colonial Office raised two critical questions. Both British and NSW legislatures were strong on political rhetoric but weak on planning further constitutional development. If decentralist federalism could only be restored with British intervention to overrule the Sydney opposition, how would the process of sub-division be maintained once the British Government granted responsible government?

Responsible government provided new opportunities for the development of Australian political ideas by devolving political authority on most 'internal' issues to existing colonial governments. The imperial Parliament retained responsibility only for those areas of policy that impinged on imperial security and was to be 'light touch' in character. In 1850, the British Parliament passed the Australian Colonies Government Act formally separating

---

[40] Clark, *Select Documents* 1, pp. 377-385 prints the 1850 Act.

Victoria from NSW in 1851. [41] It also allowed the colonies to prepare constitutions for approval by the British Parliament. The result was four Constitution Acts, intensively debated in 1853 before being submitted and approved in London for Tasmania (1854), NSW and Victoria (1855) and South Australia (1856). Any northern separation was to begin automatically with the same constitution as NSW, while thirty-five years later WA would adopt a largely identical model. [42] In arriving at their constitutions, the legislatures confronted a range of issues but in each case, the conclusion was a Sydney-led version of British national institutions, unitary in nature and more centralised than any real or preferred British constitutional forms. [43] The history of all three ex-NSW colonies was now aligned with the NSW tradition of powerful central authority. This enfeebled the prospects of any local government system comparable to America, Canada or Britain and, though it did not preclude the creation of local government, it reduced its constitutional importance.

---

[41] On the 1850 Act and its reception in Australia, see Melbourne, pp. 381-391.
[42] Melbourne, pp. 445-465, and Evans, Raymond *A History of Queensland*, (Cambridge University Press), 2007, pp. 51-77, considers the creation of Queensland in 1859.
[43] On the 1856 legislation, see Melbourne, pp. 417-441.

The Evolution of Political Boundaries in Australia to 1859

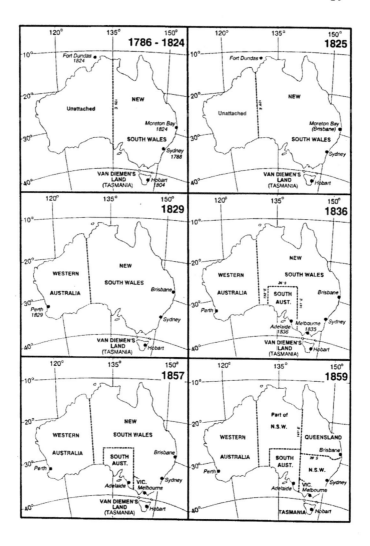

8 Settling the land

While access to native lands in North American colonies was achieved by a combination of agreement, purchase, guile and force, when the British settled at Sydney Cove in 1788 the colonial government claimed all lands for the Crown from its formal declaration of annexation on 7 February 1788.[1] The notion that Australia was *terra nullius*, unowned land was used as justification for it being settled not invaded and that the Aboriginal population had no territorial rights over it.[2] Rather than implying mere emptiness, *terra nullius* was likely to have been more broadly constructed as an absence of civilised society and English common law allowed for the legal settlement of 'uninhabited or barbarous country'. Although Australia was clearly not empty land, the presence of scattered and nomadic Aboriginal groups would have been widely perceived, through contemporary European eyes, as evidence of a barbarous country and consequently no legal impediment to settlement.

Testing terra nullius

The existence of *terra nullius* in Australia is something of a puzzle especially as imperial policy in North America had already turned away from the principle. There is no reason to assume that the British government would not have entered into treaty arrangements with the Aboriginal people as it had earlier in North America and later in NZ and

---

[1] The principle of British sovereignty over Australia was asserted on four occasions, in 1788, 1824, 1829 and 1879. See, Connor, Michael, *The Invention of Terra Nullius: Historical and Legal Fictions on the Foundation of Australia*, (Macleay Press), 2005, a contentious study.
[2] See Reynolds, Henry, *Aboriginal sovereignty: reflections on race, state, and nation*, (Allen & Unwin), 1996, pp. 1-15, 86-107, and especially Attwood, Bain, *Possession: Batman's Treaty and the Matter of History*, (Melbourne University Press), 2009, and Ford, Lisa, *Settler Sovereignty: Jurisdiction and Indigenous People in America and Australia 1788-1836*, (Harvard University Press), 2010, pp. 158-182.

elsewhere had it recognised native 'ownership' of the land. [3] The critical distinction, which originated with James Cook in 1770, was that consent to the British taking possession was unnecessary since the land seemed 'waste' and unowned. [4] In the late-eighteenth century, many believed that a society without agriculture was consequentially a society without property rights in land. The implication was that since the Aboriginal people were not farmers, they were not sovereign owners to be offered treaties. The eighteenth century jurist William Blackstone, who was regarded as authoritative on the matter in subsequent cases in several countries with legal systems based on English common law, drew a clear distinction between colonies won by conquest or treaty and those where 'lands are claimed by right of occupancy only, by finding them desert and uncultivated' (though he was unclear on whether they were uninhabited), and peopling them from the mother countries. [5] This ambiguity enabled later commentators to argue that only cultivated land was in actual possession and that in colonies of settlement English law was 'immediately there in force' on the assumption that no prior legal code and no land tenure had ever existed. Unlike most parts of the world, Britain could believe that Australia really was *terra nullius* and that there was no need to purchase it.

Terra nullius rested on a number of false empirical assertions about Aboriginal life: that the Aborigines were few in number, that they roamed throughout the land without a sense of boundaries, and that they claimed no particular territories as their own. Initially what early settlers found reinforced their view of the primitive nature of Aboriginal life but they quickly learned that the Aborigines did not lack property, and also divided land among individuals and passed property rights down from one generation to the next. This resulted in growing uncertainty as to the validity of *terra nullius* among colonial officials in NSW and in London. Both Governor King and

---

[3] See, for instance, Brown, Richard, *Resistance and Rebellion*: Brown, Richard, *Resistance and Rebellion in the British Empire, 1600-1980*, (Clio Publishing), 2013, pp. 107-124, on the Treaty of Waitangi and its immediate aftermath in NZ.
[4] See pp. 31-33.
[5] Prest, W., 'Law for Historians: William Blackstone on women, colonies and slaves', *Legal History*, Vol. 11, (2007), pp. 105-115, especially pp. 109-111.

Macquarie felt some unease about the appropriation of lands from Aborigines. By the early 1820s, there was a growing and assertive belief in Britain and Australia especially by missionaries and church organisations that *terra nullius* was an injustice towards the Aborigines and by the 1830s, criticism of *terra nullius* was widely expressed in the Colonial Office and in Parliament.

The increasingly ambivalent attitude towards the notion of *terra nullius* was reflected in a series of contradictory legal judgements in the late-1820s and 1830s.[6] The first test of *terra nullius* in Australia occurred with the decision of *R v Tommy* indicating that the native inhabitants were only subject to English law where the incident concerned both natives and settlers and not where the case concerned only natives. [7] The rationale was that Aboriginal tribal groups already operated under their own legal systems, a position supported by the decision in *R v Ballard*. Chief-Justice Forbes stated:

> I believe it has been the practice of the Courts of this country, since the Colony was settled, never to interfere with or enter into the quarrels that have taken place between or amongst the natives themselves. This I look to as matter of history, for I believe no instance is to be found on record in which the acts of conduct of the aborigines amongst themselves have been submitted to the consideration of our Courts of Justice. It has been the policy of the Judges, & I assume of the Government, in like manner with other Colonies, not to enter into or interfere with any cause of dispute or quarrel between the aboriginal natives. In all transactions between the British Settlers & the natives, the laws of the mother country have been carried into execution. [8] Aggressions by British subjects,

---

[6] Finnane, Mark, 'The Limits of Jurisdiction: Law, Governance and Indigenous Peoples in Colonized Australia', in Dorsett, Shaunnagh, and Hunter, Ian, (eds.), *Law and Politics in British Colonial Thought: Transpositions of Empire*, (Palgrave Macmillan), 2010, pp. 149-168, and Kercher, Bruce, 'The Recognition of Aboriginal Status and Laws in the Supreme Court of New South Wales under Forbes, CJ, 1824-1836', in Buck, A. R., McLaren, John, and Wright, Nancy E., (eds.), *Land and Freedom: Law, Property Rights and the British Diaspora*, (Ashgate), 2001, pp. 83-102, provide a succinct overview of the issues.

[7] *Monitor*, 26, 29 November 1827.

[8] The court had already decided that Aborigines were subject to its jurisdiction when they were in conflict with the Europeans who

upon the natives, as well as those committed by the latter upon the former, have been punished by the laws of England where the execution of those laws have been found practicable. This has been found expedient for the mutual protection of both sorts of people; but I am not aware that British laws have been applied to the aboriginal natives in transactions solely between themselves, whether of contract, tort, or crime. [9]

This position was reversed in *R v Murrell* (1836) in which Justice Burton concluded that natives had not attained sufficient numbers and civilisation as to be recognised as sovereign states governed by their own laws, and that the land was unappropriated by anyone at the time it was taken into actual possession of the King. Burton's judgement was an explicit statement of a *terra nullius* theory. [10] He also concluded that Aborigines would have been liable for murdering one another whether they were aliens or British subjects, a subtle way around the argument that they were subject only to their own customs and usages. Yet, five years later in *R v Bonjon* (1841), Justice Willis held that a single judge of the Supreme Court of NSW was not bound by the decision in *Murrell* and that it had no jurisdiction over crimes committed by Aborigines against one another. [11] They were not amenable to English law, except in cases of conflict with the British since express enactment or treaty made them subject to English law. [12] Aborigines were distinct though dependent allies, not British subjects. They had not consented to British occupation or sovereignty and were entitled to exercise their own usages and laws. [13] The strongly contrasting judgments in *Ballard* and *Bonjon* were more consistent with the

---

had come to occupy their lands. This was fully argued and decided in *R v Lowe*, 1827. See, *Australian*, 23 May 1827.
[9] *Sydney Gazette,* 23 April 1829.
[10] *Sydney Gazette*, 23 February and 12 April 1836.
[11] Davies, Susanne, 'Aborigines, Murder, and the Criminal Law in Early Port Phillip, 1841-1851', *Historical Studies*, Vol. 22, (1987), pp. 313-335.
[12] See Wilson, Alan, 'John Walpole Willis', *Dictionary of Canadian Biography*, Vol. 10, pp. 704-707, for his period in Canada that may have influenced his judgement, and Behan, H. F., *Mr. Justice J. W. Willis: with Particular Reference to his Period as First Resident Judge in Port Phillip 1841-1843*, (Glen Iris), 1979, and Barry, John V., 'Willis, John Walpole (1793-1877)', *ADB*, Vol. 2, pp. 602-604.
[13] *Port Phillip Patriot*, 20 September 1841.

writings of Vattel on the rights of nomadic peoples and, as the judgment in *Bonjon* shows, also because they were more consistent with the treatment of native peoples in other jurisdictions. [14]

In 1835, John Batman, one of the founding pioneers of Victoria, first settled at Port Phillip and made an attempt to buy the land from the Aboriginal people through a 'treaty'. [15] His treaty was signed on the banks of a creek on 16 June 1835 and was an agreement with eight Aboriginal leaders to transfer 100,000 acres of prime farming land in the Port Phillip area to Batman. However, the transaction was not as straightforward as it appeared. Batman's claim to this territory was based on the European idea of land ownership and legal contracts, a concept that was completely foreign to the native people of Victoria. For them land was not about possession, but belonging. Territories may belong to different groups, but land cannot be bought or sold. Batman also claimed that he had negotiated with Aboriginal 'chiefs' who were in charge of this land. But he was actually negotiating with tribal elders who were not in a position to sell their people's land, even if they had wanted to, and it is probable that none of the 'signatories' thought that this was what they were doing. The local Aborigines were as unable to comprehend the idea of selling their land as Batman was of appreciating the value it held for them. The exchange that took place that day, and the 'treaty' that marked it, was at best the result of a cultural misunderstanding by both sides. Inconsistencies in Batman's accounts of how the 'treaty' was signed throw his claims of legitimate purchase into doubt. The story of the treaty deeds differs from the story in Batman's journal and his report to Sir George Arthur, the VDL Lieutenant-Governor. Bain Attwood concluded:

> We will never really know how much of the [Port Phillip] Association's narrative was true because of the paucity of

---

[14] Vattel, Emeric de, *Droit des gens; ou, Principes de la loi naturelle appliqués à la conduite et aux affaires des nations et des souverains*, 2 Vols. (Abraham Droz), 1758, *The Law of Nations or the Principles of Natural Law Applied to the Conduct and to the Affairs of Nations and of Sovereigns*, (T. & J. W. Johnson), 1853, pp. 98-109.

[15] Brown, P. L., 'Batman, John (1801-1839)', *ADB*, Vol. 1, pp. 67-71. See also Bonwick, John, *John Batman, the founder of Victoria*, 2nd ed., (Fergusson and Moore), 1868, pp. 66-83.

contemporary sources. Indeed, all we have are the few accounts created by these colonisers. In respect of the famous treaty-making, we cannot even be sure it took place. Arguably, it might simply be an imaginary event that never happened. In the end, it probably doesn't matter very much whether it occurred or not. (I assume that some parts of the treaty-making did take place.) What is more important historically are the stories that have been told about it. [16]

Historians now question whether the eight Aboriginal chiefs signed their 'marks' on the contract, a theory arguably substantiated by Batman's own journal, in which he described how he had made the chiefs 'signatures' on the deeds. While radicals have largely dismissed Batman's dealings as a shameful example of colonial self-interest and perfidy, Aboriginal people, however, have cast Batman as a 'kind and just' man who established mutual understanding with their forebears and recognised their ownership of the land. In the 1930s and 1960s, the Australian Aborigines' League and the Aborigines Advancement League invoked his name in campaigning for Aboriginal rights. [17]

Both the transfer to a person rather than the Crown and its implicit recognition of native ownership and occupation of the land prompted Bourke to act. He effectively quashed the treaty with his Proclamation on 26 August 1835 and its re-publication on 3 May 1836 restating the doctrine of *terra nullius* upon which British settlement was based, reinforcing the notion that the land belonged to no one prior the British Crown taking possession of it in 1788:

> Whereas, it has been represented to me, that divers of His Majesty's Subjects have taken possession of vacant lands of the Crown, within the limits of this Colony, under the pretence of a treaty, bargain, or contract, for the purchase thereof, with the Aboriginal Natives; Now therefore, I, the Governor, in virtue and in exercise of the power and authority in me vested do hereby proclaim and notify to all His Majesty's Subjects, and others whom it may concern, that every such treaty, bargain, and contract with the Aboriginal Natives, as aforesaid, for the possession, title, or

---

[16] Doyle, Helen, *Possession: Batman's treaty and the matter of history*, (Melbourne University Press), 2009, p. 47.
[17] For the subsequent histories of the treaties, see ibid, Attwood, Bain, with Doyle, Helen, *Possession: Batman's treaty and the matter of history*.

claim to any lands lying and being within the limits of the Government of the Colony of New South Wales...and including also Norfolk Island, is void and of no effect against the rights of the Crown; and that all persons who shall be found in possession of any such Lands as aforesaid, without the license or authority of His Majesty's Government, for such purpose first had and obtained, will be considered as trespassers, and liable to be dealt with in like manner as other intruders upon the vacant lands of the Crown within the said Colony. [18]

Its publication in the colony meant that people found in possession of land without the authority of the government would be considered trespassers. [19] Although some contemporaries recognised that the Aboriginal occupants had rights in the lands, something confirmed in a House of Commons report on Aboriginal relations in 1837, the law followed and almost always applied the principles expressed in Bourke's proclamation. Glenelg supported Bourke's position completely rejecting the view that Aborigines had any rights to dispose of their land. [20] Any recognition of Batman's treaty would have had a catastrophic effect on Australian land policy virtually amounting to recognition that Australia was not the property of the Crown but of its native population. It would have been an admission that since 1788 the British had been freely disposing of land that did not belong to them. In 1847, the Supreme Court of NSW affirmed that all ungranted land in Australia belonged to the Crown: *terra nullius* had proved impossible to dislodge.

---

[18] National Archives: CO 201/247, ff411, published in the *New South Wales Government Gazette*, 2 September 1835.
[19] In practice, although Bourke's action had voided any 'treaty' that was made, it did not prevent significant movement of settlers of the Port Phillip Association from VDL and from other parts of NSW into the Port Phillip District from late 1835 onwards. In his despatch of 10 October 1835, Bourke recommended that the settlement should be recognised and, though initially the Colonial Office had doubts about doing so, Lord Glenelg supported Bourke's recommendations and on 9 September 1836 a notice recognised the existence of a settlement that had already existed for a year.
[20] *Report from the Select Committee on Aborigines (British Settlements): with the minutes of evidence*, appendix and index, 1837, pp. 10-15.

The words of the Privy Council in *Vajesingji v Secretary of State for India* in 1924 are among many other pronouncements that defined the concept of *terra nullius* unambiguously: 'territory hitherto not occupied by a recognised ruler'.[21] New Holland was considered a paradigm case of *terra nullius* because the British could identify no territorial units with a recognisable form of government, not because there had been no Aboriginal inhabitants. [22] It is the High Court that was mistaken in believing that British explorers, Whitehall officials or Australian colonists held the false belief that Australia was uninhabited or nearly so. The consistent legal doctrine from 1788 was that the original British claim of sovereignty extinguished all prior rights to property and that after 1788, 'all titles, rights, and interests whatever in land which existed' were the 'direct consequence of some grant from the Crown', and people given these grants acquired property rights through mixing their labour with the soil. Despite the growing unease about the doctrine and suggestions in the 1830s and 1840s that land policy in Australia should be changed, once established as the basis for land ownership, it would have been extremely difficult to reverse. Some of the early British perceptions that the Aborigines were very few in number and lacked a conception of property were simply incorrect. Other arguments were also employed such as they were not farmers and would not offer as much military resistance as other native peoples the British had encountered. Although the first may have been broadly correct, the extent of Aboriginal resistance was greater than anticipated. Had the British known more about the Aborigines from the start, they might have recognised Aboriginal property rights. But once *terra nullius* had been implemented, it could not be reversed, even when British opinion about the Aborigines began to change.

This state of affairs did not fundamentally change until the Australian High Court's decision in the Mabo Case in 1992 that reconceptualised the modern basis of land law in

---

[21] *Law Report*, 51 Ind. App. (1924) at 360, cit, Dawson J., in *107 Australian Law Report*, 1, p. 94.
[22] See Walters, Mark, 'Towards a 'Taxonomy' for the Common Law: Legal History and the Recognition of Aboriginal Customary Law', in Kirkby, Diane, and Coleborne, Catherine, (eds.), *Law, History, Colonialism: the Reach of Empire*, (Manchester University Press), 2001, pp. 125-139.

Australia.[23] However, despite the decision, two established features from the early colonial period were not altered. The first principle is the power of the Crown as sovereign to grant land in fee simple and to extinguish other proprietary rights inconsistent with the grant. *Mabo* reaffirmed that the doctrine of tenure is the origin of land-holding in Australia establishing the Crown as sovereign owner and entitled to grant land to private individuals on whatever conditions necessary to serve the Crown's objectives. This was evident in the instructions given to successive colonial governors before being established as a statutory power in the Imperial Land Act 1831.

Granting land 1788-1821

Australia's land policies largely originated from the British Colonial Office, but it was Australia's colonial governors who implemented and often modified the policies to fit the reality of local conditions.[24] Many of the policies emanating from London were ill-suited to the conditions of the colony and correspondence between governors and ministers in the Colonial Office demonstrate a continuing tension between London's interest in concentrating settlement and Sydney's interest in developing the country.[25] Between 1788 and 1821, land was allocated to emancipated convicts and free settlers on the basis of land grants with the intention, initially, of making the colony self-sufficient in producing its own food.[26] Underlying this policy were

---

[23] The Mabo case (Mabo v Queensland, 175 CLR 1, 1992) radically altered this position and increasingly historians view Australian colonisation as 'conquest' rather than 'settlement'. Stephenson, M. A., and Ratnapala, Suri, (ed.), *Mabo: a Judicial Revolution, The Aboriginal Land Rights Decision and its impact on Australian Law*, (University of Queensland Press), 1993.

[24] Buck, A. R., *The Making of Australian Property Law*, (Federation Press), 2006, argues that the early- and mid-nineteenth century saw the emergence of a distinct Australian property law based upon egalitarianism rather than the feudal origins of English law.

[25] Roberts, Stephen, *History of Australian Land Settlement 1788-1920*, (Melbourne University Press), 1924, reprinted 1968, remains, despite its age, the most systematic study of land policy.

[26] On the early settlement of NSW see, Perry, Thomas M., *Australia's First Frontier: The spread of settlement in New South Wales, 1788-1829*, (Melbourne University Press), 1963.

debates, especially after 1800, over whether this was best achieved by public or private farming and over whether the government or the market should be the purchaser of all products. Should the developing colonial state acting in the public interest acting as a command economy or the private sector within a free market be the basis for economic development? [27]

Land policy under Phillip

Governors of NSW were given authority to make land grants to free settlers, emancipated convicts and non-commissioned officers on terms that contributed to the sustainability of the colony, but initially not to military officers. However, in 1788, there was no land policy and little attention had been paid in the selection of men who understood farming for the First Fleet. This combined with the unproductive land round Sydney Cove initially led to food shortages and the need to import food to the new colony from South Africa, India and the Dutch colonies to the north. Phillip quickly concluded that reliance on imported food was flawed since it relied upon regular and reliable deliveries of expensive supplies by sea and that the colony should, as quickly as possible, become self-sustaining. Early exploration of the immediate area identified two possible sites both of which had good fertile soil: Rose Hill, which later became Parramatta and the valley of the Hawkesbury River.[28] However, by the end of 1788 only twenty acres had been sown, the convicts proved more adept at stealing than producing food and the government farm at Rose Hill produced insufficient grain to feed the population of convicts and marines.

---

[27] On the creation of the Australian colonial economy from scratch, see McLean, Ian W., *Why Australia Prospered: The Shifting Sources of Economic Growth*, (Princeton University Press), 2012, pp. 44-56, and Butlin, Noel, *Forming a Colonial Economy: Australia, 1810-1850*, (Cambridge University Press), 1994, pp. 96-110. 197-199. See also, Fletcher, Brian, *Land Enterprise and Penal Society: A history of farming and grazing in New South Wales before 1821*, (Sydney University Press), 1976.

[28] Ibid, Barkley-Jack, Jan, *Hawkesbury Settlement Revealed: A new look at Australia's third mainland settlement 1793-1802*, is a revisionist study that is valuable on land policy generally in the 1790s.

Phillip's solution was free settlers who, he wrote in 1790, were 'absolutely necessary'. For Phillip, free settlers meant landed proprietors who could 'bring with them people to clear and cultivate the lands, and provisions to support those they bring with them'. Effectively he wanted to transport existing English farmers to NSW rather than ordinary settlers who he thought lacked that 'spur to industry' provided by the possession of capital. Phillip was hampered by his instructions: his first commission did not mention land and his second dealt only with emancipated convicts who would be allocated 30 acres of land and a further 20 acres if married with 10 acres for each subsequent child. This established the basic allocation of 30 acres. It was not until August 1789 that encouragement should be given to marines and free settlers but 'without subjecting the public to expense'.[29] Marine privates were to be allocated 80 acres (30 acres basic allocation plus 50 acres bonus) and non-commissioned officers were entitled to 130 acres or more if they were married and had children. By providing land of a greater size to military personnel than convicts, the Crown encouraged them to remain in NSW after the completion of their military service and contribute to the external defence of the colony. The offer of free convict labour as well as provisions for their first year was also a successful policy to retain soldiers. The regulations did not provide for retired commissioned officers to receive grants and since grants for free settlers were not to exceed non-commissioner officers, the expectation in NSW was that grants around 100 acres became large farms. Population growth in NSW was also encouraged by prohibiting the re-sale of land granted by the Crown for a set period of time. This forced emancipated convicts to retain in the colony as settlers rather than returning to Britain and not to realise gains made by selling their land.

Phillip had little choice but to disobey these instructions since he had little faith in the marines as potential settlers and was forced to extend government aid for longer than was intended. In an attempt to deal with the food crisis, Phillip in November 1789 granted James Ruse, a

---

[29] Phillip's additional instructions on land grants, 20 August 1789, *HRNSW*, Vol. 1, (2), pp. 256-259, *HRA*, Series I, Vol. 1, pp. 124-128.

freed convict the land of Experiment Farm at Parramatta on the condition that he developed a viable agriculture and became the first person to grow grain successfully in Australia.[30] However, lack of transport meant that crops, when harvested, would not be readily available for Sydney.[31] Three free settlers, Phillip Schaffer perhaps the most important, soon settled at Parramatta. It is difficult to under-estimate the importance of this early farming at Parramatta since had it failed it is possible that the colony would also have failed. Phillip strictly followed his orders with regard to and grants to emancipated convicts and during 1791-1792 he allocated 63 farms to 64 emancipated convicts around Parramatta. However, he used his discretionary powers to give 60 acre basic allocation to those applicants with low social standing, such as seamen with the additional entitlement of 2 acres for a wife and 10 acres for children. Finally, Phillip allocated a minimum of 130 acres to free immigrants. The system introduced by Phillip ensured that every group of colonists (emancipated convicts, those with low social standing and free immigrants) apart from officers and serving military could receive land grants. By 1791, there were 87 settlers, emancipated convicts and seamen or marines of whom 50 were on Norfolk Island but the focus for cultivation was on the Parramatta.

---

[30] An account of Ruse's methods is given in ibid, Tench, Watkin, *A Complete Account of the Settlement at Port Jackson*, pp. 80-81. Initially Ruse was only give 1½ acres but was promised 30 acres if his experiments proved successful and on 22 February 1792 Ruse was given the first formal grant in NSW. See also, *HRA*, Series I, Vol. 1, pp. 277-282.

[31] The problem of the lack of artisans and farmers identified by Phillip was quickly acknowledged in London and 'it is advisable that twenty-five of those confined in the hulks...who are likely to be the most useful should be sent out in the ship [*Lady Juliana*] intended to convey provisions and stores': see Lord Sydney to the Lords of the Admiralty, 29 April 1789, *HRNSW*, Vol. 1, (2), pp. 230-231.

Land policy under Grose, Paterson and Hunter

By October 1792 when Phillip left the colony, some 1,700 acres were under cultivation.[32] This ensured NSW's survival but the expansion of the original settlement at Sydney Cover had thrown up new problems. Many of the early free immigrant settlers proved to be poor farmers. In addition, there was a problem of officers being granted land on which to grow food but without tenure. By mid-1791, several officers agitated to become official part-time settlers whilst remaining on full pay and doing garrison duty and in November 1791 Phillip had written to Grenville asking for approval to allow officers to own land whilst on a tour of duty.[33] Although approval did not arrive until 16 January 1793, two weeks earlier Grose had already granted 25 acres of land at Parramatta to Ensign William Cummings.[34] The problem was that Grose was given no indication of the appropriate grant size and his method of calculating this for the officers was unclear. In practice, by the beginning of 1794 almost all of the civil and military officers on the mainland had received grants around 100 acres. Although Portland had spoken decisively of a grant to an officer in the singular, under Grose second grants were also made. Of the 39 grants he issued on the mainland, only 29 officers were involved. Grose provided no explanation to London for his decision and this represented the beginnings of a land policy that advantaged officers. Under Grose, at least 157 of the free population including serving officers and soldiers received land. Some were given what the regulations dictated while others received a second grant increasing their holdings. Grose may have been generous to his officers but he also began reducing some grants without authorisation to do so. In 1794, only three of the 140 mainland grants to emancipated convicts were over 30 acres, despite many of the grantees being eligible for larger

---

[32] *HRNSW*, Vol. 1, (2), pp. 540-541, lists the 87 settlers and their grants.
[33] Phillip to Lord Grenville, 5 November 1791, *HRNSW*, Vol. 1, (2), pp. 532-539. It was approved in Dundas to Phillip, 14 July 1792, *HRNSW*, Vol. 1, (2), pp.631-632, and reached NSW on the *Bellona* on 16 January 1793.
[34] *HRNSW*, Vol. 2, p. 35, lists the grants made from 31 December 1793 to 1 April 1793.

acreages.35 This applied particularly to the developments on the Hawkesbury where ex-convicts were evidently being reduced to small farmer status.

Grose's land policy was widely and justifiable criticised by contemporaries and has subsequently been called 'anarchical'. 36 His administration was lax and the widespread lack of deeds and non-transfer of title left many poor farmers officially landless. The provision of additional large land grants, giving numbers of convict workers in excess of official entitlements and food privileges for officers ensured that a fair share of the limited resources of the colony did not flow to the poor and ex-convicts in ways that Phillip had intended.37 Through his misuse of his discretionary powers in cutting ex-convict grants while expanding land made available to officers, Grose and then Paterson began translating the elitist attitudes of the officers into a colonial reality that marginalised and disadvantaged equally ex-convicts and free poor immigrant settlers. Grose and Paterson had inadvertently given expression to the hierarchical landed structures that existed in Britain with its resultant tensions between those who saw farming as a large-scale capitalist activity that denied access to landownership to most in society and those whose vision was for an economy with a yeoman-based structure of small-holding landowners that called for an 'unlocking of the lands'.

By 1795 when Hunter arrived, there was again a food crisis in the colony. The value of much land had declined to such an extent that expenditure on seed was no longer justified and the government was no longer using convicts to clear new land for cultivation.38 Initially Hunter introduced government aid for settlers by fixing prices and promising to buy all their wheat but this had little effect and it was clear that a radical change in land policy was needed.39 The result was reversion to the policy of public

---

35 See *HRNSW*, Vol. 2, pp. 212-213.
36 Ibid, Roberts, Stephen, *History of Australian Land Settlement 1788-1920*, p. 7.
37 This is evident in the land grants between 13 December 1794 and 15 October 1795 see, *HRNSW*, Vol. 2, pp. 350-356.
38 See, Hunter to Portland, 28 April, 20 August 1796, *HRNSW*, Vol. 3, pp. 38-42, 76-79, on obstacles to progress.
39 As, for example, in the general order, 10 March 1797, *HRNSW*, Vol. 3, pp. 196-198, listing wages to be paid for particular tasks.

farming that addressed the issue of food shortages but was vigorously opposed by Portland in London.[40] In addition, by trying to evolve a flexible policy for development that satisfied both settlers and government in London, Hunter managed to alienate both. For instance, in 1799, he followed Portland's instructions to lower the price of grain but then withdrew it to conciliate the settlers.

Hunter's indecision and lack of support from London spawned settler protest that first emerged in mid-1797 when John Macarthur, a captain in the NSW Corps protested against the nationalisation of production. This resulted in the appointment of two commissioners to hear the grievances of settlers in public meetings, the first attempt to mould land policies by the collection of information instead on through generalised assumptions. The settlers' grievances were real. The government fixed the price of wheat yearly and received the settlers' produce into public granaries at that artificial price. This situation was made worse by the officers' crops going directly to the stores while settlers had to sell to 'dealers, peddlers and extortioners' at lower prices. [41] As a result, the 1798 Commission found that agriculture was being constricted. Parramatta showed signs of prosperity but many settlers had not remained on the land reducing overall output to such a degree that of the population of 4,955, 3,545 were fed by the government. Of the 388 settlers, seven out of ten supported themselves. This had not prevented Hunter from making 364 land grants, 181 to convicts covering 28,279 acres or nearly twice the area granted by his predecessors. [42]

Land policy under King and Bligh

When Philip Gidley King, Hunter's replacement arrived, he found depressed settlers, flourishing middleman, labourers demanding higher wages and farming devastated by a

---

[40] See his letter to Hunter, 31 August 1797, *HRNSW*, Vol. 3, pp. 293-298.

[41] Settlers' petition to Hunter, 19 February 1798, *HRNSW*, Vol. 3, p. 369, and settlers' appeal to Portland, 1 February 1800, *HRNSW*, Vol. 4, pp. 25-28.

[42] For the list of grants from August 1796 to 1 January 1800, see *HRNSW*, Vol. 4, pp. 38-48.

combination of flood and bush fires.[43] His immediate aim was to reverse Hunter's policies by treating all settlers equally, by reducing the number of assigned servants to two per settler and by introducing a more competitive market for grain by allocating government orders among the settlers in proportion to their crops.[44] Convict labour was also made profitable by making them work for the state rather than clearing land for settlers. Instead of dispersing labour, King concentrated it on a large government farm at Castle Hill. This resulted in a revival of individual enterprise and by 1802 cultivated land had increased by a quarter and the colony was self-sufficient. Although this resolved the immediate threat of famine, it was not a solution to the inadequacies of many settlers who were 'without either property to employ others or abilities to work themselves'. He urged that instead of sending labourers to NSW, farmers with capital should be encouraged to come to the colony believing that they could revive effective and efficient private farming. However, this faced sustained opposition from Macarthur and the officers of the NSW Corps.

The system of public farming, originally introduced by Hunter, proved remarkably successful under King to such an extent that by 1802 it was producing a surplus of grain.[45] A simple solution would have been to export any surplus but King had prohibited this. If public agriculture was efficient but settlers could not sell their surplus outside the colony, free colonisation was doomed. In 1804, Hobart ordered that government farming should be curtailed and government herds dispersed.[46] The focus was now on settlers and it was the central element of the new economic policy to aid them as much as possible. More bond labour was to be allowed, stock was to be given to successful settlers and the government was to advance loans to stimulate enterprise. This was combined with an ending of the closed market with the ending of guaranteed prices, the operation of supply and demand and the introduction of a

---

[43] See King to Portland, 25 September 1800, *HRNSW*, Vol. 4, pp. 177-186.
[44] Government and General Orders, 1 and 2 October 1800, *HRNSW*, Vol. 4, pp. 220, 222.
[45] King to Hobart, 9 November 1802, *HRNSW*, Vol. 4, pp. 899-900.
[46] King to Hobart, 1 March 1804, *HRNSW*, Vol. 5, pp. 329-330.

system of tenders with safeguards against the monopolists. This represented a shift away from government activity towards free enterprise. While control of the minutiae of life especially leading agrarian change in NSW by the governor may have been justifiable during its struggle for survival but there were limits to what government alone could achieve. By giving special terms to men with capital who could develop the colony, such as the Blaxland brothers who obtained grants of 8,000 acres in 1805 on condition that they spent £6,000 and by the development of an export trade for surplus products, Hobart and King moved NSW towards a market economy in which individual enterprise would be rewarded. [47] This resulted in a change in land policy that was for the first time linked to expansion rather than static subsistence. The NSW government wanted to group settlers round 'townships' or shires of up to 30,000 acres with farms radiating from centrally placed 'towns'. This would have the effect of gradually colonising the interior and as these lands were not retained by government but vested in certain 'Resident Trustees', chosen by settlers and other farmers in the district stimulate further growth. [48]

Under King, there was a radical transformation in land settlement. When he arrived in 1800 there were 401 proprietors with grants for 43,786 acres of land; when he left there were 646 with 84,466 acres. The settled districts had increased to below Windsor and the intervening land had in general been occupied. The area under cultivation had almost doubled and the population of the colony had increased by 4,936 to 7,052. King had played a central role in furthering these changes despite the opposition of the NSW Corps. It was, however, not until after the Rum Rebellion against King's successor William Bligh that these soldiers were demobilised and a significant obstacle to sustained expansion was eliminated.[49] While Bligh's land policy had been moderate and progressive, following his deposition there were two years of retarded development as

---

[47] See, Gregory Blaxland to Under-Secretary Cooke, 24 October 1804, *HRNSW*, Vol. 5, pp. 479-480, and Gregory Blaxland to Under-Secretary Chapman, 1 March 1805, *HRNSW*, Vol. 5, pp. 568-569.

[48] The Colonial Office approved of this and included it as part of Bligh's instructions, 25 May 1805, *HRNSW*, Vol. 5, pp. 640-641.

[49] King to Camden, 15 March 1806, *HRNSW*, Vol. 6, pp. 34-40, 43-45, provides a summary of King's achievements.

first Johnston, then Foveaux and Paterson endorsed different policies.[50] Johnston was moderate in his approach; Foveaux made few grants[51] while Paterson, revived the unstructured grants associated with Grose issuing 413 grants of 64,475 acres in a year. There are grounds to support Bligh's later assertion that the administrators gave land to individuals who they believed would support their interests. Their grants were rendered void when Macquarie took over although the Colonial Office gave him discretionary powers to confirm these grants to 'very deserving and Meritorious Persons' as he deemed fit. [52] By 1809, there were 737 settlers out of a total population of 10,482 holding 95,637 acres (an average of 128 acres each) with 7,615 acres under cultivation and 74,569 acres of pasture.

Macquarie, Bathurst and Bigge

Between 1809 and the Colonial Office's change of policy in 1817, Macquarie based his land policy largely on free settler immigration and launched a comprehensive policy of settlement in the 'interior' rather than on the more dangerous flood-plains. Military officers were no longer to receive grants and he vigorously opposed monopolists especially rich settlers such as the Blaxlands who, he argued, having turned their attention to cattle production, had violated their implicit contracts with the government in taking grants to advance arable farming. Macquarie never grasped the potential for pastoral farming but his conclusions were probably right; the rich settlers became increasingly difficult to manage and 'it seemed as if a military oligarchy were being reincarnated in the form of a civil monopoly'. [53] He concluded that if gentlemen settlers were 'difficult' and free settlers still arriving in only small numbers then emancipated convicts should be encouraged

---

[50] The decline in agriculture is evident in Civil Officers to Bligh, 18 February 1809, *HRNSW*, Vol. 7, p. 36, and in Foveaux to Castlereagh, 20 February 1809, *HRNSW*, Vol. 7, pp. 39-40.
[51] See, for example, Foveaux to Castlereagh, 20 February 1809, *HRNSW*, Vol. 7, p. 41.
[52] Proclamation, 4 January 1810, *HRNSW*, Vol. 7, pp. 256-257, *HRA*, Series I. Vol. 7, p. 268.
[53] Ibid, Roberts, Stephen, *History of Australian Land Settlement 1788-1920*, p. 21.

to farm land. In 1816, for example, of the 352 people who settled land, only 15 were free immigrants. It was important to keep out land speculators and poor settlers, who would become a burden on the colony's resources. In 1812, Macquarie included clauses in every grant forbidding their sale for five years and that the land would be cultivated.[54] Supported by Bathurst at the Colonial Office, Macquarie had developed an effective system of land settlement based on nothing more than 'a Grant of Land and Some assistance of Convict Labour'. [55]

The new system introduced in 1817 had two key features. The amount of land granted was to be determined the actual amount of capital possessed by a settler. It also sought to resolve the question of freeing the market. In 1816, Treasury officials recommended public competition and Bathurst even threatened to import Indian maize if it was cheaper. [56] Macquarie, however, postponed this development and retained the old system of government purchase. There were to be no foreign markets and this led in late 1819 to a petition by settlers who rightly claimed that 'the surplus becomes useless for want of a Market'. [57] While Macquarie had embraced the need to expand the settlement of land and had evolved effective strategies to do so, he was far less willing to welcome a free market solution. Increasingly, his land policy was under critical scrutiny. Large farmers opposed the Governor because of his failure to open up the market and the graziers joined them because he had neglected their protest against English duties. The Colonial Office was concerned by ever-increasing spending without real returns, a situation increasingly unacceptable in Britain where retrenchment after the French Wars was the dominant economic priority. In addition, Macquarie had been circumspect in his despatches with regard to land policy and for over nine years had forwarded no returns of land grants to London.

The result was the appointment of John Thomas Bigge as a Commissioner of Inquiry to fill in the details that

---

[54] This had the effect of reducing speculation in land in contrast to the speculative drive behind farming in Upper Canada.
[55] Bathurst to Macquarie, 24 July 1816, *HRA,* Vol. 9, p. 151, and Macquarie to Bathurst, 31 March 1817, outline Macquarie's change in policy.
[56] 'Henry Bathurst (1762-1834), *ADB,* Vol. 1, pp. 67-68.
[57] *HRA,* Series I, Vol. 10, p. 59.

Macquarie had omitted from his despatches.[58] Bigge arrived in NSW with certain prejudices: he was less than sympathetic to those who had been transported to the colony but leaned towards the interests and values of the large landowners. His analysis of the weaknesses of Macquarie's land policy was forensic in nature though his constructive proposals were far from original. Bigge found that many of the criticisms of Macquarie's land policy were justified. Of the 324,251 acres of land granted, convicts held more than a quarter and thousands of blocks of land were held without title. While Macquarie may have granted large tracts of land, settlers preceded surveyors who had little incentive to keep up with the rate of occupation since their profit was barely 2/6 per farm. Even where farms had been surveyed, there was a long delay in completing the deeds because registration hardly covered the cost of the parchment. At every level of land policy, there were clear abuses.[59]

Bigge proposed reviving the antiquated system of public farming in the new convict settlements of the north and the establishment of a distillery to use the surplus grain, something that had originally been proposed over a decade earlier. Instead of opening up an export trade, he relied on the building of more granaries and the conversion of the wheat into the arrack of the time. In granting land, he supported Bathurst's 1817 programme recommending that it should be allocated in proportion to capital alone. There was little new in Bigge's recommendations but they clarified the issues and justified Bathurst's policy while condemning Macquarie's administration of that policy.

Macquarie's belief that emancipated convicts could form the backbone of colonial society was bankrupt by 1820. This was reflected in his arbitrary treatment of settlers in his final years as governor, his refusal to allow any ex-soldiers to settle in 1820 and his notice, in March 1821, banning applications for land. The future that Macquarie did not recognise lay with free immigration and

---

[58] On Bigge and his reports see, pp. 82-86.
[59] Bigge's *Reports* were printed in three volumes. Vol. 2: *The State of Agriculture and Trade in the Colony of New South Wales*, The House of Lords, (Paper 119), printed, 4 July, 1823, facsimile ed., (Libraries Board of South Australia), 1971, contains his recommendations on farming.

with pastoral farming. Yet, during his governorship, he raised to NSW from a penal colony to a civil society in which there was a large free community thriving on the produce of flocks and the labour of convicts. Between 1810 and 1821, the population of NSW rose from 12,000 to nearly 40,000 cultivating 32,000 acres of land. The problem was that Macquarie's strengths in 1810 had become his weakness by 1820: 'a war-trained governor, who subjected lawyers and capitalists to his will, was admittedly suited to a convict settlement, but not for an expanding free colony'. [60]

The first official notion of land settlement was contained in Governor Phillip's instructions, in which it was assumed that a self-sustaining rural economy would make its own demand for land. Initially, settlement was linked to the feeding of the population. Grants would be made available for those who applied and small portions would be offered to emancipated convicts as it was believed that rural labour could help redeem fallen characters. The land grant system, under the direct authority of governors, was maintained until the 1820s and formed the only official means of broadening the base of settlement. Initially natural geographical features, such as the Blue Mountains, prevented the westward expansion of NSW and new settlements were made for strategic reasons by Lieutenant Collins at Port Phillip and VDL. Although Collins discounted the country at Port Phillip, VDL was settled and land grants were made at the governor's discretion.[61]

Under Macquarie the system of grants reached its peak. He held the view that rural areas should have towns constructed as service centres and places of government. Moreover, he believed that yeomen farmers should become the backbone of society and policy should be framed for their benefit. Few admitted that the Australian environment was more suited to grazing than intensive English agriculture. Large landowners and wool growers such as John Macarthur, Samuel Marsden and Gregory Blaxland sought to expand the territory available and it was the

---

[60] Ibid, Roberts, Stephen, *History of Australian Land Settlement 1788-1920*, p. 25.
[61] Wheat, barley and oats have been produced in VDL since the early days of European settlement. After starvation conditions in 1805-1807, some was exported by 1812 and in substantial quantities by the 1820s when VDL was regarded as the granary of NSW.

manoeuvring of private individuals that opened a path to new land in the west beyond the Blue Mountains. The investigations and report of Commissioner J. T. Bigge laid the foundations for altering the way in which land settlement progressed. Bigge, like Macquarie, supported the role of small farmers, but saw that wool could provide valuable export earnings encouraging a new type of settlers prepared to buy land from the Crown that gave them a permanent stake in the country.

The initial purpose of NSW and VDL was as penal settlements in which the cultivation of land was regarded as central to the economic development of the colonies. Land policy between 1788 and 1821 was based on the granting of land by NSW governors to individuals. There were definite attempts through land management to maintain and increase the population providing extra grants as an encouragement for people to raise families and supplying women to male convicts to increase the population thereby ensuring the long-term viability of the colonies. It was part of a controlled economy in which the colonial government was a major purchaser of produce and that the market forces of supply and demand generally did not operate. While this may have been justifiable in the immediate aftermath of the establishment of a penal colony where survival and basic subsistence were key priorities and where government was by military rule, it was not conducive to territorial or economic expansion. Macquarie may have laid the foundations for both between 1809 and 1821 but there were important limitations to his policies. It is no coincidence that the emergence of a new approach to land policies emerged in the 1820s at the same time that NSW moved from military to civilian rule and gubernatorial autocracy was replaced by limited representative institutions.

Land companies

When the Blue Mountains were crossed and the value of the lands beyond was appreciated, capital as well as immigration was attracted. The implementation of Bigge's report paved the way for the settlement of vast tracts of land and in the division of land into counties, hundreds, and parishes. [62] Although there were some early efforts to sell public land, grants remained the main way of allocating land until the late 1820s. The common pre-1820 practice of granting small plots of land to ex-convicts was supplemented by the allocation of substantial areas of land, typically 1,000 to 2,000 acres. Exceptionally large grants were made to the Australian Agricultural Company and the Van Diemen's Land Company, but other very substantial grants were made that resulted in the expansion of both NSW and VDL beyond their original areas of settlement along the main river systems and into the interiors of both colonies.

Australian Agricultural Company

In early 1824, the City of London was in the midst of an stock market boom and a group of British bankers, merchants and politicians saw the potential for big profits to be made in NSW. With Australian wool growing in importance, two companies, the Australian Agricultural Company and the Van Diemen's Land Company, were floated on the London Stock Exchange. The Australian Agricultural Company incorporated by Royal Charter under a special Act of Parliament, in 1824, 'for the cultivation and improvement of waste lands in the colony of NSW', obtained a grant of 500,000 acres and coal-mines at Newcastle. Part of the company's estate was selected after 1831, but when Governor Bourke energetically protested against the alienation of so huge an area, he was overruled by his official superiors. Today, listed on the Australian Stock Exchange, it is the oldest company in Australia operating under its original name. [63]

The Charter of the Australian Agricultural Company stated that most of the labour would be provided by convicts under the supervision of superintendents, overseers and skilled artisans sent from England. If, at the end of fifteen years, the company had spent £10,000 on improvements

---

[62] See, ibid, Roberts, Stephen, *History of Australian Land Settlement 1788-1920*, pp. 57-62, and King, Hazel, 'John Macarthur junior and the formation of the Australian Agricultural Company', *Journal of the Royal Australian Historical Society*, Vol. 71, (3), (1985), pp. 177-199.
[63] Gregson, Jesse, *The Australian Agricultural Company, 1824-1875*, (Angus & Robertson), 1907.

and employed 1,400 convicts, it would gain freehold title to its land. The size of the land grant was not specified in the Charter, but discussions between the company directors and the Colonial Office settled on one million acres. In London, Robert Dawson was appointed chief agent with a Colonial Committee in NSW to assist him consisting of James Macarthur, John's fourth son, his cousin Hannibal and James Bowman, the Principal Surgeon. [64] The critical decision the Committee made was the location for the land grant and its suggestion, with which Dawson concurred when he arrived in NSW in January 1826, was Port Stephens, a hundred miles north of Sydney. The area contained land suitable for growing cereals and its surrounding hills were good sheep grazing country. There was plenty of fresh water and lime (oyster shells) for building and there was a substantial sheltered harbour.

Dawson immediately recognised the economic potential of the area and decided to take the whole million acre grant between Port Stephens and the Manning River. Until April 1828, when Dawson was dismissed following growing tensions with the Colonial Committee, he explored the area and made arrangements to survey the whole land grant. [65] A series of company sheep stations stretching from Carrington in the south to the Gloucester River in the north was established. Dawson bought flocks of colonial ewes, oversaw the first shearing and sent the wool to England. The Colonial Office also approached the Company about taking over the coal mining operation at Newcastle and, despite the opposition of Governor Darling this was agreed in June 1828. Darling was instructed to hand over the coalfields and the land grant at Newcastle to the Company that was granted a thirty-one year monopoly on coal mining in NSW. [66] The Company's position was reinforced in the land regulations of 12 July 1831 containing the statement that in all grants the Crown would reserve to itself 'all mines of gold, silver and coals'. The Company was of especial

---

[64] Flowers, E., 'Dawson, Robert (1782-1866), *ADB*, Vol. 1, pp. 298-300.

[65] Dawson, Robert, *Statement of the Services of Mr Dawson, as Chief Agent of the Australian Agricultural Company*, (Smith, Elder and Co.), 1829, provided a rebuttal of the charges against Dawson for mismanagement.

[66] Murray to Darling, 25 June 1830, *HRA*: Series I, Vol. pp.

importance as an innovator in improving the quality of sheep for the British market introducing Saxon merinos and merino crosses into its flocks. Nonetheless, it was not until 1840 that the Company was sufficiently organised on the Liverpool Plains to establish its production of fine wool sheep. [67]

In late 1828, the Company directors decided to manage affairs using a commissioner and dispensed with the services of the Colonial Committee. Captain Sir Edward Parry RN, Hydrographer Royal was appointed in early 1829 and this proved to be an astute move. [68] His first tour of the company's million-acre grant at Port Stephens convinced him that at least half of it was unfit for the prime purpose of raising sheep and would have to be exchanged. Fortunately the British government was amenable and Parry's chief task in his four years in Australia was to seek out new land and secure it for the Company. He established effective pastoral and mining operations, developed the chain of sheep stations at Port Stephens and established cattle stations on the Bowman run west of Gloucester using imported shorthorn bulls to develop the Company's herds. The only problem he faced was the continuing difficulty in obtaining sufficient convict labour. In 1838, its establishment consisted of 53 free, 54 ticket-of-leave and 586 convicts 'whom it is now considered a favour to obtain'. [69] Under Colonel Henry Dumaresq, Parry's successor, the Company's lands continued to prosper and in August 1834, the directors announced their first dividend of the ten shillings per share. [70] The Warrah run was developed for fattening

---

[67] For a not uncritical account of the early years of the Company see, Mann, William, *Six Years' Residence in the Australian Provinces ending in 1839*, (Smith, Elder & Co.), 1839, pp. 216-222. See also, Campbell, J. F., 'The First Decade of the Australian Agricultural Company, 1824 to 1834', *Journal and Proceedings of the Royal Australian Historical Society*, Vol. 9, (3), (1923), pp. 113-160.

[68] *In the service of the company: Letters of Sir Edward Parry, Commissioner to the Australian Agricultural Company*, 2 Vols. (Australian National University Press), 2003. Parry, Ann 'King, 'Parry, Sir William Edward (1790-1850), *ADB*, Vol. 2, pp. 315-317.

[69] Ibid, Mann, William, *Six Years' Residence in the Australian Provinces ending in 1839*, p. 220.

[70] Gray, Nancy, 'Dumaresq, Henry (1792-1838)', *ADB*, Vol. 1, pp. 333-334.

cattle, horses were bred for the Indian army and the Company no longer needed to buy stock rather its annual sales at Sydney and Maitland proved increasingly lucrative. Annual coal sales reached £10,500 a year. But labour remained a problem, a situation made acute with the ending of transportation to NSW in 1840, and there were frequent requests to London for shepherds and miners. [71]

Dumaresq's sudden death in March 1838 led to the appointment of Captain Phillip Parker King, Governor King's son, as commissioner. [72] The collapse of the London wool market in 1836 had just begun to impact on Australia and this, combined with drought and major floods, led to a period of crisis for the Company. The ending of transportation exacerbated already acute labour shortages and the Company' agent sought with limited success to recruit families from newly arrived emigrant ships in Sydney. By the late 1840s, none of the 326 men employed in the Company's pastoral activities were convicts, though 33 were ticket-of-leave men, and all 89 miners at the Newcastle colliery were free men. In addition, there was growing colonial pressure on the Company's coal-mining monopoly from various prospecting groups that wanted to commence mining, the Australian Coal Mining Company, for instance at Illawarra in Sydney. The demand for coal was rising but skilled labour was scarce. In 1840 the company imported a hundred Irish labourers, who proved unreliable, and forty Welsh miners, who proved troublesome. Between 1842 and 1845, sales of coal dropped from 35,000 tons to 23,000 tons. King- often protested that coal was being mined elsewhere to the detriment of the company's monopoly. Although King appealed for support from the NSW government and the directors sought aid from the Colonial Office, it was clear that the monopoly had become entangled with the Company's efforts to obtain its title deeds.

The problem was that access to convict labour in NSW had altered so much since 1824 that an amending Act of Parliament received the Royal Assent in August 1846 that freed the Company's pastoral lands from the restrictions of its Charter. Although the Company had kept its side of its monopoly by raising more than 3,000 tons of coal annually,

---

[71] *Australian*, 4 October 1838, p. 4.
[72] 'King, Phillip Parker (1791-1856), *ADB*, Vol. 2, pp. 55-57.

the NSW government had failed to provide the agreed number of convicts or defended the Company's position.[73] With the growth of illegal mining and the colonial government's unwillingness to prosecute offenders, the Company agreed to relinquish its monopoly in return for receiving its freehold title at Newcastle. With the increase in immigration to NSW, the directors decided to sell part of the land. King recommended that the Liverpool Plains Grant should be divided into five sections followed by the Peel and Port Stephens grants, each divided into three sections. King suggested that if the large blocks could not be sold that each section should be auctioned in lots with a reserve price of five shillings an acre.

After ten years in NSW King was aware that the land at Port Stephens was not suitable for small-scale farming but, despite his misgivings, the directors were persuaded by James Ralfe's proposal for a private emigration scheme offering homestead lots for selection. This proved unsuccessful with only eight settlers and their families sailing from England and just 24 selection certificates issued. Local auctions sales proved more successful but by 1856, despite increasing sales for the fine wool produced at Port Stephens, the directors decided to sell all the Port Stephens sheep. Cattle breeding continued and land sales were promoted around Stroud but the Company's coal interests continued to prosper and remained an important if declining asset until its last pit closed in 1916. With increased demand for wool in the 1860s land at Warrah and later Goonoo Goonoo was restocked with sheep for both the wool and meat markets. In both locations open runs were replaced with paddocks, a process that made sheep production easier to manage and increased productivity and the number of sheep on these estates reached nearly 400,000 by 1900. However, the Closer Settlement movement from the 1890s saw the end of large-scale pastoralism in eastern NSW and the Company's focus

---

[73] An examination of its monopoly was underway by the Legislative Council in 1847 when a dispatch was received from Earl Grey that the Colonial Office and the Company had agreed to end its monopoly. Although numerous coal mines were then opened in NSW, the Company retained 2,000 acres of coal land in the colony: see Veatch, Arthur C., *Mining Laws of Australia and New Zealand*, (United States Government Printing Office), 1911, pp. 119-120.

shifted to cattle rearing for the expanding export market for frozen beef in Queensland and the Northern Territories. [74]

Van Diemen's Land Company

The Van Diemen's Land Company also worked under a Royal Charter in 1825 and secured over 250,000 acres in the north-west of VDL for a trifling quit-rent of £468.[75] It too was formed by wealthy investors in London who recognised the potential of a fine wool sheep enterprise in VDL. Exploration of the island in 1823 between the Tamar River and Circular Head by Lieutenant Charles Browne Hardwicke had revealed good agricultural land at Circular Head, something confirmed by a second expedition under Lieutenant James Hobbs. It was Hobbs' report that led the colonial authorities to insist that the new Company should take up its land grant in the north-west of the island, a decision that ultimately contributed to the failure of the venture. [76]

Formed with subscriptions of £50,000, initially the VDL Company was granted only half of the 500,000 acres requested, although this was later increased to 350,000 acres. Under its Royal Charter issued in November 1825, the Company was to select a single block from 'waste lands in His Majesty's island of Van Diemen's Land'. Edward Curr, a former Hobart merchant, was appointed the Company's chief colonial agent with responsibility for selecting the land

---

[74] Closer Settlement legislation was introduced by the NSW Parliament between 1901 and 1909 to reform land holdings and especially to break squatters' dominance of land tenure. The movement began in the 1890s and was on a smaller scale than the selection policy of the 1860s since it only involved the acquisition of land considered suitable for agriculture and was close to markets. Its aim was to produce a large and prosperous class of yeoman farmers and proved a limited success.
[75] Ibid, Roberts, Stephen, *History of Australian Land Settlement 1788-1920*, pp. 62-68, and Meston, A. L., and W. M., *The Van Diemen's Land Company: 1825-1842*, (Museum Committee, Launceston City Council), 1958
[76] Morgan, Sharon, *Land Settlement in Early Tasmania: Creating an Antipodean England*, (Cambridge University Press), 1992, examines land settlement to 1830. See also, Boyce, James, *Can Diemen's Land*, (Black Inc.), 2010, pp. 145-211, and Hartwell, R. M., *The Economic Development of Van Diemen's Land 1820-1850*, (Melbourne University Press), 1954, pp. 31-53, 58-61.

and arrived back in VDL from London in March 1826. [77] He established a base camp on the Mersey River and explored the area finding that, although there was 2,000 acres of good land, it was nowhere near the acreage the Company expected.

Although Curr requested better land, Lieutenant-Governor George Arthur refused and limited the Company to the north-west. He feared the influence of a powerful, privately owned company in the colony, and was determined to keep the more accessible good land to entice free immigrants. In 1830, Curr finally accepted the grant in six allotments covering a total of 350,000 acres. The largest, of 150,000 acres, was at Woolnorth near Cape Grim; 20,000 acres was at Circular Head, 10,000 acres at the Hampshire Hills, 10,000 acres at the Middlesex Plains, 150,000 acres at the Surrey Hills and 10,000 acres on islands off the coast.[78]

Curr's assessment of the farming potential of the grant proved astute and warned the company directors 'that our lands are not sufficiently good' and that while 250,000 acres of land almost anywhere else in VDL would support 250,000 sheep, '250,000 here would not at present keep one quarter of that number'. His concerns were well-founded. Between 1831 and 1833, more than 3,000 ewes and lambs died of cold, disease or marauding animals. Only £2,000 worth of wool was exported, carried by a ship that had cost the company £30,000. Like the Australian Agricultural Company and despite being promised convict labour and the arrangements made that agricultural labourers sentenced in England to be assigned to the Company, settlers were not provided with sufficient labour. There were 35 convicts in 1827 rising to a peak of 117 in 1835 but when these were withdrawn in 1840, the Company began leasing land to tenant farmers to cut costs. In 1842, there were 241 tenants, but by 1851 this had risen to 846. There was also diversification of farming activities including horse breeding, grazing cattle and running deer on the

---

[77] 'Curr, Edward (1798-1850), *ADB*, Vol. 1, pp. 269-271.
[78] For an early optimistic assessment of the VDL Company based primarily on its annual reports see, Bischoff, James, *Sketch of the History of Van Diemen's Land*, (John Richardson), 1832, pp. 98-155.

property and, from 1842, began to sell land. This did little to ease its financial situation.

No consideration was given to the rights of Aboriginal inhabitants by the colonial authorities in VDL and there had already been a significant reduction in their numbers because of conflict with settlers and European-introduced diseases. Those natives in the north-west had been little affected by settler incursion but this changed tragically once the VDL Company moved in. [79] The worst incident occurred at Woolnorth, on land that had once been prime hunting territory, apparently after assigned shepherds had attempted to interfere with Aboriginal women. [80] In the melee that followed, a shepherd was speared in the thigh and an Aboriginal man was shot dead. The Aborigines soon retaliated by driving 118 sheep over the Cape Grim cliff. Six weeks later, in January 1828, an expedition attacked a group of Aborigines at their campsite. There is disagreement over whether 12 or 30 Aboriginal men were killed and their bodies thrown over the cliff. Whatever the total, it demonstrated the preference of company officials to remove the native population, if necessary by exterminating them. It was not until 1842 that the last family of tribal Aborigines was taken from the Woolnorth property to Flinders Island and the 'Aboriginal problem' as white settlers saw it was deemed to have been resolved.

Between 1829 and 1852, the VDL Company realised just £20,000 from the sale of wool and shareholders had been frequently called on to prop up its operation. By the mid-1830s, the company's main income was from the sale of breeding stock in Van Diemen's Land, Port Phillip and to a lesser extent in South and Western Australia. Durham cattle and Suffolk Punch and Clydesdale horses were introduced and English grasses sown. Apart from small profits made from stock breeding in the late 1830s that led to small dividends being paid in 1837 and 1838, the company's record was one of operating losses and repeated calls on shareholders to prop it up financially. In February 1851, a

---

[79] Lennox, G., 'The Van Diemen's Land Company and the Tasmanian Aborigines: A Reappraisal', *Tasmanian Historical Research Association Papers and Proceedings*, Vol. 37, (1), (1990), pp. 65-208. See also, ibid, Morgan, Sharon, *Land Settlement in Early Tasmania: Creating an Antipodean England*, pp. 143-160.
[80] McFarlane, I., 'Cape Grim', in Manne, R., (ed.), *Whitewash*, (Black Inc. Agenda), 2003, pp. 277-298.

special general meeting in London decided to wind up the company's farming operations and lease or sell its land. All company lands were leased or sold and a part-time agent in Launceston was appointed to collect the rent. In the 1870s in an attempt to improve revenues, the Company resumed farming at Woolnorth, introducing cattle and horse breeding and also diversified its activities setting up sawmills and brickworks and operating the Mount Biscoff railway to service the west coast minerals boom. These operations continued until 1965 when Victorian pastoralist, Alan Ritchie, acquired a majority stake in the VDL Company, gaining ownership of Woolnorth. In 1993, majority ownership was bought by Tasman Agriculture Ltd., a listed New Zealand company that still owns it. Recognising the historical importance of the company, the parent company has retained the name and royal charter of the Van Diemen's Land Company.

Both the Australian Agricultural Company and the Van Diemen's Land Company failed to meet the aspirations of the corporate interests in London that saw them as a means of profiting from the expansion of the fine wool industry. But hoped for profitability in London failed to take account of the geographical and climatic problems of running sheep in NSW and VDL and, for both companies, shareholders received poor returns on their investment. What success the companies had lay less in their involvement in rearing sheep for wool or meat than in those areas of diversified activity, such as coal mining and cattle-rearing that saw production initially for the Australian market and, with the introduction of refrigeration from the 1880s, the imperial market in frozen beef and lamb. Like the land companies in British North America, these two companies only became really profitable once a global market in food production developed in the late-nineteenth century.

Surveying land and administering grants

The office of the Surveyor-General was established when the colony was founded. Augustus Alt arrived on the First Fleet holding the Office of Surveyor of Lands. [81] In his

---

[81] Dowd, Bernard T., 'Alt, Augustus Theodore Henry (1731-1815)', ADB, Vol. 1, pp. 11-12, Dowd, B. T., 'Augustus Alt, First Surveyor-

Commission, Phillip was instructed to issue a warrant to the Surveyor of Lands to make surveys of and mark out lots on any land that the colony needed. His instructions also declared that no land grants in the name of the Crown should be binding until enrolled before an officer or officers appointed for that purpose and a Grant Register was established on Phillip's orders on 22 February 1792. The registration of private legal transactions caused official concern as litigation over the buying and selling of freehold land increased. On 27 February 1802, Governor King issued a Public Order for the recoding of Assignments and other Legal Instruments in the Judge-Advocate's Office. On 6 March 1802, this resulted in the first registration of private dealings in land in the Old Register.

Alt carried out his duties until 1797 when, because of ill-health, his deputy Charles Grimes largely took over his responsibilities. [82] Alt retired in 1802 and Grimes was promoted to Surveyor-General. Between 1804 and 1806, Grimes was in England and his duties were carried out first by George Evans until dismissed for fraud and then Henry Williams. Grimes left the colony again in 1808 because of events associated with William Bligh's deposition finally resigning in 1810. Governor Macquarie recognised that a good surveyor was much needed in the colony and in 1812 John Oxley was appointed. [83] He too neglected ordinary survey work and devoted much of his time to exploration. The surveying department came in for trenchant criticism in Commissioner Bigge's report in 1822 who pointed to the failure to appoint sufficient staff to accommodate the increase in work and the disruption caused by Oxley's frequent absences. As a result, additional surveyors and draftsmen were appointed in an attempt to overcome the backlog in the survey work in the colony.

Bigge strongly recommended that the country intended to be settled should be surveyed and laid out in districts. This, he believe, would facilitate the location of land for

---

General of New South Wales', Journal and Proceedings (Royal Australian Historical Society), Vol. 48, (5), (1962), pp. 360-369.
[82] Dowd, Bernard T., 'Grimes, Charles (1772-1858)', *ADB*, Vol. 1, pp. 487-488, and 'Charles Grimes: The Second Surveyor-General of New South Wales', *Journal of the Royal Australian Historical Society*, Vol. 22, (4), (1936), pp. 247-288.
[83] Dunlop, E. W., 'Oxley, John Joseph William Molesworth (1784-1828)', ADB, Vol. 2, pp. 305-306.

settlers on their arrival from Britain. Consequently in 1825, Royal Instructions were issued to Governor Darling that ordered a general survey of the Colony and its division into counties, hundreds, and parishes. A general valuation of land throughout the Colony was also to be undertaken. Neither the survey nor the valuation of lands was to extend into those districts that lay beyond the range of any actual settlements. No land was to be granted until the survey was completed and Commissioners of Survey were appointed to put these instructions into effect. The Surveyor General was appointed as one of the Commissioners. The Deeds Registration Act 1825 (5 George IV No 22) legislated for the enrolment of land grants in the Supreme Court. This was the first time any governor of the colony had been directed specifically to enrol grants in a Court of record and introduced the principle that any deed or instrument executed bona fide and for valuable consideration should take priority according to the date of registration and not execution. The first Registrar of Deeds was appointed on 16 November 1825 and the Old System Deeds Register and Vendors' Index commenced on that date.

John Oxley died in 1828 and Major Thomas Mitchell was appointed to the position of Surveyor General. [84] The Surveyor-General's Department underwent a considerable internal reorganisation. In 1830, the Surveyor-General was given control of the Surveyor of Roads and Bridges and in the same year the Commissioners appointed by the Royal Instructions in 1825 had the Commission revoked and the Surveyor General became responsible for all arrangements connected with the survey of NSW. The Colonial Architect was also under the control of the Surveyor-General from 1833 to 1835. His responsibilities were reduced when the Colonial Secretary took responsibility for the Colonial Architect in 1835 and the supervision of roads was transferred to the Royal Engineers two years later.

On 1 January 1844, the Office of the Registrar-General was established under the Colonial Secretary with William Carter as the first Registrar-General. His functions included registration of statutes of the colonial legislature, compulsory registration of births, baptisms and burials, registration of wills, devices, deeds, the first was registered

---

[84] Baker, D. W. A., 'Mitchell, Sir Thomas Livingstone (1792-1855), *ADB*, Vol. 2, pp. 238-243.

on 5 January, conveyances and other assurances. In 1849, the Office was abolished and all duties and land records were returned to the Supreme Court but it was then re-established in 1855 with Christopher Rolleston as Registrar-General with the registration of births, deaths and marriages as its only function.

The budget of the Surveyor-General's Department was drastically reduced from £26,000 in 1842 to £12,000 in 1844 because of the economic depression and the need for retrenchment in the cost of colonial administration. Many surveyors were removed from the salaried staff of the Department and forced to work as lower-paid licensed surveyors. This left the Department ill-prepared to undertake the survey of leases under the 1847 Order in Council or to meet the demand for land in the early 1850s after the discovery of gold. Although Mitchell retained considerable if declining support from the Colonial Office in London, his relations with Gipps and Fitzroy were tense as he attempted to assert his independence from the local colonial administration while the governors stressed his subordination to it. By 1855, the Survey Department had become a public scandal since its delays prevented an increasing number of people from purchasing the land they wanted. This gave the colonial government the excuse it wanted to secure Mitchell's dismissal and on becoming governor, in July 1855 Sir William Denison appointed a Royal Commission of Inquiry into the Surveyor General's Department. Mitchell died on 5 October 1855 before the Commission reported severely criticising the methods and results of his work and his administration of the department. Although Mitchell was a poor administrator and found difficulty in delegating his responsibilities, his surveying technique achieved a high level of accuracy. Little was done to implement the recommendations of the Commission except the appointment of District Surveyors throughout the colony to supervise work of various licensed and salaried surveyors.

Restricted to unrestricted settlement

Between 1788 and the early 1820s, changes in colonial land policy were prompted largely by demographic and economic conditions. There was a change from dependence on prerogative powers to statutory legislation and regulation subject to parliamentary scrutiny. In 1826, legislation was introduced for Crown Land sales by auction while the Australian Courts Act promulgated two years later established the applicability of British common law to the Australian colonies. Free grants were abolished in 1831 in favour of grants by purchase. There was also a shift from restricted to unrestricted settlement in NSW and VDL in part caused by the development of the squatter movement beyond the limits of recognised settlement over which neither the Colonial Office nor colonial government had little control. [85] The next three decades saw expansionist exploration and settlement across the various colonies.

In July 1834, Bourke appealed to the Colonial Office to extend the limits of settlement in NSW southwards to Twofold Bay. The request was rejected:

> His Majesty's Government are not prepared to authorise a measure, the consequences of which would be to spread over a still further extent of Territory a Population, which it was the object of the late Land Regulations to concentrate, and to divert for a distant object, not immediately necessary to the prosperity of the Colony, a portion of its Revenues, the whole of which is barely sufficient to maintain in that state of efficiency, which it is so desirable, the various Establishments and Institutions required by the Inhabitants of the Districts already occupied.

The Colonial Office had consistently emphasised the importance of maintaining law and order in its penal colonies and this was easier if population was concentrated in a restricted area. Britain's interest in minimizing subsidies to its colonies justified its interest in this matter. Restricting settlement reduced the cost to government of providing protection for settlers as well as ensuring that the penal character of the colony could be maintained.

The shift towards more dispersed settlement began in the late 1820s. The intellectual trigger came in 1829 with the publication of Edward Gibbon Wakefield's tract, *Letter from Sydney* that, although initially dismissed by the British colonial establishment, won over the Colonial Office

---

[85] A relevant list of legislation in the 1830s include: Crown Lands Protection Act 1833 (4 William IV c10), Crown Lands Protection Amendment Act 1834 (5 William IV c12), Crown Land Claims Act 1835 (6 William IV c21), Validity of Grants Act 1836 (6 William IV c16), and the Crown Lands (Grants) Act 1839 (3 Victoria c1).

in the 1830s and had an enormous influence on its land policy. With the Australian economy in depression in 1828, Wakefield identified the disorganised way in which Crown Land was allocated as its primary cause. He argued that NSW lacked a sufficient labour supply because too many people were allowed to land lacking the skills necessary for colonial development. Capital could not be productively applied to the land unless labour was freely available. To prevent new immigrants from becoming landowners 'too quickly', he called for selling land at auction at a price sufficient to restrict land ownership and to increase the pool of labour available to land owners. The state would use the revenue from land sales to subsidise immigration from Britain to relieve the colony's labour shortage. The system was self-regulating, for as land sales increased, more labour would be demanded; the proceeds from the additional land sales would then be used to bring more labour to the colony to satisfy the new demands. Critical to Wakefield's ideas was the price of land: if the authorities set the price too low, then settlement would become dispersed and economic development would suffer; if the price was too high, it would act as a restraint on the colony's economic development.

The 1831 Ripon Regulations in conjunction with the 1829 restrictions on settlement reflected the decision of the Crown to restrict present use of its lands. If the Crown had been able to enforce its decision, the rapid growth of the sheep industry in NSW would not have occurred. But, the inability of the NSW government to enforce its property rights because of the enormous expanse of land, the high price of labour to the government and the growing number and wealth of squatters led to rapid growth of the pastoral industry. Once the industry became the dominant colonial industry, the question was not whether squatters' *de facto* possession of land could be controlled but how it could be converted into *de jure* ownership.

Selling and taking land

It was not until Bigge's reports were published that some English politicians recognised that land had been given away too freely. 'Large grants of land to individuals have been the bane of all our colonies,' Under-Secretary Henry Goulburn wrote in 1820, 'and it has been the main object of

Lord Bathurst's administration to prevent the extension of this evil by every means of his power.' But, the granting of land was continued after 1820 and was placed on a statutory footing with the introduction of legislation regulating the making of land grants in the 1830s. This coincided with the abolition of free grants and the shift to granting leases subject to conditional purchase. [86]

During Governor Brisbane's term between 1821 and 1825, however, land grants were more readily made. In addition to expanding the amount of land available to settlers, regulations introduced under Brisbane's enabled settlers by private tender to purchase up to 4,000 acres at 5s an acre with superior quality land priced 7s 6d.[87] During Brisbane's years in office the total amount of land in private hands virtually doubled. Lord Bathurst's spasm of moderation did not affect his successors. Governor Darling took office in December, 1825 with instructions from the Colonial Office to reduce the use of land grants and to move toward a system of land sales. In September 1826, he removed instituted a system of land grants to new settlers of moderate means and land sales at fixed prices in lots of 1,920 acres. A shortage of land surveyors forced Darling to suspend land sales in November 1826 and until 1831 grants were virtually the only mechanism for obtaining Crown Land until the Colonial Office ordered the introduction of sale by auction. By this time 3,963,705 acres had been granted either freely or at a trifling quit-rent.

In 1825, Bathurst instructed Brisbane to survey the territory to allow for more planned settlement. [88] The Instructions required the Governor to arrange for a new survey of the colony and the division of the settled districts into Counties, Hundreds and Parishes. The unoccupied lands were then to be valued and eventually sold by tender, if not otherwise reserved, at not less than the average value for that parish. There were still to be grants without purchase of between 320 acres and a maximum of 2,560

---

[86] Atkinson, James, *An Account of the State of Agriculture & Grazing in New South Wales*, (J. Cross), 1826, pp. 28-102, provides a lucid account by a 'settler'.

[87] In 1824, Brisbane approved the sale of Crown Lands in accordance with one of Bigge's recommendations. Previously only a nominal 'quit' rent was required for grants by the crown.

[88] Instructions to Governor Brisbane, 17 July 1825, *HRA*, Series I, Vol. 12, pp. 107-125.

acres unless in the immediate vicinity of a town or village. During the survey one seventh of the land in each County was to be set aside for the Church of England to provide income for an educational system under its control to be managed by the Church and Schools Corporation.[89] When Governor Darling's commission extended the NSW boundary six degrees to the west compared with the commissions issued to previous governors. In September 1826, Darling announced the boundaries within which the survey was to be conducted: the Manning River to the north, the Lachlan River to the west and the Moruya River to the south. This would allow the allocation of land grants and the boundaries, known as the limits of location, were used for other administrative purposes including police administration.[90] The nineteen counties were proclaimed by Darling in the *Sydney Gazette* of 17 October 1829.

In some places there were already squatters beyond these 'limits of location' and the prohibition on settlement was followed up with the 'Act for Protecting the Crown Lands of this Colony from Encroachment, Intrusion, and Trespass' that allowed the Governor to appoint commissioners of Crown Lands to enforce Crown property rights against squatters. There is no evidence that this stopped the flow of settlers to the bush. The graziers realised that the government had no means of enforcing its restrictions and that the few forces available to the government were more likely to be devoted to maintaining security in Sydney and its vicinity with its large convict population. Despite the uncertainty of land tenure, squatters ran large numbers of sheep and cattle beyond the boundaries. The legitimate allocation of land whether by grant or sale was upset by their unauthorised activities.

There was also considerable concern among landowners in 1835 when doubts were expressed over whether all land grants made in NSW and VDL since the beginning

---

[89] Grose, Kelvin, 'What happened to the Clergy Reserves of NSW?', *Journal of the Royal Australian Historical Society*, Vol. 72, (2), (1986), pp. 92-103, and 'Scott, Arthur and the clergy reserves of Van Diemen's Land', *Journal of the Royal Australian Historical Society*, Vol. 75, (3), (1989), pp. 153-169.

[90] Golder, Hilary, *Politics, Patronage and Public Works: The Administration of New South Wales*, Volume 1, 1842-1900, (University of New South Wales Press), 2005, pp. 52-57, considers the question of restricted settlement.

of settlement were illegal. The question was first raised in VDL that these grants had not been made in the name of the King but of the Governor, a practice that began under Phillip and had been continued by successive governors. When Crown law officers in England were consulted, they gave the opinion that all of the grants in NSW since 1788 were invalid. This insecurity was removed by legislation in 1836 (6 William IV, 16), 'to remove such doubts and to quiet the titles of His Majesty's subjects holding or entitled to hold any land in NSW.'

Squatting

Squatting, originally, in a pastoral context, was the unauthorised creation of stock stations on vacant Crown Land and largely arose when a landowner's increasing stock numbers out-grazed the land available to him by grant, purchase, lease or permit. [91] A negative view of squatting remained important through to the mid-1830s. In 1815, a witness before a House of Commons Committee commented

> These persons are almost invariably the instigators and promoters of crime, receivers of stolen property, illegal vendors of spirits, and harbourers of runaways, bushrangers, and vagrants.[92]

James Macarthur, the son of John writing in a similar strain in 1837, spoke of

> ...persons denominated squatters [were] mostly convicts holding tickets of leave or having become free by servitude who [carried on] an extensive system of depredation upon the flocks and herds and the property of the established settlers.[93]

---

[91] Weaver, John, 'Beyond the fatal shore: pastoral squatting and the occupation of Australia, 1826 to 1852', *American History Review*, Vol. 101, (1996), pp. 980-1007.

[92] Cit, Roberts, S. H., *The Squatting Age in Australia 1835-1847*, (Melbourne University Press), 1935, p. 70.

[93] Macarthur, James, *New South Wales; its Present State and Future Prospects: being A Statement, with Documentary Evidence. Submitted in support of Petitions to His Majesty and Parliament*, (D. Walther), 1837, p. 44.

Squatting, apart from these dishonest characteristics, was a natural consequence of the absence of a land policy suited to changing colonial conditions. As long as the Government gave land away to applicants possessed of capital and to others whom it wished to benefit, persons who had not benefited regarded the unoccupied areas beyond the Blue Mountains as available to those who chose to occupy them. It proved impossible to restrain settlement within prescribed limits while there were valuable grasslands stretching for hundreds of miles beyond the official boundaries. Whatever the regulations, Governor Gipps was right when he wrote in 1840

> As well might it be attempted to confine the Arabs of the Desert within a circle traced on sand, as to confine the Graziers or Wool-growers of New South Wales within bounds that can possibly be assigned to them...if they were so confined then the prosperity of the colony would be at an end. [94]

In the 1820s and 1830s, it was common for squatters to follow in the tracks of explorers such as Thomas Mitchell and Charles Sturt and grab the best-watered pasture they could find for their flocks and herds. One writer noted that 'dispersion', not confinement, was the natural law of settlement. It was not surprising that Wakefield's idea of ordered settlement and colonisation gained the attention of the British government. South Australia was settled according to his plan marrying land sales, labour and capital as an incentive to free, respectable British settlers. At Swan River settlement in WA, the attempt to use convict labour and to apportion land by grant met with a host of problems and seemed to indicate that Wakefield's ideas had merit.[95]

In eastern mainland Australia, the original impetus for squatting in the early 1820s was primarily an expanding Sydney meat market and also experimentation with wool production, with added impetus from emancipated and native-born families in search of social and economic freedom as they sought to define and consolidate their place

---

[94] Gipps to Russell, 19 December 1840, *HRA*, Series I, Vol. 21, p. 127.
[95] Oldham, W., *Land policy of South Australia: from 1830 to 1842*, (G. Hassell & Son), 1917, and Ellis, Julie-Ann, *Public land and the public mind: origins of public land policy in South Australia, 1834-1929*, (Flinders University Press), 1995.

within society. [96] Squatting took on fresh vigour in the early 1830s when the profitable British wool market strengthened pastoral diversification and drew new pastoralists from VDL and from Britain. [97] In turn, the creation of Melbourne and Adelaide expanded the meat markets for the 'Sydneyside' cattle holders, just as the goldfields populations would do on a larger scale in the 1850s. Despite a pastoral myth that sees wool as the creator of squatting, it is possible that sheep grazed no more land than did cattle in eastern Australia even as late as 1860. [98]

The first steps in establishing wool production in NSW also created an increased demand for land. From the mid-1820s, however, the occupation of Crown Land without legal title became more widespread, often carried out by those from the upper echelons of colonial society. As wool began to be exported to England and the colonial population increased, the occupation of pastoral land for raising cattle and sheep progressively became a more lucrative enterprise. By 1831, Australia was supplying 8 per cent of British wool imports. Nine years later the proportion had risen to 28 per cent and by 1850 to 53 per cent. Sheep grazing stretched out well beyond the hinterland of the first settlement, into what later became Victoria, Queensland, and South Australia, although pastoralists remained in the relatively well-watered districts. Progress was not smooth. The years between 1825 and 1828 were marked by depression, caused initially by falling wool prices in

---

[96] Fletcher, B. J., *Landed Enterprise and Penal Society: A History of Farming and Grazing in NSW before 1821* (Sydney University Press), 1976, Beever, E. A., 'The Origins of the Wool industry in NSW', *Business Archives and History*, Vol. 5, (2), (1965), pp. 91-106, Ker, Jill, 'The Wool industry in NSW 1803-1830', *Business Archives and history*, Vol. 2, (1962), pp. 18-54, Fogarty, P., 'The New South Wales Pastoral Industry in the 1820s', *Australian Economic History Review*, Vol. 8, (1968), pp. 110-122, Beever, E. A., 'Further Comments on the Origin of the Wool industry in New South Wales', *Australian Economic History Review*, Vol. 8, (1968), pp. 123-128. See also, Abbott, G. J., *The Pastoral Age: A re-examination*, (Macmillan), 1971.

[97] Ibid, Hartwell, R. M., *The Economic Development of Van Diemen's Land 1820-1850*, pp. 107-126, examines the growth of the pastoral industry.

[98] This idea that sheep were the major reason for squatting was encouraged in ibid, Roberts, S. H., *The Squatting Age in Australia 1835-1847*, pp. 35-44.

England and made worse by drought in Eastern Australia. Expansion was resumed after 1828 and continued throughout the 1830s; by 1840, however, profits were again being squeezed between rising costs and slightly falling wool prices. The optimism that had characterised the 1830s evaporated, credit was restricted, and serious depression occurred. During this period of pastoral expansion, wheat production had failed to keep pace with the growth of the population of NSW. The environment was not generally well suited to arable farming that became the occupation of farmers with inadequate resources. Supplies were imported from VDL, but by the 1840s South Australia began to supply NSW with wheat and during the next half-century emerged as the principal grain-growing region of Australia.[99]

Selling land

The experiment with land sales in 1826 foreshadowed major changes in land policy in 1831. The Colonial Office adopted many of Wakefield's ideas when the Earl of Ripon (then Viscount Goderich) issued fresh Regulations in 1831. [100] There were no more free land grants and all land within the Nineteen Counties was to be sold by public auction. [101] The Ripon Regulations instigated a new system for the sale of Crown Land in the Australian colonies that had previously been acquired through grants or sale by tender. [102] They standardised the process by introducing compulsory sale by auction and by setting a minimum sale price of 5s per acre; this rose to 12s per acre in 1839 and to £1 in 1842. The proceeds from land sales were used to fund the assisted

---

[99] Barnard, Alan, *The Australian Wool Market 1840-1900*, (Melbourne University Press), 1958, pp. 3-46, examines the extent of the wool market after 1840.
[100] Burroughs, Peter, 'Wakefield and the Ripon land regulations of 1831', *Historical Studies: Australia and New Zealand*, Vol. 11, (1965), pp. 452-466.
[101] Goderich to Darling, 9 January 1831, *HRA*, Series I, Vol. 16, p. 22.
[102] *Sydney Gazette*, 11 June 1831. The new regulations were notified in a Government Notice of 1 July 1831 and published in a Government Order dated 1 August 1831.

immigration of labourers and servants into the colonies. [103] Colonial dependence on English land law was initially rigorously maintained in the Ripon Regulations but a degree of reinvention and innovation soon became apparent as colonial administrators were forced to develop policies and legislation more suited to the uniquely Australian situation.

The Ripon Regulations, 1831

The intention of the Regulations was to concentrate settlement into compact agricultural communities but although they succeeded in raising revenue, they failed as a mechanism for concentrating population. The transition from a system of land grants to an auction system with a high upset price on land neither stopped the growth of the pastoral industry nor the rush to settle new lands. In fact, it is probable that by making marginal lands in the Nineteen Counties too expensive to settle, the new land regulations actually speeded up the exodus to the unopened lands. By 1839 there were 649 sheep 'stations' outside of the restricted area with many occupying vast areas: stations covering 20-50 square miles were not uncommon. Throughout the 1820s and 1830s, the discovery of new passes through the mountain ranges allowed settlers by 1840 to scatter over 450 miles from Sydney. While most of the best lands in NSW had been occupied by 1840, during the next two decades settlers slowly filled in the less desirable lands. The rapid growth in the sheep population, the squatting population and the value of wool exports from 4 million pounds in 1835 to 26 million pounds eleven years later transformed the squatters from a small group illegally occupying Crown Land into a major constituency of the colonial government.

'Squatting' had become so widespread by the mid-1830s that government policy in NSW towards the practice shifted from opposition to regulation and control. This resolution proved difficult. Coincidentally with their squatting march, the leading NSW landowners acquired the magisterial, executive and legislative power to preserve

---

[103] Burroughs, Peter, *Britain and Australia 1831-1855: a study in imperial relations and Crown Lands administration*, (Oxford University Press), 1967, pp. 35-75.

their hold on the land while newer immigrant squatters brought with them the matching political power of family connection and patronage. In 1836, the Legislative Council passed Bourke's Act to restrain and regulate the occupation of Crown Lands. [104] Commissioners of Crown Lands, who were also stipendiary magistrates, were appointed to protect them against unauthorised occupation as well as keeping the peace between settlers and Aborigines and monitoring ticket-of-leave convicts in the frontier districts. The Commissioners, assisted by a small police force, were to arbitrate between pastoralists over disputed sheep runs and remove unlicensed settlers on Crown Lands.

The legislation also provided that 'respectable' settlers could legally graze their stock beyond the formal limits of settlement on whatever land was available on the payment of a £10 annual licence fee. Although the 1836 Act may have been a sensible and practical means of controlling squatting, it ran counter to official British land policy on Crown Lands in NSW but was approved by the imperial government the following year. This was necessary since English law recognised 'possessory title' where individuals held a piece of land for a prolonged period of time that eventually conferred ownership on the possessor. What Bourke had recognised was that possessory title threatened the Crown's ownership of land in the squatting districts. The legislation provided security and some protection for pastoralists who took out a licence but in doing so they effectively recognised the Crown's right to issue a licence and consequently the Crown's ownership of the lands.

Despite a popular belief that squatting was a general Australian experience, squatting hardly existed in the other colonies. In VDL where there were few cattle, lax land administration in the 1820s had allowed sheep owners all the freehold land they wanted and the owners found their squatting outlets in the Port Phillip District of NSW. The Ripon Regulations had little impact in VDL since the amount of usable Crown Land that remained ungranted in 1831 was quite small. Consequently, the revenue potential of the new scheme was far less important than in NSW. In WA, massively liberal land grants, low initial stock numbers

---

[104] Fletcher, B. H., 'Governor Bourke and squatting in New South Wales', *Journal of the Royal Australian Historical Society*, Vol. 74, (4), (1989), pp. 232-251.

and a tiny domestic market, deferred for many years any perceived need to graze Crown Land. [105] The application of the Regulations produced economic collapse in the fledgling colony. The original land grants had been so extensive and the population so small that land on the private market was selling at a fraction of the price established in the Regulations. As a result, little land was sold, little revenue raised and few labourers brought to the colony. With no new labour the colony could not develop and without development land prices remained stubbornly below the set price, a situation made worse when the official reserve price was raised to £1 an acre in 1842. It was the impasse in labour supply created by the Regulations that in 1847 led colonists to petition the British government to make WA a convict colony. In South Australia in 1836, Wakefield's agriculturalist philosophy of settlement, reinforced in the 1840s and 1850s by the province's emergent agricultural and copper-mining industries, ensured that squatting did not become a major activity in the province. [106] In effect, VDL, WA, and South Australia were largely spectators of the eastern mainland's resolution of squatting.

The Regulations imposed in 1831 continued till 1838, when Lord Glenelg ordered that an increase in the price to 12s an acre because that was the minimum fixed in South Australia. It was clearly impossible to make a success of that colony if its lands were sold for more than double the price for which land could be obtained in NSW. Gipps complied with the order in January 1839. Ironically, this gave squatters added incentive to preserve their status quo, for at that price most of their land would be unattractive to buyers. This coincided with growing attention being paid to Wakefield's principle in England and this especially affected the judgement of a committee of the House of Commons before which its author gave evidence. This committee and the Land and Emigration Commissioners appointed to advise the British Government on colonial land questions,

---

[105] Forrest, Sir John, *Report on the land policy of Western Australia, from 1829-1888: accompanied by various returns, land regulations, and a map*, (Government Printer), 1889.

[106] Prest, Wilfrid, Round, Kerrie and Fort, Carol S., *The Wakefield companion to South Australian history*, (Wakefield Press), 2001, pp. 513-514, provides a succinct summary of squatter activity in the colony. See also W. L. R., *Our wool staple; or, A history of squatting in South Australia*, (John Howell), 1865.

were of opinion that all land, except town land, whatever its quality might be, ought to be sold at a fixed price of £1 per acre. Instructions were accordingly sent out that this price should be charged. [107]

The British government followed the advice of the Land and Emigration Commissioners but had failed to observe the great difference in value between country lands and lands close to a town. The Commissioners had no practical experience of colonial conditions and made the regulation that any person depositing £5,120 might have a special survey made of 5,120 acres or eight square miles of land anywhere they chose in specified districts of NSW, except within five miles of a town. A few wealthy speculators, who had a shrewd idea that lands near to Australian towns would become very valuable, at once lodged their applications and £40,960 pounds was paid before Gipps peremptorily refused to allow any more special surveys to be made. Henry Dendy obtained eight square miles in the present Melbourne suburb of Brighton for his £5,120 and was offered £15,000 before he had even had a sight of the land. Another special survey purchaser, Elgar, selected his eight square miles close to the Melbourne suburbs of Kew, Hawthorn, and Camberwell. Lord John Russell, the Colonial Secretary supported Gipps recognising that he had acted rightly in stopping the special surveys.

The failure of Gipps' land regulations

The granting of grazing licences since 1836 suited squatters because it guaranteed them in the occupation of the lands they had usurped. However, Bourke's successor, Sir George Gipps wanted to use other means to curb the chaotic spread of squatting and to introduce permanent settlement for graziers. [108] He believed that 'the occupation of land should

---

[107] For the imperial reassessment of land policy between 1838 and 1842 see, ibid, Burroughs, Peter, *Britain and Australia 1831-1855: a study in imperial relations and Crown Lands administration*, pp. 202-251.
[108] Buckley, K., 'Gipps and the Graziers of New South Wales, 1841-1846', *Historical Studies,* Vol. 7, (1956), pp. 392-407. See also Gipps' Memorandum on the disposal of Lands in the Australian Provinces', *HRA,* Series I, Vol. 21, pp. 122-134, for a cogent analysis of the defects of the existing system.

be made difficult instead of easy', and wanted to use the revenue gained from land sales to squatters for assisting immigration. [109] The government, he wrote, 'would not suffer them to be kept in perpetuity, and at a merely nominal rent, by those who may be the first to seize upon them'. [110]

The second half of the 1830s had seen a boom in squatting fuelled by the flow of investment capital from Britain and good prices for fine-wool in the British market. Critical to maintaining growth in the Australian wool industry was a continuing inflow of capital but a series of events threatened this flow. There was a manufacturing and financial crisis in Britain between 1837 and 1843, drought in NSW, a slump in wool prices and a labour shortage in the aftermath of the ending of transportation in 1840. Although wool met squatters' running costs, their real profit came from the sale of lambs. While there were potential squatters arriving in NSW with capital to invest, thousands of sheep were needed and prices remained high. However, demand abruptly fell after 1841 leading to a fall in the high price of sheep at the same time as wool prices fell: many squatters faced ruin. This economic situation underlay squatter demands in the Legislative Council during the 1840s especially when Gipps sought to rationalise the administration of Crown Lands. [111]

Gipps' plans to make the squatters pay more for their land met with organised opposition. He presented the regulations to the Legislative Council in December 1840, prompting a flood of protest from landholders and politicians.[112] In August 1841 [113] the auction system was

---

[109] 'Exportation of Capital for Importation of People', *Sydney Morning Herald*, 12 December 1843, p. 2, demonstrated the depth of opposition from the Legislative Council: 'the mismanagement on the part of the Government was one of the principal causes of the existing distress...the application of the Land Fund to immigration had been radically wrong...'

[110] Gipps to Stanley, 16 April 1844, *HRA*, Series I, Vol. 23, pp. 545-549, cit, Buckley, K., 'Gipps and the Graziers of New South Wales, 1841-6', p. 396

[111] Ibid, Golder, Hilary, *Politics, Patronage and Public Works: The Administration of New South Wales*, Volume 1, 1842-1900, pp. 69-73.

[112] 'Petition from Legislative Council', *HRA*, Series I, Vol. 21, pp. 119-121.

reinstated, but in early 1843 the colony received the news that Parliament had passed the Crown Lands Sale Act in June 1842 raising the upset price at auction to £1 per acre with no freehold grants in respect of any land in NSW outside the nineteen counties. The £1 per acre system continued to be followed until the colonies obtained representative government and were free to legislate for their lands. The legislation, however, had significant implications for the question of tenure. Select Committees of the Legislative Council in 1843 and 1844 strongly opposed the high price proposed in the 1842 Act complaining that high prices had stopped sales and encouraged further squatting by those with no vested interest in land. In 1847, a further Select Committee established to examine the minimum upset price of land concluded that it was in the squatters' interests to maintain the high price so that they could occupy land cheaply and this is supported by the reduction in the amount of land sold in auction, 371,447 acres between 1839 and 1841 when the upset price was 12 shillings an acre to only 20,250 between 1842 and 1846 when it was raised to £1.

Gipps' position on land policy was significantly weakened by the creation of an expanded Legislative Council in 1842 in which two thirds of its 36 members were elected by property owners. Squatters dominated the legislature and they strongly objected to the maintenance of British control over land policy. The Council thought the price per acre too high and objected to the provision of the Crown Lands Sale Act that gave to the Governor control over the revenue produced by the sales. At least 50 per cent of the auction proceeds had to be spent on subsidising immigration from Britain and the balance on public works. The Council considered that it should have the disposition of the money and not the Governor and the rest of Gipps' governorship was embittered by his quarrel with the Council on this question but as he retained the support of the Colonial Office, the Council did not gain control of the revenue. Gipps believed that to surrender control over Crown Lands to the Legislative Council would place the property of 'all the subjects of the Empire' at the disposal of

---

[113] Russell to Gipps, 21 August 1841, *HRA*, Series I, Vol. 21, pp. 477-480.

a group that did not represent the people of New South Wales.

Bourke's licensing system had not worked. Although it compelled squatters to acknowledge the rights of the Crown, it allowed a small number of men, who were denied any security of tenure by the Crown's claim to ownership of the land, to control huge tracts of land for a comparatively small payment. They argued that it was their hard work that made these tracts productive and that they provided exports and employment for labourers. In April 1844, Gipps made two regulations with the intention of remodelling the squatting system. The first, gazetted on 2 April, stated that from 1 July all stations were to be subject to a £10 license and an area of 20 square miles or such area that could support 4,000 sheep or 500 cattle was taken to be a separate station. The licensee could be dispossessed by the government at any time. The regulation also left their tenure uncertain and did not provide for any compensation for improvements if the land was repossessed. The second regulation allowed squatters after five years occupancy to purchase 320 acres of a run and gave purchasers security of tenure over a whole run for another 8 years. The regulations were designed to compel pastoralists to contribute revenue to the land fund of the colony and to give them some security of tenure. But Gipps was also trying to ensure that squatters did not lock up large areas of land and deny its use to future settlers by combining a licence system with a system of periodic purchase of a small portion of each station licensed.

Many squatters had not recovered from the severe depression after 1841 and it is hardly surprising that there was considerable opposition to Gipps' attempt to extract revenue from squatters who had become used to paying little for the land. He failed to recognise the importance of pastoralists to the colonial economy. They were crucial to the survival of urban merchants and financial interests who had extended them credit during the boom years. If squatters went bankrupt, then providers of credit would not recover their loans and would also face ruin. As a result urban interests opposed Gipps' regulations and supported squatters in their campaign against the Governor. More surprising was a short-lived alliance between urban working-class radicals and conservative pastoralists. With widespread unemployment and hardship among the urban working-classes, Gipps' announcement that one of the aims of the regulations was to resume assisted immigration threatened to increase already high levels of unemployment. Unwilling to move to the pastoral districts because of the poor reputation of squatters as employers, urban workers supported the pastoralists against Gipps because they saw any increase in new immigrants as a further threat to their livelihoods.

150 squatters gathered in Sydney later in the month protesting against Gipps' changes drafting a petition to the Queen and forming the Pastoral Association of NSW, the first expression of squatters as a political group. They hired a lobbyist in London to represent them before Parliament and enlisted the support of the British woollens industry that had been revived by the stimulus of cheap, high quality wool from NSW. They argued that Gipps' restructuring of the land system could seriously disrupt the flow of wool exports to British industries that were dependent on Australian supplies threatening widespread unemployment in the British woollen industry. A large squatting demonstration was held in Melbourne in June 1844 at which petitions were adopted to be sent to the British parliament and the NSW legislature requesting alterations in the law of Crown Lands and a total separation from NSW. A new association was formed at this meeting, designated the 'Pastoral Society of Australian Felix'. By lobbying in London, the squatters obtained much better terms than Gipps had offered them. Gipps found himself abandoned by the Colonial Office as Stanley, Gladstone and Grey, successive Colonial Secretaries between 1844 and 1846 distanced themselves from his policies and his regulations were never implemented.

A solution from Britain?

The Colonial Office then produced a solution of its own. The Imperial Waste Lands Act of 1846 brought into operation by Orders in Council on 9 March 1847 divided land into settled, intermediate and unsettled areas, with pastoral leases of one, eight and fourteen years respectively. Squatters were also able to purchase parts of their land as opposed to just leasing it. Leases could be granted by the NSW government for 8 and 14 years to established squatters occupying unsettled land for more than 12 months. Rent was set at £10 per year with £2 10s paid for each additional 1,000 sheep above 4,000. The Order also granted each sheep farmer a pre-emption right to conversion to freehold at £1 per acre with a minimum of 160 acres and not an excessive length of water frontage. The leases did not allow the holder to cultivate or sublet the leased land. The right of resumption was retained by the Crown. The Order established more secure rights for the squatters by providing them with long leases and they finally achieved the *de jure* property rights that had been denied them since the 1829 restrictions on settlement. The Orders remained in operation until Robertson's Land Acts of 1861 and were unaltered until 1859 when a colonial Act reclassified the intermediate districts as settled districts. The significance of the Orders, as contemporaries recognised, was the introduction of Crown leaseholds.

By 1847, there were two ways that people could acquire land. They could purchase it at auction for a minimum of £1 per acre under provisions introduced in the 1842 Crown Lands Sale Act. Or, largely in NSW, they could squat on land and obtain pastoral leases that gave their cattle or sheep runs a degree of legality. Given the scale of the squatters' holding in NSW and, after 1851, in Victoria, they formed a powerful economic and political elite that was resistant to further change in land policy and especially to calls to 'unlock the land'. By the late 1840s, nearly all the good lands were used for sheep and cattle and arable farming was located in the coastal areas. In eastern Australia not enough wheat was grown to supply local needs and VDL and then South Australia were the granaries for NSW. In South Australia, unlike in the east, the coastal lands were suited to wheat and from the 1840s it production was mechanised and transport costs were low since even though wheat-growing expanded northwards farms were still close to the sea. As a result, VDL lost out in wheat to South Australia, but diversified into the production of potatoes, oats and later fruit for the mainland. [114]

Before 1856, land disposal and settlement especially in NSW were characterised by several important elements. Successive colonial governments wanted to recreate the

---

[114] Auster, M., 'The regulation of human settlement: public ideas and public policy in New South Wales, 1788-1986', *Environmental and Planning Law Journal*, Vol. 13, (1), (1986), pp. 40-47.

colony in line with the social, economic and legal system of land use in England. This position was to a certain extent supported by the Colonial Office's desire to restrain the spread of settlement despite the development of a widespread desire for land. However, there was a failure to appreciate that the colony's land resources were different from those in the United Kingdom and that the sheer vastness of the public domain made its control and policing extremely difficult, if not impossible tasks. This situation was reinforced by a growing division between the view of English land law that the land was held in trust, that the 'owner' was merely a tenant and that the ultimate owner was the Crown and the colonial view, validated by the formation of a new form of tenure in Crown leasehold in the Imperial Waste Lands Act 1846, where landed property was seen as a mere object where ownership or occupation gave rights of exploitation without a corresponding obligation of trust. It was the discovery of gold in NSW and Victoria in 1851 that precipitated growing demands for land reform, something that after 1855-1856 was possible since the new colonial legislatures were given responsibility for the entire management and control of waste lands belonging to the Crown.[115]

'Unlocking the land'

Until 1851, squatters' privileges were not a major concern in the Port Phillip District as there was sufficient agricultural land available to meet demands. Between 1846 and 1851, more than 100,000 acres of land had been sold in the 'settled' districts near Melbourne, Geelong and the coastal towns. The Imperial Waste Lands Act 1846 and the Order-in-Council of March 1847 granted leases of up to fourteen years to squatters in the 'unsettled' districts covering the northern half of Victoria and for up to eight years in the 'intermediate' districts that included the Western District and Gippsland. In both areas, squatters had the sole or pre-emptive right to buy any part of the land during the period of their leases. To many, it seemed that the land had been 'locked up' for the benefit of the large-scale pastoralists.

---

[115] On the surrender of imperial control over land policy see, ibid, Burroughs, Peter, *Britain and Australia 1831-1855: a study in imperial relations and Crown Lands administration*, pp. 373-382.

However, a precise survey was necessary for this to have legal effect, and this had hardly begun by 1851.[116]

Once the gold rushes began in mid-1851, growing demand for farming land put pressure on the government to open some of the squatting areas. [117] As never before land ownership permeated discussion of democratic reform with demands for greater access to ownership of land to the masses rather than restricting it to the landed gentry. The question of who should occupy the land and whether it should be used for arable or pastoral farming dominated the politics of the later 1850s and 1860s in NSW and Victoria. The 'land question' proposed expanding the land market and promoting ease of transfer and sale as a means of realising the ideal of economic independence. It was in response to these economic imperatives that the Torrens legislation conceived by Sir Robert Torrens a South Australian government official and member of the provincial parliament, first introduced in South Australia through the Real Property Act (SA) 1858, aimed not at amending previous land grants but reforming the system of land transfer and other dealings through a new system of registering land grants. Within four years, Torrens statutes existed across the Australian colonies apart from WA where it was adopted in 1875. Whether this represented simply a new method of land titles registration rather than a new code of substantive real property law, the common law was considered to be sufficiently altered by the Torrens legislation to allow its express provisions to effect real change in Australian land law. [118]

Reforming the land during the Victorian gold rushes

This situation created major problems for La Trobe. Should squatters be given pre-emptive rights if leases could not be issued? Squatters were buying and selling land on the

---

[116] No leases were ever issued under this legislation and throughout the 1850s squatter occupancy of their runs continued with annual licences.

[117] Ibid, Roberts, Stephen H., *The Squatting Age in Australia 1835-1847*, pp. 350-358, is useful on the land question in the early 1850s; Clark; *Selected Documents 2*, pp. 179-180.

[118] Taylor, Greg, *The Law of the Land: The Advent of the Torrens System in Canada*, (University of Toronto Press), 2008, pp. 3-17, 35-42, considers its origins in South Australia.

assumption that pre-emptive rights existed. Equally pressing was whether the Government could sell any public land outside the 'settled' districts where there was little unsold land left. La Trobe was not a defender of the squatters and argued for a liberal interpretation of the 1846 Act believing that it was the duty of government to sell land when and more importantly where it was needed. Consequently, in March 1853, he reserved 700,000 acres 'for public purposes' where pre-emptive rights did not apply. [119] The *Argus* saw this as evidence that 'the lands are really to be unlocked at last'. [120]

Some members of the Legislative Council were highly critical of the squatters but in July 1852, they were defeated on a motion of extend the boundaries of the 'settled' districts and that leases be issued for the 'intermediate' districts so that the Government could bring forward land for sale without having to rely on its reserves. Squatters were unwilling to compromise and La Trobe's executive voted with them to demand the immediate issue of leases for all pastoral land outside the 'settled' districts. [121] This was a short-lived victory and radical members of the Council mounted a strident public campaign that led to a compromise of sorts. Protests against the squatters were bitter reflecting long established hostility and the need for outlets for capital than genuine land hunger. [122] Growing demand for land came from successful diggers and urban speculators. For miners, land signified social status; for urban businessmen it was a way to break the economic and political dominance of the 'squattocracy'.

---

[119] *Geelong Advertiser*, 24 March 1853.
[120] 'Unlock the Lands', *Argus*, 14 July 1853, reported the creation of the reserve at Kyneton on 12 July, evidence that 'the squatters shall give way, when necessary, to land purchasers and legitimate settlers'.
[121] 'Legislative Council', *Argus*, 29 July 1852, p. 6, indicates that this was defeated by 18 to 9 with 'the Nominees and Squatters coalescing in opposition to the popular representatives in the mode which is making both so odious...' See also, 'Legislative Council', *Argus*, 6 August 1852.
[122] See, for instance, 'The Squatter Swindle', *Argus*, 14 December 1852, p. 6, and 'Anti-Squatter Meeting', *Argus*, 16 September 1852, p. 6, reporting a meeting at Geelong while *Argus*, 25 August 1852 p. 6, reported a similar meeting in Melbourne two days earlier.

On 18 August 1852, La Trobe informed the Council that he did not have the power to issue leases immediately and that he would refer the issue to the Colonial Office. In the interim, squatters would be allowed to buy their homestead blocks of up to 640 acres and the existing policy of reserving land for future sale would continue.[123] While this may have satisfied many squatters, some extremists such as William Campbell reacted bitterly. In early September they restated their position and La Trobe forwarded their views to the Colonial Office along with a wordy dispatch on the issue.[124] La Trobe then gradually brought more land on to the market. With growing demands from diggers for land, in December 1852 a deputation from Castlemaine with a petition signed by thirteen hundred miners was promised that land near the diggings would be sold as soon as they were surveyed. In early 1853, the movement concentrated on the need for sales of 20, 40 and 80 acre lots near the fields. Calls for a colonial reform association were initially voiced at a conference in April 1852 but it was not until November 1852 that an association with a broad radical platform was formed.[125] Increasingly the Colonial Reform Association concentrated on the land question and the *Argus*, with monotonous regularity called on the government to 'Unlock the Lands'.

Despite criticism from the squatters, La Trobe went ahead with the sale of land and in the eighteen months from April 1853, half a million acres of land was sold. This policy, however, came too late to avert criticism caused by his indecision. Increasing land values was an inevitable result of growing demand for land: in 1851 land was about 25 shillings an acre but by 1853 this had risen to £4. The Colonial Office received La Trobe's dispatch at the end of 1852 and its response, sent to La Trobe eleven months later, approved his actions and passed the power of decision to the Victorian Government. It could establish reserves and sell land under existing legislation, could vary the classification of the districts as it thought best, and could

---

[123] 'The Leases', *Argus*, 21 August 1852, commented on La Trobe's indecision.
[124] William Campbell's position can be found best in his *The Crown Lands of Australia being an Exposition of the Land Regulations, and of the Claims and Grievances of Crown Tenants*, (John Smith & Sons), 1855, pp. 31-54.
[125] 'The Conference', *Argus*, 15 April 1852, p. 4.

issue leases to squatters but should confine pre-emptive rights to the homestead block. The news arrived in the colony in March 1854. [126] The Colonial Office had come down firmly against the squatters and the *Argus* celebrated that: 'The lands are unlocked at last!' This was over-optimistic. Many miners had simply given up or moved to the United States, South Australia or NZ where land was freely available. In reality, land remained firmly locked to the poorer farmers. The democratisation of the constitutional structures established in 1856 with electoral reform and the introduction of universal manhood suffrage in all the colonies reflected the realisation by liberals and radicals that squatter control over local politics needed to be broken before Crown Lands could be thrown open to settlement.

The Ballarat Reform League, with its main demands won in 1855, duly developed into a new organisation, the Victoria Land League, with its emblem the Southern Cross, and its motto 'Advance Australia'. [127] With the influx of population in the gold rushes, the distribution of these sheep walks to agricultural settlers became a vital political issue. The diggers and other newcomers took up politics seriously in 1857, the first year of the new parliament. At public meetings throughout the colony, they elected delegates to go to Melbourne to convene something akin to a Chartist convention. The democratic members of the Victorian Assembly provided a great stimulus to the Land League and its People's Parliament that met nightly at the Eastern Market in Melbourne for three weeks in July 1857, in close proximity to St. Patrick's Hall where parliament was sitting. 89 delegates from 32 places throughout the colony met to formulate a people's land policy and to fight for the People's Charter, especially payment of members. The Convention organisers realised that parliament, especially the Legislative Council, would not readily yield to the popular cry to 'unlock the lands'. One of the most articulate justifications of land rights was written by 'Peter Papineau',

---

[126] Lieut.-Governor La Trobe on the Squatting Question', *Argus*, 8 March 1854, p. 4, 'The Despatches on the Squatting Question', *Argus*, 17 March 1854, p. 4, 'The Despatch on Squatting', *Sydney Morning Herald*, 22 March 1854, p. 4.

[127] Serle, p. 269; *Argus,* 29 December 1856, 20 January 1857; letter by Gray in *Age*, 5 May 1857.

who published *Homesteads for the People* in Melbourne in 1855, a pamphlet that has all the hallmarks of Henry Chapman's writing. [128] Wilson Gray declared that the convention would have to fight its own battle on the hustings and led a deputation to the government to warn of 'national calamity' if land reform were delayed. [129] As David Goodman explains 'democratic politics in the 1850s...placed the issue of right to the land at the very centre of public discussion'. [130]

Despite the whiff of rebellion, the debates of the Convention, chaired by the able Wilson Gray, were fully reported in the newspapers and the League organised a monster petition signed by 70,000 people demanding that Crown Land be placed on sale to former gold miners. [131] This huge popular mobilisation had very little effect. The Legislative Council mauled the land bill and rejected the bill to pay members passed by the Assembly. Frustrated the Convention tried force and some of its supporters stormed parliament but the demonstration backfired when parliamentary supporters of the cause quickly distanced themselves from the demonstrators. To get its land policy adopted the Convention knew it needed a more democratic parliament. It demanded that members be paid and that the goldfields and the towns obtain their proper representation. Gray denounced the 'bare-faced iniquity' of the Haines government's Land Bill and advocated an alternative measure based on free selection, abolition of sale by auction and open pasturage over Crown Lands. He joined a deputation to request the government to withdraw its Land Bill and his experience of the American land system greatly helped the Convention's subcommittee on land. He also became president of the council formed after the Convention was dissolved in August.

---

[128] 'Papineau, Peter', *Homesteads for the People and Manhood Suffrage*, (S. Goode), 1855.
[129] Woods, Carole, 'Moses Wilson Gray, (1813-1875)', *ADB*, Vol. 4, pp. 287-288.
[130] Goodman, David, 'Making an Edgier History of Gold', McCalman, Iain, Cook, Alexander, and Reeves, Andrew, (eds.), *Gold: forgotten histories and lost objects of Australia*, (Cambridge University Press), 2001, p. 32.
[131] Serle, p. 272.

Free Selection

The very public discussions by the Land League had a strong impact on the Land Acts eventually passed by the Victorian Parliament in the 1860s to unlock the land from the squatters' grasp. The means for breaking the squatters' control over land was the passage of Selection Acts in the 1850s and early 1860s in the then new eastern mainland parliaments of Victoria, NSW and Queensland and South Australia. Robertson's Land Acts in NSW, Nicholson's and Duffy's Acts in Victoria, and Strangways' in South Australia attempted to put small farmers on the land. The first in Victoria in 1860 and NSW the following year were the outcome of sustained popular agitation. [132] Gold-diggers and town workers rallied to break the squatters' monopoly and give the poor man his chance; their leaders promised an Australia transformed into a pre-industrial utopia of smiling homesteads. Reformers were primarily concerned with removing squatters' privileges and providing all colonists with the opportunity to acquire land and prosper from it so that a resilient class of small yeoman arable farmers would become the backbone of Australian society. The aim of selection was to establish a free market in land.[133]

Although the development of democratically elected representation was an important element of the move towards free selection, it was recognised that the implications of democracy were entirely different in Australia than they were in England:

---

[132] 'Free Selection before Survey', *Empire*, 5 November 1860, p. 5.
[133] A selection is a small area of land rented from the Crown for agricultural or grazing purposes. From the 1850s it referred to small farmers settling on Crown Lands occupied by squatters. These smallholders (or selectors) were to pay for their land in instalments; they had to reside on the land and improve it. In NSW the selector could settle on land in the pastoral domain without prior notice or official survey: this was free selection by free selectors. Elsewhere the land was withdrawn from the pastoralist and surveyed before it was open for selection. Most types of selections are convertible i.e., they are designed to be converted to freehold tenure after a fixed number of years provided the selector fulfils certain conditions such as residence by the selector or his bailiff on the land, improvement to a set value, and payment of an annual rent.

Here it is considered synonymous with Chartism...In Australia it has a very different signification. For there the greatest extension of the suffrage must contain a conservative element which does not, and cannot exist in England. The humblest working man in Australia, possessed of the right of voting, knows well that the high rate of wages prevalent in the colony renders it a matter of certainty that with ordinary industry he must one day become the possessor of property...Men so situated may with safety be entrusted with the suffrage, where it might be dangerous to confer it on the starving Lancashire cotton spinner... [134]

With the possibility of egalitarian property relations, where all have access to the land, democracy becomes conservative in character.

It is a democracy which has no connection with socialism as a system, nor with republicanism as a force of government. There is nothing proletarian in its character, nor levelling in its object. In short, it is the natural and inevitable result of the material circumstances—the political necessities and social relations of the colony...All that can be done is to direct its operation in the minds of the people to wise and noble ends... [135]

'The land question', in the minds of contemporary English and Australian commentators, was about turning the 'poor man' into a propertied man. This aspiration, however, was not always translated into reality.

In NSW, for instance, by 1859 political reform led to the election of a Liberal government with a majority in the Legislative Assembly. [136] Led by Charles Cowper, Henry Parkes and John Robertson, Secretary for Lands, it pledged to unlock the Crown Lands and make them available for free selection. The Crown Lands Alienation Act 1861 and the Crown Lands Occupation Act 1861 were the first substantial Crown Lands legislation passed after self-government. This did not occur without opposition from the squatter-dominated Legislative Council. However, the political

---

[134] *Daily News*, 15 November 1861.
[135] Editorial, *Empire*, 24 August 1860, p 4.
[136] For the administrative context of reform in NSW in the 1860s see, ibid, Golder, Hilary, *Politics, Patronage and Public Works: The Administration of New South Wales*, Volume 1, 1842-1900, pp. 158-180.

impasse was broken when Governor Sir John Young agreed to Cowper's request that he nominate sufficient new members of the Upper House to ensure the legislation had a majority. Eventually the pastoral interest reluctantly passed the legislation if only to prevent the prospect of more radical measures. Not for the last time was the weakness of the nominated Upper House to being swamped by additional nominees demonstrated.

These Acts introduced to Parliament by John Robertson, provided for the principles of 'conditional purchase' and 'selection before survey' respectively. [137] The legislation was moderate in tone—Robertson was a landowner and squatter himself and could be relied on to protect existing property rights—and his proposal to make Crown Lands available for free selection was not without safeguards. The Crown Lands Alienation Act 1861 provided that between a minimum of 40 and maximum of 320 acres of Crown Land could be selected by anyone at a price of £1 per acre irrespective of quality. The selector was free to select his land anywhere in the rural districts, irrespective of whether it was currently part of a squatter's run or not. An initial payment of twenty-five per cent was required with the remainder repaid within three years at an interest rate of five per cent. This meant that only those urban workers who had accumulated sufficient capital had the opportunity of becoming owners of land. Robertson's vision of an Australian yeoman class had no place for the impoverished and was firmly grounded in middle-class values of self-help and individualism. The Crown Lands Occupation Act 1861 was intended to regulate the use of land for pastoral purposes and gave to persons who had acquired land by purchase, the right to lease adjoining land up to three times their purchased holdings at a rental of £2 per square mile per year. The Crown Lands Acts of 1861 divided the NSW population into two hostile camps and encouraged conflict between the squatter and selector for the purchase and possession of land. [138]

The nature of the legislation gave rise to speculation and behaviour of dubious legality by squatters and selectors

---

[137] Nairn, Bede, 'Robertson, Sir John (1816–1891)', *ADB*, Vol. 6, pp. 38-41.
[138] Morrissey, S., *Squatters and Selectors: A Social and Economic History*, (Oxford University Press), 1983.

in NSW and Victoria. This was largely absent in South Australia and Queensland where the legislation stressed actual occupation of the land. The legislation made it possible for squatters to protect their runs by careful selection of their prime sections. Squatters engaged in 'peacocking' to prevent selectors from making viable selections and selectors selected the best part of a run and then offered it for sale to squatters at outrageous prices. 'Dummying was also employed by squatters and selectors. By setting up false buyers or 'dummies', usually relatives, employees, or business associates to select land on their behalf, squatters ensured that they acquired the choicest land, especially on river frontages or lakes, and maintained their large holdings. They placed dummy huts, or flying huts as they were sometimes known, at strategic points around a property to give the appearance of activity and settlement and so to evade the regulations of compulsory residency and improvements on selections. Selectors also used dummying as a means of overcoming limitations on the size of selection blocks. Dummying' and 'peacocking' were rife, but it was twenty-two years before the 1861 Acts were officially called into question.[139]

Was free selection a success?

The 1861 Crown Lands Acts and their successors conveyed the great bulk of land alienated in NSW from the Crown into private hands and were considered by some as a 'squatting triumph'. However, this view is somewhat limited. Baker argued that the middle-class, committed to equality of opportunity and resentful of the squatters' aristocratic pretensions, were in charge of this movement and its chief beneficiaries.[140] Some historians have seen Robertson's great land reforms as necessary for the triumph of the 'middle classes', including owners of freehold land

---

[139] In 1875, amendments to the Crown Lands Acts of 1861, made dummying illegal, but made no administrative provisions to detect such a practice. Dummying continued largely unchecked mainly because the Department of Lands was not given the resources to support the provisions in the Act.

[140] Baker, D. W. A., 'The Origins of Robertson's Land Acts', *Historical Studies of Australia and New Zealand*, Vol. 8, (1958), pp. 166-182.

and urban liberals, over the squatters but that they lacked any sincere intention of concentrated land settlement.

Colonial society did not lend itself to this over-simplification. Many urban residents, of diverse occupations and financial and political interests, were squatters; many rural residents were neither freeholders nor squatters and many were liberals. Robertson himself reflected this social and political complexity: he was a country freeholder, held squatting leases and leased land to tenant farmers but he was also the most radical of the liberals. He certainly saw his gruelling campaign as an honest and balanced attempt to resolve the long-standing land problem for the benefit of all colonists, not least the landless country people. He was the great apostle of social equilibrium through land justice and he tapped city and country resentment, built up over a generation, to become one of the great land reformers of the nineteenth century: a result of his individuality and integrated colonial formation. Only he could have responded to the deeply-rooted levelling cry for easy access to land for all who wanted it and he saw in agriculture a dual opportunity for land settlement and economic differentiation. The 1861 legislation implied that the land would be thrown open to the people. Although the government passed the legislation, it did little else and the free operation of the land market benefited investors and speculators rather than the small farmer. Much of the rural poverty that was widespread in NSW and Victoria after 1865 stemmed from selectors trying to make a living on property that was too small and unsuitable for small-scale farming.

To succeed selectors needed knowledge of farming and sufficient business acumen to operate in a market economy. They are needed sufficient capital to invest in improvements in farm buildings, fences and boring wells for water. The acts produced varying results: good in South Australia; initial failure and then success in Victoria; scattered success in NSW. The wheat belt developed in NSW only after the Selection Act was amended and railways reached across the Dividing Range. In their first years the Selection Acts had exactly the opposite effect from their intention: over wide areas the squatters became the owners of lands they had formerly leased and very few smallholders established themselves. This greed and cunning and the short-sightedness and carelessness of legislators were prominent themes in the first histories of these events. Manning Clark rejected this interpretation and attributed early failure to the smallholders' lack of capital and equipment, their ignorance of agriculture and inadequate transport. [141] In addition, the small market for agriculture in the interior until the arrival of railways has been stressed much more in subsequent accounts. Local studies, most notably on the Riverina[142], western Victoria[143] and the Darling Downs[144] have explored the complex uses to which the acts were put and the part played by local circumstances and opportunities. What counts as agricultural failure might be success when a selector sold out with advantage to a squatter and selected more land elsewhere or accumulated enough land to become a small grazier. To get sufficient land, all the members of a family took up a selection, a loophole which worked in the small man's favour. The role of family in securing land and providing unpaid labour to work it has been highlighted in recent studies of gender and family.

The emphasis on the preconditions for agricultural success has had the unfortunate consequence of downplaying the significance of amendments to the legislation that put the smallholder in a stronger position. Without them, it would have been the pastoralists who exploited the new opportunities for agriculture and farmers would have been their tenants. The amendments abolished or limited open sales at auction, made dummying more difficult, gave more generous terms for repayment, and subjected the whole process to close administrative surveillance. This at last solved the dilemma which had beset legislators: if they made it easy for the small man to get land, it was also easier for the squatter's dummy. Under such provisions the modern wheat belt in South Australia and northern Victoria took shape in the 1870s with the cultivators being small freeholders. In NSW agriculture developed later, after the squatters had secured much of the good land, with the consequence that more of the wheat

---

[141] Clark, *Select Documents* 2, pp. 93-98.
[142] Buxton, G. L., *The Riverina, 1861-1891: an Australian regional study*, (Melbourne University Press), 1968.
[143] Ibid, Powell, J. M., *The public lands of Australia Felix: settlement and land appraisal in Victoria 1834-91 with special reference to the Western Plains*.
[144] Waterson, D. B., *Squatter, selector and storekeeper: a history of the Darling Downs, 1859-93*, (Sydney University Press), 1968.

farmers were tenants or share-croppers. Closer settlement Acts later provided more land for owner-cultivators.

By the 1880s, the Robertson selection process in NSW was outdated and further reform was necessary to differentiate between different categories of grazing land. The Lands Department proved unable to support the provisions of the reforms largely because it was not provided with the resources to do so. By the time free selection had been operating for ten years, confusion in the centralised system was immense, and delays for up to two years were common. Six million acres of reserves had been declared, but not surveyed. Dishonesty in the ways in which the Acts were implemented by bureaucrats, contributed to the failure of selectors to get onto the lands. The Land Committee of 1873-1874 commented on the delays within the Department but the most damning evidence suggested that some land agents actively supported the squatters. Ten years later, Messrs Morris and Ranken were appointed as Commissioners to undertake an inquiry into the state of public lands and land laws in NSW the first detailed examination of the 1861 legislation. Their report described the operation of free selection as

> ...intelligible chaos in which the rights and interests of all mainly concerned have been the sport of accident, political interest and departmental disorder. [145]

The centralisation of land administration in Sydney compounded by problems of ambiguity in the legislation were regarded as the primary causes for delays, arrears of work, individual loss and a failure to delegate responsibilities for transactions to the districts in which they arose.

Following the 1883 Commission of Inquiry, the existing Crown lands legislation was repealed by the Crown Lands Act, 1884. It also introduced a decentralised system to promote more equitable land settlement but this had little effect on the established pattern of the colony's growth. The Crown Lands Act 1884 limited free selection and

---

[145] Morris, A., and Ranken, G., *Report of the Inquiry into the State of the Public Lands and the Operation of the Land Laws*, (Thomas Richards), 1883, cit, Epps, William, *Land Systems of Australasia*, (S. Sonnenschien), 1894, p. 32.

changed its character. NSW was divided into three districts, East, Central and West. The Central and Eastern Divisions were divided into sixteen Land Board Districts with each District administered from a central Land Board Office. In East Division, selection of between 640 and 1,268 acres was allowed while in the Central Division selections of 2,560 up to four square miles were possible but selection in the Central and Western Division was limited to half the area of each pastoral lease (the Resumed Areas) that could be leased back to the lessee on an annual basis until selected. The Western Division was to have no freehold but Homestead Leases could to taken out up to 10,240 acres for a period of 28 years. This system operated for a decade but rural recession led to decline in pastoral settlement and the Resumed Areas were generally not settled. By 1893, 8 million acres of settled land had been abandoned and there was a shift to smaller sheep flocks often run in conjunction with wheat production. In 1901, however, following a Royal Commission on the condition of Crown tenants in the Western District, it was removed from the overall control of the Lands Department and places in the hands of the Western Lands Commission responsible directly to the Minister for Lands. The system established in 1884 remained the basis of Crown land legislation until 1999.

In NSW, free selection meant that selectors arrived unannounced on the squatters' runs. Without surveyed boundaries or fences, squatter and selector fought each other over water, access roads, and the straying of horses and stock. Selectors were hounded off the land by squatters or eked out a precarious existence in a place and time unsuited to agriculture. These were the experiences treated by Henry Lawson in his verse and stories. [146] Steele Rudd in *On Our Selection* also depicted poverty-stricken and blighted selectors in Queensland's Darling Downs. [147] These powerful images helped to disguise the success achieved in South Australia and Victoria from the 1870s and subsequent success elsewhere.

---

[146] See, for example, Lawson, Henry, 'The Bush Fire', *Children of the Bush*, (Angus and Robertson), 1907, pp. 131-133, and 'Settling the Land', *While the Billy Boils*, (Simpkin, Marshall, Hamilton), 1897, pp. 18-23. See also, Clark, M., *In search of Henry Lawson*, (Macmillan), 1978, pp. 50-52.

[147] Rudd, Steele, *On Our Selection*, (Bulletin Newspaper), 1899, pp. 2-16 provided a vivid account of the problems facing selectors.

Conclusions

From the foundation of the colony of NSW in 1788, the principle of *terra nullius* was adopted and all lands were vested in the Crown. Land policies were largely developed in the Colonial Office and contained in its instructions to governors. Between 1787 and 1831, governors made land grants to settlers and emancipated convicts and a private market in land sales developed as a consequence. The 1820s marked a tentative transition from land grants to the sale of land and the foundation of two chartered land companies in NSW and VDL. Between 1788 and 1831, the amount of land alienated by grants and sale by private tender amounted to just over 3.90 million acres. Following the Ripon Regulations of 1831, land grants ceased and the colonial government sold land to settlers at auction but land sales were limited due to high upset prices that increased during the 1830s. Initially the introduction of land sales did not act as a barrier to the occupation of land and between 1832 and 1838, when there was a 'mania' to occupy land for pastoral purposes, 1.45 million acres were sold by auction. However, as upset prices per acre rose to 12 shillings an acre in 1839 and then £1 in 1842, there was a dramatic reduction in the amount of land sold. [148] Parallel to the introduction of land sales, a squatter movement developed in NSW and between 1836 and 1847, the colonial government legitimised squatter holdings by issuing licenses to sheep farmers occupying Crown Lands beyond the Nineteen Counties. Finally, between 1847 and 1856 by which time the different colonies had been given responsibility for their own land policies, colonial government maintained high land prices and awarded long-term leases to holders of sheep runs.

Before the discovery of gold in 1851, land was alienated in a largely haphazard way and little regard was taken of what its best usage could be. With what most settlers regarded as unlimited land resources, there was no need for conservative land management or sustainable development and that made colonial agricultural development very different from experiences in Britain where land was less plentiful and, to maximise yields, had to be managed with considerable care. This view was at odds with the desire of

---

[148] Ibid, Buck, A. R., *The Making of Australian Property Law*, p. 81.

the Colonial Office to establish colonies that replicated the social and economic system of land use in Britain and to restrain the spread of settlement despite widespread calls for further land from settlers. There was also a significant mismatch between imperial policies and how those policies were implemented or ignored in the colonies. The sheer scale of the Crown Lands made development control and policing extremely difficult tasks while growing political consciousness among settlers saw the development of powerful political interests, especially pastoralists, who were able to oppose and obstruct imperial policies, especially after elective representation to Legislative Councils was introduced.

There were also tensions within colonial society, especially in NSW, between those who advocated an expansive agrarian ideology based on large-scale pastoral farming and those who believed in the ideal of establishing smaller-scale yeoman farming. Calls for 'unlocking the land' coincided with the demographic explosion of the 1850s and the achievement of colonial responsibility for the administration of Crown Lands. The unjustifiably famous legislation of 1861 foreshadowed the opening of lands to the people, but beyond passing this legislation the colonial government proved ineffective in implementing it and largely indifferent to the aspirations of the 'people' and laissez-faire allowed the rich to grow richer. Urban financial interests probably gained more from the Crown Lands Acts than rural settlers. Despite the introduction of 'free selection' in NSW in 1861, the big winners were not the yeoman farmers but the pastoral companies, the banks and finance companies that financed the squatters and pastoral companies and the government by way of revenue. The economic, social and political parameters of the land legislation in NSW after 1860 ultimately reflected the needs of the few at the expense of the majority.

Violence and protest

Violence accompanied the birth of NSW and was a constant presence during its formative years. Before the colony was two months old, convicts had been flogged and hung for theft. Violence, threats of violence and fear of violence were major features of the system. The convict system, intended to reduce crime through deterrence, was central to Australian experience during the first two generations of settlement. Until the 1840s, both NSW and VDL were brutalised societies in which protest of whatever form was vigorously resisted and repressed. [1]

In late 1830, the Ribbon gang led by Ralph (Ralf) Entwistle, an English convict, terrorised the Bathurst district of NSW. He had been sentenced to transportation for life to NSW for stealing clothing and was sent to work near Bathurst. In November 1829, Entwistle and another convict were given the task of driving a bullock dray to Sydney. On returning to Bathurst, they paused for a dip in Macquarie River. Unfortunately, Governor Darling was in the area to inspect the new settlement of Bathurst. The convicts were seen as they were trying to dress and were arrested by a group of soldiers led by Thomas Evernden, Bathurst's police magistrate between 1825 and his death in 1839, 'a martinet of extravagant refinery', charged with 'causing an affront' to the Governor and sentenced to a public flogging of 50 lashes. It is generally argued that Entwistle was embittered by this incident and that it led to the first major rebellion of convicts west of the Blue Mountains. [2] However, given the interval before he took any action and the lack of planning involved, this seems a less likely explanation than the actions of a landowner who deprived Entwistle of food and clothing in an attempt to maximise the profitability of his farm. [3]

---

[1] Moore, Tony, *Death or Liberty: Rebel Exiles in Australia 1788-1868*, (Murdoch Books), 2010, is a detailed survey of resistance and rebellion.

[2] On the problem of bushrangers in the 1820s and early 1830s, see, Fletcher, B. H., *Ralph Darling A Governor Maligned*, (Oxford University Press), 1984, pp. 180-182.

[3] *The Sydney Monitor*, 30 October 1830, p. 3, in an article attacking Governor Darling, suggested that the insurrection at

On 23 September 1830, Entwistle and at least four others absconded from the farm where they were assigned in Fitzgerald's Valley, some twelve miles south-west of Bathurst. 4 The men visited other properties in the following days stealing food, guns, horses and ammunition and persuading or more probably forcing other convicts to join in until the band grew to around fifty men. At one farm owned by Thomas Everden, James Greenwood, a convict overseer was killed for refusing to allow any of his convicts to join the uprising. 5 The convicts there joined the gang, bringing its membership to about 80 though few had any enthusiasm for the cause and deserted at the first opportunity. 6 A press report mentioned the leader of the gang wearing 'a profusion of white streamers in his hat', probably an attempt by Entwistle to dispel the view that he was merely leading a band of thieves. This later led to comparisons being drawn with the Ribbonmen, nationalist rebels in Ireland, though there is no evidence that the Irish members of Entwistle's band had any political agenda. 7

On 25 September, recognising that he could not rely on the majority of his men, Entwistle dismissed all but the most committed and with no more than a dozen men rode off towards the caves alongside the Abercrombie River. 8 Local landowners reacted quickly to the activities of the band and on 27 September raised a small volunteer cavalry corps of twelve men under William Suttor who, with the assistance of two Aborigine trackers, found the men the following day in a rocky glen near Captain Cook's Lookout

---

Bathurst 'had taken place on account of bad and insufficient food and clothing'.
4 *Sydney Gazette and New South Wales Advertiser*, 7 October 1830, p. 2.
5 *Sydney Gazette and New South Wales Advertiser*, 30 October 1830, p. 2, details the attack on Greenwood, the subsequent trial and executions. *The Australian*, 3 December 1830, p. 3, included a long letter on 'The Bathurst Insurgents' by an 'eye witness'.
6 *Sydney Gazette and New South Wales Advertiser*, 2 October 1830, p. 2, commented that 'the disturbances at Bathurst are, as usual, enormously exaggerated'. See also the report on *Sydney Gazette and New South Wales Advertiser*, 7 October 1830, p. 3.
7 http://www.entwistlefamily.org.uk/ribbongang.htm states that six of those eventually hanged were from Ireland.
8 Fry, Eric, (ed.), *Rebels and Radicals*, (Allen & Unwin), 1983, and Williams, Stephen, *Ralph Entwistle & the Bathurst Insurgency*, (Popinjay Publications), 1994, provide accounts of the rebellion.

and prepared to attack. The ensuing gun battle, during which an estimated 300 shots were exchanged, lasted for about an hour but with night approaching and short of ammunition, the volunteers withdrew. [9] Suttor's leadership was later criticised as lacking both energy and courage. [10] This setback led Major Donald McPherson, commandant at Bathurst to send a detachment of mounted soldiers of the 39th Regiment and mounted police on 29 September. Led by Lieutenant James Brown and reinforced with a second volunteer force, the troops sighted the rebels on 30 September at Bushrangers' Hill and set off in pursuit. But, having lost two men and five horses in the ensuing fight, Brown fell back and allowed Entwistle and his men to continue westwards. [11]

The band was active along the Lachlan River for the next few days but then dropped out of sight. Entwistle was finally located on 13 October by a detachment of ten mounted police and in a sharp exchange of fire near Borowa Plains lasting twenty minutes, four of the police were wounded and three rebels shot and captured. The rebels were again allowed to escape as the police were low on ammunition but the following day, faced with a fresh detachment of the 39th Regiment force-marched from Sydney under Captain Horatio Walpole and by various parties of volunteers, Entwistle and his six remaining men surrendered without a struggle. [12] They were charged with murder, bushranging and horse thieving in Bathurst and tried before a Special Commission consisting of Chief-Justice, Sir Francis Forbes and a jury of eight military officers, two of whom had taken part in the campaign against the rebels. The outcome was never in any doubt and on 3 November 1830, ten rebels were hanged, the first and

---

[9] Suttor's account, dated 7 October, was printed in *Sydney Gazette and New South Wales Advertiser*, 21 October 1830, pp. 2-3.
[10] *The Sydney Monitor*, 27 October 1830, p. 3, included a poem 'The Wars of Bathurst' in which Suttor was comprehensively satirised for his failure against the rebels.
[11] Darling to Sir George Murray, 5 October 1830, *HRA*, Series I: Vol. 15, pp. 769-770, provides details of the alarm among settlers and Darling's response.
[12] This was briefly reported in *Sydney Gazette and New South Wales Advertiser*, 20 October 1830, p. 2.

largest public hanging in Bathurst. [13] The Bathurst rising was one of many protests by convicts either individually or collectively as they sought to escape the vicious inequities of a penal society. [14]

The gallows stood at the apex of the system of terror. There were 260 executions between 1824 and 1860 in VDL while in NSW 1,296 persons were sentenced to death between 1826 and 1836 of whom 363 were hanged.

> On Monday, Alexander Pearce, for murder, and yesterday, John Butler, for sheep stealing, John Thompson, Patrick Connolly, James Tierney and George Lacey, for burglary and highway robbery, were executed in this town pursuant to their sentence. Pearce's body was, after it had been suspended the usual time, delivered at the hospital for dissection. We trust these awful and ignominious results of disobedience to law and humanity will act as a powerful caution; for blood must expiate blood! and the welfare of society imperatively requires, that all whose crimes are so confirmed, and systematic, as not to be redeemed by lenity, shall be pursued in vengeance and extirpated with death.[15]

One in ten convicts spent time in the various penal settlements where discipline was harsh and unremitting. The chain-gangs provided another means of brutal regimentation. At any one time in the 1830s about a thousand convicts worked in the gangs in NSW and around seven hundred in VDL. Being consigned to the gangs was meant to be a severe punishment, 'as severe a one as could be inflicted on man', according to VDL's Sir George Arthur while his NSW counterpart Richard Bourke believed that 'the condition of the convicts in the chain gangs was one of great privation and unhappiness'. [16] For fifty years the lash was the most widely used form of punishment: quick, cheap and readily available. During the 1830s, 38 per cent of VDL convicts were flogged. [17] Almost any misdemeanour could

---

[13] Hirst, J. B., *Convict Society and its Enemies: A History of Early New South Wales,* (Allen and Unwin), 1983, pp. 133-150.

[14] See, Atkinson, Alan, 'Four patterns of convict protest', *Labour History,* Vol. 37, (1979), pp. 28-51, for an important study of the nature of convict protest.

[15] 'Executions', *Hobart Town Gazette,* 24 July 1824, p. 2.

[16] Cit, Evans, L., and Nicholls, P., *Convicts and Colonial Society, 1788-1853,* (Cassell), 1976, pp. 77-78.

[17] Robson, L. L., *The Convict Settlers of Australia,* (Melbourne University Press), 1976, p. 102.

warrant the lash, 'absconding, insubordination, drunkenness, indecent conduct, neglect or wilful mismanagement of work, neglect of duty, indecent or abusive language, swearing, insolence, or other disorderly conduct'. [18] In NSW between 1830 and 1837, 42,000 floggings were administered with each victim receiving on average over 40 lashes. In just over eight years the 'cat' was laid across convict backs more than 1.6 million times. [19] Flogging deterred some but hardened and brutalised others.

The floggings are hideously frequent. On flogging mornings I have seen the ground where the men stood at the triangles saturated with blood, as if a bucket of blood had been spilled on it, covering a space three feet in diameter, and running out in various directions, in little streams two or three feet long.... Frere gave him fifty more lashes, and sent him the next day to grind cayenne pepper. This was a punishment more dreaded by the convicts than any other. The pungent dust filled their eyes and lungs, causing them the most excruciating torments. For a man with a raw back the work is one of continued agony. In four days Rufus Dawes, emaciated, blistered, blinded, broke down 'For God's sake, Captain Frere, kill me at once!', he said. [20]

By all accounts the convicts waged sullen, surreptitious resistance against the system. Occasionally resistance flared into open rebellion most seriously at Castle Hill to the west of Sydney in March 1804 but insurrection was exceptional.

Escaped convicts, or 'bolters' were of greater concern to the authorities than armed rebellion. From the earliest years of settlement convicts slipped out of the settlements and attempted to survive on the outer fringes of the

---

[18] West, J., *The History of Tasmania*, rev. ed., A. G. L. Shaw, (ed.), (Angus & Robertson), 1971, p. 414. See also, Nichol, W., 'Malingering and convict protest', *Labour History*, Vol. 47, (1984), pp. 18-27.
[19] Shaw, Alan, *Convicts and the colonies: a study of penal transportation from Great Britain and Ireland to Australia and other parts of the British Empire*, (Faber), 1966, p. 202.
[20] Clarke, Marcus, *For the Term of His Natural Life*, (George Robertson), 1874, pp. 339-340. Although the novel is made up of a series of semi-fictional accounts of actual event, its descriptions of the brutality of the convict system are generally regarded as accurate.

colonies by armed robbery. As settlers moved into the interior the scope for successful bushranging increased. The extent of bushranging is evident in over 6,800 articles published in newspapers in NSW and VDL between 1820 and 1860. These suggest that there was a dramatic increase in the 1830s (2,353 articles, over double the number printed in the 1820s), that there was a further increase in the 1840s (3,282 articles) and that its incidence did not decline significantly until the 1850s (1,780 article). In VDL between 1810 and 1825, there were as many as 100 'bolters' in the bush at any one time. The more formidable gangs led by men such as Cash and Brady were well armed and mounted and knew enough about the country frequently to elude capture, to travel rapidly from district to district and to retreat when pressed to carefully prepared hide-outs. They had well maintained networks of sympathisers and informers among the convict population. During the early 1820s, 'bolters' were so successful in their raids that settlers abandoned farms in the interior and moved into the larger towns for security. Inevitably perhaps crime was more prevalent in the convict colonies than in Britain although most felons were convicted for crime against property rather than offences against the person. In the mid-1840s, the crime rate in VDL was double that in England with convicts and ex-convicts responsible for more than 90 per cent of serious offences. [21]

Whether the violence of the convict system survived the end of transportation has been a matter of much debate but little resolution. In *Convicts and Colonies*, Shaw argued that socially, transportation did 'no great harm'. [22] By contrast, Lewis believed that 'a tradition of brutality and sadism was established at the centre of Australian life during the convict years' and that it 'has left a lasting if indefinable imprint'. [23] However, the evidence from Tasmania does not support this view. As ex-convicts died or left the colony, its crime rate fell away and by the 1880s was the lowest in Australia. Celebrating the fading of the 'hated stain' of convictism a Tasmanian statistician argued in 1891 that 'crime and pauperism' were 'simply noxious foreign

---

[21] Ibid, p. 343.
[22] Ibid, p. 358.
[23] Lewis, G., 'Violence and Nationalism in Australia', *Arena*, Vol. 43, (1976), p. 53

plants' that found 'no congenial soil in Tasmania for their propagation'. [24]

Although there were many occasions for mass political action and widespread public anger during the nineteenth century, the bloodshed at the Eureka Stockade assumed heightened significance because it was exceptional. Violence was often threatened by orators, but it rarely went further than fiery rhetoric, brawling and minor destruction of property; its nature was symbolic more than physical. Even in the outback where practically everyone was armed, guns were rarely used to settle political or even personal disputes. The struggle against imperial land policy in the 1840s, against continued transportation in VDL in the early 1850s and in favour of radical land legislation later in the decade all produced mass meetings, torch-lit processions and the implicit threat of violence. Shaw observed:

> Up to the middle of the 19th century...it seems clear enough that Australians had taken over the British tradition of threatening--and if need be of using violence, as a normal means of influencing political processes. Such methods seem to have achieved considerable success, either because the authorities thought it not worth-while to make a serious issue of what to them were somewhat petty concerns, or because they realised that the force at their disposal was relatively weak; because of these easy successes, the protests did not have to be taken so far as to create a revolutionary tradition akin to that which... [existed] in many other countries. [25]

Only a small minority of the initial convicts in NSW were convicted of political offences. Some were skilled workers, who later found their way into the early craft unions. Others were primarily Irish or drawn from the British middle-classes. In 1793, the barrister Thomas Muir and the clergyman Thomas Palmer were transported for sedition with three leaders of Scottish corresponding societies. Over the rest of the decade the authorities in Britain enacted repressive legislation against political radicals and strikers and some of those convicted were also

---

[24] Reynolds, H., "That Hated Stain': the Aftermath of Transportation in Tasmania', *Historical Studies*, Vol. 14, (1969), pp. 22-23.
[25] Shaw, Alan, 'Violent Protest in Australian History', *Historical Studies*, Vol. 15, (1973), p. 554

transported. After the 1798 Irish Rebellion, hundreds of prisoners arrived in Sydney, raising the spectre of an Irish republican revolt in the colony. The authorities, haunted from the earliest days by 'the nightmare vision of a convict republic' were prepared to take harsh measures to prevent trouble. In 1806, the convict Joseph Smallsalts was punished for extolling the revolutionary views of Thomas Paine.

> Joseph Smallsalts, a prisoner for life, was on Tuesday last brought before the Judge Advocate, charged with having uttered expressions of an inflammatory and seditious tendency...the offender was ordered 100 lashes...and sent to public labour at the Coal Mines at Newcastle. He was permitted to travel to Newcastle...with a label on his back, on which Thomas Paine was decyphered in large characters, the culprit having declared that 'he would be worse than Tom Paine if thwarted'. [26]

John Dunmore Lang later joked that in some countries the clergy might 'take the fleece' but NSW was the only place they were 'openly authorised...to take the hide also, or to flay their flock alive.' [27] Religion sometimes restrained the Irish but because of its hostility to the Roman Catholic Church, the authorities seldom allowed Catholic priests to hold mass before 1810 when they recognised priests would counsel submission to the system. However even among the Irish, probably only a minority heeded such counsel. Other clergy had very little effect. Many non-Catholic convicts were hostile to religion because, from the 'flogging parson' Samuel Marsden onwards, clergymen were part of a repressive apparatus, often serving as magistrates and ordering the lash.

Although the 'nightmare vision' did not materialise, in fact rebellion was reasonably common. The problem was that it was always fragmented, poorly organised and collapsed easily. Actual convict rebellions were betrayed with monotonous regularity and within convict society resistance took many forms short of armed uprising. The

---

[26] *Sydney Gazette and New South Wales Advertiser*, 30 March 1806.
[27] Lang, John Dunmore, *An Historical and Statistical Account of New South Wales*, 2 Vols. (Longman, Brown, Green, and Longmans), 1837, Vol. 2, p. 233.

most common response of forced labour was passive resistance:

> Early dispatches show governors almost foaming at the mouth over the difficulty of getting the convicts to raise crops. Slow-down is the meaning of the 'neglect of duty' charges that crop up so often in the punishment books. It is the situation behind respectable settlers' endless complaints about the laziness of the convicts. [28]

Such tactics often won substantial informal concessions, first limitations on the hours of work, then the right to work for pay part of the time. In addition, convicts found ways to corrupt their overseers and cheat the system: for instance, during King's governorship the convict clerks in the government stores turned to forgery on a considerable scale. These accomplishments do suggest a degree of unity among sections of the convicts that made more violent forms of resistance possible from time to time although solidarity was always very fragile. This had much to do with to the uneven and changeable circumstances of convict life:

> ...clerks and tradesmen might get to work at their usual jobs, though they might also be set to labouring; labourers might be set to quarrying stone...or following a flock of five hundred sheep around in the bush. Women would not be sent to heavy outdoor labour, but might indiscriminately find themselves doing housework in central Sydney or deep in the bush. The personal relations in which this work was done varied unpredictably in both public and private sectors...A single convict's career...might lead through all these types of situations in a few years. [29]

Middle-class radicals were effectively bought off. The small number of 'gentlemen' convicts received preferential treatment, comfortable jobs and early tickets-of-leave. Many of the political prisoners transported after the 1798 Irish Rebellion, the 1838 Canadian Rebellions and the upheavals of the Chartist movement were not really ideological rebels, while others seem to have tired of strife

---

[28] Ibid, Connell, R. W., and Irving, T. H., *Class Structure in Australian History*, p. 47.
[29] Connell, R. W., and Irving, T. H., *Class Structure in Australian History, Documents, Narrative and Argument*, (Longman Cheshire), 1980, p. 45.

by the time they reached Australia. The exceptions were the Young Irelanders transported to VDL and Fenians transported to WA for their respective involvement in the abortive 1848 and 1867 Irish Rebellions. With Irish-American assistance, some were able to escape. [30] What was clear was that the authorities emphasised the temporal and divine rightness of the punishment of those punished, that those who transgressed recognised the inevitability of punishment.

---

[30] See, Brown, Richard, *Famine, Fenians and Freedom, 1840-1882*, pp. 492-500, 521-536.

9 A convict society

Thirty years ago, Russel Ward suggested, '...the convict influence on Australian society was very much more important than has usually been supposed.' [1] For him, the unusual and discomfiting origins of Australian society had plagued Australian history and Australians' view of themselves for many years and had led people to ignore their convict heritage, to excuse it or to downplay its significance in the development of Australian identities and institutions. [2]

When sentenced to transportation, prisoners were initially imprisoned and then removed to the hulks prior to transportation but often had to wait up to two years before they were actually taken to Australia. As soon as a ship arrived, it notified the port if there were male or female convicts on board. [3] The port authorities inspected the ship and the convicts who were then brought up on deck and inspected by the Colonial Secretary or other officials. Convicts were interviewed to ascertain qualifications and previous work history and then usually assigned to free settlers or emancipated convicts as servants, farm labourers and mechanics. The more dangerous prisoners provided labour for public works such as road-making in gangs of up to 300 men guarded by the military. [4]

---

[1] Ward, Russel, *The Australian legend*, second edition, (Oxford University Press), 1978, p. 37.
[2] Smith, Babette, *Australia's Birthstain: the startling Legal of the convict era*, (Allen & Unwin), 2008, examines why Australians are still misled by myths about their convict heritage.
[3] Bateson, Charles, *The Convict Ships, 1787-1868*, (Brown), 1959, remains the best study of the sea voyage though some of his statistics have been questioned.
[4] Ibid, Shaw, Alan, *Convicts & the Colonies*, and ibid, Robson, L. L., *The Convict Settlers of Australia*, examine the process and the participants. Robson, L. L., 'The origins of the women convicts sent to Australia 1787-1852', *Historical Studies of Australia and New Zealand*, Vol. 11, (1963), pp. 43-53, and Robinson, Portia, 'From Colleen to Matilda', in Costello, Con, (ed.), *Ireland and Australia: Bicentenary Essays 1788-1988*, (Gill & Macmillan), 1986, pp. 96-110, look at the role of women.

The convict system operated on the basis of a graduated hierarchy where through good behaviour progressively rewarded convicts with increasing levels of freedom and where poor behaviour led to the removal of these privileges, restrictions on freedom, imprisonment and corporal punishment and in extreme cases capital punishment. [5] Tickets-of-leave were normally granted after four or six years allowing convicts to work for themselves outside the 'assignment' system on condition that they remained in a specified area, reported regularly to authorities and attended divine worship each Sunday. Ticket-of-leave men were also allowed to marry or bring their families from Britain and to acquire property, but they were not permitted to carry firearms or to board a ship. Minor offences could see a ticket revoked by the magistrates and the holder returned to government service. Certificates of freedom were available to convicts who had completed their sentences. Convicts serving a life sentence generally received pardons rather than tickets of leave. Conditional pardons allowed convicts their freedom as long as they remained in the colony while absolute pardons remitted the entire sentence and convicts were free within and outside the colony and could return to Britain. [6]

The attitude of Australians to their 'convict past' and the perceived ignominy of their nation's origins have changed significantly in the past half century but remains a source of some ambiguity. Unlike the United States that at least could point to the role of 'pilgrims and martyrs' in its national development, until the 1950s the criminality of Australia's founders posed a real problem since the convict past retained its immediacy. There was simply no way of ignoring Australia's origins as a penal colony but it was rationalised in different and contradictory ways. For some, British convicts were 'exiled' for trivial offences and were barely criminals at all while others saw them as thieves pure and simple whose character need not be whitewashed. Convict transportation was seen as part of the country's

---

[5] Byrne, P. J., "The public good': Competing visions of freedom in early New South Wales', *Labour History*, Vol. 58, (1990), pp. 76-83.

[6] Durston, Gregory, Magwitch's Forbears: Returning from Transportation in Eighteenth-Century London, *Australian Journal of Legal History*, Vol. 9, (2005), pp. 137-158.

economic history, a central element in producing the wealth and later 'freedom' of the colonies rather than a matter of social origins. The economic benefits of convictism outweighed moral questions about why individuals ended up on the convict ships. By the 1920s, convicts were seen as the victims of misfortune, oppressed and persecuted by those corrupt and culpable elites in Britain for whom the Australian colonies (that 'poisonous prison') epitomised aristocratic tyranny and the suffering of displaced 'Village Hampdens'. [7] Convicts may have been redeemed but historians still knew little about who they were or how they lived and worked.

In the 1950s and 1960s, Manning Clark, Alan Shaw and Lloyd Robson challenged the prevailing 'romantic' view of convicts as more sinned against than sinning. [8] Based on an analysis of a one in twenty sample of transported convicts, Robson concluded:

>...the convicts were neither 'village Hampdens' nor merely 'ne'er-do-wells from the city slums.' But if the Hampdens are placed on one side of a scale and the ne'er-do-wells on the other, the scale must tip toward the ne'er-do-wells. [9]

Robson's work formed the foundation of a view of convict transportation that became firmly entrenched for the next twenty-five years. Convicts were largely work-shy, unskilled urban thieves and prostitutes, who probably contributed little to the economy.[10] Even left-wing

---

[7] Wood, G. A., 'Convicts', *Royal Australian Historical Society: Journal and Proceedings*, Vol. 8, (4), (1922), pp. 177-208, and Roberts, D. A., "More sinned against than sinning': George Arnold Wood and the noble convict', in Gare, D., and Ritter, D., (eds.), *Making Australian History: Perspectives on the Past since 1788*, (Cengage Learning Australia), 2007

[8] Ibid, Shaw, Alan, *Convicts and the colonies*; Clark, C. M. H., 'The origins of the convicts transported to eastern Australia, 1787-1852', *Historical Studies*, Vol. 7, (1956), pp. 121-135, 314-327, and ibid, Robson, L. L., *The convict settlers of Australia*.

[9] Ibid, Robson, L. L., *The Convict Settlers of Australia*, pp. 157-158.

[10] Moore, F., *The convicts of Van Diemen's Land, (1840-1853)*, (Cat & Fiddle Press), 1976, Alexander, Alison, *Tasmania's Convicts: How Felons Built a Free Society*, (Allen & Unwin), 2010, and Hirst, J. B., *Convict society and its enemies: a history of early New South Wales*, (Allen and Unwin), 1983.

historians concluded that the bulk of the convict population was unable to combine effectively to challenge the conditions under which they toiled. [11] This tradition of historical writing reached its zenith in Robert Hughes' international bestseller, *The Fatal Shore* depicting Australia as a vast gulag populated by convicts who were largely from the ranks of a professional criminal class and produced crime in the same way that hatters produced hats and miners coal. [12] In reality, there is scope for arguing that it was industrialising Britain that was the Gulag while convict Australia, at least until 1822, represented a new and tantalisingly modern approach to work management. [13]

The publication of *Convict Workers* in 1988 had a profound impact on the way transportation was viewed, reinvigorating convict historiography towards a more nuanced approach. [14] Written by economic historians and based on quantitative analysis of a sample of nearly 20,000 convicts transported to NSW, it challenged the prevailing consensus. Historians had previously focused on qualitative accounts written by middle-class gaolers, chaplains and other moral entrepreneurs but as Sturma had already pointed, a moral ideology played an important part in controlling convict labour and this was widely reflected in middle-class nineteenth century writing about convicts. [15] The 'reformed' convict was the man or woman who made a profit for a master or mistress, while those who resisted merely confirmed their wickedness. [16]

---

[11] McQueen, H., 'Convicts and rebels', *Labour History,* Vol. 15, (1968), pp. 3-30, and Connell, R. W., and Irving, T. H., *Class Structure in Australian history: documents, narrative and argument,* (Longman Cheshire), 1982, pp. 44-50.

[12] Hughes, R., *The Fatal Shore: a history of the transportation of convicts to Australia, 1787-1868,* (Collins Harvill), 1987, p. 165.

[13] Robbins, W. M., 'Australia's First Job Descriptions and the Formalised Management of Convict Labour', p. 1, http://www.mngt.waikato.ac.nz/departments/Strategy%20and%20Human%20Resource%20Management/airaanz/proceedings/auckland2007/070.pdf

[14] Nicholas, Stephen, (ed.), *Convict workers: reinterpreting Australia's past,* (Cambridge University Press), 1988.

[15] Sturma, M., 'Eye of the beholder: the stereotype of women convicts 1788-1852', *Labour History,* Vol. 34, (1978), pp. 3-10.

[16] Garton, S., 'The Convict Origins Debate: Historians and the Problem of the 'Criminal Class'', *Australian and New Zealand Journal of Criminology,* Vol. 24, (1991), pp. 66-82.

Convict Workers found that most convicts were victims of economic conditions, were generally convicted of petty non-violent crimes especially theft and most did not re-offend at the completion of their sentence. The Proceedings of the Old Bailey Project reinforces this conclusion. Of the 30,329 verdicts between 1787 and 1868 where the punishment was transportation, 27,877 (91.92 per cent) were for theft and 654 (2.16 per cent) for violent theft. Of these, over a quarter involved simple larceny and a fifth involved pickpocketing. Bedfordshire gaol records between 1803 and 1868, during which time 633 individuals were transported, show a similar pattern of thefts though what was stolen reflected its largely rural nature. Nicholas and Robson agreed that most convicts were single, male and in their twenties, two-thirds were Protestant, one-third Catholic, most came from cities or industrialised towns and possessed skills that were broadly representative of the British and Irish working-classes. Both the Proceedings of the Old Bailey Project and the records for Bedfordshire suggest that the optimal age of offending for males was between 16 and 25 and for females 17 and 22 but also that Nicholas and Robson were broadly correct in their emphasis on the high levels of criminal activity in offenders' twenties. Nicholas pointed out that three-quarters of convicts were literate compared to 58 per cent among the English working-classes. [17]

Although convict administration was present in the main settlements, convicts were largely dispersed through the urban and rural settled areas and were involved in a range of activities. Most convict industry such as road and building construction and quarrying and timber-felling took place in non-institutional settings where convicts worked and lived in small work groups. Controversially, *Convict Workers* claimed that these skills were effectively deployed by the colonial state in a system that was marked by efficiency and in which the lash was largely silent. The extent to which the lash was deployed suggests that it was far from 'silent' but the claim for efficiency may have some merit. Rather than restricting the development of the colonial economy, cheap drafts of compliant and often skilled convict labour stimulated colonial growth rates.

---

[17] Nicholas, S., and Shergold, P. R., 'Unshackling the Past', in ibid, Nicholas, S., (ed.), *Convict Workers*, pp. 3-12.

Skilled labour was an important commodity in the new colony. Kent and Townsend claim that convicts with agricultural skills were also in high demand as supply was scarce and convicts had to be rationed. [18] For instance, the failure of the Australian Agricultural and Van Diemen's Land Companies to obtain promised levels of convict labour suggests that there is some truth in this conclusion. Given that labour shortages were an important feature of the early decades of the development of NSW and VDL and the difficulties of matching convict skills with the economic needs of the colonies, it remains unclear to what extent convict labour contributed to colonial growth rates.

Convict Workers moved the spotlight away from 'who were the convicts' and focused instead on the nature of the colonial experience of transportation. [19] This has been evident in research in the last ten years. [20] What has been highlighted was the nature of convict experience and how individual experience changed with increasing levels of freedom or repression. There has also been a growing awareness of how the practical arrangements for what constituted appropriate treatment changed over the fifty year's operation of the system in NSW and VDL. The publication of Babette Smith's *Australia's Birthstain* in 2008 and Grace Karskens' *The Colony* the following year explored and exploded some of the myths and stereotypes of the convict system and examined the part played by convicts and emancipated convicts in the formation of early Australian society highlighting especially the blurring of class lines that accompanied it. The diversity of convict work and work relations and how both changed over time has also been a fruitful area of research. Robbins has explored how convicts influenced their employment conditions negotiating and resisting the approaches adopted by the colonial state and by employers to control

---

[18] Kent, D., and Townsend, N., (eds.), *The Convicts of the Eleanor: Protest in rural England, New Lives in Australia*, (Merlin Press), 2002.
[19] Reid, K., 'Moving on: resolving the convict origins debate', *Australian Studies,* Vol. 12, (1), (1997), pp. 139-155.
[20] Gibbs, M., 'The Convict System of New South Wales: A review of archaeological research since 2001', *Archaeology in Oceania,* Vol. 47, (2012), pp. 78-83, Roberts, D., 'The 'Knotted Hands that Set is High': Labour History and the Study of Convict Australia', *Labour History*, Vol. 100, (2011), pp. 33-50.

labour and maximise profitability.[21] He dismisses the view that convict labour was not systematically structured rather he argues that convict administration under Macquarie displayed a deliberate attempt to regulate, motivate and direct labour in ways that were designed to increase productivity, something achieved by defining convict work through job descriptions and regulations. There has also been a proliferation of local studies; for instance, Walsh in his studies of the Tocal area has examined aspects of assignment and rural labour.[22] In addition, there have been developments in considering the available archaeological evidence of the convict heritage and the Internet has boosted the growth of genealogical consideration of individuals pre- and post-transportation. The result is that the convict system is now recognised as more variegated in nature and that the five decades in which it functioned in NSW and VDL saw significant alterations in the nature of convict experience and they how mediated that experience in relation to both the colonial state and employers.

Evans and Thorpe accept *Convict Workers'* broader conclusions on the nature of transportees but were critical of the book's portrayal of the colonial economy as a benign, paternalistic structure where the values of the state ruled supreme. *Convict Workers* claimed, 'The convicts speak not in words, but out of the dry dust of the statistics collected in order to regulate their convict life', but Evans and Thorpe pointed out only five transportees, all male, were named in the entire book.[23] They claimed that along with the horrors of the lash, punishment cells and penal

---

[21] Robbins, W., 'The Lumber Yards: a Case Study in the Management of Convict Labour, 1788-1832', *Labour History*, Vol. 79, (2000), pp. 141-161, 'Management and Resistance in Convict Work Gangs, 1788-1830', *Journal of Industrial Relations*, Vol. 45, (3), (2003), pp. 360-377, 'The Supervision of Convict Gangs in New South Wales, 1788-1830', *Australian Economic History Review*, Vol. 44, (1), (2004), pp. 79-100, 'Spacial Escape and the Hyde Park Barracks', *Journal of Australian Colonial History*, Vol. 7, (2005), pp. 81-96, and 'Governor Macquarie's Job Descriptions and the Bureaucratic Control of the Convict Labour Process', *Labour History*, Vol. 96, (2009), pp. 1-18.

[22] Walsh, Brian, 'Assigned convicts at Tocal: 'ne'er-do-wells' or exceptional workers?', *Journal of Australian Colonial History*, Vol. 8, (2006), pp. 67-90, provides a detailed local study.

[23] Ibid, Nicholas, S., (ed.), *Convict Workers*, p. 45.

stations, real convict voices had been largely ignored in *Convict Workers*. [24] Subsequent work has examined the way in which convicts articulated their lives, whether through resistance and other acts such as involvement in black market activities or by writing but this has raised more questions than they have answered. [25] Analysis of convict narratives uncovered a plethora of problems in interpreting these texts. Many of them were heavily shaped by middle-class editors to prepare them for wider consumption while others were at odds with archival accounts, raising questions over their reliability. [26]

For instance, when John Frost, the Chartist leader during the Newport Rebellion in 1839 was finally released in 1856, he embarked upon a speaking tour of Britain. His lectures presented as a sensational exposé of the horrors of transportation and were dominated by a tale of brutal tyranny, arbitrary rule, physical torture, human degradation and destruction faced by convicts that was neither novel nor new. Allegations of cruelty, inhumanity and the prevalence of 'unnatural' sexual acts among convicts had been central to attacks on transportation for decades, transportation to VDL had ended in 1853 and Frost's audiences were undoubtedly well aware in the 'horrors' of convict life. His *Horrors* were not a condemnation of the penal colonies *per se* but a radical allegory of a coming British anarchy. His lectures set out a

---

[24] Evans, R., and Thorpe, W., 'Power, punishment and penal labour: *Convict Workers* and Moreton Bay', *Australian Historical Studies,* Vol. 25, (1992), pp. 90-111, and Nicholas, S., and Shergold, P., 'Convicts as migrants', in ibid, Nicholas, Stephen, (ed.), *Convict workers,* p. 45.

[25] Duffield, I., 'Problematic passages: 'Jack Bushman's' Convict narrative', in Duffield, I., and Bradley, J., (eds.), *Representing convicts: New Perspectives on Convict Forced Labour Migration,* (Leicester University Press), 1997, pp. 20-42, Maxwell-Stewart, Hamish, 'The search for the convict voice', *Tasmanian Historical Studies,* Vol. 6, (1), (1998), pp. 75-89, and, Frost L., and Maxwell-Stewart, Hamish, (eds.), *Chain letters: narrating convict lives,* (Melbourne University Press), 2001. There is a brief discussion of convict literature produced by Canadian transportees in Brown, Richard, *Three Rebellions: Canada 1837-1838, South Wales 1839 and Victoria, Australia 1854,* pp. 487-488, 499-500.

[26] See, for example, Boissery, Beverley, *A deep sense of wrong: the treason, trials and transportation to NSW of Lower Canadian rebels after the 1838 rebellion,* (Dundurn Press), 1995.

nightmarish vision of the ultimate physical and spiritual degradation that tyranny would bring. [27] Just as with the convict experiences of the Patriotes from Lower Canada recounted in their memoirs, Frost was using the convict experience to re-establish a political agenda that had already, like transportation, been superseded. Attempts to use the words of convicts to create accurate windows on the past have proved as problematic as earlier endeavours to use middle-class descriptions of convict lives to try and establish who the convicts were.

The development of Australia lay in the creation of self-sustaining settlements involving convict labour that was intended to be retributive and reformative, but also economically productive. Although motivated initially by penal imperatives and imperial ambitions, Australian settlement curtailed laissez-faire ideas replacing them with strict state-controlled economic and social regulation. For much of the early colonial period, convicts dominated the colonial working population and convict labour built the colony's infrastructure and its emerging industries and businesses. Its nature, management and outcomes and its role in penal policy was integral to the ways in which the colony was administered and interpreted between 1788 and 1850.

---

[27] Frost published several versions of his account of convict life: *A Letter to the people of the United States showing the effects of aristocratic rule*, New York, 1855, *The Horrors of Convict Life: two lectures*, (Holyoake), 1856, and a reworked version published in two editions in 1857, *A Letter to the People of Great Britain and Ireland on Transportation showing the effects of Irresponsible Power on the Physical and Moral Conditions of Convicts, by John Frost, late of Van Diemen's Land*, (Holyoake), 1857. Reid, Kirsty, 'The Horrors of Convict Life: British Radical Visions of the Australian Penal Colonies', *Cultural and Social History*, Vol. 5, (4), (2008), pp. 481-495.

10 Establishing the rule of law

Elsewhere there might be the sultan's caprice, the *lit de justice,* judicial torture, the slow-grinding mills of the canon law's bureaucracy and the *auto-da-fe* of the Inquisition. In England by contrast, king and magistrates were beneath the law, which was the even-handed guardian of every Englishman's life, liberty and property. Blindfolded Justice weighed all equitably in her scales. The courts were open, and worked by known and due process. Eupeptic fanfares such as those on the unique blessings of being a free-born Englishman under the Anglo-Saxon derived common law were omnipresent background music. Anyone, from Lord Chancellors to rioters could be heard piping them (though for different purposes).[1]

In this stylish statement Roy Porter pointed to the rule of law's popularity as a rhetorical device in eighteenth century England where it was 'the central legitimising ideology, displacing the religious authority and sanctions of previous centuries.' [2] Arising out of struggles between the monarchy, Parliament and the courts, the rule of law protected the citizen, individual liberty and private property against the arbitrary actions of the State protect by placing constraints on arbitrary authority. The ruling class used the rule of law ideology to enhance their power, but it also acted as a break on that power. All citizens from the monarch to the poorest citizen became bound by the rule of law and could settle their disputes in the courts presided over by independent judges. [3]

---

[1] Porter, Roy, *English Society in the Eighteenth Century,* (Penguin), 1982, p. 149.
[2] Thompson, E. P., *Whigs and Hunters: The Origin of the Black Act,* (Penguin Books), 1977, pp. 263-264; see also Hay, Douglas, 'Property, Authority, and the Criminal Law', in Hay, Douglas, et al., (eds.), *Albion's Fatal Tree: Crime and Society in Eighteenth-Century England,* (Penguin), 1977, pp. 17-63
[3] According to Neal, the rule of law had at least three elements: 'general rules laid down in advance, rational argument from those principles to particular cases, and, at least in a developed form, a legal system independent of the executive for adjudication of disputes involving the general rules.' These elements must be applied in the everyday working of the legal system and not be used by the governing classes for rhetorical effect or only when convenient to their interests. See ibid, Neal, David, *The Rule of*

By 1800, most people in Britain and in colonial settler communities recognised that the rule of law had definition even if it was also a highly flexible notion ranging from the inherently legal to the explicitly political. What it meant in practice depended on who was employing it and for what purpose. It embraced the right to justice by the judgement of one's peers conceded in Magna Carta and trial by jury. Habeas Corpus gave people protection from detention without trial and was given a statutory basis in the 1670s. [4] Freedom from the suspension of or dispensation from laws of Parliament was secured after the Glorious Revolution of 1688. The independence of the judiciary was established by the Act of Settlement 1701 but was not fully effective in the colonies until the mid-nineteenth century. [5] This was linked with the right to trial according to law and application of established legal procedures grounded in rational principles. Finally, freedom from intrusion and arrest using general warrants was developed by the courts during the mid-eighteenth century. [6] Closely allied and overlapping with the rule of law were a series of 'constitutional rights', some of which seemed settled, at least in Britain, such as no taxation without representation and the right to petition the Crown and other protections such as freedom of the press, freedom of association, freedom of assembly and freedom of conscience.

Expediency, rhetoric and the rule of law

The ideology and practice of the rule of law were exported to Britain's colonies. According to the English jurist William Blackstone, writing in 1765:

...if an uninhabited country be discovered and planted by English subjects, all the English laws are immediately there in

---

Law in a Penal Colony: Law and Power in Early New South Wales, p. 67.

[4] This right was given legislative recognition in the Habeas Corpus Act 1679.

[5] The constitutional position of the judiciary was established in the Act of Settlement, 1701, s3.

[6] See Leach v Money (1763) 19 *State Trials*, 981; Entick v Carrington (1765) 19 *State Trials*, 1045.

force. For the law is the birthright of every subject, so wherever they go they can carry their laws with them.[7]

In practice, as David Neal has pointed out, the extent to which English law was applied in colonial courts and what the rule of leave meant depended on conditions in a particular colony. [8] The penal nature of NSW led to a practical application of the law to address the unique circumstances of a colony founded by convicts.[9] The governor was vested with autocratic power and authority, but controlling convicts meant that considerable tact and flexibility was necessary to establish effective government. Governor Phillip and his successors soon recognised the difficulty of applying some English legal doctrines if the colony was to move beyond its origins as a place of incarceration. Criminal law was applied by the Court of Criminal Jurisdiction consisting of the Judge-Advocate and six military or naval officers and by justices of the peace. It often proved harsh in its punishments with its widespread use of flogging and hanging and the introduction of internal transportation to penal settlements such as Norfolk Island. To balance this, governors introduced tickets-of-leave from 1801 and conditional pardons as rewards for good behaviour providing a way for former convicts to make the transition to civil society.

It was, however, in the civil laws where most innovation was seen and convicts, women and debtors developed rights they were denied in Britain. The Court of Civil Jurisdiction consisted of the Judge-Advocate, who with the exception of Richard Dore (1798-1799) were not legally trained until 1811, with two lay assessors and did not follow English law or precedents on a number of issues. The early Judge-Advocates were amateurs and their judgements often interpreted English law creatively based on their own attitudes to and knowledge of law. In 1788, David Collins, the first Judge-Advocate, heard a suit for damages by convicts Henry and Suzannah Kable against the

---

[7] Blackstone, William, *Commentaries on the Laws of England*, (University of Chicago Press), 1979, Vol. 1, pp. 104-105.
[8] Ibid, Neal, David, *The Rule of Law in a Penal Colony: Law and Power in Early New South Wales*, pp. xii, 15, 32 and 64.
[9] McLaren, John, *Dewigged, Bothered & Bewildered: British Colonial Judges in Trial, 1800-1900*, (University of Toronto Press), 2011, pp. 122-125.

captain of the vessel they sailed in for the loss of their effects.[10] Collins found in their favour awarding them £15, a decision that meant that suits could be brought by and against convicts and recognition of their commercial and land transactions, something that would not have been allowed in Britain. Under the early governors, the court recognised the right of women to enter into contracts and permitted them a share in property left in NSW when wives and children were deserted by their husbands or cohabiters who had returned to England. This represented a radical shift from the limitations on married women's status in English law. Collins and Richard Atkins also reduced the harsher features of the law of debt by allowing payment in kind by crops or livestock with extended periods to pay rather than imprisoning the debtor. It was far better to have farmers producing food and paying off their debts than languishing in prison.

As convicts, emancipated convicts, and their children formed a large proportion of the population until the 1840–87 per cent in 1828 falling to 63 per cent by 1841–British governments wanted civil liberty to be restricted by the colonial administration and that placed restrictions on the rule of law. Until 1823, governors, even if good governance necessitated an element of rule by consent, had extensive prerogative and discretionary powers. They agreed with the British government that the transported criminals needed to be kept under close surveillance and punished firmly and quickly if they broke the rules. [11] The problem with this was that colonists, whether free settlers or emancipated convicts, felt they were too closely watched and demanded that the rule of law be recognised as protection against the arbitrary rule of the governor. While the colonists waged their campaign for civil and legal rights, the courts became 'a sort of broking house of power.' [12] Colonists expressed their opposition to the actions of governors, while governors

---

[10] Nagle, John F., *Collins, the courts & the colony: law & society in colonial New South Wales 1788-1796*, (Indiana Press), 1996.
[11] For the debate on the kind of convicts sent to Australia, see Garton, Stephen, 'The Convict Origins Debate: Historians and the Problem of the 'Criminal Class,"* Australian and New Zealand Journal of Criminology*, Vol. 24 (1991), pp. 24-82, and Dyster, Barrie, 'Convicts', *Labour History*, Vol. 67, (1994), pp. 74-83.
[12] Ibid, Neal, David, *The Rule of Law in a Penal Colony: Law and Power in Early New South Wales*, p. 190.

sought to have their actions and authority legitimised by judicial process.

Neal argues that the political ideas and discourse of the colonists were based on their English legal inheritance as systematised by Blackstone in his *Commentaries on the Laws of England*. [13] They claimed 'no more than their rights as free-born Britons, rights guaranteed by Magna Carta, Habeas Corpus, the Bill of Rights, [and] the Act of Settlement.' Seeking 'to forge a new social and political order out of the penal colony', they demanded an independent judiciary, trial by civilian, not military, jury, and representative government. [14] The first important step in establishing the rule of law in NSW occurred in 1824 when the newly established Supreme Court began to hear cases. It was staffed by judges appointed in England who supported the principles of the rule of law and were a major counterweight to the power of the governors. The achievement of a nominated legislature, the development of a free press and the introduction of civilian jury trials were significant landmarks in entrenching the rule of law. But it was not until a partially elected legislature was formed in 1842 that, Neal argues, NSW finally changed from a penal colony to a free society, a situation helped by the ending of transportation to the colony.

NSW was by any standards a different sort of colony, like Newfoundland 'an anomalous society too divided and too backward to be able to work the old representative system'.[15] In its early decades the lack of conventional legislative bodies and the single-minded commitment of governors to establishing and maintaining a convict colony meant little open debate over the meaning of the rule of law. This occurred, despite the fact that Lord Sydney, the intellectual planner of the colony seems to have imagined it as a society of freemen. Under the practical disciplinary guidance of Governor Phillip and his successors various forms of radicalism including republicanism were entertained by some convicts, especially those transported

---

[13] Ibid, Neal, David, *The Rule of Law in a Penal Colony: Law and Power in Early New South Wales*, pp. 23 and 25.

[14] See, Blakeney, Michael, 'The reception of Magna Carta in NSW', *Journal of the Royal Australian Historical Society*, Vol. 65, (2), 1979, pp. 124-142.

[15] Ward, J. M., *Colonial self-government: the British experience 1759-1856*, (Macmillan), 1976, p. 130.

for political crimes, such as Maurice Margarot and 'General' Joseph Holt, one of the many United Irishmen to be transported. [16] However, as long as these people were subject to penal law, most had no accepted public forum for voicing their views.

After 1800, the discourse and rhetoric of the rule of law began to be invoked more openly by groups in the colony who stood outside the executive and judiciary. Convicts were pardoned and emancipated. Some of these, such as Margarot, continued to nurse their radical views while others deployed the rule of law out of pure self-interest. George Crossley, a former attorney transported for perjury, appealed to both English law and the rule of law to vindicate his own dubious machinations in the court room, whether as litigant or legal adviser.[17] As Governor Philip Gidley King discovered convicts or emancipated convicts who were literate, gentlemanly and with influential friends in Britain, could cause problems when they invoked the Ancient Constitution, Magna Carta and the rights of freeborn English men in their correspondence with the executive. King was well aware that his predecessor John Hunter had been recalled after complaints about the Governor's alleged fiscal mismanagement of the colony to the Colonial Office by Thomas Fyshe Palmer, Scottish Martyr turned colonial businessman.[18]

It was self-protective instincts at work then that caused King to react sourly to being castigated for abusing the rule of law by John Grant, in 1805. [19] Grant was transported in 1803 after being sentenced to death for the attempted

---

[16] Ibid, Silver, Lynette, R., *The Battle of Vinegar Hill: Australia's Irish Rebellion*, pp. 128-130 contains pen portraits of several convicts, including Maurice Margarot and Thomas Fyshe Palmer ('Scottish Martyrs'). See also, Roe, Michael, 'Margarot, Maurice (1745-1815)', *ADB*, Vol. 2, pp. 206-207.

[17] Allars, K. G., 'Crossley, George (1749-1823)', *ADB*, Vol. 1, pp. 262-263, and 'George Crossley: An Unusual Attorney', *Journal and Proceedings of Royal Australian Historical Society*, Vol. 44, (5), 1958, pp. 261-300.

[18] Earnshaw, John, 'Palmer, Thomas Fyshe (1747-1802)', *ADB*, Vol. 2, pp. 312-313.

[19] On this see Cramer, Yvonne, (ed.), *This Beauteous and Wicked Place: Letter and Journals of John Grant, Gentleman Convict*, (National Library of Australia), 2000, pp. 89-153, and Lynravn, N. S., 'Grant, John (1776 -)', *ADB*, Vol. 1, pp. 469-470.

murder of a solicitor who had warned him off an heiress with whom he was obsessed. He had arrived in the colony with 50 hogsheads of brandy purchased in Rio and expected, given his social status, to be put on the government pay roll. Governor King, possibly distracted by the aftermath of the Castle Hill Rebellion, was unresponsive to Grant's pleas to be allowed to land his brandy and to be granted a job. The gentleman convict reacted unfavourably when King granted him a conditional pardon in 1805, which he found did not allow him to return to England until the close of his sentence. Irritated, he wrote to the governor quoting Blackstone on the rights of English subjects in 'uninhabited' lands and briefly referring to Magna Carta, argued:

> Now Sir! I ask you as an Independent Englishman, witnessing with astonishment the miserable state to which Thousands of Unfortunate Men are reduced in this country, by what Authority do those in power at home, by what Right do *you, make Slaves of Britons* in this distant corner of the Globe? ... [A]t your Door lies all the blood spilt in the struggle of half-starved Men for Personal Liberty in this Country. [20]

Even though Grant and political prisoners, including Margarot were re-transported for accusing the governor of despotism, they can be said to have kept the discourse and rhetoric of the rule of law alive in the colony, at least in providing a benchmark against which governmental actions should be judged. [21] Grant had also directed similar sentiments to Judge-Advocate Richard Atkins[22] and was called before the judge on the direction of King, convicted of sedition and sentenced to five years hard labour on Norfolk Island and in VDL suggesting that the executive recognised

---

[20] Ibid, Cramer, Yvonne, (ed.), *This Beauteous and Wicked Place: Letter and Journals of John Grant, Gentleman Convict*, p. 105; Grant to King, 1 May 1805, *HRA*, Series I, Vol. 5, p. 537.

[21] King to Under Secretary Cooke, 20 July 1805, *HRA*, Series I, Vol. 5, pp. 534-536, referred to separating Margarot, Henry Haynes, Michael Robinson and William Maum for sowing 'discord in this Settlement'.

[22] Bennett, J. M., 'Atkins, Richard (1745-1820)', *ADB*, Vol. 1, pp. 38-40.

the potential power, and, for them, the subversive quality of this rhetoric.²³

Growing opposition to the arbitrary authority of successive governors came from an emerging colonial elite ready to impress its image of governance and society on the colony. Free settlers, led by John Macarthur, sought to secure their own social and economic interests. While they received a set-back in the wake of the Rum Rebellion of 1808, their disgrace was only short-lived. Free settlers cultivated strong connections with conservative politicians in Britain and sought to exercise their influence both with the imperial government and in NSW.²⁴ They were the group from whom the magistracy was selected and, as a result, this gave them considerable power at a local level. Moreover, with varying degrees of success they sought to put pressure on governors to further their ultimate aim of involvement in government of the colony. Lachlan Macquarie who sought the full inclusion of emancipated convicts in colonial society was not well disposed to them. ²⁵ They fared better with his successors, Sir Thomas Brisbane and Ralph Darling, who faced attacks from the emancipated convicts and their champions.²⁶ The NSW 'Family Compact', 'a snug coterie' and 'a family party' as W. C. Wentworth once described them, was not as consistently influential as its Upper Canadian counterpart because it lacked the executive and legislative bodies through which to influence the political process. Its pressure operated at a vicarious level in that it had to secure its ends through allies in the expatriate colonial administration or through political friends in London.²⁷

---

²³ Ibid, Cramer, Yvonne, (ed.), *This Beauteous and Wicked Place: Letter and Journals of John Grant, Gentleman Convict*, p. 116.
²⁴ Eddy, J. J., *Britain and the Australian Colonies 1818-1831: The Technique of Government*, (Oxford University Press), 1969, pp. 68-70.
²⁵ Ward, J. M., *James Macarthur: Colonial Conservative 1798-1867*, (Sydney University Press), 1981, pp. 20-33.
²⁶ Ibid, Neal, David, *The Rule of Law in a Penal Society: Law and Power in Early New South Wales*, p. 108. See also, Fletcher, B. H., *Ralph Darling, A Governor Maligned*, pp. 103-130, 257-275.
²⁷ Ibid, Wentworth W. C., *Statistical, Historical and Political Description of the Colony of New South Wales, and its dependent Settlements in Van Diemen's Land*, p. 383.

A professional colonial judiciary

The 'creative' development of local law in NSW was not without its critics in Britain. For Jeremy Bentham and his disciples, what they saw as the almost anarchic approach to punishment and rewards was offensive while the perceived immorality of convict and free society were denounced by William Wilberforce and the evangelical movement. It was, however, the Rum Rebellion in 1808 that focused thinking in London on the future administrative and legal nature of the colony. It was important to replace the rebellious military clique with effective administration that had no links with local interests. A decision was also made to replace Richard Atkins, compromised during the rebellion, by a Judge-Advocate who was a lawyer.

The establishment of a professional colonial judiciary in NSW posed a series of problems. Until representative institutions were introduced in 1823 and, arguably until those institutions included an element of election in the 1840s and given the highly personal nature of the gubernatorial power, the judiciary was the only body that could effectively question the authority and actions of governors. Tensions between the judiciary and the colonial authorities emerged from the early 1810s and intensified in the 1820s and early 1830s. Since the Colonial Office also played a major role in the appointment of the colonial judiciary, there was a perhaps inevitable ambiguity in its attitude to judicial decisions especially when those that challenged the authority of colonial governors. Successive Colonial Secretaries found themselves having either to support their governor or their judges reflecting the potential conflict between their political and legal roles. The Colonial Office could and did refer the decisions of the colonial judiciary to English law officers and appeal courts but since colonial judges had yet to achieve the judicial independence that existed in Britain, it was also prepared to recall judges whose actions it found politically unacceptable. This did not prevent their subsequent reappointment in other parts of the empire though the causes of their initial dismissal often reappeared. For instance, Justice John Walpole Willis was dismissed from his position in Upper Canada because he was considered too sympathetic to reformist sentiment in the colony and was prepared to make the administration accountable for its actions. [28] Willis held office in Victoria in the early 1840s with similar results. [29] Similarly, Jeffrey Bent was dismissed as a judge in NSW, largely because of his awkward relationship with Governor Macquarie but reappeared and caused problems in the West Indies first in Grenada then Trinidad and St Lucia and finally British Guiana.[30] Finally, there were continuing tensions between free settlers and emancipated convicts over legal and political rights. Although conservative in attitude, settlers sought to increase their political control over the colony by calling for representative institutions and by restricting the rights of emancipated convicts. For emancipated convicts, the critical issue was how, having served their sentences, they should assert their rights as free citizens and be accorded the same legal rights as free settlers.

The Bents and Macquarie

Although Richard Dore had legal qualifications, the next legally qualified Judge-Advocate, Ellis Bent [31] was not appointed until 1810. [32] His official duties as Judge-Advocate were diverse, extensive and exacting and he presided over the Civil and Criminal Courts. At this time there were emancipated attorneys in the colony who had

---

[28] Wilson, Alan, 'John Walpole Willis', *Dictionary of Canadian Biography*, Vol. 10, 1871-1880, (University of Toronto Press and the Université Laval), 1972, pp. 704-707.

[29] Behan, H. F., *Mr. Justice J. W. Willis: with particular reference to his period as first resident judge in Port Phillip 1841-1843*, (Glen Iris), 1979. See also, ibid, McLaren, John, *Dewigged, Bothered & Bewildered: British Colonial Judges in Trial, 1800-1900*, pp. 170-189.

[30] The commentary in *HRA* stated that Bent was not considered 'blameworthy' by the British government that chose to employ him elsewhere: *HRA*, Series I, Vol. 9, p, 864

[31] Currey, C. H., 'Bent, Ellis (1783-1815)' and 'Bent, Jeffrey (1781-1852)', *ADB*, Vol. 1, pp. 87-92. See also, ibid, McLaren, John, *Dewigged, Bothered & Bewildered: British Colonial Judges in Trial, 1800-1900*, pp. 125-130.

[32] Castlereagh to Macquarie, 14 May 1809, *HRA*, Series I, Vol. 7, p. 81, deals with Bent's appointment following the suspension of Richard Aitkins. Macquarie granted him 1,265 acres of land in the Bringelly District in 1810: Macquarie to Liverpool, 18 October 1811, *HRA*, Series I, Vol. 7, p. 440.

been struck off the rolls when convicted of the offences that had led to their transportation. To prevent litigants bringing their personal enmities and passions into the court, Bent adopted a pragmatic stance permitting three of these ex-convict lawyers to practice in the Court of Civil Jurisdiction; but he admitted them, as he was careful to say, not as attorneys, but only as the specially appointed agents for their clients. [33] He recommended that some attorneys should be encouraged by the government to move to NSW and if and when they arrived, he made it clear he would withdraw the tentative permission given to the ex-convict attorneys to appear in his court.[34] It was not until January 1815 that two attorneys William Moore and Frederick Garling arrived in NSW. [35] Bent's decision reflected his general attitude to the controversy over the status of emancipated convicts and he was prepared to admit to the jury box 'the more respectable and affluent of those who, [having] been transported to this country, had either satisfied the full sentence of the law or received a free pardon'. However, he thought that the appointment of emancipated convicts to more important offices should be decided, 'not on any theoretical grounds, but on a sober and minute consideration of its most remote practical consequences.'

The Colonial Office was disinclined to limit the governor's powers and Bent's proposed reforms were not well received, though a number of them were later incorporated in the New South Wales Act in 1823. [36]

---

[33] His brother Jeffrey took a more conventional stance objecting to the admission of ex-convicts as attorneys: see Macquarie to Bathurst, 22 June 1815, *HRA*, Series I, Vol. 8, pp. 480-483.

[34] Bathurst to Macquarie, 13 February 1814, *HRA*, Series I, Vol. 8, p. 139: Bathurst informed Macquarie that he had selected 'two Solicitors of highly respectable Characters to proceed by an early Opportunity to the Colony', their salaries of £300 per year were to 'become a Charge upon the Colony'.

[35] See, Mckay, R. J., 'Moore, William Henry (1788-1854)', *ADB*, Vol. 2, pp. 255-257 and McIntyre, Joanna, 'Garling, Frederick (1775-1848)', *ADB*, Vol. 1, pp. 426-427. See also, Bathurst to Macquarie, 13 February 1814, *HRA*, Series I, Vol. 8, p. 139, stated that, following Jeffrey Bent's recommendation, two solicitors would be proceeding to NSW.

[36] See, Bent to Liverpool, 19 October 1811, *HRA*, Series I, Vol. 7, pp. 814-821, prints Bent's proposals sent to Lord Liverpool.

Bathurst thought there were 'many advantages' in 'the continuance of a judicial officer who bore a commission exclusively military'. The provision originally introduced in 1787 for the administration of the criminal law was unchanged and Ellis Bent retained the military title of Judge-Advocate. For civil cases, a Supreme Court was established composed of a judge and two assessors, with a jurisdiction in equity, probate and all common law matters except where the cause of action was below £50. When the amount involved was less, cases were to be heard by a tribunal called the Governor's Court, over which the Judge-Advocate was to preside. Bent was acutely critical of these changes. By the time these Letters Patent were promulgated on 12 August 1814, Macquarie and his Judge-Advocate had become estranged because of their opposed views on the status of the judiciary in relation to the executive in NSW. Macquarie took the words of Bent's commission, 'you are to observe and follow such orders and directions from time to time as you should receive from our governor', to mean precisely what they said. Apart from his strong views on the independence of the judiciary, Bent interpreted these words as requiring obedience to lawful orders and he refused to comply with directions that he considered were repugnant to the laws of England or involved his doing or officially agreeing to an illegal act. This was particular evident when Macquarie wished to revise the port regulations initially issued in 1810 to prevent the landing of undesirable individuals from ships in the harbour, smuggling and the escape of convicts. He asked Bent to put his revisions into the appropriate legal language which he did after a significant delay. [37] Bent had concluded that some of the provisions were already covered by British legislation relating to plantations, that others were so broad that they threatened the freedom of innocent people and were consequently illegal, contrary to statutory plantation legislation and repugnant to the laws of England. Macquarie, having modified his original proposals, then ordered the judge to revise and frame the regulations but Bent again refused arguing:

---

[37] Macquarie to Bathurst, 24 February 1815, *HRA*, Series I, Vol. 8, pp. 394-396, 400-424.

I cannot consistently with my ideas of my duty to my Sovereign, or to my own Conscience, undertake to frame the Port Regulations in the Manner and on the Principle proposed by Your Excellency... [38]

The relationship between Bent and Macquarie was made more difficult by Bent's growing ill-health that led to his early death in 1815.

The situation was exacerbated by the arrival, in mid-1814, of Jeffrey Bent who had been appointed as Chief Judge of the Supreme Court of Civil Judicature, created by the Letters Patent on 4 February 1814. [39] Like his brother, Jeffrey had cordial relations with the free settler elite because of mutually conservative views and distaste for Macquarie and his policies.[40] He was unwilling to open his court until lawyers arrived from Britain [41] and as he held his office under the Crown and was not required, like the Judge-Advocate, to obey the orders of the Governor, Macquarie could only report the whole matter to the Colonial Office.[42] These mounting differences led Macquarie to request Bathurst to accept his resignation unless the Bents were removed. [43] Bathurst decided in January 1816 to support his governor and recall the judges. They seemed, he wrote, 'too much disposed to resent the authority of the Governor and to withhold from him that cordial co-operation without which the business of the colony could

---

[38] Bent to Macquarie, 11 January 1815, *HRA*, Series I, Vol. 8, p. 423.

[39] Macquarie to Bathurst, 28 June 1813, *HRA*, Series I, Vol. 7, p. 777, recommending Bent's appointment as a puisne judge: '...of Mr. Jeffery Bent to be the Assistant Judge Could not fail of producing so desireable an Object, when United with the Mild and Conciliatory Manners of his Brother, Mr. Ellis Bent.'

[40] See, ibid, McLaren, John, *Dewigged, Bothered & Bewildered: British Colonial Judges in Trial, 1800-1900*, pp. 130-141.

[41] See, Macquarie to Bathurst, 24 March 1815, *HRA*, Series I, Vol. 8, p. 466: '...frivolous and ridiculous Reason' for not opening his court.

[42] See his complaints in Macquarie to Bathurst, 7 October 1814, Macquarie to Bathurst, 30 November 1814, and Macquarie to Bathurst, 24 February 1815, *HRA*, Series I, Vol. 8, pp. 301-302, 380-383, 389-399.

[43] Macquarie to Bathurst, 1 July 1815, *HRA*, Series I, Vol. 8, pp. 620-622.

not be satisfied'. [44] Bathurst based his dismissal of Jeffery on the latter's closure of his court, even though as a general principle he approved the judge's attitude to convict attorneys. [45]

The disputes between Macquarie and the Bents, aggravated by their abrasive personalities, marked the beginning of tensions between the executive and judiciary that lasted until the late 1820s. Macquarie, as an army officer unused to having his orders questioned, was convinced he was doing the right thing in blending running a penal colony firmly with a more liberal interpretation of how the colony's economy and social structure should develop in which the emancipated convict should have an important role. The Bents were committed to the primacy of English law in the colony at the expense of working with the executive authority and committed to a society in which only free settlers could hold political power. As society moved from its penal origins towards becoming a civil society, there was increasing incompatibility between quasi-military government and a colonial judiciary that asserted its independence from political control.

Barron Field, John Wylde and John Thomas Bigge

Macquarie may have won his battle with the Bents but his success proved short-lived. His administration of NSW, already subject to criticism from within, now found itself under concerted attack in London. The Home Office was critical of Macquarie's desire to incorporate emancipated convicts into colonial society as diluting the punitive and deterrent effect of transportation. The Treasury was, as ever, concerned about rising costs in NSW when there was retrenchment at home. English law officers were critical of Macquarie's assumption of powers that were outside his commission and beyond the law. The Colonial Office was under pressure from these institutions to rein in the perceived excesses of colonial administration. Bathurst's response, in part to satisfy these institutional pressures was a commission of inquiry under John Thomas Bigge, a

---

[44] Bathurst to Macquarie, 18 April 1816, *HRA*, Series I, Vol. 9, pp. 107-108
[45] Bathurst to Jeffrey Bent, 12 April 1816, *HRA*, Series I, Vol. 9, pp. 112-113.

skilled judge and lawyer and effective administrator, to determine the situation in NSW. This included considering the administration of civil and criminal justice and the conduct of individuals in NSW against whom complaints had been made. [46]

Convinced that it would vindicate his actions, Macquarie was initially enthusiastic about the inquiry but soon realised that Bigge was opposed to his attempts to liberalise social relations. Bigge's examination of the administration of justice exposed tensions between colonial government and the law especially problems with the existing court structure and the actions of Barron Field, Chief-Justice of the Supreme Court of Civil Jurisdiction appointed in May 1816 and John Wylde, Bent's successor as Judge-Advocate. [47] Both Field and Wylde were sympathetic to the ideas of the wealthy free settlers in their disputes with wealthy emancipated convicts over the future development of the colony. Field, for instance, was opposed to the introduction of trial by jury and a legislative assembly in NSW. Their legal judgement was often questioned and they disagreed over Field's desire to introduce the complex procedures of English law into a colonial context for which they were ill-suited.

Most importantly, in 1820 Field declared that all who had been pardoned in the colony were still convict attaint, arguing that Governor Phillip and his successors had not followed the correct procedure when applying the royal clemency. This meant that emancipated convicts were declared incapable of being granted or of buying land, holding or conveying any property, suing in a Court of Justice or giving evidence in any court. For Field, the argument that local law had allowed suits by emancipated convicts was of no importance. What mattered was the primary of English law and procedures. Bigge thought that Field was incorrect in his conclusions about the legal status of pardons granted in NSW and that this needed intervention from London. He also saw Field as a divisive figure in the colony agreeing with Macquarie who, in 1821,

---

[46] See, ibid, McLaren, John, *Dewigged, Bothered & Bewildered: British Colonial Judges in Trial, 1800-1900*, pp. 142-149.
[47] Currey, C. H., 'Field, Barron (1786-1846)', *ADB*, Vol. 1, pp. 373-376, and McKay, R. J., 'Wylde, Sir John (1781-1859)', *ADB*, Vol. 2, pp. 627-629.

included him in the list of 'factious and dissatisfied in New South Wales'.

Bigge rejected calls for representative government with a legislative assembly and trial by jury arguing that the nature of the colony made it unprepared for such reforms. His report on the judicial establishment in NSW became the basis of changes in the machinery for the administration of justice made in 1823 by the New South Wales Act and the Charter of Justice. Such changes involved the creation of a new Supreme Court under a new Chief-Justice with both civil and criminal jurisdiction replacing the two previous courts. The problem with the formation of the unified Supreme Court was that it represented evolution from the existing system rather than fundamental reform. The judges in the criminal court still sat with military assessors even if their powers were now limited to matters of fact. In civil cases, trials continued to be heard by a judge and lay assessors drawn from the magistracy or a jury where the parties involved agreed. The legislation ended Wylde's and Field's appointments but Field had already sailed for England in the *Competitor* in February 1824 without waiting for the arrival of his successor or for the reconstitution of the Supreme Court. Governor Brisbane was not sorry to see him go.

Forbes and Darling

Appointed in 1823 [48] and first Chief-Justice of the Supreme Court of NSW until 1837, Francis Forbes already had considerable experience of the administration of justice in Bermuda and Newfoundland where he had proved effective in balancing the principles of English law with particular local economic and social circumstances. [49] He took the view that it was important for NSW to move away from its

---

[48] Bathurst to Brisbane, 4 August 1823, *HRA*, Series I, Vol. 11, p. 102

[49] Bennett, J. M., *Sir Francis Forbes: First Chief Justice on New South Wales 1824-1837*, (Federation Press), 2001, pp. 16-37. See also, Currey, C. H., 'Forbes, Sir Francis (1784-1841)', *ADB*, Vol. 1, pp. 392-399, Holloway, Ian, 'Sir Francis Forbes and the Earliest Australian Public Law Cases', *Law and History Review*, Vol. 22, (2004), pp. 209-242 and ibid, McLaren, John, *Dewigged, Bothered & Bewildered: British Colonial Judges in Trial, 1800-1900*, pp. 149-156.

authoritarian origins and that English law should apply except where doing so would produce irrational decisions and adopted a broadly liberal interpretation of the meaning of the rule of law in the colony. Forbes had significant powers as head of the judiciary but also as a member of the Legislative Council and, ex officio, of the later Executive Council. [50] The 1823 Act stated that the governor could not submit any local bill to the Legislative Council until the Chief-Justice had certificated that the proposed measure was not repugnant to the laws of England. [51] This meant that local laws had to conform to imperial legislation that expressly applied to the colony or by implications to imperial legislation because of its general nature; so, for instance, NSW could not introduce a local free trade law since it would have been repugnant to the Navigation Acts that limited colonial trade. The situation with regards to repugnancy and the Common Law in colonies was less clear: should colonial laws conform to the corpus of judgements of the Common Law or simply certain 'fundamental principles' of the system? The approach adopted in other colonies for deciding whether laws were repugnant or not was whether they were, in the circumstances, appropriate to local conditions. This placed an important constraint upon what governors could and could not do and brought Forbes into conflict especially with Ralph Darling.

Forbes' relationship with his first governor, Sir Thomas Brisbane was good. The new Legislative Council first met on 25 August 1824 and as Brisbane thought it wise not to attend its sittings Forbes was virtually its president. He established the criteria by which the governor was guided in nominating unofficial members and temporarily became the

---

[50] Warrant appointing a Council in NSW, 19 January 1824, *HRA*, Series I, Vol. 11, pp. 195-196.
[51] See, New South Wales Act (1823) 4 Geo IV, c 96, s29: 'And be it further enacted that no law or ordinance shall by the said governor or acting governor be laid before the said council for their advice or approbation or be passed into a law unless a copy thereof shall have been first laid before the chief justice of the supreme court of New South Wales and unless such chief justice shall have transmitted to the said governor or acting governor a certificate under the hand of such chief justice that such proposed law is not repugnant to the laws of England but is consistent with such laws so far as the circumstances of the said colony will admit.'

parliamentary draughtsman when Saxe Bannister, the Attorney-General proved incompetent. [52] Although he approved criticism of Macquarie's policy of including emancipated convicts in key roles in government and the law, he did not agree with wealthy free settlers who saw themselves as the only group in the colony with the right to rule. Trial by jury, he believed, should be introduced as quickly as possible and on 14 October 1824, trial by common jury of twelve inhabitants, who had come to the colony as free men or had been born in it, was instituted for the first time in Australia, though it was initially limited to the Quarter Sessions. On the same day the *Australian*, the colony's first independent newspaper, was published by Robert Wardell and William Charles Wentworth who had qualified as barristers in England and practised as attorneys in NSW where there was no division in the profession. [53] In November, the charter of the Australian Agricultural Company was issued and the Macarthurs, especially Hannibal were strongly represented on its local committee. Invited by Sir Robert Wilmot-Horton, Permanent Secretary at the Colonial Office to comment on the wisdom of the Company's million-acre grant, Forbes reported adversely on the formation of large estates and favoured 'unlocking the land' for settlers. He was also critical of members of the local committee who sold their stock to the company at high prices.

Forbes had already earned the reproach of the Macarthurs over his advice to Brisbane in a quarrel between Henry Grattan Douglass and magistrates at Parramatta. [54]

---

[52] Currey, C. H., 'Bannister, Saxe (1790-1877)', ADB, Vol. 1, pp. 55-56.

[53] See, Currey, C. H., 'Wardell, Robert (1793-1834)', *ADB*, Vol. 2, pp. 570-572, and Persse, Michael, 'Wentworth, William Charles (1790-1872)', *ADB*, Vol. 2, pp. 582-589.

[54] Brisbane to Bathurst, 6 September 1822, HRA, Series I, Vol. 10, pp. 744-780, Bathurst to Brisbane, 1 April 1823, *HRA*, Series I, Vol. 11, pp. 73-74, approved Brisbane's actions. When Governor Sir Thomas Brisbane arrived in November 1821, Douglass became a regular visitor at his residence, an association that brought him into conflict with his colleagues on the Parramatta bench. The first clash came in August 1822 over a convict girl, Ann Rumsby, whom he had taken into his home. Dr James Hall, surgeon superintendent of the *Maria Ann* in which she had been transported, alleged that Douglass was behaving improperly with

At the Colonial Office Forbes had read the reports relevant to Brisbane's removal of the names of Samuel Marsden and Hannibal Macarthur and three others of the Parramatta bench from the Commission of the Peace and had agreed with James Stephen that the magistrates' proceedings were indefensible. However, Marsden had retaliated against Brisbane's action by sending defamatory letters to Sir Robert Peel and Wilberforce accusing Douglass of punishing convicts illegally. These letters were passed on to Bathurst who ordered an inquiry to be conducted in the colony by Brisbane, Forbes and Archdeacon Thomas Scott.[55] Their finding exonerated Douglass and reflected scathingly upon Marsden. The grand jury of Parramatta, of which

---

her. Samuel Marsden, Hannibal Macarthur and three other magistrates held a meeting, to which Douglass was summoned but failed to appear. The magistrates then had Ann arrested and she was sentenced to imprisonment for perjury at Port Macquarie. Brisbane intervened, gave her a free pardon, threatened to remove the Parramatta magistrates who had not only refused to sit with Douglass on the bench but also called a secret general meeting of justices to support their action and complained to London of a conspiracy against Douglass. Douglass, however, soon showed that he could defend himself. In April 1823, he brought an action for libel against Hall, claiming damages of £5,000 but was awarded £2 and costs. Next month with William Lawson he fined Marsden for allowing one of his convict servants to be at large and, when Marsden refused to pay, had his piano seized and sold. Marsden promptly sued him for damages of £250, but the court awarded him only the amount of the fine. Marsden then complained to the bishop of London that Douglass was preventing inmates of the Female Factory from taking their infants to church for baptism and connived with Hannibal Macarthur in a letter to Robert Peel at the Home Office, charging Douglass with drunkenness, torture of prisoners and other disreputable official conduct. These letters, forwarded to the Colonial Office, brought orders for an inquiry which exonerated Douglass but provided a loophole for Macarthur as foreman of the Grand Jury to publish further complaints against Douglass in the *Sydney Gazette*. Brisbane's reports extolled his virtues with increasing warmth after each attack and in February 1824 he nominated him as commissioner of the Court of Requests and sent him to London to consult the Colonial Office on the functions of the new court: Brisbane to Bathurst, 21 February 1824, *HRA*, Series I, Vol. 11, p. 230. See, Noad, K. B., 'Douglass, Henry Grattan (1790-1865)', *ADB*, Vol. 1, pp. 314-316.
[55] Bathurst to Governor of NSW, 2 September 1824, *HRA*, Series I, Vol. 11, pp. 351-353, 462-465, 717-807.

Hannibal Macarthur was foreman, then indicted Douglass and two other justices for imposing what the jury considered an illegal sentence: daily flogging of a convicted thief until he disclosed the whereabouts of stolen goods. The men so indicted sought government intervention. On Forbes's advice, Brisbane remitted the matter to the Legislative Council, which in turn searched all the available bench proceedings and found many precedents for the sentence imposed by the indicted justices, including some imposed by Marsden and Macarthur. Forbes then proposed an Act of Indemnity that was duly passed in October 1825. Meanwhile Bathurst had severely censured Hannibal Macarthur for his conduct and 'from that time', wrote Forbes, 'I have been a marked man and no efforts have been spared to get me out of the colony.' [56] The free settler clique he had offended subjected Brisbane to a vitriolic attack unfairly alleging his weakness and laziness in his rule of the colony and in 1825 he was relieved of his command and replaced by Ralph Darling. [57]

Darling's governorship coincided with the culmination of the decade-long political infighting between emancipated convicts who pressed for acceptance of their ideals of government and justice and wealthy free settlers who resisted those demands. With political power still firmly in the hands of a strong executive, the colonial press was unflinching in its criticisms of those officials and free settlers who it saw as obstructing progress towards a more egalitarian civil society. Tensions between the governor and the judiciary reached a peak in the late 1820s reflecting their different personalities and political ideologies. Darling was a former general with some skill in that role but Forbes found him 'quite unacquainted with civil business' and possessed of 'less knowledge of the laws of his country than any gentleman filling his high official station whom it was ever [his] fortune to meet'. Although ready to improve the efficiency of the administrative and fiscal affairs of the colony, he had a conservative's suspicion and mistrust of political and social change and was quick to judge others

---

[56] Forbes to Wilmot-Horton, 30 October 1823, *HRA*, Series IV, Vol. 1, pp. 731-743, at p. 741.
[57] 'Sir Ralph Darling (1772-1858), *ADB*, Vol. 1, 1966, pp. 282-286, and ibid, Fletcher, B. H., *Ralph Darling: A Governor Maligned*, provide biographical material.

unfavourably, especially if they disagreed with him and was unreceptive to criticism. At the same time, as a military man he was impatient with lack of action and the niceties of legal process. Darling also lacked sound legal advice from the law officers of the Crown that might have curbed his enthusiasm for executive initiatives of dubious legality. Francis Forbes by contrast was a liberal in political and legal terms. He was born not in England but in Bermuda.[58] Forbes had been educated and trained as barrister in London, and before going to Sydney had been Attorney-General in Bermuda and Chief-Justice of Newfoundland. [59] In that latter role he had developed a reputation as a liberal; for Governor Sir Charles Hamilton too liberal, because of the judge's belief that law should to some extent reflect and respond to local conditions and needs and in the necessity of constraining inferior courts. Forbes recognised the need to bring English law and the rule of law more fully into the operation of justice and governance in NSW. At the same time, as a sophisticated observer of British imperialism, he was aware of the importance of balancing concerns over centralisation with appreciation of the realities of the particular colony, its history and population. In his judicial role he was perhaps too detached from an executive that needed sound legal advice.

A major area of conflict between Darling and Forbes was freedom of the press and the governor's increasing petulance towards radicalism in the colony, inspired in particular by Wentworth, the leading advocate of the emancipist cause. Not satisfied with the conservative reforms to the constitution and justice system of NSW in the late 1810s and early 1820s, Wentworth was vigorous and vocal in his campaign for both trial by jury and a representative legislative assembly. Only these changes, he argued, would give colonists, including emancipated convicts, a voice in both the administration of justice and their own governance. It was a combination of Wentworth and his journalistic colleagues, Wardell and Edward Smith

---

[58] On Forbes, see Castles, Alex C., *An Australian Legal History*, (Law Book Co.), 1982, pp. 182-184.
[59] On his period in Newfoundland see, O'Flaherty, Patrick, 'Sir Francis Forbes', *Canadian Dictionary of Biography*, Vol. 7, (University of Toronto and the Université Laval), 1988, pp. 301-304.

Hall[60] advocating these views while labelling Darling as a tyrant that baited the governor. [61] Darling's initial move was to instruct the Attorney-General, Saxe Bannister to launch a seditious defamation prosecution against Edward Hall for libel of several members of the administration in *The Monitor* only to abandon the action on the grounds that the newspaper had altered its tone. As a result relations between Darling and Bannister deteriorated to such an extent that Bannister resigned. He then unsuccessfully instituted private prosecutions against Wardell of the *Australian* and Robert Howe of the *Gazette* for their critical comments on his resignation. The failed prosecution of the newspapermen for seditious libel, an offence open to repressive use even in England, left Darling frustrated by the inability of the courts to curb the power of the press.

Darling then sought to muzzle the press by other means. Instructions for controlling the press had been framed by James Stephen in the light of suggestions from Lieutenant-Governor Sir George Arthur in VDL. Arthur's proposal of a licence revocable at the governor's will had already been submitted to Brisbane who on Forbes' advice declined to sanction it. [62] Darling was anxious to placate the press, although Arthur, on receiving similar instructions, promptly had bills prepared providing for licenses and imposing a stamp duty and sent them to Sydney for parallel action. Darling delayed until, angered by the criticisms of the *Monitor* and the *Australian* submitted these bills to Forbes for his certificate as prescribed in the 1823 Act. Forbes refused his certificate to the six clauses relating to a licence in the first bill because he believed them inconsistent with English law, a view later upheld by the law officers of the Crown. Giving what can only be described as a broad interpretation to existing constitutional doctrine and a political construction to the rule of law, the Chief-Justice denied certification to the licensing law as

---

[60] See, Kenny, M. J. B., 'Hall, Edward Smith (1786-1860)', *ADB*, Vol. 1, pp. 500-502, and Ferguson, J. A., 'Edward Smith Hall and the "Monitor"', *Journal of the Royal Australian Historical Society*, Vol. 17, (3), (1931), pp. 163-200.

[61] On this see Darling's comments in a letter to Under Secretary Horton 15 December 1826, *HRA*, Series I, Vol. 12, pp. 761-762.

[62] Darling to Under Secretary Hay 4 December 1826, *HRA*, Series I, Vol. 12, pp. 725-729.

repugnant to the freedom of the press. [63] He went so far as to describe this freedom as a constitutional privilege. Bruce Kercher suggested: 'that [it] was as much a statement of political aspiration as law, given the repressive nature of English press laws'.[64] However, he did certify the other clauses and they became law as the Newspaper Regulating Act. [65]

The second bill did not include the amount of stamp duty to be imposed, but Forbes found no objection in law to a newspaper tax and gave his certificate, expecting that, when the crucial amount was determined, the bill would be returned to him for further certification. This was not done. A duty of 4d was inserted, the bill was passed, the governor assented and it was promulgated. Forbes maintained that these actions contravened sections 27 and 29 of the 1823 Act and that the 4d tax was too high. He therefore intimated that, if the Act were challenged before the Supreme Court, he would declare it invalid. [66] Darling then proclaimed that 'a certain Bill purporting to be an Act', was suspended; later the authorities at Westminster upheld Forbes' opinion and the Act was disallowed. [67] In 1828, when bills to license auctioneers and places of public entertainment were submitted to Forbes, they too were found by him to be open to the same legal objection that had been fatal to the first six clauses of the Newspaper Regulating Act, but this time amendments were made and the requisite certificates were given. [68] Forbes was not prepared to allow the colony to

---

[63] Darling to Bathurst, 8 May 1827, *HRA*, Series I, Vol. 13, pp. 285-287, covers the disallowed clauses; see also Forbes to Bathurst, 1 May 1827, pp. 289-297 for Forbes' reasons.
[64] Kercher, Bruce, *An Unruly Child: A History of Law in Australia*, (Allen & Unwin), 1995, pp. 85-86; see also, Edgeworth, Brendan, 'Defamation Law and the Emergence of a Critical Press in Colonial New South Wales (1824-1831), *Australian Journal of Law and Society*, Vol. 6, (1990-91), pp. 67-70.
[65] Ibid, *The Public General Statutes of New South Wales from 5th Geo IV to 8th Will, IV, inclusive, (1824-1837)*, pp. 50-59.
[66] Darling to Bathurst 29 May 1827, *HRA*, Series I, Vol. 13, pp. 374-379; Darling to Bathurst 30 May 1827, pp. 380-387.
[67] Ibid, *The Public General Statutes of New South Wales from 5th Geo IV to 8th Will, IV, inclusive, (1824-1837)*, pp. 59-62. The stamp duty legislation was suspended by Government Notice on 31 May 1827 and was never enforced.
[68] Ibid, *The Public General Statutes of New South Wales from 5th Geo IV to 8th Will, IV, inclusive, (1824-1837)*, pp. 149-154.

continue with a form of government that allowed repressive action and in which the governor was not subject to any local authority other than his own. He did so by invoking a liberal view of constitutional rights and of the rule of law that reflected the reformist sentiments he held, and caused him to support trial by jury and to muse about a legislative assembly in the colony.

Irritation at Government House was made worse when Forbes notified Darling that certain regulations issued on 30 July 1827 for the assignment of convicts and the granting of tickets-of-leave were *ultra vires*. In Forbes' opinion, masters had a legal right of property in the service of convicts assigned to them and, although he approved the principle of tickets-of-leave as inducements to reformation, he considered that they could not be given legally to assigned servants or granted at all except under an authority conferred by parliament.[69] Again his opinions were upheld by the Crown law officers, much to the annoyance of Darling, who, on advice from the Home Office and his own legal officers, had revoked the assignment of certain servants of the editors of the *Monitor* and the *Australian*, with the avowed intention of restricting his critics' output. In his frustration Darling suspected that the Chief-Justice was colluding with Wardell, the editor of the *Australian* and saw Forbes unjustifiably as the main cause of his problems.[70] The fault rested with Darling and his legal officers, none of whom was a match for Wardell or Wentworth. The governor's bitterness was intensified by a series of defeats in prosecutions for criminal libel instituted by the Attorney-General. Although Wardell had a serious case to answer, Forbes thought his acquittals were probably due to the knowledge of at least some of the jury that the prosecutions had been ordered and they themselves nominated by the governor. In his dispatches Darling attributed these setbacks to the Chief-Justice's bias in favour of Wardell, an aspersion that Forbes convincingly rebutted.[71]

---

[69] Forbes to Darling, 1 August 1827, *HRA*, Series I, Vol. 13, p. 489.
[70] On the Wardell libel case, see, Darling to Hay, 1 August 1827, *HRA*, Series I, Vol. 13, pp. 477-484.
[71] See, for example, Darling to Goderich, 10 September 1827, *HRA*, Series I, Vol. 13, pp. 509-510: '...Mr Forbes's endeavours to assume a power of controlling generally the measures and acts of the Government....' and Darling to Hay, 15 December 1827, *HRA*,

Darling was to get into a further notable scrape with the Chief-Justice and his colleagues over his distaste for dissent before he was recalled in 1831. The issue was whether the undoubted executive power exercised by previous governors to assign and release convicts was now subject to the demands of the rule of law and examination by the Supreme Court. Darling in attacking one of his newspaper critics, Edward Hall, tried another tack.[72] By gubernatorial order he sought to deprive Hall of Peter Tyler, one of his assigned convicts. The Supreme Court had already determined that the revocation power did not give the governor unfettered discretion, because a decision had to be connected to a proper purpose, for example to grant a genuine indulgence to the convict or protect him from an abusive master. The Court, led by Forbes, concluded that Darling had abused his discretion in this instance, a decision that held even though the court's interpretation was initially rejected in the Colonial Office.[73] Once again Forbes showed himself to be an opponent of arbitrary government, elevating the rule of law in the process.

The Hall case is also interesting in that, although the Supreme Court fought shy of issuing criminal information against the Sydney magistrates who had convicted Hall of harbouring a runaway convict, the judges criticised the magistrates for their decision warning them against contempt of the superior institution. Furthermore, Hall ultimately secured damages against the magistrates in a civil action before the Supreme Court. This episode illustrates another point of tension within the administration of governance and justice in the colony, the identification of the magistracy with the conservative elite. In NSW, conservative exclusionists were able to exercise significant power through their control of local government and justice. In the Hall case and other decisions of the Forbes court, judicial review of executive and administrative action took firm root in Australia.

Chief-Justice Forbes was genuinely committed to impartiality in the judicial role and was a broadly liberal

---

Series I, Vol. 13, pp. 648-649: '...he has endeavoured to raise an Opposition to the Government.'
[72] There had been a succession of disputes between Hall and Darling dating back to 1826: see, *HRA*, Series I, Vol. 14, pp. vi-xiii.
[73] *HRA*, Series I, Vol. 16, pp. 292-294.

advocate of the rule of law. Despite the personal attacks by opponents such as John Macarthur, he avoided strong ties with particular interests in the colony. He could relate the tradition of which he was a part to both the present and future needs of the colonies in which he served. However, Forbes was not infallible and he may be criticised for taking an excessively disinterested position in relation to the need of Darling for sound and considered legal advice. Moreover, as Bruce Kercher had observed, he could be exasperatingly illiberal in certain context in, for instance, legislation relating to bushrangers and indecisive in others, as he seems to have been in relation to Aboriginal rights. He was, however, guided by a strong belief that 'the judicial office…bowed to no other power but the supremacy of law'.[74] He stood out in being singularly adept at balancing a respect for English legal tradition with a recognition that the law needed to accommodate colonial constitutional change.

This cautious approach to reform sought to define the powers of the governor and establish the principle of separation of powers in which the authority of the governor was constrained by the supervisory authority of the courts. Australian reformers drew on the history and traditions of the British constitution in their demands for a free press, trial by jury and taxation by representation. The passage of the Australian Court Act in 1828 made the NSW Supreme Court independent of the executive. It was not that governors such as Ralph Darling and Richard Bourke were opposed to notions of the free-born Englishmen, the issue was when the Australia colonies would be ready to assume greater responsibility for their own affairs in the form of further representative institutions and how governors responded to demands for those institutions.

Conclusions

The appointments of Richard Bourke as Governor of NSW in 1831 and Sir John Franklin as Governor of VDL in 1837

---

[74] Kercher, Bruce, 'The Recognition of Aboriginal Status and Laws in the Supreme Court of New South Wales under Forbes CJ, 1824-1836', in Buck, A. R., McLaren, John and Wright, Nancy, (eds.), *Land and Freedom: Law, Property Rights and the British Diaspora*, (Ashgate), 2001, pp. 83-102.

indicated that reform in Britain would be extended to the colonies. This was especially evident in the position of the jury system seen by Enlightenment thinkers as sanctioned not only by tradition but as an inalienable right of Englishmen. [75] The introduction of criminal and civil jury trials occurred gradually and faced stubborn resistance from the British Government. The campaign for trial by jury had been taken up by free settlers as early as 1791 and by several governors including Hunter, King, Bligh and Macquarie. Edward Hall, editor of the reformist *Monitor* wrote in *The rights of juries*:

> ...self-defence and love of power, induce governments, even the best of them, to take little pleasure in enlightening the people, because such enlightenment make the people *prying* and *impertinent*, that is to say, freedom-loving people. [76]

In his reports, Bigge did not support the efforts of the emancipated convicts to establish a right to trial by jury and gave three main reasons for this conclusion: tensions between the free and freed settlers meant the system would not operate impartially; there were insufficient competent jurors to implement the system; and, finally, serving on the jury would greatly inconvenience people. [77] Nevertheless, juries were soon allowed with the 1823 Act providing for a judge and jury of seven commissioned officers, nominated by the governor to try criminal issues before the Supreme Court. In civil cases, provision was made for a tribunal system where a judge and two assessors, who were magistrates nominated by the governor, would determine the case. Where property valued at £500 or more was involved a jury trial could occur where both parties agreed. Legislation in 1829 permitted the Supreme Court to order trial by jury in civil cases if either side requested it though this was rarely used and most trials continued to be heard by judges sitting with assessors. The 1830s saw further

---

[75] Bennett, J. M., 'The establishment of jury trial in New South Wales', *Sydney Law Review*, Vol. 3, (1959-1961), pp. 463, 464-465.

[76] Hall, Edward, *The Rights of Juries, In Ten Essays*, (Printed at the Sydney Monitor office), 1835, p. 70.

[77] Bigge, J. T., *The Report on the Judicial Establishments of New South Wales and Van Diemen's Land*, 21 February 1823, (Cmnd. 33).

reforms. In 1832, the NSW Legislative Council, with much prompting from Governor Bourke passed legislation stating that trials of all civil matters were to be heard before a civil jury of twelve. Significantly, it also allowed limited use of trial by jury for criminal cases. In 1839, military trials were finally abolished followed by the use of military juries in 1840 and trial by assessors in 1844. The assessors were replaced by a jury of four in civil cases although the parties had the option of seeking a jury of twelve. These developments became permanent features of the administration of justice in NSW in 1847 and the campaign for full jury trial had finally succeeded.

In NSW the judges were necessarily drawn from England during this period. Although, those men varied in their political and social philosophies and their attitudes towards colonial conditions, it was possible and perhaps inevitable that some would see the value of independence and detachment in the judicial role, especially after 1820 when there was a conscious attempt to introduce more clearly the substance and values of English law to the colony. With responsible government constitutional argument and the protection of rights shifted more clearly into the legislative sphere in Australia as it had in Canada. Consequently, the rule of law became more clearly a court-based and legal doctrine, despite the idiosyncratic attempts of Justice Benjamin Boothby in South Australia to give the judges primacy over colonial legislation.[78] However, it may well be that disputes between upper and lower houses within several Australian colonies that periodically produced legislative stalemate helped to preserve a more clearly political role for the courts in Australia than was true in Canada at the same time. [79]

---

[78] Castles, Alex C., and Harris, Michael C., *Lawyers and Wayward Whigs: Government and Law in South Australia 1836-1986*, (Wakefield Press), 1987, pp. 126-134 and ibid, McLaren, John, *Dewigged, Bothered & Bewildered: British Colonial Judges in Trial, 1800-1900*, pp. 193-216.

[79] See, Davidson, Alastair, *The Invisible State: The Formation of the Australian State 1788-1901*, (Cambridge University Press), 1991.

11 Policing

There was a fundamental tension at the heart of the colony in NSW in the first decades of the nineteenth century. It was to be a penal colony, governed through executive military rule but in which the principles of the rule of law applied. Although the British intended to transport English law and legal proceedings along with the convicts, in practice there were significant departures from English law in the new and distant colony. Notably, the first civil case heard in Australia, in July 1788, was brought by the Kables, a convict couple. They successfully sued the captain of the ship in which they had been transported, for the loss of a parcel during the voyage. In Britain, as convicts, they would have had no rights to bring such a case. The question of how to police a society that was both penal and free posed major problems for colonial government after 1823. This was exacerbated by the sub-division of NSW after 1824 with the separation of VDL and Victoria and the establishment of South Australia, by the growing numbers of free settlers arriving in the colonies especially after the discovery of gold in 1851 and the gradual ending of transportation from the 1840s.

The British context

Colonists, initially in NSW but later in the newer colonies, were influenced by established English traditions in determining their policing arrangements. The English were suspicious of any notion of a powerful police, which they equated with the Catholic absolutism of France. This led to the development of decentralised model of policing where the administration of justice and the policing of towns and villages were placed under local control. The gentry acted as unpaid magistrates dispensing justice through the local Bench and property owners devoted some time to the duties of the unpaid parish constabulary. [1] The traditional

---

[1] Philips, David, "A New Engine of Power and Authority': The Institutionalization of Law-Enforcement in England, 1780-1830', in Gatrell, V. A. C., Lenman, Bruce, and Parker, Geoffrey, (eds.), *Crime and the Law: The Social History of Crime in Western Europe Since 1500*, (Europa), 1980, pp. 155-189; Hay, Douglas,

view of policing before 1829 was that it was inefficient and corrupt and by the late-eighteenth century had begun to break down when faced with the increasing incidence of urban unrest and property crime especially in London and that the 'real' history of policing for London and England begins with the setting up of the Metropolitan Police in 1829. This was certainly the view of contemporary critics such as Patrick Colquhoun but Quarter Sessions and other local records suggest that to view policing simply from Westminster slanted the issue of law enforcement in the eighteenth and early-nineteenth century unjustifiably in favour of reformers. [2] Although there was ineffective policing before 1829, the same inefficiency was also evident after 1829. Magistrates and local administration in the eighteenth century was not hopelessly ineffective and local leaders in parochial and county administration were prepared to adopt effective methods of policing and this proved pivotal to the implementation of national policies. [3] There was:

---

and Snyder, Francis, (eds.), *Policing and Prosecution in Britain, 1750-1850*, (Clarendon Press), 1989; Emsley, Clive, *The English Police: A Political and Social History*, 2nd ed., (Longman), 1996, pp. 15-23; McMullan, J. L., 'The Arresting Eye: Discourse, Surveillance, and Disciplinary Administration in Early English Police Thinking', *Social and Legal Studies*, Vol. 7, (1998), pp. 97-128. Gattrell, V. A. C., 'Crime, authority and the policeman-state', in Thompson, F. M. L., (ed.), *The Cambridge Social History of Britain 1750-1950, Vol. 3: Social Agencies and Institutions*, (Cambridge University Press), 1990, pp. 243-310, provides a good overview.

[2] For 'traditional' teleological accounts of policing history, see Reith, Charles, *A Short History of the British Police*, (Oxford University Press), 1948, Ascoli, David, *The Queen's Peace: the Origins and Development of the Metropolitan Police 1829-1979*, (Hamish Hamilton), 1979, and Critchley, T. A., *A History of Police in England and Wales*, (Constable), 1978.

[3] See, for example, Kent, Joan R., 'The centre and the localities: state formation and parish government in England, circa 1640-1740', *Historical Journal*, Vol. 38, (1995), pp. 363-404, considers state formation at the base of the governmental system and examines the extent of, and reasons for, support of national policies at the parochial level. See also, Innes, Joanna, *Inferior Politics: Social Problems and Social Policies in Eighteenth-Century Britain*, (Oxford University Press), 2010, and Davies, Stephen, 'The Private Provision of Police during the Eighteenth

>...a significant degree of continuity between the old and the new—the 'bobbies' of Scotland Yard carried on what the 'Charlies' on the night watch had begun. [4]

Police reformers, such as John Fielding and Patrick Colquhoun and the commercial and propertied middle-classes increasingly advocated rigorous control and surveillance of the lower classes by a more systematically organised and coordinated police force. Such proposals were vehemently opposed by the gentry and the emerging industrial working-classes, who feared that the government would form a powerful, centralised police force to ride roughshod over their liberties. With the crucial support of Tory backbenchers, they resisted efforts to establish French-style police methods in England. The most important development was the Middlesex Justices Act of 1792 that appointed stipendiary or paid magistrates in charge of small police forces. But the predominantly local system of policing was still in place in the 1820s.

There was less resistance to stern measures against agrarian protest and violence in Ireland. The Peace Preservation Act of 1814 and the Irish Constabulary Act of 1822 established police forces in county areas and created a more militarised and centralised form of policing. [5] The author of these statutes, Sir Robert Peel, when Home Secretary used arguments based on the efficiency of the Irish police and the threat to liberty from disorder and crime to achieve police reform in England. Peel pushed the Metropolitan Police Act through Parliament in 1829 creating a paid, uniformed, preventive police for London headed by commissioners without magisterial duties and under central direction. The example of uniformed, professional police subsequently spread throughout England over the following decades, but they remained subject to local control and the extent to which the new

---

and Nineteenth Centuries', in Beito, David T., Gordon, Peter, and Tabarrok, Alexander, (eds.), *The Voluntary City: Choice, Community and Civil Society*, (University of Michigan Press), 2002, pp. 151-181.

[4] Reynolds, E. A., *Before the Bobbies: The Night Watch and Police Reform in Metropolitan London, 1720-1830*, (Stanford University Press), 1998, p. 5, see also, pp. 148-166.

[5] Palmer, S. H., *Police and Protest in England and Ireland, 1780-1850*, (Cambridge University Press), 1988, pp. 193-271.

police differed from the existing watchmen and constables should not be exaggerated.[6]

These developments provided two different models for colonial policing. A centralised, military-styled and armed force of Ireland kept away from the local community in barracks and a consciously non-military, unarmed, preventive English police supposedly working in partnership with and with the consent of the local community.[7] More often than not elements from both models were employed by colonial police forces and adapted to suit local circumstances. Where the security of the state was threatened, the Irish approach was deployed, while English methods were more pervasive and influenced day-to-day policing of all aspects of social life.[8]

Consensus and conflict

During the 1950s and 1960s, historians of English policing argued that the introduction of the 'new police' received widespread community support. The few individuals, who opposed its introduction, it was argued, were soon won over by the force's ability to prevent crime and maintain social order, securing it 'the confidence and the lasting admiration

---

[6] Styles, John, 'The Emergence of the Police: Explaining Police Reform in Eighteenth- and Nineteenth-Century England', *British Journal of Criminology*, Vol. 27, (1987), pp. 15-22.

[7] Jeffries, Sir Charles, *The Colonial Police*, (Max Parrish), 1952, is despite its limitations, the only general history. For more revisionist studies, see, Brogden, Michael, 'An Act to Colonise the Internal Lands of the Island: Empire and the Origins of the Professional Police', *International Journal of the Sociology of Law*, Vol. 15, (1987), pp. 179-208; Anderson, D. M., and Killingray, David, (eds.), *Policing and the Empire: Government, Authority, and Control, 1830-1940*, (Manchester University Press), 1991, and Emsley, Clive, *The Great British Bobby: A history of British policing from the 18th century to the present*, (Quercus), 2009, pp. 104-111.

[8] See, ibid, Emsley, Clive, *The Great British Bobby*, pp. 91-92, for a succinct discussion of the two models and Hawkins, Richard, 'The 'Irish Model' and the Empire: A Case for Reassessment', in ibid, Anderson, D. M., and Killingray, David, (eds.), *Policing and the Empire*, pp. 18-32, makes a powerful case that there was no real 'Irish model'.

of the British people'.[9] The smooth transition from a locally based 'inefficient' parish constable system to an efficient and professional body of law enforcers formed the basis of this 'consensus' view. [10] During the 1970s, historians using conflict and social control theories challenged the consensus view of widespread public acceptance. Concentrating on working-class responses, they argued that the 'new police' were resisted as an instrument of repression developed by the propertied classes. The 'new police', it was argued, were developed to destroy existing working-class culture in order to impose 'alien values and an increasingly alien law on the urban poor'.[11] Conflict historians argued that a preventive police system was developed in response to changes in the social and economic structure of English society. Robert Storch, the foremost proponent of this interpretation contended that, the formation 'of the new police was a symptom of both a profound social change and deep rupture in class relations'.[12] The working-classes questioned the legitimacy of the 'new police' and responded to their interference in a variety of ways ranging from subtle defiance to open and, on occasions, violent resistance.

More recently the level of support that the 'new police' received from the propertied classes has been questioned.

---

[9] Jones, David, 'The New Police, Crime and People in England and Wales, 1829-1888,' *Transactions of the Royal Historical Society*, Vol. 33, (1983), p. 153. For discussions of this debate see, Emsley, Clive, *Policing and its Context, 1750-1870*, (Macmillan), 1987, pp. 4-7; Bailey, V., 'Introduction', in Bailey, V., (ed.), *Policing and Punishment in Nineteenth Century Britain*, (Croom Helm), 1981, pp. 12-14; Fyfe, N. R., 'The Police, Space and Society: The Geography of Policing', *Progress in Human Geography*, Vol. 15, (3), (1991), pp. 250-252; Taylor, David, *The new police: crime, conflict, and control in 19th-century England*, (Manchester University Press), 1997, ibid, Brogden, M., 'An Act to Colonise the Internal Lands of the Island: Empire and the Origins of the Professional Police', pp. 181-183.

[10] King, H., 'Some Aspects of Police Administration in New South Wales, 1825-1851', *Royal Australian Historical Society*, Vol. 42, (4), (1956), p. 207.

[11] Ibid, Jones, David, 'The New Police, Crime and People in England and Wales, 1829-1888', p. 153.

[12] Storch, R., 'The Plague of the Blue Lotus: Police Reform and Popular Resistance in Northern England, 1840-57', *International Review of Social History*, Vol. 20, (1975), p. 62.

Barbara Weinberger argues that opposition to the 'new police'

> ...was part of a 'rejectionist' front ranging from Tory gentry to working class radicals against an increasing number of government measures seeking to regulate and control more and more aspects of productive and social life. [13]

Palmer also argues that conflict historians 'have tended to ignore or down play the resistance within the elite to the establishment of a powerful police' and have over-emphasised the threat from below. [14] While accepting that the introduction of the 'new police' involved a clash of moral standards, he argues that it should not be exaggerated.[15] These more recent studies therefore suggest that opposition to the 'new police' was also, but not equally, evident in the responses of the English upper- and middle-classes.

A subtle historiography

Broad generalisations about the public's opposition to or acceptance of the 'new police' have tended to obscure the subtleties in community responses. Opposition did exist, at times resulting from police enforcement of 'unpopular edicts' or attempts to 'prevent mass meetings,' although they were also used and supported by many people 'as a fact of life' in their preventive and social order capacities.[16] While these studies have concentrated predominantly on the public's negative responses to the introduction of the 'new police', Stephen Inwood has considered how the police, administratively and functionally, dealt with the

---

[13] Weinberger, B., 'The Police and the Public in Mid-nineteenth-century Warwickshire', in ibid, Bailey, V., (ed.), *Policing and Punishment in Nineteenth Century Britain*, p. 66.
[14] Ibid, Storch R., 'The Plague of the Blue Lotus: Police Reform and Popular Resistance in Northern England, 1840-57', p. 61; ibid, Palmer S. *Police and Protest in England and Ireland, 1780-1850*, p. 8.
[15] Storch, R., 'Policeman as Domestic Missionary: Urban Discipline and Popular Culture in Northern England, 1850-1880', *Journal of Social History*, Vol. 9, (4), (1976), pp. 481-502.
[16] Ibid, Jones, David, 'The New Police, Crime and People in England and Wales, 1829-1888', p. 166; ibid, Emsley, Clive, *The English Police*, pp. 5-6.

public. Too great a reliance on social control theories has led to over-simplification of the complex inter-relationships between the 'new police' and the wider community. While the 'new police' sought 'to establish minimum standards of public order,' it was not in their own interests 'to provoke social conflict by aspiring to unattainable ideals'. [17] Inwood sees relations between the police and the public as based on a calculated pragmatism in which it was acknowledged that attempts to impose unpopular laws rigidly would ultimately meet with resistance resulting in 'damage to the rule of law'.[18] Police administrators and the constables on their beats were required to tread carefully between the demands and expectations of 'respectable' society and the practical need for good relations with the working-classes.[19]

While there has been a re-examination of public responses to the 'new police' and police responses to the public, these studies maintain that the police were, amongst particular groups, for varying reasons and at certain times, unpopular. Weinberger argues that this unpopularity stemmed from public

> ...suspicion of the police as an alien force outside the control of the community; resentment at police interference in attempting to regulate traditionally sanctioned behaviour; [and] objections to expense.[20]

Reacting to policing in the colonies

How did the public respond to the introduction of the 'new police' in the Australian colonies? Did the police encounter opposition at either an organisational or operational level and if so, by whom and what form did this opposition take? In NSW until the 1820s, policing was largely decentralised with magistrates in rural areas controlling the police and

---

[17] Inwood, S., 'Policing London's Morals: The Metropolitan Police and Popular Culture, 1829-1850', *London Journal*, Vol. 15, (2), (1990), p. 144.
[18] Ibid, Inwood, S., 'Policing London's Morals: The Metropolitan Police and Popular Culture, 1829-1850', p. 134.
[19] Ibid, Inwood, S., 'Policing London's Morals: The Metropolitan Police and Popular Culture, 1829-1850', p. 131
[20] Ibid, Weinberger, B., 'The Police and the Public in Mid-nineteenth-century Warwickshire', p. 65.

deciding 'what would and would not be policed.' [21] They used their authority to protect their class interests and relied upon flogging and secondary internal transportation to enforce order. The assistance of the military was necessary to quell large-scale disorder, but it was not used for ordinary policing duties. Reflecting the characteristics of the population, most policemen were convicts. In 1823, J. T. Bigge, charged with making transportation more of a deterrent for English criminals, reported to the Colonial Office that police organisation was defective and recommended centralised control rather than retaining local control by unpaid magistrates.[22]

New South Wales and Van Diemen's Land

In the 1820s and 1830s, police reform in NSW was a compromise between the English and Irish models, modified to meet the exigencies of a large convict population, the activities of bushrangers, the resistance of the Aborigines and a growing urban population.[23] Bigge, in his report on the administration of justice, had recommended that the police across NSW should be centralised under one authority. Bathurst intended to implement this but Brisbane and Darling postponed the change, hampered by inadequate funds and recruits of poor quality. Magistrates outside Sydney were unwilling to relinquish control of the police creating a system of divided control with a mounted police, composed mainly of soldiers, formed to deal with bushrangers and Aborigines. In 1825, Captain F. N. Rossi became the head of the Sydney police, whose existence was made official by the Sydney Police Act in 1833, a statute based on the London Metropolitan Police

---

[21] Ibid, Neal, David, *The Rule of Law in a Penal Colony: Law and Power in Early New South Wales*, p. 163.
[22] Ibid, Neal, David, *The Rule of Law in a Penal Colony: Law and Power in Early New South Wales*, pp. 148-149.
[23] Ibid, King, Hazel, 'Some Aspects of Police Administration in New South Wales, 1825-1851', pp. 205-30; Sturma, Michael, 'Policing the Criminal Frontier in Mid-Century Australia, Britain, and America', in Finnane, Mark, (ed.), *Policing in Australia: Historical Perspectives*, (University of New South Wales Press), 1987, pp. 15-34; Finnane, Mark, *Police and Government: Histories of Policing in Australia*, (Oxford University Press), 1994, chapter 1.

Act of 1829. [24] In the absence of local government, the Sydney police were required to assume a range of urban functions. In addition to the police, overseers, masters and private informers ensured that the colonists enjoyed 'a level of surveillance more akin to a penal colony than the society they knew in England.' [25]

Bigge's report influenced thinking about police arrangements in VDL far more than in NSW. [26] Lieutenant-Governor George Arthur created a more highly centralised policing system and controlled the police, mainly comprised of convicts, through paid magistrates, responsible directly to him. [27] His police reforms and their operation made VDL a more intensively policed society than NSW. He saw himself as the servant of empire, answerable only to the British government and not local colonists and was the foremost supporter of the benefits of transportation. [28] Feeling that a penal colony was 'an unnatural condition' because 'virtue' was subordinate to 'crime', Arthur believed he had no choice but to rule the colony as a jail. There were 254 police in August 1828, increasing to 346 in December

---

[24] King, Hazel, 'Rossi, Francis Nicholas (1776-1851)', *ADB*, Vol. 2, pp. 399-401.
[25] Ibid, Neal, David, *The Rule of Law in a Penal Colony: Law and Power in Early New South Wales*, p. 54.
[26] Petrow, Stefan, 'Policing in a Penal Colony: Governor Arthur's Police System in Van Diemen's Land, 1826-1836', *Law and History Review*, Vol. 18, (2000), pp. 351-395, and 'After Arthur: Policing in Van Diemen's Land 1837-46', in Enders, Mike and Dupont, Benoît, (eds.), *Policing the lucky country*, (Hawkins Press), 2002, pp. 176-198. See also, Easton, Greg, *Tasmanian Police: From Force to Service*, (Connect Credit Union), 1999.
[27] Boyce, James, *Van Diemen's Land*, (Black Inc.), 2008, pp. 145-212 provides the most recent discussion of Arthur's rule. See also, Stephenson, Richard, 'The Rise of Governor Arthur's Police State', *Historical Records of Australia: A Documentary Periodical*, number 1, (1990), pp. 11-15.
[28] *Report from the Select Committee on Transportation, Together with the Minutes of Evidence, Appendix, and Index*, (Irish University Press), 1968, Vol. 2, Appendix, p. 2, Arthur, George, *Defence of Transportation, in Reply to the Remarks of the Archbishop of Dublin in His Second Letter to Earl Grey*, (Gowie), 1835, Arthur to Howick, 18 February 1832; Chapman, Peter, 'The Island Panopticon', *Historical Records of Australia: A Documentary Periodical*, number 1, (1990), pp. 6-10.

1833 and 453 in April 1835. [29] In 1835, the population has been estimated at 40,172, giving a ratio of one policeman for every 88.7 people; in Sydney and the settled districts, the ratio in 1836 was 1 policeman for every 133 people. [30] In rural England, the ratio was not more than 1 to every 1,000 people. The ratio in VDL was not only much more than the colonists had been used to in England but was also significantly higher than in the heavily policed society of NSW. This meant that convicts and colonists were always under the surveillance of the police and made collision with them difficult to avoid, especially in the towns. The police were more concerned to enforce order than protect liberty and were generally supported by the magistrates. The police could use their discretionary powers to harass and arbitrarily arrest free citizens, who were required to buy their freedom with bribes or other favours. On the other hand, if properly supervised, the police were a protection against property crime and violence and many colonists welcomed their protection.

Making order his aim, Arthur expected colonists to sacrifice their rights and liberties in the interests of making transportation a feared punishment and in exchange for the security of person and property that he provided. [31] Those who 'knowingly' emigrated to a convict colony, which was in effect 'an immense Gaol or Penitentiary,' should not he argued expect 'to retain every immunity and privilege' they enjoyed in England and should 'abide cheerfully by the rules and customs of the Prison.' There could be:

>...no happiness nor prosperity without personal security,' and this could only be secured by '*severe discipline*'.[32]

---

[29] Police Serving on 1 August 1828; CO 280, Return of Police Establishment in Van Diemen's Land, 31 December 1833, and Quarterly Return of Police in Van Diemen's Land, 1 April 1835.
[30] Population figures for VDL might have been underestimated. See ibid, Hartwell, R. M., *The Economic Development of Van Diemen's Land, 1820-1850*, p. 68; ibid, Neal, David, *The Rule of Law in a Penal Colony: Law and Power in Early New South Wales*, pp. 54, 155.
[31] Giblin, R. W., *The Early History of Tasmania*, 2 Vols. (Melbourne University Press), 1939, Vol. 2, p. 629.
[32] CO 280, Arthur to Hanley, 4 April 1834, emphasis in original.

The majority of colonists, especially those in the interior, resigned themselves to this policy and were constrained to obey his commands for two reasons.[33] They appreciated the security, funded not by local taxes but by the Crown that Arthur provided after years of anarchy. Given the shortage of free labourers, they also feared losing the cheap convict labour that Arthur could withdraw whenever he liked. But those colonists who did not rely on convict servants for their wealth or who had fallen out with Arthur, mainly the residents of the colony's capital Hobart Town, felt that the benefits of transportation were purchased at too high a price and became hostile to attacks on their liberty.[34]

As its central aim was to strengthen the authority of the governor and enforce order, the rule of law as a protection of free citizens was compromised at all levels of the legal system in VDL. Under Arthur's authoritarian rule, the nominated Legislative Council, paid magistrates and the police generally placed the orderly management of the convict system ahead of rights and liberties. He also expected the Supreme Court, formed in 1824 with the arrival of John Pedder as Chief-Justice, to uphold his autocratic rule, even where his powers might 'trench upon the privileges or conveniences of the free.' [35] With a seat on the Executive Council until 1836 and on the Legislative Council, Pedder subordinated the judicial arm of government to the executive and destroyed confidence in his impartiality. [36]

This view antagonised many free settlers, especially in Hobart Town. They echoed their NSW counterparts by demanding a greater say in determining the colony's future

---

[33] Forsyth, W. D., *Governor Arthur's Convict System: Van Diemen's Land, 1824-36*, (Sydney University Press), 1970, pp. 109, 126-129.

[34] Ibid, *Report from the Select Committee on Transportation; together with Minutes of Evidence, Appendix, and Index*, pp. 117, 225; ibid, West, John, *The History of Tasmania*, Vol. 1, p. 122; ibid, Giblin R. W., *The Early History of Tasmania*, Vol. 2, pp. 420-421, 605.

[35] CO 280, Arthur to Hanley, 4 April 1834.

[36] For a sympathetic view of Pedder, see Bennett, J. M., *Sir John Pedder: First Chief Justice*, (University of Tasmania), 1977. See also, Howell, P. A., 'Pedder, Sir John Lewes (1793-1859)', *ADB*, Vol. 2, pp. 319-320.

and the rights of freeborn Englishmen railing against what they saw as arbitrary and unjust government interference. The press in Hobart Town and Launceston was the watchdog of arbitrary government and outspoken proponents of the rights of the people. In 1826, the *Colonial Times that* regularly referred to 'free-born British subjects,' wrote:

> It must be recollected that we are in these Colonies, as far as our rights go, in England. By the privileges of our birth, the British Law is the only one to which we are subjected. Every immunity possessed by our brethren in England is also equally possessed by us *de jure,* notwithstanding many of them are withheld *de facto.* But when they are withheld, it is by the effect of the Law, specially enacted for that purpose. [37]

In 1827, a petition from free settlers to the British government called for trial by jury and a representative assembly, 'the pride and the birth-right' and 'the safeguard of every Briton.' [38] In the courts, colonists contested arbitrary uses of police power and employed the language of the rule of law when arguing for their rights or defending their liberties. They were 'not to be put off with the shadow of Liberty, after having once known the fullness of its enjoyments.' [39] But they realised that the paid magistrates gave prime consideration to convict order and discipline and supported police action unless the evidence clearly demonstrated they had acted illegally or arbitrarily. Police work had an important bearing on whether in practice the rule of law could curb arbitrary power. Not only did the police threaten liberty by treating colonists unequally and unjustly, they also enforced the law, made 'its orders meaningful' and constituted its 'coercive function'.[40]

The police exploited any statute allocating fines to an informer, but some statutes, such as the Dog, Impounding

---

[37] *Colonial Times,* 28 April 1826, p. 2.
[38] *Colonial Times,* 16 March 1827, p. 2. As in NSW these were only gradually conceded: in 1830, jury trials could be used in civil cases where both parties agreed; military juries were not removed from criminal cases until 1840; and it was a decade later that a partially elected Legislative Assembly was secured.
[39] *Colonial Times,* 2 March 1827, p. 2.
[40] Ibid, Neal, David, *The Rule of Law in a Penal Colony: Law and Power in Early New South Wales,* p. 143.

and Licensing Acts, were particularly lucrative and their irritating application intensely annoyed free settlers. The Dog Act aimed to halt further increases in the numbers of dogs that roamed the colony ravaging sheep and annoying town residents. [41] Owners, who did not pay a duty on all dogs, failed to describe their dogs correctly or failed to control their dogs, could be heavily fined up to £25, with part of fines going to informers. Constables also enforced the provision that rewarded them with five shillings for every dog destroyed for indiscriminately killing valuable sheep and cattle dogs.[42] The result was corruption. In 1831, for instance, a constable provoked a dog to break its chain, laid information against the owner for letting his dog off the chain, and secured part of the fine. In Hobart Town, constables allegedly walked down the street, each with a bitch on a lead and a number of ropes with nooses, which they threw around the neck of any dogs that stopped to make acquaintance with the bitches.[43] After thirty minutes, the constables had caught thirteen dogs. Their owners preferred to pay the constables £1 or £2 rather than appear in court, where they could not prove their dogs had been 'seduced' by the policemen's bitches. [44] A number of landed proprietors, stockholders, and inhabitants of Bothwell petitioned for the repeal of the Dog Act because of its misuse by constables. Colonial Secretary Burnett responded by directing the Bothwell police magistrate to take 'strong measures' against 'improper and vexatious' proceedings. [45]

Although there were widespread complaints about policing methods under Arthur in urban areas, in the interior, settlers welcomed the security and order imposed by Arthur's measures against bushrangers and Aborigines, which enabled them to concentrate on developing their land holdings. Policemen in rural areas were scattered and the chances of clashing with settlers were minimised. Settlers might complain if police interfered with their property or

---

[41] *Hobart Town Gazette,* 20 February 1830, p. 62; Morgan, Sharon, *Land Settlement in Early Tasmania: Creating an Antipodean England,* (Cambridge University Press), 1992, pp. 62, 118.
[42] *True Colonist,* 22 April 1836.
[43] *Cornwall Chronicle,* 12 December 1835.
[44] *Cornwall Chronicle,* 12 December 1835; emphasis in original.
[45] Eldershaw, P. R., 'Burnett, John (1781-1860)', *ADB,* Vol. 1, pp. 182-183.

failed energetically to stop stock stealing, but they did not normally attack the management of the convict system or question Arthur's authority. Their prosperity depended on the imposition of order and, fearing the loss of convict servants, they did not want to alienate Arthur or his magistrates.

Arthur's successors, Sir John Franklin [46] and Sir John Eardley-Wilmot [47] lacked his autocratic personality and the administrative ability to make the convict system run effectively. [48] From 1 July 1836, the British Government refused to fund the heavy police costs and required Franklin and Eardley-Wilmot to pay for the police and gaols from local taxation and land sales. This created tension with both the Legislative Council and the colonists and made police funding a controversial issue. Franklin and Eardley-Wilmot grappled with this problem but it was not resolved until 1846 when the Colonial Office finally agreed to pay two-thirds of the cost of police and gaols. There were also changes in the management of convicts. Under the assignment system, convicts were usually assigned to work for private employers, who provided shelter, food, clothing, and food according to government regulation. [49] In response to criticisms that this was too lenient, the British government introduced the probation system in 1842. [50] At

---

[46] Fitzpatrick, Kathleen, *Sir John Franklin in Tasmania 1837-1843*, (Melbourne University Press), 1949, and 'Franklin, Sir John (1786-1847), *ADB*, Vol. 1, pp. 412-415.

[47] Roe, Michael, 'Eardley-Wilmot, Sir John Eardley (1783-1847)', *ADB*, Vol. 1, pp. 345-346; Shaw, A. G. L., 'Three Knights: Sir James Stephen, Sir John Franklin, and Sir John Eardley-Wilmot', *Tasmanian Historical Research Association Papers and Proceedings*, Vol. 36, (1989), pp. 141-153.

[48] Ibid, Boyce, James, *Van Diemen's Land*, pp. 213-235 considers the late 1830s and 1840s.

[49] Shaw, A. G. L., The Origins of the Probation System in Van Diemen's Land', *Historical Studies, Australia and New Zealand*, Vol. 6, (1953), pp. 16-28 and 'Sir John Eardley-Wilmot and the Probation System in Tasmania', *Tasmanian Historical Research Association Papers and Proceedings*, Vol. 11, (1963), pp. 5-19.

[50] Under this system male convicts worked in probation gangs scattered throughout the penal colony for at least two years. For the following two years convicts received a probation pass, allowing them to work for wages while reporting to the police. If well behaved, they became eligible for a ticket-of-leave and later a conditional pardon. See, Brand, Ian, *The Convict Probation*

the same time, the British Government flooded the colony with convicts, including those from NSW where transportation ended in 1840. The annual population of convicts increased from 17,661 in 1836 to 30,279 in 1846.[51] This had a marked effect of levels of crime in the colony and bushranging, subdued under Arthur, became a much greater threat. Finally, in the 1840s VDL experienced an economic depression and the large numbers of convicts on release and the increasing numbers of free immigrants found work scarce. All sources of public revenue, especially land sales, declined and by 1844 the colony was virtually bankrupt.

VDL was an often brutal and brutalised society in which transported or emancipated convicts made up a substantial proportion of the population. Free settlers were in a minority and often saw themselves as under attack from the indigenous Aboriginal population as well as by absconded convicts, bushrangers and by criminals in general. Maintaining security was a critical issue and this raised fundamental questions about the nature of the judicial system and how society should be policed. Arthur, Franklin and Eardley-Wilmot tried largely without success to square the need to make VDL a penal colony in which those transported were punished with the demands of free settler society for judicial and political liberty and, from the late 1830s, with calls for an end of transportation. Such was the antipathy felt by many towards the centralised police system introduced by Arthur and maintained by his successors that, in 1858, the settlers adopted a decentralised model for policing. Police forces were controlled by municipal councils and lay magistrates replaced paid magistrates. Local accountability did not necessarily herald the end of arbitrary government. The elites who controlled the councils and the local courts used their power to protect their own interests, often to the detriment of the rule of law but they also resisted the intrusions of the central government for the rest of the century. Municipal councils finally relinquished control and the Police Regulation Act in

---

System: Van Diemen's Land, 1839-1854, (Blubber Head Press), 1990.
[51] Eldershaw, P. R., *Guide to the Public Records of Tasmania, Section Three: Convict Department Record Group*, (State Library of Tasmania), 1966, p. 64.

1898 created a Tasmanian-wide organisation under a police commissioner who reported to the Attorney-General, who answered to a democratically elected parliament.

South Australia

South Australia was founded as a society of free settlers and not as a penal settlement.[52] It was hoped that a respectable society would develop and there would be no need for an organised Police Force. [53] Initially some protection for settlers was provided by employing a few retired soldiers and special volunteer constables and the settlers also brought the ancient office of Constable, never a popular office. By late 1837, it was recognised that a permanent police force was necessary largely because of the influx of criminals from the NSW, VDL and the Port Phillip District who considered the 'free settlers' to be 'easy game' and this was not opposed by the colony's middle-classes. [54] On 28 April 1838, a Police Force was established by Governor Hindmarsh though it was not until the following year that it was authorised by the Legislative Council. [55]

In Britain, the local upper- and middle-classes objected to their 'new police' on the grounds that it undermined their traditional powers as magistrates, but this was not the case in South Australia where magistrates were not men of substantial means. Their duties were often time consuming impinging on other business activities and the removal of some of those duties in favour of bureaucratic institutions

---

[52] Pike, D., *Paradise of Dissent: South Australia 1829-1857*, (Melbourne University Press), 1957. See also, Blacket, John, *History of South Australia: A Romantic and Successful Experiment in Colonization*, 2nd ed., (Hussey & Gillingham Ltd.), 1911, pp. 51-90, 121-136, for the precarious nature of settlement before 1840.

[53] This section draws heavily on, Mackay, David, 'Public Responses to the 'New Police' in South Australia, The 1840s', *Flinders Journal of History and Politics*, Vol. 18, (1996), pp. 19-41.

[54] There are two recent studies of the South Australian police: Hopkins, Chas, *South Australia Police 1838-2003: a history of the development and operations of the force from its establishment*, 2nd ed., (South Australian Police Historical Society), 2005, and Cunningham, Col, (ed.), *South Australia Police: A Pictorial History 1838-2008: proudly serving South Australia over 170 years*, (South Australia Police), 2008.

[55] 'Hindmarsh, Sir John (1785-1860)', *ADB*, Vol. 1, pp. 538-541.

was welcomed rather than resisted. Middle-class objections to the 'new police' in Britain stemmed primarily from the cost of preventive policing while in South Australia, costs were met from government revenue rather than a local police rate. English rate-payers sought to minimise police expenditure while South Australians appear to have been enthusiastic about the force's expansion and public expenditure generally. This is clearly evident in the force's expenditure of £17,200 in 1840 and the three-fold increase in police personnel after the force's initial formation, peaking at 118 in the first and second quarters of 1841. [56]

The financial cost associated with the functioning of the 'new police' remained unchallenged until Governor George Grey [57] instituted cuts in government expenditure in mid-1841. [58] His economies led to a reduction in the police force and proved unpopular. In late 1842, the *Adelaide Examiner* reflected middle-class attitudes in commenting:

> Economy is one thing and reduction is another; there is such a thing as being 'pound wise and penny foolish' which, in our opinion, is the proper term by which we ought to designate the policy of his Excellency. [59]

The formation of a preventive police force in South Australia was generally embraced by the middle-classes. Its expansion was accepted as necessary and subsequent reductions were viewed with considerable concern and anger by many colonists. If there was middle-class opposition to a preventive police force, it was not reported in the local press nor was it the subject of petitions to the Colonial Secretary's Office. In reality, the police rarely came into contact with members of the middle-classes in either a

---

[56] Public expenditure proved a major problem in the first decade of South Australia. In 1838, public revenue was £1,448 while public expenditure £16,580. By 1840, public revenue reached £30,618 but public expenditure £171,430 and the total debt chargeable on the revenue of the colony stood at £305,328 2s 7d on 1 May 1840.
[57] 'Grey, Sir George (1812-1898), *ADB*, Vol. 1, pp. 476-480.
[58] In 1841 and 1842, public expenditure was cut resulting in considerable unemployment, a situation exacerbated by the depressed economy This was reflected in the fall in public revenue to £25,329 in 1841 as well as a reduction of public expenditure £89,999. It was not until 1846 that revenue exceeded expenditure.
[59] *Adelaide Examiner*, 31 December 1842, p. 2.

public order or criminal capacity. On the rare occasions that they did, the middle-classes displayed a similar degree of indignation as members of the working-classes. This stemmed principally from the belief that it was not the task of the police to supervise or control their behaviour. [60] The responses of Osmond Gilles and his counsel to police interference in their activities illustrates the middle-class belief that the police were present to maintain order amongst the working-classes and should not 'interfere' in the activities of 'gentlemen'.

The responses of the working-classes were more varied and critical because of their greater level of interaction with the police during the course of their daily lives. The police, apart from their social control and crime prevention functions, had a variety of other duties such as acting as firemen and inspectors of weights and measures, caring for lost children and taking the sick and injured to hospital. These activities brought them into close and persistent contact with the working-classes helping to influence public attitudes towards the police and serving, to some extent, to legitimise their operations within the community. The working-classes showed some reticence about the activities of the 'new police' but this should did not mean any reluctance on their part to use the police or that they necessarily saw them 'as an arm of the bureaucracy' whose aim was the suppression of working-class activities.[61]

---

[60] For instance, in early 1847, Osmond Gilles, previously Colonial Treasurer and wealthy entrepreneur, who was notorious for his almost ungovernable temper, was arrested by PC Nolan after exiting a public house and while being conveyed to the police station was described as being 'very violent both in language and actions'. The duty sergeant at the Adelaide police station stated that he thought Mr Gilles drunk 'as he did not like being searched, and having his property taken from him. He resisted it, and it was taken with much difficulty.' The opinion of Gilles' counsel, however, provides a clearer indication of middle-class attitudes to police interference in their activities. In his pleadings to the magistrate, Gilles' counsel stated that, it was to be 'regretted that the matter had come before their Worships, both on Mr Gilles' account and because it was one which but for the interference of the police might have been so easily avoided': *Register*, 30 January 1847, p. 3.
[61] Ibid, Weinberger, B., 'The Police and the Public in Mid-nineteenth-century Warwickshire', p. 75.

The relationship between the police and the working-classes never reached the levels of fractiousness evident in VDL. The police force was subject to Grey's economies in 1841 and 1842 and its manpower was severely reduced while those who remained on the force suffered reductions in both wages and rations. Police opposition to Grey's policies was responsible for reducing tensions between police and disaffected settlers. The police were restrained in their approach to settler protest gather information about meetings but making no attempt to disband them. As a result, the period most likely to erupt with violence against the police was marked by considerable inaction. Assaults on the police, though their significance should not be overstated, provide one measure of the unpopularity of the police. Between 1839 and 1849, there were only 301 assaults on the police accounting for about 1 in 20 of all arrests. A breakdown of these arrests shows that the assaulters were drawn from a relatively small section of the working-classes supporting Weinberger's argument that: 'It is to their position in particular trades and in their propensity to drink (the two often being associated) that one must look to find real differences between assaulters and the rest' and that alcohol consumption was a particularly important contributing factor. [62]

Police behaviour was subject to widespread public scrutiny as, for instance, in the *South Australian* editorial response to the coroner's inquest on William Brust who had bayoneted by the police at Port Adelaide. [63] The finding that

---

[62] Ibid, Weinberger, B., 'The Police and the Public in Mid-nineteenth-century Warwickshire', p. 73: of the 161 assaults against the police between 1839 and 1845, 54 per cent occurred when offenders were being arrested for drunkenness.

[63] In 1848, the passengers and crew of *Princess Royal* had taken to the hotels of Port Adelaide to celebrate their arrival. Inspector Litchfield, expecting a disturbance, had taken the precaution 'two hours before of placing three police constables together', who were later joined by a fourth. A seaman from *Princess Royal* was arrested for drunken and riotous behaviour and lodged in a police cell. John Hood, the third mate of the vessel, sought the release of the prisoner by offering bail but was refused. The arrest of the third mate incited the gathering crowd who started to break the windows of the station and 'threatened to pull the place down.' The four constables armed with muskets with bayonets fixed charged the crowd, during which William Brust, a seaman from *Princess Royal* was stabbed in the abdomen and later died. The

Brust had 'died of the effects of a bayonet wound, but by whom inflicted is unknown' caused some disquiet as it was felt that the coroner had unduly favoured the police in his verdict. The failure to investigate the matter adequately, the paper claimed, was undermining public confidence in the police:

> As the matter stands at present, there is a rooted conviction in the public mind that had the attack with bayonets and the wound been *vice versa* - had a policeman received the wound, and died - the inquest and subsequent proceedings would have been conducted in a very different manner and with a very different result. [64]

The small number of assaults against police, as a measure of opposition and the occupations from which a substantial proportion of the assaulters were drawn, provides further support for this. Robert Storch argues that the introduction of the 'new police' 'called forth a bitter and often violent response' from the working-classes. [65] The South Australian experience suggests that during the 'new police's' first decade of operation, it was not so much the institution that caused opposition but the way in which the powers of that institution were used that led to working-class criticism.

Conclusion

How far colonial authorities adopted the English or Irish model of policing or a combination of the two and whether policing was centralised or decentralised depended primarily on the nature of particular colonies. In NSW, policing evolved gradually leading to structures dominated by a landed magistracy that resisted attempts to centralise the system or decentralise it based on a system of local government. Control was exerted through the lash and,

---

assault by the seamen of *Princess Royal* and their attempts to inflict grievous bodily harm were responded to with active and immediate intervention in favour of the police but this did not preclude criticism of their actions: *South Australian*, 30 June 1848, p. 2, 14 July 1848, p. 2.

[64] *South Australian*, 14 July 1848, p. 2.

[65] Ibid, Storch R., 'The Plague of the Blue Lotus: Police Reform and Popular Resistance in Northern England, 1840-57', p. 87.

when necessary, secondary internal transportation to penal settlements. By contrast, in VDL where the penal dimension remained dominant until the early 1850s and where free settlers' rights were regarded as subservient to the needs of a penitential system, policing was firmly centralised and intrusive on the behaviour of both convicts, those emancipated and free settlers. There was no attempt to establish a system of policing based on a consensual, preventative model rather the police were regarded as a militarised instrument of the surveillance state. In the first decade of South Australia, the notion of policing by consent was clearly evident reflecting widespread public support, if on occasions critical across social classes for the institution even though the police's broader welfare role in colonial society was significant. That South Australia was a free settler colony may explain why this occurred but so too may the relatively low number of arrests.

This was not the case in Victoria where the police were not primarily a protective or preventative force but instead a repressive institution used first to overcome Aboriginal resistance to dispossession and later to put down agitation by independent gold miners, small farmers, workers and others opposing government policy. [66] In Victoria, the 'ideal' of a police service operating with the consent and cooperation of the community was not achieved for much of the nineteenth century. Far from being a politically neutral force, police consistently regarded sections of the community as 'the enemy' and sided with wealthy economic and political elites to repress challenges to privilege. [67] Police at times used excessive force, escalated conflict and disorder and failed to protect those in need of protection. 'Keeping the peace' was frequently used as a euphemism to justify restricting individual rights.

Centralisation was adopted in all the mainland Australian colonies by 1863 (Tasmania had introduced a decentralised system in 1858 and retained in until 1898) and by New Zealand in stages in 1867 and 1877. [68] The

---

[66] On the problem of policing during the gold rushes in Victoria see, Brown, Richard, *Settler Australia, 1780-1880, Volume 2: Eureka and Democracy*, (CreateSpace), 2013, pp. 68-73.
[67] For the role of the police in the Kelly outbreak, see pp. 343-348.
[68] On policing the NZ, see the work of Hill, R. S., *Policing the Colonial Frontier: The Theory and Practice of Coercive Social and Racial Control in New Zealand, 1767-1867*, (Historical Branch,

existence of a large convict and ex-convict population, a refractory native population, the problems caused by the discovery of gold and the persistent problem of bushrangers led to the formation of powerful centralised forces that were key agents of the colonial state in establishing social order.

How a colonial society was policed depended on who was being policed. When it was citizens with civil and political rights, the approach that evolved was cautious and arguably increasingly consensual but when dealing with non-citizens such as convicts or Aborigines, the police was often free to exercise naked coercive power. They were often the symbols and instruments of colonial rule and the imposition of policing was an integral part of 'empire building'. Relations with settlers were based on a calculated pragmatism in which it was acknowledged that attempts to impose unpopular laws rigidly would ultimately meet with resistance resulting in 'damage to the rule of law'.[69] Police administrators and the constables on their beats were required to tread carefully between the demands and expectations of 'respectable' society and the practical need for good relations with the working-classes. [70] Police work had an important bearing on whether in practice the rule of law could curb arbitrary power. Not only did the police threaten liberty by treating colonists unequally and unjustly, they also enforced the law, made 'its orders meaningful' and constituted its 'coercive function'. [71]

Dept. of Internal Affairs), 1986, *The Colonial Frontier Tamed: New Zealand Policing in Transition, 1867-1886*, (Historical Branch, Dept. of Internal Affairs), 1989, and *The Iron Hand in the Velvet Glove: The Modernisation of Policing in New Zealand, 1886-1917*, (Historical Branch, Dept. of Internal Affairs), 1995.

[69] Inwood, S., 'Policing London's Morals: The Metropolitan Police and Popular Culture, 1829-1850', p. 134.

[70] Ibid, Inwood, S., 'Policing London's Morals: The Metropolitan Police and Popular Culture, 1829-1850', p. 131.

[71] Ibid, Neal, David, *The Rule of Law in a Penal Colony: Law and Power in Early New South Wales*, p. 143.

12 Bushrangers and women in rebellion

Whether they were what Eric Hobsbawm christened 'social bandits', bushrangers operated in the shadows, often on the fringes of society, in geographically isolated areas. [1] Their lives and actions, like those of other frontier figures, remain shrouded in mystery and legend. Some have been lionised and romanticised in popular fiction. These individuals were admired for flaunting authority and championing the interests of the masses against elite oppression and were often seen by ordinary people as beacons of popular resistance. The *Colonial Times* reported in August 1825 that a poem had been found in the pocket of a bushranger 'written in blood':

> We are the boys that fears no dangers,
> And what you term us is bush-rangers; If it is our lives you do demand,
> True to our guns, then we must stand. We all are young and in our prime,
> To meet our hardships we incline And if our blood you mean to shed,
> Life for life before we yield.
> 'Tis in the bush we are forced to go-
> You settlers prove our overthrow :
> To rob and plunder is against our will.
> But we must have a living still. Now to this country we are come,
> Banished from our native home, And if we can't go back no more,
> We will rob the rich to feed the poor. [2]

In reality, however, banditry often involved violent acts by brutal common criminals for whom theft was simply an economic expedient. Contemporary sources tend to focus on individual bushrangers and often projected the

---

[1] The notion of the 'social bandit' originated in Hobsbawm, Eric, *Primitive Rebels: Studies in Archaic Forms of Social Movement in the 19th and 20th Centuries*, (Manchester University Press), 1959, and was fleshed out a decade later in *Bandits*, (Weidenfeld & Nicholson), 1969, revised edition, (Pantheon), 1981.
[2] *Colonial Times*, 25 August 1825, p. 3

urban middle-class views of writers who romanticised often oral traditions for their own literary and political reasons. [3]

Bushranging in a penal society

Bushrangers were the natural consequence of a system that assigned convicts to forced labour in remote locations across a sparsely occupied countryside. They first became extensive in VDL, where hunting rather than farming became for a time the basis of the economy. For survival the colony had to give guns to convicts and send them out to hunt kangaroos. Initially they had to return to Hobart or Port Dalrymple to sell the meat and get more ammunition. But once settlement proceeded beyond the initial beachheads and settlers became dispersed, the hunters had alternative sources of supply and could operate independently as outlaws. Settlers had an interest in protecting them and trading with them, and often they had the sympathy of emancipated convicts and assigned servants. They were colourful figures with 'long ratty hair, thick beards, roughly sewn garments and moccasins of kangaroo hide, a pistol stuck in a rope belt, a stolen musket, a polecat's stench'. [4] By 1814, they were such a problem that Macquarie offered an amnesty to those bushrangers who turned themselves in by 1 December 1814. This foolhardy proclamation seemed to suggest that all crimes except murder could be committed with impunity until that date; it provoked a carnival of robbery and mayhem. Few surrendered and there was panic in Hobart, prompting Lieutenant-Governor Davey, who lacked a criminal court to try bushrangers or sufficient troops, to declare martial law in 1815. [5] Several were executed after trial by court martial

---

[3] Bonwick, James, *The Bushrangers: Illustrating the Early Days of Van Diemen's Land*, (George Robertson), 1856, White, Charles, *History of Australian Bushranging: Early days to 1862*, (Angus and Robertson), 1900, and Boxall, George, *The story of the Australian bush-rangers*, (Swan Sonnenschein & Co., Ltd.), 1899, still provide the best early narrative accounts of bushrangers. See also, Karskens, Grace, *The Colony: A History of Early Sydney*, (Allen & Unwin), 2009, pp. 300-309.
[4] Ibid, Hughes, Robert, *The Fatal Shore*, p. 227.
[5] Eldershaw, P. R., 'Davey, Thomas (1758-1823)', *ADB*, Vol. 1, pp. 288-289.

before Governor Macquarie revoked martial law. But the problem did not go away. [6]

William Sorell was appointed Lieutenant-Governor of VDL in 1817 in the hope that he would be able to restore order and bring direction and organisation into its government.[7] He immediately proceeded to try to reform the abuses prevalent on the Derwent. He found much disorder in the administration, government activities were not co-ordinated and corruption was common. [8] The convicts were under little control and bushranging had almost reached open armed revolt against the colonial authorities. Sorell firmly met the challenge of Michael Howe, the leader of the bushrangers and self-styled 'Governor of the Woods'. [9] Howe already had a gang of 28 by 1814 and had excellent intelligence about troop movements from small farmers and convicts. Well-planned and executed military operations quickly ended Howe's career and sent most of his followers to the gallows. The stern warning was not lost on those runaway convicts who sought to emulate Howe. [10] Sorell knew that large-scale bushranging was only possible where help was given by outwardly law-abiding free colonists and, in less than eighteen months after taking office, he had arrested all known sympathisers of the bushrangers and those who

---

[6] See, for instance, reports of bushranging in *Hobart Town Gazette and Southern Reporter*, 5 October 1816, p. 1, 19 October 1816, p. 1, 23 November 1816, p. 1, 14 December 1816, p. 1.
[7] Reynolds, John, 'Sorell, William (1775-1848)', *ADB*, Vol. 2, pp. 459-462.
[8] See discussion by Curnow, R., 'What's Past is Prologue: Administrative Corruption in Australia', in Tiihonen, Seppo, (ed.), *The history of corruption in central government*, (IOS Press), 2003, pp. 37-64, especially pp. 39-46.
[9] Von Stieglitz, K. R., 'Howe, Michael (1787-1818)', *ADB*, Vol. 1, pp. 560-561. See also, the pamphlet by Sorell's secretary: Wells, Thomas, *Michael Howe, the Last and Worst of the Bushrangers*, (Andrew Bent, Hobart), 1818, and ibid, Bonwick, James, *The Bushrangers: Illustrating the Early Days of Van Diemen's Land*, pp. 47-57.
[10] On Proclamation offering 100 guineas for Howe's apprehension was issued in *Hobart Town Gazette and Southern Reporter*, 6 September 1817, p. 1. The reward was extended to include a free pardon for any convict following Howe's involvement in the murder of William Drew, *Hobart Town Gazette and Southern Reporter*, 27 December 1817, p. 1.

assisted them. [11] Macquarie optimistically but inaccurately ventured the hope that the 'Bush-Ranging System' was now in decline. [12]

In addition to the soldiers sent against the bushrangers, a force of field police was raised composed largely of convict volunteers, motivated by promises of freedom, money, free passages back home or grants of land. Soldiers and police were assisted by male and female Aboriginal trackers, such as Musquito, an Aboriginal convict from NSW who had helped track and kill Michael Howe in 1818. [13] He was denied his promised reward of being allowed to return home and walked into the bush joining a 'tame gang' that was linked to the Oyster Bay Aborigines. However, the spread of settlement in VDL increasingly threatened their lands and some of his band became progressively more antagonistic towards settlers, attacking several shopkeepers in raids on the east coast in November 1823 and in 1824.[14] Trained by their leader in the use of firearms, they became a formidable force. In August 1824, Musquito was shot and captured by Teague, a Tasmanian Aborigine, but Teague was not given the boat promised as a reward, so he too took to the bush and led a band of Aboriginal bushrangers. No action was taken against him when he came in, but Musquito, convicted on dubious evidence as it is unclear whether he committed any of the murders, was hanged in February 1825.[15] In 1830, a Committee into the Military Operations against Aborigines questioned settlers about the origins of Aboriginal hostility and it concluded, though it makes only the briefest mention of Musquito that the hanging of the four Aborigines in 1825 and 1826 contributed to the permanent rift between the

---

[11] *Hobart Town Gazette and Southern Reporter*, 18 August 1821, p. 2, reported that a melodrama called 'Michael Howe, the Terror of Van Diemen's Land' was performed at the Cobourg Theatre in London

[12] *HRA*, Series I, Vol. 14, p. 292.

[13] Parry, Naomi, 'Musquito (1780-1825)', *ADB*, Supplementary Volume, p. 299.

[14] Melville, Henry, *The History of the Island of Van Diemen's Land from the year 1824 to 1835*, (Smith and Elder), 1835, pp. 32-35, provides later evidence for Sorell's broken promises initially given in 1817.

[15] *Hobart Town Gazette and Van Diemen's Land Advertiser*, 25 February 1825, p. 2, reported his execution.

Aborigines and settler society. There remains some disagreement about the significance of Musquito and whether he was a resistance leader or simply a criminal. [16]

In 1824, Colonel George Arthur, a strict disciplinarian was appointed Lieutenant-Governor and seeking to increase the deterrent effect of transportation on criminals in Britain, he increased convict discipline and ensured that punishment was uniform and assured. [17] The British government responded by increasing the annual average of convicts sent to VDL from about 800 between 1817 and 1827 to about 1,800 between 1828 and 1835; between 1830 and 1836, convicts formed around 44 per cent of the population. [18] The increase in convicts and free settlers swelled the total population from 5,468 in 1820 to 24,279 by 1830. Arthur imposed severe punishments and floggings on convicts who disobeyed his regulations and many were hanged for committing serious crimes, but order was also

---

[16] West, John, *The History of Tasmania*, 2 Vols. (Henry Dowling), 1852, Vol. 2, pp. 11-16, and Bonwick, James, *The Last of the Tasmanians: or, the Black War of Van Diemen's Land*, (Samson Low), 1870, pp. 93-107, and *The Lost Tasmanian Race*, (Samson Low), 1884, pp. 78-83, discuss Musquito within the view that the destruction of the Tasmanian Aborigines was inevitable. By contrast and often overlooked Calder, James Erskine, *Some Account of the Wars, Extirpation, Habits etc. of the Native Tribes of Tasmania*, (Henn & Co.), 1875, pp. 47-56, took a more sympathetic view of Musquito and did not see the destruction of the Tasmanian Aborigines as either inevitable or necessary. Attempts by historians in the 1970s to elevate Musquito to the status of a resistance leader were rebuffed by Windschuttle, Keith, *The Fabrication of Aboriginal History: Volume 1, Van Diemen's Land*, (Macleay Press), 2002, pp. 61-82, an inherently flawed study that views him as a bushranger whose criminal behaviour was inimical to resistance. See also the discussion of the extirpation of the Tasmanian Aborigines see, Brown, Richard, *Resistance and Rebellion in the British Empire, 1600-1980*, (Clio Publishing), 2013, pp. 91-95.
[17] Shaw, A. G. L., *Sir George Arthur, Bart, 1784-1854*, (Melbourne University Press), 1980, and Shaw, A. G. L., 'Sir George Arthur, (1784-1854)', *ADB*, Vol. 1, pp. 32-38.
[18] Ibid, Shaw Alan, *Convicts and Colonies*, pp. 365-367, Forsyth, W. D., *Governor Arthur's Convict System: Van Diemen's Land, 1824-36*, (Sydney University Press), 1970, p. 150, ibid, Alexander, Alison, *Tasmania's Convicts: How Felons Built a Free Society*, pp. 34-89, and Hartwell, R. M., *The Economic Development of Van Diemen's Land, 1820-1850*, (Oxford University Press), 1954, p. 68.

encouraged by offering inducements, such as a tickets-of-leave and pardons, to those who behaved correctly and showed signs of reformation. [19] There could be:

>...no happiness nor prosperity without personal security,' and this could only be secured by 'severe discipline'. [20]

Although Arthur was instructed by the British government to establish 'a stricter surveillance and discipline' over convicts, on his arrival in 1824, he first had to deal with a number of threats to effective government. [21] Of particular concern was 'a vast amount of crime amongst the Prisoners—Murders, constant Robberies, and other atrocious acts,' perpetrated especially by bushrangers. [22] Given his 'exceedingly limited' military force, and his 'inadequate means of punishing offences,' Arthur was thankful that crime was not more widespread, but it was 'truly distressing' to the settlers on isolated farms.[23] The activities of Matthew Brady and thirteen other convicts who had escaped from the brutality of Macquarie Harbour in June 1824 demonstrate the problem of suppressing

---

[19] Arthur, George, *Defence of Transportation, in Reply to the Remarks of the Archbishop of Dublin in His Second Letter to Earl Grey*, (Gowie), 1835, pp. 48, 96-100, ibid, Shaw Alan, *Convicts and Colonies*, pp. 217-48, and Davis, R. P., *The Tasmanian Gallows: A Study of Capital Punishment*, (Cat and Fiddle Press), 1974, pp. 13-33.
[20] CO 280, Arthur to Hanley, 4 April 1834, emphasis in original.
[21] Arthur to Bathurst, 14 September 1825, Arthur to Huskisson, 21 April 1828, minute by Arthur, 26 February 1828, Arthur to Murray, 25 May 1829, *HRA*, Resumed Series III, Vol. 8, pp. 367-371.
[22] Arthur to Bathurst, 3 July 1825, ibid, Levy, M. C. I., *Governor George Arthur*, pp. 90-96, and Maxwell-Stewart, Hamish, "I Could Not Blame the Rangers...': Tasmanian Bushranging, Convicts and Convict Management', *Tasmanian Historical Research Association Papers and Proceedings*, Vol. 42, (1995), pp. 109-126.
[23] Examples of bushranging in VDL are taken from, Petrow, Stefan, 'Policing in a Penal Colony: Governor Arthur's Police System in Van Diemen's Land, 1826-1836', *Law and History Review*, Vol. 18, (2000), pp. 351-395, and 'After Arthur: Policing in Van Diemen's Land 1837-46', in Enders, Mike, and Dupont, Benoît, (eds.), *Policing the Lucky Country*, (Hawkins Press), 2002, pp. 176-198.

bushranging. [24] Arthur's methodical police methods, rewards and spies eventually wore down the Brady gang, and Brady himself was captured in 1826. [25] It now became clear to what extent the bushrangers symbolised popular hostility to the rulers and dozens of petitions arrived at Government House seeking clemency but Brady was still hanged. [26] For the remainder of his period in office, Arthur sought to limit bushranger activity by reducing levels of convict escapes but, with growing convict numbers, he had limited success.

Under Arthur's successors, Sir John Franklin [27] and Sir John Eardley-Wilmot, [28] bushranging still posed a potent threat. In 1838, Franklin reported 'several daring outrages, attended with personal violence, robbery, and murder' committed by four armed convicts. [29] Reacting to the 'alarm' of settlers, Franklin took 'the most vigorous measures' to catch the bushrangers. He sent all able-bodied constables in pursuit and offered 'extraordinary rewards' for their capture and free pardons to convict servants who defended their masters. Convicts who helped capture bushrangers were liable to be killed for their betrayal and were often given free passage to England. [30] Franklin encouraged settlers to defend themselves resolutely, to tell the nearest Police Magistrate of the appearance of bushrangers as quickly as they could and to scour the country for signs of bushrangers. [31] Four bushrangers were captured, but magistrates remained vigilant. [32] Most

---

[24] Robson, L. L., 'Brady, Matthew (1799?-1826)', *ADB*, Vol. 1, pp. 147-148, ibid, Bonwick, James, *The Bushrangers: Illustrating the Early Days of Van Diemen's Land*, pp. 67-86.
[25] 'Brady, the Bush-ranger', *Colonial Times and Tasmanian Advertiser*, 17 March 1826, p. 3.
[26] *Hobart Town Gazette*, 6 May 1826, p. 2.
[27] Fitzpatrick, Kathleen, *Sir John Franklin in Tasmania 1837-1843*, (Melbourne University Press), 1949, and 'Franklin, Sir John (1786-1847), *ADB*, Vol. 1, pp. 412-415.
[28] Roe, Michael, 'Eardley-Wilmot, Sir John Eardley (1783-1847)', *ADB*, Vol. 1, pp. 345-346, Shaw, A. G. L., 'Three Knights: Sir James Stephen, Sir John Franklin, and Sir John Eardley-Wilmot', *Tasmanian Historical Research Association Papers and Proceedings*, Vol. 36, (1989), pp. 141-153.
[29] Franklin to Glenelg, 14 May 1838.
[30] Franklin to Stanley, 21 July 1843.
[31] *Hobart Town Gazette*, 18 May 1838, p. 2..
[32] Forster to Police Magistrates, 6 July 1838.

landholders willingly defended themselves but had farms to work and relied on 'the protecting care of the Government'.[33] This protection was weakened by the withdrawal of regular troops and in November 1840, Franklin reported that he had three companies of infantry less than in May 1839. He protested that, as the convict population increased and spread throughout the island on public works and roads, absconding would increase unless the military could be located at each probation station.[34]

In 1843, bushranging reached especially dangerous levels. The *Cornwall Chronicle* identified seven gangs of bushrangers comprised of from two to fifteen men operating in the north alone.[35] Three 'very determined' bushrangers, including Martin Cash and Laurence Kavenagh, escaped from Port Arthur, committed various acts of robbery and eluded capture. [36] Cash had experience as a splitter in 'the most intricate and impenetrable districts' and knew where to hide. [37] Kangaroo hunters and shepherds allegedly harboured bushrangers and supplied them with ammunition and provisions. [38] Cash used a telescope to watch from the hills and attacked farms at the most vulnerable times, when men were in the fields or constables were not in the vicinity. [39] Bushrangers laughed at the ineffective efforts of convict constables to find them and their 'overweening confidence' encouraged others to abscond to the bush. According to the *Hobart Town Advertiser*, colonists faced a more numerous, desperate and dangerous breed of convicts than the petty thieves of the past. The most desperate were the 'dark, stern, and determined' Irish prisoners, whose crimes had imperilled the lives of others and risked their own. [40] Convicts who

---

[33] Memorial from landholders at Swanport, 25 August 1838.
[34] Franklin to Russell, 3 April 1840, Franklin to Russell, 18 November 1840.
[35] *Cornwall Chronicle*, 6 May 1843, p. 3.
[36] Franklin to Stanley, 3 June 1843.
[37] Cash, M., *Martin Cash: The Bushranger of Van Diemen's Land in 1843-4*, (Walch and Sons), 1870.
[38] *Launceston Advertiser*, 14 September 1843, p. 2. .
[39] *Hobart Town Courier*, 17, 24 February, 31 March 1843.
[40] *Hobart Town Advertiser*, 28 March 1843, p. 2; compare this claim with an analysis of offences by Irish convicts in VDL, see Williams, J., *Ordered to the Island: Irish Convicts and Van Diemen's Land*, (Crossing Press), 1994.

had spent time at Norfolk Island and who were 'anxious for plunder, and, if necessary, bloodshed', were especially feared. [41]

Franklin was sensitive to charges of inefficiency and despite the large numbers of convicts dispersed throughout the colony and a relatively small police force, he pointed out that few convicts absconded and, when they did, committed a 'small amount of crime' and were usually quickly recaptured. [42] Only Riley Jeffs and John Conway, who shot District Constable Ward at Avoca and the Cash gang retained their freedom for long periods. In July 1844, Burgess reported that, during the first half year of his tenure, the average period of freedom was twenty-four days. [43] The police adopted various measures to recapture bushrangers. In July 1843, each magistrate selected four constables as Field Police, men of 'good conduct' with knowledge of the bush. They were stationed at the headquarters of each district ready for immediate deployment and were trained in the use of firearms by the military stationed in their districts. Between January and March 1844, 90 constables were taken from other stations to pursue absconders.

The move to bushranging was a form of protest and on occasions an organised one. Indeed, there are cases where bushranging was a clear consequence of failed collective protest. The most infamous of these occurred at the Castle Forbes Estate in the Hunter Valley, north of Sydney in 1833. [44] Responding to repeated ill-treatment such as striking men and bringing them before magistrates to be flogged for trivial offences, the convict servants sent a representative to the Governor with a petition. However, as his application was irregular and his absence unauthorised, the man was put in chains and flogged at which point the men rose in revolt, robbed the estate and sought to murder the estate manager. At their trial and in speeches on the scaffold prior to being hanged, the men implored the governor to prevent cruelties that had led to their act of

---

[41] *Colonial Times*, 2 April 1844, p. 2..
[42] Franklin to Stanley, 3 June 1843, *Hobart Town Courier*, 12 May 1843, p. 3.
[43] Burgess to Colonial Secretary, 22 July 1844.
[44] This is fully explored in Brown, Richard, *Famine, Fenians and Freedom 1840-1882,* pp. 484-488, and above pp. 368-374.

desperation. In 1846, a gang of probationer convicts employed at Deloraine went on strike when the superintendent refused to make up for rations stolen by several absconding colleagues. Punished for their refusal to work, the men absconded and raided neighbouring properties until they were apprehended and charged with armed robbery. At the resulting trial 12 of the 21 involved were sentenced to death, but this was commuted and all were sent to Port Arthur. [45] Such cases highlighted the risks of overt collective action. In a number of other cases, groups of convicts in chain gangs attacked their supervisor in response to harsh treatment or poor rations even at the almost certain risk of being executed and there are also cases where the murder of a fellow prisoner was reportedly instigated as an extreme means of escaping conditions that were no longer seen as endurable by those involved. [46]

As a form of rebellion bushranging was fragmented with individuals or gangs operating largely independently of each other. Although they posed a threat of public order and were especially feared in the poorly policed frontier areas, their ability to threaten the colonial authorities was limited. They may have been seen by some contemporaries and by later historians as social bandits, but contemporary evidence suggests that many were simply criminals and often very brutal ones. Only in rare cases, such as that of Matthew Brady and Daniel Priest 'the friendly bushranger', did bushrangers gain significant public sympathy. Priest, for instance, was spared execution by the intercession of several clergymen and a petition signed by many country people. [47] Their support within local communities was

---

[45] *Launceston Examiner*, 14 January 1846, p. 3. For a detailed account see Dunning, Tom, and Maxwell-Stewart, Hamish, 'Mutiny at Deloraine: Ganging and Convict Resistance in 1840s Van Diemen's Land', *Labour History*, Vol. 82, (2002), pp. 35-47.

[46] The assaults often involved more than three workers and the role of employment conditions as the underlying cause is not only raised but in many cases widely acknowledged at the subsequent court proceedings. For references to several such cases tried in the Supreme Court of New South Wales, see *Australian*, 21 April 1829, (*R. v. Burgen, Allen, Mathews and Sullivan*); *Sydney Gazette*, 11 November 1833, (*R. v. Smith and others*); and *Sydney Herald*, 6 August 1835, (*R. v. Cassidy and Bagley*).

[47] A reward for Priest's capture dated 12 April 1843 was reported in *Courier*, 21 April 1843, p. 4. This was increased to £100 as well as a

based on their ability to terrorise isolated homesteads or small rural communities and they had little impact on larger centres of colonial power though Brady captured the township of Sorell for a night. From the 1820s, better organised military forces and police led to the quicker capture of escaped convicts but bushranging remained a problem until transportation ended. It continued during the 1850s in VDL but had virtually ceased by 1859 though two youths were hanged in 1883 for terrorising people in Epping Forest shooting two people dead and burning a cottage.

Bushranging in a free society

From the 1850s, especially with the discovery of gold, the character of bushranging changed from an often vapid expression of rebellious liberation by brutalised convicts to criminal activity by native born free men who held up travellers, local landowners and coaches transporting gold and cash. The growth of the electric telegraph in the 1860s and the growth of illustrated newspapers in the 1880s made bushrangers a popular subject in British and Australian newspapers. In some cases their activities involved a search for social justice but for most they were simply criminal acts and they continued to be a persistent problem for the forces of law and order across Australia for the remainder of the century.

Armed highway robbery increased as a result of the transport of gold but also because the introduction of better roads increased people's mobility. In 1864, the Hall gang concentrated its attentions on the Sydney-Melbourne road south of Goulburn. Such were the concerns of the colonial government about Hall's activities that, in 1865 it introduced the Felons' Apprehension Act that allowed those named as 'outlaws' to be shot on sight. Outlaws were legally considered guilty without the usual formality of a trial. Similar legislation, which expired on 26 June 1880,

---

conditional pardon 19 May 1845, *Courier*, 22 May 1845, p. 2. His arrest followed in September 1845, 'Further Particulars of Priest', *Courier*, 27 September 1845, p. 2. His trial took place on 8 October, *Cornwall Chronicle*, 11 October 1845, pp. 235-236, and he was condemned to hang but the Lieutenant-Governor agreed to the petition on 'condition of transportation for life', *Launceston Examiner*, 1 November 1845, p. 4. Priest died in 1883.

was introduced in Victoria in 1878 in response to the shooting of three police at Stringybark Creek on 26 October by the Kelly gang. The Victorian legislation also included a clause that any person harbouring the outlaws, or aiding them with information or supplies or withholding or giving false information to the police, made him or her susceptible to a heavy prison sentence. Its aim was to cut the gang off from its supplies and information. In both NSW and Victoria, the legislation was a pragmatic response to specific problems of criminality that it was difficult to resolve through conventional policing and judicial methods. [48]

In NSW, cattle stealing had long been common in squatting districts but by the 1860s, there was more wealth in rural districts attracting systematic banditry. Bushrangers such as Ben Hall and Frank Gardiner survived partly because small squatters assisted and protected them, as did rural workers. [49] For instance, when Hall's gang violently confronted two larger squatters, Henry Keightley and David Campbell in October 1863, station workers did not aid their employers. Bushrangers proved able to outwit the NSW police—Hall often used stolen race-horses that easily outpaced the police nags—they also became heroes to much of the population of Sydney. There were tumultuous scenes at the conclusion of Gardiner's trial in 1864 when the jury found guilty of two non-capital offences rather than the capital offenses pursued by the authorities though he was still sentenced to a cumulative sentence of thirty-two years' hard labour. Over just two days in the previous year, 14,000 people had signed petitions in an attempt to save two other young bandits from the gallows. In 1874, following petitions to the Governor Sir Hercules Robinson to use his prerogative of mercy, Gardiner was released subject to exile dying in the United States in 1903. This proved a controversial decision and resulted in the fall of Henry Parkes' government. [50]

---

[48] Eburn, Michael, 'Outlawry in Colonial Australia: The Felons Apprehension Acts 1865-1899', *ANZLH E-Journal*, (2005), pp. 80-93, reviews legislation in NSW, Victoria and Queensland.
[49] Penzig, Edgar F., 'Hall, Ben (1837-1865)', *ADB*, Vol. 4, p. 322, and Penzig, Edgar F., 'Gardiner, Francis (Frank) (1830-1903)', *ADB*, Vol. 4, p. 229.
[50] Parkes, Henry et al, *Debates on the Prerogative of Pardon as Involved in the Release of Gardiner & Other Prisoners*, (Gibbs,

In Victoria, where selection was most successful, hardships faced by small farmers in the north-east led to the Kelly outbreak at the end of the 1870s. [51] With the decline of the Ovens gold fields, large numbers of generally under-capitalised ex-diggers sought to establish themselves on small farms in north-eastern Victoria, in the region around Benalla, Wangaratta and Beechworth. In this area the land under cultivation increased from 22,000 acres in 1860 to 163,000 in 1883, yet small farmers fell into such arrears that over 70 per cent of the land selected after 1872 took more than two decades to purchase. Families lived in poorly constructed dwellings and necessity drove them to evade the provision of the Selection Acts that were supposed to help them. After poor harvests or when farm prices were low, men violated the residency requirements of the legislation, introduced in an attempt to prevent land speculation, to find temporary jobs such as shearing that could take them away for up to five months. This overlapped with the most important time for farming and women and children were left to cope. [52]

Economic hardship drove the selectors to other forms of lawlessness such as burning squatters' fences and 'rescuing' impounded livestock. The region's remoteness from Melbourne bred a sense of indifference and hostility toward the colonial authorities while farmers' isolation from each other inhibited effective political organisation to press for resolution of their grievances. Politicians who won their votes lost interest in selector interests upon election, while farmers' unions were ineffective before the 1880s. In 1878, when the Kelly outbreak began, grain prices were

---

Shallard & Co.), 1874?, and Parkes, Henry, *The Case of the Prisoner Gardiner: The Prerogative of Pardon*, (George Robertson), 1876.

[51] Molony, J., *I am Ned Kelly*, (Allen Lane), 1980, 2nd ed., (Melbourne University Press), 2001.

[52] O'Malley, Pat, 'Social bandits, modern capitalism and the traditional peasantry: a critique of Hobsbawm', *Journal of Peasant Studies*, Vol. 6, (4), (1979), pp. 489-501, demonstrates the importance of the presence of class conflict and the absence of effective, institutionalised political organisation of producers' interests in the context of the Kelly outbreak. See also, O'Malley, Pat, 'Class Conflict, Land and Social Banditry: Bushranging in Nineteenth Century Australia', *Social Problems*, Vol. 26, (1979), pp. 271-283.

falling and bad weather had damaged crops. Police in rural areas, like those previously deployed on the goldfields, were paramilitary in style and drew heavily on the Royal Irish Constabulary as a model. [53] They generally came from outside the area, knew nothing of local habits and made little effort to find out. The police were closely allied with the squatters; officers mixed with them socially and the force was always willing to pursue alleged cattle rustlers because of the substantial rewards on offer. Selectors suffered from police corruption, intimidation, incompetence and brutality. They could complain about police but the complaints were never heard or dismissed. Tensions in the rural community came to a head with the Kelly outbreak, and many unpalatable features of policing were brought to public light.

Ned Kelly's family was part of a wider clan with a history of horse theft and clashes with the police, while the authorities for their part conducted a campaign of harassment against the Kellys. Kelly was born in Beveridge, Victoria in 1854 or 1855, the eldest son of John 'Red' Kelly, an Irish-Catholic who was reputedly transported for stealing two pigs and died in 1866. He spent much of his adult life evading police facing charges of stealing, robbery, assault and murder. The police station at Greta, the setting for the Kelly outbreak, was established in 1869 at the request of local squatters, who wanted selector stock thieves dealt with. Hall, the police officer placed in charge of the station, set up a system of spies and used threats and intimidation to control the district's 'criminal classes'. An incentive to corruption was supplied by the local Stock Protection Association, comprised of squatters that supplied rewards for the arrest of suspected stock thieves. Hall vigorously pursued the rewards and arrests were often indiscriminate.

In 1871, Hall arrested the then sixteen year old Ned Kelly, a member of a selector family over use of a horse. In the process he tried, more than once, to shoot Kelly, who was unarmed and administered a severe pistol whipping when his gun failed. The arrest triggered resentment throughout the selector community in the district and Kelly was subsequently sentenced to three years hard labour on

---

[53] Victoria Police, *Police in Victoria 1836-1980*, (Victoria Police), 1980, and Haldane, R., *The People's Force: A history of the Victoria Police*, (Melbourne University Press), 1986, pp. 78-93.

perjured police evidence. Hall's successor, Flood, later threatened to give Kelly 'worse than Hall did'. The whole Kelly family, including women and children, were harassed by local police. These incidents provided the background for the events at Stringybark Creek in 1878, where three police officers were shot and killed by Kelly and his gang. Four police set out on Kelly's trail after an altercation at the Kelly family home in which a police officer was slightly injured. Although Kelly was later found guilty of murder by a Supreme Court jury, there is evidence supporting Kelly's claim that the police were shot in self-defence. The police hunt for the gang over the following twenty months and its climax at the 'siege of Glenrowan', demonstrate both the militaristic style of policing in the area and the extent of police alienation from the community.

Local people generally thought Kelly was 'a man-made outlaw by persecution and injustice' and refused to cooperate with police in the hunt. [54] However, the authorities were alarmed at the degree of public sympathy for this gang of outlaws. One local newspaper reported that three out of every four of the men in the area were on Kelly's side and the sympathy cut across racial divisions, with local Chinese helping to supply the gang. [55] There are claims that the Victorian Aboriginal trackers first employed in the pursuit were sympathetic to the Kellys and led the police around in circles though other accounts suggest the trackers simply wanted to avoid shoot-outs. Chief-Commissioner Standish shared this view, lamenting:

> The Gang were secure of the good will of a great proportion of the inhabitants of these regions...Indeed the outlaws are considered heroes by a large proportion of the population of the North Eastern district who...look upon the police as their natural enemies.

Unable to count on local people's help, police resorted to spies and arresting 'Kelly sympathisers' under the Felons' Apprehension legislation. The Kelly gang had a very effective 'bush telegraph' and were supplied with information and provisions, and in return paid their supporters from the proceeds of their bank robberies. In

---

[54] Morrissey, Doug, 'Ned Kelly's sympathisers', *Historical Studies*, Vol. 18, (1978), pp. 288-296.
[55] *Pastoral Times*, 10 July 1880.

early January 1879, the police arrested 30 'suspected' Kelly sympathisers and detained them in Beechworth gaol. Twenty-three were subsequently charged, and over the next four months were repeatedly remanded in custody while the court awaited the presentation of police evidence against them. By 22 April, eleven men were still inside the gaol without having an opportunity to defend themselves. The suspected sympathisers were farmers and confined at a time when crops needed harvesting. However, the police disregarded such concerns; the higher priority was to capture the gang and stem the gang's access to supplies. It was thought that by breaking their supply line, the gang would need to find alternate sources and that in doing this they would need to come out of hiding. Neither of these objectives appeared to have worked. The action gave the impression that law was neither fair nor equitable. In fact, the police and government's perceived misuse of the power given to them by the Felons' Apprehension Act, ultimately influenced public opinion against them and sympathy for the gang increased.

In addition, search parties were heavily armed. Police finally caught up with Kelly and his gang at Glenrowan. During a siege lasting several hours police blazed away at an inn containing the gang and sixty-two unarmed civilians. Police bullets fatally wounded three civilians, including an old man and a child and injured others, one a teenage boy shot in the back after he tried to escape the potential death trap. While the police showed little regard for the civilians' safety, the gang tried unsuccessfully to negotiate safe passage for those trapped inside. After the siege one journalist wrote:

> The want of judgement displayed by them [the police] was criminal. The indiscriminate firing into a house filled with women and children was a most disgraceful act. [56]

Nevertheless the government paid the police involved in Kelly's capture substantial rewards.

Portrayals of Ned Kelly as a political figure rely on oral sources and the merging of elements of Irish republicanism with contemporary land grievances provided at least a

---

[56] 'Destruction of the Kelly Gang', *Argus*, 29 June 1880, pp. 5-6.

quasi-political rationale for the Kelly outbreak. Ned's Jerilderie letter harked back to the penal settlements where

> ...many a blooming Irishman...was flogged to death and bravely died in servile chains but true to the shamrock and a credit to Paddy Land. [57]

On the other hand, sympathisers came from a diversity of nationalities with differing political views. Following the gang's capture, the Melbourne populace showed its sympathy with demonstrations, including a meeting of 8,000 supporters at the Hippodrome Theatre demanding a reprieve. [58] Shortly after Ned's execution on 11 November 1880 someone fired a shot during a demonstration outside the Glenrowan police station. The demise of the Kelly gang did not remove deeply felt grievances in north-eastern Victoria and for several years, tensions remained high between Kelly sympathisers and the authorities. Official policy denied sympathisers the right to select land and this nearly led to a second rebellion. Later the policy softened and the economic prosperity of the 1880s saw tensions dissipate. Those selectors who managed to survive as farmers gradually became a conservative social force in the following decades.

The seminal place Ned Kelly and other bushrangers have in Australian history suggests that they symbolised

---

[57] The 'Jerilderie Letter' is Kelly's 56-page confession and manifesto in which he admits his crimes but seeks to justify them by saying that he had been forced into them by the corrupt police and he demanded that squatters share their property with the poor. Written in early 1879, it was left with the bank's accountant Edwin Living after the Kelly Gang took about £2,000 from the bank at Jerilderie (8-10 February). Kelly unsuccessfully sought the town's newspaper editor but Living accepted the letter offering to pass it on to the editor. In fact, Living and the bank's manager took it the Melbourne office of the Bank of New South Wales. The police made a 'copy' and placed it 'on file' where it remained largely ignored until the 1930s. See, Elliott, William, 'The Kelly Raid on Jerilderie by One Who Was There', *The Jerilderie Herald and Urana Advertiser*, 4 July 1913.

[58] 'The Execution of Edward Kelly', *Argus*, 11 November 1880, p. 6, includes a narrative of the Kelly gang's exploits as well as a description of the execution itself.

more than individual criminality. [59] The Kelly outbreak was linked to a broader struggle over land and challenges to squatter privilege. Hancock maintained that after the gold rushes and reforms to the democratic process

> Australian nationalism took definite form in the class struggle between the landless majority and the land monopolising squatters. [60]

Because police were at the forefront of repressing selector agitation, they were inevitably part of that struggle. One contemporary police officer described the Kelly outbreak as a form of 'guerrilla warfare' and that the police in the region was 'an army of occupation'. The unpopularity of rural policing assured the hero status of bushrangers in Australian history. It is true that Kelly's 'enemies, even more than his allies, helped make him a legend'.

Women in rebellion

Although much has been written about male convict resistance, contemporaries were equally concerned by the activities of female convicts. Governor Hunter described female convicts as a

> ...disgrace to their sex, are far worse than the men, and are generally found at the bottom of every infamous transaction committed in the colony. [61]

Popular attitudes towards women were expressed in the Molesworth Report:

> ...that society had fixed the standard of the average moral excellence required of women much higher than that which it had erected for men...a higher degree of reformation is required in the

---

[59] Basu, Laura, 'Towards a Memory Dispositif: Truth, Myth and the Ned Kelly lieu de mémoire', in Eril, Astrid, and Rigney, Ann, (eds.), *Mediation, Remediation and the Dynamics of Cultural Memory*, (Walter de Gruyter GmbH & Co.), 2009. pp. 139-156, and Basu, Laura, 'Memory *dispositifs* and national identities: The case of Ned Kelly', *Memory Studies*, Vol. 4, (2011), pp. 33-41.
[60] Hancock, W. K., *Australia*, (Hutchinson's University Library), 1952, p. 60.
[61] Hunter to Portland, 3 July 1799, *HRA*, Series I, Vol. 4, p. 586.

case of a female, before society will concede to her that she has reformed at all. [62]

Anne Summers, writing during a wave of Australian feminism in the mid-1970s, attempted to explain the common perception of women convicts as almost universally immoral:

> The whore stereotype was devised as a calculated sexist means of social control and then...characterized as being the fault of the women who were damned by it.[63]

In contrast, free settler women were characterised as 'God's police' in Summers' work, as these women, with no criminal past, have been seen by both their contemporaries and historians as more moral and upright than the convict women.

The life of female convicts was dominated by two unequal relationships, with the colonial authorities and with men. [64] Women were not subjected to the same levels of physical punishment as male convicts but there was a strong belief in discipline to reform women and the ways in which this operated was of considerable import.[65] Contemporaries tended to view convict women in two contrasting ways, moral dichotomies that pervade current

---

[62] *Report from the Select Committee on Transportation*, (Ordered to be Printed by the House of Commons), 1837.

[63] Summers, Anne, *Damned Whores and God's Police: The Colonization of Women in Australia*, (Penguin), 1975, p. 286.

[64] For women as convicts, see, Daniels, Kay, *Convict Women*, (Allen & Unwin), 1998, Oxley, Deborah, *Convict Maids: The Forced Migration of Women to Australia*, (Cambridge University Press), 1996, Damousi, Joy, *Depraved and disorderly: female convicts, sexuality and gender in Colonial Australia*, (Cambridge University Press), 1997, Reid, Kirsty, *Gender, Crime and Empire: Convicts, settlers and the state in early colonial Australia*, (Manchester University Press), 2007, and the discussion in Brown, Richard, *Three Rebellions: Canada 1837-1838, South Wales 1839 and Victoria, Australia 1854*, pp. 806-807, 821-822.

[65] Women who challenged male authority were punished severely. Though these punishments involved physical pain, more important was their visibility and humiliating nature. Floggings were used but rarely more than 25 lashes. More common were hard labour, fines and occasionally the stocks. Most hated by women was having their heads shaved.

historiography on female convicts. [66] Some observers saw all convict women as 'whores', immoral, degraded and irredeemable. In 1843, for instance, Lucretia Dunkley and Martin Beech, her lover were executed for the murder of her husband:

> A wife – the drunken polluter of the rites of Hymen, the violator of every tie by which the scared institution of marriage can unite in holy wedlock, yielding to brutal lust, and with her paramour consummating her guilty passion in the blood of her husband. [67]

Others, however, made a distinction between those women who could be 'reformed' and became ordinary wives and mothers and those of 'bad character' who were 'incorrigible' in their anti-social behaviour and who could or would not be reformed. [68]

> It is sometimes said, that there is no medium with respect the female character, that either they are all that's good and virtuous, or that they are depraved and abandoned in the extreme; how then is it that in a place like this, where the most profligate and wicked of the female sex are to be found how is it, we say, that the proportionate number of females suffering the severe penalty of the law, should be so comparatively small, when compared with the number of male malefactor. [69]

Female factories had a multiple role acting as arrival depots where women were held before assignment or re-assignment and as places of refuge for women when ill or pregnant or when conditions outside became intolerable. They were also places of imprisonment where women served out sentences for colonial crimes. Termed 'factories', a variety of work was carried out in them, but employment it appears was the least of their roles. Although the factories at Parramatta and the Cascades in Hobart were the largest and attracted most public

---

[66] Ibid, Daniels, Kay, *Convict Women*, pp. 31-48, provides a good summary of the pervading historiography in the late 1990s.
[67] *Sydney Morning Herald*, 15 September 1843, p. 3.
[68] Ibid, Reid, Kirsty, *Gender, Crime and Empire: Convicts, settlers and the state in early colonial Australia*, pp. 17-52, examines the relationship between gender and 'visions of order'.
[69] *Colonial Times*, 23 April 1830, p. 3.

attention, there were institutions at Newcastle, Port Macquarie and Moreton Bay in NSW and at Launceston, George Town and Ross in VDL. [70] They may have been seen by some women as an escape from the dominant male culture of the colonies but most were there because their 'bad behaviour' that was seen as an affront to male authority especially what employers characterised as insolence.

The position of convict women in NSW and VDL, whether inside factories or not, resulted in resistance and rebellion. Damousi identified three different types of resistance. [71] Female sexuality and especially promiscuity limited the extent to which the colonial authorities could mould these women in 'respectable' colonists. Overstepping spatial boundaries and moving into uncontrolled space through drunkenness, abusive language, insolence or petty crime challenged colonial authorities. Finally, there were occasions when women took collective action and rebelled. This was frequently represented by observers as a spectacle, and there were elements of 'rough music' in their actions, and as bizarre or absurd. [72] The press characterised their actions as expressions of wild emotions and those involved in suppressing women's rebellions were seen as 'taming' their recalcitrant excesses.

The Female Factory in Parramatta was a frequent centre of rebellion. [73] Its inmates were divided into three

---

[70] There was, for instance, widespread public concern and criticism about the mismanagement of the Cascades Factory following the death of child were evident in the Hobart *Colonial Times*, 13 March 1838, p. 5, with calls on 27 March 1838 for Governor Sir John Franklin to 'dismiss the persons under whose carelessness or indolence these shocking occurrences take place' and a damning coroner's court verdict reported on 3 April 1838. Despite this, the *Colonial Times*, 29 May 1838, reported a further fatality in the factory nursery.

[71] Ibid, Damousi, Joy, *Depraved and disorderly: female convicts, sexuality and gender in Colonial Australia*, pp. 65-66.

[72] On this issue see, Thompson, E. P., 'Rough Music' in his *Customs in Common*, (Merlin Press), 1991, pp. 467-538, an extended version of 'Rough Music: Le Charivari anglais', *Annales: Économies, Sociétés, Civilisations*, Vol. 27, (1972), pp. 285-315.

[73] On female factories generally and the issue of rebellion, see, ibid, Daniels, Kay, Convict Women, pp. 103-156, and Salt, Annette.

classes. The first was women returned from assignment without complaint and eligible for re-assignment; the second for those pregnant or nursing or moved up from the third-class on probation; the third was a criminal division.

The factory operated as a prison, a maternity home, a marriage bureau, an employment exchange and a hostel or refuge for women in transit between jobs. All its inmates, however, were strictly speaking prisoners... [74]

Originally intended for 300 occupants, by 1830 the factory rarely contained fewer than 500 adults and 100 or so children. There were never enough places to assign female convicts, so a larger proportion of females than males remained in government employment, primarily in wool manufacture. In addition, women returned to the factory over and over because of mistreatment during assignment or were returned there as vagrants because they were unable to find respectable employment. Some committed offences in order to get back to the factory. Females, unlike males, were chosen for assignment individually by settlers, and were likely to be selected on the basis of physical appearance as their skills or previous work history. Apart from the male settlers' sexual intentions, this highlighted the low value placed on female convict labour. Women convicts were seen as immoral and troublesome and as hampered by children; penal authorities regarded their work as a cost saving rather than a source of income for the Crown. Yet the Parramatta factory did profit from their labour. Between 1838 and 1842, there was a return of over £5,000, probably an underestimate. [75]

Exploitation provoked resistance: the go-slow was as common among women as men. When Governor Gipps visited in 1838, he found the third-class women idle because they had no handles for their hammers; they had

---

These outcast women: the Parramatta Female Factory, 1821-1848, (Hale & Iremonger), 1984.
[74] Smith, Babette, *A Cargo of Women: Susannah Watson and the Convicts of the Princess Royal*, (New South Wales University Press) 1988, p. 53.
[75] Alford, Katrina, *Production or Reproduction? An Economic History of Women in Australia*, (Oxford University Press), 1984, p. 164.

simply broken the handles as soon as they were provided. [76] The Parramatta factory was also famous for its riots especially over food and comparisons have been drawn with the actions of women in food riots in Britain. [77] In October 1827, the authorities reduced the inmates' ration of bread and sugar, provoking 100 women to break out and march to Parramatta for provisions. [78]

> A numerous party again assailed the gates, with pick axes, axes, iron crows...and the inmates were quickly poured forth, thick as bees from a hive...About one hundred came into town...Constables were seen running in all directions. A captain, a Lieutenant, two serjents; and about forty rank and file...were seen flying in all directions with fixed bayonets...and so violent were the Amazonian banditti, that nothing less was expected but that the soldiers would be obliged to commence firing on them...[the convict women] Went along, carrying with them their aprons loaded with bread and meat. [79]

The press viewed this event with a combination of amazement and whimsy, trivialising what was a potentially dangerous rebellion. [80] In 1831, a crowd of several hundred women broke out, seized a particularly hated overseer and shaved her head, threatening to go to Sydney and shave the head of 'the Governor and his mob' as well. One of their leaders suggested they demolish the press of the *Sydney Monitor* to punish its editor, who had portrayed the female convicts as 'the worst and vilest of their sex'. [81] Soldiers were called in to round the women up on both occasions and all of Parramatta was amused by the sight of the local

---

[76] *Sydney Herald*, 1 March 1838, 'Our New Governor', *Sydney Gazette and New South Wales Advertiser*, 8 March 1838.
[77] Dunn, Judith, *Colonial Ladies, lovely, lively, and lamentably loose: Crime reports from the Sydney Herald relating to the Female Factory, Parramatta, 1831-1835*, (Judith Dunn), 2008, a useful collation of primary material.
[78] Kent, D., 'Customary Behaviour Transported: A Note on the Parramatta Female Factory Riot of 1827', *Journal of Australian Studies*, No. 40, (March 1994), pp. 75-79.
[79] 'Riot at the Female Factor', *Sydney Gazette and New South Wales Advertiser*, 31 October 1827.
[80] 'The Factory', *Sydney Gazette and New South Wales Advertiser*, 2 November 1827.
[81] 'Female Insurrection at the Factory', *Sydney Monitor*, 5 February 1831.

police and military chasing the women replete with provisions in their aprons. The troops turned out again in 1832 to quell 'extremely unruly' behaviour. [82]

Prisoners bitterly resented having their hair cropped and staged a further riot in 1833 on a day set for hair-cutting.[83] The Reverend Samuel Marsden himself appeared to confront them later lamenting:

> The women had collected large heaps of stones and as soon as we entered the 3rd Class they threw a shower of stones as fast as they possibly could and at the whole of us...It will never do to show them any clemency...I have no doubt but all the officers who saw their riotous conduct will be convinced of the necessity of keeping them under the hand of power. [84]

Yet keeping them under the 'hand of power' seldom proved easy. 1836 saw further problems and in 1852 a visiting writer recorded stories of another riot in 1839 over cropping convicts' hair that apparently achieved a relaxation of the 'depilatory laws':

> ...it is not many years ago that the Amazonian inmates, amounting to seven or eight hundred, and headed by a ferocious giantess...rose upon the guards and turnkeys, and made a desperate attempt to escape by burning the building. The officer commanding... sent a subaltern with a hundred men, half of them armed only with sticks...They laughed at the cane carrying soldiers, refuting their argumentum baculinum by a furious charge upon the gates, in which one man was knocked over by a brickbat...This unladylike ebullition was considered, as I am assured, the most formidable convict that ever occurred in the colony, not even excepting that of Castle Hill, in the year 1804! [85]

---

[82] 'Police Report', *Sydney Gazette and New South Wales Advertiser*, 5 March 1832.
[83] Ibid, Damousi, Joy, *Depraved and disorderly: female convicts, sexuality and gender in Colonial Australia,* pp. 86-87, views head-shaving as a 'process of defeminisation', and as 'a lasting sign of punishment and an outward sign of moral corruption and weak character.' It also denoted 'feminine shame as those so punished were de-sexed and defeminised with their vanity undermined.'
[84] Samuel Marsden to Colonial Secretary, 7 March 1833, cit, ibid, Smith, Babette, *A Cargo of Women: Susannah Watson and the Convicts of the Princess Royal*, pp. 54-55.
[85] Mundy, Godfrey Charles, *Our Antipodes; or, Residence and rambles in the Australian colonies: With a glimpse of the gold fields*, 2 Vols. (R. Bentley), 1852, Vol. 1, p. 137.

Similar events also occurred in VDL. [86] In 1838, on a visit to the Cascades Factory in Hobart, Sir John Franklin, his wife and guests were subjected to a direct action by 300 female inmates who bared their buttocks which they then slapped in front of the governor's party. Though some of the females in the party 'could not control their laughing', expressions of jest or 'play' were punishable offences for convict women. Franklin, by contrast, was horrified by the event and vowed never to visit the institution again. In 1841, a prisoner in the Female Factory at Launceston asked to be released from solitary confinement on grounds of illness and when the Surgeon refused, a group of inmates seized and held the Sub-Matron while releasing the prisoner. Eighty-five women barricaded themselves in a section of the Factory beating off police attacks by arming themselves with parts of their spinning wheels, bricks, knives and bottles. After the authorities refused to make concessions, they 'became very outrageous, breaking the Furniture and windows and attempting to burn the Building'. When the ringleaders were eventually brought to trial they continued to 'exhibit the most outrageous Conducts abusing and threatening the Magistrates to their face.' [87]

Resistance by convict women received less attention by contemporaries and subsequently by historians than convict rebellions by men. The important difference from male convict rebellions lay in the ways in which women's actions were regarded by the press. Rebellion was seen in two contrasting ways: on the one hand there was the fear engendered by the 'unruly mob'; on the other, rebellions by women were seen as less threatening than those by men, more of a 'frolic' or spectacle. In extreme cases, however, the rioters were de-sexed or masculinised by the press, as

---

[86] See Daniels, K., 'The Flash Mob: Rebellion, Rough Culture and Sexuality in the Female Factories of Van Diemen's Land', *Australian Feminist Studies*, Vol. 18, (1993), pp. 133-150, and Reid, Kirsty, "Contumacious, ungovernable and incorrigible': convict women and workplace resistance, Van Diemen's Land 1820-1839', in Duffield, Ian and Bradley, James, (eds.), *Representing Convicts: New Perspectives on Convict Forced Labour Migration*, (Leicester University Press), 1997, pp. 88-105.
[87] Daniels, Kay, and Murnane, Mary, *Uphill All the Way, A Documentary History of Women in Australia*, (University of Queensland Press), 1980, p. 20.

their actions overtly crossed the boundary between socially acceptable and unacceptable female behaviour in their challenge to male hegemony.

13 Hell in Paradise

Convict resistance was widespread in NSW and then VDL in the decades following the unsuccessful rebellion in 1804. The major reason why there were no further large-scale rebellions on mainland Australia was that recalcitrant convicts were increasingly isolated in punishment settlements. The discovery of coal in NSW resulted in the development of Newcastle and its example was later following in VDL with the establishment of the prison settlement at Port Arthur. However, the most feared and infamous settlement was on Norfolk Island that lay about a thousand miles from both Australia and NZ and covers an area of just over thirteen square miles and was represented as all that was bad about the convict system. Bathurst's 1824 proclamation stated that the 'worst description' of convicts from NSW and VDL would be sent to the Island. [1] Its isolation and the draconian nature of its administration, especially after 1825, made it one of the most brutal penal settlements of the nineteenth century and it was the location for the other major convict rebellion in 1834. [2] In 1840, Charles Dickens volunteered to write a cheap government-sanctioned narrative of Norfolk Island to ensure that the lower orders held it in sufficient dread. [3] Such a work was

---

[1] Bathurst to Brisbane, 22 July 1824, *HRA*, Series I, Vol. 11, p. 322.
[2] See, Hoare, Merval, *Norfolk Island; An outline of its history 1774-1968*, fifth edition, (University of Queensland Press), 1999, Hazzard, Margaret, *Punishment Short of Death: A History of the Penal Settlement at Norfolk Island*, (Hyland House), 1984, Treadgold, M. L., *Bounteous Bestowal: The economic history of Norfolk Island*, (Australian National University), 1988, and O'Collins, Maev, *An Uneasy Relationship: Norfolk Island and the Commonwealth of Australia*, (ANU Press), 2002, pp. 1-19. Benton, Laura, *A Search for Sovereignty: Law and Geography in European Empires, 1400-1900*, (Cambridge University Press), 2010, pp. 197-208, examines the uses made of extra-legal disciplinary systems.
[3] Dickens to Normanby, 3 July 1840, in Storey, Graham, Tillotson, Kathleen, and Easson, Angus, (eds.), *The Letters of Charles Dickens, Volume 7, 1853-1855*, (Oxford University Press), 1993, p. 818. The letter was referred to in the context of *Hard Times*, (Bradbury & Evans), 1854, p. 178, where Norfolk Island is briefly mentioned.

unnecessary since the Island was already a byword for criminality and perversity.

Settling Norfolk Island

Sighted and named by Captain Cook in 1774, Norfolk Island was included as an auxiliary settlement in the British government's plan for colonisation of NSW in 1786 and initially settled in March 1788. The decision to settle Norfolk Island, as well as the main settlement at Botany Bay, was based on its natural resources: tall, straight Norfolk Island pines and the NZ flax plant. [4] Cook had taken samples back to Britain and reported on their potential uses for the Royal Navy. Britain was heavily dependent on flax for sails and hemp for ropes largely imported from Russia through the Baltic Sea ports and also on timbers for mainmasts from New England. Relying on potentially erratic imports of these supplies posed a threat to Britain's naval supremacy. Norfolk Island offered an alternative source and some historians, notably Geoffrey Blainey, have argued that this was a major reason for the founding of the convict settlement of NSW in 1788. The *Universal Daily Register* revealed the plan for a dual colonisation of Norfolk Island and Botany Bay:

> The ships for Botany Bay are not to leave all the convicts there; some of them are to be taken to Norfolk Island, which is about eight hundred miles East of Botany Bay, and about four hundred miles short of New Zealand. [5]

The advantage of a non-Russian source of flax and hemp for naval supplies was referred to in *Lloyd's Evening Post*:

> It is undoubtedly the interest of Great-Britain to remain neutral in the present contest between the Russians and the Turks...Should England cease to render her services to the Empress of Russia, in a war against the Turks, there can be little of nothing to fear from her ill-will. England will speedily be

---

[4] See, Nobbs, R., (ed.), *Norfolk Island and its First Settlement, 1788-1814*, (Library of Australian History), 1988, and Donohoe, J. H., *Norfolk Island, 1788-1813: the people and their families*, (J. H. Donohoe), 1986.
[5] *Universal Daily Register*, 23 December 1786.

enabled to draw from her colony of New South Wales, the staple of Russia, hemp and flax. [6]

Governor Arthur Phillip's final instructions, given him in April 1787 less than three weeks before sailing, included the requirement to colonise Norfolk Island to prevent it falling into the hands of France, whose naval leaders were also showing interest in the Pacific. [7]

...as soon as Circumstances may admit of it...to prevent its being occupied by the Subjects of any other European Power. [8]

Phillip had chosen King as second lieutenant on HMS *Sirius* for the expedition to establish a convict settlement in NSW. King had served with Phillip before the First Fleet and was regarded as his protégé. Phillip certainly had a high opinion of King and consciously promoted his interests throughout the late 1780s and 1790s. Despite his lowly rank, soon after the settlement was established at Sydney Cove, King was selected to lead a small party of convicts and guards to set up a settlement at Norfolk Island. On 14 February 1788, he sailed for his new post with a party of twenty-three, including fifteen convicts. [9] On 6 March 1788, King and his party landed with difficulty, owing to the lack of a suitable harbour and set about building huts, clearing the land, planting crops and resisting the ravages of grubs, salt air and hurricanes. [10]

---

[6] *Lloyd's Evening Post*, 5 October 1787.
[7] Dyer, Colin, *The French Explorers and Sydney*, (University of Queensland Press), 2009, draws on French observations of the British convict settlement in NSW.
[8] *HRNSW*, Vol. 1, (2), pp. 84-91, *HRA*, Series I: Vol. 1, pp. 2-9.
[9] Crittenden, Victor, *King of Norfolk Island: The Story of Philip Gidley King as Commandant and Lieutenant-Governor of Norfolk Island*, (Mulini Press), 1993. For King's appointment and instructions see, *HRNSW*, Vol. 1, (2), pp. 136-138. Fidlon, P. G., and Ryan, R. J., (eds.), *The Journal of Philip Gidley King: Lieutenant, R.N., 1787-1790*, (Australian Documents Library), 1980, gives King's view of his governance of Norfolk Island until 1790.
[10] Phillip to Sydney, 28 September 1788, *HRNSW*, Vol. 1, (2), pp. 185-187, provides analysis of the resources of Norfolk Island. See also, Phillip, Arthur, *The voyage of Governor Phillip to Botany Bay: with an account of the establishment of the colonies of Port Jackson & Norfolk Island*, 3rd ed., (Printed for J. Stockdale), 1790.

More convicts were sent and these proved occasionally troublesome. Early in 1789, King prevented a mutiny when some of the convicts planned to take him and the other officers prisoner and escape on the next boat to arrive. [11] Despite the lack of a safe harbour, of lime and timbered land, there was plenty of fish, the stock flourished and the soil was good. It could maintain 'at least one hundred families', King told Phillip. Impressed by his work, the governor several times recommended his subordinate for naval promotion, but this would have raised difficulties because of King's lack of seniority. To resolve the problem the Secretary of State announced in December 1789 that King would be appointed Lieutenant-Governor of Norfolk Island at a salary of £250. [12]

Following the wreck of *Sirius* at Norfolk Island in March 1790, King left and returned to England to report on the difficulties facing the settlements in NSW. During his twenty months absence, the island was under the command of Lieutenant-Governor Robert Ross [13] but Ross was not an easy commandant and convicts, settlers, soldiers and officials had become discontented under his rule. [14] King found 'discord and strife on every person's countenance'

Ross to Phillip, 11 February 1791, gives a detailed discussion of problems encountered, *HRNSW*, Vol. 1, (2), pp. 434-450.

[11] Phillip to Sydney, 12 February 1790, *HRNSW*, Vol. 1, (2), pp. 293-294. Since Phillip had corresponded with Sydney during 1789, it is difficult to explain why he left it a year before informing him of the mutiny.

[12] For King's commission dated 28 January 1790, see, *HRNSW*, Vol. 1, (2), pp. 287-288.

[13] For Ross' instruction dated 2 March 1790, see, *HRNSW*, Vol. 1, (2), pp. 314-316. See also his observations on the island in December 1790, *HRNSW*, Vol. 1, (2), pp. 416-420, and the contrast with King's observations in January 1791 when he was in London, *HRNSW*, Vol. 1, (2), pp. 428-431. See also, Macmillan, David S., 'Ross, Robert (1740?-1794)', *ADB*, Vol. 2, pp. 397-398.

[14] Ross had introduced martial law almost as soon as he arrived at Norfolk Island because of the loss of the *Sirius*; see, Ross to Phillip, 22 March 1790, *HRNSW*, Vol. 1, (2), pp. 319-320, and also the enclosures pp. 321-323, in which Ross laid down the standards that would now operate on the island. Phillip informed Grenville in a letter dated 14 July 1790, *HRNSW*, Vol. 1, (2), pp. 357-358. Food shortages on Norfolk Island led Ross to introduce draconian measures to conserve supplies in proclamations on 7 August 1790, *HRNSW*, Vol. 1, (2), pp. 390-393.

and was 'pestered with complaints, bitter revilings, backbiting'. [15] Tools and skilled labour were both in short supply. Thefts were common and there was still no criminal court on the island, despite the representations he had made in London on the need for better judicial arrangements.[16] However, King's guidance helped to improve conditions. The regulations he issued in 1792 encouraged the settlers, who were drawn from ex-marines and ex-convicts, and he was willing to listen to their advice on fixing wages and prices and other things. Unfortunately King had no success with growing the flax that so interested the British government. [17] The pine timber was found to be not durable enough for masts and this industry was also abandoned. By 1794, the island was self-sufficient in grain and had a surplus of swine that it could send to Sydney. Maize, wheat, potatoes, cabbage, timber, flax and fruit of all kinds grew well, the population grew to more than 1,100 and about a quarter of the island was cleared. Suffering from gout, King returned to England in October 1796, and after regaining his health, he resumed his naval career.

Between 1796 and 1800, Norfolk Island was ruled by Captain John Townson and then briefly by Captain Thomas Rowley. Townson spent six years on Norfolk Island between late 1791 and 1799 and received a twenty acre lease. [18] His administration was generally capable and he seems to have had a steadying influence on both convicts and settlers. When Townson left prematurely in November 1799, Rowley, as the senior officer, took charge of the settlement. He ordered liquor stills to be demolished to reduce the drunkenness on the island, and this move

---

[15] King to Under Secretary Evan Nepean, 23 November 1791, *HRNSW*, Vol. 1, (2), p. 562; see also King to Phillip, 29 December 1791, *HRNSW*, Vol. 1, (2), pp. 572-580.

[16] See Phillip to Dundas, 4 October 1791, *HRNSW*, Vol. 1, (2), p. 655, on the inconveniences of the lack of a criminal court on Norfolk Island. Legislation was finally passed in London establishing a criminal court on Norfolk Island on 9 May 1794, *HRNSW*, Vol. 2, pp. 235-236.

[17] King to Dundas, 19 November 1793, *HRNSW*, Vol. 2, pp. 86-98, details the voyage to NZ to obtain Maori help with flax production. This failed and the natives returned to NZ, *HRNSW*, Vol. 2, p. 174.

[18] Austin, M., 'Townson, John (1759?-1835)', *ADB*, Vol. 2, pp. 536-537.

brought threats of prosecution from their owners. [19] King returned to NSW in early 1800 as Governor. [20] He appointed Major Joseph Foveaux as Lieutenant-Governor of Norfolk Island in June 1800. [21]

Foveaux found the settlement quite run down, little maintenance having been carried out in the previous four years. Its population consisted of 519 men, 165 women and 269 children and had an unusually high ratio of free settlers to convicts: not including children, there were 308 free settlers and 272 convicts. Foveaux was unimpressed with his civil administration regarding the NSW Corps officers generally unfavourably. [22] He set about building up the community, particularly through public works and attempted to improve education. By 1800, Norfolk Island was a regular stop from the increasing number of whaling ships from the United States and Britain. Whale oil was much in demand, not least as a means of street lighting and by 1802 almost a hundred ships were involved in the Southern Ocean fishery. Whalers made lengthy voyages, often lasting two or three years and they found that wood and food were cheaper on Norfolk Island than in Sydney. This gave a welcome boost to the island's economy. Whaling captains were often of assistance to Foveaux, selling tools and other goods needed on the island and carrying despatches to and from England. However, on occasions Foveaux complained that whalers overcharged for taking goods and passengers to Sydney and demanded

---

[19] Fletcher, B. H., 'Rowley, Thomas (1748?-1806)', *ADB*, Vol. 2, p. 403.

[20] King arrived in NSW with the letter (Portland to Hunter, 5 November 1799, *HRNSW*, Vol. 3, pp. 733-738, *HRA*, Series I: Vol. 2, pp. 387-392, recalling Governor John Hunter was received on 16 April 1800, but he did not hand over the government to King until 28 September.

[21] See, King to Portland, 29 April 1800, *HRNSW*, vol. 4, p. 79, makes clear King's decision and King to Foveaux, 26 June 1800, *HRNSW*, Vol. 4, pp. 96-108, details Foveaux's appointment and instructions. See also, Fletcher, B. H., 'Foveaux, Joseph (1767-1846)', *ADB*, Vol. 1, pp. 407-409, and Whitaker, Ann-Maree, *Joseph Foveaux: power and patronage in early New South Wales*, (University of New South Wales Press), 2000, pp. 55-80, for his years on Norfolk Island.

[22] State of the Settlement in Norfolk Island, 6 November 1800, *HRNSW*, Vol. 4, pp. 252-253.

urgent repairs that interfered with his plans for public works and farming. [23]

Foveaux and rebellion in 1800

There had been attempted convict rebellions in 1789 and 1794 and this situation intensified with the arrival on the island in early November 1800 of a group of United Irish prisoners, several of whom had been implicated in conspiracies in Sydney in September and October. Although Foveaux was aware of the need for surveillance over the convicts, he believed that lenient treatment and the isolation of the island would discourage any attempts at escape. The United Irishmen were allowed free association with each other and with earlier arrivals. In particular, Farrell Cuffe, a school teacher and United Irishman from County Offaly struck up or possibly renewed a friendship with Peter McLean, a political prisoner from County Cavan who had arrived with Foveaux in July. The result was preparations for an armed escape. Convicts began making pikes and Cockerton Ross, an expiree, promised to give them 15 muskets. McLean was also in correspondence with Thomas Pyshe Palmer in Sydney who promised that a ship would come to take them away once the conspirators had seized the settlement. [24]

The rebellion was originally planned for Christmas Day when McLean and sympathetic soldiers would open the barracks and the rebels would seize weapons and proceed to the guardhouse, magazine and gaol. The fraternisation of several of the soldiers with the Irish convicts had already caused some concern in the garrison but no action had been taken. However, preparations were so advanced that the plan was brought forward to the night of Saturday 13 December but was deferred for twenty-four hours following a meeting at which the rebels disagreed about whether the officers, their wives and children should be killed or not. In the interim, the conspiracy was

---

[23] On the development of the South Sea whale-fishery, see, minutes of the Board of Trade, 4 December 1801, *HRNSW*, Vol. 4, p. 630. See also, Little, B., 'Sealing and Whaling in Australia Before 1850', *Australian Economic History Review*, Vol. 9, (1969), pp. 109-127.
[24] Earnshaw, John, 'Palmer, Thomas Fyshe (1747-1802)', *ADB*, Vol. 2, pp. 312-313.

betrayed to Foveaux by Henry Grady, a reluctant rebel and Thomas Hodges. Foveaux acted decisively and with his civil and military officers agreed that capital punishment should be used, perhaps angered that his leniency had been abused or by the threat of violence to women and children.[25] McLean and John Houlahan, named as the chief organiser of the pike-making were arrested on the Sunday morning and hanged in the afternoon before the assembled convicts and soldiers. The four soldiers involved were ceremoniously drummed out of the NSW Corps and received 500 lashes each. Although there were some questions about the legality of summary executions, King agreed with Foveaux's actions and submitted a favourable report to London. [26]

Until severe asthma forced him to return first to Sydney in September 1803 and to London a year later, Foveaux concentrated his efforts on improving conditions on Norfolk Island, paying particular attention to public works, with results that earned high praise from both King and Lord Hobart, the Secretary of State. More questionable, however, was the dubious morality of allowing the sale of female convicts to settlers. Despite these advances, the future of Norfolk Island as a penal settlement, initially questioned by King as early as 1794, had already been decided before Foveaux left. It was too remote, too costly to maintain and the lack of a harbour made it difficult for shipping and, with the establishment of a settlement in VDL in 1803, there was now an alternative location for a penal settlement for difficult convicts. By 1803, Lord Hobart called for the removal of part of the Norfolk Island military establishment, settlers and convicts to VDL, due to its great expense and the difficulties of communication with Sydney. [27] Foveaux made his view clear to the Colonial Office that Norfolk Island should be abandoned in favour of VDL on his leave in England. [28]

John Houston, a naval lieutenant, was sent from Sydney to take over as Lieutenant-Governor and arrived at

---

[25] *HRNSW*, Vol. 4, pp. 266-267, details the meeting
[26] King to Portland, 10 March 1801, *HRNSW*, Vol. 4, p. 319, 325,
[27] Hobart to King, 24 June 1803, *HRNSW*, Vol. 5, pp. 157-159; this was not received by King until May 1804.
[28] See, Lieutenant-Governor Foveaux's Observations concerning the Removal of the Settlement at Norfolk Island, 25 March 1805, *HRNSW*, Vol. 5, pp. 581-585.

Norfolk Island on 13 February 1804 with Captain John Piper of the NSW Corps. Foveaux also returned to the island in February and continued with his plans for improvement but in July 1804 received a despatch from King ordering evacuation of the island. [29] Houston returned to Sydney and Piper became Lieutenant-Governor, a position he held until January 1810. [30] The duty of carrying out the frequently altered instructions fell to Piper and he appears to have exhibited both tact and organising ability. The evacuation was achieved more slowly than anticipated because of the reluctance of settlers to uproot themselves from the land they had struggled to tame and compensation claims for loss of stock. It was also delayed by King who insisted on the importance of the island for the whaling industry and probably his own personal attachment to it. [31] The first group of 159 left in February 1805 and comprised mainly convicts and their families and military personnel, only four settlers departing. [32] Between November 1807 and September 1808, five groups of 554 people left. Only about 200 remained, forming a small settlement until the remnants were removed in 1813. A small party led by a trusted emancipated convict William Hutchinson, which finally left on 15 February 1814, remained to slaughter stock and destroy all buildings so that there would be no incentive for anyone, especially from another European power, to visit or attempt to colonise it. [33]

'Hell in Paradise'

The ways in which Norfolk Island was regarded in the nineteenth century have led to stories to be told that do not

---

[29] King to Foveaux, 20 July 1804, *HRNSW*, Vol. 5, pp. 403-406, detailed how the partial evacuation was to be managed.
[30] Barnard, Marjorie, 'Piper, John (1773-1851)', *ADB*, Vol. 2, pp. 334-335.
[31] King to Sir Joseph Banks, 14 August 1804, *HRNSW*, Vol. 5, pp. 447-448, expressed King's belief in the importance of Norfolk Island and King to Camden, 30 April 1805, *HRNSW*, Vol. 5, pp. 600-601, concerning the whalers.
[32] See King to Camden, 30 April 1805, *HRNSW*, Vol. 5, pp. 600-601, on the first tranche of the removal.
[33] Le Roy, Paul Edwin, 'Hutchinson, William (1772-1846)', *ADB*, Vol. 1, pp. 574-575.

correspond to its reality. The Norfolk Island legend has several defining characteristics that include assumptions that the prisoners were universally brutalised and had no hope, that commandants and their subordinates were sadists, sexual violence was widespread, and that 'unnatural crimes'–Victorian shorthand for homosexuality–were rampant.

During Norfolk Island's second settlement between 1825 and 1855, it was indeed the 'Hell of the Pacific', a place dominated by death and despair. [34] In 1824, the Governor of NSW, Sir Thomas Brisbane, [35] received a directive from Lord Bathurst, the Colonial Secretary that Norfolk Island was again to be turned into a penitentiary. [36] Its remoteness, seen previously as a disadvantage, was now viewed as an asset for the detention of those 'twice-convicted', men who had committed further crimes since arriving in NSW and VDL. Brisbane decided that it was the best place to send the worst felons 'forever to be excluded from all hope of return'. Norfolk Island would be 'the *nec plus ultra* of Convict degradation'.[37]

His successor, Governor Ralph Darling, [38] was even more severe than Brisbane, and made it clear in 1827 that he wished that 'every man should be worked in irons that the example may deter others from the commission of crime' [39] and that 'My object was to hold out [Norfolk Island] as a place of the extremest punishment short of death'. [40] Governor George Arthur, in VDL, also believed that 'when prisoners are sent to Norfolk Island, they should

---

[34] See, Nobbs, R., (ed.), *Norfolk Island and its Second Settlement, 1825-1855*, (Library of Australian History), 1991.
[35] Heydon, J. D., 'Brisbane, Sir Thomas Makdougall (1773-1860)', *ADB*, Vol. 1, pp. 151-155, and Brisbane, Sir Thomas Makdougall, *Reminiscences of General Sir Thomas Makdougall Brisbane*, (T. Constable), 1860, pp. 43-60.
[36] Bathurst to Brisbane, 22 July 1824, *HRA*, Series I: Vol. 11, pp. 321-322, acknowledged by Brisbane, 21 May 1825.
[37] Brisbane to Under-Secretary Horton, 24 March 1825, *HRA*, Series I: Vol. 11, p. 553.
[38] 'Sir Ralph Darling (1772-1858), *ADB*, Vol. 1, 1966, pp. 282-286, and ibid, Fletcher, Brian, *Ralph Darling: A Governor Maligned*, provide biographical material.
[39] Darling to Under-Secretary Hay, 10 February 1827, *HRA*, Series I: Vol. 13, p. 106.
[40] Cit, ibid, Hazzard, Margaret, *Punishment Short of Death*, p. 111.

on no account be permitted to return. Transportation thither should be considered as the ultimate limit and a punishment short only of death'. Sir Richard Bourke instructed Major Joseph Anderson, the notorious Commandant of Norfolk Island from 1834 to 1839, to keep prisoners working manually in irons even though it was expensive and inefficient, as the penal settlement was considered a place of punishment. He deliberately warned him against implementing any more efficient methods of production, such as mills that were not 'urged by the labour of convicts'. [41] Despite the reliance on manual labour, prisoners on Norfolk Island were cheaper to keep than chained convicts in NSW and the existence of the place at all was considered by many in Britain to be part of the 'moral cost' of the transportation system. Convicts so feared Norfolk Island that Elliott one of the prisoners declared that he would rather hang than be sent there. [42] The Norfolk Island penal settlement was not primarily for the reformation of convicts.

Conditions for convicts, many of them Irish Catholics, were unrelentingly brutal. A large percentage of the convicts were sentenced to remain in heavy chains for the terms of their natural lives and most convicts were chained during the day. Convicts were used primarily as farm labourers or in building much of what today is Kingston. Stone was quarried for building from Nepean Island, a rock close to shore and coral rubble was rendered with lime and sand. Norfolk Pine was used for joinery and roofs and floors were made from thin stone slabs. Flogging was common, sometimes up to 500 strokes. Dumb-cells were constructed to exclude light and sound in which some lost their sanity. Solitary confinement, increased workloads and decreased rations were also common forms of punishment. Michael Burns, for instance, suffered a total of 2,210 lashes

---

[41] See, Bourke to Stanley, 15 January 1834, *HRA*, Series I: Vol. 17, pp. 319-320, 327-328.

[42] *R. v. Jones, Giles and Elliot*: report of execution, *Australian*, 13 September 1833. For other declarations of preference for death over transportation to Norfolk Island, see *R v Gough, Watson and Muir*, 1827, Therry, R., *Reminiscences of Thirty Years' Residence in New South Wales and Victoria: with a supplementary chapter on transportation and the ticket-of-leave system,* (Sampson Low, Son, and Co.), 1863, pp. 19, 24, and *R v Pegg*, 1831, who preferred death to 14 years' transportation.

and almost two years in confinement, much of it in solitary with at least six months of those two years on a diet of bread and water. His crimes were insolence, suspected robbery and neglect of work, striking a fellow prisoner, bushranging, singing a song, calling for a doctor, attempted escape and inability to work due to incapacity caused by his punishments. [43] Thomas Bunbury, briefly commandant in 1839 after the brief mutiny by the 80th Regiment on the island, [44] wrote that he could not understand why 'a villain who has been guilty of every enormity, should feel shame at having his back scratched with the cat-o-nine-tails when he felt none for his atrocious crimes' and that 'if a man is too sick to work he is too sick to eat'. [45]

Such was the harshness of both hard labour and punishment that for some death was preferable to continued torment though contemporary evidence for this is limited. When Father William Ullathorne, Vicar general of Sydney, visited Norfolk Island to comfort those due for execution after the 1834 rebellion, he found it 'the most heartrending scene that I ever witnessed'. Having the duty of informing the prisoners as to who was reprieved and who was to die, he was shocked to record as 'a literal fact that each man who heard his reprieve wept bitterly, and that each man who heard of his condemnation to death went down on his knees with dry eyes, and thanked God.' [46] John Frederick Mortlock, who wrote about his own

---

[43] Cook, Thomas, *The exile's lamentations or biographical sketch of Thomas Cook who was convicted at the Assizes held at Shrewsbury in March 1831 for 'writing threatening letters' and sentenced 14 yrs transportation and re-convicted for forgery and sentenced to Norfolk Island for life*, 1840, reprinted, (Library of Australian History), 1978, p. 48.

[44] Sargent, Clem, 'The British Garrison in Australia 1788-1841: the mutiny of the 80th Regiment on Norfolk Island', *Sabretache*, Vol. 59, (3), (2005), pp. 5-22, is essential on this neglected rebellion.

[45] Bunbury, Thomas, *Reminiscences of a Veteran: being personal and military adventures in Portugal, Spain, France, Malta, New South Wales, Norfolk Island, New Zealand, Andaman Islands, and India*, 3 Vols. (C.J. Skeet), 1861, reprinted (N & M Press), 2009, cit. ibid, Hazzard, Margaret, *Punishment Short of Death*, p. 152

[46] Cit, Birt, Henry Norbert, *Benedictine Pioneers in Australia*, 2 Vols. (Herbert & Daniel), Vol. 1, 1911, p. 178, and Butler, Edward Cuthbert, *The life & times of Bishop Ullathorne, 1806-1889*, 2 Vols. (Burns, Oates, and Washbourne, Ltd.), 1926, Vol. 1, p. 94.

treatment at various settlements around Australia and arrived on Norfolk Island in 1845, explained:

> ...instead of awakening moral responsibility, it [injudicious severity] strengthens the Devil, and makes men more difficult to manage—more likely to be dangerous when restored to society. [47]

There is evidence that some men committed capital offences with 'suicidal intent' so that they would be executed. For instance, William Westwood, one of the leaders of the 1846 riot suggested in a conversation with Stipendiary Magistrate Samuel Barrow that he 'became careless and reckless of life' and that 'the death I am going to suffer could be preferable to Norfolk Island.' [48] However, an attempted escape from gaol suggests that his claims should be treated with some scepticism. These incidents were embellished into stories of 'suicide lotteries' by some contemporary writers. John West, for instance, argued that men at Macquarie Harbour 'gambled for life'. [49] The Norfolk Island suicide lottery myth relies on an extremely limited number of sources and despite the continued currency of these tales, the suicide rate on the Island was extremely low with only three recorded attempted suicides, a consequence Causer argues 'that convicts were averse to suicide for explicitly religious reasons'. [50]

By the mid-1840s, there was increasing concern among humanitarians and those concerned with managing convicts that the regime on Norfolk Island was too brutal and that it left no room for rehabilitation. In 1846, Robert Pringle Stuart, a magistrate in the VDL Convict Department exposed the scarcity and poor quality of food, inadequacy of housing, horrors of torture and incessant flogging, insubordination of convicts and corruption of

---

[47] Mortlock, J. F., *Experiences of a convict transported for twenty one years: an autobiographical memoir*, (Richard Barrett, Printers), 1864, p. 67.
[48] Barrow to Comptroller-General of Convicts 2 November 1846, cit, Causer, Tim, 'Norfolk Island's 'suicide lotteries': myth and reality', unpublished paper, p. 5.
http://www.academia.edu/1109987/Norfolk_Islands_suicide_lotteries_myth_and_reality
[49] Ibid, West, John, *The History of Tasmania*, p. 397.
[50] Causer, Tim, 'Norfolk Island's 'suicide lotteries': myth and reality', unpublished paper, pp. 5-6.

overseers. [51] Robert Willson, Catholic bishop of Hobart visited Norfolk Island from VDL on three occasions. Following his first visit in 1846, he reported to the House of Lords who, for the first time, came to realise the enormity of the cruelty perpetrated under the British flag and attempted to remedy the evils. [52] A number of days before his visit 34 men were flogged; the day after his arrival, another 14; and at the service he held on the island, 218 of the 270 men attending were in chains. He returned three years later and found that many of the reforms had been implemented. However, rumours of resumed brutality brought him back in 1852 and this visit resulted in a damning report, listing atrocities and blaming the system that gave successive commandants absolute power over so many people. [53] He observed:

...the state of the yard, from the blood running down men's backs, mingled with the water used in washing them when taken down from the triangle - the degrading scene of a large number of men...waiting their turn to be tortured, and the more humiliating spectacle presented by those who had undergone the scourging...were painful to listen to. [54]

In the thirty years that Norfolk Island was settled for a second time, there were sixteen commandants, most of whom lasted less than a year. [55] Lieutenant-Colonel James Thomas Morisset (1829-1834), Major Joseph Anderson (1834-1839), [56] Captain Alexander Maconochie (1840-

---

[51] Stuart, Robert Pringle, and Naylor, Thomas Beagley, *Norfolk Island, 1846: the accounts of Robert Pringle Stuart and Thomas Beagley Naylor*, (Sullivan's Cove), 1979, pp. 9, 12, 18, 23, 27.
[52] *Hobart Courier*, 29 December 1847, printed the evidence Willson gave to the Select Committee in the previous June.
[53] 'Norfolk Island Prisoners', *Colonial Times* (Hobart), 15 October 1852.
[54] Robert Willson to Sir William Denison, Governor of VDL, 22 May 1852, Convict Discipline and Transportation, Further Correspondence, *Parliamentary Papers*, Vol. LXXXII, (1852-1853), p. 89.
[55] Britts, M. G., *The Commandants: The Tyrants Who Ruled Norfolk Island*, (Herron Publications), 1980.
[56] Barry, John V., 'Anderson, Joseph (1790-1877)', *ADB*, Vol. 1, pp. 13-14. Atkins, Thomas, *Reminiscences of Twelve Years' Residence in Tasmania and New South Wales*, (Printed and published at the *Advertiser* Office, Malvern) 1869, pp. 21-57, gives a very critical

1844) and John Giles Price (1846-1853) [57] lasted significantly longer and of them Morisset and Price were regarded as exceptionally harsh. Only Maconochie concluded that brutality bred defiance and attempted to apply his theories of penal reform, providing incentives as well as punishment. [58] His methods were criticised by many in the settler community as being too lenient and, although he had the support of Sir George Gipps, the NSW Governor who briefly visited the island in 1843, he was recalled by the Colonial Secretary Lord Stanley who stated that 'Norfolk Island would again become a place of the severest punishment'. [59] Apart from Price, all the commandants were military officers, brought up in a system where discipline was severe and they relied on a large number of military guards, civil overseers, ex-convict constables, and convict informers to provide them with intelligence and carry out their orders. They ruled a brutalised and brutalising society.

Recent research provides a more nuanced view of the convicts who were transported to Norfolk Island between 1825 and 1855. [60] This has called into question the

---

account of Anderson's brutality from the viewpoint of the Church of England chaplain on the island from November 1836 to January 1837.
[57] Barry, John V., *The life and death of John Price: a study of the exercise of naked power*, (Melbourne University Press), 1964, and more succinctly 'Price, John Giles (1808-1857)', *ADB*, Vol. 2, pp. 351-352.
[58] Barry, John V., 'Maconochie, Alexander (1787-1860)', *ADB*, Vol. 2, pp. 185-186. See also, Ward, Gerard, 'Captain Alexander Maconochie, R.N., K.H., 1787-1860', *Geographical Journal*, Vol. 126, (4), (1960), pp. 459-468. Maconochie, Alexander, *Norfolk Island*, (J. Hatchard), 1847, gives a brief overview of his experience. Morris, Norval, *Maconochie's gentlemen: the story of Norfolk Island & the roots of modern prison reform*, (Oxford University Press), 2004, pp. 1-160, details Maconochie's period as commandant using a unique combination of fictionalised history and critical commentary.
[59] On Gipps' visit to Norfolk Island, see *The Australian*, 13 February 1843, *Australasian Chronicle*, 2 March 1843
[60] What follows draws on Causer, Tim, 'The worst types of sub-human beings'?: The myth and reality of the convicts of the Norfolk Island penal settlement, 1825-1855', unpublished paper. http://www.academia.edu/1109979/The_worst_types_of_sub-

accuracy of the received interpretation that the convicts were the most incorrigible men transported to NSW and VDL and that they had been re-transported to Norfolk Island as a result of further offences. Causer's database of 6,458 Norfolk Island convicts shows that 3,860 were originally transported to NSW or VDL and also 165 men were either free or native-born, but that 2,403 men were transported directly from England immediately challenging the theory that all the prisoners were doubly convicted. [61] The age, marital status, occupation and literacy of the Norfolk Island convicts broadly corresponded with the conclusions reached in *Convict Workers*: transportees were generally of prime working age, most were single and most were functionally literate although Norfolk Island men were slightly less skilled overall largely because of the greater proportion of unskilled rural workers essential for the labour-intensive farming on Norfolk Island. [62]

The strongly expressed views of contemporaries, something reinforced by later historians is that the penal settlement on Norfolk Island was established to detain a particularly dangerous sub-stratum of depraved criminals. In fact, few of them had originally been transported for explicitly violent offences and 70 per cent were convicted of non-violent crimes against property, a conclusion that accords with the sample used in *Convict Workers*. Why then did these men eventually end up on Norfolk Island? [63] Of the 3,840 men sent from NSW and VDL to Norfolk Island, only 2,258 men were recorded as being detained under a colonial conviction. The majority (66.5 per cent) were reconvicted of non-violent property offences, mostly burglary, housebreaking, highway robbery and stock theft.

---

human_beings_The_myth_and_reality_of_the_convicts_of_the _Norfolk_Island_penal_settlement_1825-1855

[61] 730 men were transported from England and Ireland in 1840 for Alexander Maconochie's experimental system while 1,703 were transported from England between 1844 and 1846 to undergo a period of probation.

[62] Causer, Tim, 'The worst types of sub-human beings'?: The myth and reality of the convicts of the Norfolk Island penal settlement, 1825-1855', pp. 4-17. On the conclusions of *Convict Workers*, see above pp. 276-280.

[63] Causer, Tim, 'The worst types of sub-human beings'?: The myth and reality of the convicts of the Norfolk Island penal settlement, 1825-1855', pp. 17-30.

Just over a fifth of Norfolk Island convicts were detained for explicitly violent offences, a much lower proportion than might be expected. Beyond those transported to Norfolk Island by order of a colonial court, the fate of the remaining NSW and VDL men exposed the system's arbitrariness. A number were removed from other penal stations to Norfolk Island; for instance, 60 capital respites and lifers were transferred from Port Macquarie in July 1830 and 109 men from Cockatoo Island in two drafts during early 1844 and 1848. Nearly 55 per cent of the convicts were sent to Norfolk Island either under their original sentence of transportation or without being subject to a colonial conviction. The 'deviancy' of Norfolk Island's convicts was and is embedded in the public imagination but Causer's research demonstrates that the convicts were not necessarily the most depraved in the colonies. This, however, does not alter the fact that the conditions in which they lived were regarded as unremittingly brutal.

Rebellion in 1834

Convict rebellions were a feature of Norfolk Island almost from its foundation but their incidence intensified after 1825. In September 1826, an attempt was made by convicts to escape from the island by boat, having been told that there was an island within a hundred miles where they could safely hide and never be found. While most of the soldiers were chasing two absconders, about thirty prisoners seized and bound their overseers, robbed the Stores for provisions and weapons and put three boats to sea, killing a soldier. The commandant, Captain Vance Young Donaldson and soldiers followed them to the nearby small and uninhabited Phillip Island, where they were captured. The ringleaders were sent to Sydney for trial, where they were sentenced to death. [64]

Lieutenant-Colonel James Thomas Morisset was appointed commandant of Norfolk Island in 1829. [65] During his period in office, the convict population grew

---

[64] *HRA*, Series I: Vol. 15, pp. 596-597.
[65] Parsons, Vivienne, 'Morisset, James Thomas (1780-1852)', *ADB*, Vol. 2, pp. 260-261. See, Huskisson to Darling, 19 May 1828, *HRA*, Series I: Vol. 14, pp. 192-193, and Darling to Sir George Murray, 12 February 1829, *HRA*, Series I: Vol. 14, pp. 641-642.

from about 200 to over 700 by 1832 and there were several attempts at rebellion that were strenuously suppressed. Governor Darling was supportive of Morisset, regarding him 'a very Zealous Officer' whose duties were of 'a most arduous nature' observing that 'the Conduct of the Prisoners has of late been outrageous in the extreme, having repeatedly avowed...to Murder every one employed at the Settlement, and it is only by the utmost vigilance that they have been prevented accomplishing their object.' [66] There was, however, growing criticism of Morisset's rule within the more radical sections of NSW society. In 1832, Edward Hall, editor of the *Sydney Gazette*, wrote that the convicts on Norfolk Island had been

> ...made the prey of hunger and nakedness at the caprice of monsters in human form...and cut to pieces by the scourge...have no redress or the least enquiry made into their suffering. [67]

By the beginning of 1834, there were widespread rumours of rebellion across the island. [68] According to a convict named Laurence Frayne, Morisset was about to flog confessions out of the convicts, as the Reverend Samuel Marsden had done to Irish convicts thirty years earlier. Morisset was increasingly incapacitated by a head wound he had received during the Peninsular War in 1811 and had already decided to sell his commission. In practice, the running of the island was devolved to his second-in-command, Captain Foster Fyans. [69] Fyans was an experienced officer having served in Portugal and Spain between 1811 and 1814 and in India and Mauritius from

---

[66] Darling to Goderich, 26 August 1831, *HRA*, Series I: Vol. 16, p. 339
[67] *Sydney Gazette*, 4 December 1832.
[68] Kercher, Bruce, *Outsiders: tales from the Supreme Court of NSW, 1824-1836*, (Australian Scholarly Publishing), 2006, pp. 109-124 considers violence on Norfolk Island. *R v. Douglas and others*, Supreme Court of NSW, July 1834, printed in *Sydney Gazette*, 13, 20, 27 September, 1834, provides the detail, http://www.law.mq.edu.au/scnsw/Cases1834/html/r_v_douglas_and_others__1834.htm
[69] Brown, P. L., 'Fyans, Foster (1790-1870)', *ADB*, Vol. 1, pp. 422-424. See also, *Memoirs recorded at Geelong, Victoria, Australia by Captain Foster Fyans, 1790-1870: transcribed from his holograph manuscript given by descendants to the State Library, Melbourne 1962*, (Geelong Advertiser), 1986.

1818 until he arrived in Sydney in 1833. He was firm but fair in his attitude to convicts and later wrote of his experience as commandant of the Moreton Bay penal colony:

> Five hundred convicts on this establishment were well and usefully employed; there was none of that lurking feeling in the men, and I may add that the settlement appeared to me not unlike a free overgrown establishment...I was always of opinion that mitigation to the deserving tended to good, and feel not sorry to acknowledge that I was instrumental to mitigating to a great extent seventy convicts, and well pleased often I have been in meeting some of these men doing well in the world as respectable citizens, and only in one solitary instance I failed in my hope. [70]

However, his view of Norfolk Island was emphatic: 'to the latest hour [it] was a disgrace to England...the true discipline of the penal settlement subverted.'

Fyans was right to be concerned as an anonymous note, left in the soldiers' barracks warned them to 'beware of poison'. He had clear memories of a plot hatched by fifteen convicts two years before on the *Governor Phillip* to poison the ship's company with arsenic in their food on the voyage to Norfolk Island. Fortunately this attempt was prevented by one of his fellow prisoners turning informer. Fyans was especially concerned by John Knatchbull in whose cabin a pound of arsenic was found though neither he nor the other convicts were charged. [71] Knatchbull came from a privileged landed background, the son of Sir Edward Knatchbull and his second wife. Educated at Winchester School, he had volunteered for the navy in 1804 becoming a lieutenant in 1810 and retiring on full-pay after Napoleon's defeat at Waterloo. [72] The Admiralty stopped his pay in 1818 because of a debt he incurred in the Azores. Convicted of stealing with force and arms in 1824, he was sentenced to transportation for fourteen years and arrived in NSW in

---

[70] Cit, ibid, Brown, P. L., 'Fyans, Foster (1790-1870)', p. 424.
[71] *Sydney Gazette*, 4 December 1832, detailed the 'diabolical conspiracy'.
[72] 'Knatchbull, John (1792?-1844)', *ADB*, Vol. 2, pp. 65-66, and Knatchbull, John, *Life of John Knatchbull. Written by Himself, 23rd January-13th February, 1844, in Darlinghurst Gaol*, first pub., Roderick, Colin, (ed.), *John Knatchbull from Quarterdeck to Gallows*, (Angus and Robertson), 1963.

April 1825. Initially, he adapted well to the colonial environment and was given his ticket-of-leave in 1829. However, two years later, he was successfully prosecuted for forgery but his death sentence was commuted to transportation for seven years to Norfolk Island where he arrived on the *Governor Phillip* in late 1832. [73] Knatchbull was central to the rebellion as the only way off the island was by ship and claimed that although he was unable to take part, he had offered to command a ship to South America if one could be captured.

On 1 August 1833, Knatchbull, George Farrell and Dominick McCoy agreed on a complex plan. First, it linked the convicts in the lumberyard and sawpits to those at the lime-burners' kiln and the stone quarry and called for a simultaneous rebellion. At the dawn muster in the convict barracks yard, they would rush Fyans and his soldiers and overpower them. If any of the guard managed to barricade themselves in the guardhouse, the prisoners would set fire to it and flush them out. Meanwhile the gaol gang, made up of prisoners under special punishment, would also rush their own guard as they were being mustered for work in the stone quarry. The rebels would then seize the apparatus of colonial rule. The two columns of convicts would then advance on Government House and capture Morisset, seize the 18-pound cannon there and turn it on the military barracks. If the soldiers surrendered they would be spared; if not, they would hang with the hated convict constables, overseers and informers. Finally, the convicts would escape from the island. They would force Morisset to hand over his codebook of signals, so that they could flag false messages to the next ship to anchor off the reef. They would get on board by wearing the overseers' blue jackets and seize the vessel that Knatchbull would pilot to America, for 'if he once got there, the Americans would not allow them to be given up again.' In the months between the formulation of the plan and the rebellion, Redmond Moss successfully carried messages between the different gangs.

---

[73] See, 'Diabolical Conspiracy to murder the crew and guard of the *Governor Philip* transport on her passage to Norfolk Island', *Sydney Gazette and New South Wales Advertiser*, 4 December 1832, and the report in *Hobart Town Courier*, 4 January 1833.

Shortly after 5 am on Wednesday 15 January 1834, men in the military barracks heard a ragged volley of musket fire. The rebellion had begun. At the dawn muster in the prisoners' barracks thirty-eight men, an unusually large number, had reported sick and were marched off to hospital by John Higgins, a warder. Once inside the hospital lockup, they overpowered Higgins and locked him in a sickroom. The prisoners struck off each other's irons, burst into the wards and armed themselves with weapons ranging from chair legs to scalpels and a poker. Some even found axes. They massed in the entrance of the hospital in silence, ready to fall on the guard when it came by. A hundred yards away this guard was mustering the gaol gang, about thirty convicts under the eye of a corporal and twelve privates of the 4th King's Own Regiment. The guard corporal ordered the prisoners to march, but they would not budge. They stood there, rattling their chains. The signal was given. At that moment, Frayne looked toward the sawpits and cried, 'Are you ready?' Seconds later, forty convicts from the sawpits attacked the guards from behind, while the hospital gang burst from hiding and attacked their front. Taken completely by surprise, the soldiers could not get their weapons to their shoulders. The convicts 'were within the bayonets of the Guard, before they were aware of them' and for a few moments the convicts and guards locked, grappling for their guns. After a brief melee, military discipline prevailed and the guards now began firing as they backed into the gateway of the gaol, frantically loading and firing while their comrades kept the lunging convicts back at sabre-point. Several convicts, including Henry Drummond, one of the ringleaders went down and, as suddenly as it began, the fracas broke up.

Half a mile away in Quality Row, where the barracks and officers' houses stood, Foster Fyans and his reacted quickly to the situation. They double-timed down the road to intercept the mutineers and when they charged again. Fyans gave the order to fire and, when the black-powder smoke cleared fifteen rebels were stretched on the ground while most of the others had plunged into the sugar cane that grew beside the road. Only the remnants of the gaol gang, hampered by their irons stood dumbly in surrender. Soldiers followed the escapees into the vegetable gardens and sugar cane. Fyans then led a detachment up the hill to deal with the convicts at the agricultural station at

Longridge. They had lookouts where they could see the Kingston gaol buildings and signal the start of the mutiny. Convicts crowded exultantly around and Walter Bourke, their leader smashed the lock on the main tool chest and started passing out axes and pitchforks to the men. Crying 'Liberty or Death!' about eighty convicts followed him down the road to Flagstaff Hill. They expected to see a victorious crowd of fellow rebels surging to meet them. Instead they saw two men stumbling up the hill, one of them wounded pursued by redcoats. The soldiers fired a few rounds at the rebels, but the range was too great. Soon, they closed in and beat the rebels back to Longridge, taking twenty-eight prisoners on the way. With difficulty, Fyans kept the soldiers from bayoneting them to death on the spot, but felt later that 'perhaps such lenity is ill bestowed'. Within a couple of hours, all the Longridge rebels were subdued and bound together with rope in a line, the soldiers marched them down the hill to Kingston.

By noon, Fyans had the mutineers confined in the main prison barracks, 'nearly one thousand Ruffians', he wrote later. A few were still missing, among them Robert Douglas, who was found later on the other side of the island at Anson's Bay, still carrying a musket with ninety rounds of ammunition wrapped in a palm leaf. A bayonet thrust had destroyed his left eye and infection blinded the other a few days later. Fyans interrogated him daily in the hospital, but Douglas refused to say anything about the rebellion. The final tally of casualties was nine rebels dead and about fifty wounded. No guard was killed until the night of 17 January, when two military search parties met in a cornfield while looking for rebels still at large and, each believing the other to be convicts, opened fire. One fluke shot killed both a civilian constable and Thomas York a young private of the 4th Regiment.

Captain Fyans adopted harsh measures against the rebels. Blacksmiths took nine days to make new irons for the prisoners. Rebels locked in the gaol awaiting trial were kept naked in a yard so crowded that not a third of them could sit at a time. For the next five months, while the reports went back to Sydney and arrangements were being made to send a judge to Norfolk Island, the rebels were kept locked to a chain cable. Mass floggings went on into the evening, until the 'desperate lawless and listless mob' had been scourged into submission. Some convicts, weary of their 'acute and intolerable sufferings', according to Fyans alone, planned to commit group suicide, but never put their plan into action. It took Fyans and his staff five months to interrogate all the witnesses and take their depositions for trial. In this, Fyans was supported from March 1834 by Joseph Anderson, the new commandant of the island. Of those charged with mutiny, half were lifers and another third had sentences of fourteen years. In the course of the rebellion's suppression, Knatchbull turned informer. 162 rebels were charged but the Attorney-General ruled that only 59 should be tried. The trials took place on Norfolk Island in July and twenty-nine rebels were sentenced to death. [74] Thirteen were eventually executed in front of their fellows on 22 and 23 September.

After the trials, Judge Sir William Burton severely reprimanded Fyans:

> Most improperly, Sir, did you act as a magistrate, in accepting a confession from Knatchbull; neither should any deposition have been taken from him. Throughout the trials his name has been connected in every case: he was the chief of the mutineers, the man you should have named first in the Calendar. You have saved his life, or prolonged it. He never can do good.

Fyans blamed himself for saving Knatchbull's neck by accepting his depositions and 'for so gross an act, in setting this monster loose on society.' Burton was proved right. Knatchbull returned from Norfolk Island in May 1839 [75]

---

[74] The trial of the rebels, *R v. Douglas and others*, Supreme Court of NSW, July 1834, printed in *Sydney Gazette*, 13, 20, 27 September, 1834. The *Sydney Herald* and *Australian* gave no formal reports of these trials, although the *Australian* listed them on 22 August 1834. The *Sydney Herald* reported the second to seventh trials on 27 September 1834. Bourke to Spring Rice, 15 January 1835, *HRA*, Series I: Vol. 17, pp. 638-639, provides the only 'official' discussion of the rebellion and trials.

[75] By 1839, fifteen years had elapsed since his initial sentence and Knatchbull assumed that his absolute pardon would follow when he wrote a most eloquent petition informing Governor Gipps after his return from Norfolk Island. His hopes were dashed by the note the Barracks clerk, Thomas Ryan, penned on the back of the document, repeating the unproven claim that Knatchbull had tried to poison the ship's crew on the *Governor Phillip*. Ryan also drew the governor's attention to the regulation that recommended a colonial conviction should not be served concurrently but be added

and gained his second ticket-of-leave in July 1842 but was hanged early in 1844 for the murder of Ellen Jamieson, a shopkeeper. [76] There had been little surprise at the outcome of his trial since he had been caught red-handed with £17 taken from the victim and the public called for hime to be hanged. Defended by Robert Lowe, later British Home Secretary, the trial was not delayed by Lowe's attempt to get an adjournment to seek medical opinion on Knatchbull's sanity. Since Lowe could not offer a defence questioning what happened, he chose to argue a novel case for moral insanity. [77] This was rejected both by Judge Burton and the jury that found him guilty, a verdict widely supported in the press and by the public. [78] His execution on 13 February 1844 was attended by at least 5,000 people with *The Australian* putting the figure at double that amount. [79]

A final flourish

There were minor disturbances in 1841, 1842 and 1843 but a violent affair in 1846. [80] Joseph Childs, commandant from 1844 to 1846, proved to be no match for the hardened convicts largely because he had no experience of life in a penal settlement. [81] When Robert Pringle Stuart visited Norfolk Island, he reported that Childs was 'a most amiable benevolent gentleman and honourable officer' but that

---

to the original sentence. Rather than being released, Knatchbull was re-transported to Port Macquarie

[76] See, NSW State Archives, Supreme Court: Police report on John Knatchbull, 1844, 9/6329, No. 135.

[77] *Sydney Morning Herald*, 25 January 1844. See also, 'Mental Epidemics', *The Australian*, 1 February 1844, and 'Monomania', *Sydney Morning Chronicle*, 3 February 1844. The debate over Lowe's novel defence continued after the execution, see *Morning Chronicle*, 8 June 1844,

[78] On *R v. Knatchbull* and the defence of 'moral insanity', see Woods, Gregory D., *A history of criminal law in New South Wales: the colonial period 1788-1900*, (Federation Press), 2002, pp. 159-162.

[79] The execution was reported in *Sydney Morning Herald*, 14 February 1844, and *The Australian*, 15 February 1844.

[80] On the attempted escape on the *Governor Phillip*, see Gipps to Lord Stanley, 15 August 1842, *HRA* Series I: Vol. 22, pp. 200-201.

[81] Barry, John V., 'Childs, Joseph (1787-1870)', *ADB*, Vol. 1, pp. 220-221.

what was needed to avoid anarchy and insubordination was 'an officer of experience in, or capacity for, government, judgement, energy, decision and firmness'. [82] Childs was recalled but, before he left, a group of convicts revolted in July 1846, murdering four officials.[83]

As was usual with new commandants, Childs had cracked down on discipline and removed some privileges that convicts had become accustomed to. On 1 July 1846, William Westwood, a convicted bushranger also known as 'Jackey Jackey' led a mutiny provoked by Childs' decision the previous day to remove the prisoners' tins and knives and other utensils used for cooking their food and that all food would in future be cooked for them. [84] He attacked and brutally killed two overseers, a guard who called out that he had seen it all and another guard who was asleep. In half an hour, the military restored order at the point of the bayonet and convicts who had joined the riot quickly returned to their cells. Sentenced to death with twelve others, Westwood was hanged on 13 October 1846 by Childs' successor, John Price, who considered Childs responsible for the state of affairs that led to the revolt. [85] A contemporary report blamed the situation on Childs' 'utter imbecility'. [86] There was one last act of convict defiance when, in March 1853, some convicts seized a government launch and attempted to row to freedom. In July, news was received that the launch had reached the coast of NSW and some of the runaways had been captured.

From the mid-1840s, there was growing pressure to end transportation to VDL, something that was finally achieved in 1853. The cost of maintaining the penal settlement on Norfolk Island was growing and Port Arthur in VDL was seen as a less costly alternative. This combined

---

[82] Ibid, Stuart, Robert Pringle, and Naylor, Thomas Beagley, *Norfolk Island, 1846: the accounts of Robert Pringle Stuart and Thomas Beagley Naylor*, p. 69.
[83] 'Disturbances at Norfolk Island', *The Australian*, 8 August 1846, provides an account of events.
[84] Rutledge, Martha, 'Westwood, William [Jackey Jackey] (1820-1846)', *ADB*, Supplementary Volume, pp. 404-405.
[85] *The Australian*, 14 November 1846.
[86] Rogers, Henry, (ed.), *Essays, Selected from Contributions to the Edinburgh Review*, 2 Vols. (Longman, Brown, Green and Longmans), 1850, Vol. 2, 'Treatment of Criminals', p. 506. The article was originally published in 1847.

with increasing criticism by magistrates and clergymen of the nature of penal rule on Norfolk Island led to the decision to abandon the island for a second time. [87] The process began in 1847 and was completed in May 1855 when the last convicts were moved to VDL. [88] There was a further factor that played a part in this decision. With some irony, Earl Grey, the Colonial Secretary, saw Norfolk as a possible home for the inhabitants of Pitcairn Islands, descendants of the mutineers from the *Bounty* and their Tahitian-Polynesian wives. [89]

---

[87] 'Norfolk Island and Transportation', *The Australian*, 18 February 1847, indicated that the 'island establishment is to be immediately reduced to a very small scale'.

[88] Earl Grey to Sir Charles Fitzroy, 27 February 1847, *HRA*, Series I: Vol. 25, pp. 375-376.

[89] Murray, Thomas Boyles, *Pitcairn, the island, the people, and the pastor: to which is added a short notice of the original settlement and present condition of Norfolk Island*, (Society for Promoting Christian Knowledge), 1857, pp. 363-428, provides a valuable contemporary account of this process. See also, Belcher, Lady, (Diana Joliffe), *The Mutineers of the Bounty and Their Descendants in Pitcairn and Norfolk Islands*, (Harmer & Brothers Publishers), 1871.

14 Fearing the Irish, 1800-1807

From the early 1790s through to the last group of convicts transported to WA in 1868, Australia was frequently the destination for Ireland's political prisoners. The Defenders and United Irishmen were transported to NSW in the 1790s and early 1800s, the rural rebels and defeated members of Young Ireland to VDL between the 1820s and early 1850s and Fenians to WA. [1] These convicts brought the conflicts from Ireland with them and especially their struggle against 'Imperial' Britain. As a result, they were among the most fractious and, from the perspective of the colonial authorities, the most dangerous and disruptive group in the emerging colonies. Between 1800 and 1807, there were at least three planned rebellions that were thwarted before they could break out and the Castle Hill Rising of 1804 when a convict rebellion was put down with considerable ferocity.

An Irish context

During the eighteenth and nineteenth centuries, the fundamental division in Ireland was religious. [2] To be a full member of Irish civil society, individuals had to be members of the Anglican Church of Ireland. Until 1829, Irish Roman Catholics and Protestant Dissenters were barred from certain professions such as law, the judiciary and the army and had restrictions on inheriting land. Catholics could not bear arms or exercise their religion publicly. With papal recognition of the Hanoverian dynasty in 1766, the threat to the ruling Protestant Ascendancy eased and many Penal Laws were relaxed or lightly enforced. From 1766, Catholics favoured reform and their views were represented by the 'Catholic Committees', a moderate organisation of Catholic gentry and clergy in each county that called for the repeal of the Penal Laws and

---

[1] Whitaker, Anne-Maree, 'Swords to ploughshares? The 1798 Irish rebels in New South Wales', *Labour History*, Vol. 75, (1998), pp. 9-32.
[2] Elliott, Marianne, *When God Took Sides: Religion and Identity in Irish History*, (Oxford University Press), 2009, considers this division through to the twenty-first century.

emphasised their loyalty. Calls for change were also evident among the Irish Protestant élite that had come to see Ireland as their native country. Politically active Irishmen were far from disinterested when arguing about issues such as Irish independence or parliamentary reform. [3] During the American War of Independence, the government in London needed the support of Ireland and as a result, a Parliamentary faction led by Henry Grattan agitated for more favourable political and trading relationships with England. [4] Many of their demands were met in 1782, when Free Trade was granted between Ireland and England and legislative powers devolved to Dublin. Partly as a result of the trade laws being liberalised, Ireland went through an economic boom in the 1780s. Canals extended from Dublin westwards and the Four Courts and Post Office were established. Dublin's granite-lined quays were built and it boasted that it was the 'second city of the Empire'. Corn Laws were introduced in 1784 to give a bounty on flour shipped to Dublin promoting the spread of mills and tillage.

The French Revolution had a dramatic impact on Irish politics. [5] In 1792, Grattan succeeded in carrying an Act conferring the franchise on the Roman Catholics; in 1794, he introduced a reform bill that sought to retain legislative power in the hands of men of property. He had a strong conviction that while Ireland could best be governed by Irish hands, democracy in Ireland would inevitably turn to plunder and anarchy. The defeat of Grattan's mild proposals helped to promote more extreme opinions.

---

[3] Small, Stephen, *Political Thought in Ireland 1776-1798: Republicanism, Patriotism and Radicalism*, (Oxford University Press), 2002, provides a detailed analysis of the development of Irish Patriotism into radical republicanism.
[4] On Grattan see, Madden, D. O., (ed.), *The speeches of the Right Hon. Henry Grattan: to which is added his letter on the union, with a commentary on his career and character*, 2 Vols. (J. Duffy), 1822, Grattan, Henry, *Memoirs of the life and times of the Rt. Hon. Henry Grattan by his son*, 2 Vols. (H. Colburn), 1839, 1846. See also, Mansergh D., *Grattan's Failure: Parliamentary Opposition and the People in Ireland*, (Irish Academic Press), 2005.
[5] Smyth, Jim, (ed.), *Revolution, counter-revolution, and union: Ireland in the 1790s*, (Cambridge University Press), 2000, especially pp. 1-38.

Conservative loyalists such as John Foster, John Fitzgibbon and John Beresford remained opposed to further concessions to Catholics and argued that the 'Protestant Interest' could only be secured by maintaining the connection with Britain. In particular, the French Revolution prompted relentless action against the radical United Irishmen and deprived the Patriot movement of solidarity and unity.

The United Irishmen movement, formed in 1791, was based on an non-sectarian alliance between the Dissenter and Catholic bourgeoisie including Northern manufacturers, merchants and professionals, Belfast and Dublin artisans and Catholic peasants (the Defenders), against an entrenched Protestant Ascendancy that had many features of the French pre-revolutionary 'Ancien regime'. Initially the United Irishmen campaigned for the end to religious discrimination and the widening of the right to vote. With this route effectively blocked by the mid-1790s, the group soon radicalised its aims and sought to overthrow British rule and found a non-sectarian republic.[6] The United Irishmen spread quickly throughout the country. Republicanism was particularly attractive to the largely literate Ulster Presbyterian community, who were also discriminated against for their religion. Many Catholics, particularly the emergent Catholic middle-class, were also attracted to the movement and it claimed over 200,000 members by 1798. Violence and disorder became widespread and in 1795, hardening loyalist attitudes led to the foundation of the Orange Order, an uncompromising Protestant grouping.

The United Irishmen now dedicated to armed revolution, forged links with the Defenders, a militant Catholic society. [7] Wolfe Tone, the United Irish leader, went

---

[6] Elliott, Marianne, *Partners in Revolution: the United Irishmen and France*, (Yale University Press), 1990, Dickson, David Keogh, Dáire and Whelan, Kevin, (eds.), *The United Irishmen: republicanism, radicalism, and rebellion*, (Lilliput Press), 1993, and Curtin, Nancy, *The United Irishmen: popular politics in Ulster and Dublin, 1791-1798*, (Oxford University Press), 1998

[7] From its origins in Armagh in 1784 as the Catholic faction in a local sectarian feud, the Defender movement had gradually spread along lines of religious cleavage or cultural frontiers into County Down, Louth and south Ulster. Stimulated by the news and controversy about the French revolution and encouraged by the

to France to seek French military support and a French expeditionary force of 15,000 troops arrived off Bantry Bay in December 1796, but failed to land due to a combination of indecisiveness, poor seamanship and storms off the Bantry coast. [8] The government began a campaign of repression targeted against the United Irishmen, including executions, routine use of torture, transportation to penal colonies and house burnings. As the repression began to bite, the United Irishmen decided to go ahead with an insurrection without French help. Their activity culminated in the Irish Rebellion of 1798. [9] The uprising in Dublin failed but the rebellion then spread in an apparently random fashion firstly around Dublin, then briefly in Kildare [10] Meath, Carlow and Wicklow. [11] County Wexford [12]

Catholic agitation, the Defenders were transformed into a politicised secret society. This process was then reinforced and the Defender organisation expanded from Meath across the north midlands into Connaught, by the continuing economic, political, and law-and-order crisis. By 1795, Defenderism had a presence in at least sixteen counties and in Dublin. They had successfully infiltrated the militia and knit far-flung lodges into a co-ordinated, if not well-disciplined, organisation. Defenderism had evolved a chameleon ideology infinitely adaptable to varying local conditions: on some occasions sectarian, then agrarian, always francophile and anti-ascendancy. With the emergence of a recognisable regional command structure in Ulster and a Catholic leadership aligned to the radical northern wing of the United Irishmen, the stage had been set for the making of a revolutionary coalition.

[8] Elliott, Marianne, *Wolfe Tone: Prophet of Irish Independence*, (Yale University Press), 1991.

[9] Pakenham, T., *The Year of Liberty: the great Irish rebellion of 1798*, (Weidenfeld & Nicholson), 1998, remains an excellent narrative. See also, Bartlett, Thomas, (ed.), *1798: a bicentenary perspective*, (Four Courts), 2003.

[10] Chambers, Liam, *Rebellion in Kildare 1790-1803*, (Four Courts), 1998.

[11] O'Donnell, Ruán, *The rebellion in Wicklow, 1798*, (Irish Academic Press), 2003.

[12] Hay, Edward, *History of the Insurrection of County Wexford*, (J. Stockdale), 1803, Wheeler, H. F. B., & Broadley, A. M., *The war in Wexford: an account of the rebellion in the south of Ireland in 1798, told from original documents*, (J. Lane), 1910, Dickson, Charles, *The Wexford Rising in 1798: its causes and course*, (The Kerryman), 1955, and Keogh, Dáire, and Furlong, Nicholas, (eds.),

in the southeast saw the most sustained fighting, to be briefly joined by rebels who took to the field in Antrim and Down in the north. [13] A small French force landed in Killala Bay in Mayo leading to a last outbreak of rebellion in counties Mayo, Leitrim and Longford. The rebellion lasted three months before it was suppressed, but claimed up to an estimated 25,000 lives.

Irish Transportation

Most rebels became fiercely republican after having seen the successful creation of the United States and the changes caused by the French Revolution. Republican notions such as natural rights and a popularly elected upper house were a major threat to those whose power rested on established monarchical and oligarchic institutions. Political dissidents were regarded and treated as a threat to British society and Oldfield suggests:

> There is a case for contending that Britain (unlike many other European nations) escaped outright revolution in the nineteenth century by being able to siphon off its radicals (as convicts) and its paupers (as assisted immigrants) to the other side of the world. [14]

The British Government preferred deporting or exiling political prisoners to Botany Bay rather than risk creating martyrs if they were executed, something that was largely confined to leaders. [15] This proved an effective policy for the

---

The Mighty Wave: the 1798 rebellion in Wexford, (Four Courts), 1996.
[13] Stewart, A. T. Q., *The Summer Soldiers: the 1798 Rebellion in Antrim and Down*, (Blackstaff Press), 1995.
[14] Oldfield, Audrey, *The Great Republic of the Southern Seas: Republicans in Nineteenth-Century Australia*, (Hale & Iremonger), 1999, p. 212.
[15] Retribution for the rebel leaders in 1798 was swift and largely uncompromising. Bagenal Harvey, Cornelius Grogan, Mathew Keogh, and Anthony Perry, all Wexford commanders and all Protestants were executed; their heads stuck on spikes outside the courthouse in Wexford town. Father John Murphy, the hero of Oulart and Enniscorthy was captured in Tullow, County Carlow. He was stripped, flogged, hanged and beheaded: his corpse was burned in a barrel. With an eye for detail, the local Yeomanry spiked his head on a building directly opposite the local Catholic

British and the manner in which they dealt with all political dissent in England, Scotland and the British colonies. [16]

The precise number of Defenders and United Irishmen transported to NSW before 1800 cannot be resolved conclusively from the available sources. [17] Whitaker argues that about 400 of the several thousand United Irishmen sentenced to transportation actually reached NSW; a total 58 less than Shaw's figure but 75 more than Rudé. [18] However, of the 519 male prisoners disembarked in NSW from four ships between 1793 and 1797, between 200 and 300 convicts were probably Defenders and they made up at least half of all the Irish political prisoners who arrived in NSW before 1806. While it seems that there were very few political prisoners on the *Queen* in 1791, an unknown number were put on board the *Boddingtons* and *Sugar Cane* in 1793. The 233 men landed in Port Jackson from the *Boddingtons* and *Sugar Cane* had all been sentenced in or before 1793, predating the merger with the United Irishmen. [19] As 60-70 men on the *Boddingtons* were convicted in counties where Defender disturbances had occurred it can be assumed, following Shaw's rule of thumb, that many of them were members of that organisation. [20] The *Sugar Cane* carried fewer prisoners from these districts and a higher proportion of Dubliners,

---

church. By the end of the rebellion between 10,000 and 25,000 rebels including a high proportion of non-combatants had been killed, most summarily.

[16] Ibid, Moore, Tony, *Death or Liberty*, pp. 67-133, considers Irish rebels in Ireland and Australia.

[17] The discussion of Defenders draws heavily on O'Donnell, Ruán, 'Desperate and Diabolical': Defenders and United Irishmen in early NSW', unpublished paper.

[18] Whitaker, Anne-Maree, *Unfinished Revolution: United Irishmen in New South Wales, 1800-1810*, (Crossing Press), 1994, p. 29, Rudé, George, 'Early Irish Rebels in Australia', *Historical Studies*, Vol. 16, (1974-1975), p. 23, and ibid, Shaw, Alan, *Convicts & the Colonies*, p. 170.

[19] Hall, Barbara, *Of Infamous Character: The Convicts of the Boddingtons, Ireland to Botany Bay, 1793*, (B. Hall), 2004, Hall, Barbara, *A Nimble Fingered Tribe: The Convicts of the Sugar Cane, Ireland to Botany Bay, 1793*, (B. Hall), 2002, second edition, 2009.

[20] Ibid, Shaw, Alan, *Convicts & the Colonies*, p. 171.

an area not significantly affected by Defenderism at that time. [21]

There were many Defenders among the 286 male convicts transported on the *Marquis Cornwallis* and *Britannia* in 1796-1797. [22] They were, however, described as United Irishmen and although they did not take part in the 1798 Rebellion, there was little to distinguish them from later political prisoners. [23] There is no reason to assume that the political prisoners of the *Marquis Cornwallis* and *Britannia* would have been regarded as anything but comrades by rebels arriving on the *Minerva* and *Friendship* in 1800. Close ideological ties are also likely to have existed between them and the Defenders of the *Boddingtons* and *Sugar Cane*. Information on these two ships is more conclusive and Rudé agreed with Shaw's identification of 'about' 100 Defenders on these Ships. [24] However, a close comparison of disturbed districts with trial locations yields a figure only slightly lower than the total male complement of 163 men on the *Marquis Cornwallis*. Sufficient numbers of Defenders were sentenced in 1793 to fill several ships but relatively few were actually transported NSW. Of the 25 Louth Defenders sentenced to transportation at Dundalk Assizes in March 1793, only four embarked. Similarly, only two of the twelve sentenced at the Cork City and County Assizes in March 1794 actually arrived.

In 1795, the *Marquis Cornwallis* was seen as a 'political' ship; contemporary accounts stated it left Cork on

---

[21] There were 53 county and city Dubliners on the *Sugar Cane* as opposed to 36 on the *Boddingtons* and 12 Corconians up from 3. Only one convict on *Sugar Cane* came from Louth and Monaghan and none from Donegal.

[22] Hall, Barbara, *A Desperate Set of Villains: The Convicts of the Marquis Cornwallis, Ireland to Botany Bay, 1796*, (B. Hall), 2000, third edition, 2005, Hall, Barbara, *Death or Liberty: The Convicts of the Britannia, Ireland to Botany Bay, 1797*, (B. Hall), 2006.

[23] *Boddingtons* arrived 7 August 1793, *Sugar Cane* 17 September 1793, *Marquis Cornwallis* in February 1796, and *Britannia* on 27 May 1797. See also, *HRA*, Series I: Vol. 1, pp. 446, 454, and Vol. 2, p. 31.

[24] See, ibid, Shaw, Alan, *Convicts & the Colonies*, p. 171, and ibid, Rudé, George, 'Early Irish Rebels in Australia', p. 19.

9 August with 'seventy...Defenders' on board. [25] The *Britannia* also embarked substantial numbers of Defender/United Irish convicts given the turmoil in which that year's assizes had taken place. A county breakdown of the most likely Defender prisoners on the *Britannia* gives a figure of 145 men that included some criminals and omitted political prisoners from less disturbed counties. That 60 of the 107 non-Dubliners received life sentences, a marked increase on the 40 per cent rate on the non-political *Queen*, may indicate a high incidence of seditious crimes. *Britannia* was also the first ship to leave Ireland after the passage of the draconian Insurrection Act in 1796 that may explain a Dublin press report of August 1796 stating 'fifty convicts...[were] shipped from the North Wall for Botany Bay' of whom 'three quarters' were Defenders. As the *Britannia* landed only 39 male convicts from Dublin City and County in Port Jackson in May 1797, it would appear that it too was a 'political' ship.

The intriguing and ill-discipline of the exiled Defenders that concerned Governor Hunter and frightened Governor King was very apparent during the voyages of the ships with Defender convicts. [26] One man was summarily executed for mutiny on the *Sugar Cane* and some details of a plot on the *Boddingtons* reached the colony. [27] While mutiny and escape were common topics of conversation among all convicts, the Defender/United Irishmen of the *Britannia* and *Marquis Cornwallis* planned uprisings that resulted in the deaths of about 26 men and two official enquiries in Port Jackson. [28] The rebellious conduct of the convicts on the *Britannia* and *Marquis Cornwallis* before and after arrival in NSW seems to have prejudiced the colonial administration against later shipments of prisoners who had taken part in the 1798 rebellion. That two mutinies of a similar nature had been suppressed on successive voyages must have struck Hunter as the probable consequence of transporting Defenders and United Irishmen en masse. Serious problems also occurred

---

[25] *New Cork Evening Post*, 10 August 1795.
[26] Ibid, Shaw, Alan, *Convicts & the Colonies*, p. 168.
[27] Ibid, Bateson, Charles, *The Convict Ships, 1787-1868*, pp. 129-130.
[28] Hunter to Portland, 5 September 1796, *HRA*, Series I: Vol. 1, p. 653, *HRNSW*, Vol. 3, pp. 102-111.

on the *Anne, Hercules, Atlas I* and *Minerva* in 1800-1802 but not among the largely criminal cargo on the *Queen* and *Rolla* further highlighting the combustible nature of 'political' ships. The *Minerva* contained amongst the Irish rebels, Joseph Holt and James Harold. [29] Joseph Holt had struck up a friendship with the landowner William Cox on the ship and was given a job managing Cox's Dundas farm in western Sydney. Many of the United Irishmen on the *Minerva* were sent off to Norfolk Island in an attempt to disperse them. Although Hunter and his successor Governor King expressed considerable opposition to such transports, neither had any real control over the numbers or type of prisoners embarked for NSW. [30] The Governors were also remarkably ill-informed as to the character of Irish prisoners as documents setting down their names and crimes and sentences generally only arrived after the ships had docked if at all. [31] This created an atmosphere of paranoia in the colony that was accentuated by the United Irish plots of 1800 and the Castle Hill rebellion in March 1804. [32]

---

[29] Joseph Holt was born in Ireland in 1756 and became a tenant farmer and as a trusted Protestant loyalist held some minor local positions. About 1797, he joined the United Irishmen in part because of a private feud with the landlord Thomas Hugo. In 1798, the Fermanagh Militia burned his house down on Hugo's orders. Holt fought in the Wexford County rebellion before successfully leading a rebel guerrilla group in Wicklow County. Eventually he came to the conclusion that it was in his interests to surrender in order to get the best terms he could for himself and his wife. This led to exile without trial in the colony of NSW. After the 1804 Rebellion, he was exiled again to Norfolk Island and then VDL. He returned to Sydney and was given a land grant in order to farm. Holt was granted a pardon in 1809 before returning to Ireland in 1812. He wrote a personnel account of the rebellions in Wicklow and NSW: Croker, T. C., (ed.), *Memoirs of Joseph Holt: general of the Irish rebels, in 1798*, 2 Vols. (H. Colburn), 1838, Vol. 2, covers his life in Australia. See also, Bolton, G. C., 'Holt, Joseph (1756-1826)', *ADB*, Vol. 1, pp. 550-551.
[30] King to Portland, 21 May 1802, *HRA*, Series I: Vol. 3, p. 489.
[31] Portland to Hunter, 2 March 1797, *HRA*, Series I: Vol. 2, p. 9. King to Castlereagh, 24 July 1798, and Hunter to Portland, 1 November 1798, *HRA*, Series I: Vol. 2, pp. 234-236.
[32] King came to regard virtually all Irish male prisoners sent to New South Wales after 1793 as dangerous as the 'diabolical characters' of the *Anne*: King to Portland, 28 September 1800,

Discussion of rank and file Defenders in the Australian context has hitherto centred on a series of oft quoted comments made by Governor Hunter [33] in 1796 regarding 'those turbulent and worthless characters called Irish Defenders' who had boldly 'threatened resistance to all orders'. [34] As no such opinions were expressed by Hunter's predecessor in relation to the Defenders sent out in 1793, it would appear that his blanket hostility was a response to the ability of the convicts on the *Britannia* and *Marquis Cornwallis* to destabilise the colony and his knowledge of their plotting on the voyages from Ireland. To the Governor's intense annoyance, the Defenders who arrived in 1796-1797 not only disaffected otherwise peaceable English convicts but escaped both frequently and in large numbers. Hunter complained they had 'completely ruined... [those] formerly received from England' and threatened 'that order so highly essential to our well being'.[35] One of the more serious and disruptive breakouts involved a twenty strong 'gang of...Defenders' who were so obstinate when apprehended that Hunter had two executed.[36] Hunter's exasperation with the 'Defenders' moved him to suggest that they should not be sent to NSW but rather to 'Africa, or some other place as fit for them'. [37]

Uncovering insurrection

Anti-authoritarianism was characteristic of republican subversives and part of a pattern of behaviour established

---

HRA, Series I: Vol. 2, p. 614. See also King to Portland, 10 March 1801, *HRA*, Series I: Vol. 3, p. 9.

[33] For Hunter, see Hoyle, Arthur, *The Life of John Hunter, Navigator, Governor, Admiral*, (Mulini Press), 2001, Auchmuty, J. J., 'Hunter, John (1737-1821)', *ADB*, Vol. 1, pp 566-572. See also, Wood, G. A., 'Governor Hunter', *Journal and Proceedings* (Royal Australian Historical Society), Vol. 14, (6), (1928), pp. 344-362.

[34] Hunter to Portland, 12 November 1796, *HRA*, Series I: Vol. 1, p. 674.

[35] Hunter to Portland, 10 January 1798, *HRA*, Series I: Vol. 2, p. 118.

[36] Hunter to Portland, 15 February 1798, *HRA*, Series I: Vol. 2, p. 129, *HRNSW*, Vol. 3, pp. 359-360.

[37] Hunter to Portland, 12 November 1796, *HRA*, Series I: Vol. 1, p. 675.

in Ireland. To see their sustained defiance of the colonial government simply as a reaction to the prospects of overdue emancipation greatly underestimates their shared ideology and paramilitary experience that provided a firm grounding for undercover activities. Many urban criminals would also have possessed skills of this type but it was primarily the Irish convicts with political associations who were credited with unsettling the colony. Hunter was right to worry; in 1800 just six months after the arrival of the *Minerva* a rebellion was being planned on the Government Farm at Toongabbie. [38]

The rebellion involved taking Parramatta and killing Samuel Marsden who had earned a reputation as the 'flogging parson'.[39] The rebels would then pike the soldiers in their beds, take their muskets and march on Sydney. Its leaders had planned for pikes to be manufactured and hidden to ensure the rebels were well armed. The plan was betrayed by informants who gave Marsden word of the insurrection. When the leaders of the rebellion learned this they quickly cancelled the uprising. Governor Hunter led an inquiry into the insurrection in which Marsden overzealously pursued the issue of the hidden pikes. He threatened the Irish Catholic preacher James Harold over of the location of the pikes. [40] Harold prevaricated but under pressure finally revealed the name of a supposed pike maker, Bryan Furey. Furey denied making the pikes but later told Marsden that Harold had contacted him to make some fake ones to get Marsden off Harold's back. Marsden eventually sent Harold to Norfolk Island and Furey to gaol despite the lack of evidence against them. [41]

The failed insurrection of August 1800 and the removal of the suspected Irish leaders to remote parts of the colony did not dampen the convicts' enthusiasm for

---

[38] Hunter to Officers, 4 September 1800, *HRNSW*, Vol. 4, pp. 119-130, details the enquiry into the insurrection.
[39] Yarwood, A. T., 'Marsden, Samuel (1765-1838)', *ADB*, Vol. 2, pp. 207-212.
[40] Perkins, Harold, 'Harold, James (1744-1830)', *ADB*, Vol. 1, pp. 512-513.
[41] Hunter to Officers, 4 September 1800, *HRNSW*, Vol. 4, pp. 119-130, details the inquiry into an Irish plot in 1800 and King to Banks, 8 October 1800, on a threatened rebellion by United Irishmen at Parramatta, *HRNSW*, Vol. 4, p. 229 and pp. 235-238

organised rebellion. [42] In September 1800, another insurrection was planned. [43] The rebels were to assemble at Parramatta on a Sunday morning when the local authorities and hierarchies would be in Church service. There the rebels would overpower the soldiers and then march on Sydney. The leaders used an escaped convict, John Lewis to send messages from farm to farm. Unfortunately Lewis was captured, gaoled and eventually talked of the rebellion. From the information Lewis gave, Captain John Macarthur of the NSW Corps received a shakily written letter that relayed that a 'Croppie' uprising was about to occur. MacArthur's advice to the governor was to wait for the convicts to rebel and once they were out in the open deal with them. The rebel leaders learned that their plan had been discovered and halted their operations. Marsden once again zealously set about trying to discover the hidden pikes. Several more informants came forward and one named the still gaoled Bryan Furey as a pike maker. This enabled the NSW Corps to round up the ringleaders; William Silk, Micheal Quintan, Maurice Wood, John Burke and Thomas Brannon. They were flogged and isolated from the general convict population on the hulk *Supply* in Sydney Harbour. The remainder of the rebels were given either two hundred or five hundred lashes.

The authorities seem to have feared that Holt, an experienced rebel leader, would be a centre of disaffection, but nothing was farther from his plans. As a lower middle-class Irish Protestant with firm notions of respectability, Holt wanted to better his position by thrift and hard work and remained divorced from what he saw as impractical insurrection. Despite this, he was implicated as a leader in the rebellion but without substantial proof of his involvement he was spared the lash as was Harold. [44] As a

---

[42] Most of the Irish rebellions took place during King's term of office. For biographical information, see Shaw, A. G. L., 'King, Philip Gidley (1758-1808)', *ADB*, Vol. 2, pp. 55-61; King, J., and J., *Philip Gidley King: a biography of the third governor of New South Wales*, (Methuen), 1981.
[43] King to Portland, 12 October 1800, *HRNSW*, Vol. 4, pp. 234-238. See also the detailed papers relating to the Irish conspiracy in 1800 in, *HRA*, Series I: Vol. 2, pp. 575-583, 637- 651, and King to Banks, 8 October 1800, *HRNSW*, Vol. 4, pp. 235-238.
[44] Despite his vigorous protests Holt was arrested twice more for suspected complicity in plans for an Irish rising. On Christmas Eve

form of punishment for their suspected complicity with the rebels both Holt and Harold, who were still being detained from the previous insurrection, were made to watch the floggings of two convicted offenders, Maurice Fitzgerald and Paddy Galvin on the orders of Judge-Advocate Richard Atkins and Marsden. Holt left a vivid account:

> The place they flogged them their arms pulled around a large tree and their breasts squeezed against the trunk so the men had no power to cringe ... There was two floggers, Richard Rice and John Johnson the Hangman from Sydney. Rice was left-handed man and Johnson was right-handed, so they stood at each side, and I never saw two threchers in a barn move their strokes more handier than those two man-killers did....
>
> I [Holt] was to the leeward of the floggers...I was two perches from them. The flesh and skin blew in my face as it shook off the cats. Fitzgerald received his 300 lashes. Doctor Mason - I will never forget him - he used to go feel his pulse, and he smiled, and said: 'This man will tire you before he will fail - Go on.'...During this time [Fitzgerald] was getting his punishment he never gave so much as a word - only one, and that was saying, 'Don't strike me on the neck, flog me fair.' ...Next was tied up Paddy Galvin, a young boy about 20 years of age. He was ordered to get 300 lashes. He got one hundred on the back, and you could see his backbone between his shoulder blades. Then the Doctor ordered him to get another hundred on his bottom. He got it, and then his haunches were in such a jelly that the Doctor ordered him to be flogged on the calves of his legs. He got one hundred there and as much as a whimper he never gave. They asked him if he would tell where the pikes were hid. He said he did not know, and would not tell. 'You may as well hang me now,' he said, 'for you

---

1803 he was hauled before Atkins on a false accusation of plotting his murder, but was again cleared. Three months later, however, he was detained after the Castle Hill rising and transported to Norfolk Island, where he remained until November 1805. Nevertheless he seems to have held aloof from conspiracies, having a lively fear of informers and contempt for the amateurish tactics of the disaffected Irish Catholics. Returning to his farm, Holt met no further trouble except the confiscation of an illicit still in 1806. Through Major Edward Abbott he secured a free pardon from Lieutenant-Governor William Paterson in 1809, confirmed by Governor Lachlan Macquarie in 1811. Next year, Holt sold his properties for over £1,800 and returned to Ireland often lamenting that he had left NSW.

never will get any music from me so.' They put him in the cart and sent him to the Hospital. 45

No aspect of Marsden's activities did more harm to his reputation than his severity as a magistrate. This particular action was scarcely defensible, but Marsden was not the only magistrate who ordered the infliction of illegal punishments.

In 1801, the transport ship *Anne* arrived at Sydney with 69 United Irishmen out of the 178 convicts on-board. Governor King was disturbed as the rebel leaders from the previous rebellions had been uncovered and sent to remote parts of the colony. 46 The arrival of the *Anne* promised another group of United Irishmen leaders who could cause problems in the convict population, a view reinforced by the convict mutiny on the ship en route. The *Anne* brought news of Irish Union and King hoped that this would persuade the Irish convicts to accept their fate in Australia. This proved a forlorn hope. The Irish political prisoners had been fighting against English rule for several years and wanted to go home. The main opponent preventing this was the British authorities in Sydney and Parramatta. During the next year four more rebellion plots were uncovered. All were foiled by informants in the convict population. Two of the plots involved escaping by ship, either by seizing a ship or seeking passage on a French ship. The Governor was so concerned that convicts would escape by sea that in 1804 with word of a possible convict uprising, several American ships were sent out of Sydney Harbour because King suspected that they would be sympathetic to the rebelling Irish convicts. 47

In 1803, there were still outstanding issues for the Irish convicts. The idents stating the term the prisoners were to remain exiled in NSW still had not arrived from England. 48 Until the idents arrived all Irish prisoners were stuck in the penal colony. There continued to be escape

---

45 Ibid, Croker, T. C., (ed.), *Memoirs of Joseph Holt: general of the Irish rebels, in 1798*, Vol. 2, pp. 119-122.
46 King to Portland, 10 March 1801, *HRNSW*, Vol. 4, pp. 325-326.
47 This was followed up in the Government and General Order, 31 March 1805, *HRNSW*, Vol. 5, pp. 588-589, that laid down penalties for helping convicts to abscond.
48 King had commented on this problem earlier in, Portland, 21 August 1801, *HRNSW*, Vol. 4, pp. 463-464.

attempts by convicts both English and Irish. Inevitably the escapees would raid nearby farms for liquor and firearms. In February 1803, fifteen convicts escaped from a farm at Castle Hill and raided the farm of Verincourt de Clambe for liquor, silverware and firearms. [49] Two of the convicts, Patrick Gannan and Francis Simpson went on to the farmhouse of James Bean and raped his seventeen year old daughter but were captured two days later asleep in the bush and hanged. [50] The *Sydney Gazette* commented:

> Justice to the Prisoners at large in the Colony requires that we should here observe, that this banditti is entirely composed of Irish prisoners, brought by the *Hercules* and *Atlas*. [51]

Rebellion at Castle Hill in 1804

By 1800, the colony at Sydney was not yet self-sufficient in food and was dependent on imported food. [52] In an effort to remove this dependency King expanded the Government farm at Castle Hill and by 1804, there was a significant concentration of 474 convicts on the farm. [53] It was rare for so many convicts to live and work together and there is little doubt that this situation aided preparations for insurrection by bringing together seasoned campaigners in rebellion. The previous year, King, influenced by the uneasiness of the Irish convicts, had allowed the Roman Catholic clergyman Father James Dixon to preach Mass to the Irish. [54] The first public mass was celebrated in Sydney

---

[49] Details of this can be found in George Caley's account of the colony of NSW from 1800 to 1803, *HRNSW*, Vol. 5, p. 300, and in King to Hobart, 9 May 1803, *HRA*, Series I: Vol. 4, pp. 84-85.
[50] Additional soldiers were sent to Castle Hill as a result; see Government and General Order, 16 February 1803, *HRNSW*, Vol. 5, p. 22. See also *Sydney Gazette*, 5, 19 March 1803. The executions occurred on 23 March, *HRNSW*, Vol. 5, p. 74.
[51] *Sydney Gazette*, 5 March 1803.
[52] The system of public farming, originally introduced by Hunter, proved remarkably successful under King to such an extent that by 1802 it was producing a surplus of grain: King to Hobart, 9 November 1802, *HRNSW*, Vol. 4, pp. 899-900.
[53] King to Major Johnston, 25 February 1803, *HRNSW*, Vol. 5, pp. 51-51, suggests that there were already problems at Castle Hill with only '200 refractory convicts'.
[54] Parsons, Vivienne, 'Dixon, James (1758-1840)', *ADB*, Vol. 1, p. 309. For, King's proclamation and regulations governing Roman

on 15 May 1803 and others followed later at Parramatta and the Hawkesbury. In doing so, King gave the Irish the legal means of coming together. King was so pleased at the salutary effect on the Irish Catholics that he decided to pay Dixon a salary of £60. But after praising the experiment in a dispatch of 1 March 1804, he soon ended it determined to enforce the convicts' attendance at Anglican services because he believed that, especially after the rising of Irish convicts, seditious meetings took place when Catholics met to attend Mass.[55] In part the Irish rebels were fired by news arriving in the colony of Robert Emmett's uprising in Dublin in 1803.

By 1804, most of the Irish leaders of the previous attempts at rebellion had been imprisoned and moved to outlying areas of the colony such as Norfolk Island. Dispersal had worked well for the authorities but with each new rebellion plan, new Irish leaders rose among the convicts more aware of what not to do next time. The leaders of rebellion on 4 March 1804 were Phillip Cunningham and William Johnston. Cunningham was a veteran of the 1798 conflict in Ireland and the mutiny of the convict transport ship *Anne*. From his experiences in Ireland and NSW, he understood that secrecy and a non-traceable but effective system of communication were essential to a successful rebellion. [56] Cunningham's emphasis on secrecy was so successful that it was not until the day before the rebellion that the authorities knew of its existence. On the evening of 3 March, one of the Irish convict overseers turned informant. On Sunday 4 March, the day of the rebellion, two more informants came forward and provided names. John Griffen was one of the informants and had been relaying a message to the pike-maker Bryan Furey that the rebellion was on for Sunday night. Since Furey did not get the message the areas of

---

Catholic congregations, 19 April 1803, see, *HRNSW*, Vol. 5, pp. 97-98, and King to Hobart, 9 May 1803, *HRA*, Series I: Vol. 3, pp. 104-105; King to Hobart, 9 May 1803, *HRNSW*, Vol. 5, p. 116.
[55] King to Hobart, 1 March 1804, *HRNSW*, Vol. 5, p. 324.
[56] Silver, Lynette Ramsay, *The Battle of Vinegar Hill: Australia's Irish Rebellion*, (Doubleday), 1989, (Watermark Press), 2002 remains the only substantial study. *Sydney Gazette*, 11 March 1804, contained a detailed account based on King's despatch. See also, ibid, Karskens, Grace, *The Colony: A History of Early Sydney*, pp. 292-297.

Sydney, Parramatta and Windsor did not rebel. Castle Hill was the only district that rose in rebellion.

Despite this intelligence, the authorities in Parramatta and Sydney did not act immediately and on 4 March 1804, John Cavenah set fire to his hut in Castle Hill at 8.00 pm. This was the signal for the rebellion to begin. With Cunningham leading, 200 rebels broke into the Government Farm's buildings, taking firearms, ammunition and other weapons. Initially there was mayhem as buildings were ransacked to cries of 'Death or Liberty'. Two English convicts dragged the Hills District flogger, Robert Duggan from under his bed and George Harrington an English convict beat him unconscious. A constable was saved from a musket ball in the face when the musket of John Brannon misfired. Another constable was saved in similar circumstances when Jonathon Place's musket also misfired. Cunningham gathered the rebels and reprimanded them for their lack of disciplined behaviour. The rebels then went from farm to farm on their way to Constitution Hill at Parramatta gathering firearms, supplies and drinking any liquor they found. The looting of farms gave the rebels over 180 swords, muskets and pistols that accounted for a third of the colony's entire armoury. [57]

Within an hour of Cavenah firing his hut, word of the rebellion had reached Parramatta causing considerable panic and by 11.00 pm Governor King in Sydney was aware of the situation. In Parramatta, Samuel Marsden, an obvious target for the rebels, fled the town by boat with his and John Macarthur's family. [58] In Sydney, Major George Johnston rounded up a NSW Corps contingent of twenty-nine soldiers and force marched them through the night to

---

[57] W. Pascoe Crook, a missionary provided a detailed account of the early stage of the rebellion, *HRNSW*, Vol. 5, pp. 314-315, while George Suttor to Sir Joseph Banks, 10 March 1804, *HRNSW*, Vol. 5, pp. 350-352, is more detailed on its aftermath.

[58] Surgeon Thomas Arndell had written from the Hawkesbury to 'the Reverend Mr. Marsden, or in his absence, the Officer commanding at Parramatta', 4 March, 1804: 'Revr. Sir, From Strong and confirmed information I have every reason to believe that many of those deluded prisoners that call themselves United Irishmen and others had an Insurrection in project this night, and I beg you will be so kind as to forward some ammunition with the bearer sent on purpose for our Defence here' *HRA* Series I: Vol. 4, p. 567. This warning may account for Marsden's escape.

Parramatta.⁵⁹ Governor King immediately set off for Parramatta and arrived around 4 am on 5 March where one of his first actions was to declare martial law in the affected districts. ⁶⁰

> I do therefore proclaim the Districts of Parramatta, Castle Hill, Toongabbie, Prospect, Seven and Baulkham Hills, Hawkesbury and Nepean to be in a STATE of REBELLION; and to establish Martial Law throughout those Districts.... ⁶¹

Cunningham's plan involved burning the Macsrthur property of 'Elizabeth Farm' in order to draw the Parramatta garrison out of the town. Once this was done the rebels in Parramatta would rise up and set fire to the town as a signal. The Castle Hill rebels would gather at Constitution Hill and then raid the barracks for more arms and ammunition. From there the rebels would march to Windsor and join up with the rebels in the Hawkesbury before marching on Sydney. At dawn on 5 March, rebels were still straggling in to Constitution Hill. Phillip Cunningham and William Johnston were busy drilling the rebels on the hill while they were waiting for the signal from the uprising rebels in Parramatta. The signal never came. Cunningham's messages to the Parramatta and Windsor rebels had not got through and he decided that the rebels would head down the Hawkesbury Road to Windsor to meet up with the rebels from the Hawkesbury. Had Cunningham effected this, King maintained it would have increased his force by a further hundred rebels. ⁶²

Major Johnston's group of twenty nine soldiers of the NSW Corps and fifty members of the 'Active Defence' militia pursued the rebels through Toongabbie and Sugar Loaf Hill until they were only a few miles away from the rebels. ⁶³ Major Johnston sent Father Dixon ahead in an

---

⁵⁹ For Johnston's account of events see his succinct report to Lieutenant-Colonel Paterson, 9 March 1804, *HRNSW*, Vol. 5, pp. 348-349.
⁶⁰ See, King's proclamation of martial law, 5 March 1804, *HRNSW*, Vol. 5, pp. 345-346. The statement in the *Sydney Gazette* is more of a summary.
⁶¹ *HRNSW*, Vol. 5, p. 346.
⁶² King to Hobart, 12 March 1804, *HRNSW*, Vol. 5, pp. 355-356.
⁶³ Sydney and Parramatta also raised militias to defend the towns from the rebels but neither of these forces took part in the Battle of

effort to convince the rebels to surrender but he also wanted Father Dixon to slow the rebels down so his foot soldiers could make up the few miles difference. When Father Dixon failed to halt the rebels, Major Johnston and Trooper Anlezark attempted to persuade them to take the Governor's offer of clemency. After Major Johnston challenged the rebel leaders to come forward, Phillip Cunningham and William Johnston separated from the 233 rebels and spoke with the Major. It was agreed that Major Johnston would bring back Father Dixon to talk with them again. This delay gave sufficient time for the NSW Corps soldiers and militia to catch up to the rebels. When Major Johnston and Trooper Anlezark returned with Father Dixon they knew that their troops were not far behind. Once again Phillip Cunningham and William Johnston walked out to meet them while the rebels formed ranks. Johnson asked the rebel leaders what they really wanted and Cunningham replied 'Death or Liberty' adding, according to one account, 'and a ship to take us home'. With these words Major Johnston held a pistol to William Johnston's head and ordered him to move toward the soldiers and militia that had appeared over the rise. Anlezark did the same with Cunningham.

Major Johnston without any other preliminaries, ordered his men to charge and open fire. Over fifty armed civilians, a mounted trooper, and 29 military men, most capable of firing 780 prepared rounds of ammunition in 10 to 15 minutes, were pitted against 233 rebels. Although the odds were technically with the rebels, with the precision and economy of movement that came from practice and military training, the soldiers formed ranks and for fifteen minutes carried out their duty precisely as ordered. Leaderless, caught completely unawares and totally unprepared, the rebels weakly returned fire before fleeing in all directions leaving fifteen dead that are said to have been left to rot on the ground where they fell. After the battle, several prisoners were murdered by the soldiers and militia until Major Johnston intervened and threatened his troops with his pistol. During the battle, William Johnston

---

Vinegar Hill. The 'Parramatta Loyalists' militia numbered thirty six and remained in Parramatta. The 'Sydney Loyalists' did not march with Major Johnston and remained in Sydney during the rebellion.

escaped his captor's attention and fled into the bush. Cunningham was not so lucky and was struck by the sword of Quartermaster Thomas Laycock and left for dead as the soldiers rounded up the rebels. Amazingly Cunningham survived the blow and, critically wounded, was picked up by soldiers and dragged to the Hawkesbury. In the official reports that followed the battle neither Major Johnston's actions nor Laycock's was mentioned. [64]

Retribution was swift as King believed that punishing the leaders would pacify the convicts who had followed them. The 1804 Rebellion is referred to as an Irish rebellion or 'Australia's Irish rebellion'. This is misleading as the group of rebels on Vinegar Hill included convicts and free men of different nationalities such as Charles Hill. Of those hanged, several were English convicts. King's decision meant that most of the rebels were not punished, a pragmatic decision as the captured rebels were still needed to work the Government Farm. Phillip Cunningham was summarily hanged from the staircase of the public store at Windsor on 6 March. It has been suggested that Cunningham was already dead prior to his 'execution' as all the other leaders faced a court martial four days later. The

---

[64] Vinegar Hill was not a formal location in 1804. The battle between the rebels and the soldiers became commonly known as the 'Battle of Vinegar Hill' after the Irish battle in 1798. Common usage of the name Vinegar Hill began to appear in the 1810s and 1830s in the Rouse Hill area. But Vinegar Hill is not on a map. There have been competing views on the location of Vinegar Hill. Originally thought to be Rouse Hill, George Mackanass challenged this in the 1950s marking the location of Vinegar Hill as the crossroads between Windsor Road and Schofields Road. In the 1980s, several other local historians came to the same conclusion as did the NSW Commissioner for the Department of Planning and the Environment in 1982. Lynette Ramsay Silver points to the letter of Major Johnston which talks of his troops turning at the 'Government Stock Fence' to the second hill from Half Way Pond. By her reckoning the Government Stock Fence is where Old Windsor Road and Windsor Road meet today and Old Ponds Creek is known today as Second Ponds Creek. For Silver, the location of the battle is approximately at the crossroads of Schofields Road and Windsor Road. The area occupied by Castlebrook Lawn Cemetery satisfies the criteria in every respect and in 1988 a sculpture commemorating the battle was dedicated at Castlebrook Lawn Cemetery by former Australian Prime Minister Gough Whitlam.

other possible explanation is that he was not expected to survive the trip to Parramatta and he was executed before he could die of his wounds, a position possibly supported in correspondence between Johnston and King.[65] The rest of the leaders were brought before a court martial. William Johnston who had surrendered to the authorities pleaded guilty. John Neale admitted he was in the rebel group. Jonathon Place denied all charges and the rest claimed they had been forced to join the rebellion. William Johnston and Samuel Humes as leaders in the rebellion were ordered hung in a public place and then for their bodies to be hung in chains. One was hanged from a tree on the road to Prospect near Parramatta, the other probably near Johnston's Bridge at Toongabbie on the road to Hawkesbury. Six others were executed: Charles Hill and Jonathon Place at Parramatta on 8 March, John Neale and George Harrington at Castle Hill the following day and John Brannan and Timothy Hogan in Sydney on 10 March. The *Sydney Gazette* of 18 March 1804 reported on the background of the 'Principal Offenders':

> Philip Cunningham the Principal Rebel leader, who was executed at Hawkesbury, was one of the Prisoners by the Ann, and was remarkably active in the mutinous transactions on board that vessel which rendered a recourse to rigorous exertions necessary to the safety of the Officers and crew. Some time after his arrival he was sent up to the Settlement at Castle Hill, whence he was appointed overseer of the Government Stone-masons and such was the...indulgence shown him, that in the Course of little more than a twelvemonth he had nearly erected on his own account, a stone building of considerable value.
>
> Samuel Humes officiated as overseer of the Carpenters, and had a convenient house, and received also many indulgences that might have awakened a sentiment of gratitude in his breast which would have prevented his disgrace and untimely exit.
>
> John Place was the only survivor of the three who embarked on the fatal enterprise of crossing the Mountains, under the ludicrous supposition of an unknown Settlement there existing, and was pardoned on account of the pitiable and deplorable plight in which he was found. He was afterwards corporally punished for

---

[65] Johnson to King, 6 March 1804, *HRNSW*, Vol. 5, p. 345, states that 'C_____, who is one of the rebel chiefs, who was supposed to be dead on the field, was brought in here alive, and I immediately - with the opinion of the officers - ordered him to be hung up.'

a second time absconding in order to subsist in the woods, and his restless and relentless disposition at length drew down upon him the provoked vengeance of the Law.

Charles Hill, although several years a free man had lost all sight of character, and was in consequence frequently implicated in theft and misdemeanour. He rented a farm, and might have procured an honest and comfortable livelihood, but the hope of plunder could alone induce him to join the infatuated people, and his atrocious designs obtained their due reward.

The same edition also reported:

Francois Girault, a Frenchman, in obedience to HIS EXCELLENCY'S positive command, quitted the Colony, in His Majesty's ship Calcutta, having been charged on evidence strongly presumptive with secretly abetting and encouraging the late Revolt. This man resided at Parramatta, and had for several months past devoted much of his time to trafficking as a pedlar to and from Castle Hill during which intercourse he too probably obtained an undue influence among the people at the Settlement, and availing himself of an unhappy credulity, disseminated gradually the seeds of dissention and discontent, but ingeniously in the end found means to avoid open detection and to escape condign punishment.[66]

Many of the remaining leaders were flogged with either 200 or 500 lashes and then sent to the new penal settlement at Coal River (Newcastle). [67] Finally, Joseph Holt and Maurice Margarot were arrested on suspicion of involvement. Holt was kept in gaol before sent to Norfolk Island on 19 April, on the instructions of the magistrates who decided that, although there was insufficient evidence to convict him of treason before a criminal court, 'the tranquillity of the colony' required such a measure. Margarot also joined Holt in exile at Norfolk Island. Other suspected rebels who had not been openly involved in the rebellion were also sent to Norfolk Island without proof of

---

[66] The same edition of the *Sydney Gazette* included a report that war between Britain and France had restarted. There is an unproven, but significant implication that Girault was a French agent.

[67] Lieutenant Menzies to King, 15 June 1804, *HRNSW*, Vol. 5, pp. 385-386, gives brief details of a conspiracy at Newcastle. See also, King to Hobart, 14 August 1804, *HRA*, Series I: Vol. 5, pp. 1-2.

their involvement.⁶⁸ By August 1804, King was sufficiently confident to write to Lord Hobart:

> I am happy to inform your Lordship that no late circumstances of that kind have occurred to disturb the tranquillity of the colony, notwithstanding which I rather hope than am confident that anything of the kind may never happen again-nothing so daring I think ever will; yet, altho' every exertion is made to counteract their being misled, I am sorry to say that a few disaffected characters will always be endeavouring to poison the minds of the greater part of those who have been sent here for sedition and rebellion in Ireland, who, notwithstanding the lenity shewn them so lately, have been endeavouring to resume their wild plans, which has rendered it necessary to put the worst of that class under greater restrictions than has hitherto been the case.⁶⁹

However, Johnston took a more sanguine view, if only to support his argument that the NSW Corps should be reinforced:

> Should Insurrection again appear, it may not be in the feeble way in which the last broke out; therefore, a stronger hand must be applied to put it down; or should it be found necessary to form other Settlements where a Military Force would be required, or to augment the Detached Posts already out, the King's Service must materially suffer, either by weakening Head Quarters so as to render due subordination to the Government unfortified, or deferring that Service till a representation was made Home.⁷⁰

A possible insurrection in 1807

Michael Dwyer had been involved in the 1798 rebellion and later made contact with Robert Emmet but was reluctant to commit his followers to march to Dublin unless the rebellion showed some initial success. The subsequent failure of Emmet's rising in 1803 led to a period of repression and renewed attempts by the Government to wipe out Dwyer's forces. In December 1803, Dwyer finally capitulated on terms that would allow him safe passage to

---

⁶⁸ King to Under-Secretary Cooke, 20 July 1805, *HRNSW*, Vol. 5, pp. 663-667, detailed how political prisoners and especially Margarot were treated.
⁶⁹ King to Hobart, 14 August 1804, *HRA*, Series I: Vol. 5, p. 1.
⁷⁰ Johnston to King, 24 April 1805, *HRA*, Series I: Vol. 5, p. 448.

America but the government reneged on the agreement holding him in Kilmainham Jail until August 1805, when they transported him to NSW as an unsentenced exile.

Dwyer arrived in Sydney on 14 February 1806 in the *Tellicherry* and was given free settler status. [71] He arrived with his wife and two children. He was given a grant of 100 acres of land on Cabramatta Creek in Sydney adjacent to grants to his comrades Hugh 'Vesty' B . Michael Dwyer was quoted as saying that all Irish would be free in this new country. This statement had been used against him and he and several others in the group were arrested in February 1807 and imprisoned. [72] Bligh reported to William Windham, on 19 March, 1807:

> No arms have been found, or any positive overt act committed, our information leading only to declared plans which were to be put into execution by the Irish convicts, headed by O'Dwyer and some of the Irish state prisoners, as they are here called.
>
> It appears that, in order to avoid detection, they determined to rest their success on seizing the arms of the loyal inhabitants ; and to effect this, the Irish servants of the inhabitants were on a certain time fixed to massacre their respective masters, and the principal persons of the colony, and then to possess themselves of their arms.
>
> Of this determination, I continued to have proofs more or less, when I determined on seizing the persons represented as the ring-leaders, and effected my purpose. O'Dwyer I have put on board the Porpoise. Byrn (sic), Burke, and some others are in jail for trial, and will be brought forward as soon as our evidences are all arranged and prepared.[73]

On 11 May 1807, Dwyer was charged with conspiring to mount an Irish insurrection against British rule. An Irish convict stated in court that Michael Dwyer had plans to march on Parramatta. Dwyer did not deny that he had said

---

[71] See, O'Donnell, Ruan, 'Dwyer, Michael (1772?-1825)', *ADB*, Supplementary Vol. p. 110, and Lawlor, Chris, *In search of Michael Dwyer*, (Chris Lawlor), 2003.

[72] O'Dwyer, B. W., 'Michael Dwyer and the 1807 plan of insurrection', *Journal of the Royal Australian Historical Society*, Vol. 69, (1983), pp. 73-82, remains the only account of the supposed insurrection.

[73] Bligh to Windham, 19 March 1807, *HRNSW*, Vol. 6, pp. 259-260.

that all Irish will be free but he did deny the charges of organising an Irish insurrection in Sydney. On 18 May 1807, Dwyer was found not guilty of the charges of organising an Irish insurrection in Sydney. Bligh informed Windham of his actions on 31 October 1807:

> ...they have since been tried, and the fact, in my opinion, proved, yet they were acquitted - except two, who were sentenced to corporeal (sic) punishment. The whole being prisoners for life I immediately divided the gang and sent two of each to the settlements of Norfolk Island, the Derwent, and Port Dalrymple, and kept two here. The two men who informed of this conspiracy gave their evidence so steadily as to induce me to give them free pardons, and they remain here without any apprehension of being molested by the disaffected Irishmen. [74]

Bligh regarded the Irish and many other nationalities with contempt and disregarded the first trial acquittal of Michael Dwyer. Dwyer was stripped of his free settler status and transported to Norfolk Island and later to VDL. On 27 May, 1807, Bligh sent Dwyer and Morris to Norfolk Island with instructions to the Commandant, Captain Piper:

> Michael O'Dwyer and William Morris, two convicts for life, being found to be persons necessary to be removed from this settlement, you are hereby required and directed to receive the two said men, and victual them accordingly, taking care that they are not suffered to quit Norfolk Island unless by authority from under my hand. And the said William Morris, having received five hundred and twenty-five lashes, pursuant to his sentence of one thousand, you are hereby required to direct the remaining part of four hundred and seventy-five lashes to be inflicted according to the warrant sent herein by the Judge-Advocate. [75]

After Governor Bligh was deposed in 1808, the acting Governor of NSW, George Johnston who was present at Dwyer's acquittal in the first trial ordered that he should be freed. Michael Dwyer later became Chief of Police in 1813 at Liverpool, NSW but was dismissed in October 1820 for drunken conduct and mislaying important documents. In December 1822, he was sued for aggrandising his farm with Ann Stroud's. This spurred Daniel Cooper to demand

---

[74] Bligh to Windham, 31 October 1807, *HRNSW*, Vol. 6, p. 363.
[75] Bligh to Windham, 31 October 1807, *HRNSW*, Vol. 6, p. 354.

restitution of some £2,000 invested in Dwyer's popular Harrow Inn. Bankrupted, Dwyer was forced to sell off most of his assets but this did not save him from several weeks' imprisonment in the Sydney debtors' prison in May 1825 where he evidently contracted dysentery from which he died in August 1825.

Conclusion

Unlike the Eureka rebellion in 1854, Australian historians have been slow to see the 1804 convict revolt as a legitimate expression of political resistance. Established in 1788, the fledgling British colony of NSW was small and isolated, but with a significant cadre of political rebels among its convict population. As a result, it had a strong undercurrent of republicanism and a persistent anti-authoritarianism to British rule. To O'Farrell, the Irish were led to rebel by semi-mystical impulses, 'frustrations, sickness of heart, and impulses of affront: in a word pride' and Silver also implies that the rebels were merely homesick romantics. [76] More recently historians Ann-Maree Whitaker and Ruan O'Donnell have recognised the political imperatives that shaped rebellion. Although it is easy to dismiss rebellions as wild and absurd, they generally involved detailed planning but there was also a wider vision that transcended ethnicity. Those planning rebellions believed that all disaffected men, free and convict, would join them to throw off their shared oppression and that together they would seize a ship and sail to freedom.

With the exception of Joseph Holt's *Memoirs*, published in 1838 twelve years after his death and decidedly critical of seditious activities, the accounts of the planned or actual Irish rebellions in the first decade of the nineteenth century were written by those who sympathised with or supported the actions of the authorities. The rebels themselves have little or no voice and where it is evident it is generally mediated through the voice of the authorities in despatches, reports and accounts. Reliance on 'official' sources poses particular problems especially since official attitudes towards Irish 'politicals' from the early 1790s was broadly negative. This can be seen David Collins'

---

[76] O'Farrell, Patrick, *The Irish in Australia: 1788 to the Present*, (University of New South Wales Press), 2000, p. 38.

comments on the fractious character of Irish convicts in 1798 and 1799 and of the need to take firm action against them:

> The Irish prisoners who had arrived in the last ships from that country had about this period become so turbulent and refractory, and so dissatisfied with their situation, that, without the most rigid and severe punishment, it was impossible to derive from them any labour whatever. [77]
>
> A numerous body of the Irish convicts, many of whom had but lately arrived, insisted that 'their times were out', and could not be persuaded that they were mistaken by any remonstrance or argument. They grew noisy and insolent, and even made use of threats; upon which a few of the most forward and daring were secured, and instantly punished; after which they were ordered to go back to their work. They had also taken up the idea that Ireland had shaken off its connection with England, and they were no longer to be considered as convicts under the British government. This was a most pernicious idea to be entertained by such a lawless set of people, and requiring the strong arm of government to eradicate it. [78]

More problematic was the political ideas circulating among Irish convicts especially their belief in their ultimate liberation through French intervention. To the authorities, isolated in NSW, this posed a major threat.

> A report prevailed at this time among the labouring people, particularly the Irish, who were always foremost in every mischief and discontent, that an old woman had prophesied the arrival of several French frigates, or large ships of war, who were, after destroying the settlement, to liberate and take off the whole of the convicts. The rapidity with which this ridiculous tale was circulated is incredible. The effect was such as might be expected. One refractory fellow, while working...at Toongabbie, threw down his hoe, advancing before the rest, and gave three cheers for liberty. This for a while seemed well received; but, a magistrate fortunately being at hand, the business was put to an end, by

---

[77] Collins, David, *An account of the English colony in New South Wales from its first settlement in January 1788, to August 1801: with remarks on the dispositions, customs, manners, &c., of the native inhabitants of that country*, 2 Vols. (T. Cadell and W. Davies), 1798, Vol. 2, p. 54.

[78] Ibid, Collins, David, *An account of the English colony in New South Wales*, Vol. 2, pp. 102-103.

securing the advocate for liberty, tying him up in the field, and giving him a severe flogging. [79]

Colonial paranoia increased once evidence of planned rebellion became evident after 1800 but how real was the threat from Irish convicts? The Defenders and United Irishmen transported between 1795 and 1806 provided leadership to those convicts, who were prepared to take direct action to overthrow the colonial authorities. Although it was the Irish convicts who were a particular concern to Hunter, King and Bligh, it is important not to over-exaggerate their significance while underestimating the involvement of convicts of other nationalities. The Irish convict leadership had considerable experience in planning and implementing rebellious activities. This explains why successive governors sent leaders or presumed leaders, whether there was concrete evidence of sedition or not, to the more isolated penal settlements on Norfolk Island and VDL. This had the effect of disrupting any planning for insurrection. Finally, the hatred of the British in Ireland was transposed to NSW and Irish leaders had a willing supply of convicts prepared to support their actions. That support came from non-Irish convicts is a reflection of the punitive and arbitrary nature of convict life. Where they were concentrated in one area, as on the Castle Hill farm, Ireland's cause helped bind these men together.

However, there were major problems for those seeking rebellion. Keeping planning secret was a major difficulty and only the Castle Hill revolt in 1804 saw planning converted into action. Convicts were always willing to 'split upon each other' and this allowed the authorities to intervene before matters spiralled out of control. The objectives of rebellion such as the rallying cry of 'Death or Liberty' or demands for a ship to go home were idealistic and unrealistic. Although these may have been the aims of rebel leaders, there is little evidence that they were widely held by the rank-and-file, many of whom claimed that they had been forced into rebellion. [80] As in Ireland during the

---

[79] Ibid, Collins, David, *An account of the English colony in New South Wales*, Vol. 2, p. 77.
[80] The major source for the attitudes of ordinary rebels comes from after the rebellion had failed. Faced with possible hanging, it is hardly surprising that many claimed they had been coerced into

1798 rebellion, when faced with even inferior military force, the rebels could not translate numerical strength into military advantage. Finally, the hoped for French aid was illusory: it was never part of French strategy and, during the critical years between 1801 and 1804, war in Europe had been suspended.

It was the British government that was constantly afraid of convict rebellion and disorder though this did not stop it sending political prisoners to NSW despite the concerns of successive governors. For the authorities, a colony composed largely of convicts was inevitably turbulent and rebellious, something reflected in Hunter's and King's despatches. In his reports on NSW and VDL in the early 1820s, Bigge considered that the best security against rebellion was the higher standard of living that convicts generally enjoyed in NSW than in Britain and the opportunities and rewards open to those with industry and skill. Some convicts 'bolted' but only a few rebelled.

---

rebelling. This was evident in other rebellions, for example, after the Chartist rebellion at Newport in 1839, many of those arrested claimed coercion as a defence.

15 Irish Political Prisoners, 1790-1876

From the early 1790s through to the last group of convicts transported to WA in 1868, Australia was frequently the destination for Ireland's political prisoners. The Defenders and United Irishmen were transported to NSW in the 1790s and early 1800s, rural rebels and defeated members of Young Ireland to VDL between the 1820s and early 1850s and Fenians to WA. These convicts brought the conflicts from Ireland with them and especially their struggle against 'Imperial' Britain. As a result, they were among the most fractious and, from the perspective of the colonial authorities, the most dangerous and disruptive group in the emerging colonies.

NSW had a strong undercurrent of republicanism and a persistent anti-authoritarianism to British rule. Between 1800 and 1807, there were at least three planned rebellions that were thwarted before they could break out and the Castle Hill Rising of 1804 when a substantial convict rebellion was put down with considerable ferocity.[1] Lynette Ramsay Silver implies that the rebels were merely homesick romantics. More recently Ann-Maree Whitaker and Ruan O'Donnell have recognised the political imperatives that shaped rebellion.[2] Although it is easy to dismiss rebellions as wild and absurd, they generally involved detailed planning but there was also a wider vision that transcended ethnicity. Those planning rebellions believed that all disaffected men, free and convict, would join them to throw off their shared oppression of the colonial authorities and that together they would seize a ship and sail to freedom.

---

[1] Silver, Lynette Ramsay, *The Battle of Vinegar Hill: Australia's Irish Rebellion*, (Doubleday), 1989, (Watermark Press), 2002, remains the only substantial study.

[2] Moore, Tony, *Death or Liberty: Rebel Exiles in Australia 1788-1868*, (Murdoch Books), 2010, includes a general survey of resistance and rebellion. Whitaker, Anne-Maree, *Unfinished Revolution: United Irishmen in New South Wales, 1800-1810*, (Crossing Press), 1994, and O'Donnell, Ruán, 'Desperate and Diabolical': Defenders and United Irishmen in early NSW', unpublished paper.

The convicts had no desire to rule NSW merely to escape from it.

Convict resistance was widespread in NSW and then VDL in the decades following the unsuccessful rebellion in 1804. The major reason why there were no further large-scale rebellions on mainland Australia was that refractory convicts were increasingly isolated in punishment settlements. The discovery of coal in NSW resulted in the development of Newcastle and its example was later following in VDL with the establishment of the prison settlement at Port Arthur. However, the most feared and infamous settlement was on Norfolk Island that lay about a thousand miles from both Australia and New Zealand and covers an area of just over thirteen square miles. Its isolation and the draconian nature of its administration, especially after 1825, made it one of the most brutal penal settlements of the nineteenth century.

By the 1830s, the numbers of Irish convicts transported for political offences declined and the nature of resistance to the colonial authorities took on a more anti-authoritarian character. This was evident in the Castle Forbes incident in late 1833. Although not caused by specifically Irish issues, it did involve Richard Bourke, the Irish-born governor of NSW, Roger Therry, an Irish Catholic barrister who defended the rebels and John Hubert Plunkett, the Irish Catholic Solicitor-General of NSW and three of the rebels were from Ireland. Unlike the 1804 rebellion, what occurred at Castle Forbes in 1833 or on Norfolk Island the following year had little to do with politics. In both cases, convicts were trying to escape from intolerable conditions.

In 1822, James Mudie, a retired military officer and bankrupt bookseller, arrived in NSW. He and his family had been given free passage to the colony largely through the support of his patron Sir Charles Forbes and the Colonial Office.[3] He had an order for a land grant and was given 2,150 acres on the Hunter River that he named Castle Forbes after his patron acquiring 2,000 adjoining acres in 1825. With the assistance of assigned convicts and his overseer, John Larnach, later his son-in-law and partner, Castle Forbes was turned into one of the finest farms in the

---

[3] Dowd, Bernard T., and Fink, Averil F., 'Mudie, James (1779-1852)', *ADB*, Vol. 2, pp. 264-266.

colony, producing substantial quantities of wool, meat and wheat. [4] About 1830, Mudie was appointed a justice of the peace by Governor Sir Ralph Darling and served on the bench at Maitland, where he became greatly feared by convicts because of his excessive use of flogging for even minor offences. He had fixed ideas on the reasons for transportation and felt that:

> Indulgence merely impairs their usefulness. Prolongation of punishment is justified, even when reformation has been achieved, because it acts as a deterrent to the lower classes in England. [5]

Mudie later claimed that he introduced this harsh policy to counter the lenient policy of Governor Richard Bourke, who after his arrival in December 1831 took steps to reduce the magistrates' powers to inflict summary punishments.[6] For instance, Bourke passed a law restricting punishment of convicts to 50 lashes. By showing himself to be sympathetic to convicts, Mudie argued that the governor had set the stage for rebellion.[7] According to the *Sydney Herald*, Bourke's 'soothing system for convicts' was responsible for a great increase in crime. Mudie and a few other magistrates on the Hunter River shared this belief and secretly began to collect signatures for what their opponents later called the 'Hole and Corner Petition', copies of which, according to Bourke in September 1834, were sent to England 'for circulation in quarters where it is hoped an impression unfavourable to my Government may be produced'. [8] Later that year the gross exaggeration and inhuman attitudes of the petitioners were denounced in a

---

[4] See, Dowd, Bernard T., and Fink, Averil F., 'Larnach, John (1805-1869)', *ADB*, Vol. 2, p. 86.
[5] *Scone and Upper Hunter Historical Society Journal*, Vol. 1, (1), (1959), p. 106.
[6] See King, Hazel, 'Bourke, Sir Richard (1777-1855)', *ADB*, Vol. 1, pp. 128-133, and King, Hazel, *Richard Bourke*, (Oxford University Press), 1971, pp. 160-165, on the Castle Forbes affair. See also, McKenzie, Kirsten, *A Swindler's Progress: Nobles and Convicts in the Age of Liberty*, (Harvard University Press), 2009, pp. 170-175.
[7] Mudie, James, *The Felony of New South Wales*, (Whaley and Co.), 1837, p. 70.
[8] The petition signed by 127 free settlers on Hunter's River against the 'dangerous and injurious tendency' of Bourke's legislation is printed in *Sydney Herald*, 26 August 1833, p. 2.

pamphlet by 'An Unpaid Magistrate', thought to be Roger Therry. [9]

Responding to repeated ill-treatment such as striking men and bringing them before magistrates to be flogged for trivial offences by Larnach who was in charge of the estate, the convicts sent one of their number to the Governor with a petition. However, as this application was irregular and his absence unauthorised, the man was put in chains and flogged. In early November 1833, six convicts took to the bush after stealing supplies, guns, ammunition and horses. [10] Anthony Hitchcock, John Poole, James Riley, David Jones, John Perry and the youngest, seventeen year old James Ryan claimed they had absconded after brutal mistreatment. Larnach, who was washing sheep in a near-by stream and was shot at but not injured. A group of men including Larnach went in pursuit of the escaped convicts, located the escapees camping in a steep ravine and successfully captured them. [11]

There was widespread press comment on the rebellion before the trial that displayed how divided the colony was over the fate of the rebels. The *Sydney Monitor*, for instance, objected to a four day delay on the start of the trial because of public cost for maintaining the witnesses already in Sydney. [12] At their trial, they were defended by Roger Therry, a fellow countryman and committed supporter of Bourke.[13] Mudie later suggested that Bourke had retained Therry to conduct the defence. In fact, he did so at the request of Father John Joseph Therry who

---

[9] Currey, C. H., 'Therry, Sir Roger (1800-1874)', *ADB*, Vol. 2, pp. 512-513.

[10] *New South Wales Government Gazette*, 13 November 1833, p. 477, gives details of items stolen and descriptions of the six men involved. John Poole and James Riley were from Dublin and James Ryan from County Tipperary.

[11] *Sydney Monitor*, 16 November 1833, p. 2, prints a letter, with editorial comment, from Mudie dated 11 November that is critical of Bourke and what Mudie saw as his lenient policies towards convicts. See also, 'The Bushrangers at the Hunter', in the same issue.

[12] 'Private Justice and Economy sacrificed to Private Convenience', *Sydney Monitor*, 7 December 1833, p. 2

[13] For a detailed report of the case, which was tried before the Supreme Court of New South Wales, see *Sydney Herald*, 12 December 1833, p. 2, and *Sydney Monitor*, 14 December 1833, p. 2.

believed that some of the accused were guilty of no more than desertion and that they might escape capital punishment if well defended. Despite arguing in mitigation that the accused had suffered appalling treatment from Larnach and Mudie, they were found guilty.

The men were in utter hopelessness of their escape from conviction. They had repeatedly declared before the trial that they would prefer death to return to Castle Forces. [14]

Five were executed and David Jones was exiled to Norfolk Island for life. Perry, Riley and the young James Ryan were hanged on 21 December 1833 and Hitchcock and Poole were sent to the Hunter River, to be executed there. This trial was one of the most controversial in NSW convict history. Mudie and Larnarh's mistreatment resulted in public outcry at the execution of the men. At their trial and their speeches on the gallows, the men implored the Governor to prevent cruelties that led to their act of desperation.[15]

Bourke appointed a government inquiry consisting of John Hubert Plunkett [16] and Frederick Hely [17] to investigate charges made at the trial against Mudie and Larnach for the treatment of their assigned servants. [18] The commission

---

[14] Therry, Roger, *Reminiscences of 30 Years Residence in New South Wales and Victoria*, (Sampson Law, Son & Co.), 1863, p. 168; see pp. 164-176, for Therry's comments on the whole affair.

[15] For the Castle Forbes incident see *Sydney Gazette*, 26 November 1833, 9, 10 December 1833, White, Charles, *Convict Life in New South Wales and Van Diemen's Land*, (C. & G. S. White), 1889, pp. 397-402. ibid, Hirst, J. B., *Convict Society and its Enemies*, pp. 144, 182-183, Blair, Sandra, 'The Revolt at Castle Forbes: A Catalyst to Emancipist Emigrant Confrontation', *Journal of the Royal Australian Historical Society*, Vol. 64, (1978), pp. 89-107.

[16] Suttor, T. L., 'Plunkett, John Hubert (1802-1869)', *ADB*, Vol. 2, pp. 337-340, and Molony, John N., *An Architect of Freedom: John Hubert Plunkett in New South Wales, 1832-1869*, (Australian National University Press), 1973, pp. 9-21.

[17] Pike, F., 'Hely, Frederick Augustus (1794-1836)', *ADB*, Vol. 1, pp. 529-530.

[18] Bourke to Lord Stanley, 15 April 1834, *HRA*, Series I, Vol. 17, pp. 409-410, briefly outlined events at Castle Forbes and the appointment of the investigation. *Sydney Monitor*, 21 January 1834, Supplement, pp. 1-2, *Sydney Monitor*, 28 January 1834,

report led to criticism of Bourke's approach to managing convicts in the *Sydney Herald* and led to calls for an ending of penal settlement. [19] Mudie and Larnach were exonerated of ill-treatment but criticised for the rations they supplied to convicts. In April 1834, it was reported that six more of Major Mudie's men had absconded and 'taken to the bush'. They included Stephen Parrott who had refused to join the rebels the previous year but:

> ...he had been again flogged since, and has frequently declared that he wished he had been hanged with the others rather than remain in the Major's service. In all probability the alternative he preferred awaits him. [20]

Angered by the report the two men prepared a joint protest and asked Bourke to send it to London. [21] The Governor refused and in September 1834 with help from Edward Smith Hall, of the *Monitor*, they printed *Vindication of James Mudie and John Larnach, from Certain Reflections ...Relative to the Treatment by Them of Their Convict Servants*. This pamphlet was sent direct to the Colonial Office. At the same time William Watt, a ticket-of-leave convict employed as a sub-editor in the *Sydney Gazette* that had aligned itself with Bourke's reformist administration, attacked Mudie for his cruelty to convicts in a pamphlet *Party Politics Exposed*. Mudie in turn charged Watt with serious misdemeanours. [22] Brought to trial in

---

Supplement, pp. 1-2, *Sydney Monitor*, 31 January 1834, Supplement, p. 1, *Sydney Monitor*, 4 February 1834, Supplement, pp. 1-2, *Sydney Monitor*, 7 February 1834, p. 5, prints the evidence collected by the Commission.

[19] *Sydney Herald*, 24 February 1834, p. 2.
[20] 'Any Thing but the 'Major', *Sydney Gazette*, 10 April 1834, p. 2.
[21] Bourke to Lord Stanley, 20 September 1834, *HRA*, Series I, Vol. 17, pp. 542-543, details Mudie's charges of maladministration against Bourke. See Glenelg to Bourke, 31 August 1835, *HRA*, Series I, Vol. 18, p. 88, approving Bourke's action against Mudie.
[22] Bourke to Glenelg, 28 February 1836, *HRA*, Series I, Vol. 18, pp. 306-307, 314-330, details Mudie's private prosecution of Watt. See, *Sydney Herald*, 27 July 1835, p. 3, *Sydney Herald*, 30 July 1835, p. 3, *Sydney Herald*, 3 August 1835, p. 2, on Watt's committal trial before magistrates for receiving a printed proof slip knowing it had been 'feloniously stolen', *Sydney Gazette*, 20 August 1835, p. 2, *Sydney Gazette*, 22 August 1835, p. 2, *Sydney Gazette*, 25 August 1835, p. 3, for his civil jury trial, and *Sydney*

Sydney, Bourke removed Watt to Port Macquarie where, despite Mudie's attempts to prevent it, he married Ann Howe the proprietor of the *Gazette* in 1836, but drowned the following year. Mudie also attacked Roger Therry for defending the mutineers at their trial and Bourke for showing favouritism to convicts. These tactics proved ineffectual but Mudie induced Campbell Riddell, the Colonial Treasurer to stand against Therry, the governor's nominee for election to the chairmanship of the Quarter Sessions. Riddell's victory by one vote, later shown to be irregular, was upheld by the Colonial Office. Bourke regarded this ruling as a personal affront and decided to confirm the resignation he had already submitted.

In 1836, Mudie was not reappointed to the Commission of the Peace. [23] Sickened with colonial affairs, he sold Castle Forbes for £7,000 and in March sailed for England determined on retribution. In 1837, he published *The Felonry of New South Wales*, an attack on those he believed had opposed him in the colony especially Chief-Justice Forbes and Therry:

> ...what a sink of corruption and iniquity, detestable profligacy and disgusting filth, is presented by the whole system of the law courts and the actual state of the legal profession, in New South Wales. [24]

In 1840, Mudie returned to Sydney to a frosty reception; his malicious comments in *The Felonry of New South Wales* had lost him old friends. John Kinchela, son of the judge who had been maligned in the book, publicly horsewhipped Mudie in Sydney, and, when Mudie sued him, the £50 damages imposed on Kinchela were promptly paid by a subscription in the court. It is possible that as a Calvinistic Presbyterian, Mudie's antagonism towards Bourke, Therry and Watt was an expression of his anti-Catholicism. Watt and Therry were Catholics and although Bourke was a Protestant he was renowned for his religious tolerance. Mudie attacked Bourke's Irish ancestry and

---

Herald, 24 August 1835, p. 2, and Blair, S., 'The Convict Press: William Blair and the Sydney Gazette in the 1830s', *The Push from the Bush*, Vol. 5, (1979), pp. 98-119.
[23] Bourke to Glenelg, 28 February 1836, *HRA*, Series I, Vol. 18, p. 308, gives Bourke's reasons for not reappointing Mudie.
[24] Ibid, Mudie, James, *The Felonry of New South Wales*, p. 151.

Roman Catholic convicts who, he maintained, used their religion as a means for planning rebellion. [25] With no future in NSW in 1842, Mudie returned to London, where he lived until his death a decade later.

The Men of '48

Events in Europe and in Ireland in 1848 did not have the same impact on Irish-Australians as they did on their compatriots in the United States. The tyranny of distance proved an insuperable obstacle to any meaningful involvement in the affairs of Ireland and this isolation bred a degree of disinterest and, in many cases, apathy. The news that eventually reached the colonies and that was disseminated through the Australian press was filtered and sanitised and contained little to excite the passions of the local Irish population. The arrival of the Young Ireland leaders in VDL did not appreciably alter this situation.[26] Given the importance of Daniel O'Connell in the early- and mid-1840s in developing working-class Irish nationalism, it may appear surprising that the Young Ireland rebellion had such a small impact on Australia. For Irish-Australians, the violence of 1848 was insignificant when compared to the enormity of the Famine and the ideas of Young Ireland had yet to make any real inroads into Australian thinking. [27] Even the conservative *Sydney Herald* acknowledged that events in Europe washed over Australia and Australians no

---

[25] Ibid, Mudie, James, *The Felonry of New South Wales*, pp. viii, 99-100, 188.
[26] Campbell, Malcolm, *Ireland's New Worlds: Immigrants, Politics and Society in the United States and Australia, 1815-1922*, (University of Wisconsin Press), 2008, pp. 43-46.
[27] Cullen, Rev. J. H., *Young Ireland in Exile: The Story of the Men of '48 in Tasmania*, (The Talbot Press), 1928, Touhill, Blanche, M., *William Smith O'Brien and His Irish Revolutionary Companions in Penal Exile*, (University of Missouri Press), 1981, Kiely, Brendan, *The Waterford rebels of 1849: the last young Irelanders and their lives in America, Bermuda and Van Diemen's Land*, (Geography Publications), 1999, and McConville, Sean, *Irish political prisoners, 1848-1922: Theatres of War*, (Routledge), 2003, pp. 45-106 tell the collective story. See also, http://www.youngirelanders.utas.edu.au/ an excellent site on the Young Irelanders in VDL on which I have strongly relied.

longer saw themselves as a penal settlement but as a community in which they enjoyed rights and liberties:

> There are, it is true, some few restrictions upon our local right which we have reason to complain [but] when we remember the infancy of our settlement, and the recency of our deliverance from penal thraldom, we should rather rejoice that our advancement has been so considerable. All the solid benefits pertaining to a free people are already ours. [28]

The development of the Repeal Association in the early 1840s, the catastrophic impact of the Famine after 1845 and the unwillingness of successive Conservative and Whig governments to countenance any devolution of political power from Westminster to Dublin combined in the revolutionary spring and summer of 1848 to create growing tensions within the Irish nationalist movement that hinted at possible insurrection. When this occurred in briefly in 1848 and 1849, it proved short-lived, poorly organised, lacking support or arms and failed miserably. Fifteen Young Irelanders were, as a consequence, transported to VDL between 1849 and 1850. [29] John Mitchel, John Martin, Kevin Izod O'Doherty and William Paul Dowling were transported for treason-felony or seditious journalism. William Smith O'Brien, Thomas Meagher, Terence Bellew McManus and Patrick O'Donohoe were transported for the unsuccessful rebellion at Ballingarry in July 1848. [30] The remaining seven were transported for their involvement in

---

[28] *Sydney Herald*, 26 July 1848, cit, ibid, Campbell, Malcolm, *Ireland's New Worlds: Immigrants, Politics and Society in the United States and Australia, 1815-1922*, p. 46.

[29] The Clonmel trials were widely reported in VDL in both the Hobart *Colonial Times* and the *Courier*. Originally Martin and O'Doherty were to depart with O'Brien, Meagher, McManus and O'Donohoe. Because of a delay in the transportation orders, Martin and O'Doherty were dispatched first. On 28 June 1849, Martin and O'Doherty set sail on the four-month voyage to VDL: see 'The Exiles Traitors' a letter by O'Doherty on this: *Launceston Examiner*, 8 June 1850, p. 4

[30] For Ballingarry and the sequence of events leading up to this abortive episode see, Brown, Richard, *Famine, Fenians and Freedom, 1840-1882*, pp. 166-197.

an attack on the Cappoquin Police Barracks in Waterford in July 1849 and tried the following year. [31]

Life in Van Diemen's Land

With the exception of Smith O'Brien, all had accepted conditional 'tickets-of-leave' and had been placed in different police districts across the eastern half of the island. [32] Meagher,[33] McManus, O'Doherty and Martin were respectively allocated to Campbell Town, New Norfolk, Oatlands and Bothwell districts. O'Donohoe lacked private financial means and was allowed to live in Hobart Town where the colonial authorities thought he might find work more easily. [34] John Mitchel finally arrived in Hobart Town from Bermuda in November 1850. [35] The colonial press in VDL, NSW and Victoria abounded with comments about the 'Irish Exiles' over the next six years reporting their activities and escapes, organising subscriptions for their support in exile and calling for them to be pardoned.

Convicts living under a ticket-of-leave in VDL could normally live where they liked in relative freedom on condition that they reported to government authorities, though not necessarily in person, twice a year.[36] As political prisoners, the Young Irelanders were given conditional tickets-of-leave that imposed certain limitations on their

---

[31] For the County Wexford Rising in 1849 see, ibid, Brown, Richard, *Famine, Fenians and Freedom, 1840-1882*, pp. 207-211.
[32] *Colonial Times*, 30 October 1849.
[33] Wylie, Paul R., *The Irish general: Thomas Francis Meagher*, (University of Oklahoma Press), 2007, pp. 66-84, and O'Sullivan, Elaine, 'O'Meagher in Australia', in Hearne, John M., and Cornish, Rory T., (eds.), *Thomas Francis Meagher: the making of an Irish American*, (Irish Academic Press), 2006, pp. 106-122, consider his exile in VDL.
[34] Davis, Richard, 'Patrick O'Donohoe: Outcast of the Exiles', in Reece, R. H. W., (ed.), *Exiles from Erin: Convict Lives in Ireland and Australia*, (Macmillan), 1991, pp. 96-103.
[35] On VDL in the early 1850s see, ibid, Robson, Lloyd, *A History of Tasmania: Vol. 1, Van Diemen's Land from the Earliest Times to 1855*, pp. 441-512, and ibid, Boyce, James, *Van Diemen's Land*, pp. 213-250.
[36] Alexander, Alison, *Tasmania's Convicts: How Felons Built a Free Society*, (Allen & Unwin), 2010, and Brand, Ian, *The Convict Probation System: Van Diemen's Land, 1839-1854*, (Blubber Head Press), 1990, examine how the convict system worked.

freedom. They gave their *parole* or word of honour not to escape but could not leave the police districts allotted to them or vacate their own homes after 10 pm. Changes of address within their local districts had to be reported to the authorities and they were required to report to their district Police Magistrate in person once a month. Most significantly, they were not to communicate with each other.[37] Despite pleas from the authorities, as well as from family and friends, Smith O'Brien refused to give his parole to obtain a ticket-of-leave, was kept on board the *Swift* and not allowed to land at Hobart Town, before being transferred to Maria Island, the convict probation station on the east coast of VDL.[38] There he was imprisoned in a small cottage, within the convict precinct until August 1850.[39]

Mitchel followed the example of his fellow Young Irelanders and accepted a ticket-of-leave when he arrived in VDL.[40] His poor health, one of the reasons why he was transferred from Bermuda, led the authorities to allow him to join Martin in Bothwell where they shared lodgings.[41] On 15 August 1850, a week after he arrived in Bothwell, Martin took Mitchel to meet Meagher and O'Doherty where their

---

[37] On this issue see, Petrow, Stefan, 'Men of Honour?: The Escape of the Young Irelanders from Van Diemen's Land', *Journal of Australian Colonial History*, Vol. 7, (2005), pp. 139-160, at p. 143.
[38] Sloan, Robert, *William Smith O'Brien and the Young Ireland Rebellion of 1848*, (Four Courts Press), 2000, pp. 300-302, deals cursorily with O'Brien's exile and later life. Morton, Caroline, *Maria Island: Its Past, Present and Probable Future*, (Printed at The Mercury Office), 1889, provides near contemporary context.
[39] O'Brien's treatment was highlighted in a public meeting held in Sydney and reported in the *Colonial Times*, 25 March 1851, p. 2. His plight had already been reported in the *Colonial Times*, 1 November 1850, p. 3.
[40] Petrow, S., 'Island Prison: John Mitchel in Van Diemen's Land', *Australian Journal of Irish Studies*, Vol. 3, (2003), pp. 62-78. Mitchel, John, *Jail Journal, or, Five Years in British Prisons*, (Office of the 'Citizen'), 1854, pp. 227-342, gives details of his life in VDL. See also, O'Shaughnessy, P., *The gardens of hell: John Mitchel in Van Diemen's Land 1850-1853*, (Kangaroo Press), 1988.
[41] Ibid, Mitchel, John, *Jail Journal, or, Five Years in British Prisons*, pp. 241-255, provides Mitchel's early views of Bothwell. See also, 'John Mitchel', *Launceston Examiner*, 15 March 1851, p. 4.

allotted police districts overlapped so they did not break their boundary restrictions on the shore of Lake Sorell. Martin, Meagher and O'Doherty had met there before but the meetings became more covert after Mitchel's arrival. [42] Further meetings followed and the authorities soon gave up trying to keep them apart. Mitchel lived in Bothwell with Martin for fourteen months and during this time sent word back to Ireland for his wife Jenny to join him. She travelled from Ireland with their five children on the brig *Union* and arrived in VDL in June 1851.[43] Mitchel and his family moved to a 200 acre property, three miles from Bothwell on the Clyde River that he stocked with sheep and cattle. Martin, invited to live with the Mitchels spent his time writing letters to friends and family in Ireland. O'Doherty settled at Oatlands where he continued his study of medicine and made friends with Father Bond, the local Catholic clergyman. He became manager of the dispensary in Hobart in November 1850 and in January 1851 was acting surgeon at St Mary's Hospital. [44]

Mitchel, Martin, Meagher and O'Doherty were enduring a comfortable exile but conditions for Smith O'Brien, who still refused to accept a ticket-of-leave, were less congenial. He planned to escape recognising that to break his parole would have severely compromised his integrity as both an Irish aristocrat and a gentleman. Four months after Mitchel's arrival, he attempted to escape on the *Victoria* a trading vessel that was due to call at Maria Island on one of its regular visits before leaving for California. Smith O'Brien noted in his private diary that he could not reveal all the particulars of the escape attempt, since his journal could be 'seized at any moment'. [45] The escape attempt was planned and financed by the Irish Directory, a secret organisation of New York Irish nationalists. [46] However, the plan was known to the

---

[42] Ibid, p. 235.
[43] Ibid, p. 269. *Colonial Times*, 6 June 1851, p. 3.
[44] Patrick, Ross, and Dawson, T., 'A Dublin Young Irelander in Australia: Kevin O'Doherty and Eva of 'The Nation", *Dublin Historical Record*, Vol. 35, (1982), pp. 56-70.
[45] Davis, R., (ed.), *'To Solitude Consigned': The Tasmanian Journal of William Smith O'Brien 1849-1853*, (Crossing Press), 1995, p. 142.
[46] *The Courier*, 17 August 1850, p. 2, suggested that the British government would have been 'glad to hear of his escape as

authorities and Smith O'Brien was apprehended as he waded out to the dinghy taking him to the *Victoria*. Governor Sir William Denison promptly removed him to Port Arthur as punishment where he remained for the next three months. [47] Smith O'Brien then agreed to accept a ticket-of-leave with a promise not to escape for a period of six months. On approval of these conditions, he was then assigned to the New Norfolk district and took up residence at Elwin's Hotel on 20 November 1850 where he enjoyed the company of the local gentry.

Mitchel visited Smith O'Brien several times and was introduced to Smith O'Brien's friends. To celebrate his move from Port Arthur to New Norfolk, Meagher, McManus, O'Doherty and O'Donohoe each paid visits to Smith O'Brien but they proved controversial. Meagher managed to elude capture, but McManus, O'Doherty and O'Donohoe were all observed crossing their restriction boundaries and were consequently punished with three months' hard labour at Port Arthur probation stations. [48] McManus and O'Doherty were released for two months, but O'Donohoe, who on the advice of Earl Grey, the Colonial Secretary had been particularly targeted for punishment because of his outspoken activities with the *Irish Exile*, served the full three months. This episode had a profound impact on the exiles' view of their detention in VDL and their subsequent attitudes towards escape.

Escapes

The question of escape posed a dilemma for the Young Irelanders. They had given their parole and, as gentlemen they would have regarded breaking their word as socially

---

calculated to relieve them of much annoyance and embarrassment.' On 7 September 1850, p. 3, it included an account of Smith O'Brien's arrest while attempting to escape on the *Victoria*.

[47] Currey, C. H., 'Denison, Sir William Thomas (1804-1871)', *ADB*, Vol. 4, pp. 46-53. Denison, Sir William, and Lady, *Varieties of Vice-Regal Life*, 2 Vols. (Longman, Green and Co.), 1870, Vol. 1, pp. 1-279 deals with his period in VDL; see pp. 133-137, 146-148, 179, 182-183, 248, for references to Young Irelanders in his journal.

[48] 'The State Prisoners', *Courier*, 28 December 1850, pp. 2-3, details the hearing before they were removed to Port Arthur.

unacceptable and an attack on their honour. However, the punishment imposed after they breached their restriction boundaries led to a change in attitude and they decided that their word to the penal authorities was invalid and consequently that escape was now acceptable.

McManus

With the help of a petition organised by the Catholic Bishop Robert Wilson, O'Doherty was released early. McManus was involved in a legal controversy over Denison's legal right to detain him at Port Arthur and was released shortly after O'Doherty. Later, government lawyers sought to overturn the court's findings and advised Denison that the government had cause to re-arrest McManus and return him to Port Arthur where he was assigned to a labour gang.[49] McManus' health had suffered considerably while at the Cascades and he had no qualms about keeping his word not to escape. Sympathisers in Launceston devised an imaginative plan. John Galvin, a farmer who looked like McManus, providing an alibi for McManus by feigning sickness while McManus himself hid in the home of Father Butler, an Irish priest. At the end of February 1851, McManus made his way to George Town and was rowed to the clipper the *Elizabeth Thompson* and smuggled aboard after the ship had been searched.[50] He then made his way to San Francisco arriving on 5 June gloating that he had outwitted his captors and 'left them in utter confusion' by escaping without breaking his parole.[51]

Meagher

While O'Doherty, McManus and O'Donohoe were at Port Arthur, Thomas Meagher was planning his forthcoming marriage to nineteen-year-old Catherine Bennett. The daughter of Brian Bennett, an ex-convict living in New Norfolk, Catherine was governess to the six children of Dr Edward Hall of Ross. Meagher met Catherine and the Halls when their vehicle broke down while travelling to Ross.

---

[49] *Cornwall Chronicle*, 15 January 1851, p. 29, *Launceston Examiner*, 1 March 1851, p. 7, *The Courier*, November 1851, p. 3.
[50] *Launceston Examiner*, 15 March 1851, p. 5.
[51] Ibid, Cullen, Rev. J. H., *Young Ireland in Exile: The Story of the Men of '48 in Tasmania*, p. 99.

Meagher, ever the gentleman, helped Dr Hall make the repairs. After assisting the children's attractive young governess from the conveyance, he evidently became captivated by her. His fellow Young Irelanders believed that Catherine was far below Meagher's social class but Meagher was determined. The marriage was scheduled for 22 February 1851 and McManus, released from Port Arthur and on his way back to Launceston, attended the wedding. Meagher and Catherine settled on the shores of Lake Sorell in a cottage that Meagher built with a generous contribution from his father and he farmed a small island in the middle of the Lake . For the few months after their wedding, Meagher and Catherine were evidently happy and three months into their married life Catherine became pregnant. However, she soon began experiencing problems with the pregnancy that caused some concern but despite her condition and her isolation, Catherine elected to remain at the cottage with Meagher.

During 1851, Meagher became increasingly restless about his life in VDL. When finally he decided to escape to America, Catherine supported him, despite her pregnancy and planned to join him when he was free. The question of whether his escape was honourable shadowed Meagher for many years. On 3 January 1852, Meagher advised the local magistrate Thomas Mason by letter that he was withdrawing his parole and unless arrested would shortly leave VDL. [52] Whether Meagher had given the police sufficient time to arrest him or whether he had actually escaped early and therefore acted without honour proved contentious. Had the latter been the case, Mitchel said that Meagher had raised doubts about the Irish exiles' good faith and therefore done a 'grievous wrong to us and to our cause'. [53] Meagher fled to Waterhouse Island, just off the northeast coast of VDL, where he waited for a rendezvous with the *Elizabeth Thompson*, the same vessel that collected McManus. He escaped first to Brazil and at

---

[52] Comment on this was contained in an article in *The Courier*, 23 August 1853, p. 2.
[53] Ibid, Petrow, Stefan, 'Men of Honour?', pp. 151-152. See also, 'O'Meagher's Escape', *Launceston Examiner*, 14 February 1852, p. 6.

Pernambuco boarded the schooner *Acorn* heading for New York where he received a rapturous welcome.[54]

What happened to Catherine is less clear. After Meagher's departure she went to stay with her parents at Ross giving birth to a baby boy she named Henry Emmett Fitzgerald Meagher a month after Meagher escaped. The child was short-lived and died on 15 June. In 1853, Catherine travelled to New York with Thomas Meagher senior to join her husband. There were growing tensions in the marriage and four months later Catherine, who was again pregnant, returned to Ireland with Thomas Meagher senior. The birth of Thomas Francis Meagher III weakened Catherine and she died from typhus on 9 May 1854 and was buried not far from Waterford in the Meagher family vault. However, an unpublished biography of P.J. Smyth gave a different version of events. According to this biography, Catherine died and was buried in Tasmania and Smyth arranged passage for her surviving son to Ireland to be raised by the Meagher family.[55]

O'Donohoe

O'Donohoe had been allowed to live in Hobart Town to search for work but he found this difficult. On the advice of several colonists he founded a weekly newspaper called the *Irish Exile and Freedom's Advocate* that first appeared on the streets of Hobart Town on 26 January 1850. The newspaper gave O'Donohoe the opportunity to develop a latent talent for writing. Over the next twelve months he capitalised on this talent by combining 'radical theology' and 'explosive politics' that evidently contributed to the paper's success. The Anti-Transportation League had organised in VDL the previous year and anxious to rid themselves of the stigma of living in a penal colony, a large majority of the free settlers were anxious to end

---

[54] Ibid, Mitchel, John, *Jail Journal, or, Five Years in British Prisons*, p. 290. *Colonial Times*, 7 December 1852, printed an effusive biography of Meagher from the *Irish American* while the *Courier*, 11 September 1852, p. 3, reported Meagher's arrival in New York. See also, 'Thomas Francis Meagher in America', *Launceston Advertiser*, 20, 24, 27 November, 1852, pp. 2, 4, 4, and 1, 4, 8 December 1852, pp. 4, 4, 4.

[55] See, http://www.youngirelanders.utas.edu.au/memoire.pdf

transportation and achieve self-government.[56] Through his newspaper O'Donohoe contributed to their growing voice and also championed the rights of the convicts and workers of VDL, who did not have a voice. Although Denison was unimpressed by the *Irish Exile*, he did not shut it down perhaps because he hoped to enlist its support for his own pro-transportation cause. But had this been the case, it was unsuccessful: O'Donohoe's newspaper survived only twelve months.[57]

On 3 December 1850, when McManus, O'Donohoe and O'Doherty visited William Smith O'Brien at Elwin's Hotel in New Norfolk, they were observed crossing their restriction boundaries, technically breaching their parole. While O'Donohoe, unlike McManus and O'Doherty, was never tried for that particular offence, a further visit to Smith O'Brien on 17 December, organised by Meagher, led the colonial authorities to act. On that occasion Meagher invited both O'Donohoe and the editor of the *Hobart Guardian*, John Moore, to accompany him. But en route to Elwin's Hotel O'Donohoe and Moore got drunk, exchanged words and came to blows.[58] O'Donohoe was tried on 19 December for being drunk and disorderly and fined 10 shillings. The entire episode might have finished there, but it seems that Denison decided to use the occasion to close the *Irish Exile* and on 8 January 1851, revoked his ticket-of-leave, as well as those of McManus and O'Doherty.[59] O'Donohoe was despatched by government steamer to Saltwater River Probation Station at Port Arthur where he was employed for the next three months in hard labour.[60]

---

[56] For Mitchel's comments on the transportation question in VDL see, ibid, Mitchel, John, *Jail Journal, or, Five Years in British Prisons*, pp. 274-276, and a letter in *Colonial Times*, 16 April 1852. See also, *New York Herald*, 20 July 1852.

[57] For more on the *Irish Exile* see, Howell, P. A., 'The *Irish Exile and Freedom's Advocate*, The Rise and Fall of a Convict Newspaper in the Denison Period', *Tasmanian Historical Research Association Papers and Proceedings*, Vol. 26, (4), (1979), pp. 115-131.

[58] The incident was reported in 'Domestic Intelligence', *Sydney Morning Herald*, 11 January 1851, p. 4.

[59] *Southern Australian*, 31 January 1851, p. 2.

[60] *Colonial Times*, 10 January 1851, p. 2.

On his release from Port Arthur, Governor Denison sent O'Donohoe to Oatlands for assignment.[61] Denison believed that the remoteness of the Island's interior would restrict O'Donohoe's 'trouble-making' capacity. O'Donohoe's deeply resented Denison for the treatment he endured at Saltwater River and back in Oatlands he once again created problems in his attacks on John Donellan Balfe's appointment as Assistant Comptroller General of convicts.[62] In the anti-transportation ferment in 1850, a number of newspaper articles in support of Denison's pro-transportation stance written by Balfe appeared under the pseudonym 'Dion', something he continued doing until 1853. The Young Irelanders were shocked to learn of Balfe's presence on the Island, particularly when they heard that he had authority over them within the convict department. Meagher under the name 'Virginius' attacked Balfe in a series of letters to the anti-transportationist paper *Launceston Examiner* detailing Balfe's alleged career as a spy in Ireland and his treachery against the cause of Irish nationalism.[63] O'Donohoe also decided to contribute his own knowledge of Balfe's Irish spying activities to the colonists at large. Exasperated by O'Donohoe's outburst, Denison once again accused him of breaching the conditions of his ticket-of-leave and on 20 August sent him back to Port Arthur.[64]

---

[61] The motives for and legitimacy of Denison's peevish actions is considered in *Maitland Mercury*, 12 February 1851, p. 2. The *Launceston Examiner* and the *Colonial Times* were particularly critical of Denison's action but there was also critical comment from the NSW and Victorian press.

[62] Robson, L. L., 'Balfe, John Donnellan (1816-1880)', *ADB*, Vol. 3, pp. 79-80, and Petrow, S., 'Idealism Betrayed: John Donnellan Balfe, Supergrass of 1848', in ibid, Davis, Richard, and Petrow, Stefan, (eds.), *Ireland & Tasmanian 1848: Sesquicentenary Papers*, pp. 70-95.

[63] *Launceston Examiner*, 13 September 1851, pp. 4-5, *Launceston Examiner*, 16 September 1851, p. 4, *Launceston Examiner*, 24 September 1851, p. 7, *Launceston Examiner*, 30 September 1851, p. 5, *Launceston Examiner*, 1 October 1851, p. 5, *Launceston Examiner*, 8 October 1851, p. 5, *Launceston Examiner*, 6 October 1851, p. 5, *Launceston Examiner*, 7 October 1851, p. 5, and *Launceston Examiner*, 26 November 1851, p. 4. See also, 'Who is Dion?', *Colonial Times*, 16 September 1851.

[64] On O'Donohoe's contribution to the transportation debate see, Davis, R. P., 'The Liberal Catholicism of Patrick O'Donohoe and

Denison restored his ticket-of-leave three months later but O'Donohoe had had enough. His recent experiences weakened his resolve to maintain any gentlemanly code-of-honour and this was reinforced by friends in Launceston who agreed that his harsh treatment by the authorities absolved him of any requirement to keep his word not to escape. With his conscience clear, O'Donohoe colluded with local sympathisers on a plan that would deliver him from Denison and penal exile forever. On 20 December 1852, he was boarded the steamer *Yarra Yarra* for Melbourne. He then travelled to Sydney, Tahiti and finally reached San Francisco on 22 June 1853. From San Francisco, he travelled to New York to join Meagher and Mitchel but they received him coolly since they did not regard O'Donohoe's escape as honourable. O'Donohoe died broken and destitute on 22 January 1854 only days before he could be reunited with his wife and child.

Mitchel

Reports of Meagher, McManus and O'Donohoe's reception and activities in America made Mitchel restless. The catalyst for his decision to escape from VDL was prominent Young Irelander Patrick James Smyth.[65] Smyth was one of the Young Irelanders who had escaped arrest after the rebellion at Ballingarry by fleeing to America, where he joined the Irish Directory, a group of well-off sympathetic Irish Nationalists in New York. At their request Smyth travelled to VDL to help plan further escapes arriving in early January 1853. After an initial meeting with Mitchel, and a meeting later with Mitchel and Smith O'Brien, Mitchel elected at Smith O'Brien's insistence to escape. Smith O'Brien claimed that he had already had his chance and said he was still hopeful that at some point the British Government would pardon him so that he would be free to

---

the Tasmanian Crisis of 1850', *Journal of Religious History*, Vol. 5, (1969), pp. 314-330.
[65] Born in Dublin, Smyth was the son of a prosperous merchant and an old school friend of Thomas Meagher, although three years older. Smyth joined the Repeal Association but seceded with the Young Irelanders in 1846 and became a leading member of the Irish Confederation.

return to Ireland.66 With the decision made, Smyth returned with Mitchel to Bothwell to make plans. It took Smyth six months to organise the escape. All involved agreed that the escape must be honourable at all costs and that Mitchel must transparently inform the authorities of his intention to give up his parole. To this end the escape committee executed the plan down to the last detail. They examined the layout of the police station at Bothwell where Mitchel was to formally withdraw his ticket-of-leave and then inspected the route of his departure. Mitchel was to walk into the police office, formally withdraw his parole and then leave before the police could catch him. 67

On 8 June, the day chosen for his escape, Bothwell was 'so full of police' that the planned escape appeared compromised and was postponed until the following day. Smyth used the opportunity to bribe as many of the local police as possible to ensure success. James, Mitchel's son was sent to Hobart Town to advise the shipping agents of the delay. The following day, Mitchel and Smyth made their way on horseback to the police station in Bothwell but encountered James returning from Hobart with news that the shipping agents could not hold the ship any longer without causing undue suspicion and the ship had to sail without him. Mitchel had no intention of backing out of the escape and was prepared for 'life on the run' until passage could be arranged on another ship. Mitchel and Smyth thus continued on their way to the Bothwell Police Station. Mitchel handed G. A. Davis, the Assistant Police Magistrate at Bothwell a letter dated 8 June 1853 formally resigning his ticket-of-leave and retracting his promise not to escape. 68 Before Davis could arrest him, Mitchel strode out the door, leapt onto his horse and, accompanied by Smyth, rode off down the main street of Bothwell to freedom.69

---

66 Ibid, Mitchel, John, *Jail Journal, or, Five Years in British Prisons*, pp. 309-312.
67 *Colonial Times*, 11 June 1853, p. 2.
68 The letter is printed in *Launceston Examiner*, 5 July 1853, p. 2.
69 For events leading to the first abortive attempt at escape see, ibid, Mitchel, John, *Jail Journal, or, Five Years in British Prisons*, pp. 313-320. *Hobart Courier*, 10 June 1853, p. 2, and *Launceston Examiner*, 5 July 1853, p. 5, reported his escape; *Hobart Courier*, 1 July 1853, printed a letter from Mitchel detailing his escapades. *Cornwall Chronicle*, 15 June 1853, p. 2, stated that 'it is rumoured that Mr Mitchell has effected his escape from the colony...'

For the next six weeks Mitchel was a fugitive in the Tasmanian bush while Smyth sought a vessel to collect him from the colony.[70] The first and second attempts to escape from the north of VDL in early July 1853 failed because of the poor weather and the vigilance of the police. Mitchel then travelled to Launceston where friends concealed him in Father Butler's home. Consensus among Mitchel's friends was that the north was 'too hot to hold him' and he decided to travel south to Hobart Town for a third attempt to escape. It was decided that Mitchel should escape on the regular passenger brig the *Emma* scheduled to sail for Sydney within the week and on the evening of 20 July the ship sailed out of VDL's waters.[71]

Pardons

Smith O'Brien, Martin and O'Doherty were thrilled to hear that Mitchel had been received in San Francisco and New York as a hero. Smith O'Brien continued to participate in the social life that he had carved for himself at New Norfolk. Martin, with the Mitchels gone, took up a teaching position in the home of the Jackson family, a job he did not particularly relish. O'Doherty established a medical practice, though with little initial success. All three appeared reasonably content to await their freedom through administrative channels rather through any further escape attempts. Escape had become more difficult because Mitchel's departure had led to increase police vigilance.

On 22 February 1854, Lord Palmerston, Home Secretary in the Aberdeen Cabinet announced a conditional pardon for Smith O'Brien and the following month, Martin and O'Doherty were also pardoned. [72] The pardons meant that, although they could not return to the United Kingdom, they were free to travel anywhere else in his Majesty's Dominions. By the time the news of the pardons reached

---

[70] Ibid, Mitchel, John, *Jail Journal, or, Five Years in British Prisons*, pp. 321-236, details the first two abortive escape attempts.

[71] Ibid, Mitchel, John, *Jail Journal, or, Five Years in British Prisons*, pp. 338-347, deals with his final successful escape. *Colonial Times*, 19 July 1853, p. 4.

[72] 'House of Commons—February 22, Mr Smith O'Brien', *Courier*, 19 May 1854, p. 2, *Colonial Times*, 19 May 1854, p. 2, 'Release of WM. Smith O' Brien', *Colonial Times*, 23 May 1854, p. 2.

Australia, P. J. Smyth was already in Melbourne with instructions from the New York Directory to arrange further escape plans for Smith O'Brien, Martin and O'Doherty. The pardons, however, made this unnecessary. On 16 May 1854, Smyth wrote to Smith O'Brien congratulating him on the announcement and advised that he would arrive in VDL shortly with the intention of making their departure from the island a celebrated event. Subsequently, Smith O'Brien was much feted by the local dignitaries who had befriended him and on 6 July finally left the island. [73] Festivities were arranged in Melbourne to celebrate the pardon of the three Young Irelanders and each of them spoke at the celebrations held in their honour.[74]

Of the Young Irelanders transported to VDL in 1849, William Paul Dowling, born in Dublin in 1824, is the least known. He was arrested in London in August 1848 in possession of Young Irelander documents, was convicted of treason-felony, the first case under a new law that did not include the death penalty and was transported to VDL for life.[75] On arrival in VDL he was granted a ticket-of-leave. Initially assigned to a 'gentlemanly little man' called Robin Hood, Dowling quickly established himself as a self-employed portrait painter. He married his Irish fiancé in Hobart in 1850, received a full pardon in 1857 and was joined by his brother Matthew in Launceston, Tasmania, where the two set up a reasonably successful photography and lithography business. He missed his Dublin family deeply and saw himself as 'a solitary exiled artist' writing that he and his wife Julia felt themselves living in 'in a land of strangers'. Dowling and his family returned to Ireland in

---

[73] 'Mr W. S. O'Brien', *Courier*, 6 July 1854, p. 3. Seed also, 'Presentation of Address to Mr W. S. O'Brien', *Courier*, 5 July 1854, p. 2, 'The Irish Political Exiles: Presentation of an Address to Mr Smith O'Brien', *Colonial Times*, 5 July 1854, p. 2, and 'The Launceston Address to Mr W. S. O'Brien', *Courier*, 10 July 1854, p. 2.

[74] 'Victoria—The Smith O'Brien Demonstration', *Courier*, 26 May 1854, p. 2, 'The Victoria Testimonial to Mr O'Brien', *Courier*, 10 July 1854, p. 2, 'Presentation of Addresses and Testimonials to Messrs Smith O'Brien, Martin and O'Doherty', *Argus*, 24 July 1854, p. 4,

[75] Glover, Margaret, and Maclochlainn, Alf, (eds.), *Letters of an Irish Patriot: William Paul Dowling in Tasmania*, (Tasmanian Historical Research Association), 2005.

late 1866 and set up shop in Dublin, but the business failed and he returned to Tasmania in early 1869. He died in Launceston in 1877. His laudatory obituary in Launceston newspapers tactfully omitted any reference to his early career as a rebel or transported convict.

The fate of the Cappoquin Seven is largely unknown.[76] They were tried at Waterford on 13 July 1850 for their involvement in either attacking or soliciting to attack the Barracks and were sentenced to transportation to VDL for either seven or fourteen years. They were transported on the *Hyderabad* and arrived in VDL on 13 December 1850 where they worked on the probation gangs and were allowed to progress to pass-holder status. In 1854, just before leaving the island, John Martin made a plea for clemency on their behalf. The seven were all conditionally pardoned between 1854 and 1855 and apparently remained in Australia.

The Young Irelanders had little impact on Irish nationalism in Australia and few in VDL embraced Young Ireland. They remained at the margins of Australian life, largely aloof from the population of VDL and disparaging of the convict-tainted society into which they had been removed. O'Donohoe and Meagher made a slight contribution to the anti-transportation movement and Smith O'Brien drafted a new constitution for VDL during his confinement on Maria Island and submitted it to the *Launceston Examiner* for public discussion but in neither area were their contributions seminal. Yet, Mitchel and Martin, in particular seem to have developed some affection for the landscape of the island and looked back on their exile with a degree of fondness. However, everywhere in the writings of the Young Irelanders was an underlying tension and sense of discontent at their contact with colonial Australia.[77] They felt cut off from Ireland and this, as much as anything, explains why they were keen to escape. For them, Australia was simply too remote and, with the exception of O'Doherty, they made no real

---

[76] Davis, Richard, 'Unpublicised Young Ireland Prisoners in Van Diemen's Land', *Tasmanian Historical Research Association Papers and Proceedings*, Vol. 38, (1991), pp. 131-137, examines what can be known.
[77] Ibid, Campbell, Malcolm, *Ireland's New Worlds: Immigrants, Politics and Society in the United States and Australia, 1815-1922*, pp. 44-45.

contribution to the later development of Irish nationalism in the colonies.

After Van Diemen's Land

Although the Young Irelanders on occasions met after leaving VDL, their subsequent careers were largely separate. On 26 July 1854, Smith O'Brien and Martin finally left Australia for Ceylon, where they separated. Smith O'Brien continued on to Malta via Madras, where he visited his brother-in-law and then travelled to Europe, settled for a period in Brussels and completed his book *Principles of Government*. [78] In May 1856, a free pardon was announced for the exiles and on 8 July, after further travelling in Europe, Smith O'Brien returned to Ireland where he continued to uphold the ideals of Young Ireland. [79] Smith O'Brien was invited to re-enter politics but preferred to pursue public involvement through scholarship. He was a member of several learned societies, often dealing with Irish language and culture. He was active as a publicist on political matters with addresses to the Irish nation, though he did not attend public demonstrations. He travelled widely including the United States and Canada in 1859 where he reunited with Mitchel and Meagher and was generally feted as a major public figure.[80] He returned to Ireland, but after his wife Lucy died in 1861 continued his travels on the Continent. On 18 June 1864, Smith O'Brien died in Bangor, Wales and was given a large public funeral.[81]

After leaving Smith O'Brien in Ceylon, Martin continued on to Paris where he settled for several years. In 1858, he returned to Ireland and again became involved in politics helping to establish the 'National League' that sought the legislative independence of Ireland. In May 1870, he joined the 'Home Government Association of Ireland' and the following year was returned to Parliament as MP for County Meath continuing to advocate the

---

[78] O'Brien, William Smith, *Principles of Government or Meditations in Exile*, 2 Vols. (James Duffy), 1856.
[79] 'English News to the 21st May', *Courier*, 14 August 1856, p. 2.
[80] *New York Times*, 26 February 1859, *Chicago Tribune*, 1 March 1859.
[81] McMahon, Jerry, 'The funeral of William Smith O'Brien', *Newcastle West Historical Society*, Vol. 1, (1990), pp. 36-38.

political freedom of the Irish people. He died on 29 March 1875, aged 63, from bronchitis made worse by attending his brother-in-law John Mitchel's funeral. He had collapsed at the graveside and died nine days after Mitchel and in the same house at Dromalane.[82]

Kevin O'Doherty decided to try his luck at gold prospecting in the Victorian goldfields. He travelled to Paris where he continued to study medicine and married Irish nationalist poet Mary Eva Kelly. After his full pardon, O'Doherty returned to Ireland completing his medical studies in Dublin in 1857. O'Doherty returned to Victoria in 1860 and after a short stay in Geelong moved to Sydney and settled at Brisbane in 1865 where he became a leading physician.[83] He was one of the first presidents of the Queensland Medical Society and carried out extensive honorary work at Catholic hospitals. A member for Brisbane in the Legislative Assembly between 1867 and 1873 and from 1877 to 1884 a member of the Legislative Council, he had wide interests. In 1872, he was responsible for the first Health Act in Queensland and in 1875-1877 gave evidence to many commissions on medical matters.

In 1886, O'Doherty was elected to the House of Commons as member for North Meath but resigned after the split in Parnell's party and returned to Brisbane. Unable to set up practice again, he was finally appointed secretary to the Central Board of Health and supervisor of the quarantine station. He died in Brisbane on 15 July 1905.[84] P.J. Smyth returned to Ireland and remained active in politics. Smyth was elected a Home Rule Party MP for Westmeath at a by-election in 1871 and was re-elected in 1874. At the 1880 general election, he did not seek re-election in Westmeath, but stood instead in Tipperary, where he was elected unopposed. He left the House of Commons at the end of 1884, when he was appointed as Secretary to the Irish Loan Fund Board and died the following year.

---

[82] 'John Martin', *Newry Journal*, 30 August 2005, is useful on his career after VDL.
[83] Rude, G., 'O'Doherty, Kevin Izod (1823-1905)', *ADB*, Vol. 5, p. 355; see also ibid, Patrick, Ross, and Heather, *Exiles Undaunted: The Irish rebels Kevin and Eva O'Doherty*.
[84] 'Death of Dr K. I. O'Doherty: Well Known Queenslander Gone', *Brisbane Telegraph*, 17 July 1905.

In America, McManus, Meagher and Mitchel pursued their lives with varying success. McManus attempted to return to the world of commerce resuming his former business of a shipping agent. His efforts met with little success and he died in San Francisco in 1860 impoverished and disillusioned. Meagher employed his talents as an orator and became a success on the public lecture circuit. In 1855, he was admitted to the New York bar and practised as a lawyer. At the outbreak of Civil War he served with the army during the first campaign in Virginia. Towards the end of 1861, he organised the 'Irish Brigade' and was elected colonel of the first regiment from which he rose to the rank of Brigadier General.[85] At the end of the war in 1865, Meagher was nominated secretary of Montana territory and in September 1866 became temporary governor.[86] The following year, on 1 July 1867 aged 43 he drowned in mysterious circumstances on the Missouri River near Fort Benton, Montana. His body was never recovered and some believed he was murdered and buried in an unmarked grave.[87]

Of all the Young Irelanders' careers after leaving VDL, Mitchel's was arguably the most infamous.[88] He was the most widely read and highly regarded in the nationalist

---

[85] Cornish, Rory T., 'An Irish republican abroad: Thomas Francis Meagher in the United States, 1852-1865', in ibid, Hearne, John M., and Cornish, Rory T., (eds.), *Thomas Francis Meagher: the making of an Irish American*, pp. 139-162. See also, Cullinane, Jim, 'T. F. Meagher and the Irish Brigade', *Decies*, Vol. 59, (2003), pp. 81-99.

[86] Thane, James L., 'An active acting-governor: Thomas Francis Meagher's administration in Montana territory', *Journal of the West*, Vol. 9, (1971), pp. 537-555, Axline, Jon, "With courage and undaunted obstinacy': Meagher in Montana, 1865-1867', in ibid, Hearne, John M., and Cornish, Rory T., (eds.), *Thomas Francis Meagher: the making of an Irish American*, pp. 176-194, and Axline, Jon, 'In a fierce and frightful region: Thomas Francis Meagher's Montana adventure, 1865-1867', *Decies*, Vol. 59, (2003), pp. 119-138.

[87] Emmons, David M., 'The strange death of Thomas Francis Meagher: tribal politics in territorial Montana', in ibid, Hearne, John M., and Cornish, Rory T., (eds.), *Thomas Francis Meagher: the making of an Irish American*, pp. 223-239.

[88] McGovern, Bryan P., *John Mitchel: Irish Nationalist, Southern Secessionist*, (University of Tennessee Press), 2009, is particularly useful on his exile in the United States.

community. After his escape and arrival in New York, he founded a newspaper called *The Citizen*, in which he serialised his experiences as a convicted felon since leaving Ireland. He opposed the abolition movement and from October 1857 to August 1859 published a weekly journal called the *Southern Citizen* in the interests of the slaveholders. At the conclusion of the Civil War, he returned to New York where he became editor of the *Daily News* and was arrested for articles supporting slavery, subsequently spending five months in prison. On release he became involved with the Fenian movement and in October 1867 established a newspaper called the *Irish Citizen*, which was published until July 1872. Nominated in 1874, while still in America to represent Tipperary Mitchel was unsuccessful but was then controversially elected unopposed in February 1875. Characteristically, Mitchel announced his intention of 'discrediting and exploding the fraudulent pretence of Irish representation by declining to attend the sittings of Parliament' but his political career was cut short aged fifty-nine by his untimely death at Dromalane on 20 March 1875.

The Men of '67

In the mid-1860s, hundreds of men were arrested in Ireland on suspicion of complicity in Fenian activity. There were two elements among those charged and convicted: those who were civilians and those who were currently serving in the British military forces. The civilian element was treated as political prisoners but those from the military were treated as ordinary criminals. The sheer numbers involved posed a major problem for the British government especially as Irish nationalism had tactical allies in the House of Commons and the Irish diaspora had created sizeable communities in the United States and Australia that too were capable of exerting diplomatic pressure on Britain. [89]

In 1848, transportation had been the usual penalty for convicted felons but by the mid-1860s the situation had been reversed. Only a minority of offenders were now removed to WA, the only Australian colony that still

---

[89] Ibid, McConville, Sean, *Irish political prisoners, 1848-1922: Theatres of War,* pp. 140-144, provides a useful context.

accepted convicts. The critical question for the government was what to do with the most serious Fenian offenders. At least some of the prisoners given long sentence were removed to English convict prisons. However, after Irish representation especially from the Roman Catholic hierarchy, consideration was given to sending the Fenians to WA. Unusually, some of the men were asked whether they were willing to be transported though it is unclear the extent to which this was the result of prisoner initiatives. This may have had certain attractions and Fenians would have remembered that many of the Young Irelanders transported to VDL escaped to the United States. British convict prison conditions were harsh and sentences were longer while in Australia, time was spent in labour gangs while working for a ticket-of-leave. Throughout September 1867, the Home Office recruited the transportation party consisting of ordinary criminals and Fenians that, it was decided, would be the last to be sent. In September 1867, the *Hougoumont* left Portland and, because of fears of a possible Fenian rescue, was escorted by the steam warship *Earnest* until clear of the Channel. [90]

The sixty-two Fenians consisted of 45 civilians accommodated in quarters on the main lower deck astern and 17 military Fenians quartered with the 218 criminal prisoners in the mid-ship section of the lower deck though they were allowed to associate during the day. The isolation of prison cells was gone and was replaced by unlimited association and conversation. There was regular and extended access to the upper decks for air and exercise and there were frequent religious services. Concerts were staged every second night and the *Wild Goose*, a ship's journal (that ran to seven issues) was produced. Prison diet was replaced by ship's rations that were a considerable improvement on the fare provided in Portland and Millbank. Relations between the crew and the Fenians were amiable and on arrival in Australia, the Captain described the men's behaviour as 'exemplary'. [91]

---

[90] The fear of an attempted rescue persisted once they arrived in WA and not only in WA, but also in South Australia and Victoria, the presence of a warship was requested from Sydney.

[91] Amos, Keith, *The Fenians in Australia, 1865-1880*, (New South Wales University Press), 1988, pp. 100-121, provides a detailed account of the voyage making good use of the diary kept by Denis Cashman since published: Sullivan, C. W., (ed.), *Fenian Diary:*

Despite this, the arrival of the Fenians at Fremantle was viewed by some colonists with considerable suspicion that was heightened by rumours of Fenian privateers threatening the colony.[92] With no naval forces, colonists justifiably believed that a single privateer armed with a single heavy gun could reduce Fremantle to rubble in a matter of hours.[93] Since Fenians had already invaded Canada in 1866, it was widely believed that there was no reason why they should not invade WA to rescue their compatriots. There was also widespread resentment that the imperial government had violated its pledge to end transportation.[94] This placed considerable pressure on the colonial administration in WA that only knew the Fenians were coming three weeks before they arrived.[95] Responsibility for managing both the Fenians and fractious colonists fell on Dr John Hampton, the colony's governor since 1862 who had been Comptroller-General of Convicts in VDL when the Young Irelanders were transported.[96] Hampton was supported by Francis Lochee, one of the most influential men in WA.[97] Hampton was fully aware of the widespread fear of the Fenians among colonists and although he thought the threat to the colony was exaggerated, he asked for the support of a warship from Commodore Lambert of the Australian squadron in Sydney. The potential threat posed by the Fenians was taken seriously and two companies of the 14th Regiment were immediately sent from Tasmania and *HMS Brisk*, a

---

Denis B. Cashman on board the Hougoumont, 1867-68, (Wolfhound Press), 2001.
[92] Fenian issues were widely reported in the colony based largely on British and occasionally American newspapers: for instance in 1867, *Perth Gazette & Western Australian Times*, 4, 11 January, 15 February, 15 March, 19 April, 17 May, 14 June, 12 July, 19 July, 9 August, 16 August, 1 November, 15 November, 20 December.
[93] *Perth Gazette & Western Australian Times*, 20 December 1867.
[94] In May 1865, WA was advised of the change in Britain's policy to transportation and that one convict ships would be sent in 1865, 1866 and 1867 after which transportation would cease.
[95] *Perth Gazette & Western Australian Times*, 20 December 1867.
[96] Boyce, Peter, 'Hampton, John Stephen (1810?-1869)', *ADB*, Vol. 1, pp. 508-509.
[97] Tauman, Merab Harris, 'Lochée, Francis (1811-1893)', *ADB*, Vol. 2, pp. 121-122.

corvette of 16 guns was despatched from Sydney.[98] There was some justification for this as a letter written in 1876 suggests that in both NSW and New Zealand tentative plans were made for a rescue attempt.[99]

As in NSW and Victoria in the aftermath of the attempted assassination of Alfred, Duke of Edinburgh by Henry O'Farrell, the most strenuous opposition in WA came largely from Anglo-Irish Protestants who were implacably opposed to Fenian notions of Irish self-determination and other British-minded loyalists who were influenced by them.[100] Their concerns were reinforced by the large Irish element in the colony including 60 per cent of the colony's military.[101] By contrast, Irish Catholic immigrants in WA regarded the concerns of respectable middle-class English and Irish-born Protestants with a combination of amusement and scorn and dismissed the Fenian scare as loyalist panic and anti-Irish prejudice.[102] As long as the Fenians were treated reasonably, liberal Irish Catholic and non-Irish opinion maintained, they would not pose any threat to the colony and that the Fenian panic had

---

[98] Hasluck, Alexandra, *Unwilling Emigrants: A Study of the Convict Period in Western Australia*, (Oxford University Press), 1959, remains an important study on transportation. See also, Stannage, C. T., (ed.), *Studies in Western Australian History, Vol. 4: Convictism in Western Australia*, (University of Western Australia Press), 1981, and Sherriff, Jacqui, and Brake, Anne, (eds.), *Studies in Western Australian History, Vol. 24: Building a Colony: The Convict Legal*, (University of Western Australia Press), 2000.

[99] Kelly to O'Donovan Rossa, 8 April 1876, Archives of the Catholic University of America, Fenian Brotherhood Collection, Box 1, Folder 14, Item 2.

[100] The O'Farrell affair was widely reported: *Perth Gazette & Western Australian Times*, 17 April, 1 May, 8 May 1868. See also, Brown, Richard, *Famine, Fenians and Freedom*, pp. 515-521

[101] Editorial, *Perth Gazette & Western Australian Times*, 21 February 1868, commented on there being 'no lack of Fenian sympathisers among our population'.

[102] *Perth Gazette & Western Australian Times*, 28 February 1868 commented that 'Fenians in Swan River are no longer Fenians' suggesting that the threat felt by some in the colony was exaggerated.

been manufactured by a minority of wealthy Irish-born landowners and some English immigrants. [103]

Convict life

On Friday 10 January 1868, all the convicts on the *Hougoumont* were moved to the prison in Fremantle known to all as 'The Establishment'. [104] The Fenians were probationary convicts, the second stage in the convict system designed to speed progress to rehabilitation. The first, six months solitary confinement, had already been served by most in British prisons. Probation usually lasted for half the convict's sentence at the end of which a ticket-of-leave would be granted that allowed convicts to take employment with free settlers and marry if he wished. Misconduct could result in the ticket being withdrawn and the resumption of probation. The *Hougoumont* convicts were allowed two days rest and began road-work on the outskirts of Fremantle the following Monday. Civilian Fenians were separated from other convicts while the military Fenians were scattered among different working parties. Around six Fenians remained in Fremantle prison where their skills enabled them to be used to do clerical work. Despite hard work and conditions, the Fenians indicated that they preferred conditions in Fremantle to those in Britain.[105] Although the Fenians were generally well-behaved, reports of misconduct increased as the year progressed. These were for relatively minor transgressions of the rules, such as being inattentive on parade. However, constraints on their communication with comrades in other locations and with friends in Ireland proved a more difficult issue for the authorities.

---

[103] Bolton, G. C., 'The Fenians are coming, the Fenians are coming!', in ibid, Stannage, C. T., (ed.), *Studies in Western Australian History, Vol. 4: Convictism in Western Australia*, pp. 62-67.
[104] Ibid, Amos, Keith, *The Fenians in Australia, 1865-1880*, pp. 122-146, examines the period of Fenian convict servitude.
[105] On conditions for Fenian prisoners see, Casey, John Sarsfield, *The Mingling of Swans*, (University College Dublin Press), 2010, includes Casey's unpublished account of his experiences as a convict on roadwork parties, as well as correspondence by Casey and other Fenians and some articles on his impressions of WA which were published in Dublin separatist newspapers.

Controlling prisoners' mail and suppressing 'improper matter' was seen by the authorities as central to the whole rationale of imprisonment. For Fenians, it represented censorship preventing truthful communication about convict conditions and they sought to get round it by whatever means possible and this brought them into conflict with the authorities. Between April and November 1868, ten letters were confiscated and fifteen letters suppressed because, for instance, a letter appears not to have been written to a bona fide relative or a decision was made not to allow a prisoner to write letters to particular individuals. Although there were no restrictions on the number a letters convicts could receive, they were only allowed to write a letter every two months. This meant that if a letter was confiscated or suppressed, the next opportunity to write a letter was forfeited meaning that four months could elapse between letters if there had been any breach of acceptable conduct. Several Fenians were punished by solitary confinement for breaches of the rules while others were brought before the magistrates charged with writing clandestine letters. The colonial authorities, however, sought to mitigate these sentences largely because they did not want to make the situation worse by a draconian enforcement of rules. After the problems Hampton had with loyalists before the Fenians arrived, he did not want to revive their agitation by allowing hints of problems with the prisoners becoming public.

The danger of this occurring became clear in May 1868 in the reaction of conservative loyalists to Hampton agreeing to British requests to reduce the troop presence in the colony. A petition followed in which the Home Government was accused of putting the colony at risk and then not providing sufficient military protection. As the petitioners provided no evidence to support their fears, the reduction in forces went ahead. The critical question for the authorities was how Fenian good behaviour could be rewarded and Governor Hampton recommended that there should be some reduction in the length of the probationary period before ticket-of-leave status should be granted. This was the only part of his Fenian policy with which Whitehall disagreed. In many respects, over the ten months Hampton was responsible for the Fenians, he had adopted an even-handed policy that had successfully kept both the Fenians and their loyalist opponents under control.

Within a few weeks of Hampton's departure from the colony, his successor Acting-Governor Lieutenant-Colonel John Bruce was confronted by a Fenian 'mutiny' involving the whole of Assistant Warder Howard's work party.[106] The problem arose because of Howard's officious attempts to enforce the regulations especially his attempts to control mail and prevent communication with some of their comrades already released on tickets-of-leave. Niggling conflict persisted between the authorities and the civilian Fenians for the next two months. In an attempt to calm the situation, all the troublesome Fenians in Howard's camp were brought under escort to Perth prison to face charges but this precipitated a 'mutiny' when they then refused to work. This coincided with the belated royal visit of Prince Alfred in early February 1869 and, concerns for his safety, meant that his stay lasted only three days. For the next two months, despite being sentenced to solitary confinement or being sent to new work gangs, the Fenians maintained their refusal to work and were then all sent to Fremantle prison. Fortunately, the authorities recognised that increasing punishment of the fractious Fenians would prove counter-productive especially when applied to men who were principled in their stance. Conciliation proved successful and after Assistant Warden Howard was reassigned, the Fenians returned to work.

Pardons

In April 1869, news reached the colony that more than half of the Fenian convicts, coincidentally including most of the rebellious group, had been granted a Queen's pardon that was to be put into effect without delay. [107] The men listed for a free pardon included all but nine of the civilian Fenians including all those with tickets-of-leave and 12 of the 14 mutineers. This suited all parties. Gladstone's government was seen 'pacifying' Ireland, Bruce rid himself of an awkward disciplinary problem and 34 Fenians could now return to Ireland if they wanted to. The British convict

---

[106] Wieck, George F., 'Bruce, John (1808-1870)', *ADB*, Vol. 3, pp. 275-276.
[107] The issue had been raised in the House of Commons on 22 February 1869: *Perth Gazette & Western Australian Times*, 16 April 1869.

system had adopted a fairly lenient approach to the Fenians in an attempt to help their moral reformation but it had failed to overcome their deeply held view that they had never been guilty of criminal conduct. More than half of the Fenians had now been released but the mainly military Fenians remained incarcerated as a result of long term sentences.

The initial problem facing the pardoned Fenians was whether to remain in Australia, return to Ireland or go elsewhere especially to America. Of those who received a free pardon in 1869, 15 went to San Francisco immediately with a further 2 in the 1870s, 9 remained in Australia (4 in Victoria, 4 in WA and 1 in NSW) while only 10 returned to Ireland.[108] The free pardons permitted Fenians to return to Ireland if they wished but not at the expense of the British government. As a result, a widespread move to assist pardoned Fenians was organised especially among Irish diggers on goldfields in Victoria, NSW and New Zealand mobilised by Irish-Australian newspapers in Melbourne and Sydney. £1,400 was collected in NSW and about £5,000 in Victoria. Although sufficient to meet expected needs, wealthier Irish colonists made little contribution for the same reasons it did not contribute to the Irish State Prisoners Fund three years before: they were opposed to Fenians methods and did not want to offend loyalists by sympathising with Fenian objectives. Nonetheless, there were numerous, small donations generally ten shillings or less.

Parts of Australia's Protestant establishment were bitterly opposed to the pardoned Fenians. The *Argus* denounced the *Advocate* as a 'Fenian' newspaper and warned readers that 34 Fenians would soon land in Melbourne unless something was done about it. [109] Both Victoria and South Australia had introduced legislation in 1854 and 1858 that prevented freed felons from entering their territories and the main ports for transit to the United States and Ireland were from Adelaide, Melbourne and

---

[108] Ibid, Amos, Keith, *The Fenians in Australia, 1865-1880*, pp. 289-290, lists all Fenians with brief details of their lives. See also, pp. 174-199.
[109] *Argus*, 17 June 1869.

Sydney.[110] John Kenealy a pardoned Fenian was arrested in Melbourne under the Influx of Criminals Prevention Act. [111] He agreed to leave in the allotted time and went initially to Adelaide, where he was not allowed to land, returned to Melbourne and then to Sydney and finally San Francisco.[112] Although Kenealy would later repent his physical force past, he nonetheless invested in the *Catalpa*, an American whaling vessel, to rescue six Fenians from WA on Easter Monday 1876. Representation was made on behalf of other Fenians that they might at least be allowed to collect money waiting them and to make arrangements for journeys home or elsewhere and the matter was discussed in the Victorian Parliament. Although not passed to deal with those receiving a Royal Pardon but those with conditional pardons, the Victorian Attorney-General said that this distinction did not matter in law.[113] The Victorian solution was temporarily not to be applied to allow Fenians to make arrangements for proceeding elsewhere.[114] The Adelaide *Register* expressed the widespread feeling of relief felt by many across Australia and not simply the conservative loyalists:

> Fenianism is not yet extinct in Australia... [but] than goodness some of it is going away. [115]

---

[110] Gunn, Tom, 'Objectionable on the grounds of equity and Policy': The 'free' Australian colonies and anti-convict legislation', *ANZLH E-Journal*, (2006), examines the development of these policies.
http://www.anzlhsejournal.auckland.ac.nz/pdfs_2006/Others_1_Gunn.pdf

[111] An Act to prevent the influx of criminals into Victoria was originally passed in 1854 largely to prevent the influx of criminals into the goldfields: *Government Gazette*, 17 November 1854. The legislation had been allowed to lapse in 1862 but was revive the following year: *Argus*, 6 March 1862, and 15 September 1863.

[112] *Perth Gazette & Western Australian Times*, 3 September, 24 September, 29 October 1869.

[113] *Age*, 7 August 1869, details the case against Kenealy. See also ibid, Amos, Keith, *The Fenians in Australia, 1865-1880*, pp. 176-185.

[114] *Age*, 1 November 1869. The recidivist question continued to be reported in the Victorian press throughout the 1870s and the 1880s long after transportation had ended.

[115] Cit, *Advocate*, 30 April 1870.

Those Fenians who remained in WA established new lives in which their earlier involvement in Irish radicalism played no part. Hugh Brophy and Joseph Noonan ran a successful building firm for three years before Brophy left for Melbourne in May 1872. Initially arrested under the Influx of Criminals Prevention Act, he was bailed and then released when it was recognised that, having been free for three years, he was exempted from the legislation. He settled in Melbourne and became a successful building contractor. Noonan remained in WA as a builder and architect and married into one of the most respectable Catholic families in the colony.[116] Cornelius O'Mahony and Thomas Duggan became teachers. Luke and Lawrence Fullam became boot-makers but both died young of consumption. Jeremiah Aher and John Goulding found work as carpenters, though Aher went to San Francisco in 1876.

Nine civilian Fenians were denied pardons in May 1869 because of their more important roles in the movement.[117] In July 1869, a petition that sought their release was sent to London and though unsuccessful it provided support for the activities of the Fenian Amnesty Association. To put pressure on Gladstone's government, the Association held 31 public meetings in Ireland during the second half of 1869 and 1870 that were attended by many thousands. In December 1870, Gladstone finally agreed that all Fenian prisoners who had not been British soldiers should be released on condition that they did not return to the United Kingdom before their sentences had expired. Eight conditional pardons were handed out on 13 March 1871 but only James Kearney settled in WA working as an itinerant boot-maker. John Flood, Thomas Baines, Thomas Fennell and J. Edward Kelly left WA on 11 May 1871 bound for New Zealand from where they intended to continue on to America. Since 1867, New Zealand also no longer accepted conditionally pardoned convicts and the Fenians were arrested and threatened with deportation

---

[116] Taylor, Robyn, 'Nunan, Joseph Denis (1842-1885)', *ADB*, Supplementary Volume, pp. 308-309.

[117] *Perth Gazette & Western Australian Times*, 18 June 1869, listed the civilian Fenians still incarcerated as Edward John Kelly, James Dunne, John Flood, Thomas Baines, David Bradley, Thomas Fennell, George Francis Connolly and James Kearney.

back to WA.[118] They were then given passage to NSW aboard a cargo vessel bound for Newcastle. Flood and Kelly decided to remain in NSW while Baines and Fennell departed for San Francisco.[119] Flood and Kelly stayed several years in Sydney working in journalism before Flood first tried his hand as a digger, where he may have been recruiting Fenian sympathisers before settling permanently in Queensland where he was for many decades the newspaper editor and owner in Gympie. Kelly remained in Sydney until 1875 when he left for San Francisco.

Of the Fenians who remained in Australia, most were quickly assimilated into their adopted land and had no further truck with Irish radicalism. However, Flood, Michael Cody and Kelly appear, on the basis of slight evidence, to have been instrumental in establishing a tentative Fenian organisation in the Irish community in NSW and in New Zealand. In April 1876, Kelly wrote a letter to O'Donovan Rossa in which he outlined details of his Fenian organisational work undertaken with Flood and Cody.[120] Keith Amos accepts the veracity of the report pointing to its lack of exaggeration of the organisation's modest following in Sydney and its recognition of the reluctance of 'respectable' Irish to be associated with Fenianism. The Fenian Brotherhood's (FB) Convention in Philadelphia in 1876 suggested that Fenianism was numerically as strong in NSW and Victoria as it was in the United States, giving a figure of 7,000 members though Kelly's report also suggests that it was never a strong as the Fenians in the United States thought it was. The figure is doubtful and may rely on the strength of the Australian response to fund collections for Fenian prisoners and the

---

[118] Coverage in New Zealand press: *Evening Post*, 9 June 1871, p. 2, *West Coast Times*, 3 July 1871, p. 2.
[119] Fennell, Philip, and King, Marie, (eds.), *Voyage on the Hougoumont and Life at Fremantle*, (Xlibris Corporation), 2000, prints Thomas Fennell's journal of his three years in WA in Fremantle Prison and on a chain gang.
[120] Kelly to O'Donovan Rossa, 8 April 1876, Archives of the Catholic University of America, Fenian Brotherhood Collection, Box 1, Folder 14, Item 2; ibid, Amos, Keith, *The Fenians in Australia, 1865-1880*, p. 196 prints Kelly's report.

Catalpa expedition but it is possible to conclude that a Fenian organisation in NSW existed in the 1870s.[121]

Escape

Between 1868 and 1876, eight Fenians attempted to escape from WA; seven succeeded. The earliest escape was by John Boyle O'Reilly in 1869. What was important about his escape and one of the major reasons why it was successful was the level of assistance he received from a Catholic priest, a number of free settlers and several American sailors. O'Reilly was an NCO in the 10th Hussars when arrested in 1866 for assisting fellow soldiers to join the Fenian movement.[122] Found guilty at his court martial, his death sentence was commuted to 20 years penal servitude. After two years in English prisons, O'Reilly was transported on the *Hougoumont*. In his first weeks at the Convict Establishment in Fremantle he worked with the chaplain, Father Lynch, in the prison library. O'Reilly was transferred to a road party at Bunbury but was soon given clerical duties and entrusted to deliver the weekly report to the local convict depot. During 1868, he developed a close relationship with the local clergyman, the Rev. Patrick McCabe and confided in the priest his plans to escape, but McCabe dissuaded him from putting them into effect. In February 1869, through McCabe, O'Reilly met Jim Maguire, an Irish settler in the district working on land clearance for the Bunbury racecourse. Foiled in his first attempt, he hid on Maguire's farm until he could board the American

---

[121] Ibid, Amos, Keith, *The Fenians in Australia, 1865-1880*, pp. 197-199.
[122] Roche, J. J., *Life of John Boyle O'Reilly, Together with his Complete Poems and Speeches*, edited by Mrs J. B. O'Reilly, (Cassell), 1891, was published a year after his death and although generally reliable, it is obtuse on aspects of his life in WA. Barry, Liam, (ed.), *Selected Poems, Speeches, Dedications and Letters of John Boyle O'Reilly*, (National Gaelic Publications), 1994, included sections from O'Reilly's recently discovered 1868 diary. Birman, Wendy, 'O'Reilly, John Boyle (1844-1890)', *ADB*, Vol. 5, pp. 371-372, and Evans, A. G., *Fanatic Heart: a life of John Boyle O'Reilly 1844-1890*, (University of Western Australia Press), 1997.

whaler *Gazelle* that was replenishing its supplies in the area on 18 February 1869.[123]

After narrowly escaping capture at Roderiquez Island, transferring to the American *Sapphire* at St Helena and joining the *Bombay* as a deck-hand at Liverpool, he arrived at Philadelphia on 23 November. Eventually O'Reilly made his way to Boston where he worked as a journalist and his first major assignment was the New York Fenian convention in 1870 and subsequent unsuccessful invasion of Canada.[124] This experience prompted O'Reilly to reverse his opinion on military Fenianism and he rejected militancy seeking to achieve Ireland's independence by raising the status and self-esteem of the Irish people. His views were well received by Boston's large Irish-born population and *The Pilot*'s readership grew until it was one of the most read newspapers in the country.[125] O'Reilly soon became its editor and eventually part-owner. For many nationalists, *The Pilot* was too closely associated with the Catholic Church that denounced Fenianism and its successor Clan na Gael, an organisation O'Reilly never joined.[126] This did not prevent John Devoy and other Clan na Gael leaders seeking O'Reilly's advice.

---

[123] For O'Reilly's escape see, ibid, Amos, Keith, *The Fenians in Australia, 1865-1880*, pp. 147-173, Buddee, Paul, *The Escape of John O' Reilly*, (Longman), 1973, and Barry, Liam, *Western Australia's Great Escape: the dramatic escape of Fenian John Boyle O'Reilly*, (C. F. N. Publications), 1992.

[124] McManamin, F. G., *The American Years of John Boyle O'Reilly, 1870-1890*, (Catholic University of America), 1959. See also, Walsh, Francis R., 'John Boyle O'Reilly, the *Boston Pilot* and Irish-American Assimilation, 1870-1890', in Tager, Jack, and Ifkovic, John W., (eds.), *Massachusetts in the Gilded Age*, (University of Massachusetts Press), 1985, pp. 148-163, and Schneider, Mark, 'Irish Americans and the Legacy of John Boyle O'Reilly', in Schneider, Mark, *Boston Confronts Jim Crow, 1890-1920*, (North-eastern University Press), 1997, pp. 161-186.

[125] This was evident in Boston City Council, *A Memorial of John Boyle O'Reilly from the City of Boston*, (printed by order of the Board of Aldermen), 1891.

[126] For O'Reilly and the Catholic Church in Boston see, O'Connor, Thomas H., *Boston Catholics: A History of the Church and its People*, (Northeastern University Press), 1998, pp. 143-147.

The military Fenians

The 17 military Fenians were, both on the voyage on the *Hougoumont* and in Fremantle, subjected to harsher treatment than the civilian Fenians. They were regarded by the authorities as doubly disloyal to both the Queen's uniform and to her government in Ireland and were excluded from the 42 pardons granted to the Fenian convicts between 1869 and 1871. Three military Fenians were given only five years penal servitude in 1866 but none received a pardon largely because, though Gladstone was prepared to pardon all Fenians without exception in 1871, the Duke of Cambridge, Commander-in-Chief objected and was supported by the Queen. This left the remaining Fenians with two options: they could follow O'Reilly's example and try to escape or serve out their sentences.[127]

James Keilley and Thomas Hassett attempted to escape in 1869 and 1870-1871. Keilley, a soldier from Tipperary serving a life sentence, made two attempts to abscond from his road party in July 1869 but was recaptured on both occasions. He appears not to have made any real plans but made his bids for freedom on impulse. After 1870, he appears to have become a reformed character earning two years remission of his sentence and a promotion to convict constable. Thomas Hassett made a more concerted, if ultimately unsuccessful effort to escape in 1870. His convict record was marred only by one incident of insolence and his escape from a work party in June 1870 took the authorities by surprise. He remained at liberty in WA until April 1871 when he was discovered by the water police stowed away on a ship bound for London. He was sentenced to three years hard labour within Fremantle Prison with the first six months in strict solitary confinement. Both the sources for his escape place the blame of its failure with Noonan, Brophy and O'Mahony who had been pardoned in 1869 for their failure to send or withhold money due to Hassett in the Fenian relief fund.[128]

---

[127] Ibid, Amos, Keith, *The Fenians in Australia, 1865-1880*, pp. 200-210, examines attempts to secure the release of the military Fenians to 1874.
[128] James Wilson to John Devoy, September 1873, and Martin Hogan to Dublin-based Amnesty International, August 1875, provides detailed accounts of Hassett's escape attempt but no later

Having gained their freedom and achieved a degree of respectability in the colony, it appears that the freed Fenians were not prepared to jeopardise their new positions. Hassett finally escaped on the *Catalpa* in 1876.

From 1869, several of the military Fenians achieved a measure of freedom. John Donoghue, John Lynch and William Foley, who had been sentenced to five years, were given tickets-of-leave between May and July 1869. Donoghue then worked as a labourer and stockman and settled permanently in the colony when his sentence expired in August 1871. Lynch also worked as a labourer until he received his conditional release in November 1870. Like his comrades, Lynch also worked as a labourer and received his certificate of freedom in August 1871. Four further Fenians, Patrick Killeen, John Foley, John Shine and Thomas Delaney received their tickets-of-leave in 1871. Killeen remained in the colony after he was granted his certificate of freedom in June 1874. John Foley initially remained in WA but made his way to Adelaide in August 1878. John Shine and Thomas Delaney did not receive their certificates of freedom until 1878 and embarked for the United States from Melbourne in 1882. They were probably accompanied to the United States by James McCoy who received his ticket-of-leave in mid-1874 and his conditional pardon in March 1878. The final Fenian to receive a ticket-of-leave was Patrick Keating primarily on the grounds of ill-health in July 1873 and he died in late January the following year.[129] For the seven remaining Fenian convicts, all serving life sentences, it was clear that any attempt to escape was futile since the pardoned Fenians remaining in the colony were unwilling or unable to provide the necessary outside support.[130] Their only

---

Fenian reminiscences enlarged on the escape. See, ibid, Amos, Keith, *The Fenians in Australia, 1865-1880*, pp. 201-203.

[129] Ibid, Amos, Keith, *The Fenians in Australia, 1865-1880*, pp. 206-208, examines the reasons behind this decision and suggests that his treatment showed that the convict authorities could adopt a caring and considerate attitude. By contrast, James Wilson, one of those remaining in prison, suggested in a letter to Devoy that Keating's condition deteriorated because of indifferent treatment.

[130] Thomas Darragh, Martin Hogan, Michael Harrington, Thomas Hassett, Robert Cranston and James Wilson were the six Fenians who escaped in 1876. Two Fenians were not included. Thomas Delaney was under close confinement within the prison and there

alternative was seeking help from Fenians in America and Ireland.

The Catalpa escape

The escape of six military Fenians from WA on the whaling barque *Catalpa* and their subsequent successful voyage to freedom in the United States was one of the greatest and certainly more dramatic achievements of the Fenian movement.[131] In September 1873, James Wilson smuggled a letter John Devoy entitled *A Voice from the Tomb* asking American Fenians to aid the escape of the remaining convicts. Devoy had unsuccessfully approached the Fenian Brotherhood's executive in 1872 and 1873 about a rescue attempt but he persisted and at the convention of the Clan na Gael at Baltimore in July 1874, he was in a more influential position and was finally successful. An Australian Prisoners' Rescue Fund to finance the operation was launched immediately and about $7,000 was raised without giving any details of the mission. Devoy sought advice from O'Reilly and Thomas Fennell, both former prisoners at Fremantle on how this might be accomplished. O'Reilly particularly stressed that the plan had to be absolutely clandestine, as lack of secrecy had been the undoing of many Fenian operations in the past. The initial plan had been to land a small party of men who would

---

was no practical way he could have joined the escapees. James Keilley had been exposed as an informer in 1866, but although his comrades appeared to have forgiven him he was still regarded as a risk and was not included in the escape. He received a conditional pardon in 1878 and remained in WA dying in 1918. Ibid, Amos, Keith, *The Fenians in Australia, 1865-1880*, pp. 230-231.

[131] Ibid, Amos, Keith, *The Fenians in Australia, 1865-1880*, pp. 210-257, provides a detailed account placing the escape in the context of Irish-Australian nationalism. Pease, Z. W., *The Catalpa Expedition*, (Hesperian Press), 1897, pp. 66-185, is based on Captain Anthony's account of the plot and voyage while Fennell, Philip, and King, Marie, (eds.), *John Devoy's Catalpa Expedition*, (New York University Press), 2006, prints Devoy's account and other contemporary sources. Laudenstein, William J., *The Emerald Whaler*, (Andre Deutch), 1961, and Stevens, Peter, *The Voyage of the Catalpa*, (Carroll and Graf), 2002, give modern, dramatic accounts. See also, Golway, Terry, *Irish Rebel: John Devoy and America's Fight for Ireland's Freedom*, (St. Martin's Press), 1998, pp. 71-86.

release the Fenians, if necessary, by force of arms. This was a high risk strategy given the strength of the garrison at Fremantle Prison. O'Reilly and Fennell rejected this plan instead suggesting that the rescue party pick up the escapees according to a prearranged plan using a whaling ship that laden with a legitimate cargo could sail to WA where it would be seen to be on legitimate business venture. In February 1875, Devoy then approached whaling agent John T. Richardson, who told them to contact his son-in-law, 29 year-old, whaling captain George Smith Anthony, a nonconformist, temperance Protestant who agreed to take part in the operation. Neither Richardson nor Anthony were Fenians or Irish but they believed in the rightness of the rescue, a position reinforced by Britain's support of the South during the Civil War.

James Reynolds, a member of the Clan and on the committee to rescue the prisoners, bought under his name for the Clan the *Catalpa* for $5,200 and George Anthony recruited twenty-two sailors. The *Catalpa* was a three-masted barque, slow moving but sound and sailed to New Bedford for conversion into a whaler, complete with coppered hull and was then fitted out and provisioned for a whaling expedition. On 29 April 1875, the *Catalpa* sailed from New Bedford, Massachusetts. The only ones on board who knew its ultimate mission were Captain Anthony, and Dennis Duggan a representative of the conspirators who posed as the ship's carpenter. At the end of October 1875, it put in to Fayal, in the Azores, where it discharged 210 barrels of sperm oil from its whaling operations, took on stores and replaced some faulty navigational equipment. Desertion by crews during port calls was a common occurrence in the nineteenth century and the crew of the *Catalpa* proved no exception. This allowed a new, undocumented crew to be recruited and eventually the vessel sailed for Bunbury in WA. In February 1876, during the voyage, they met the *Ocean Beauty* out of Liverpool bound for New Zealand. Anthony went on board and learnt of the coincidence that its captain had once been master of the *Hougoumont*. When Anthony explained that he was thinking of whaling off the Western Australian coast, the *Ocean Beauty*'s master provided him with copies of valuable navigational charts of the waters.

Key to the success of the rescue was having Fenian support in WA to plan and coordinate the escape. Having successfully freed Fenian leader James Stephens from a British jail, John J. Breslin was recruited in the United States to take charge of the rescue mission. He left New York on 18 July 1875 and arrived in San Francisco a week later where the Californian branches of the Fenian Brotherhood, which had raised nearly half of the rescue fund, sought to have at least one of their own men on the expedition. Captain Thomas Desmond was suggested and Breslin, who liked and trusted him from the outset, agreed. The two men left for Sydney on 13 September intending to contact Edward Kelly, a freed Fenian and they arrived on 15 October. Support for the mission was secretly organised in Sydney and New Zealand after Breslin arrived and this supports the existence of the Fenian organisation Kelly later described in his letter to O'Donovan Rossa. Breslin and Desmond then continued to Fremantle arriving on 13 November.

While in California, Breslin and Desmond had created new identities. Breslin was disguised as the American millionaire businessman, 'James Collins' with land and mining interests in Nevada and other states while Desmond became an Illinois-born American, Thomas Johnson. Breslin won the confidence of the authorities in Fremantle who believed that he was in the colony to spend large amounts of money buying land for forestry and mining interests. The subterfuge worked and in December, Breslin was taken on a guided tour of Fremantle Prison to view the labour that would be available to him for his enterprise. This tour of the prison convinced Breslin that the prison was so heavily guarded that he could only rescue the Fenians when they were working outside of the jail. Finally, he made contact with the Fenian prisoners who were to be in work parties outside the Prison, telling them when the escape was to take place. Desmond took a job in Perth as a carriage-maker and wheelwright. By mid-January 1876, Breslin had determined the plan of escape and but was a further two months before the *Catalpa* arrived. The *Catalpa* fell behind its intended schedule because of bad weather in which she lost her foremast but finally dropped anchor off Bunbury on 29 March 1876.[132] Captain Anthony

---

[132] *Western Australian News*, 21 April 1876, is the first Australian paper to mention the *Catalpa* on a 'whaling cruise' and also gives

sailed to Fremantle on the coastal steamer the *Georgette* with the Fenian agent John Breslin.

Originally, the escape was scheduled for 6 April but the appearance of the gunboat *HMS Convict* led to a postponement. The gunboat visited the colony each year, stayed for about a week and then proceeded to Adelaide or Sydney. A further complication arose when Breslin learned that two Fenian agents had arrived from Britain with the same objective and who were unaware of the American mission.[133] The IRB (Irish Republican Brotherhood) mission was a response to appeals for help from Martin Hogan in mid-1875. Breslin was unsure whether the two agents were in fact British spies and sought to establish their credentials without disclosing his plans. Once this was done, the IRB agents placed themselves at Breslin's disposal. What he did not know was that the IRB mission had already been compromised and a secret warning had already been sent to the WA Governor but there were no signs that the authorities were aware of the American plan. Had the governor been advised by London to have the Fenians placed in strict custody, then both the IRB and American attempts would have failed.

The escape was rearranged for Easter Monday, 17 April, when most of the Convict Establishment garrison would be watching the Royal Perth Yacht Club regatta. The plan was to bring six Fenian prisoners, who had escaped from work parties to Rockingham, then by longboat to the *Catalpa* waiting 10-12 miles at sea. This involved good organisation, good communication and good planning. On Sunday evening, one of the IRB agents cut the telegraph wires linking Perth and Fremantle with King George's Sound to prevent the authorities attempting to send the *Conflict* in pursuit of the *Catalpa*. The telegraph lines linking Australia with Britain went down on 24 April some 45 miles from Port Darwin, a short distance from the shore. Whether this was done by Fenian sympathisers from the town or not is unclear though when Devoy heard from Britain that the line had been cut he assumed a connection

---

a detailed account of the escape. See also, *Western Australian News*, 28 April 1876.
[133] Ibid, Amos, Keith, *The Fenians in Australia, 1865-1880*, pp. 222-224.

to the escape. [134] The six convicts easily effected their escape using two horse drawn buggies and drove them to Rockingham where Anthony and Breslin were waiting with a whaleboat moored at the Jarrah Timber Company's jetty. James Bell, a worker with the Company, saw them arrive at around 10 am and asked them what should be done with the horses and carts they had abandoned. When they replied that they did not much care what he did, Bell's suspicions were aroused and he decided to ride to Fremantle and alert the authorities, arriving there at 1 pm.

The Water Police sent their fast police cutter to Rockingham that arrived in time to observe the *Catalpa's* whaleboat heading towards the horizon. The cutter returned to Fremantle where its coxswain, Mills, reported that they needed assistance. The coastal steamer *Georgette*, still in port, was commissioned to help in attempts to recapture the escapees. The whaleboat sighted the *Catalpa* in the distance at 5.30 pm, but by 7 pm a squall caused them to lose contact in the gathering darkness. This meant that the crew and passengers of the open boat were forced to spend an unwelcome, uncomfortable and unscheduled night at sea. Both the cutter and the coastal steamer returned to the Rockingham area the following morning The *Georgette* carried a force of Pensioner Guards commanded by Major Finnerty but the Superintendent of Water Police, J. F. Stone, was in charge of the whole operation. Around 7am, when the storm subsided, the whaleboat again made for the *Catalpa* but an hour later spotted the *Georgette*. Stone hailed the *Catalpa* and requested to come aboard to check for escapees but this was refused. The *Georgette* followed the *Catalpa* for several hours but running low on coal, was forced to break off the engagement and return to Fremantle for fuel. As the whaleboat again made for the ship, a police cutter was spotted. The two boats raced to reach the *Catalpa* first, with the whaleboat winning and the men climbing aboard as the police cutter passed by. The *Catalpa* set sail immediately, heading for the open waters of the Indian Ocean.[135]

---

[134] Ibid, Amos, Keith, *The Fenians in Australia, 1865-1880*, pp. 253-255, concludes that there was 'at least a strong likelihood the cable was cut on Breslin's instructions...'
[135] News of the escape spread slowly across Australia and was reported in Victoria, *Argus*, 4 May 1876, in Tasmania, *The Hobart*

It was not, however, until 8 am on 19 April that the *Georgette*, now also armed with a 9-pound howitzer canon on its front deck, overtook its quarry. It came alongside the whaler, demanding the surrender of the prisoners and attempting to herd the ship back into Australian waters and fired a warning shot across its bow. The *Catalpa* hove to, but its master claimed they were in international waters under the American flag and challenged the police superintendent to create a diplomatic incident.[136] Stone, uncertain whether they were in international waters or not, felt he had no choice and reluctantly let the *Catalpa* sail away. On 19 August 1876 the *Catalpa*, after trying unsuccessfully to hunt whales for a short period and successfully avoiding Royal Navy ships, arrived triumphantly in New York, carrying the Fenian escapees.[137]

Reactions in WA to the escape ranged from those who sympathised with the escapees and those who felt angered that the colony had been fooled by an American captain. An official board of inquiry examined the circumstances of Fenian prison supervision that resulted in the retirement or dismissal of several senior figures in the WA convict service and the police sought evidence of outside assistance. The two IRB agents were still in the colony and it was believed that they might attempt to free the remaining Fenian prisoners, Keilly, Delaney, McCoy and Shine, a position reinforced by the arrival of an American schooner at Fremantle in early May. Although there is no evidence that a second Fenian escape was planned, it seems highly

---

Mercury, 13 May 1876, and in the *Sydney Morning Herald* on the same day but not until 14 June in the *Brisbane Courier* in Queensland.

[136] The governor of WA had instructed Stone not to attempt to board the vessel if more than three miles from the Australian coast. However, the legal opinion later produced by the British Law Office in London suggested that the vessel was 'liable to be pursued and stopped anywhere on the high seas', cit, ibid, Amos, Keith, *The Fenians in Australia, 1865-1880*, p. 241.

[137] *Argus*, 4 September 1876, gives 10 August 1876 as the date the *Catalpa* reached New York and this was replicated in other Australian newspapers. It is clear from Anthony's account in ibid, Pease, Z. W., *The Catalpa Expedition*, p. 167, that 19 August is the correct date. See also, Fennell, Philip A., 'History into Myth: The *Catalpa*'s Long Voyage', *New Hibernia Review*, Vol. 9, (2005), pp. 77-94.

probable that it was contemplated but security had been increased and success would have been unlikely. For O'Farrell, Fenianism 'was too strong a meat for the average Irish-Australian stomach' and that the Fenians sailed out of Australian history in 1876 and dropped out of Australian history, even Irish-Australian history, for over a century. [138]

Conclusion

Although Fenianism in Australia tends to be seen largely in relation to the arrival and later escape of some of the men of '67 and the attempted assassination of the Duke of Edinburgh in 1868, the existence of Fenian organisation in NSW, Victoria and WA is supported by the available evidence and there were links between Fenian sympathisers and Fenian organisation in the United States and Britain. Among some Irish immigrants from the early 1860s were Fenians. Much as with Chartism in the 1840s and 1850s, we do not know the extent to which Irish immigrants from the early 1860s were imbued with Fenian ideas and whether those ideas survived the voyage to a new life.

Like Chartism in the early 1850s, Fenian ideas were imported to Australia from the early 1860s. Unlike Chartist ideas that had a direct application to the emerging colonial constitutions in the mid-1850s, Fenianism had little to offer most in the Irish-Australian community and its impact on emerging Irish-Australian nationalism was limited despite attempts, especially in NSW, to construct an Australian Fenian conspiracy and to see all Irish-Australians in a Fenian hue. In both Australia and New Zealand, the Fenian threat was grossly exaggerated but in a more hostile sectarian context than had existed for several decades in 'isolation, remoteness and colonial fragility bred fear and paroxysm', it was credible.[139] Yet transported Fenians were almost universally critical of Irish nationalism in Australia. Edward Kelly observed 'Irish nationalist stinks in the nostrils of the 'respectable' community, but they glory in being Catholic and loyal to their Queen'. He regarded the

---

[138] Ibid, O'Farrell, Patrick, *The Irish in Australia: 1788 to the Present*, p. 215.
[139] Ibid, Campbell, Malcolm, 'A 'Successful Experiment' No More: The Intensification of Religious Bigotry in Eastern Australia, 1865-1885', p. 72.

Sydney Hibernian Society as weak, Catholic and not truly Irish and as sucking up to the English. Kelly was a Protestant and found the clericalism and Catholic exclusivity of the Irish-Australians stifling, offensive and unnatural.[140]

It was not the impact of Fenianism on Australia that really mattered, but the impact that Australia had on Fenianism. Most Irish-Australians chose not to rally to Fenianism. Those bold Fenian men who had arrived in the *Hougoumont* in early 1868 either escaped to the United States retaining their radical zeal or they remained in the colonies and became infected by Australian respectability or decided that they had no quarrel there and that Australian freedoms should be applied in Ireland. Yet for many conservative Australian colonists the threat posed by Irish nationalist remained whether from a nationalist rising within Australia or in the form of an attack on Australia's exposed colonies by an Irish-American filibustering warship that was given credence by the success of the *Catalpa* mission. This was evident in 1868-1869, 1876 and especially during the Fenian scares of 1880 and 1881 in WA.[141] There may not have been consensus over the future status of Ireland but the development of militant revolutionary Irish nationalism or moves towards Orange violence had been largely rejected by colonists of whatever religious persuasion. There was Irish support when it appeared that famine had returned in 1879-1880. Irish politicians and agitators who toured the colonies were generally well received and interest was maintained about what was taking place in Ireland. Sectarian division persisted and there were undoubtedly tensions over race and culture and over individual loyalties, but a large part of the population was beginning to see themselves as a new race of Anglo-Celtic Australians. Irish nationality remained importance and was celebrated especially on St. Patrick's Day but being a White Australian was increasingly regarded as a unifying ideology.

---

[140] Cit, ibid, O'Farrell, P., *The Irish in Australia*, p. 214.
[141] Ibid, Amos, Keith, *The Fenians in Australia, 1865-1880*, pp. 259-267, considers the panics of 1880 and 1881.

Appendix: Who ran colonial government?

Prime Ministers (1783-1886)

1783-1801	William Pitt (1759-1806): Tory
1801-1804	Henry Addington (1757-1844); Tory
1804-1806	William Pitt (1759-1806); Tory
1806-1807	William Wyndham Grenville, Baron Grenville (1759-1834); Whig
1807-1809	William Henry Cavendish Cavendish-Bentinck, 3rd Duke of Portland (1738-1809); Whig
1809-1812	Spencer Perceval (1762-1812); Tory
1812-1827	Robert Banks Jenkinson, 2nd Earl of Liverpool (1770-1828); Tory
1827 (April-Aug)	George Canning (1770-1827); Tory
1827-1828	Frederick John Robinson, Viscount Goderich (1782-1859); Tory
1828-1830	Arthur Wellesley, Duke of Wellington (1769-1852); Tory
1830-1834	Charles Grey, 2nd Earl Grey (1764-1845); Whig
1834 (July-Nov)	William Lamb, 2nd Viscount Melbourne (1779-1848); Whig
1834 (Nov-Dec)	Arthur Wellesley, Duke of Wellington (1769-1852); Tory
1834-1835	Sir Robert Peel, 2nd Baronet (1788-1850); Conservative
1835-1841	William Lamb, 2nd Viscount Melbourne (1779-1848); Whig
1841-1846	Sir Robert Peel, 2nd Baronet (1788-1850); Conservative
1846-1852	Lord John Russell (1792-1878); Whig-Liberal
1852 (Feb-Dec)	Edward George Geoffrey Smith Stanley, 14th Earl of Derby (1799-1869); Conservative
1852-1855	George Hamilton-Gordon, 4th Earl of Aberdeen (1784-1860); Peelite-Whig

APPENDIX

1855-1858	Henry John Temple, 3rd Viscount Palmerston (1784-1865); Liberal
1858-1859	Edward George Geoffrey Smith Stanley, 14th Earl of Derby (1799-1869); Conservative
1859-1865	Henry John Temple, 3rd Viscount Palmerston (1784-1865); Liberal
1865-1866	Lord John Russell (1792-1878); Liberal
1866-1868	Edward George Geoffrey Smith Stanley, 14th Earl of Derby (1799-1869); Conservative
1868	Benjamin Disraeli (1804-1881); Conservative
1868-1874	William Ewart Gladstone (1809-1898); Liberal
1874-1880	Benjamin Disraeli (1804-1881); Conservative
1880-1885	William Ewart Gladstone (1809-1898); Liberal
1885-1886	Robert Cecil, 3rd Marquess of Salisbury (1830-1903); Conservative

Secretaries of State for War and the Colonies (1812-1886)

1812-1827	Henry Bathurst, 3rd Earl Bathurst (1762-1834)
1827 (April-Sept)	Frederick John Robinson, Viscount Goderich (1782-1859)
1827-1828	William Huskisson (1770-1830)
1828-1830	Sir George Murray (1772-1846)
1830-1833	Frederick John Robinson, Viscount Goderich (1782-1859)
1833-1834	Edward George Geoffrey Smith Stanley, Lord Stanley, 14th Earl of Derby (1799-1869)
1834 (June-Nov)	Thomas Spring Rice (1790-1866)
1834-1835	George Hamilton-Gordon, 4th Earl of Aberdeen (1784-1860)
1835-1839	Charles Grant, Baron Glenelg (1778-1866)
1839 (Feb-	Constantine Henry Phipps, Marquess

Aug)	of Normanby (1797-1863)
1839-1841	Lord John Russell (1792-1878)
1841-1845	Edward George Geoffrey Smith Stanley, Lord Stanley, 14th Earl of Derby (1799-1869)
1845-1846	William Ewart Gladstone (1809-1898)
1846-1852	Henry George Grey, 3rd Earl Grey (1802-1894)
1852 (Feb-Dec)	Sir John Somerset Pakington, 1st Baronet (1799-1880)
1852-1854	Henry Pelham Fiennes Pelham-Clinton, 5th Duke of Newcastle under Lyme (1811-1864)
1854-1855	Sir George Grey, 2nd Baronet (1799-1882)
1855 (Feb)	Sidney Herbert (1810-1861)
1855 (Feb-July)	Lord John Russell (1792-1878)
1855 (July-Nov)	Sir William Molesworth, 8th Baronet (1810-1855)
1855-1858	Henry Labouchere (1798-1869)
1858	Edward Henry Stanley, 15th Earl of Derby (1826-1893)
1858-1859	Sir Edward Bulwer-Lytton (1803-1873)
1859-1864	Duke of Newcastle (1811-1864)
1864-1866	Edward Cardwell (1813-1886)
1866-1867	Earl of Carnarvon (1831-1890)
1867-1868	Duke of Buckingham and Chandos (1823-1889)
1868-1870	Earl Granville (1815-1891)
1870-1874	Earl of Kimberley (1826-1902)
1874-1878	Earl of Carnarvon (1831-1890)
1878-1880	Sir Michael Hicks Beach (1837-1916)
1880-1882	Earl of Kimberley (1826-1902)
1882-1885	Edward Henry Stanley, 15th Earl of Derby (1826-1893)
1885-1886	Frederick Stanley (1841-1903)

Appendix

Governors of New South Wales (1788-1861)

1788-1792: Arthur Phillip (1738-1814)
1792-1794: Francis Grose (1756-1814); Acting Governor
1794-1795: William Paterson (1755-1810); Acting Governor
1795-1800: John Hunter (1737-1821)
1800-1806: Philip Gidley King (1758-1808)
1806-1808: William Bligh (1754-1817)
1808 (Jan-July): George Johnston (1764-1823); Acting Governor
1808-1809: Joseph Foveaux (baptised 1767, d. 1846); Acting Governor
1809-1810: William Paterson (1755-1810); Acting Governor
1810-1821: Lachlan Macquarie (1761-1824)
1821-1825: Sir Thomas Brisbane (1773-1860)
1825 (Dec): William Stewart (1769-1854); Acting Governor
1825-1831: Ralph Darling (1772-1858)
1831 (Oct-Dec): Patrick Lindesay (1778-1839); Acting Governor
1831-1837: Sir Richard Bourke (1777-1855)
1837-1838: Kenneth Snodgrass (1784-1853); Acting Governor
1838-1846: Sir George Gipps (1791-1847)
1846 (July-Aug): Sir Maurice Charles Philip O'Connell (1768-1848); Acting Governor
1846-1855: Sir Charles Augustus Fitzroy (1796-1858)
1855-1861: Sir William Thomas Denison (1804-1871)

Governors of Van Diemen's Land (1824-1855)

1824-1836: George Arthur (1784-1854); Lieutenant-Governor from 1824
1836-1837: Kenneth Snodgrass (1784-1853); Acting Lieutenant-Governor
1837-1843: Sir John Franklin (1786-1847); Lieutenant-Governor
1843-1846: Sir John Eardley Eardley-Wilmot, first baronet (1783-1847); Lieutenant-Governor
1846-1847: Charles Joseph La Trobe (1801-1875); Acting Lieutenant-Governor
1847-1855: Sir William Thomas Denison (1804-1871); Lieutenant-Governor

Appendix

Lieutenant-Governors and Governors of Victoria (1851-1863)

1851-1854: Charles Joseph La Trobe (1801-1875); Lieutenant-Governor
1854-1855: Sir Charles Hotham (1806-1855); Lieutenant-Governor
1855-1856: Edward MacArthur (1789-1872); Acting Governor
1856-1863: Sir Henry Barkly (1815-1898); Governor

Further Reading

The bibliography provides a general guide to relevant books. More detailed references can be found in the footnotes. Many of the references to primary sources are available on Google Books or Internet Archive either to be read or downloaded.

Bibliographies

Ferguson, John Alexander, *Bibliography of Australia*, 7 Vols. and *Addenda*, facsimile edition, (National Library of Australia), 1975-1986, and Brown, L. M., and Christie, I. R., *Bibliography of British History 1789-1851*, (Oxford University Press), 1977, and Hanham, H. J., *Bibliography of British History 1851-1914*, (Oxford University Press), 1976. Porter, Andrew, (ed.), *Bibliography of Imperial, Colonial and Commonwealth History since 1600*, (Oxford University Press), 2002, is the standard bibliography.

See also, *Bibliography of British and Irish History* (BBIH) http://apps.brepolis.net/BrepolisPortal/default.aspx

Biographies

Australian Dictionary of Biography, 17 Vols. (Melbourne University Press), 1966-, an *Index Volume* for Vols. 1-12, (plus consolidated corrigenda), and the *Supplement* that also includes a name index to all published volumes. http://www.adb.online.anu.edu.au/adbonline.htm

The Dictionary of National Biography (DNB), though old, is still worth consulting and is on CD. *The Oxford Dictionary of National Biography*, 60 Vols. (Oxford University Press), 2004, replaces and extends the original DNB.
Available on subscription: http://www.oxforddnb.com/

Further Reading

General histories

There are many general surveys of Australian history. The following examples represent different ways of approaching the subject: Atkinson, Alan, *The Europeans in Australia: A History*, 2 Vols. (Melbourne University Press), 1997, 2004, Macintyre, Stuart, *A Concise History of Australia*, 3rd ed., (Cambridge University Press), 2009, Day, David, *Claiming a Continent: A New History of Australia*, (Harper Collins), 1996, and Molony, John, *The Penguin History of Australia*, (Penguin, 1988). Clark, Manning, *A History of Australia*, Vols. I-IV, (Melbourne University Press), 1962-1978 is magisterial, idiosyncratic and readable. Russell, Penny, and White, Richard, (eds.), *Pastiche I: Reflections on Nineteenth Century Australia*, (Allen & Unwin), 1994, and Schreuder, Deryck M., and Ward, Stuart, (eds.), *Australia's Empire*, (Oxford University Press), 2008, are useful collections of papers.

Davison, Graeme, Hirst, John, and Macintyre, Stuart, (eds.), *The Oxford Companion to Australian History*, 2nd ed., (Oxford University Press), 2001, is a valuable reference books.

Index

A

Aborigines, 33, 34, 73, 87, 110, 122, 132, 185, 196, 197, 198, 199, 200, 201, 202, 203, 204, 225, 239, 307, 317, 322, 324, 330, 331, 335, 336, 346

Anderson, Joseph, 28, 368, 371, 372, 380

Arthur, Sir George, 1, 19, 35, 49, 60, 94, 97, 137, 138, 181, 200, 224, 266, 303, 318, 319, 320, 322, 323, 324, 336, 337, 338, 339, 358, 360, 367, 425, 426, 465

Atkins, Richard, 143, 155, 156, 157, 160, 163, 164, 170, 285, 288, 290, 396

Australian colonies

New South Wales, vi, vii, viii, 1, 2, 3, 4, 5, 6, 7, 9, 10, 11, 12, 13, 15, 16, 17, 18, 19, 26, 27, 30, 32, 33, 34, 35, 36, 37, 39, 40, 41, 43, 45, 46, 47, 48, 49, 50, 51, 52, 53, 54, 55, 57, 58, 60, 61, 63, 65, 69, 70, 74, 77, 80, 82, 83, 84, 86, 87, 89, 90, 91, 92, 93, 94, 95, 96, 98, 99, 100, 101, 102, 103, 104, 105, 106, 107, 108, 118, 120, 121, 123, 124, 125, 126, 127, 128, 131, 132, 136, 138, 139, 140, 141, 145, 146, 149, 150, 152, 153, 155, 156, 160, 162, 164, 171, 172, 173, 175, 176, 177, 178, 179, 180, 181, 182, 183, 184, 185, 186, 187, 188, 189, 191, 192, 193, 194, 197, 199, 202, 204, 205, 206, 207, 208, 210, 211, 212, 215, 216, 217, 218, 219, 221, 222, 223, 226, 227, 228, 230, 231, 233, 234, 235, 236, 237, 238, 239, 240, 241, 242, 243, 244, 245, 246, 247, 253, 254, 255, 256, 257, 258, 259, 260, 261, 262, 263, 264, 265, 266, 267, 268, 269, 270, 274, 275, 276, 278, 279, 280, 283, 284, 285, 286, 289, 290, 291, 292, 293, 295, 296, 297, 298, 299, 300, 302, 306, 307, 308, 309, 310, 317, 318, 319, 320, 321, 324, 325, 329, 335, 341, 343, 354, 355, 358, 359, 360, 361, 363, 367, 368, 369, 371, 372, 373, 374, 375, 376, 377, 380, 381, 382, 384, 389, 390, 391, 392, 393, 397, 398, 399, 407, 409, 411, 412, 413,

414, 416, 417, 419, 420, 422, 430, 442, 446, 449, 450, 460, 465
Port Phillip District, 70, 107, 110, 179, 185, 186, 187, 188, 189, 191, 193
Queensland, vii, 17, 22, 32, 60, 173, 194, 204, 223, 236, 253, 256, 260, 343, 360, 437, 449, 459
South Australia, vii, 7, 89, 108, 109, 113, 118, 120, 179, 182, 183, 184, 185, 186, 187, 189, 191, 194, 235, 236, 237, 240, 246, 248, 251, 253, 256, 257, 258, 260, 309, 310, 325, 326, 330, 440, 446
Van Diemen's Land, vi, vii, viii, 5, 77, 79, 82, 94, 96, 173, 223, 224, 226, 275, 289, 308, 317, 318, 319, 323, 333, 334, 335, 336, 337, 341, 356, 417, 420, 422, 423, 435, 436, 465
Van Diemen's Land, 3, 4, 7, 20, 70, 73, 77, 79, 82, 83, 84, 86, 87, 89, 91, 92, 93, 94, 96, 97, 118, 119, 120, 160, 172, 179, 180, 181, 182, 183, 184, 185, 202, 216, 217, 218, 223, 224, 225, 226, 230, 233, 234, 236, 237, 239, 240, 246, 261, 263, 266, 268, 269, 272, 278, 279, 280, 288, 303, 307, 310, 318, 319, 320, 324, 325, 328, 330, 333, 334, 335, 336, 337, 339, 342, 352, 356, 358, 365, 367, 370, 371, 373, 374, 382, 383, 384, 392, 408, 411, 413, 414, 420, 421, 422, 423, 424, 425, 427, 428, 429, 431, 433, 434, 435, 436, 437, 438, 440, 441
Victoria, vii, viii, 3, 8, 9, 108, 109, 112, 118, 119, 120, 173, 179, 185, 191, 192, 193, 194, 200, 236, 246, 247, 248, 251, 253, 256, 257, 258, 260, 291, 310, 330, 343, 344, 345, 348, 368, 417, 422, 424, 425, 434, 437, 440, 442, 446, 447, 449, 458, 460, 466
Western Australia, vii, 3, 7, 89, 108, 109, 118, 119, 179, 182, 183, 188, 189, 191, 194, 225, 235, 239, 240, 248, 272, 384, 413, 439, 440, 441, 442, 443, 446, 447, 448, 449, 450, 452, 453, 454, 455, 457, 459, 460, 461

B

Balfe, John Donellan, 430
Ballingarry, 421, 431

Banks, Sir Joseph, 1, 11, 12, 13, 21, 32, 35, 63, 65, 70, 71, 140, 141, 142, 143, 171, 366, 394, 395, 400
Bannister, Saxe, 299, 303
Bathurst rebellion 1830, 263–66
Bathurst, Lord, 79, 82, 85, 86, 90, 91, 94, 95, 97, 98, 99, 100, 101, 102, 103, 129, 130, 146, 213, 214, 215, 232, 292, 293, 294, 295, 297, 299, 300, 301, 304, 317, 337, 358, 367, 463
Batman, John, 185, 196, 200, 201, 202
Baughan, John, 52, 57, 58
Bent, Ellis, 81, 86, 291, 293, 294
Bent. Jeffery, 81, 294
Bentham, Jeremy, 176, 177, 290
Bigge, John Thomas, 81, 82, 83, 84, 85, 86, 87, 91, 93, 98, 102, 180, 213, 214, 215, 217, 227, 231, 232, 295, 296, 297, 308, 317, 318, 412
reports, 84–87
Blackstone, William, 197, 283, 284, 286, 288
Blainey, Geoffrey, 11, 17, 18, 359
Botany Bay, i, vi, 1, 2, 10, 11, 12, 13, 14, 15, 17, 18, 19, 20, 21, 22, 32, 33, 35, 36, 69, 123, 179, 359, 360, 388, 389, 390, 391
alternatives to, 10–11
as 'dumping ground', 11–16
for trade, 16–18
why choose Botany Bay?, 18
Brady, Matthew, 268, 337, 338, 341, 342
Breslin, John J., 456, 457, 458
British Empire, 11, 83, 104, 111, 180, 197, 267
British government, vi, 7, 14, 41, 44, 47, 48, 54, 56, 62, 69, 71, 72, 73, 82, 103, 108, 113, 114, 120, 137, 140, 196, 220, 235, 240, 241, 285, 291, 318, 321, 323, 336, 337, 359, 362, 410, 412, 424, 439, 446
Admiralty, 19, 24, 28, 31, 41, 50, 63, 77, 142, 172, 183, 207, 376
Colonial Office, vi, 7, 66, 83, 85, 93, 99, 104, 106, 108, 110, 111, 112, 117, 118, 144, 145, 167, 169, 181, 182, 183, 184, 185, 187, 188, 190, 191, 192, 193, 198, 202, 204, 212, 213, 214, 219, 221, 222, 229, 230, 232, 237, 243, 245, 247, 250, 251, 261, 262, 287, 290, 292, 294, 295, 299, 300, 306, 317, 323, 365, 414, 418, 419
Home Office, 19, 36, 39, 40, 44, 47, 48, 49, 50, 295, 300, 305, 440
Parliament, vii, 7, 9, 33, 89, 93, 94, 95, 97,

103, 106, 108, 118, 119, 120, 121, 122, 179, 184, 193, 194, 198, 218, 221, 223, 243, 245, 251, 253, 255, 282, 283, 312, 436, 439, 447
  Treasury, 12, 13, 19, 41, 48, 50, 54, 72, 138, 214, 295
Burke, Edmund, 103, 111, 407
Bushrangers, 5, 234, 263, 307, 317, 322, 324, 331, 332, 333, 334, 335, 337, 338, 339, 340, 341, 342, 348, 349
  Felons' Apprehension Acts, 342, 346, 347
  in free societies, 342–49
  in penal colonies, 333–42

C

Campbell, Robert, 70, 154, 167, 174, 421
Canada, 10, 13, 110, 111, 113, 115, 116, 118, 169, 180, 184, 188, 194, 199, 214, 248, 281, 290, 309, 436, 441, 451
Cash, Martin, 339, 340
Castle Forbes, 105, 340, 414–20
Castle Hill, vii, 211, 267, 288, 355, 384, 392, 396, 398, 400, 401, 404, 405, 411, 413
Castlereagh, Lord, 75, 77, 78, 79, 81, 127, 142, 145, 146, 147, 156, 161, 162, 164, 165, 166, 167, 168, 169, 170, 171, 172, 213, 291, 392
Catalpa escape 1876, 454–60
Clan na Gael, 451, 454
Collins, David, 19, 29, 30, 36, 37, 42, 70, 124, 126, 133, 160, 167, 168, 169, 172, 284, 285, 409, 410, 411
Colonial government
  Colonial Secretary, 123–32, 273
  colonial state, i, vi, ix, 1, 205, 277, 278, 279, 331
  Colonial Treasurer, 92, 327, 419
  Executive Council, 95, 102, 121, 298, 320
  Governor's Secretary, 123
  judiciary, 102, 104, 283, 286, 287, 290, 293, 295, 298, 301
  Legislative Assembly, 92, 121, 254, 321, 437
  Legislative Council, 84, 94, 95, 96, 99, 100, 104, 105, 106, 107, 111, 112, 113, 114, 115, 116, 117, 118, 119, 120, 121, 180, 189, 222, 239, 242, 243, 249, 251, 252, 254, 298, 301, 309, 320, 323, 325, 437
  local government, 101, 189, 191, 194, 306, 318, 329
  NSW Constitution Act 1842, 113–15
  Surveyor-General, 92, 95, 154, 163, 164,

184, 226, 227, 228, 229
Convict Workers, 276, 277, 278, 279, 280, 373
Cook, Captain James, 1, 13, 15, 16, 17, 21, 22, 23, 31, 32, 33, 140, 197, 359
   discovery of NSW, 31–33
Cowper, Charles, 115, 134, 254, 255
Crime, 4, 50, 56, 106, 139, 199, 234, 263, 268, 276, 311, 312, 313, 314, 318, 319, 324, 327, 337, 340, 352, 367, 415
   forgery, 271, 369, 377
   larceny, 36, 277
   murder, 28, 36, 43, 48, 265, 266, 288, 333, 334, 338, 340, 341, 345, 346, 351, 377, 381, 396
   robbery, 266, 268, 333, 338, 339, 341, 342, 345, 369, 373
   theft, 44, 56, 85, 263, 277, 332, 345, 373, 405
Crossley, George, 162, 163, 287
Cunningham, Phillip, 399, 400, 401, 402, 403, 404

D

Denison, Sir William, 4, 120, 229, 371, 425, 426, 429, 430, 431, 465
Devoy, John, 451, 452, 453, 454, 455, 457
Dixon, Father James, 71, 398, 399, 401, 402

Dore, Richard, 58, 124, 125, 133, 284, 291
Douglass, Henry Grattan, 299, 300, 301
Dwyer, Michael, 406, 407, 408, 409

E

Eardley-Wilmot, Sir John, 323, 324, 338, 465
Economy
   capitalist, 175, 209
   coal, 5, 68, 69, 162, 178, 218, 219, 221, 222, 226, 276, 358, 414
   currency, 66, 78, 123, 138, 370
   farming, 23, 42, 44, 47, 48, 49, 54, 68, 74, 86, 99, 144, 153, 175, 200, 205, 207, 209, 210, 211, 213, 214, 215, 216, 222, 224, 226, 237, 246, 248, 257, 262, 333, 344, 364, 373, 398
   pastoral farming, 180, 185, 187, 192, 213, 216, 220, 221, 231, 234, 236, 237, 238, 245, 246, 248, 249, 253, 255, 260, 261, 262
   population, viii, 3, 6, 30, 42, 52, 63, 72, 84, 87, 90, 105, 106, 107, 113, 116, 121, 149, 180, 182, 184, 185, 189, 192, 196, 202, 205, 208, 210, 212, 213, 216, 217, 225, 230, 233, 236,

237, 238, 240, 251, 255, 268, 276, 281, 285, 302, 317, 319, 324, 331, 336, 339, 343, 346, 362, 363, 374, 395, 397, 409, 420, 435, 451, 461
prices, 55, 56, 58, 62, 66, 68, 82, 123, 138, 144, 209, 210, 211, 232, 236, 237, 240, 242, 243, 256, 261, 299, 344, 362
sheep, 52, 53, 67, 68, 74, 140, 141, 154, 185, 219, 220, 222, 223, 224, 225, 226, 231, 233, 236, 238, 239, 242, 244, 246, 251, 260, 261, 266, 271, 322, 416, 424
spirits, 45, 46, 48, 50, 55, 58, 59, 65, 66, 72, 73, 74, 139, 140, 144, 145, 146, 234
wages, 56, 62, 66, 123, 209, 210, 254, 323, 328, 362
whaling, 16, 18, 45, 69, 70, 89, 363, 366, 447, 454, 455, 456
wool, 83, 87, 107, 140, 153, 175, 216, 217, 218, 219, 220, 221, 222, 223, 224, 225, 226, 235, 236, 237, 238, 240, 242, 245, 353, 415
Education, 72, 78, 85, 93, 103, 106, 115, 116, 132, 363
Entwistle, Ralph, 263, 264, 265

Evatt, H. V., 145, 146, 159, 173, 175

F

Fenians, iv, vi, vii, 272, 384, 413, 421, 422, 440, 441, 442, 443, 444, 445, 446, 447, 448, 449, 450, 451, 452, 453, 454, 456, 457, 458, 459, 460, 461, 484
Field, Barron, 85, 86, 295, 296, 297
Forbes, Sir Francis, 95, 102, 103, 104, 198, 265, 297, 298, 299, 300, 301, 302, 303, 304, 305, 306, 307, 419
Franklin, Sir John, 307, 323, 324, 338, 339, 340, 352, 356, 465
Fremantle, 441, 443, 445, 449, 450, 452, 454, 456, 457, 458, 459
Furey, Bryan, 394, 395, 399
Fyans, Captain Foster, 375, 376, 377, 378, 379, 380

G

Gardiner, Frank, 343, 344
Glenelg, Lord, 108, 202, 240, 338, 418, 419, 463
Gold, viii, 3, 117, 120, 173, 193, 219, 229, 247, 248, 251, 252, 261, 310, 330, 331, 342, 344, 349, 437
Governors of NSW
    Bligh, William, vii, 60, 70, 73, 75, 76, 77, 126, 127, 136, 137,

INDEX

140, 141, 142, 143, 144, 145, 146, 147, 148, 149, 150, 151, 152, 153, 154, 155, 156, 157, 158, 159, 160, 161, 162, 163, 164, 165, 166, 167, 168, 169, 170, 171, 172, 173, 174, 175, 176, 177, 210, 212, 213, 227, 308, 407, 408, 411, 465

Bourke, Sir Richard, 89, 102, 103, 104, 105, 106, 107, 108, 110, 116, 131, 201, 202, 218, 230, 239, 241, 244, 266, 307, 309, 368, 380, 414, 415, 416, 417, 418, 419, 465

Brisbane, Sir Thomas, 5, 89, 90, 91, 94, 95, 98, 99, 100, 101, 102, 108, 129, 130, 232, 289, 297, 298, 299, 300, 301, 303, 317, 358, 367, 437, 465

Darling, Sir Ralph, 89, 95, 100, 101, 102, 103, 104, 107, 108, 130, 131, 146, 181, 192, 219, 228, 232, 233, 237, 263, 265, 289, 297, 298, 301, 302, 303, 304, 305, 306, 307, 317, 367, 374, 375, 415, 465

FitzRoy, Sir Charles, 116, 117, 118, 121, 190

Foveaux, Major Joseph, 52, 64, 127, 134, 138, 164, 165, 166, 167, 168, 172, 173, 174, 175, 213, 363, 364, 365, 366, 465

Gipps, Sir George, 89, 110, 111, 113, 114, 115, 116, 117, 131, 187, 189, 191, 229, 235, 240, 241, 242, 243, 244, 245, 353, 372, 380, 381, 465

Grose, Major Francis, 30, 45, 46, 47, 48, 49, 50, 51, 54, 62, 63, 137, 138, 208, 209, 213, 465

Hunter, Captain John, 2, 19, 22, 23, 25, 34, 45, 46, 49, 50, 51, 52, 53, 54, 55, 56, 57, 58, 59, 60, 63, 64, 65, 66, 69, 71, 72, 73, 74, 75, 76, 77, 124, 125, 133, 137, 138, 139, 140, 151, 153, 208, 209, 210, 211, 287, 308, 349, 363, 391, 392, 393, 394, 398, 411, 412, 465

King, Philip Gidley, 5, 23, 25, 26, 31, 32, 33, 34, 39, 42, 44, 45, 49, 51, 59, 60, 61, 62, 63, 64, 65, 66, 67, 68, 69, 70, 71, 72, 73, 74, 75, 76, 77, 89, 125, 126, 138, 139, 140, 141, 143, 146, 148, 149, 151, 153, 154, 156, 157, 197, 210, 211, 212, 221, 227, 271, 287, 288, 308, 360, 361, 362, 363, 365, 366, 391, 392, 393, 394,

395, 397, 398, 399, 400, 401, 403, 404, 405, 406, 411, 412, 465
Macquarie, Lachlan, 5, 6, 35, 68, 76, 77, 78, 79, 80, 81, 82, 83, 84, 85, 86, 87, 89, 91, 98, 100, 127, 128, 129, 136, 148, 150, 163, 165, 167, 168, 169, 170, 172, 173, 174, 177, 179, 198, 213, 214, 215, 216, 217, 227, 279, 289, 291, 292, 293, 294, 295, 296, 299, 300, 308, 333, 334, 335, 337, 370, 374, 381, 396, 419, 465
Paterson, Captain William, 46, 49, 51, 52, 57, 58, 65, 74, 127, 134, 137, 160, 165, 167, 168, 169, 170, 174, 175, 208, 209, 213, 396, 401, 465
Phillip, Captain Arthur, viii, 1, 4, 7, 14, 15, 16, 19, 20, 21, 22, 23, 24, 25, 27, 29, 30, 33, 34, 35, 36, 38, 39, 40, 41, 42, 43, 44, 45, 46, 47, 53, 60, 61, 62, 63, 72, 76, 84, 90, 108, 123, 124, 137, 147, 148, 154, 184, 189, 200, 202, 205, 206, 207, 208, 209, 216, 227, 234, 239, 247, 284, 286, 291, 296, 325, 360, 361, 362, 376, 465

Grey, Earl, Henry George Grey, 3rd, 117, 118, 190, 191, 192, 193, 222, 245, 318, 337, 383, 425, 464
Grey, Sir George, 326, 328
Griffin, Edmund, 126, 133, 157
Grimes, Charles, 154, 163, 164, 227

H

Hall, Ben, 343
Hawkesbury, 24, 47, 49, 51, 68, 76, 80, 143, 144, 146, 152, 154, 159, 160, 174, 205, 209, 399, 400, 401, 403, 404
Holt, Joseph, 287, 392, 395, 396, 397, 405, 409
Howe, Michael, 334, 335

I

Immigration, 81, 87, 107, 132, 213, 215, 217, 222, 231, 238, 242, 243, 245
assisted, 7, 81, 107, 128, 192, 237, 239, 245, 335, 343, 388
bounty scheme, 45, 107
India, 10, 16, 18, 19, 54, 66, 68, 69, 70, 108, 139, 203, 205, 369, 375
Irish convicts, i, 3, 58, 71, 147, 164, 264, 269, 270, 271, 272, 317, 339, 364, 368, 375, 384, 385, 391, 392, 393, 394, 395, 396, 397, 398, 399, 407, 408, 410, 411, 413, 414, 420, 421, 422, 424, 430, 434, 435,

436, 437, 438, 439, 442, 443, 446, 448, 455
Castle Hill 1804, 398–406
context, 384–88
Defenders, 384, 386, 387, 389, 390, 391, 393, 411, 413
Dwyer and rebellion, 409
rebellions 1800-1803, 393–98
transportation, 388–93
United Irishmen, 58, 71, 287, 364, 384, 386, 387, 389, 390, 391, 392, 394, 397, 400, 411, 413

J

Jamison, Thomas, 147, 164, 165
Johnson, Richard, 48, 56
Johnston, George, 58, 71, 73, 127, 133, 136, 143, 149, 150, 155, 156, 157, 158, 159, 160, 161, 162, 163, 164, 165, 166, 167, 168, 169, 170, 171, 172, 174, 175, 213, 398, 400, 401, 402, 403, 404, 406, 408, 465
Johnston, William, 399, 401, 402, 404

K

Kelly, Edward (Ned), 344–49
Knatchbull, John, 376, 377, 380, 381

L

La Trobe, Charles Joseph, viii, 110, 186, 248, 249, 250, 251, 465, 466
Land companies, 217–26
Australian Agricultural Company, 218, 219, 220, 224, 226, 299
Van Diemen's Land Company, 180, 218, 223–26
Land policy
Crown Land, 9, 44, 102, 107, 114, 120, 230, 231, 232, 233, 234, 236, 237, 238, 239, 240, 242, 243, 245, 251, 252, 253, 254, 255, 256, 259, 261, 262
Crown Lands Alienation Act 1861, 254, 255
Crown Lands Sale Act 1842, 243, 246
Deeds Registration Act 1825, 228
free selection, 252, 253, 254, 255, 256, 259, 260, 253–60, 262
Gipps and squatters, 241–45
granting land 1788-1821, 204–17
land and gold, 248–52
land grants, 1, 34, 35, 36, 38, 40, 42, 44, 46, 47, 48, 49, 50, 67, 68, 74, 76, 78, 87, 102, 119, 125, 130, 138, 140, 142, 146, 150, 154, 163, 166, 170, 176, 185, 203,

204, 205, 206, 207, 208, 209, 210, 212, 213, 214, 216, 217, 218, 219, 220, 223, 224, 226, 227, 228, 230, 231, 232, 233, 234, 235, 237, 238, 239, 240, 243, 248, 261, 299, 306, 335, 392, 407, 414
land regulations 1844, 244
land sales, 7, 102, 222, 231, 232, 235, 237, 242, 261, 323, 324
land surveying, 226–29
leases, 78, 125, 148, 149, 151, 154, 175, 176, 229, 232, 245, 246, 247, 248, 249, 250, 251, 257, 261
pre-emptive rights, 248, 249, 251
restricted to unrestricted settlement, 229–31
Ripon Regulations 1831, 231, 237, 238, 239, 261
Torrens legislation, 248
Waste Lands Act 1846, 245, 247
Legal system
Attorney-General, 114, 299, 302, 303, 305, 325, 380, 447
Australian Courts Act 1828, 96–98, 230
Charter of Justice, 36, 37, 81, 93, 94, 97, 297
Chief-Justice, 94, 95, 96, 102, 109, 198, 265, 296, 297, 298, 302, 303, 305, 306, 320, 419
Civil Court, 36, 37
Court of Criminal and Civil Jurisdiction, 36
English law, 37, 97, 197, 198, 199, 204, 239, 284, 285, 287, 290, 295, 296, 297, 298, 302, 303, 309, 310
Judge-Advocate, 36, 37, 74, 75, 85, 86, 123, 124, 155, 156, 157, 163, 164, 227, 284, 288, 290, 291, 293, 294, 296, 396, 408
jury, 28, 86, 94, 96, 99, 104, 111, 116, 265, 283, 286, 292, 296, 297, 299, 300, 301, 302, 305, 307, 308, 309, 321, 343, 346, 381, 418
Kable v Sinclair 1788, 37, 284
lawyer, 81, 83, 86, 162, 290, 296
magistrates, 43, 46, 57, 67, 76, 79, 83, 94, 105, 126, 147, 153, 155, 157, 158, 164, 186, 239, 263, 270, 274, 282, 299, 300, 306, 308, 310, 312, 316, 317, 318, 319, 320, 321, 322, 323, 324, 325, 327, 338, 340, 370, 380, 383, 397, 405, 410, 415, 416, 418, 427, 444
New South Wales Act 1823, 93–95

New South Wales Courts Act 1787, 36
pardons, 5, 6, 90, 91, 288, 292, 300, 323, 334, 342, 380, 392, 396, 431, 433, 434, 436, 437, 445, 446, 452, 453, 454
Quarter Sessions, 94, 96, 99, 299, 419
repugnancy, 95, 97, 102, 118, 293, 298, 304
rule of law, i, viii, 37, 76, 86, 88, 102, 109, 162, 163, 176, 177, 178, 282, 283, 285, 286, 287, 288, 298, 302, 303, 305, 306, 307, 309, 310, 316, 320, 321, 324, 331
Supreme Court, 81, 93, 94, 95, 96, 97, 98, 198, 199, 202, 228, 229, 286, 293, 294, 296, 297, 304, 306, 307, 308, 320, 341, 346, 375, 380, 381, 416
Locke, John, 137, 156, 176
Lord, Simeon, 2, 78, 81, 92, 174
Lowe, Robert, 115, 116, 381

M

Macarthur, Hannibal, 219, 299, 300, 301
Macarthur, James, 106, 219, 234
Macarthur, John, 27, 46, 47, 50, 52, 54, 55, 56, 58, 68, 74, 83, 127, 133, 139, 140, 141, 143, 146, 147, 150, 152, 153, 154, 155, 156, 157, 158, 159, 160, 161, 162, 164, 165, 166, 168, 169, 170, 171, 172, 173, 174, 175, 210, 211, 216, 289, 307
Maconochie, Alexander, 371, 372, 373
Magna Carta, 283, 286, 287, 288
Margarot, Maurice, 75, 287, 288, 405, 406
Marsden, Samuel, 48, 56, 81, 85, 216, 270, 300, 301, 355, 375, 394, 395, 396, 397, 400
Matra, James, 1, 12, 13, 14
Mitchell, Thomas, 73, 228, 229
Moreton Bay, 98, 280, 352, 376
Morisset, Thomas, 371, 372, 374, 375, 377
Mudie, James, 105, 414, 415, 416, 417, 418, 419, 420
Musquito, 335, 336

N

New York, 424, 428, 429, 431, 433, 434, 436, 438, 439, 451, 456, 459
New Zealand, 11, 31, 32, 44, 62, 69, 77, 196, 197, 222, 226, 251, 330, 358, 359, 362, 369, 414, 442, 446, 448, 449, 455, 456, 460
Newcastle, 72, 79, 163, 164, 218, 219, 221, 222, 270, 352, 358, 405, 414, 449, 464

479

Norfolk Island, vii, 2, 15, 19, 23, 24, 25, 27, 30, 35, 39, 42, 45, 60, 61, 62, 64, 66, 69, 72, 73, 98, 125, 126, 166, 202, 207, 284, 288, 340, 358, 359, 360, 361, 362, 363, 365, 366, 367, 369, 370, 371, 372, 373, 374, 375, 376, 379, 380, 381, 382, 383, 392, 394, 396, 399, 405, 408, 411, 414, 417
  conditions, 366–74
  penal colony established, 359–64
  rebellion 1800, 366
  rebellion 1834, 374–81
  rebellion 1840-1855, 381–83
NSW Corps, 26, 27, 43, 46, 47, 49, 52, 54, 55, 57, 58, 59, 62, 71, 73, 74, 75, 76, 77, 125, 127, 132, 136, 137, 138, 139, 140, 141, 144, 146, 147, 149, 150, 151, 153, 154, 155, 156, 157, 158, 159, 160, 162, 163, 165, 166, 169, 170, 171, 173, 174, 175, 210, 211, 212, 363, 365, 366, 395, 400, 401, 402, 406

O

O'Reilly, John Boyle, 450, 451, 452, 454, 455

P

Pakington, Sir John, 120, 193, 464
Parkes, Henry, 254, 343, 344

Parramatta, 24, 27, 29, 30, 42, 46, 53, 68, 71, 80, 81, 85, 98, 146, 168, 205, 207, 208, 210, 299, 351, 352, 353, 354, 394, 395, 397, 399, 400, 401, 404, 405, 407
Pastoralists, 184, 189, 236, 239, 244, 245, 247, 258, 262
Peel, Sir Robert, 185, 300, 312, 462
Pitt, William, 11, 12, 15, 17, 49, 462
Plunkett, John Hubert, 114, 414, 417
Policing, 310–31
  British context, 310–13
  colonial policing, 331
  historiography, 313–16
Political prisoners, vii, 71, 271, 288, 384, 388, 389, 390, 391, 397, 406, 412, 413, 420, 422, 439
  Fenians, 439–61
  Young Irelanders, 420–39
Port Arthur, 341, 414, 425, 426, 429, 430
Portland, Lord, 49, 50, 51, 52, 53, 54, 55, 56, 57, 58, 59, 60, 62, 63, 64, 66, 67, 69, 74, 125, 139, 208, 209, 210, 211, 349, 363, 365, 391, 392, 393, 395, 397, 440, 462
Price, John Giles, 372

R

Redfern, William, 83

Religion
  Anglican, 105, 106, 384, 399
  Nonconformist, 105
  Protestant, 103, 104, 106, 277, 384, 385, 386, 392, 395, 419, 446, 455, 461
  Roman Catholic, 104, 105, 106, 270, 277, 310, 345, 371, 384, 386, 387, 388, 394, 398, 399, 414, 420, 424, 426, 437, 440, 442, 448, 450, 451, 460, 461
  sectarianism, 104, 105, 116, 386, 387, 460
Representative government, 93, 95, 112, 119, 131, 243, 286, 297
Responsible government, i, vi, vii, viii, 9, 89, 110, 111, 113, 114, 115, 117, 118, 119, 120, 121, 131, 188, 189, 190, 193, 309
  achieving, 118–22
Robertson, John, 246, 253, 254, 255, 256, 257, 259
Robson, Lloyd, 266, 273, 275, 277, 338, 422, 430
Rose Hill, 24, 25, 205
Ross, Major Robert, 22, 23, 25, 34, 38, 39, 45, 61, 62, 77, 124, 158, 173, 361, 428
Rum Rebellion, vi, 126, 137, 144, 146, 158, 160, 173, 177, 136–78, 212, 289, 290
Ruse, James, 24, 206, 207

S

Selectors, 253, 255, 256, 257, 259, 260, 344, 348
Settlement of Australia, 25, 33–46
Smyth, Patrick James, 428, 431, 432, 433, 434, 437
Social class
  middle-classes, 256, 269, 312, 315, 325, 326, 327
  working-classes, 93, 245, 277, 312, 314, 316, 327, 328, 329, 331
Society
  artisans, 24, 41, 90, 92, 207, 218, 386
  convicts, vi, vii, 1, 2, 3, 4, 5, 10, 11, 12, 13, 14, 15, 18, 20, 21, 22, 23, 24, 25, 26, 27, 28, 29, 34, 35, 36, 37, 38, 39, 40, 41, 42, 43, 44, 45, 46, 47, 48, 50, 51, 52, 53, 54, 55, 56, 58, 60, 61, 62, 65, 66, 67, 71, 74, 76, 78, 80, 81, 82, 84, 85, 87, 89, 90, 91, 92, 95, 96, 98, 99, 104, 105, 107, 112, 119, 120, 123, 125, 126, 128, 144, 146, 147, 150, 164, 174, 176, 180, 191, 192, 205, 206, 209, 210, 215, 216, 217, 218, 219, 220, 221, 222, 224, 234, 239, 263, 264, 266, 267, 268, 269, 270, 271, 273, 274, 275, 276, 277,

278, 279, 280, 281, 284, 285, 286, 287, 292, 293, 300, 305, 306, 310, 317, 318, 319, 323, 324, 330, 331, 333, 334, 336, 337, 338, 339, 340, 341, 342, 350, 358, 359, 360, 361, 362, 363, 364, 365, 366, 368, 370, 372, 373, 374, 375, 376, 377, 378, 379, 381, 382, 383, 384, 388, 389, 390, 391, 393, 394, 395, 397, 398, 403, 408, 410, 411, 412, 413, 414, 415, 416, 418, 419, 429, 440, 443, 444, 445, 448, 452, 453, 454, 458
emancipated convicts, vi, 38, 44, 47, 51, 71, 76, 78, 81, 82, 84, 87, 88, 89, 90, 91, 92, 100, 101, 106, 176, 188, 189, 204, 205, 206, 207, 208, 213, 215, 216, 261, 273, 278, 285, 287, 289, 291, 292, 295, 296, 299, 301, 302, 308, 324, 333
emancipist, 2, 78, 81, 83, 84, 90, 148, 302
exclusives, 83, 88, 90, 91
free settlers, vi, vii, ix, 3, 6, 7, 10, 13, 14, 28, 30, 35, 40, 41, 46, 47, 51, 52, 53, 54, 55, 61, 62, 66, 68, 76, 78, 81, 84, 87, 89, 90, 91, 92, 93, 100, 102, 103,

105, 106, 107, 110, 111, 123, 126, 143, 144, 146, 151, 160, 166, 176, 177, 179, 185, 189, 197, 198, 202, 204, 205, 206, 207, 208, 209, 210, 211, 212, 213, 214, 215, 217, 222, 224, 225, 228, 230, 232, 233, 234, 235, 238, 239, 244, 249, 251, 261, 262, 265, 268, 271, 273, 275, 285, 289, 291, 295, 296, 299, 301, 308, 310, 320, 321, 322, 324, 325, 328, 330, 331, 332, 333, 335, 336, 337, 338, 350, 353, 361, 362, 363, 365, 366, 415, 428, 443, 450
gender, 93, 258, 350, 351, 352, 355
landowner, 4, 103, 234, 255, 263, 392
respectability, 54, 91, 92, 93, 101, 395, 453, 461
smallholders, 47, 53, 166, 253, 257, 258
squatters, 107, 188, 192, 223, 231, 233, 234, 235, 238, 239, 240, 241, 242, 243, 244, 245, 246, 247, 248, 249, 250, 251, 253, 255, 256, 257, 258, 259, 260, 262, 343, 344, 345, 348, 349
Sorell, William, 334, 335, 342, 427

Squatters, 249
Squatting, 185, 234, 235, 236, 234–37, 238, 239, 240, 241, 242, 243, 244, 245, 248, 256, 257, 343
Stephen, James, 70, 159, 181, 188, 189, 190, 323, 418
Swan River, 109, 182, 183, 184, 235, 442
Sydney, Lord, 1, 12, 13, 17, 19, 20, 21, 22, 23, 24, 25, 34, 39, 41, 43, 44, 207, 286

T

Terra nullius, 34, 196, 197, 198, 199, 201, 202, 203, 261
Territorial fragmentation, 179–94
Therry, Roger, 368, 414, 416, 417, 419
Thomson, Edward Deas, 114, 117, 131, 134
Transportation, vii, 1, 2, 3, 10, 11, 27, 28, 37, 82, 87, 97, 98, 106, 107, 115, 119, 120, 164, 187, 188, 189, 191, 192, 221, 242, 263, 267, 268, 269, 273, 274, 275, 276, 277, 278, 280, 281, 284, 286, 292, 295, 310, 317, 318, 319, 320, 324, 330, 336, 342, 368, 369, 374, 376, 377, 382, 387, 389, 390, 415, 421, 429, 430, 435, 439, 440, 441, 442
assignment system, 82, 102, 323

convict labour, 10, 15, 18, 49, 82, 102, 187, 192, 206, 220, 221, 224, 235, 276, 277, 278, 279, 281, 320, 353
female convicts, 275–80
First Fleet, 1, 11, 14, 15, 17, 19, 21, 19–22, 22, 23, 24, 25, 26, 27, 36, 39, 57, 60, 90, 136, 147, 205, 226, 360
numbers transported, 3, 82, 90, 269, 277, 372, 373, 384, 421, 441
Second Fleet, 3, 17, 23, 25, 26, 27, 28, 25–28, 28, 29, 41
Third Fleet, 28–29
tickets-of-leave, 98, 99, 271, 284, 305, 337, 422, 445, 453

U

United States, 65, 66, 89, 169, 181, 182, 186, 222, 251, 274, 343, 363, 388, 420, 421, 436, 438, 439, 440, 446, 449, 453, 454, 456, 460, 461

V

Violence, vi, vii, 84, 170, 263, 268, 269, 312, 319, 328, 338, 365, 367, 375, 420, 461

W

Wakefield, Edward, 183, 184, 230, 231, 235, 237, 240
Wardell, Robert, 299, 302, 303, 305
Wentworth, D'Arcy, 27, 65, 78, 82, 147
Wentworth, William Charles, 65, 82, 99, 102, 104, 111, 112, 114, 115, 120, 147, 289, 299, 302, 305
West Indies, 10, 83, 110, 111, 291
Westwood, William, 370, 382
Wilberforce, William, 26, 81, 290, 300
Willis, John Walpole, 199, 290, 291
Wylde, Sir John, 85, 295, 296, 297

Y

Young Ireland, 384, 413, 420, 423, 435, 436
Cappoquin Seven, 435
Dowling, William Paul, 421, 434
Martin, John, 12, 13, 14, 16, 17, 167, 173, 339, 421, 422, 423, 424, 433, 434, 435, 436, 437, 453
McManus, Terence Bellew, 421, 422, 425, 426, 427, 429, 431, 438
Meagher, Thomas, 421, 422, 423, 424, 425, 426, 427, 428, 429, 430, 431, 435, 436, 438
Mitchel, John, 421, 422, 423, 424, 425, 427, 428, 429, 431, 432, 433, 435, 436, 437, 438, 439
O'Brien, William Smith, 3, 420, 421, 422, 423, 424, 425, 429, 431, 433, 434, 435, 436
O'Doherty, Kevin Izod, 421, 422, 423, 424, 425, 426, 429, 433, 434, 435, 437
O'Donohoe, Patrick, 421, 422, 425, 426, 428, 429, 430, 431, 435

About the Author

Richard Brown was, until he retired, Head of History and Citizenship at Manshead School in Dunstable, and has published twenty-eight print and Kindle books and 50 articles and papers on nineteenth century history. He is the author of a successful blog, The History Zone that has a wide audience among students and researchers. Having completed his Rebellions Trilogy; *Three Rebellions: Canada 1837-1838, South Wales 1839 and Victoria, Australia 1854, Famine, Fenians and Freedom, 1840-1882*, and *Resistance and Rebellion in the British Empire, 1600-1980* and two volumes on Rebellion in Canada, he has now embarked on a study on Chartism.

Visit the author's website:
https://sites.google.com/site/lookingathistory/

Visit the author's blogs:
http://richardjohnbr.wordpress.com/ or
http://richardjohnbr.blogspot.com/

Or contact him on Twitter: https://twitter.com/#!/

Other recent books by Richard Brown

Rebellion in Canada, 1837-1885, Volume 1: Autocracy, Rebellion and Liberty, (CreateSpace), 2012.
Rebellion in Canada, 1837-1885, Volume 2: The Irish, the Fenians and the Metis, (CreateSpace), 2012.
Sex, Work and Politics: Women in Britain, 1830-1918, (CreateSpace), 2012; also available in a Kindle version.
Society under Pressure: Britain 1830-1914, (Nineteenth Century British Society series), 2012. Kindle version
Three Rebellions: Canada 1837-1838, South Wales 1839 and Victoria, Australia 1854, (Clio Publishing), 2010, also available in a Kindle version.

Lightning Source UK Ltd.
Milton Keynes UK
UKOW05f2259170414

230197UK00007B/113/P